THE SUNDAY TIMES
Book of the Countryside

THE SUNDAY TIMES

Book of the Countryside

—— Including One Thousand Days Out in —— Great Britain and Ireland

EDITORS

Philip Clarke

Brian Jackman

Derrik Mercer

ART DIRECTOR

Clive Crook

Macdonald

Macdonald Futura Publishers

London

CONTRIBUTORS

Rosemary Atkins
Alec Clifton-Taylor
A.W. Coysh
Barry Dennis, editor, *Angling Times*
Professor David Dineley, Professor of Geology, University of Bristol
Andrew Gilg, lecturer in geography, University of Exeter
Richard Girling, editor, Scene, *The Sunday Times*
Mark Girouard, formerly Slade Professor of Art, University of Oxford
Anthony Greenbank
Francesca Greenoak
Christopher Hall, director, Council for the Protection of Rural England
Arthur Hellyer, formerly editor of *Gardening Illustrated* and *Amateur Gardening*
Suzanne Hodgart
Roy Milward, reader in geography, University of Leicester
John Prizeman
Dr Adrian Robinson, reader in geography, University of Leicester
Graham Rose, agricultural and gardening correspondent, *The Sunday Times*
Bryan Silcock, science correspondent, *The Sunday Times*
Robert Troop, property correspondent, *The Sunday Times*
John Watney
Dr John Whittow, senior lecturer in geography, University of Reading
Geoffrey Young, director, WATCH Trust for Environmental Education

The books which have helped to establish the reputation
of many of our contributors are detailed in the bibliography on page 339;
the names of other contributors appear in the
acknowledgements on page 337.

CONSULTANTS

Professor T.W. Freeman, Emeritus Professor of Geography, University of Manchester
Sir Emrys Jones, formerly Principal, Royal Agricultural College and Chief Scientific Adviser to
the Minister of Agriculture
Professor H.H. Lamb, Emeritus Professor, Climatic Research Unit, University of East Anglia
Grenville Lucas, deputy keeper, Herbarium, Royal Botanic Gardens, Kew
Graham Moss, director, Community Resources and Planning Group

In addition to the consultants named above, several contributors acted also as consultants,
notably Alec Clifton-Taylor, Roy Milward, Dr Adrian Robinson and Dr John Whittow. Many
organisations were also particularly helpful and our debt to these sources, along with other
acknowledgments, appears on page 337

DESIGNER
Pedro Silmon

PICTURE EDITOR
June Stanier

First published in Great Britain in 1980 by
Macdonald · London and Sydney

reprinted with corrections 1980, 1981

Macdonald Futura Publishers
Paulton House
8 Shepherdess Walk
London N1 7LW

ISBN 0 354 04441 9

Filmset in Monophoto Baskerville by Servis Filmsetting Limited, Manchester

Colour separations by Excel Lithoplates Limited, Slough

Printed in Great Britain by Purnell & Son Limited, Paulton, Bristol

Contents

Foreword

Forewords are supposed to sing praises, but
wine like this needs no bush. A look at the formidably
distinguished list of contributors, at the wealth
of illustration and subject-matter, and not least at the price, is
recommendation enough. Such a comprehensive
introduction to the pleasures of rural and 'wild' Britain – and Ireland –
has long been needed. But now I am going to break rules,
because I suspect the book's very excellence and attractiveness requires
a warning to the unwary. The greatest threat to our countrysides
is less the physical harm we do them than our growing detachment from
their reality. For two centuries now we have become
increasingly an urban culture, increasingly in exile from
what exists outside our cities. A major danger of such exile is
that one can fall in love with pictures of things.
But pictures of things, as Henry VIII found with some of his brides,
can be insidiously more seductive than things in the flesh.
Real countrysides are sometimes much more secretive and 'difficult'
than they may appear from an armchair.
The essential passport to all things rural is patience,
and patience is not a town virtue. Much urban ingenuity
is devoted to artificially concentrating pleasure in time and space.
But this is a trick nature never learnt.
Rarities never occur there as in a film, one crowding on another,
all in perfect close-up. Very little yields to the passing glance,
nothing is displayed and labelled as in a zoo or a museum.
The wild will always stay closed to those who cannot learn to wait,
and to see the commonplace with fresh eyes.
I am a heretic too about the labelling. Never be brainwashed
into thinking that the countryside is like
some fiendish identification test, which you fail if you cannot
name everything you meet. Seeing and feeling
are just as important, and too many names act like blinkers:
they narrow vision. Truly knowing any form of life –
or way of life – is always as much an art as a science. In this we are all
amateurs, and start equal. Of course some names and explanations,
such as this book will give you, are necessary for the hard knowledge
that must underlie genuine feeling and affection, as opposed to
mere sentiment. What you have here is a key to a door, behind which lies
a secret land; it will let you in, but it is not the land itself.
No book, however thorough, however well-intentioned,
can be that. Once beyond the door, only you can find it –
its place in you, your place in it. Discovering this, one's own nature
in the mirror of nature, remains one of the most rewarding
experiences that life has to give, as strange and fertile as a journey to
another, and greener, planet. You may read
this invitation to it, and still decline; but you cannot claim it
was not handsomely offered.

John Fowles

Chapter One
The Making of the Countryside: the Natural Landscape

The British Isles possess a diversity of landscape which is unsurpassed; nowhere of comparable size has such variety. This scenic richness is a reflection of a complex, immensely long and, at times, mysterious geological history. To build the land has taken 3000 million years in which there were periods of convulsive upheaval, unceasing attrition and undisturbed calm. Only in the last 26 million years has this group of islands acquired the shape we know today. The sweep and scale of these great episodes is described here. So are the major Earth movements and Earth processes which have determined the scenery we see today, such as this view of Langdale in the Lake District

The British Isles do not go in for brash extremes. There are no deserts, no glaciers; no Niagaras nor Matterhorns (though it was not always so). But that is not to say the landscape lacks drama. For a demonstration of elemental savagery, walk out along any Cornish headland when a heavy sea is running. When heavy rollers charge the bays head on, and the shock of their fall, the suck and grind of pebbles swept up in their terrible undertow booms in the zawns and chasms of the shaken cliffs, then the entire coast from Hartland to Sennen seems the wildest place on earth.

And there are other places, as in the Black Cuillins of Skye, where even on a calm day, the silence of those implacable summits, the feeling of being watched by unseen eyes, is overpoweringly eerie.

The same prickle of unease can be felt among the lonely plains of Mayo, where bleached skeletons of long dead tree trunks protrude forlornly from the peat bogs, like the relics of a lost world.

Mostly, though, the face of the land responds to gentler rhythms. Its variations are more subtle, its contours softer. Connoisseur's country, often secretive, its sweet surprises walled about by hedgerow trees or lost in a fold of the hills. Then, just as you feel you are getting the measure of a particular stretch of countryside it suddenly changes pace, throws up some topographical *trompe l'oeil* that stops you in your tracks: Cheddar Gorge, the Wrekin, the Wye from Symonds Yat, the cliffs of Moher falling sheer into the sea.

Often it is a man-made feature which dominates the view; Bamburgh's hoary sea castle crouched on its rock above the Northumbrian dunes; or the Uffington White Horse, that free-flowing piece of pagan graffiti carved in the turf of the Berkshire Downs. It could hardly be otherwise in islands where man has been tilling, building, scratching and burrowing since the last Ice Age.

The much-maligned British climate has also played a vital part in the shaping of the landscape (see Chapter 9). The ice has been gone 10,000 years but, as will be explained later, the insidious forces of wind, frost and rain are still chipping away at the land, splintering the mountain summits, punching holes in the sea cliffs and carrying sediment down to the estuaries.

This temperate climate on the edge of Europe has determined the range of plant and animal habitats which can survive (see Chapter 4). Some localities within the British Isles have their own micro-climates. For instance, what could be more different than the sub-arctic tundra of the Cairngorm plateau and the Gulf Stream gardens of Tresco in the Isles of Scilly? But overall, it is a climate of moderation. The prevailing south-westerlies that sweep in from the Atlantic give a rain-washed, water-colour landscape, but it sparkles between the showers, matching its moods to the skies.

What we see when we look at the British Isles is a countryside of man's making. But to understand what is happening on the surface, to read the landscape and unravel its mysteries, you must first look to the rocks beneath.

The land underfoot is a rock hound's paradise, a complex mosaic running right through the geological spectrum (see p 18) from volcanic magmas forged in the crucible of the Earth's core (Edinburgh Castle is built on the plug of an eroded volcano which belched its last some 350 million years ago), to Ice Age moraines dumped by dying glaciers.

Fire and ice, and in between the slow laying down of the sedimentary rocks; downland chalk, red Devon sandstone; the clays and marls of the Midland vales; Pennine gritstone, cornbrash, limestone; each layer an epitaph to its own epoch, the burying ground of long dead seas and lost continents going back to the age of dinosaurs and beyond.

And all this time the part of the Earth's crust we call the British Isles was slowly drifting around the globe. Some 300 million years ago, when the coal forests were growing, it was a tropical Everglade straddling the Equator. Since then it has been nudged slowly north all the way to the present latitude, a pawn in the battle of the restless continents.

It was not a smooth ride. The land rose and fell, tilted, bent and buckled as it lurched from one geological era to the next. At one point, some 400 million years ago, the ponderous jockeying of the great land masses threw up a mountain chain that stretched across Scotland into Northern Ireland and down into Cumbria and Snowdonia. In their prime these peaks rivalled the Himalayas, but weather and the slow drip of time has ground them down to mere stumps of their former grandeur.

Even the most cursory glance at the structure of these islands reveals the scars of those cataclysmic spasms – fault, fold and fracture – in all their terrifying beauty (see p 14). It was a violent birth, subjected to unimaginable forces which

The oldest rocks in the British Isles are in north-west Scotland. Suilven (above) is a hulking 1000-million-year-old mountain of Torridonian sandstone. It sits upon even older rock, the Lewisian gneiss, which pre-dates it by a further 1800 million years

split Scotland from coast to coast, creating the Great Glen in which Loch Ness lies, and caused entire seas to vanish.

In southern Britain rocks of igneous origin are rare. They crop up as no more than a few pre-Cambrian hiccups among the Midland clays; Charnwood Forest in Leicestershire, Shropshire's Long Mynd, the switchback humps of the Malvern Hills (see p 12), each with its own distinctive micro-landscape flung up in sharp relief above the encircling vales.

But in the far south-west of Britain it is a different story. There, erosion and ancient earth movements have laid bare the cupolas of a plutonic underworld formed 290 million years ago (see illustration), and the dark glitter of granite is everywhere. From the tors of the Dartmoor skyline to the natural rock castles of the Penwith peninsula, this toughest of rocks adds its own obdurate qualities to the West Country landscape.

Granites also make distinctive contributions to the Scottish and Irish skylines. The bare summit plateaux of the Cairngorms are matched by the rolling Wicklow Mountains south of Dublin; the lonely Scottish heights of Arran are echoed by the Mountains of Mourne.

Elsewhere, the British Isles are mostly an accumulation of mud, sand and shell, a huge spoil heap stuffed with the residue of the vanished deserts, oceans and deltas in which life evolved and whose countless dead, themselves turned to stone long ago, lie buried in deep swathes from Durham to Dorset. Under the skin, much of the land is little more than a boneyard (see p 26).

Life in its earliest forms appeared in Cambrian times 570 million years ago,

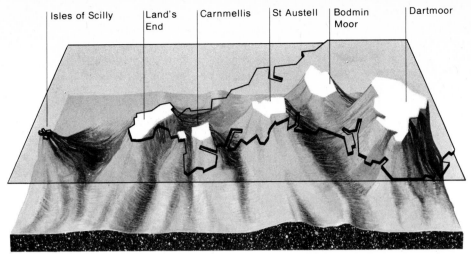

Devon and Cornwall owe much of their scenic appeal to the huge 'stocks' of granite which rise from a single elongated core, or batholith, which reaches down to unknown depths beneath the surface. The upper parts of these 'stocks' appear as rugged coastal and moorland areas like Land's End and Dartmoor. The white areas indicate the proportions of surface exposure. These granite masses were pushed up and intruded into the overlying sedimentary rocks 290 million years ago. Dartmoor is the largest of the five shown. The Isles of Scilly are the surviving remnants of a sixth

slowly evolving in the warm Ordovician and Silurian seas which then covered much of eastern Ireland, southern Scotland, Wales and the Welsh border country. Relics of those primeval seas are the Silurian coral reefs and fossil trilobites – primitive crustaceans – of Wenlock Edge and Ludlow.

In the Devonian period 400 million years ago the British Isles became a prehistoric Arizona, a sandstone furnace of desolate badlands and painted deserts whose fierce red colours still glow from the sea-cliffs and fields of Devon and the mountains above Killarney. This was the age of fishes, barbaric creatures with armour-plated snouts and bony scales, who evolved in warm lagoons and left their fossil remains in the sandstone beds of the Caithness cliffs.

In time the deserts were drowned by invading seas which laid down the limestone carcass of the Pennines, added the gaunt Millstone Grits of the High Peak and gave rise to the Coal Measures, fossil relics of the world's first forests. These were the Carboniferous rocks, whose limestones form almost two-thirds of Ireland's present surface, including the rocky wilderness of the Burren in County Clare.

Then followed the Mesozoic era, the day of the dinosaur, when fierce ichthyosaurs surged through Britain's tropical seas, and the primitive life forms which had crawled from the Devonian ooze now walked the earth in the shape of giant reptiles.

The ichthyosaurs left their skeletons, entombed among myriads of coiled ammonite shells in the crumbling Blue Lias clays of Lyme Regis, and the dinosaurs

their footprints embedded in the Purbeck ledges. But the richest treasure of the epoch was the great stripe of Jurassic limestone that runs from Dorset through the Cotswolds and on up to Yorkshire. This is the stone, sometimes silvery grey, sometimes weathered to a deep honeygold, whose mellow beauty embellishes a long line of towns from Chipping Campden to Stamford.

During the final 60 million years of Mesozoic time, further subsidence led to deep inroads of the Cretaceous seas, their waters teeming with tiny marine organisms whose shelly skeletons fell like an endless snowstorm to build the English chalklands.

Where they fell they buried other corpses, including shoals of primitive sponges which, in the fullness of time became the flint nodules from which early man would fashion his tools.

The Tertiary era, which had tiptoed in after the Cretaceous to the whisper of drifting silt, went out to the apocalyptic crunch of the 'Alpine Storm', the global shudder which lasted 20 million years and which created the Alps and raised a crumpled England from the waves.

By now another remarkable change had taken place. Gone at last were the great reptiles, the primitive tree-ferns and giant horsetails of the coal forests. In their place came plants and animals more closely related to the flora and fauna of today.

In Northern Ireland and Western Scotland volcanoes were still pouring out lava which contracted as it cooled, forming in places the strange pencil columns of the Giant's Causeway and Fingal's Cave. But elsewhere Britain was becom-

ing more docile in old age. London was laying down the clays from which so many of her houses would be dug; and sabre-toothed tigers roamed the Home Counties.

The two or three million years of the Pleistocene period, which ended only 10,000 years ago, form the last chapter in the natural shaping of the British Isles, and in many ways it is the most important.

This was the period during which these islands lay deep frozen in the grip of the Great Ice Age which made several forays far into Western Europe. Glaciers gouged out the Lakeland dales and scalloped cwms and corries from the summits of Snowdon and Helvellyn; ice sheets disgorged their debris in vast outpourings of sands and gravels like those which now cover parts of Cheshire and the Norfolk Breckland (see p 15).

The power of the ice planed smooth the mountainsides, its meltwaters fed a 240ft (73m) high Niagara in Yorkshire where Malham Cove's grey cliffs now rise, and its presence diverted the Thames, which used to flow across East Anglia.

This, then, was the finishing touch, nature's final polish to the landscape we see today. When the ice retreated for the last time, the climate improved. The sealevel rose, creating the drowned *rias* or river valleys of Milford Haven, the Fal and Bantry Bay, and forests spread north as if to blot out the bleak memory of the post-glacial permafrost. And in the wake of the woods, as we shall see in Chapter 2, came man.

Forging of a landscape.
Six hundred million years to make it

The Malvern Hills are one of the few places in the British Isles where much of the story of landscape can be seen in a single, explicit 'georama'. The view looking south-south-eastwards from Worcestershire Beacon (1394ft, 425m), highest point on the hump-backed crest line of the Malverns, takes the eye over the middle reaches of the River Severn and the Vale of Gloucester to the distant limestone escarpment of the Cotswolds.

To the east, fertile and fruitful, lie the Vales of Worcester and Evesham and the north-eastern extension of the escarpment with its isolated outlying hills; to the north the red rocks and soils of the Midland Plain; and to the west a swathe of undulating country which runs beyond Hereford to the hills of Wales.

From this one point the viewer, turn-

Millstone grit country. The strange shapes of Yorkshire's Brimham Rocks weathered by rain and frost into a landscape which suggests an alien world

ing full circle, sees scenery which is based on rocks of almost every geological period, except for the chalk and a few younger formations; which has been subjected to the spasms and turbulence of huge earth movements; and which has been fashioned by the unremitting work of natural forces. All this represents a time span of 540 million years, 90 per cent of the Earth history of southern Britain.

Here the rich, rolling farmlands of the English Midlands, with neatly hedged fields and water-threaded meadows, epitomise the landscapes of lowland Britain. Rivers like the Severn have, over the past few million years, gradually etched the gently tilted land surface into a series of scarps and vales. At the same time the red sandstones and clays of the Midlands have been slowly exposed and lowered by the constant incision of running water.

The same forces of erosion and weathering have caused the Cotswold escarpment to retreat slowly south-eastwards, leaving behind the outlier (see opposite) of Bredon Hill to show something of its former extent.

In contrast to these lowlands the Malvern Hills rise dramatically from the Midland Plain, a rugged exposure of Britain's primeval skeleton which was once blanketed by younger rocks. This narrow line of hills, running north to south, possessed of a complicated geology of its own and made from ancient and harder rocks, belongs to the oldest of the great geological ages, the Pre-Cambrian.

The Malverns are a bony massif of ancient lavas and granite-like materials which protrudes through layers of younger calcareous muds, sands and clays laid down in the tranquil seas which once covered the country.

These venerable foundation stones of basement Britain were forged in the fires of early Earth over 600 million years ago.

The Malvern Hills. Here older rocks of basement Britain protrude through the lowland floor. Snow on the summits is a reminder that these are the first foothills of the mountain land

Chalk country. The rounded, rolling green of Wiltshire downland with a farm set in a sheltering fold in the hill and woods marching the crest above

Since then they have been crushed, folded and faulted by gigantic earth movements which punctuated the quieter episodes when sedimentary layers were gently accumulating.

Like their Welsh, Scottish and Irish counterparts, the Malverns are mere shadows of their former selves; no more than stumps of an ancient mountain chain worn down by the same forces – water, sun, wind and ice – which are still inexorably at work, fashioning the scenery of the British Isles.

Yet still they stand, by man's time scale permanent and enduring, geological milestones upon the Midland Plain,

providing a scenic boundary between lowland and highland Britain – the first foothills of the mountain land.

The hill that was left behind. Remnant of the Cotswold scarp

Bredon Hill (961ft, 293m), to the north of the A435 road between Evesham and Tewkesbury, is an outlier of the main Cotswold escarpment. An outlier is a mass of rock separated from its main outcrop, the intervening strata having been destroyed by weathering and stream erosion (see illustration below).

The scarp summit is of hard limestone. Beneath are softer clays which are worn

away more rapidly. Rain, and spring water rising along the junction of the two rocks carries the clay downhill.

This action undercuts the limestone to form a steep scarp slope. As it is undermined portions slip down and are gradually broken up. The process is repeated unceasingly, but faster in some places than others, to give an uneven scarp line. As new surfaces are attacked the scarp edge retreats, slowly and irregularly.

The Bredon bastion, isolated from the main escarpment several million years ago, is now being reduced more rapidly as it is assaulted on all sides by the forces of erosion. One day it will disappear.

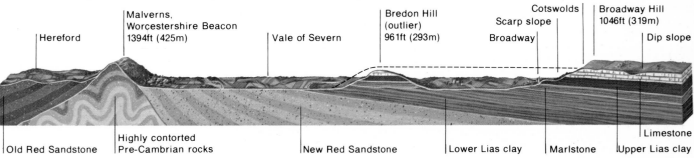

This stretch of countryside has been in the making for 540 million years, a span of geological time which nearly covers the complete Earth history of southern Britain. The scenery, based on rocks of almost every geological

age, has been shaped by natural forces. Thus Bredon Hill is an isolated remnant of the Cotswold Scarp which has retreated (marked by dotted line) before the continuous onslaught of rain and stream erosion

The land in spasm. How violent upheaval changed the terrain

The Great Glen slashes through the highlands of Scotland for almost a hundred miles (160km) from Inverness to the island of Lismore near Oban. It is one of the most remarkable topographical boundaries in the British Isles. To one side are the North-West Highlands, to the other the Grampians. Within it, between Loch Linnhe and the Moray Firth, runs a chain of lochs – long, straight and deep. One is Loch Ness.

The Glen's scenery is outstanding, its mysteries compelling. Whatever it is which is supposed to lurk in the depths of Loch Ness has excited the interest of investigators for years. Geologists, however, are trying to unravel a different mystery. The Great Glen (also known as Glen Mor and the Great Glen of Albyn) is a major landscape feature which is the product of one of those periods in the geological past when scenery changed dramatically in relatively short spans of time. The gigantic fractures which have cracked the rocks of the British Isles are legacies of these great periods of flux. Of these fractures, or faults, the Great Glen is the most notable.

How was it formed? Periodically the world's tectonic plates shift position (see map below). The plates are major structural elements of the Earth's crust. They are like enormous floes of pack-ice which move in relation to each other.

Sometimes, as they shift, they collide head on. Such collisions which cause considerable crumpling or folding of the rocks are the very stuff of mountain building. At other times the plates grind slowly past each other along so-called tear, or wrench faults. The Great Glen is the best example in the British Isles of this sort of large scale lateral movement (see opposite). In this instance it began during an earlier phase of plate tectonics, some 350 million years ago, when the plate boundaries were quite different (see map below).

How much movement there has been, or even in what direction, is a matter of argument. The most likely case is that the North-West Highlands have been moving slowly south-westwards relative to the Grampians for the past 350 million years. In that time they have travelled about 65 miles (104km). Then, of course, the shape of Scotland was totally different to what it is today, and the country was part of a continent which included Greenland and Newfoundland. So the idea of Inverness once sitting somewhere near to where Wick is now may be amusing but is misleading. An even larger movement, up to 200 miles (320km), has been suggested by some authorities. Others argue a movement of 60-odd miles (100km) in the opposite direction, north-eastwards. Whatever the answer, the line of the fault is now lost beneath a chain of lochs.

The largest faults in the British Isles are found in Scotland. So are all the main types of fault which geologists identify. Indeed, it was here that one of these types was first discovered. The Moine Thrust in the North-West Highlands follows a line from Skye to Loch Eriboll on the north coast. This line marks the north-west edge of a huge block of the Earth's crust which was driven bodily over another, along an oblique plane of sliding called a thrust fault (see opposite).

To the west of the Moine Thrust is the oldest landscape in the British Isles where mountains of sandstone rise abruptly from a lake-dotted, ice-scoured basement of Lewisian gneiss. To the east is a landscape of hills and plateaux built upon Moinian rocks, dark coloured, flaky schists produced by the action of intense heat and pressure on sands and muds.

Here, a century ago, geologists were puzzled because the normal order in which beds of rock appear, lying in sequence according to their age, with the oldest at the bottom and the most recently formed at the top, was reversed. It was the search for an answer to this apparent anomaly which led to the discovery and understanding of the thrust fault, one of the fundamental principles of structural geology. The complexities of this can be seen and more easily understood at the Nature Conservancy Council's Knockan Cliff Geological Trail between Ullapool and Inchnadamph.

Farther south, near Stirling, another major Scottish fracture, the Ochil Fault, has brought tough, resistant volcanic lavas hard up against relatively soft rocks. This happened when there was a large displacement, or downthrow, of rocks towards the south which left a cliff-like formation. This has been accentuated by erosion and weathering, the softer rocks being worn away at a faster rate than the harder ones. The result is the fault line escarpment of the Ochil Hills which runs from Blairlogie eastwards to beyond Dollar. It extends for some 20 miles (30 km) and viewed from the south appears as a straight mountain-front rising steeply from the Clackmannan plain. This type of fracture is described as a normal fault (see illustration opposite).

Earth movements such as these are not completed. Minor earth tremors still occur along the Great Glen and Ochil Faults. In the last 200 years sixty have been recorded along the Great Glen.

In other parts of the British Isles the rocks, instead of fracturing, have crumpled under pressure. The main forms of this crumpling, or folding, are shown on the opposite page. There have been three

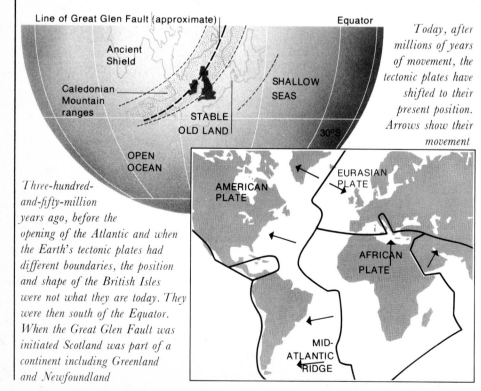

Line of Great Glen Fault (approximate)

Equator

Ancient Shield

Caledonian Mountain ranges

STABLE OLD LAND

OPEN OCEAN

SHALLOW SEAS

30°S

AMERICAN PLATE

EURASIAN PLATE

AFRICAN PLATE

MID-ATLANTIC RIDGE

Three-hundred-and-fifty-million years ago, before the opening of the Atlantic and when the Earth's tectonic plates had different boundaries, the position and shape of the British Isles were not what they are today. They were then south of the Equator. When the Great Glen Fault was initiated Scotland was part of a continent including Greenland and Newfoundland

Today, after millions of years of movement, the tectonic plates have shifted to their present position. Arrows show their movement

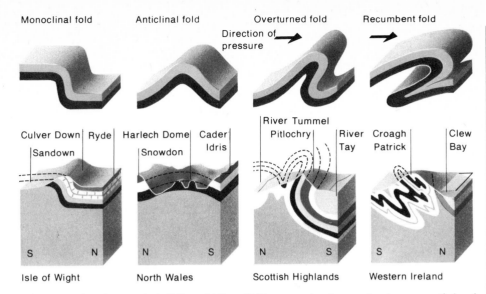

Monoclinal fold   Anticlinal fold   Overturned fold   Recumbent fold

Direction of pressure

Culver Down | Ryde   Harlech Dome | Cader Idris   River Tummel / Pitlochry | River Tay   Croagh Patrick | Clew Bay

Sandown   Snowdon

S   N   N   S   N   S   S   N

Isle of Wight   North Wales   Scottish Highlands   Western Ireland

The mechanics of mountain building: folding. Folds occur when layers of rock are crumpled and buckled into a series of wave-like structures. They are usually produced by horizontal compression and result in a variety of forms which influence scenery. The simple syncline, where rock layers are folded downwards, is not illustrated. The last period of British Folding was 90 million years ago

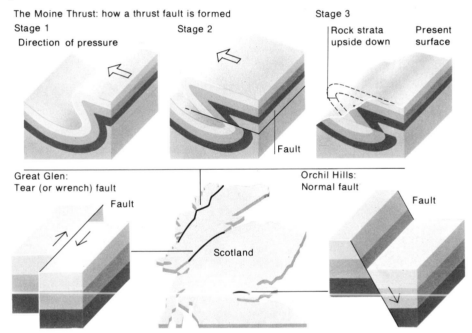

The Moine Thrust: how a thrust fault is formed

Stage 1   Stage 2   Stage 3

Direction of pressure   Rock strata upside down   Present surface

Fault

Great Glen: Tear (or wrench) fault   Orchil Hills: Normal fault

Fault   Fault

Scotland

The mechanics of mountain building: faulting. Faults are fractures produced by pressure and tension in the Earth's crust which cause rocks to be displaced. They have a marked influence on landscape. Scotland's Moine Fault, Great Glen and Ochil Hills are examples of three different types of fault

major episodes of this. Episode one, 400 million years ago, formed the fold mountains of Scotland (the Grampians and Southern Uplands), the Lake District, North Wales and Northern Ireland.

Episode two, 300 million years ago, created the spectacular folding of Munster in Southern Ireland, the tight folds of Pembrokeshire and South-West England and those of the Pennines.

Episode three, a mere 30 million years ago, represented the outer ripples of the maelstrom which threw up the European Alps and also folded the sedimentary rocks of Dorset and stood the chalk and its neighbouring rocks on end in the Isle of Wight.

Scotland's Great Glen. A 100-mile-long (160km) fault which has made one of the most dramatic boundaries in the British Isles

The mighty power of ice. A major force in moulding scenery

On the seashore at Porthleven, Cornwall, stands a block of rock. It is estimated to weigh 60 tons. How it came to be there is a geological puzzle. For it is entirely foreign to its surroundings, unlike any other rocks in the vicinity. Geologists think it may have originated from Scotland since it is a form of very ancient material called gneiss which is common to the North-West Highlands and the Hebrides.

Only ice sheets, with their immense power, seem to have the capability to have transported it to Cornwall's Channel coast. In successive ice ages they did move enormous quantities of material from the highlands to the lowlands. Ice carried rocks from North Wales to Birmingham and from Scandinavia to East Anglia and Yorkshire. Boulders and pebbles from Cumbria's Shap Granite have been found far to the south and east in lowland boulder clays and gravels. It has even been suggested that the famous blue stones of Stonehenge were transported from Pembrokeshire, not by men, but by ice sheets!

These alien rocks, or erratics as geologists call them, are useful in helping map the routes of the ice sheets. The examples mentioned are located in areas which were within the southern limits of the ice. Porthleven, however, lies south of the generally accepted line of the great glaciations (see map overleaf).

How then did its large erratic rock, the Giant's Block, get there? The most likely explanation is that it was 'rafted' there on a floating iceberg and then dumped as the iceberg melted. Other erratics along the Channel coast are thought to have been transported in the same way. Ice rafting is a process common in higher latitudes and can be seen happening in Canada's Gulf of St Lawrence today.

In the British Isles the legacy of the Ice Age, which lasted, with warmer interruptions, for two million years, is seen almost everywhere. The rugged magnificence of highland scenery, the smooth lowland spreads of clays, gravels and sands and even some features of chalk downland can be explained in terms of this cold period. Although the last ice caps disappeared 10,000 years ago, this in geological time is only yesterday.

To understand the Ice Age imagine British winters, such as that of 1962–63 or 1978–79, becoming commonplace

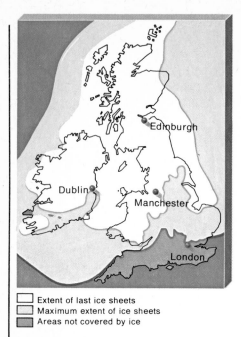

The British Isles under ice. In the last 2½ million years there have been periods of intense arctic cold when glaciers formed in the mountains, later coalesced and spread out, across the lowlands. The map shows how the earliest glaciations reached farthest south. The ice sheets also filled the basins of the Irish and North Seas. It was over 3000ft (914m) thick

Extent of last ice sheets
Maximum extent of ice sheets
Areas not covered by ice

and even more prolonged. Eventually the heavy snowfalls survive the shorter, cooler summers. Glaciers begin to form in the Scottish, Welsh and Irish mountains. Ultimately these combine to form ice sheets completely burying even the highest mountain tops (as in Greenland today). They then surge outwards into the British and Irish lowlands.

Ireland had two such ice caps, a large one in the north and a smaller one centred on the mountains of Kerry and Cork, but their coalescence just failed to submerge the highest peaks of the Dingle Peninsula and the Galty Mountains.

All Scotland and Wales disappeared as ice lobes reached as far south as the Thames, the Bristol Channel and the Isles of Scilly. In front of the ice sheets, in unglaciated southern England, a severe climate prevailed, similar to that of Canada's modern Arctic. For most of the year the ground was frozen and snow covered, even in summer still frozen just beneath the surface.

In what is now Devon and Cornwall frost action helped fashion the distinctive moorland tors. These granite rocks were sharpened by frost splitting them along their joints; and the fallen blocks, or clitters, were moved down the gentle slopes by solifluxion, a movement which occurs with the continuous freezing and thawing of the ground.

The seasonal surface melting of the frozen terrain sent surface water coursing over the barren landscape. This was swollen by the meltwaters of nearby ice sheets and streams were able to flow across the frozen subsoil of the formerly permeable chalk. The chalk downlands were therefore quite drastically modified. Most of the dry valleys of the chalklands are thought to have been formed in this way.

The main river valleys were quickly filled with a detritus of chalky mud, sands and gravels, which was later carved by rivers into river terraces such

as those of the Thames and the River Severn.

Elsewhere the glacial meltwaters either left spreads of sandy gravel in places such as Thetford Chase in Norfolk or they carved out gorges across hill barriers. Of these the Ironbridge Gorge in Shropshire, now followed by the River Severn, is the most spectacular although the streamless Valley of the Rocks, near Lynton, North Devon, and winding Newtondale on the North Yorkshire Moors are also noteworthy.

In Ireland the dumping ground of the ice sheets was the Central Plain where spreads of boulder clay, sand and gravel totally buried the solid rocks. These, in turn, have been mantled by post-glacial peat bogs.

The effects of the Ice Age are more marked in Ireland than in Britain, so much so that Irish terminology has been adopted internationally to describe certain glacial landforms, such as eskers and drumlins.

The first are sinuous gravelly ridges marking the former courses of glacial streams which ran in tunnels beneath the ice. The second are low, whale-backed

U-shaped glacial trough
Horn peak
Pinnacle ridge (Arête)
Corrie moraine
Corrie lake
Hanging valley
Corrie
Truncated spurs
Perched blocks

How ice shapes the land surface. At the peak of the last Ice Age, 50,000 to 30,000 years ago, a glacier bulldozed down a highland valley (see inset) carving out a U-shaped trough. When the ice melted it left behind this and other distinctive features of glacial erosion. Today ice and frost are still at work in winter cutting back the corries and sharpening the high ridges

At the lower end of Snowdonia's Llyn Ogwen (above) the waters of the lake escape down a high cliff where the Nant Ffrancon pass makes a sharp bend. Beyond is a typical glaciated valley, U-shaped, with truncated spurs and ice-smoothed rocks. Some have ice scratch marks, like those shown (top left) from the Lake District. Here the huge Bowder Stone (above left) was carried down valley by ice

hills of boulder clay, fluted by the over-riding ice and likened to a basket of eggs. There are superb examples of these in the Central Plain, and in Antrim and Armagh. Drumlins can also be seen in north Anglesey, Cumbria's Vale of Eden and in the Tweed Valley.

At the close of the Ice Age, glaciers in the mountains of Scotland, Ireland, Wales and the Lake District bulldozed remorselessly from their rocky, arm-chair-shaped hollows, known as cor-ries or cwms, into the adjoining valleys (see illustration). The erosive power of these ice streams is exemplified by the ice-polished and scratched rocks of many Scottish glens and the overdeepened U-shaped troughs of Cumbria's Langdale, Snowdonia's Nant Ffrancon and

Ireland's Glendalough.

In the Llanberis Pass in North Wales truncated spurs – spurs which have been partly shaved off by the glacier as it moved down the valley – testify to the amount of rock that has been removed. Here, too, perched blocks, erratics which have been left in an exposed position, teeter on the edge of the abyss. The height from the floor of the pass to their precarious resting place shows how thick the ice was.

Some large blocks, such as the Bowder Stone on the lower slopes of the fell overlooking the entrance to Borrowdale in the Lake District, were moved far down the valleys. This block is estimated to weigh nearly 2,000 tons.

Sometimes these blocks are associated with piles of hummocky, glacial 'rubbish' termed moraines. These mark the termi-nation or recessional stages of a valley glacier.

The majority of moraines, however, are found high up in the corries. They are remnants of the very last cold phase 10,000 years ago and frequently these bouldery ridges impound circular lakes beneath the rocky headwalls of the

corrie. Snowdonia's Llyn Idwal and Cumbria's Stickle Tarn are among the best known.

Other waters occupy the long, gla-cially overdeepened hollows of the neigh-bouring valleys. Cumbria's lakes, Scotland's numerous lochs, especially Skye's Loch Coruisk and Loch Avon in the Cairngorms, and the renowned Lakes of Killarney are outstanding examples.

On the mountain tops the work of frost is everywhere: in the splintered summits, the ever-growing cliff-foot screes and the knife-edged ridges or arêtes. When the headwalls of adjoining corries retreat, eaten back by glacial plucking, the pul-ling away of rock by moving ice, the intervening ridges are narrowed or even breached. The pinnacle ridges of The Cuillins, the Crib Goch ridge of Snowdon and Helvellyn's Striding Edge testify to the sharpness of these almost Alpine landforms. Although most of the frost shattering took place in the Ice Age the highest summits in the British Isles still experience an Alpine climate, so that plateau tops like the Cairngorms are mantled with freshly broken rock waste.

Rocks of the British Isles

How they were formed

The look of a piece of landscape is determined largely by the nature of the rocks beneath it. In the British Isles the variety of scenery reflects the presence of rocks of almost every age in the Earth's history. Geologically, these islands are almost a museum model.

The three main groups of rocks are all present. The igneous rocks are formed from molten rock or magma brought up from deep below the Earth's surface. When magma cools slowly beneath the surface it forms rocks with large crystals such as granite. When it cools rapidly on the surface – as, for example, volcanic lava – it forms finely crystalline rocks such as basalt.

The sedimentary rocks have their beginnings in the weathering or breaking down of the other rocks by frost, rain, sun, wind and chemical processes. The weathered material is transported by water and deposited in rivers, lakes and the sea. As these loose sediments are cemented together by mineral matter, or are compressed by the pressure of overlying material, sedimentary rocks are formed. Some like coal and limestone are the remains of once living organisms. Others form from chemicals dissolved in water. Shales and sandstones are other examples of sedimentary rocks. All these rocks are layered.

Metamorphic rocks are those igneous or sedimentary rocks which have been changed from their original form by heat, pressure and chemical action. This happens most commonly when molten magma is intruded into layers of sedimentary rocks. Limestone, for example, becomes marble. Shale is compacted into slate.

How to recognise rocks
Sedimentary

Oolitic limestone. This is a build-up of small calcareous spheres like fish roe, cemented together. Its creamy colour and durability has led to its popularity as an English building stone.

Chalk. Probably the best known of all rocks, and the material which makes up the White Cliffs of Dover. It is a pure form of limestone. Dazzling white when freshly exposed. Fine grained and permeable. Often has flints and fossils.

Sandstone. Composed of small rounded glassy quartz granules plus some reddish feldspar minerals cemented together. The commonest red and brown sandstones are stained by iron oxides but there are white and grey varieties.

Conglomerate. Composed of rounded pebbles derived from all rock types in a fine grained matrix of sand or silt cemented by silica or calcite. These consolidated pebble or gravel beds are formed mainly along sea and lake shores.

Shale. A fine-grained rock of silty or muddy particles, characterised by the ease with which it splits along its thin bedding planes. In section it appears like the pages of a closed book.

Journeys through geological time

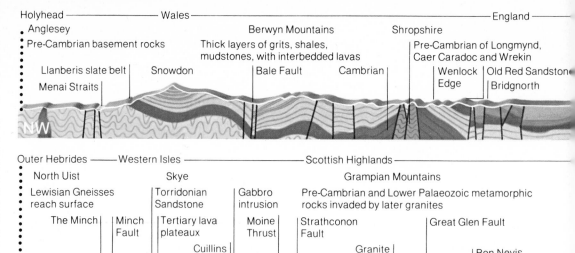

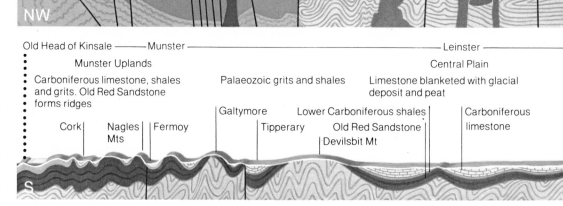

Igneous

Basalt. This is a black fine-grained rock, created by the solidification of a former lava. Often weathers into hexagonal columns, as at the Giant's Causeway and Fingal's Cave.

Rhyolite. Is a yellowish-buff coloured, fine grained lava. This rock is found especially in Snowdonia.

Granite. The most common igneous rock. Distinguished by its large crystalline grains of mica, quartz and feldspar. Formed at very great depths and exposed only in the highlands of Britain and Ireland and as Dartmoor's tors.

Metamorphic

Mica Schist. Rocks which have silvery or bronze flakes of mica are found in the north-west of Scotland and western Ireland. They split easily but unlike slates their splitting surfaces are often irregular not flat.

Slate. A stone produced by metamorphism of shales and mudstones. Can be black or shades of blue, green, brown or buff. Easily splits into slabs and very thin sheets, but unlike a shale it splits obliquely across the bedding planes.

Gneiss. Rocks which have undergone considerable change by heat and pressure. Is often striped into black and white or black and red crystalline layers which sometimes occur draped around glassy aggregates or 'eyes' of quartz.

Quartzite. Occurs when great pressure closes up the pore spaces of a sandstone. It thus becomes very hard and because of its almost 100% silica is usually white or light-coloured and medium grained.

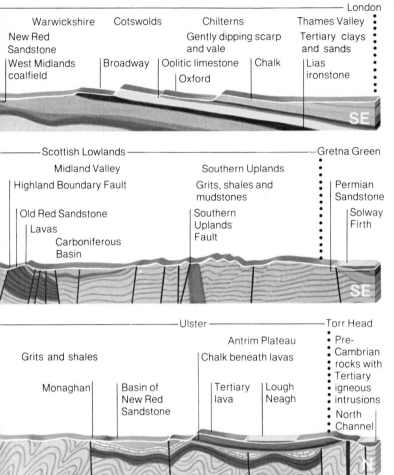

Journey 1. London–Holyhead.

Following this 230 mile (370km) line the traveller cuts across the grain of the country (see geological map below). The cross-section shows how after leaving the young clays and sands of the London Basin the surface rocks get progressively older north-westwards until the ancient metamorphics of Anglesey are reached. In the south, limestone scarp and clay vale succeed each other as far as the red sandstone plain of The Midlands. The ancient rocks of Shropshire break up the orderly progression but beyond the Border, Welsh grits and mudstones form a rolling, dissected plateau which rises gently to the high peaks of Snowdonia.

Journey 2. Gretna Green–Outer Hebrides.

Here the line, 260 miles (418km) long, (see map) crosses from one of Scotland's youngest rocks – the New Red Sandstone of the Solway – to Britain's oldest rocks, the Lewisian gneiss of the Outer Hebrides. In between lie the rolling hills of the Southern Uplands, the coalfields and the sandstones and limestones of the Central Valley, the gentler scenery of which is punctuated by scarps of tougher, interbedded lavas. To the north lie the incomparable Highlands where ice has worked on a variety of old igneous and metamorphic rocks to create a landscape of deep glens and rugged mountains. Skye's mountains and plateaux are built from much younger igneous rocks.

Journey 3. Old Head of Kinsale–Torr Head.

From south to north the line of the section (see map) is 270 miles (434km). The well folded sandstones and limestones of southern Ireland have been greatly denuded – enough to uncover the underlying Silurian grits and shales which form some of Ireland's highest mountains. Lying to the north the gently folded Carboniferous limestone, with its blanket of glacial drift and peat, creates the featureless, lake-dotted Central Plain which rises northwards to the older hill country of Northern Ireland. Here some younger clays, sandstones and even chalk occur but they have been almost swamped by thick basalt lava flows – now forming the Antrim Plateau in the central hollow of which is Lough Neagh.

Geological map of British Isles. This shows sedimentary rocks classified according to their age of deposition and igneous rocks according to their mode of origin. The map is simplified. At this scale it is not possible to show the detail which appears in the geological sections above. This is why the colour coding on it is different to that used in the sections. The lines on the map correspond to the sections. Following these lines on the ground, even approximately, takes the traveller on three incredible journeys through geological time. The figures indicate age in millions of years.

Sedimentary rocks
Cenozoic
Tertiary and marine Pleistocene. Mainly clays and sands. Glacial drift not shown .... up to 65

Mesozoic
Cretaceous. Mainly chalk, clays and sands 65–140

Jurassic. Mainly limestones and clays 140–195

Triassic. Marls, sandstones and conglomerates 195–230

Palaeozoic
Permian. Mainly magnesian limestones, marls and sandstones 230–280

Carboniferous. Limestones, sandstones, shales and coal seams 280–345

Devonian. Sandstones, shales, conglomerates (Old Red Standstone); slates and limestones.. 345–395
Silurian. Shales, mudstones, greywacke, limestones 395–445

Ordovician. Mainly shales and mudstones; limestone in Scotland 445–510

Cambrian. Mainly shales, slate and sandstones; limestone in Scotland 510–570

Upper Proterozoic
Late Pre-Cambrian. Mainly sandstones, conglomerates and siltstones 600–1000

Metamorphic rocks
Lower Palaeozoic and Proterozoic. Mainly schists and gneisses 500–1000

Early Pre-Cambrian (Lewisian). Mainly gneisses 1500–3000

Igneous rocks
Intrusive. Mainly granite, gabbro and dolerite } .... { Rocks of
Volcanic. Mainly basalt, rhyolite, andesite and tuffs } .... { all ages

A pattern of rivers. Their waters lend beauty to the land

The University of Keele in North Staffordshire, is both a well of learning and a watershed. Perched at 600ft (183m) on its sandstone ridge, it is in a remarkable location on one of England's major drainage divides (see map below).

Water from a bucket emptied upon its campus will have as its final destination the sea. But which sea? For Keele sits at the hub of three great river systems. Northwards the streams drain towards the River Mersey and thence to the Irish Sea; the south-east flowing streams are the headwaters of the River Trent which empties into the North Sea; and to the south-west they are part of the River Severn system which carries water to the Bristol Channel.

These three great rivers, like others in the British Isles, are part of a drainage pattern which is the product of a long and complex evolution. No less important to the overall pattern are other substantial rivers: the Thames, the longest river wholly in England; Fenland's Witham, Welland, Nene and Great Ouse, a run of rivers which drain one of the most singular of landscapes; the Tyne, Tees and Wear, the flows of which are soon to be regulated by man with the 2,700 acre reservoir of the Kielder Water Scheme in the North Tyne Valley; Scotland's Forth, Tay, Clyde and fast flowing Spey; and the Shannon which drains a vast tract of Ireland.

There is no sensible answer to how old these rivers are. For throughout the geological history of the British Isles rivers have existed whenever there was land. Some flow today following a pattern which was broadly set millions of years ago. Others follow courses the carving of which can be counted in mere thousands of years. The latter only flow where they do because of the Ice Age; and the sweeps and curves they follow on their inevitable downhill journey to the sea may bear little relation to the paths they took before the ice sheets over-

whelmed their courses.

The Thames, although there is argument about it, is thought to have followed a more northerly course across Essex and Suffolk than it does today. At one time, perhaps, its mouth was at the Wash; at another where the estuary of the River Blackwater is now. But the ice sheets and their debris pushed it south, deflecting it to its present course.

The Severn also has had a dramatic and permanent change of route. It used to flow northwards from near Shrewsbury, possibly taking the Dee as a tributary, and emptying into the Irish Sea where the Dee estuary is now.

Then, during one of the Ice Age's recessional phases when the ice sheets retreated northwards they uncovered a rocky ridge near to Shropshire's Wrekin. The melt waters, trapped between ice and ridge, were unable to escape. A lake formed and its level rose until it overflowed, cutting through the ridge to form the Ironbridge Gorge, the waters moving southwards to the Bristol Channel. Eventually the lake was emptied but the Severn never regained its previous course. For now it was blocked by mounds of debris left by the ice sheets.

These are two dramatic instances of Ice Age river diversion. There were many changes to river scenery in that period which were only superficial. Often meltwater channels were cut beneath or alongside the ice. Temporary lakes formed, grew in depth and made their own overflow channels. Many of these channels are now dry. The streams which trickle through them are so small that they are obviously incapable of having carved out the wide deep valleys in which they flow. Newtondale in North Yorkshire is an example.

In fact most of the major scenic features of England and Wales, rivers included, have developed in the last 26 million years since Miocene times. The rivers then were beginning to adopt the lines they occupy at present. The Miocene marked the climax of the Alpine storm which had great influence

on Britain, among other things creating the newly formed trough which is now known as the London Basin. Into this the drainage of the lower Thames was collected. It is also thought to have given the Lake District the domed form on which its rivers were developed, the very earliest stages in the making of a marked radial drainage pattern. Much, much later Wordsworth, in his 'Description of the Scenery of the Lakes', was to write of a number of valleys diverging 'like spokes from the nave of a wheel'.

Before the onset of the Ice Age, many coastal areas which had been cut into wide, level platforms by both rivers and the sea, were uplifted. This gave the rivers which flowed across them a new lease of life enabling them once more to cut down, incising new and deeper valleys. This rejuvenation created many gorge-like valleys and meanders like those on the River Wye.

It has given the Wye outstanding scenic appeal. The river swings in big curves up to four miles in amplitude, and in several it almost forms a complete loop, as at Symond's Yat and the great turn under Wynd Cliff, near Chepstow. Here the river's progress to the sea is through a narrow, steep-sided gorge.

The Wye works to shape the landscape in its own particular way. Equally the character of the river itself, its vigour and power, depends upon the kind of land surface across which it flows. The Wye is a river which belongs to the western hills and mountains, where the coastal plains, unlike those of the south and east, are narrow or missing altogether. Rivers and streams are fast flowing, often short, plunging directly into the sea.

In most of eastern, lowland Britain very broad plains intervene between the hills and the sea. Rivers now seem larger but lazier, gliding through broad valleys and far-spreading flood plains, giving a very different texture to the landscape. Nowhere is this more apparent than in the vast shallow basin of the Fenlands.

Here the Fenland rivers concentrate an enormous volume of fresh water; and man since Roman times has been trying to temper its worst excesses with large and impressive drainage schemes. The soil, the economy and the history of Fenland stem from one salient, natural phenomenon – an excess of water. As Daniel Defoe put it: 'All the water of the middle part of England which does not run into the Thames or Trent comes down into these fens'.

It is a happy benefit that a river's work

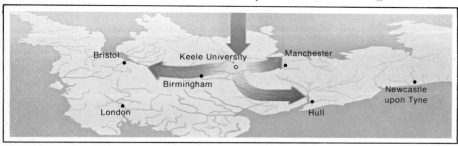

Where the water flows. One of England's great drainage divides is centred on Keele University, North Staffordshire, which is at the hub of three major river systems

Running water enriches the green of meadow and woodland on the Wye (above) and at Lower Slaughter in the Cotswolds (below left) where bridge and buildings are of local stone. At High Force (below right) the peaty waters of the Tees foam against dark blue-grey Whin Sill rock

enhances and nourishes the visual appeal of the landscape. Constable painting by the Stour understood this well. The opportunities for paint and canvas are rich and varied: the Thames making its spectacular cut through the hills at Goring Gap, the only river crossing a six-mile wide (9.6km) belt of waterless chalk; the coalescence at Dartmeet of the East and West rivers to make one incomparable Dart; the surprise of a tiny tributary of Scotland's river Dee called

Vat Burn cutting a deep gorge and gigantic circular pothole 50ft (15m) into solid granite.

History, of course, is much lubricated by rivers. Their banks have served as settlement sites, their running waters as power for mills, their broad expanses as barriers and boundaries.

Yet their greatest work is that which springs from their power as natural forces. There is no better example than the valley of the Severn seen from the

Cotswolds or the Malverns.

When the Severn started the work, which lasted millions of years, of making this great vale it is unlikely that much of a depression existed. Now the immensity of the valley is so impressive that it is hard to believe that it and its tributaries have been able to carry away the vast amount of material which once filled it. It is a panorama which helps one grasp the astonishing power of rivers in shaping the land.

How running water shapes the countryside

Despite its apparent tranquillity and sense of permanence the scenery of the British Isles is constantly changing. The clatter of a pebble bouncing along a river bed is a reminder of this dynamic quality of landscape. Indeed, it is running water, among all the agents engaged in shaping scenery, which is the most effective. It whittles away mountains and hills and carries away the loosened material.

Thus a river is a powerful work-horse – and the work it does is demonstrated by these powers of erosion, transport and deposition. The load of transported material it carries, either by rolling or bouncing, as in the case of the pebble, or as fine particles suspended in the water, depends on its energy.

In its upper course a river is engaged primarily in erosion. In these steep upper gradients boulders, cobbles and pebbles are quickly dumped, to be moved again only in times of flood. But the fine sands and clays stay with the river longer, constantly being carried downstream to the lowlands, or swept out to sea.

Therefore it is easy to distinguish between the cascading clear waters of the boulder-strewn Scottish, Welsh and Cumbrian streams and the slow, muddy waters of the Thames in London.

Because of the geological diversity of the British Isles, rivers rarely complete their journeys without encountering rock strata of differing hardness. So instead of a theoretical smooth curve a river's long profile – what its slope looks like in section from source to sea – is really a succession of gentle reaches interspersed with rapids or even falls.

Many of these steps occur where the river flows over a band of hard rock such as that which creates the High Force falls in Upper Teesdale. Some waterfalls occur at fault-lines. The Clyde Falls and the Pennine stream of Gordale Scar are two of the finest examples.

In the mountains the majority of waterfalls result from the severe over-deepening of the main trunk valleys by ice. This leaves subsidiary streams to plummet from the high, hanging tributary valleys. Lodore Falls in the Lake District is a good example and so is the Powerscourt Fall, near Dublin.

The rivers of the limestone and chalk-lands possess special features. These rocks are so permeable that surface drainage is generally absent unless the rock is mantled with boulder clay, as in Ireland's Central Plain.

In the Pennines the drainage of Ingleborough disappears underground when it crosses from impervious rocks on to the Carboniferous limestone. Ireland's famous Burren has virtually streamless landscapes for the same reason, although it possesses miles of subterranean channels (see illustration below).

The chalk downlands of England are also notoriously waterless. Nevertheless they have a remarkable network of dry valleys probably formed in the Ice Age.

The latter are called bournes. The amount of water flowing in them fluctuates according to seasonal rainfall. They are drainage features which have given distinctive names, such as Winterbourne, to chalk localities.

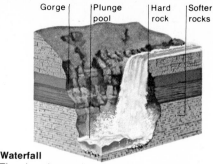

Waterfall
The river is running over hard rock. Beneath this are softer rocks. The falling water wears back these softer layers leaving the hard rock unsupported. Fragments break away and slowly the fall recedes, leaving a gorge

Anatomy of a river.
Its journey from source to sea

In the hills a river is born. Water rises from a spring. Or trickles as meltwater from snow and ice. Or runs in tiny runnels down a rain-lashed slope.

From such modest beginnings great rivers flow. But, in the course of their journeys from source to sea, they change their character dramatically. As they do so, they also change the character of the landscape.

As the youthful stream tumbles through the mountains, instead of following a straight course, it winds round minor obstacles, then between overlap-

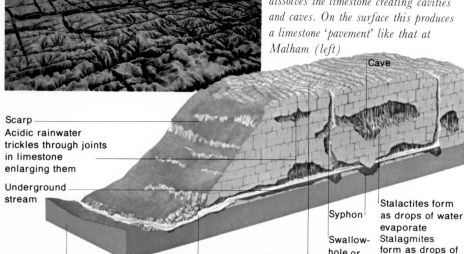

Limestone is riddled with vertical and horizontal cracks through which water percolates. The water, which falls as rain, picks up carbon dioxide which turns it into weak carbonic acid. This dissolves the limestone creating cavities and caves. On the surface this produces a limestone 'pavement' like that at Malham (left)

Scarp
Acidic rainwater trickles through joints in limestone enlarging them

Underground stream

Cave

Syphon

Swallow-hole or pot-hole

Stalactites form as drops of water evaporate
Stalagmites form as drops of water fall on cave floor

Older, harder impervious rock

Underground stream re-emerges

Clints (blocks of rock) and grikes (dissolved joints) form limestone 'pavement'

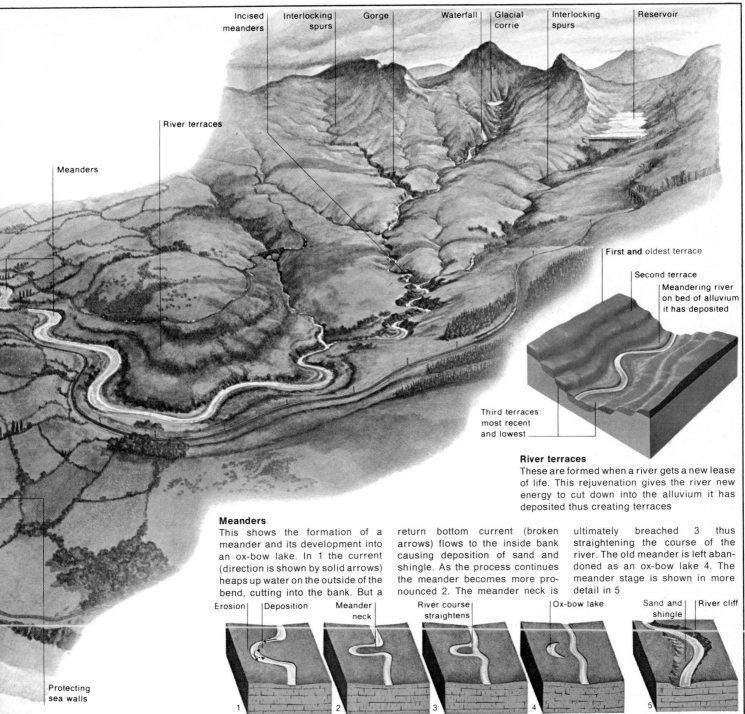

Incised meanders · Interlocking spurs · Gorge · Waterfall · Glacial corrie · Interlocking spurs · Reservoir

River terraces

Meanders

Protecting sea walls

First and oldest terrace

Second terrace

Meandering river on bed of alluvium it has deposited

Third terraces: most recent and lowest

River terraces
These are formed when a river gets a new lease of life. This rejuvenation gives the river new energy to cut down into the alluvium it has deposited thus creating terraces

Meanders
This shows the formation of a meander and its development into an ox-bow lake. In 1 the current (direction is shown by solid arrows) heaps up water on the outside of the bend, cutting into the bank. But a return bottom current (broken arrows) flows to the inside bank causing deposition of sand and shingle. As the process continues the meander becomes more pronounced 2. The meander neck is ultimately breached 3 thus straightening the course of the river. The old meander is left abandoned as an ox-bow lake 4. The meander stage is shown in more detail in 5

Erosion | Deposition — Meander neck — River course straightens — Ox-bow lake — Sand and shingle | River cliff

1   2   3   4   5

ping or interlocking hill spurs. This happens because some of the rocks it encounters are more resistant than others to the wearing action of running water.

All the time the river cuts deeper into the land surface, but as it does so it may encounter a formerly buried, tough band of rock. It cuts through this as well, but takes longer. Then steep-sided gorges are formed. Their shape is influenced by the well-jointed hard rocks which make their walls. The beautiful wooded Dove Dale in the Peak District, Scotland's lonely Corrieshalloch Gorge Near Ullapool and the romantic Fairy Glen on the Conwy River in Wales are examples.

On leaving the mountains the river's volume increases as the number of its tributaries grows. It now begins to swing from side to side in its ever-widening valley. These swings become meanders.

Meanders are clearly visible on most of our major rivers: the Severn near Shrewsbury, the Trent at Nottingham, the Forth at Stirling.

Sometimes the river acquires a new lease of life. This happens when earth movements uplift the land, or when the level of the sea falls. The re-energised river then cuts down deep into its existing valley creating incised meanders. These can be seen on the Wye above Chepstow or on the Dee near Llangollen.

At the same time the river cuts down into its former valley deposits, the thick layers of mud, sand and gravel, or alluvium, which it laid down in its lower reaches, thus creating a series of terraces above the newly entrenched channel. Without such re-energising much of the load it is carrying would be deposited, as downcutting has virtually ceased.

A river's lower reaches are the widest part of its valley and are very susceptible to floods since the floodplain is protected only by artificial embankments built following early inundations.

Finally the river arrives at the seawalls of the estuary where there are wide, sweeping mudflats and tidal marshes. Here its work is taken over by the sea.

23

Birth of the lakes. Ice gouged the hollows, meltwater filled them

Lough Neagh in Northern Ireland is the oldest and largest sheet of fresh water in the British Isles. Yet, seen for the first time, it seems unspectacular. Its very size, 155sq miles (40,145 hectares), its lack of islands and woodlands, its regular shape and the low levels of the surrounding countryside scarcely produce a scenic triumph. It is fascinating, however, for other reasons. It is the only lake in the British Isles which has its origin in a major earth movement.

Forty million years ago the basalt rocks of the central part of the Antrim Plateau gradually sank. This great down-sagging is thought to have brought the basalt surface some 2000ft (610m) below the surrounding rim of the basalt plateau. In this great hollow Lough Neagh was formed. Since then the basin has been substantially filled with sand, gravel and clay sediments. Lough Neagh itself, with eight rivers draining into it but only one flowing out, is now quite shallow, only 40–50ft (12–15m) deep.

Unlike Lough Neagh, the majority of British lakes were created in the last 50,000 years as a result of glacial activity. Even the lakes of Scotland's Great Glen (Lochs Ness, Oich and Lochy) and Lake Bala in Wales, although influenced in their direction by geological faults, occupy glacier-deepened troughs.

Elsewhere the mountainsides are dotted with hundreds of llyns (Welsh) or tarns (English) formed where corrie glaciers have scooped out rocky hollows. Where ice has scoured and over-deepened the valleys into glacial troughs, rock basin lakes occur. Loch Coruisk, below the main ridge of the Cuillins in the Isle of Skye, is a spectacular example. The rocky hollow of Loch Morar, south of Mallaig, contains Britain's deepest lake (1017ft, 310m). Yet its surface, like that of Loch Coruisk, is only a few feet above sea level.

Sometimes lakes impose curious patterns on the landscape. In the Western Highlands of Scotland and the Lake District they exhibit a radial formation. These areas were former centres of ice caps from which glaciers streamed out in all directions. Some of the long, narrow finger-lakes such as Windermere, Wastwater and Loch Lomond have been in part impounded behind terminal moraines of the last valley glaciers, but they all occupy ice-deepened rock basins.

In other places some smaller lakes

have formed in what are described as kettle holes. These occurred when large blocks of stagnant ice, buried in the tumultuous outwash sands and gravels and moraines of glaciers, finally melted, creating an enclosed hollow. The material which lay above the ice collapsed and the hollow was filled by water. Shropshire's meres at Ellesmere were formed in this way.

The curious shapes of Ireland's Lough Oughter and Upper Lough Erne reflect the fact that they have partly submerged a drumlin landscape. Of all the landscapes in the British Isles Ireland's is the richest in lakes.

Here the presence of Carboniferous limestone has had a profound influence on lake formation, for some of the largest lakes occupy enormous solution hollows. These are hollows produced by the solvent action of water on limestone. Because the level of groundwater – water below the surface stored in openings, spaces and cavities in the rocks – is high, the subterranean limestone is waterlogged and surface water does not drain through it. So Loughs Derg, Mask and Corrib and Lower Lough Erne are all

permanent features.

Some of the largest bodies of water in the British Isles are man-made, either as sources of drinking water or to serve hydro-electric schemes. The Lackan Reservoir in Ireland's Wicklow Mountains, Scotland's Blackwater Reservoir, Hawes Water in Cumbria and the Elan, Vyrnwy and Trawsfynydd lakes in Wales all fall into these categories. The Kielder Water Scheme, in the North Tyne Valley, will create when completed one of the biggest man-made lakes in Western Europe.

Other waters have been created inadvertently – subsidence lakes in the coalfields or the Cheshire 'flashes' of the Northwich salt mining area. The Thames valley is scarred with lakes in old gravel workings. Even the famous Norfolk Broads are man-made.

Norfolk's Broadland with its marshes, meandering, reed-fringed rivers and wide, shallow lakes – the 'Broads' themselves – is one of the best known and most unusual areas of East Anglia.

For many years it was thought of as the remains of a large river estuary which was gradually silting up. Some Broads

have disappeared since the first Ordnance Survey map of the area was published; others are getting smaller. Now the combined researches of historian, geographer, archaeologist and botanist have resulted in the spectacular discovery that these large lakes are the works of man – flooded medieval peat diggings. Their scale makes them one of the more astonishing modifications to a natural landscape.

There was a time when Broadland was indeed a wide open estuary with exits to the sea near Horsey and at Yarmouth and Lowestoft. This estuary probably existed as late as Roman and Anglo-Saxon times. Silting must have taken place in the quieter waters within it, especially at the seaward end. This produced brackish, swampy conditions with thick vegetation. Over the years this led to the formation of thick layers of peat.

Norwich, a thriving city in medieval times, provided a ready markét for peat fuel. Digging started in the 11th century and lasted about 200 years. In this time over 2500 acres of peat were excavated. The diggings were possible because at this time there was a rise in the land

relative to sea level which produced drier conditions.

But from the 13th century this changed. There was a gradual rise in sea level, possibly coupled with a downward tilting of the land surface. This caused the flooding, over a long period, of the old peat workings. This process, still continuing today, formed the Broads as we know them.

Norfolk's Broadland (above left) represents one of man's more remarkable unplanned modifications to the landscape. In contrast Loch Coruisk (above) in the Isle of Skye owes its genesis to natural forces, to the enormous erosive power of ice. The wholesale excavation of the valley in which the loch lies is the work of a glacier on a grand scale. Lake Vyrnwy (below) in Wales is an example of a man-made lake created to ensure a supply of drinking water

Fossils. Once living organisms, now date-stamps of geological time

Fossils, so common in many British rocks, are links with the unimaginably distant past. They are the remains of things once living, mostly the hard parts of animals or the woodier tissues of plants, which became entombed in sand and mud.

In time these soft sediments were compressed and hardened into stone; and fragments of bone, shell, leaves or wood within them were permeated by mineral matter. This resulted in fossils being formed, sometimes as large as a dinosaur skeleton or so small as to be invisible to the eye.

Once buried, a sedimentary rock and its fossils may not be returned to the surface of the Earth for millions of years, perhaps washed out from the face of a sea cliff, or revealed by quarrying.

Fossil-rich sea cliffs near Charmouth, Dorset. For many miles on this coast the cliffs are cut in nearly horizontal rocks, limestones and shales in blue and yellow. Storms wash fossils from them

During the time it is buried the world evolves new forms of life and the whole face of the Earth and its climate change. Many living things become extinct, and the only remaining evidence of their existence may be fossils. The geological map of the British Isles, with its complicated arrangement of rock strata, reflects the immense series of changes which have gone on over the last 600 million years.

Many of the British rock formations have been adopted as 'milestones' along the geological way, and the time they represent is marked by the kind of fossils they contain. By using various fossils as 'date stamps' geologists are able to correlate rocks of the same age over wide geographical areas.

Thousands of different species of fossils have been found in the British Isles. The small selection shown here are fairly common and represent a time span of 400 million years.

All the drawings are produced at half scale except for those of *Trinucleus* and *Atrypa* which are to size.

Trinucleus (*Trinucleus fimbriatus*). Age: 425 to 465 million years. Common in Ordovician period.
One of a large diverse group known as trilobites of which woodlice and king crabs are among recent living relatives. *Trinucleus* had a large, three-lobed head, segmented body and tail. Its many pairs of legs on underside of body are rarely preserved. Trilobites swam, floated, crawled on the bottom or burrowed. Some, like *Trinucleus*, were blind, probably scavengers and browsers. As trilobites grew, they shed their tough skins and these are frequently found as fossils. The earliest trilobites are found in Lower Cambrian rocks, the last in Permian rocks, so they lasted perhaps 355 million years.
Where found: this one at Builth Wells. They occur in north and south Wales, the Welsh Borderlands, the Lake District and south Scotland.

Atrypa (*Atrypa reticularis*). Age: 400 to 435 million years. Abundant in Silurian period.
This is the shell of a brachiopod, a small marine creature, rather like a nut, which lived in shallow warm water and fed by collecting tiny particles of food from the water drawn into the space within the shells. It is often associated with fossil corals. It suffered an eclipse 225 million years ago when many kinds of bivalves (cockles, mussels, clams) began to colonise the sea floors. Since then brachiopods seem to have survived only in deeper and cooler parts of the seas and oceans, usually firmly attached to seaweed or the sea floor.
Where found: common in the Wenlock and associated rocks of the Welsh Borderlands and West Midlands.

Dictyoclostus (*Dictyoclostus semireticulatus*). Age: 325 to 370 million years. Flourished in early Carboniferous period.
A large, relatively thick-shelled and robust brachiopod shellfish recognised by its almost hemi-

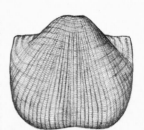

spherical shape and the regular pattern of surface lines and ridges. It lived in the shallow, clear, warm waters of the early Carboniferous period, building up shell banks and spreads of shell debris.
Where found: typical member of fossil assemblages in Carboniferous limestones of Wales, the Pennines, Ireland and parts of Scotland.

Gryphaea (*Gryphaea arcuata*). Age: about 200 million years. Common in the Jurassic period.
Known in some localities as Devil's Toenail, this is a distant relative of the oysters. It is a bivalve with one very curved shell and one less so.
As the animal grew the left valve became curved and developed into a form of cup in which the soft parts lay, covered by the small right valve. Conspicuous growth ridges emphasise the curvature. *Gryphaea* abounded on the relatively shallow sea floor over much of Britain in Jurassic times. In adult life it lay free on the silty clay or silt. By the end of the Jurassic period it was replaced by the early true oysters. This was about 140 millions years ago.
Where found: in the grey shales, clays and limestones of the Liassic rocks from Dorset to Yorkshire.

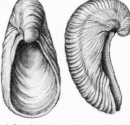

Dactylioceras (*Dactylioceras commune*). Age: about 170–180 million years. Also of the Jurassic period.
This coiled and chambered shell is typical of one of the most common British ammonites, extinct sea animals akin to living squid and nautilus. It floated in open water and probably fed on small invertebrate creatures, and in its turn, may have been eaten by fish, ichthyosaurs or plesiosaurs. When the animal died gas in the chambers of the shell may have kept it floating for some time, but very large numbers of these shells accumulated on the sea floor. Sediment there was rich in partially decomposed organic matter and in due course this became bituminous black shale. *Dactyliocera* shells in it are beautifully preserved, commonly in full relief rather than squashed flat. Many have been replaced by iron pyrite (iron sulphide) and appear to be made of brass.
Where found: in the Upper Liassic rocks of Yorkshire around Whitby.

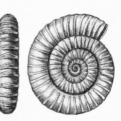

Micraster (*Micraster cor-anguincum*) Age: about 75 million years. Common in the Cretaceous period.
This inhabitant of the Chalk sea is not unlike some modern sea-urchins found round the shores of the British Isles today. It belongs to a group known as the echinoids and is rather bun-shaped, covered in small spines like its modern relatives and has the five-rays or feeding grooves that most echinoids have. It lived on, and burrowed just below, the soft chalky surface mud of the sea floor, feeding on a rich supply of microscopic organic debris. Being buried so much in life, it was well placed to become a fossil. Many were preserved by the replacement of their shell and the chalk mud within it by silica (flint). Flint echinoids occur in soils over much of the chalk land of the British Isles long after the chalk itself has been eroded away.
Where found: in the Upper Chalk from southern England to Yorkshire. Also in Northern Ireland.

Cardita (*Cardita planicosta*). Age: about 60 million years. Lived in the Tertiary period.
To all intents and purposes *Cardita* is a modern bivalve but more conspicuous with a thick shell and robust hingeing of the two valves. The shell was not only a protection from the waves and currents but also from shellfish-eating sharks and rays. *Cardita* was shallow burrowing and fed on small food particles in the water which it drew into its shell. It lived, with a large population of other bivalves, all looking remarkably like living species, not far from shore and probably in sub-tropical conditions, on the silty floor of the Eocene sea which covered south east England. Also present in the sea were snails, tusk shells, limpets and other forms of shellfish.
Where found: in the Bracklesham Beds of Sussex and the Isle of Wight.

Great British landscapes

This guide to the classic landscapes of the British Isles shows the underlying rocks which makes them what they are; how natural forces have fashioned them; and the way man has modelled them to his particular purpose

Glaciated Nant Ffrancon valley, Snowdonia

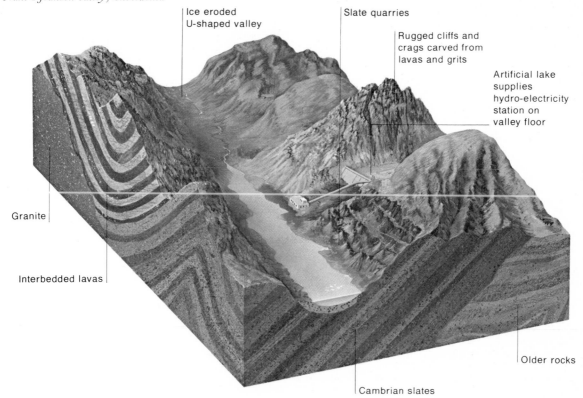

Ice eroded
U-shaped valley

Slate quarries

Rugged cliffs and
crags carved from
lavas and grits

Artificial lake
supplies
hydro-electricity
station on
valley floor

Granite

Interbedded lavas

Cambrian slates

Older rocks

Snowdonia, North Wales

Snowdonia, where grey peaks rise dramatically above the coastal plains of Gwynedd, is one of the best-known mountain lands in the British Isles. A great variety of rocks has helped build a complex massif which has been folded, faulted and uplifted on countless occasions.

The most spectacular peaks, with ice-eroded cliffs and jagged pinnacle ridges, are generally found where volcanic rocks abound. These often came from sub-marine volcanoes and the lavas and ashes are interbedded with coarse grits and finer-grained mudstones of the former sea bed sediments. Later earth-movements, accompanied by enormous pressures, created the slatey rocks. It is these more easily weathered rocks which build the smoother, dome-like mountains.

Because of the Ice Age few deep soils have survived. Some of the earlier valley lakes, however, have been slowly filled with peaty sediments in post-glacial times, allowing some rudimentary farming on the valley floors at lower altitudes. Elsewhere, the countryside is given over to rough grassland, scattered broadleaf woodlands in the sheltered hollows and conifer plantations on the plateaux.

But the works of industrial man are also apparent. Slate quarrying has left gigantic scars in certain valleys.

☐ Where to see similar scenery: also in Wales in the vicinity of Cader Idris and in the area of Tal-y-llyn.

The Highlands of Scotland

The Highlands of Scotland are composed of a great variety of rocks, most of which are extremely old, highly fractured, tightly folded and altered by numerous intrusive igneous rocks such as granite. The Outer Hebrides are the home of the oldest rocks in the British Isles.

Gashed by deep, often fault-guided corridors, the upland massifs offer towering cliffs and sweeping ice-steepened slopes to challenge climber and skier. Less adventurous travellers will be content to marvel at waterfalls, beautiful lochs and seemingly endless forests. Many of the glens have been so deepened by glaciers that they are now occupied by Britain's deepest waters, such as Loch Ness and Loch Morar. In places the sea has flooded some of the western valleys to create long, winding fjords which penetrate far into the mountains.

Scattered remnants of the once-ubiquitous Scots pine forests survive. But in the far north birchwoods predominate

and newly-planted ranks of exotic conifers now clothe many of the formerly open moorlands. These contrasting habitats harbour a rich wild life.

Amid the generally barren and rocky terrain, good farming land is at a premium – except for the widely dispersed crofting communities of the northwest who cling to the small pockets of productive land, particularly on the shelly, sandy soils of the old uplifted shorelines.

☐ Where to see similar scenery: the Highlands have a character all their own.

The Craven Uplands of the Pennines

Some of the highest summits in the Pennine backbone of England occur in the Craven Uplands where such peaks as Ingleborough, Penyghent and Whernside rear their flat-topped heads above the surrounding limestone moorlands and the intervening valleys. Few other uplands exist with such contrasts of colour. The limestone cliffs, or 'scars', gleam white in the sunshine with a mantle of bright green grassland. The peaks, however, are built

of terraced layers of hard gritstone and softer shales. These weather to dark aprons of scree and give thin, barren soils below the black, peat-crowned summit plateaux.

Streams rise on these windswept upper slopes, then plunge rapidly into great vertical shafts once they cross on to the permeable limestone.

The uplands are sometimes terminated abruptly by escarpments which may have been fashioned along a geological fracture or fault. Contrasting rocks and different soils on the lower side of the fault lead to a different type of land use. The Craven Lowlands, for example, are an area of improved farming land with trees, scattered farms and villages, very different from the treeless uplands.

☐ Where to see similar scenery: in Derbyshire at Matlock and on the border with Staffordshire at Dovedale. Also isolated examples in the Mendips, at Llandudno (The Great Orme) and the Marble Arch area of County Fermanagh.

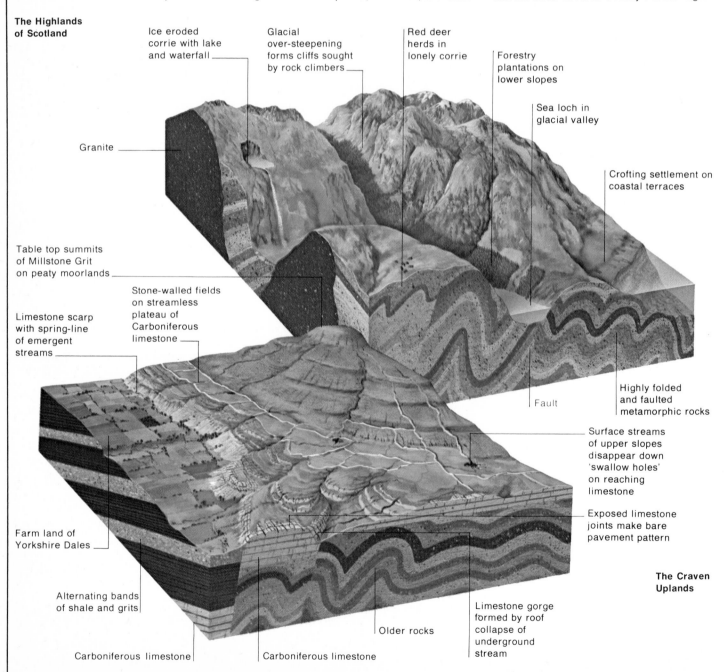

The Highlands of Scotland

Ice eroded corrie with lake and waterfall

Glacial over-steepening forms cliffs sought by rock climbers

Red deer herds in lonely corrie

Forestry plantations on lower slopes

Sea loch in glacial valley

Granite

Crofting settlement on coastal terraces

Table top summits of Millstone Grit on peaty moorlands

Stone-walled fields on streamless plateau of Carboniferous limestone

Limestone scarp with spring-line of emergent streams

Highly folded and faulted metamorphic rocks

Fault

Surface streams of upper slopes disappear down 'swallow holes' on reaching limestone

Exposed limestone joints make bare pavement pattern

Farm land of Yorkshire Dales

The Craven Uplands

Alternating bands of shale and grits

Limestone gorge formed by roof collapse of underground stream

Older rocks

Carboniferous limestone

Carboniferous limestone

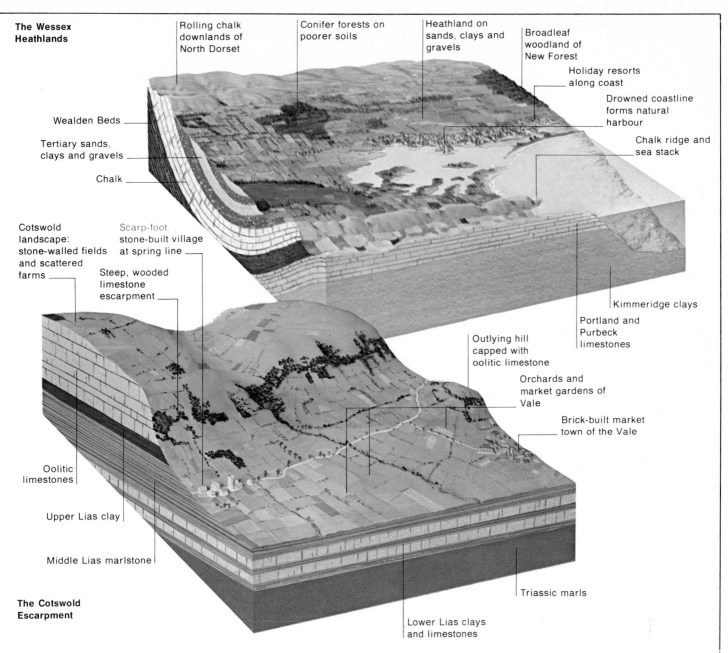

The Wessex Heathlands

Rolling chalk downlands of North Dorset

Conifer forests on poorer soils

Heathland on sands, clays and gravels

Broadleaf woodland of New Forest

Holiday resorts along coast

Drowned coastline forms natural harbour

Chalk ridge and sea stack

Wealden Beds

Tertiary sands, clays and gravels

Chalk

Cotswold landscape: stone-walled fields and scattered farms

Scarp-foot stone-built village at spring line

Steep, wooded limestone escarpment

Kimmeridge clays

Portland and Purbeck limestones

Outlying hill capped with oolitic limestone

Orchards and market gardens of Vale

Brick-built market town of the Vale

Oolitic limestones

Upper Lias clay

Middle Lias marlstone

Triassic marls

The Cotswold Escarpment

Lower Lias clays and limestones

The Cotswold Escarpment and Vale of Evesham

The mellow, creamy-coloured stone villages of the Cotswolds reflect the excellence of the locally-quarried building material. The Cotswolds are formed of limestones which are older than chalk and different in character. The most important are the Great and Inferior Oolitic limestones – the harder rocks which create the prominent escarpment and include the famous Bath Stone, one of England's foremost free-stones, fine grained and easily sawn. Oolitic limestone consists of minute, tightly-cemented spheres of calcium carbonate, resembling the roe of a fish, from which it derives its name.

As with chalk, limestone allows rainwater to permeate rapidly. Uplands are virtually streamless and only the deepest valleys and the scarp-foot springlines provide sufficient surface water to maintain permanent settlements. Underlying the limestones are thick beds of marlstone and clay. Surface water abounds in the clay vale where these gently tilted older rocks emerge from beneath the limestone escarpment. The escarpment is generally too steep for farming and is either left in rough grassland and scrub or planted in thick woodlands.

The chestnut brown soils of the limestone terrain give way rapidly to the grey and red soils of the vale, with extensive fruit orchards and market gardens adding variety to the field patterns.

☐ Where to see similar scenery: the Stone Belt extends north-east to Oxfordshire and Northants.

The Wessex Heathlands

The heathlands of Dorset and Hampshire occupy a lowland basin which has been partly flooded by the sea to form the landlocked harbour of Poole. They are bounded on the north by the rolling chalk downlands of Dorset's Cranbourne Chase and on the south by the open grassland plateaux and ridges of the Isle of Purbeck.

To the layman the sands, clays and gravels of the heathlands hardly merit the term 'rocks', but they were laid down as some of Britain's youngest rocks within the last 70 million years. Their acid soils can maintain only a heathland flora of heather, gorse and occasional clumps of Scots pine, which are unusual in the well-farmed English Lowlands. Only in the more fertile east – in the New Forest – are there remnants of primeval oakwoods. Elsewhere, the Forestry Commission has utilised the poorer soils for extensive conifer plantations.

The sandy heathlands have a remoteness and charm of their own, for this is Thomas Hardy country where Puddletown Heath has been immortalised as the famous 'Egdon Heath'. At Poole Harbour the heathlands reach the coast. This is the habitat of the red squirrel and such rare birds as the Dartford warbler and the red-backed shrike. Here, too, are sandy beaches and coastal resorts.

The impact of modern man and the implicit threat to wildlife and lonely beauty is beginning to change the Wessex heathlands. The pipeclays of Poole have long been the basis of a pottery but the Winfrith atomic energy station and the recently discovered oilfield of the Arne peninsula pose new hazards to the heathlands.

☐ Where to see similar scenery: around Aldershot and Bagshot. London's Hampstead Heath is a watered-down version of this type of landscape.

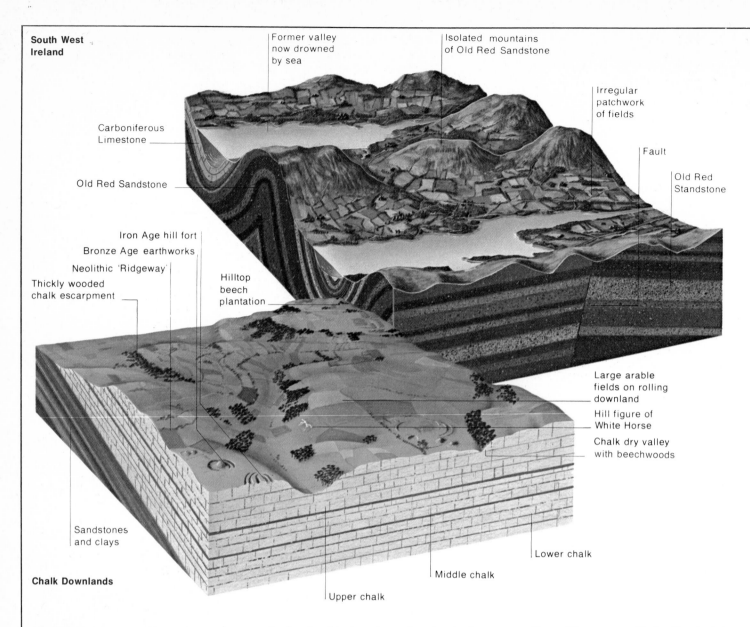

South West Ireland

Former valley now drowned by sea

Isolated mountains of Old Red Sandstone

Irregular patchwork of fields

Carboniferous Limestone

Fault

Old Red Standstone

Old Red Sandstone

Iron Age hill fort

Bronze Age earthworks

Neolithic 'Ridgeway'

Hilltop beech plantation

Thickly wooded chalk escarpment

Large arable fields on rolling downland

Hill figure of White Horse

Chalk dry valley with beechwoods

Sandstones and clays

Chalk Downlands

Lower chalk

Middle chalk

Upper chalk

Chalk Downlands of Southern England

The Chalk Downlands are often taken as the epitome of Lowland England. They stretch from the Channel coast of Devon, eastwards to Kent, and north-eastwards to beyond the Wash.

Although some of its beds are harder than others, chalk is soft by comparison with its flints, but resistant when compared with its neighbouring clay rocks. Thus, where it has been gently folded or tilted, chalk creates distinctive hills and escarpments overlooking the clay vales.

Chalk's permeability means that surface water is rarely found on the downlands, although the rocks act like a giant sponge by retaining subterranean water and releasing it slowly at springs which mark the 'water table'.

Largely due to the scarcity of water, villages are dotted along the spring-line in the valley bottoms, while flint-built farms are scattered on the downs. Impressive prehistoric earthworks and standing stones, linked by ancient trackways, such as The Ridgeway, illustrate the former importance of chalk uplands at a time when the clay vales were too marshy and forested for easy settlement.

The short, springy grassland was the basis of extensive sheep farming in the Middle Ages, but today it has frequently been ploughed, so that large, hedgeless fields of corn have replaced much of the livestock. Except where younger clays mantle the surface, woodland is generally confined to the steeper slopes of the dry valleys and scarps.

☐ Where to see similar scenery: the Chilterns, for a chalk landscape with a thick covering of clay supporting beechwoods. For open downland, the North and South Downs, the Berkshire Downs, Salisbury Plain, Cranbourne Chase.

South West Ireland

The sea-girt mountainlands of Kerry and west Cork have long been famed for their scenery. Atlantic rollers bite deeply into the fertile valleys, leaving the bony fingers of the gaunt hills as intervening peninsulas. Geology and scenery are at their most simple here, for the Old Red Sandstone survives in the 300 million year-old upfolds (anticlines) while the less resistant Carboniferous shales and limestones of the downfolds (synclines) are picked out by the linear valleys, now partially submerged by the sea.

Ice sheets have scoured the uplands, leaving the massive red, purple and green grits as bare slabs and crags along the crestlines. These are pitted with glacial hollows and dotted with lakes, such as the beautiful Barley Lake. Some of the sheltered valleys, especially Glengarriff, support thick woodlands, but in the main these windswept coasts are treeless, with the heather and gorse-strewn slopes of the sandstone giving way to the brighter green fields of the shale and limestone valleys floors. Here, surrounded by fuchsia hedges, are the few scattered farms and the tiny market towns, some of which have become modern tourist centres. The deep waters of Bantry Bay are famed not only as a text book example of a ria (drowned river valley) but also for their value as an oil tanker terminal.

On the headlands good farming land is at a premium, especially near Kenmare which was the centre of a former ice cap. Here soils have been swept away from the ice-scrubbed hills. Only Mizen Head (the Land's End of Ireland) appears less barren than its neighbouring peninsulas, partly due to its lower elevation and its less glaciated terrain.

☐ Where to see similar scenery: geological structures and related topography of this kind are rare in the British Isles, but ria coastlines typify south-west England and Pembrokeshire.

Dartmoor

Dartmoor is made of granite, just one exposure of a gigantic, subterranean, dome-shaped mass of granite which stretches laterally for 120 miles beneath Devon and Cornwall. Its various outcrops also form Bodmin Moor, St Austell, Falmouth, Land's End and the Isles of Scilly granites.

Some 300 million years ago this granite, then molten rock, or magma, was forced up from within the earth, into the existing slates and sandstones. Since then the forces of erosion have stripped away the overlying rocks to reveal the granite rising above the surrounding lowlands. Despite its hardness, granite weathers in a particular way, along its planes of weakness, to form weirdly-shaped grey tors, such as Haytor, which crown the skyline.

According to season these dark peaty moors, with their dangerous bright-green mires, are carpeted with purple heather or golden gorse. In a few remote river valleys remnants of ancient oakwoods, such as Wistman's Wood, survive. Coniferous plantations cover many lower slopes.

The moorlands are almost devoid of modern settlement, although prehistoric earthworks testify to the presence of early man. Today villages are tucked in sheltered valleys around the perimeter of the moor, leaving the trackless uplands to buzzard, curlew, fox and deer.

☐ Where to see similar scenery: in Galloway, Southern Scotland. Granite also produces higher mountain areas in the Isle of Arran, the Cairngorms, Cheviots and Mountains of Mourne.

The Antrim Coast, Northern Ireland

The north-eastern corner of Northern Ireland boasts scenery which is uncommon in the British Isles, for here layer upon layer of basaltic lavas, poured out some 60 million years ago, have buried a landscape of chalk. Where the two rocks are exposed in juxtaposition at the coast the contrasts of black and white cliff scenery are startling.

Unlike the deep-seated, intrusive granites, the dark basalts cooled quickly as they were forced out from surface fissures. Thus, their crystals are smaller and their columnar jointing much more marked owing to the different rates of cooling. Nowhere are the basaltic columns as well displayed as at the Giant's Causeway. Here the hexagons are so perfectly fashioned that in 1694 a paper read to the Royal Society acknowledged that they were not man-made owing to the lack of mortar between the columns!

Inland from the coastal cliffs there are deep valleys in the rolling, moorland-covered surface of the plateau. These valleys, known as the Glens of Antrim, bring bright green farmland into the sombre bog landscapes of the interior where the dark peat cuttings contrast with the white painted cottages and farms. The narrow walled fields climb the slopes with such regularity that their patterns have been referred to as 'ladder farms'.

Underlying the extensive peat bogs are thick layers of boulder clay deposited by former ice-sheets. In places this clay has been fahioned by the glacier ice into streamlined hillocks known as drumlins.

☐ Where to see similar scenery: on a smaller scale there are columnar basalts in Scotland on the Isle of Staffa (Fingal's Cave) and on Mull.

Dartmoor

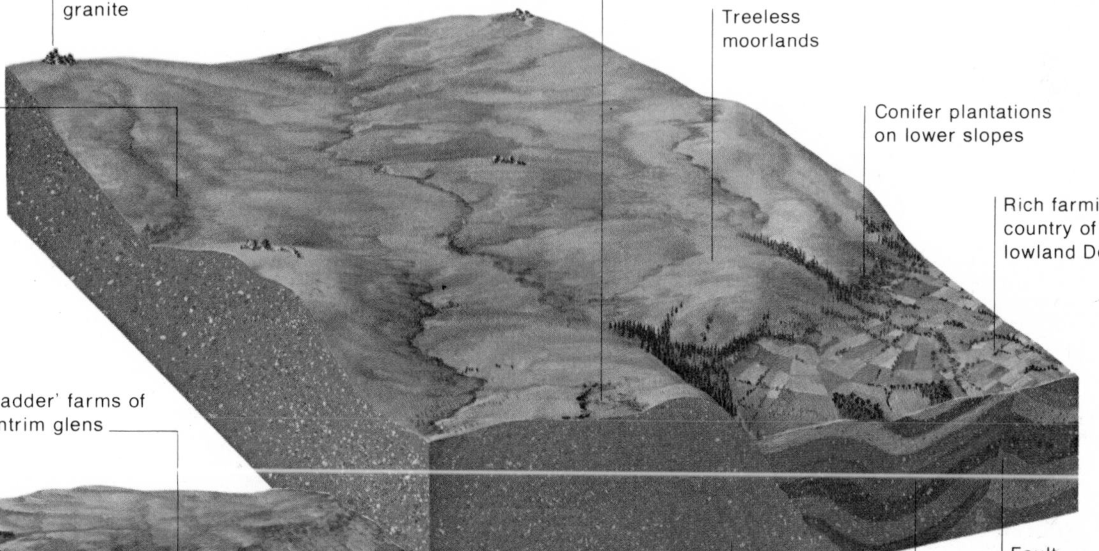

Natural broadleaf woodland surviving in remote valley

Summit tors on granite

Mire

Treeless moorlands

Conifer plantations on lower slopes

Rich farming country of lowland Devon

Stepped landforms created by layers of basaltic lava

Basalt columns on coast

'Ladder' farms of Antrim glens

Fault

Devonian slates and sandstones

Granite

Peat cuttings in extensive bogs

Whaleback hills in boulder clay known as drumlins

The Antrim Coast

Clays

Sandstones

Older rocks

Chalk

Boulder clay

Basaltic lavas

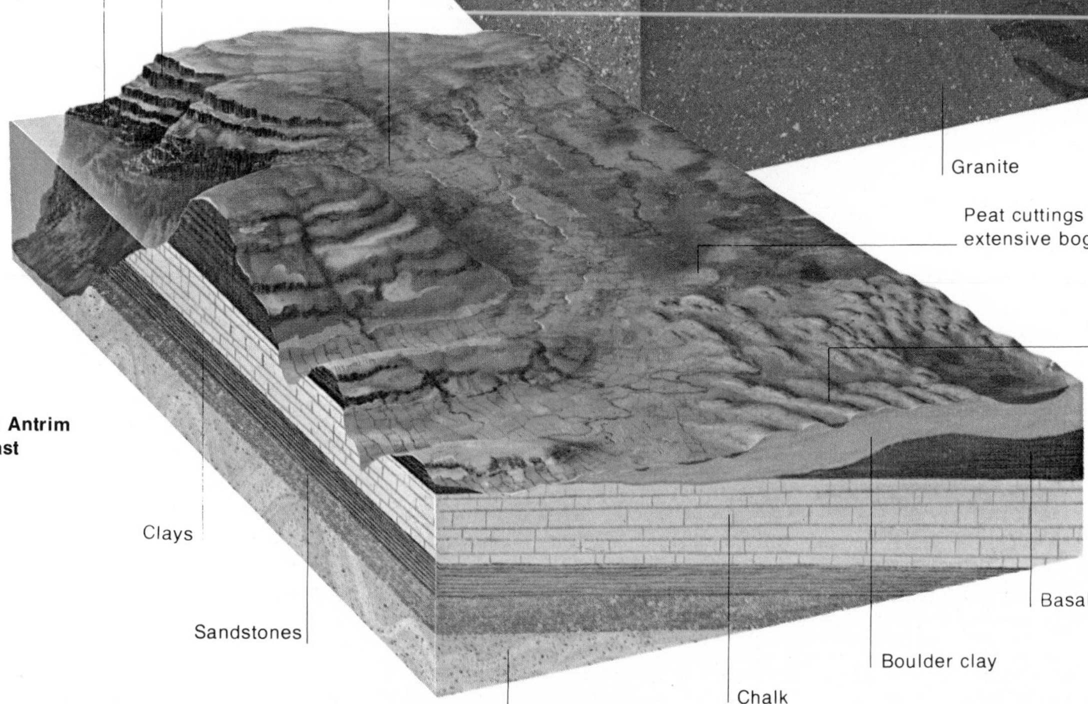

Chapter Two
The Making of the Countryside: the Mark of Man

The ruins of Corfe Castle dominate the village to which it has given its name in the Purbeck Hills of Dorset. But it is not the only legacy of earlier generations to be seen in this photograph.
The country lane winding between hedgerows is one of many features often regarded as intrinsic elements of traditional or 'unspoilt' countryside which originate from the work of man moulding the landscape. How man contributed to the diversity of the British Isles through six broad periods of history is the theme of this chapter

Prehistoric Britain: Man begins to change the natural landscape

Man arrived late in the British Isles, barely yesterday in a geological calendar that measures time in millions of years. And it is only in the last 5000 years that he has been able to shape the landscape. Up to then the forces of nature, the long-term processes of geology and the rhythms of climatic change, discussed elsewhere in this book, were the dominant factors. It was they that determined the topography, soils and vegetation which combined to form the habitat of this relative newcomer to Earth, *homo sapiens*.

The first human evidence of Man's life in the British Isles came from a gravel pit at Swanscombe in the Thames valley 20 miles (32km) from what is now the heart of London. Three fragments of a skull and thousands of flint tools dating back around 150,000 years ago to the Palaeolithic Age (see panel, opposite) were found there.

Even older worked flints have been found indicating that man was living in the British Isles possibly 200,000 years ago. Palaeolithic Man seems most likely to have lived primarily in the lowlands of southern Britain, although the absence of flints in upland areas could also be a consequence of the Ice Age obliterating evidence of earlier cultures in northern Britain. Archaeologists simply do not know for certain. But wherever he lived it was a life of hunting, fishing and food-gathering that continued well into the Mesolithic era.

It was in Neolithic or the New Stone Age, from about 3250 BC, that the first dramatic change occurred: forest dwellers – hunters and fishermen – turned to the first primitive forms of farming. The first communities of farmers still hunted animals for food but they also began to cultivate grain crops such as wheat and barley. And botanists, who have analysed the pollen preserved in peat bogs and muds gathered over the centuries on lake beds, have shown that the Neolithic farmers made the first inroads into the great forests which had covered most of Britain since the Ice Age finally ended around 10,000 BC. Thus, for the first time, man became an intrusive force in shaping the landscape.

Man's exploitation of the land grew through the Bronze and Iron Ages which preceded the Roman occupation and the first *written* account of the British Isles – prehistoric is so-called where there is

Chysauster in Cornwall is one of the few Iron Age villages in Britain to survive in anything like its original form – largely because it was built of local stone. It was occupied from 100 BC to 300 AD

only archaeological rather than written evidence of the past. By the time of the late Iron Age, when the Romans first set eyes on Britain, considerable areas had been cleared of their original woodland.

The complex succession of cultures that existed in Britain during those final prehistoric eras also left their mark in ways which, although faint and indistinct, can still be seen today. Outlines of ancient field patterns pick out areas of earliest settlement; disturbed ground along the Downs and the heathlands of southern England betray sites of ancient flint workings; and, most striking of all, burial places, stone circles and hill forts remain as testimony to societies whose complexity is still far from understood.

Clearing the forests

Over most of the British Isles the continuous farming of the last 1,000 years or more has erased all traces of prehistoric agriculture from the countryside. Yet aerial photography and botanical analysis have proved that the first farmers had altered the landscape substantially by the time of the Roman conquest.

After the end of the Ice Age forests grew to cover all but the highest mountain tops. But when the Romans first encountered the ancient areas of settlement on Salisbury Plain and its neigh-

bouring chalk uplands, for instance, they saw not woodland but a patchwork pattern of fields and extensive pastures for the grazing of cattle and, to a lesser extent, sheep.

The same process of forest clearances – accomplished mainly by burning and maintained by the grazing of livestock – has been traced through pollen analysis in the lake muds and peat bogs of the Lake District. There it has been proved that extensive tracts of moorland, particularly above the 1000ft (305m) contour, had come into being as early as the later centuries of the Bronze Age. Likewise the mantle of forest had been pushed back in the limestone upland of the Peak District ever since the intrusion of the first Neolithic farmers to whose presence, almost 5000 years ago, the landscape of Derbyshire still bears silent witness in the ruined monoliths of their burial places at Five Wells and Minninglow.

How prehistoric man actually farmed can be seen through aerial photography which has revealed patterns of ancient fields still inscribed upon the contemporary designs of arable and pasture land. For instance, in the chalk lands of southern England, especially in the South Downs, fields are visible which have been dated back 3000 years to the early Bronze Age. These small fields have even smaller rectangular or oblong plots separated from each other on sloping ground by lynchets – see below right.

But in highland Britain, at places ranging from the hill masses of southwest England to the Shetlands, abundant proof of land clearing and cultivation as well as settlement can still be detected by the human eye. Most of this evidence, on the fringes of Bodmin Moor and Dartmoor, for instance, survives at heights above the present levels of farming. Clusters of cairns, low overgrown heaps of stone on what are today heather-covered moors, are a legacy of the original stone-by-stone clearance of the land. And on the ground faint markings of hut circles show where the Bronze Age cultivators of such upland field systems in the North Yorkshire Moors lived and worked.

From the Bronze Age onwards man's primitive farming was greatly aided by more efficient tools. Archaeological investigation of ancient field sites at Overton Down, Wiltshire, and Gwithian, Cornwall, has even revealed the marks of prehistoric ploughing. In the downland of Wiltshire the ploughlines are scored into the chalk subsoil while wind-blown sand has preserved a whole series of ploughing layers at Gwithian.

Small and irregular fields thus seem to have been part of the rural economy of the British Isles from the earliest Neolithic farmers through to the Iron Age. But the fragmentary and widely scattered evidence suggests that these early landscape elements have played little part in the subsequent evolution of field patterns – even in Ireland.

There it was long believed that the present pattern of fields was largely a legacy of the Celtic world, linked with ancient pastoral traditions. It is certainly true that in western Ireland archaeologists have traced more than 30 prehistoric field boundaries of stones that had been preserved under thick growths of peat. But recent research has shown that the patterns of the Irish rural landscape have evolved largely since the 17th century.

However there may be one small area where the honeycomb pattern of tiny fields has survived virtually intact since Iron Age times – around the hamlets of the Penwith peninsula in Western Cornwall. Otherwise it was through the first clearing of the forests that the prehistoric farmers most effectively put their stamp on the face of the British Isles.

Five Ages of Prehistoric Britain

Palaeolithic: before 8000 BC. Man lived by hunting, fishing and food gathering (eg nuts, roots and berries), often dwelling in caves. Much evidence destroyed by Ice Age, but many animals known to have existed that are now extinct in the British Isles such as bison, bear, rhinoceros and hyaena. No firm evidence of any settlement in Ireland.

Mesolithic: 8000 to 3250 BC. Man still practised a shifting culture, not strictly nomadic but no permanent settlement. Increasing evidence of population in northern England, Scotland and Ireland. First evidence of temporary woodland clearances in areas such as Dartmoor and the Cleveland Hills.

Neolithic: 3250 to 1700 BC. Forest clearances became more widespread as man began to farm the land with grain crops. Settlements were generally on high ground where many long barrow burial chambers can still be found. Extensive trade in stone axes around Britain. Early embanked sanctuaries or 'henges', sometimes with stone, although these were mostly of a later period.

Bronze Age: 1700 to 500 BC: Metallurgical skills developed sufficiently to make bronze weapons and ornamental objects, but stone and wooden implements (including a primitive plough in the late Bronze Age) were still used in agriculture. More forest clearing. Stone circles tend to date from this period, as do round barrows (*tumuli*) and cairns. Ireland's gold brought new settlers and trade, not only with Britain but with continental Europe. Increasing evidence of lowland settlements, notably in the English Midlands.

Iron Age: 500 BC to 43 AD. Many hilltop settlements were developed into hill 'forts', often defended by vast ramparts and serving as tribal capitals. Settlement patterns become more varied with farmsteads and small villages or hamlets as well as the larger communities associated with the biggest hill-forts. Cattle and sheep grazing became more common and trade routes expanded. Much of Scotland and Ireland remained in the Bronze Age for several centuries, but may have entered the Iron Age with the builders of hill forts, possibly about 200 BC. Many facets of Iron Age or Celtic society survived the Roman centuries, particularly in highland Britain and Ireland which were largely or totally unaffected by Roman influences.

☐ All dates are approximate and there were often important regional variations from the generalised summaries above.

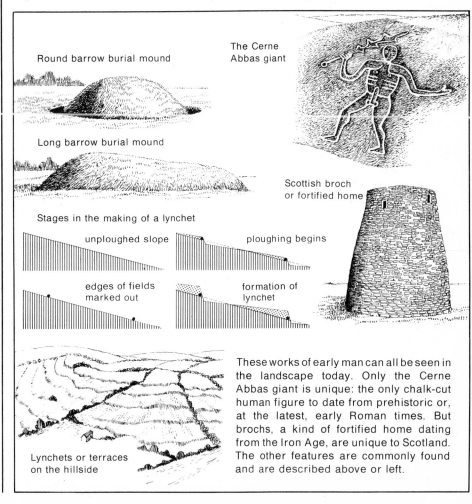

Round barrow burial mound

Long barrow burial mound

Stages in the making of a lynchet

unploughed slope

ploughing begins

edges of fields marked out

formation of lynchet

The Cerne Abbas giant

Scottish broch or fortified home

Lynchets or terraces on the hillside

These works of early man can all be seen in the landscape today. Only the Cerne Abbas giant is unique: the only chalk-cut human figure to date from prehistoric or, at the latest, early Roman times. But brochs, a kind of fortified home dating from the Iron Age, are unique to Scotland. The other features are commonly found and are described above or left.

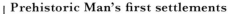

*Above: Pentre Ifan cromlech in
Dyfed, South Wales. Originally the
large capstone, so elegantly poised
on the supporting slabs, formed the
roof of a Neolithic burial chamber
but the covering mound of earth
has eroded away. Cromlechs are
also known as quoits or dolmens*

*Left: Hambledon Hill Iron Age hill
fort in Dorset. The long and
winding double ramparts enclose
earlier fortifications and a
substantial Neolithic long barrow
can be seen clearly on the hilltop*
*Right: Long Meg and Her
Daughters stone circle in Cumbria.
Long Meg herself is a standing stone
12ft (3.6m) high just outside this
Bronze Age circle of 59 stones which
represents 'her' daughters. There
were originally 70 stones and of
those which survive only 27 are still
standing upright*

Prehistoric Man's first settlements

Many of the most striking examples of
the prehistoric centuries surviving in the
present landscapes are monuments to the
dead: the Neolithic burial chambers, or
long barrows, sometimes guarded at
their entrance by massive stones that
each weigh several tons. They have survived long after the mud-and-wattle
stockades of the earliest settlements dis-
integrated. But their locations, as well as
their size, give the first clues as to where
early man lived. Where these burial
chambers were also near great stone
monuments, such as at Avebury and
Stonehenge in Wiltshire and Callanish
on the Isle of Lewis, we may take it that
these were areas of abiding settlement
even in times of shifting agriculture when
people were neither strictly nomadic nor
settling permanently in one particular
location within an area.

Burial chambers date from not only
the Neolithic Age but also the Bronze
Age when most of the many barrows on
Salisbury Plain were constructed. There
may once have been more circles of
standing stones but these survive only
where they are elaborate, as at Stonehenge and Avebury, or remote, as at
Castlerigg in the Lake District.

It is in the more remote parts of the
British Isles that the relics of earlier
centuries have best escaped plundering
and destruction. In the heart of Mainland, the chief island of Orkney, for
instance, stand three relics all gathered
together close to the shores of an inland
loch: the Ring of Brodgar, the gaunt
stones of Stenness and the severe formal
architecture of Maes Howe, a chambered tomb. Together they must have
formed an important core of population
in this far outpost of northern Britain.

Other great monuments from the prehistoric ages include the tombs of Newgrange, north-west from Dublin in the
central plain of Ireland. These predate
Stonehenge by around 1000 years, indicating an advanced and sizeable settlement for that time. And Arbor Low, the
great 'henge' monument of recumbent
stones whose site forms a focal point for
the limestone country of the Peak District near Buxton, may well have acted as
a ritual centre for the prehistoric popula-

tion of the southern Pennines.

It is only possible to surmise that this might be so since few relics of actual living accommodation survive anywhere from prehistoric times. Those that do, such as the clusters of stone huts and paved courtyards at Chysauster in Cornwall and Skara Brae in the Orkneys, were small farming or fishing communities which survive because they were built in local stone rather than the more common timber. However, Skara Brae's remarkable quality of preservation is also due to being buried beneath sand-dunes until these were exposed by a gale in the 19th century.

More numerous, however, are the hill forts which developed during the Iron Age. Altogether, if small examples are

excluded, no fewer than 600 such forts have been found in England and Wales alone. To some extent the name 'fort' is misleading. Some were simply places on exposed hill-tops where cattle and sheep were penned, probably overnight to give protection from wild animals during the summer months when upland pastures were grazed. Many hill forts contained only a single farm and thus were entirely rural in their functions.

But many were the true precursors of towns with a pattern of streets, evidence of industries such as metal-working and pottery and temples in a few sites. Some were very large – 100 acres (40 hectares) or more – and, surrounded by vast ramparts, served as tribal capitals. In Ireland forts were built with more elab-

orate defences in the west than the east of the country and, as in Scotland, some sites are coastal promontories as well as hill tops. Notable examples are Maiden Castle and Hambledon Hill (above, left) in Dorset: Tre'r Ceiri on Llyn peninsula, North Wales: An Sgurr on the island of Eigg in the Inner Hebrides; and Dun Aengus on Inishmore, one of the Aran islands in Galway Bay.

Even now the work (genius, perhaps) of prehistoric man, whether it be barrows, stone circles or hill forts, manages to convey the feeling of earlier cultures – of nameless people whose engineering knowledge and skills have been discerned only in the most recent research and whose work survives to be a marvel even in the Space Age.

The first industrial revolution

If prehistoric farmers contributed to the making of the landscape, it is equally true that the earliest industries – stone quarrying and the extraction of metallic ores – have left their marks on the countryside.

Rocks which could be shaped to give hard cutting edges to tools and weapons were exploited with increasing effect through prehistoric times. The chief sources for these earliest industries were: 1. Flint which was abundant in the chalklands of southern and eastern Britain and also on the coast of Antrim, in glacial deposits and on the beaches; 2. Volcanic rocks among the ancient uplands of the north and west of the British Isles.

Probably the most impressive and exciting of the early industrial sites is Grimes Graves near Thetford, Norfolk. Here 35 acres (14 hectares) of tumbled ground, hollows and hillocks of chalk waste, conceal the entrances to mine shafts that were worked for at least 500 years in the extraction of flint. More than 800 separate pits have been counted, some 30 or 40ft (9–12m) deep while, at the surface, 100 'chipping' floors where the raw material was shaped into tools have been recognised.

More than 4000 years ago the area around Grimes Graves was suffering from the side-effects of mining more commonly associated with the last industrial revolution: its shafts and underground galleries had caused subsidence, its waste materials had buried good pastureland to create the first derelict land and maybe the first tips of waste.

So far it has been impossible to trace the extent of the traffic in implements made from the Norfolk flint, although it doubtless extended all over southern Britain and perhaps to the continent. But tools made from igneous rocks, whose sources are clearly established under microscopic analysis, have shown that there was widespread and long-distance trade from the 'axe-factories' in western and northern Britain.

Such factories have been found as far apart as Land's End and Shetland while high up on the Langdale Pikes in the Lake District, a distinctive grey-green volcanic rock was quarried for more than 1000 years in order to make stone axes. Langdale axes have been found in archaeological investigations in the Peak District, the East Midlands and Hampshire to name but a few places.

Their discovery bears witness to widespread trade that helped to establish the first lines of communication across the British Isles. It is likely that the earliest tracks from the valleys into the hills were traced by Neolithic farmers following their livestock in the annual migrations to the summer pastures. By the early Bronze Age several long-distance routes had been established.

Many of these tracks were often used centuries later, in Tudor and Stuart times, by the cattle drovers making their way to the lush fattening pastures and cattle fairs of the Midlands. The most famous prehistoric road is the Icknield Way – also known as the Ridgeway for part of its course – which follows the long belt of the chalk hills from Salisbury Plain across the Chilterns into the flint rich Norfolk Breckland around Grime's Graves described above.

Roman Britain: the legacy of conquest and civilisation

The Roman occupation of the British Isles lasted just under 400 years. It began with the invasion of south-east England in AD 43 and ended about 410 when the last of the Roman armies withdrew to continental Europe. Their conquest had never been complete. Ireland had always remained outside the sphere of the Empire, while many costly military expeditions had failed to achieve an effective and lasting occupation of Scotland.

Agricola's invasion of northern Britain in the last quarter of the 1st century brought the Romans as close as ever they came to the incorporation of Caledonia. His army reached as far north as the lowlands flanking the Moray Firth and it is believed that a fleet was based in Orkney. Agricola established a series of forts between the Forth and the Clyde, a line of defences that in AD 142 incorporated in the frontier works of the Antonine Wall, a chain of signal stations, camps and roads along a defensive line built of turf and stone that extended for 37 miles (see map).

The Antonine Wall functioned as an effective occupied frontier for only short periods of time, scarcely more than a decade on three separate occasions in the Roman centuries. By the end of the 2nd century all effective Roman control had ceased to the north of the Solway Firth: Hadrian's Wall, built between AD 123–128, marked the northern limit of the empire, and its impact on the countryside, within the British Isles.

The first towns

The establishment of towns was probably the most profound change wrought by the Roman occupation. There had been a few large settlements before and in places the Romans had built on earlier sites, as at Colchester. But the earlier Iron Age communities never had the urban character associated with Roman towns.

English county towns, the basis of regional life for so many centuries, reveal in many places a beginning as provincial centres in Roman Britain: Gloucester, Chester and Cirencester, for instance, betray their origins in their name (-cester originating in *castra*, meaning camp) but Lincoln and York as well as London were also Roman towns. But the Romans did not leave behind an unalterable blueprint for urban evolution; in most places the rectangular Roman street pattern did not survive to any extent.

The prehistoric flint mines of Grimes Graves in Norfolk: man's first industrial landscape

Roman road at Blackstone Edge in the Pennines: the best-preserved in Britain

Furthermore, some of the greatest Roman towns were to be extinguished either altogether at their original sites, as at Viroconium, Calleva and Verulamium which are short distances away from the modern village of Wroxeter, Silchester and St Albans respectively.

Many Roman settlements were military rather than civilian in nature. Within the confines of Dover Castle, above the famous white cliffs, is a unique survival of such a settlement: a Saxon church whose tower was originally built as a Roman lighthouse. It still stands 40ft (12m) high and is the sole surviving relic of the most important Roman naval base in England, *Portus Dubris*.

Dover was one of a line of ports that stretched from the Wash to the Solent, the so-called Forts of the Saxon Shore. Richborough (*Portus Rutupis*) was the main port of entry but Lympne (*Portus Lemanis*) and Dover were close rivals. In addition to commanding the sea routes across the Channel to Gaul, the forts were in some cases also ports with an important commercial role in the movement of minerals, grain, hides – and slaves.

Nine of the Roman forts still survive to some degree and in many cases their walls have remained remarkably intact, particularly at Portchester, the most westerly of the Roman Forts. Portchester is still on the coast unlike former ports and forts such as Pevensey, Richborough and Stutfall Castle at Lympne all of which are now some distance inland. Only Dover of the Kentish Roman forts and ports has remained immune to subsequent changes in the coastline.

The towns, whether military or civilian, were linked by an elaborate network of brilliantly-engineered roads (see map). At Blackstone Edge (above) on the Pennine Moors above Littleborough it is still possible to walk along a few yards of Roman road.

Only rarely does the original Roman pavement still exist – Blackpool Bridge in the Forest of Dean, Gloucestershire, is another site – but the routes chosen and laid down by the Romans have often survived. Sometimes they can be located only through the spade of an archaeologist or the observant eye of a local historian. But for many miles in many different parts of the country the routes are still used today. Even some of their names are as familiar as their characteristic straightness: Watling Street, Fosse Way and Stane Street.

Gold in the hills

The chief aim of the Roman conquest of Britain lay in the exploitation of the natural resources of these islands, above all its mineral resources of lead, gold, silver, iron, copper and tin. As one historian of the Roman period has written 'they came not to develop the country but to take from it what it already produced'. The legacy of Roman mining in the countryside of the 20th century is not easily recognised after so many centuries of later exploitation.

At Dolaucothi, in the gentle hills of south-west Wales, however, there are some remains of Roman mining that are unique in western Europe. Here gold occurs as a primary deposit in veins of quartz. Although the gold mines were worked as recently as the late 19th century, when new shafts were dug and engine houses and processing plant installed, the evidence of Roman operations is still to be seen. A seven-mile-long (11km) aqueduct, carefully engineered to take water from a narrow gorge in the River Cothi to tanks above the gold mine, can still be clearly traced. And some of the tunnels, too, in this deserted labyrinth are reminiscent in their form of Roman mines in the south of Spain with tool marks on the roof and walls suggesting that they were cut by hand.

Other areas likely to have been sites of Roman mining are the lead-rich hills around Matlock and the Forest of Dean, for centuries the most prolific source of iron ore in Britain. Roman mining in the Forest is well attested but the location of any particular working cannot be proved; among the likeliest places, however, is the Scowles, a wooded maze of

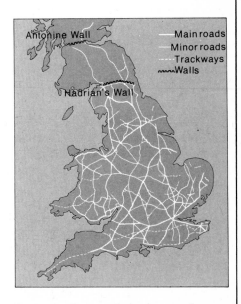

Roman roads covered the country far more extensively than is generally known

Hadrian's Wall in Northumberland: no monument to the 400 years of the Roman occupation of Britain is more enduring, no posting for the Roma...

hillocks and deep rock-encircled, over-grown pits.

Villas and the middle classes

In the countryside of lowland England the effect of four centuries of Roman rule on the subsequent evolution of the land-scape is hard to define. The sites of 620 villas are known, but of these fewer than 100 could be described as luxurious country houses with the rooms, baths, heating systems and mosaics commonly associated with the term 'villa'.

Most villas were farm buildings, laid out on a rectangular Roman plan with no more than six rooms. It is believed that these were occupied by native Britons, a kind of rural middle class who were descendants of the builders of Iron Age forts and who had adopted the habits of nearby Roman towns. The excavation of several villas has revealed the existence of an older Iron Age farm. Excavation has also shown how villas were rebuilt during the Roman years as their owners prospered.

In the parts of England most favoured by fertile soil, climate and topography there was therefore a continuity in farm-ing. The Roman villa and its estate represented essentially a modification of an older British farming system to the architectural fashions and market economy of the Mediterranean world. The North and South Downs, the Cotswolds and the area north of London are examples of areas where, although farming was intensified during the Roman centuries, it remained basically a development of ancient systems.

Elsewhere there is evidence that im-perial estates were established where Roman experts pioneered the colonis-ation of fresh land for agriculture. Their most ambitious project was in the Fens where land was reclaimed early in the 2nd century AD. A canal called the Car Dyke was also cut from the edge of the Fens near Peterborough to the River Witham at Lincoln. The cargoes of corn destined for the huge garrison at York then passed by another Roman water-way, the Fossdyke, into the Trent before heading northwards via the rivers con-verging on the Humber.

Today, like the fields and farms of the imperial estates, the Car Dyke has all but vanished from the landscape. It appears

...gionnaires could possibly have seemed more bleak

The Dark Ages: the arrival of Saxons, Danes and Christianity

Almost 700 years separate the end of Roman government in the British Isles from the Norman invasion of 1066 – the Anglo-Saxon centuries or the Dark Ages as they are commonly known. The latter term reflects both the ignorance that once shrouded these centuries and the pagan years that followed the fall of Rome. But it is altogether too pejorative a description. By the time the Normans arrived these so-called Dark Ages had witnessed the founding of nearly every village which is on the map of England today and many of its county towns were flourishing. By then, too, Britain had been Christian for several centuries.

Political historians have established a degree of unity in this long span of time through the genealogies or family histories of the lines of Saxon kings, among whom the rulers of Wessex were to become supreme during the closing two centuries. But the epoch of the Anglo-Saxons has a lot to do with native Britons, peoples who were alien to the invaders and settlers from northern Europe who took over the south-east lowlands in the fifth century. Even the Romans had failed to incorporate the whole of Britain within their imperial territories so it was hardly surprising that the Saxons effectively occupied a much smaller part of the British Isles than their predecessors. A study of the scattering of the earliest Anglo-Saxon names across the English landscape suggests that the majority of their settlements early in the first half of the sixth century were to be found south-east of a line drawn from the Wash to the Solent.

There is no accurate means of telling the numbers of settlers who came to the British Isles from across the North Sea. Once it was believed that the great invasion swept all before it: that the British population of the lowlands fled to the west or was wiped out in the confusion of a savage military conquest. Now a somewhat different view is taken of these events. Archaeological research has shown recently that some Saxons were settled in Britain in the latter part of the 4th century – perhaps a generation and more *before* the Roman withdrawal.

Even more important in understanding the development of the landscape over the decades of transition from the Romans to the Saxons is the realisation that there was a continuity of British patterns of life into the middle years of the fifth century. Romano-British communities and pagan Anglo-Saxon settlers have been shown to be living side-by-side within the town walls of Canterbury, Dorchester-on-Thames and London long after the Roman troops had withdrawn to Europe.

And there is growing proof of a continuity of life in the countryside, too. For instance, a recently excavated villa at Shakenoak, in Oxfordshire, has shown that the farm was still inhabited, and presumably the estate was still productive, in the middle of the fifth century by people of a mixed Romano-British and Anglo-Saxon origin. In many places estates of the Roman centuries seem to have evolved into Anglo-Saxon manors. At Withington, in the Cotswolds, it has been argued that the present parish boundary and the lands of the medieval

on the ground as a scarcely perceptible hollow and embankment which wanders across lush pastures and meadows or else as a line drawn across the soils of freshly-ploughed land.

But knowledge of the countryside of Roman Britain is far from complete and never will be. Valuable evidence from villas, discovered in years gone by, has often been lost. New finds, especially in the past quarter century, have added greatly to our knowledge. Perhaps the most striking was the discovery in the 1960s of a Roman villa, till then unsuspected, at Fishbourne near Chichester. Nothing can compare with it elsewhere in Britain. Fishbourne, with its numerous mosaics has about 100 rooms, and has been described as a palace.

Offa's Dyke, photographed here near Clun in Shropshire, remains an impressive earthwork today 1200 years after it was erected as a Saxon boundary and barrier against the Welsh – *see page 43*

manor outline the extent and the limits of the much older Roman villa estate.

The Anglo-Saxon settlements of eastern and southern England and the emergence of a series of kingdoms from Northumbria to Wessex led to a sharp division of the British Isles into a Celtic west – a mostly upland Britain facing the Atlantic and focused upon the Irish Sea – and the lowlands of England facing the North Sea and the narrows of the Channel. Their development affected the landscape in different ways – as will be explained on the opposite page – but one common underlying factor was the movement towards political unity.

By the first half of the 10th century a new political order was emerging in the British Isles. Where 300 years before there had been 11 Saxon states, there was just Wessex as sole ruler of lowland England. The princedom of Gwynedd, based on its mountain stronghold of Snowdonia, was giving a sense of unity to Wales. Further north the medieval shape of Scotland was also emerging and in Ireland there were signs of lordships that were the beginnings of the four provinces of Ulster, Leinster, Munster and Connaught, with Meath on the Central Lowland.

The most striking consequence of this political unification in terms of the geography of Britain was the renewal of life in the towns. Yet urban ways had never been totally forgotten. There is now increasing evidence for the survival of communities through the early Saxon centuries in London, Canterbury, Bath and perhaps also in as remote a Roman town as Carlisle.

Greater impetus came, however, in the 9th and 10th centuries with the founding of *burhs*. By the time of Alfred the Great's death in 899, he had established 30 *burhs* which had all been fortified against attack from the Danes. All but one of these settlements – Buckingham – were south of the Thames, but by the first quarter of the 10th century defended towns were also established in the Midlands – at Warwick, Tamworth, Stafford and Bakewell to give but four examples. Recent archaeological research has also shown that streets and town centres were replanned during this time at Lewes and in the Wessex capital of Winchester. There was one other influence which encouraged the development of urban life at this time – the Danes, Scandinavians, Norsemen or, as they are most popularly if erroneously known, the Vikings.

The peaceful and linguistic legacy of the Viking conquest

The Vikings contributed far more to the development of the British Isles than the rape and plunder raids of popular legend. The last two centuries before the Norman conquest saw large-scale settlement in eastern England by Scandinavians. There were also substantial areas of Viking or Danish strength in the more exposed parts of Scotland, eastern Ireland, the Lake District and the Isle of Man (where a line of Norse kings reigned).

Scandinavian political power in England stretched east from a line running roughly between the estuaries of the Thames and the Dee – the so-called Danelaw. Wessex had regained control of virtually the whole of England by the middle of the 10th century, but the extent of Scandinavian influence is evident in the survival of many place-names. Among the most common of these are *by* (meaning a village), *thwaite* (a clearing) and *thorpe* (also village or a farmstead). See below for a glossary of some common place-names.

Norse influence had been particularly important in the development of urban life in many parts of the British Isles. Within the area of the Danelaw the new settlers developed existing Saxon towns into thriving *burhs* or boroughs that served as regional and trading centres. Recent excavations at York, for instance, have suggested that the city owes its importance almost as much to its revival under Norse influence as to its earlier Roman foundations. The success of these *burhs* led the kings of Wessex to develop their towns along similar defensive and commercial lines.

Around the coasts of Ireland the Vikings, having been fierce raiders early in the 9th century, began to exert a more positive influence. Some historians believe they introduced coinage to Ireland and they certainly founded the first towns in the trading ports of Dublin, Wexford, Waterford, Cork and Limerick. On the other side of the Irish sea Cardiff, Swansea and Chester (which had been almost desolate since Roman days) also owe much to the trade encouraged by Norse merchants. Far to the north Shetland, Orkney and the Hebrides were to remain part of the Scandinavian world for 400 years.

A glossary of some common placenames with Saxon or Norse origins*

MODERN FORM	MEANING
Barrow-; Bar-; -berry; -burgh	Hill, mound, tumulus
Barton	Corn farm, outlying grange
Beck	Stream
Brock-; Brough-; -brook; -broke	Brook, stream
Brough-; -burgh; -bury; -borough	Fortified place
-bourne; -borne	Stream, spring
-by	Village, settlement, farm
Cleve-; Clif-; -cliff; -ley	Cliff, bank
Coate; Coton; -cot; -cote	Cottage
Deane; Den-; -dean; -den	Valley
Dun-; -den; -don; -ton	Down, hill
Ea-; E-; -ey; -eau	Stream, river, island
Frith	Woodland
Hale; Hal-; -all; -hall	Nook, narrow valley
-ham	Village, manor, homestead, meadow, enclosure
-hampton	Home farm
-hanger	Slope
-hay; -hey	Fence, enclosure
Had-; Hat-; Hed-; Heath-	Heath, heather
Holt-; -hurst	Wood
Lea-; -leigh; -ley; -low	Forest, wood, glade, clearing
Med-; -mede	Meadow
-mond; -mont	Mount, hill
-stead; -sted	Place, religious site
Stret-; Sturt-; Stred-; Strat-	Street
Thwaite-; -thwaite	Clearing or meadow
-ton; -tone	Enclosure, farmstead, village
Wick-; Wig-; wich; -wick	Dwelling, farm
-worth; -worthy	Enclosure

*Selections of common placenames with Gaelic origins appear in the Days Out sections of this book

Landscapes of Anglo-Saxon England

The colonisation of lowland, southeastern Britain by the Anglo-Saxons left its mark indelibly on the landscape. The newcomers from across the North Sea continued the attack upon the forests and established villages as the nuclei of their agricultural economies. Apart from some churches, or remnants of churches, Saxon buildings have long since vanished; they were too flimsy to forestall either decay or rebuilding in later centuries. But the great majority of villages on the map of England today were in existence by 1066.

The impact of the Saxon farmer and his English speaking descendants on the countryside is most evident in the abundance and distribution of place-names; see glossary of some common place-names on opposite page. It has long been accepted that many places whose names end in *ham* or *ing* belong to the earliest stages of the Anglo-Saxon settlement. The suffix *ham* is taken to mean anything from village to homestead or enclosure, and when *ing* occurs it is usually coupled with a personal name, one who perhaps acted as a tribal leader. For instance Hastings, it is believed, was founded by 'the followers of Haesta'. Sussex – which itself means the territory of the South Saxons – contains about 50 place-names ending with the suffix *-ing*.

Some places hark back to the earliest period of colonisation, before the conversion of the Anglo-Saxons to Christianity, in their commemoration of the pagan gods of northern Europe. Thus the Staffordshire Black Country remembers the god Woden at Wednesbury and Wednesfield. And in East Kent we find Woodnesborough meaning 'the *bury* or defended place of Woden'. There the church stands on a mound, slightly raised above the surrounding fields and lanes. Is this perhaps the last faint relic in the landscape of an Iron Age earthwork, a site that was taken over and dedicated to the worship of Woden by the earliest Anglo-Saxon settlers?

Place-names are also testimony to the agricultural activities of the Saxons. Their inroads into the forests are recorded for all time in such terms as *ley*, *hurst*, *holt*, *hey* and *field*. All are suffixes indicating clearings or places where log huts were raised and cattle pastured in the wild wood. And Chorley, a name that occurs in several parts of England, means 'the clearing of the peasants', suggesting long forgotten communal efforts in pushing back the frontiers of the

Skellig Michael: Dark Age monastic cells on a bleak island without worldly temptations

forests which covered the land.

The most impressive individual landmarks of the first four centuries of the Anglo-Saxon epoch are some huge linear earthworks of which Offa's Dyke, shown on the previous page near Clun in Shropshire, is the greatest.

Offa's Dyke is as magnificent in its conception as Hadrian's Wall, extending from the estuary of the Dee in the north to the mouth of the Wye – a distance of 120 miles (193km) which formed the western frontier of the kingdom of Mercia. It was raised in the reign of King Offa (757–795) and, unlike many lesser earthworks, remains an impressive feature of the landscape today.

To walk the length of the dyke, which now forms the basis for much of a long-distance footpath, is to discover insights into the landscape and society of the long-vanished society of Mercia. The strategic intentions of the earthwork are evident in the sections where the dyke strides across the slopes of westward-facing hills with long views into Wales. In Powys an Iron Age hill-fort, Burfa Camp, was incorporated in the line of the earthwork. A missing link in the line of the dyke in the plain of Hereford suggests that the dense primeval woodland that then existed there made the creation of a man-made frontier, with its raised banks and deep ditches, an unnecessary further protection.

Other Anglo-Saxon earthworks were less grand and today, except where they serve as parish boundaries or define the line of a footpath, they seem to be meaningless features in the landscape. Not so 1500 years ago when they marked boundaries of large estates as well as frontiers or defensive lines of kingdoms. Grim's Dyke in Cranborne Chase, Dorset, for instance, probably marked the boundary of a cattle ranch.

Landscapes of Celtic Britain

The influence of seven centuries of Dark Age history in the making of the landscapes of western and northern Britain seems remarkably slight. The early Christian church formed the most revolutionary element among peoples whose way of life, both socially and economically, essentially represented a continuation of the ways of the Iron Age.

St Patrick had converted most of Ireland to Christianity in the middle years of the fifth century and by the sixth century the gospel was also being spread in Scotland by the missionary activity of St Columba and St Moluag from their island monasteries on Iona and Lismore. Monasteries were the initial fulcrum of the church in Celtic Britain, whereas the later Christianity of Saxon England was organised territorially through bishops based on dioceses.

Most monasteries were centres of worship, learning and farming, but some monks sought special austerities and a few were hermits. Remains of normal monasteries, including churches, living quarters and Round Towers built to guard treasures against Norse raiders, survive in many places, for example Glendalough in Co Wicklow and Clonmacnoise beside the Shannon. Worldly temptations could be avoided in such places as Skellig Michael, a tiny rocky island 700ft (213m) high, in the Atlantic eight miles (13km) off the south-west coast of Ireland. The lack of any timber on the island meant that the monastery was built of stone and this, allied to its inaccessibility, has meant that small beehive-shaped cells and oratories still survive today.

Although people settled around monasteries, few villages developed. In this separate Celtic world of Wales, Scotland and Ireland farming was developing inside enclosures. In Ireland these were known as *raths*, if surrounded by earth banks, or *cashels*, if inside walls of stone; in all there is estimated to have been between 30,000 and 40,000 of these enclosures, each occupied by a farmer with perhaps 70 acres of land.

From the end of the 9th century the Church was absorbed into the Roman allegiance, centred as in England on dioceses with a bishop rather than on separate monasteries. But although archaeology has so far revealed little of the life of the monasteries, there can be no doubt that they had been the great centres of culture in Celtic Britain. In Ireland their cultural legacy is immense.

From top to bottom: the castles of Ludlow in Shropshire, Castle Rising in Norfolk and Harlech in Gwynedd. With the castles often came new towns. The streets of Ludlow still largely follow the grid-iron plan characteristic of Norman settlements established in the 12th century

Cistercian monks sought isolation and bequeathed abbey

The Middle Ages: the citadels of conquest and the years of decline

The landscape of the Middle Ages can be detected without the assistance of either archaeology or aerial photography. It is evident in the 'fossilised' strips of open fields, in ruins of castles and monasteries, in the street plans of many market towns and cities, in the narrow winding lanes which join village to village and, above all, in the thousands of names of fields, farms and city streets.

Indeed the medieval centuries contributed so much to the visual wealth of England especially – in the shape of castles, monasteries, cathedrals and the domestic architecture of prosperous wool

to match the beauty of their surroundings. Above is Rievaulx Abbey, North Yorkshire, and below right, Melrose Abbey in the Scottish Borders

towns – that this has become the prime tourist image of the British Isles. But it is a mistake to regard the entire period as a golden age of expansion. The two centuries up to 1300 were ones of growth, although this was most marked in England and southern and eastern England at that. The years that followed, however, witnessed a fall in population caused largely by the effects of climatic change, plague and wars, especially with the French and Scots. By 1485, and the founding of the Tudor dynasty in England, a slow recovery was under way.

But the story begins in the decades after 1066 with the building of castles to help the Normans control their newly-conquered lands.

A great wave of castle-building followed the Norman Conquest during the reign of William I. Most of these were raised in the hearts of Saxon towns which already formed regional centres. The Domesday Book tells us that at Lincoln 166 houses were destroyed for the building of the castle while at Norwich 98 houses were pulled down in clearing the site for a huge earth motte, crowned by a forbidding stone keep.

Elsewhere the building of the castle preceded the creation of a town. The Domesday Book again records, for instance, the erection of a gigantic motte on the lip of the steep-sided Kensey valley in Cornwall; on the slopes beneath the castle the borough of Launceston was soon to come into being. The same process was repeated at many places in the Welsh Marches, an uneasy frontier zone ever open to raids from the west and border strife between the 100 and more territories of earls, barons and bishops that formed a mosaic of little states between the Bristol Channel and the Dee estuary. The building of Ludlow Castle along this frontier soon after 1085 was particularly remarkable since it also involved the creation of a planned town at the gates of the castle that retains its basic shape to this day.

The border territories where the claims of the English, Welsh and Scots were perpetually in conflict are inevitably rich in medieval castles and boroughs. North Wales has Conwy and Caernarfon castles, for instance, and in Northumberland the Normans established almost 20 'motte and bailey' castles. Some of these have faded into the countryside as no more than overgrown mounds and ditches but others, as at Alnwick and Warkworth for instance, were extended and elaborated throughout the medieval centuries to survive as some of the finest examples of the redundant technology of military architecture to be seen in Britain. Many Norman castles in Ireland were humble structures but most of the towns which developed around them had walls which in some places, including Dublin, can still be seen today.

The motte and bailey style of Norman castle

The 'ridge and furrow' of medieval farming remains visible near Southam in Warwickshire

Years of prosperity and growth

The population of England grew about threefold in the first two centuries after the Norman conquest: from about $1\frac{1}{2}$ million at the time of the Domesday Book in 1086 – an incomplete record since it did not cover all of England, let alone the rest of the British Isles – to around $4\frac{1}{2}$ million in 1300.

This growth was not evenly spread throughout the country. In the long settled tracts of southern and central England, where the opportunities for the expansion of farming at the expense of unreclaimed woodland were by then slight, the growth of population was negligible. Where wasteland, forest and fen were still available for colonisation, population grew rapidly.

In the south of Warwickshire, for instance, medieval records show some villages to have been the same size in 1279 as they had been in 1086. But to the north of the county beyond the River Avon in the densely-forested district of Arden the population grew dramatically as tiny clusters of farms and moated manor houses were planted in newly-cleared land. Remarkably high increases in population between 1086 and the early years of the 14th century have also been detected in the Fenland where the first extensive reclamation was carried out since Roman times. The number of tenants in Spalding, for instance, increased by $6\frac{1}{2}$ times over that period.

This age of expansion left its mark on both the countryside and the towns. In the country it was the heyday of open-field farming. This involved two, three and maybe more huge fields grouped around the nucleus of a village. Each field was then laid out in strips to be farmed by the individual farmers living in the village. The farmers ploughed up and down the strips with the plough throwing the soil towards the centre of the strip to form a ridge. Each strip was separated from its neighbour by a double furrow – hence the 'ridge and furrow' pattern that can still be seen not only through aerial photography but also on the ground, especially in winter when vegetation is bare.

The origins of this method of farming are obscure. It has traditionally been associated with the Saxons but some historians and geographers argue that it only came into being after the Norman conquest – perhaps as a consequence of the rising population and the need to work the land more intensively. There is, for instance, only one reference in the Domesday Book to strip farming – at Garsington in Oxfordshire – amid the endless statistics about plough-teams and ploughlands. What is certain is that this method of farming became much more widespread in the 12th and 13th centuries.

The wealth of these centuries is reflected in other changes. They saw the rebuilding of hundreds of parish churches as wooden Saxon churches were reconstructed in stone. However, an even more striking sign of the times was the founding of new towns and the granting of borough charters to already established settlements. By 1334 there were more than 200 boroughs in England alone. Some places which received charters were successful and continued down the centuries to form market towns or the great cities of the present day; others faltered in the economic decline of the later medieval centuries and not a few were failures from the beginning. In Lancashire, for instance, 23 boroughs were founded, but only four of them – Lancaster, Liverpool, Preston and Wigan – could be described as towns at the end of the Middle Ages.

Some of Britain's most prosperous ports were founded during these two centuries of expansion; Boston, King's Lynn and Newcastle came into existence about 1100. Harwich, Liverpool and Portsmouth were founded about a century later and Kingston-upon-Hull was established about 1300.

The prosperous centuries of the early Middle Ages owe not a little to the numerous monastic foundations of the Plantagenet kings and private landowners. In particular the coming of the new order of the Cistercians in the 12th century broke new ground over many acres of upland Britain, since it was an order that insisted upon isolated life in wild and lonely places. The Cistercian houses provide many of the finest ruins in Britain; among them are Rievaulx and

Fountains Abbeys in Yorkshire, Tintern on the banks of the Wye and Melrose in the Borders. Their influence was more than architectural: they became vast landowners, invariably using their land for sheep rearing. Furness Abbey, for instance, owned thousands of acres above Eskdale and Borrowdale in the Lake District as well as the entire Furness peninsula between lakes Windermere and Coniston. The word 'grange' is a widespread reminder of monastic power since it originally meant an outlying monastic farm.

In Wales, Scotland and Ireland the pace of change was slower and the most remote parts remained unaffected by the patterns of development in the lowland areas of southern Britain. Nevertheless towns still grew up around Norman castles and churches with markets that became increasingly prosperous. Craftsmen were located mainly in the towns (most of which had a cornmill) but some, notably blacksmiths, were spread more widely through the countryside. A few even penetrated areas far from Norman influence, such as the Orkneys, where the 12th century cathedral at Kirkwall reflects the Norman skills of masons, glaziers and carpenters. At the same time continental masons were imported into Ireland to invigorate native customs and to produce at Cashel a church reflecting both prehistoric and medieval traditions.

Cashel was outside the area of the

greatest Norman influence in Ireland. This was confined to the more fertile part of the country, mainly in the eastern part of the Central Lowland and in such valleys as the Nore, Suir and Barrow, all of which join to flow through Waterford Harbour. They made little impact west of the Shannon or in Ulster.

Norman political power also failed to encompass the greater part of Wales but the Welsh princes, the rulers of Gwynedd, encouraged the great Norman monastic orders to acquire property. For instance, towards the end of the 12th century, the Cistercians were endowed with Aberconwy, a place of high strategic importance which a century later was to be taken over by Edward I for the founding of the new town and castle of Conwy.

In the lowlands of Scotland, too, a strong centralised monarchy followed many Norman principles of organisation. Towns grew up around castles – such as Edinburgh in the 12th century – markets established to encourage trade, foreign monastic orders endowed with vast tracts of land which sometimes became centres of agricultural expansion. But the highlands and islands remained, largely immune from such changes and therefore continued to be dominated by clan rule.

☐ See page 24 for the making of the Norfolk Broads.

The Round Tower of Kilmacduagh, Co Galway, leans slightly out of the perpendicular. These towers are peculiar to Ireland and were used variously as hiding places and defences against Norse raiders. Here the tower stands next to cathedral ruins dating back to the 10th century

The years of deserted villages

The great divide in the Middle Ages came at the beginning of the 14th century. Population ceased to grow, indeed by the middle of the century, when the Black Death spreading from India wrought havoc all over Europe, there was a catastrophic decline of numbers in some parts of the country. As the plague raged between 1348 and 1350 it is estimated that between a third and a half of the population of the British Isles died, many of them in the towns.

The Black Death has been blamed for the economic stagnation, the abandonment of agricultural land, the desertion of hundreds of villages (see below) and the decline of population that is a characteristic of the 15th century. No doubt the Black Death and the succeeding epidemics of 1361, 1369 and 1374 were important factors in the economic and social changes of the late Middle Ages, but research has also shown that the long period of expansion and prosperity had come to a close a generation before the plague ever reached the British Isles.

Two severe periods of famine from 1315–1317 and again in 1321 seem to mark a turning point in the population history of medieval England. The onslaught of these famines which severely reduced the corn harvest, and consequently the stock of seed-corn for the next year, may well be explained by a deterioration in the climate of western Europe that set in at the beginning of the 14th century. It was a time of cool, sunless wet autumns when the corn failed to ripen. The Black Death came as the ultimate scourge among the troubles of those times. And, ironically, some villages were to die as a result of reviving prosperity rather than plague.

Ingarsby in east Leicestershire is one of more than 2000 deserted village sites in England alone. But it is unusual since it is known exactly when, and why, it became deserted. The year was 1469. The village had contained a dozen families according to a tax survey in 1377 but it became deserted overnight when it was bought and razed to the ground by Leicester Abbey.

The monks wanted the land as sheep pasture for the booming wool trade. Vast numbers of village desertions were caused by acquisitive landlords with interests in the wool trade that flourished from the second half of the 15th century.

The continued use of the Ingarsby site as pasture as opposed to arable land has meant that it is still possible to walk along the hollows of the former lanes between the grassy platforms where the farmsteads once stood. In the valley below, the earth dam which collected the waters of a brook in a large mill-pond can still be seen, as can the faint lines of 'ridge-and-furrow' field patterns encircling the old settlement.

It was once thought that the Black Death of 1348–50 had caused many village desertions but nowhere was this the sole factor. A great number of desertions occurred between 1450 and 1520 at a time when population in England was slowly rising once more and when the plague must have passed into the folklore of the nation. The motives for desertion in these latter decades were largely economic, determined above all by the movements in corn and wool prices.

The booming wool exports to Flanders and Italy and the rise of the cloth industry in Coventry, Norwich, the Cotswolds and the little towns of Suffolk brought about a rise in wool prices that ensured high profits to the landlord who could convert the open arable fields to pasture. The many village desertions in the counties of eastern England, therefore, are related to the location of the chief cloth-making centres, hence the scores of abandoned sites in Norfolk and south Warwickshire which offered not only good grazing land but also easy access to such wool-exporting ports as Boston and King's Lynn or the busy cloth town of Coventry.

The years of decline were most marked in Ireland, large areas of which retreated into fighting and traditional Celtic ways. The Celtic lifestyle was based on small self-sufficient hamlets without any of the commercial interdependence between town and country that had seen the birth of market towns in England. This was at its most deep-rooted in Ireland since it had initially survived for 1000 years without occupation by the Romans or their successors from the continent.

The Vikings had established the first towns – even the name Ireland has Norse origins – and the Anglo-Norman invasion of 1169 added more towns as well as the mixed farming methods of England to large areas of Ireland, particularly the south and east. But there were too few colonisers for the Anglo-Norman influence to withstand the difficulties of the 15th century. Even the towns with their castles fell into disrepair while outside the town walls Celtic influence reasserted itself as the widespread existence of Gaelic placenames still testifies.

The landscape revolution of the Tudor to Georgian years

The victory won by Henry Tudor on the open fields of the village of Bosworth in Leicestershire in 1485 saw the beginning of an era of unparalleled change in the landscape. Many of the features now regarded as integral elements in the 'traditional' countryside have their origins in the three centuries from 1485 that preceded the Industrial Revolution.

The fields were enclosed by hedgerows, country houses laid out in landscaped parkland, villages rebuilt in their local stone with sufficient solidity to survive to the present day. Industry, too, gathered momentum from small scale enterprises such as iron-smelting and glass-making in the Weald of Kent. Trade flourished and with it towns grew and communication routes improved – on land and water.

The impact of these changes was most marked in England and with good reason for these were centuries in which England emerged as a major political force in the world. And as English power came to dominate Wales, Scotland and, to a lesser degree, Ireland, so too did the fashions and practices of the English conquerors. Architectural styles and farming methods were thus implanted on vast tracts of the British Isles.

Quite when this English Revolution led into the Industrial Revolution is impossible to say. The 18th century saw the first stirrings of the Industrial Revolution in some parts of the British Isles while others, notably Ireland, were still adjusting to the agricultural changes of the previous two centuries. Improvements in road and water communications were also under way during these centuries, but their impact will be examined in the next section on the Industrial Revolution when their significance became most apparent.

But another revolution was slowly producing its own far-reaching transformation of the landscape. Piecemeal enclosure of the old open fields around the villages of England had been going on since the 14th century, particularly in the south-west and south-east of the country.

Improved techniques of animal husbandry offered wealthy landowners far more valuable returns than accrued from traditional farming. Many tenants of the open field therefore found themselves evicted and great hedged fields of pasture were created on their rich clay lands.

Field enclosures came later to upland areas like the Peak District (above) with drystone walls rather than hedgerows acting as boundaries

Kersey, Suffolk: the prosperity of the Tudor to Georgian years enabled quite humble cottages to be rebuilt in sturdy local materials

By the end of the 16th century only the shire counties of the English Midlands still had a high proportion of cultivated land farmed in unenclosed strips. And when the Parliamentary Commissioners set about completing the task of enclosures in the middle of the 18th century they found that in many areas it was only a mopping-up operation. The change-over to a landscape of hedged fields – to be so mourned when threatened with destruction in the 20th century – had been largely accomplished by private agreements.

Where the Commissioners did have a job to do, as in the Midlands and eastern England, they left behind a new country-side of large regular fields with straight hedges of hawthorn with perhaps the occasional ash or elm set within to give variety. New straight roads of specified width, and nowadays having wide grass verges, were another of the Commissioners' innovations. New farmhouses were also built and in many cases they were set within the new pattern of fields rather than standing next to the roadway as was characteristic of older dwellings.

The enclosure movement spread, albeit more slowly, to the less fertile uplands of Britain where local stone was often used to form field boundaries rather than specially-planted hedge-rows. But the planting of hedgerows was not the only break with the 3000-year tradition of cutting down woodland for agricultural purposes. Many landowners planted new trees as copses during the 17th century, particularly after the poet John Evelyn had aroused concern among the intelligentsia about the wan-ton destruction of so much of the natural forests of Britain. Many of these copses were planted in the deer parks that surrounded country houses and which, as at Burghley, were sometimes destined to be landscaped by later generations of owners. Not all landowners planted trees for strictly selfless motives: many trees provided cover for foxes who were hunt-ed enthusiastically by the new squires.

In Ireland trees were still being cut down. The 16th and 17th centuries were the years of the great 'plantation' move-ment with profound changes in the land-scape. During these two centuries English and Scottish settlers made new towns, villages and farms. In Ulster, what had previously been a countryside ravaged by strife became prosperous, with domestic industry in the homes. In the remoter areas, especially the up-lands, clusters of houses remained with

Glamis Castle in Tayside: rebuilt in the 17th century with the flavour of a French chateau

the land farmed in strips, but generally new fields were laid out, houses built, woods cleared and marshes or bogs drained. Hedgerows were grown in the lowlands though stone walls formed field boundaries in the mountains and in the west of Ireland from Donegal to Kerry. Some are of massive height to protect oats and potatoes from Atlantic gales. Traditionally the Protestants have had the largest and most fertile farms. Planta-tion thus had profound repercussions on the political history as well as the land-scape of Ireland.

Country houses lose their defences

The stately homes of the 20th century tourist industry are often the country houses of the 16th century. The Tudor years saw the emergence of many such houses surrounded by private estates and many survive in largely unaltered form today. Rich people had always had their great private houses. Sometimes they were so rich and powerful that these were castles, but even lesser nobility had their manor houses.

But the country houses of the 16th and 17th centuries were a new phenomenon. They reflect more than the general pros-perity of the age and more to, too, than the improvement in building skills; they are related directly to some of the key political acts of Tudor times. Henry VIII's onslaught on the Church and the dissolution of the monasteries released hundreds of thousands of acres. Much passed to the crown itself but the former monastic land also gave rise to a new breed of landed gentry, often royal favourites or those holding high offices of state. Burghley House near Stamford, for instance, was built by William Cecil, the

first Lord Burghley and Treasurer to Elizabeth I. It also reflects the Renaissance influence that had accom-panied increased trade from Europe.

The Act of Union of 1536 which finally linked England and Wales had also encouraged the development of country houses. Greater political stability meant that new buildings could be less defensive in nature and more aesthetic in nature and appeal. Even former strongholds like Powis Castle, above the Severn near Welshpool, were transformed into com-fortable country houses with formal gar-dens and a surrounding parkland.

Scotland and Ireland did not ex-perience the same political stability and therefore lagged a century or more behind England in terms of country house building. Elizabethan Scotland still concerned itself with building forti-fied houses, only slightly more homely than the medieval castles. As late as 1680 Glamis in Tayside was rebuilt with an array of conical turrets and impressive massive stone walls. In the border centres like Jedburgh, even town houses had their architectural style influenced by the needs of defence. In Ireland it was much the same story with what were effectively 'castles' built by the powerful families who came in as planters and were given estates of several thousand acres; some, such as Kilkenny and Cahir in Co Tipperary, were already fortified centres of the Anglo-Norman period. As peaceful conditions developed the tradi-tion of building fine country houses became stronger, with many outstanding examples dating from the Georgian years.

☐ *See also pages 80–85 about country houses.*

Reclaiming the Fens

The greatest single act of change in the 17th century as it affected the countryside was undoubtedly the reclamation of the Fens. For centuries this inherently rich area of fertile peaty and silty soils near the Wash had never realised its full potential. Despite Roman and other reclamation efforts, the area was still regularly flooded, particularly during winter months as rivers such as the Ouse, Granta, Nene, Welland and Witham overflowed their banks and spread out over vast areas of surrounding land.

The architect of the great reclamation was Cornelius Vermuyden, a Dutchman. He first made his name as a drainage expert when he tackled the draining of Hatfield Chase near Doncaster. This work, important though it was, proved to be only an essential preliminary to the much greater task of draining the Great Level of the Fens. The problem, as Vermuyden saw it, was to get the water of the rivers draining into the peat 'bowl' away to the sea as quickly as possible. The Ouse, in particular, wandered seemingly without aim or purpose over vast tracts in a series of great meander loops. A shorter straightened course would give a more rapid run off and minimise the danger of flooding.

To achieve this a great artificial cut or canal known as the Bedford River was dug between Earith and Denver. It was 21 miles (34km) long and 70ft (21m) wide – a tremendous achievement to be accomplished only with the spade. The Civil War interrupted further work but in 1650 another period of draining began. This led to the cutting of a second artificial channel, now known as the New Bedford River. Water then had to be pumped from drains in the fields into these major drainage channels. This was done at first by windmills which became a characteristic feature of the Fenland scene. They were ultimately replaced by steam engines – the first of which appeared near Denver in 1820 – but one windmill has been restored and re-erected at Wicken Fen where some of the 'original' reed and sedge fen has been preserved in a nature reserve.

Reclamation has continued after Vermuyden's time so that large-scale flooding is now most unlikely. But some problems remain. Dust storms can occur during a dry spring and carry away the whole top surface of the soil while the peat itself is shrinking as the water level sinks due to drainage schemes.

An iron post from the Great Exhibition of 1851 was sunk into the peat of Holme Fen that year. Its top was then level with the surface at that time but now about 13ft (4m) is exposed. This wastage of the peat fen poses considerable problems, not least in the building of houses and roads on such an unstable foundation. In spite of this the Fens remain as an outstanding example of a man-made countryside where nature's endowment has been turned to advantage by the farmer. (Other areas of agricultural wealth, reclaimed at various times up to present times, include Holderness in east Yorkshire, the meres of south and west Lancashire, and the Somerset 'levels'.)

Harnessing the rivers

Such industry as existed during these centuries was on a small scale and dependent on local raw materials and the availability of water power. In the heavily-forested Weald of Kent and Sussex a rural iron industry flourished throughout the medieval period – its origins in fact go back to the Romans – with the ironmasters turning out a whole range of products from nails and horseshoes to firebacks and cannons. The industry really came alive in Tudor times when skilled workers from the continent brought in new techniques of smelting and casting. Using local iron ore and charcoal from the Wealden forests, furnaces and forges grew up at sites where it was possible to create a head of water by damming a narrow valley. It is these 'hammer' ponds of Kent, Sussex and Surrey which are the most obvious survivals in the countryside of the former industry, though the more observant and searching can still find pieces of bloomery iron around furnace sites like Lamberhurst and Ashburnham.

In upland Britain the power problem was solved by directly harnessing the swiftly flowing rivers. In 25 miles (40km) of the River Kent in the Lake District, for instance, there were no fewer than 90 watermills during the late 18th century. For a brief period at the turn of the 19th century this quiet corner of the Westmorland countryside had a more industrial society than the heart of the Midlands around Birmingham. Bobbins, textiles, paper and snuff mills, as well as the ubiquitous corn-grinding mill, were all using the ample power supplied by the Kent and its tributaries.

Only the advent of steam power and the coming of the railways with their cheap coal brought these essentially rural industries into decline.

Improving the uplands

The countryside of the British Isles on the eve of the industrial revolution in the 18th century was still intensely rural in character. Towns had grown, in England especially, but farming remained the main occupation. Many villages were simply collections of farms, perhaps looking out onto a central green where most of the social life was enacted. These smaller villages or hamlets are particularly associated with upland areas of Britain where agricultural advance in the Tudor and Georgian years was less dramatic.

The higher and wetter parts of Britain posed more intractable problems for agriculture. The soils were generally thinner and intensely leached by the heavy rain and rapid drainage over the steep slopes so that they did not readily respond to the efforts of the small band of 'improvers'. But despite these unfavourable and discouraging circumstances some attempts were made to reclaim even the upland wastes in the latter half of the 18th century. This has been explained by a variety of circumstances, including a favourable climatic period, expanding demand for farm produce, the growth of home spinning and weaving of wool, and an increasing population in all parts of the British Isles. Among the instances of upland development, large and small, were:

England. One of the last and perhaps the greatest attempts at landscape betterment was made on the heathery wastes of Exmoor well above the 1000ft (308m) contour. In 1818 John Knight, who had made his wealth as a Shropshire ironmaster, bought an estate of 15,000 acres centred on Simonsbath. In a generation he and his son Frederic brought about a complete transformation. The flat plateau tops were drained, ploughed and limed and then converted into fine pastures. A wall of stone 29 miles (47km) long was built to enclose the moorland property and 15 new farmhouses sprinkled over the vast area of his landholding. High earthbanks planted with hazel and shelter belts of beech and sycamore were all part of the scheme to tame part of Exmoor. How successful Knight was can be judged today by comparing the rich farmlands he created with the barren wastes of Dartmoor or Bodmin Moor at much the same height.

Wales. Thomas Johnes was the most notable pioneer with his country house, formal gardens and 'natural' landscaping of the Ystwyth valley inland from

Aberystwyth. More than four million trees were planted, mainly larch but also oak and beech in more sheltered places of a valley where the original wood cover had been destroyed by lead mining. Although some of the deciduous trees were quite foreign to the Welsh hillsides, the arboriculture was on the whole a success and Johnes' Hafod estate became 'one of the wonders of Wales' drawing visitors such as J.W. Turner who has left us with a painting of the now demolished house with its two long wings added by John Nash to the original design. Remnants of the estate survive today under the protection of the Forestry Commission.

Scotland. Sir John Sinclair adopted a slightly less eccentric approach to improving the wastes of his native Sutherland. The move from arable to pastoral farming was causing conflict between landlords and tenants as huge highland estates were increasingly turned into more profitable sheep runs. Sinclair, as a paternal landlord, tried to soften the blow by resettling his tenants in new coastal villages like Badbea and Sarclett near Wick where fishing could be combined with farming and craft industries. More successful, though, were his farm improvement schemes around the ancestral home of Thurso Castle and the 'new' village of Halkirk. Most landlords were not so benevolent and the great highland clearances caused great hardship as well as a complete transformation of vast areas of northern Scotland.

Ireland. Many landlords in upland areas planted fine estates (demesnes) with landscaped grounds, kept in order by numerous labourers housed in the villages. A few landlords, like Richard Edgeworth in Longford and Lord Altamont of Westport, tried to reclaim mountain land as well as bog and brought in new breeds of cattle to graze the improved pastures. But many landlords did little or nothing to improve the lot of their tenants; absentee landlords living off rents were regarded with particular odium. Generally the tenants had no security of tenure – the northern areas were more of an exception – and evictions were frequent. People without land became squatters on common land either on hillsides above the area generally farmed or on the edges of bogs. The overcrowding on the land became increasingly severe and with only a small proportion of the landless and jobless able to find work in the towns, emigration to Britain and America was increasing by the end of the 18th century.

The Industrial Revolution: Man leaves the land for the towns

There had been industry in the British Isles since prehistoric man first scoured the ground for flints. It had changed the landscape of areas like the Weald in Kent and Sussex where the iron industry had been so strong and around the Tyne where coal had long been mined or dug from open pits.

But the impact of these early industries on the overall landscape was small. Britain remained a predominantly agricultural country in the middle of the 18th century. Yet within 100 years a majority of the population lived in towns and depended on industry for their livelihood. Vast cities had grown, sometimes out of nothing, Vast mining enterprises littered and transformed the landscape with their residue.

The purpose of this book is neither to provide an economic history of the British Isles nor to dwell on the development of Britain's cities. The importance of the Industrial Revolution is treated here strictly in terms of its impact upon the countryside of the British Isles. This impact was considerable, not merely in the once unspoilt landscape that was devoured or disfigured by the new industries and towns but also in the vast tracts of the countryside apparently unaffected by industrialisation. Few areas, for instance, were immune to the influence of canals and railways. The legacy of the Industrial Revolution on the face of Britain is as varied as it is visible. Steam power transformed the British Isles, first by enabling large factories to be built – often alongside the rivers and canals initially used for trade – in the centre of towns and then through the railway age.

From the 1840s, when the railways covered almost the whole country, the growth of industry and towns was rapid, especially in coalfield areas. Older industrial areas, notably London with its growing port, Liverpool, Birmingham, Hull and central Scotland shared in this industrial growth. People left the land, particularly in upland Wales, Scotland and Ireland, to seek a new life in the towns so that only in Ireland was a majority of the population still dependent on agriculture at the close of the 19th century. Industry has continued to transform the landscape during the 20th century, but that is a story taken up in the final chapter of this book: The Future of the Countryside. It is a story that is far from being over.

Ironbridge: the first iron bridge in the world was erected in 1779 across the River Severn near Coalbrookdale: an area regarded as the birthplace of the Industrial Revolution

The birthplace of the revolution

If one area can claim to have been the birthplace of the Industrial Revolution, then it is the middle Severn valley around Coalbrookdale. Here, in a quiet corner of the Shropshire countryside, there was a fine river waterway available for transport, steep banks clothed with woodland ideal for making charcoal, deposits of iron and clay and accessible coal seams – all the ingredients to develop a whole group of industries.

It was a largely rural landscape in 1707 when Abraham Darby became ironmaster of a small blast furnace at Coalbrookdale in one of the steep-sided valleys running down to the Severn. It was here that Darby began experiments using coke to smelt the local iron ore. Since what there was of an iron 'industry' was gravely threatened by a shortage of charcoal, Darby's success ultimately re-volutionised the manufacture of iron and steel and thus provided a firm foundation for widespread industrial growth. At first Darby used the local coal straight from the mine but when this did not answer his purpose he converted it into coke on a spot close to the furnace. Gradually the more readily available coke replaced charcoal in the manufacture of cast iron, though it was not until 1775 that char-coal ceased to be used in the forge where other forms of iron and steel were made.

Abraham Darby's family inherited his pioneering spirit: Abraham Darby II was to build the nearby Horsehay iron-works in 1755 and in 1779 Abraham Darby III built the first iron bridge in the world high across the Severn one mile (1.6km) downstream from Coalbrooke-dale. The bridge is no longer used for traffic but was an engineering master-piece which served an important prac-tical as well as symbolic purpose: it allowed raw materials and finished pro-ducts to pass freely across the Severn so that new industries like the tile works at Jackfield were set up on the other bank.

The area around Ironbridge remained important throughout the 19th century. It was, for instance, to Coalbrookedale that Richard Trevithick came in 1802 when building his steam engine. Isambard Kingdom Brunel also used iron rolled at the Horsehay works for his ship, the *Great Britain*. But the focus of the industrialisation shifted elsewhere leav-ing the Ironbridge area largely neglected and forgotten. Luckily, however, many remains of these birthpangs of the Indus-trial Revolution can now be seen under the aegis of the Ironbridge Gorge Trust.

The first factories and slums

Cromford in Derbyshire was to the textile industry what Coalbrookdale was to the iron industry. It was at Cromford that Richard Arkwright established his first textile mill in 1771 and began a social revolution that was to have far-reaching effects well beyond the Derwent Valley. It marked the beginning of a changeover from cotton industry to the factory system of production.

Previously such industry as existed had been mostly a small-scale affair. Even inventions like Hargreaves's spinning jenny in 1767 had initially aided home-based textile workers. And the dependence on water power had meant that industries were sited high up remote river valleys rather than in city centres or lowland plains; many of these are still visible, though generally in ruins, in Pennine valleys of Lancashire and Yorkshire.

Arkwright also relied on water power for his Cromford mill, but the sheer scale of the enterprise was revolutionary. More than 800 people were employed, many of them working at night. By then further mills had been built by Arkwright and others in the Peak District and Josiah Wedgwood had opened his first factory in the Potteries. The movement of people from the land to the factories was under way.

By the middle of the 19th century steam had replaced water power as the driving force of the industrial revolution and factory growth was swift. No longer were factories confined to the relatively remote banks of fast-flowing rivers. Now they could be built in the heart of cities, alongside the railways and canals that served their needs. And builders erected houses around these new factories whose quality was often epitomised in one 19th century word – slums.

In older towns open spaces were devoured by builders as populations grew rapidly. Birmingham, for instance, grew from 35,000 in 1760 to 73,000 in 1801 and 233,000 in 1851. Elsewhere in the industrial Midlands and North of England new cities were created out of tiny hamlets. A single farmhouse near the banks of the Tees in 1830 became the basis of Middlesbrough and a population of 50,000 just 50 years later. There were already signs by the mid-19th century that industrial towns were growing into one another, eventually to form 'conurbations'. A new landscape was being born.

It was least evident in Ireland which had hardly any coal and only a limited industrial development. Without the stimulus of industry, except in Belfast after the 1850s and other Ulster cities, emigration to either Britain or America remained the only hope for people in much of famine-afflicted Ireland.

Mining ravages the landscape

Industry's voracious appetite for raw materials, especially metals, led to a determined exploitation of the potential mineral wealth of the country. As most of the ores were located in the older rocks of the British Isles, upland areas bore the brunt of much exploitation.

Quiet rural areas could be changed overnight following the discovery of a rich lode of copper, lead or tin and the lives of the local people altered completely. Unfortunately most mineral working, being a robber industry, brought only a short period of prosperity so that today many, if not all, the 19th century workings are abandoned. Although there has been considerable reclamation, especially since 1945, the legacy often remains in old buildings, mountains of waste, disused pit shafts, sheets of water known as 'flashes' caused by subsidence, and disintegrating workers' cottages.

These features are also typical of the landscape of coal mining, the longest-lasting and most extensive form of mineral extraction within Britain. But they can be found, too, outside the areas generally associated with coal mining and the Industrial Revolution.

Parys Mountain in Anglesey, for instance, is today a scene of great desolation with its multi-coloured waste tips, great open caverns, settling pits and ruined engine houses. And yet, in the latter half of the 18th century, this was the site of the greatest copper mine in the world.

Cornwall, which still has some tin mines and china clay quarries, also has a rash of industrial remains, particularly the distinctive engine house and its adjacent chimney. Many dot the skyline of the rising ground between Redruth and Camborne where the mining for copper and tin was most intense. The famous coastal site of Botallack, not far from Land's End, is one particularly spectacular abandoned industrial site. But in Cornwall, as in the rest of Britain, much remains to be done to clear up the rape of the landscape which took place during the period of intense mining activity in the 19th century.

Cottage industry: weavers' homes at High Ogden, near Rochdale, in Lancashire

The Lady Isabella water wheel at Laxey in the Isle of Man is now a major feature of a 20th century industry – tourism. The 72ft (22m) wheel was built in 1854 to drain the rich but deep-seated lead mines of the Laxey Valley by using the waters draining off Snaefell. It was in use until the end of the First World War. It is the world's largest surviving water wheel

Transport: opening up Britain

Nearly 2000 years of transport can be seen in a 300-yard (270m) stretch of countryside three miles east of Daventry in the Midlands. The oldest of four lines of communication that run next to each other at this point is the A5 road which follows the line of the Roman Watling Street. Then, from the last 200 years, there are the Grand Union Canal, the main railway line between London and North-West England and, finally, the M1 motorway.

All forms of communication leave distinctive marks on the landscape. Whether these are regarded as 'good' or 'bad' tends to change with the passage of time. The architecture and earthworks associated with railways and canals were once regarded with the kind of horror modern conservationists often reserve for motorways. What is certain is that a radical improvement in transport was an essential element in the Industrial Revolution of the late 18th and early 19th centuries.

Until then rivers had formed the main arteries of communication for carrying bulky commodities – river ports such as Bewdley on the Severn and Totnes on the Dart still have long wharves and large warehouses as reminders of their former importance. Roads had been poor until the Turnpike Acts of the 17th and early 18th centuries. A road network did exist, however, and some routes dated back to prehistoric times, such as the Icknield Way across Southern England. There were also many drovers' trails for driving sheep and cattle from upland pastures to markets. These wide grassy paths can still be seen in many areas, especially in the northern Pennines, mid-Wales and Border country. Isolated pubs sometimes have their origins as drovers' inns.

The turnpikes improved road standards but left few reminders of their existence other than the occasional tollhouse which can be seen alongside the road. But the better roads did increase travel during the Georgian years. This was the great coaching era and many fine country inns date from this period (see Chapter Three). It was not until the early 19th century that engineers like Macadam and Telford made great advances in improving the quality of the roads themselves. Telford, for instance, remodelled the old Watling Street route between London and Holyhead to provide a firm, well-drained surface and fewer sharp gradients. Telford's new road – now the modern A5 – crossed into Anglesey over the Menai suspension bridge. This bridge was completed in 1825, and thus coincided with the start of the railway era. It was only in the 20th century that the pioneering work of men like Telford and Macadam would assume major importance. And before railways had been born, another form of transport had achieved a far greater impact on the economic history and landscape of Britain – canals.

Artificial waterways had existed since Roman times, with their Car Dyke near Peterborough and Fossdyke between the Trent and Witham. But apart from the isolated 16th century exception of the canal between Exeter and the sea, they were phenomena of the late 18th and early 19th centuries when an intricate network of canals was dug across Britain.

History tends to credit James Brindley as the father of this canal movement following the construction of the Bridgewater canal to carry coal from mines at Worsley into Manchester. The first long-distance canal, however, was in Ireland and ran for $18\frac{1}{2}$ miles (30km) between the Upper Bann and Newry harbour. Building lasted from 1729 to 1742 and involved 14 locks to cope with changes of level.

Early canals tended to follow the contours but later, as engineering skills improved, they became much more direct plunging through hillsides in tunnels or across valleys in aqueducts. The distinctive features that canals brought to the landscape can nearly all be seen near the stretch of the Grand Union Canal referred to earlier: here there are wharves, locks, cuttings, tunnels, lock-keeper's cottages and canalside inns.

Elsewhere there are still great aqueducts (such as that built by Telford to take his Shropshire Union Canal across the Dee valley near Llangollen) and lifts (as at Anderton on the Trent and Mersey Canal). When the wharves and warehouses seem strangely large for tranquil spots, they are often remnants of the former importance of once major canal ports, as at Shardlow, at the junction of the Grand Trunk Canal and the Trent, and at Braunston, where the Grand Junction and Oxford canals met.

Cities and towns alike began to develop canal quarters with massive brick warehouses lining the bank of the waterway. One town, Stourport, was the sole creation of the canal age. It developed where the Staffordshire and Worcestershire Canal joined the Severn. A pair of dock basins was dug out in 1771 where craft could lie safely at anchor, away from the flood waters of the river. A new town quickly followed and its canal basins as well as the town itself, with its Georgian warehouses, inns and rows of terrace cottages, remain a worthy reminder of the past.

Some canals decayed as well as declined but many survived intact to find a new role today. Canals have become major leisure centres for boating, fishing and simply rambling along towpaths. They are often also important for wildlife and are particularly valuable in the high plateau area of the English Midlands which otherwise has few watery landscapes.

Railways have also become much loved, even as nature reserves along some disused lines. The shrunken railway network of today is not very different from the picture that had emerged by the middle of the last century. In their heyday railways fulfilled all the requirements of the Industrial Revolution, making it possible for heavy and bulky materials to be transported quickly from one part of the country to another. Among these materials were not only the fuels needed to fire the factories but also cheap building materials which greatly diminished the variety previously associated with vernacular architecture. The impact of railways on the landscape was also immense, of course. Vast cuttings were made – one at Tring, Hertfordshire, was $2\frac{1}{2}$ miles (4km) long and up to 60ft (18m) deep – and tunnels hewn across far wider areas of Britain than had ever been affected by canals. Ironically, Victorian railway architecture is now widely admired and cherished.

If railways did much to further the industrialisation of Britain, other than Ireland and northern Scotland, they also provided the means for town-dwellers to get out into the countryside and to the coast. Excursion trains quickly grew in popularity during the 19th century and accounted for the rapid growth in seaside resorts such as Brighton and Blackpool. Travellers with more rarified tastes could also use the railways to penetrate once remote parts of Wales and Scotland – railways reached Mallaig and Kyle of Lochalsh during the 1890s, for instance. Hotels sprang up in secluded parts to cater for a new class of tourist interested in 'country' pursuits like angling or hill walking that for previous generations had been often part of everyday life. For the first time the countryside was becoming the playground of urban man.

Sh

Do

cottage

Chapter Three

Living in the Countryside

Hill in Shaftesbury comes close to many people's image of the quintessential village street. Thatch and mellow brick cottages huddle together along a steeply-cobbled twisting street. ry is more a market town than a village but the countryside is never far away. Gold Hill mains as much a monument to the prime of pre-industrial Britain as those green hills of et beneath the apparent simplicity of country life, so alluring to modern urban man, is epth of history which few cities can match. There is a complexity too which belies the re postcard image of places such as Gold Hill. And there is continuing change as 20th century man shapes the landscape for his needs. From villages to market towns, untry houses, churches to pubs, this chapter highlights country life – past and present

Villages: the alluring yet complex antiquity of country life

A dream village reeks more of nostalgia than the farmyard. The dream is potent but unreal. There is no quintessential village. There never has been. In many parts of the British Isles there are not even villages at all. The hamlet is the characteristic form of rural settlement for much of Britain; and in the hills and mountains even hamlets are secondary to a scattering of individual farmsteads.

Each settlement, whether village or hamlet, tells its own story. The clues are visible in position and shape, architecture and agriculture. Its very name can indicate age and original function. The longevity of settlement over much of the British Isles remains evident alongside 20th century phenomena as diverse as 'gentrification' and dereliction.

Where a hamlet ends and a village begins is as difficult to define as where a village ends and a town begins. It is not simply a question of size: what would now be classed as a hamlet in strictly population terms – fewer than 200 people – once would have been regarded as a village. A more satisfactory, and subtle, yardstick is that of the services and buildings which each community can support.

A church, school and craftsmen such as a blacksmith were an integral part of a village yet beyond the scope of a hamlet. A village was therefore largely self-supporting with only the weekly trip to the local market town required for trade. But if this traditional conception of a village is to be fulfilled today it requires a far greater population than it did 100 years ago, let alone before then.

With a population of 1000 people it might just be possible to maintain a single-form primary school but it would need 2500 people to ensure sufficient support for a doctor, shop, pub and bus services. Some villages may be luckier and, blessed by richness of either setting or inhabitants, be able to support adequate services on smaller numbers. But can less favoured villages grow much beyond 2500 people without losing their traditional character?

It is an academic question. The traditional character of villages has changed already and changed irreparably: they are no longer necessarily dependent on the land. There are villages now which live on tourism, villages which house mostly commuters or weekenders, even villages with 'light' industry. Yet apart

Village idyll: thatched cottages, Perpendicular church and green at Cavendish, Suffolk

Market town: the market-place (here with a fair) at the heart of Richmond, North Yorkshire

from the special case of fishing communities it was the land which not only gave life to all villages but also shaped the fundamental differences between types of rural communities.

Food, water, shelter and security have been the motivating forces of all communities ever since rudimentary advances in his primitive agriculture first enabled prehistoric man to settle in one place (hence 'settlement') for any length of time. And the form of agriculture he practised largely dictated the nature of the settlements in which man lived.

Quite how agriculture developed within the British Isles is far from fully understood and the subject of sometimes arcane dispute among academics. It used to be thought that arable or crop farming was predominant only in the lowlands of

southern and eastern Britain. But archaeological research and aerial photography over the last 30 years have demonstrated that quite extensive tracts of upland Scotland, Wales and the south-west peninsula of England were arable land in prehistoric times.

Geology, climate and the varying skills of the peoples who occupied different parts of the British Isles have all contributed to considerable agricultural diversity. Consequently this complexity – and, indeed, mystery – is reflected in the nature of rural settlements.

Two broad conclusions can be made, although each is subject to detailed qualifications and numerous exceptions:
1. Arable farming is more widespread in the lowland areas of the British Isles; pastoral farming is most common in the

Showpiece village: Lacock, Wiltshire, grew around the gates of an abbey, later a country house

ance of such factors as flat land, natural fertility and water supply. Thus what attracted the Romans to a particular site often attracted the Saxons and the Danes when they came to colonise the land in the centuries before the Norman Conquest. Professor W.G. Hoskins, author of *The Making of the English Landscape*, believes that many thriving villages still stand on sites first chosen by Bronze Age or Neolithic farmers.

These are most likely to be those on hill tops, sufficiently high above the forests for both protection and primitive agriculture. However it is now far from certain that Neolithic and Bronze Age settlements were confined to hills such as Salisbury Plain, the North and South Downs or the Cotswolds. Aerial photography in the past 20 years has revealed hundreds of lowland sites in the valley of the Warwickshire Avon, the Nene in Northamptonshire and the Trent.

Is it likely that prehistoric settlements existed only where they were later abandoned? The answer lies buried beneath the fabric of villages that have survived. Only unsuccessful settlements are generally traced archaeologically and even then the stone of Roman settlements is detected more readily than the wood and thatch of earlier communities.

Claims that some villages must have existed in the same place since prehistoric times are therefore plausible, but as yet unproven. It is the Domesday survey, a mammoth stock-taking of their newly-conquered lands completed by the Normans in 1086, that provides the first indisputable record of rural antiquity. But by then many, if not most, of the villages recorded in the Domesday book were already several hundred years old. Their names are the clues to their age and history.

Most place-names predate early documentary records of settlements, such as Domesday, and thus are often the only evidence available for reconstructing the ebb and flow of history across the landscape. Roman, Saxon, Celtic and Scandinavian names can all be identified within the British Isles, although few have escaped a degree of corruption as spellings and pronunciations have changed over the centuries.

This corruption means that names which are now identical may have had very different origins. Nevertheless scholars have established some general principles that have greatly increased understanding of the Dark Ages. The suffixes *-ley*, *-hurst* and *holt*, for instance, all indi-

upland areas of the North and West.
2. Villages are most characteristic of arable areas; hamlets and scatterings of individual farmsteads predominate in pastoral regions.

The reason for this difference is simple enough. Pastoral farming needs land more than it needs people and cannot support the larger concentrations of people found in the villages of predominantly arable areas. (Before mechanisation arable farming *required* relatively large numbers of people to pool their resources, especially at harvest time.)

Obviously geology and the fertility of the soil were important factors in determining these differences in agriculture and therefore settlement. Geography has also influenced the location of settlements, regardless of their size or form.

The defensive nature of hill forts was mentioned in the preceding chapter but settlements are also found at passes between hills, fords, bridging points and natural crossroads.

Another prerequisite for success was a natural source of water. The village pond or the well upon the green may now seem no more than a picturesque curiosity in places like Finchingfield, Essex, and Ashmore, Dorset, but they were once the very basis of the village's existence. Not even a community as powerful as Old Sarum, the precursor of modern Salisbury, could survive its lack of natural water.

Is it any wonder then that so many villages have such ancient antecedents? It is only the agricultural revolution of this century that has lessened the import-

Town and country: the Pennine mill town of Hebden Bridge, W. Yorkshire (above) and the fishing community of Robin Hood's Bay, N. Yorkshire (below)

Border country: the planned 18th century village of Blanchland, Northumberland (above) and the softer charms of Cardington, Shropshire (below)

cate the former existence of clearings in the woodland established by Saxon farmers as they pushed back the frontiers of the forests. A common Scandinavian equivalent in northern and eastern England is -*thwaite*, also meaning a clearing. Saxon and Scandinavian elements often take the form of prefixes and suffixes – see glossary of some common place-names on page 42.

The Domesday picture was one of an overwhelmingly rural England – which is all it covered – with just one in ten of its $1\frac{1}{2}$ million population living in what could loosely be called towns. The village was the basis of English life and many, perhaps most, villages on the map of England today existed by the time of Domesday. There were exceptions, most notably in the northern counties more sketchily covered by the survey and those destined to be in the forefront of the Industrial Revolution.

There were also villages which would grow into market towns or great cities like Birmingham or Liverpool. And there were villages recorded in the Domesday survey which would die and that survive today only as names of individual farms, churches or at best hamlets. Some 2,000 sites of deserted villages have been identified in England alone (see page 48).

Coastal villages are often more recent than inland ones – it was only in the 15th century, for instance, that improved building techniques enabled large-scale construction of quays and jetties. Nevertheless, for England especially, the pattern of rural settlement was largely established 1000 years ago. And it is neither accident nor divine intervention that the church is invariably the oldest surviving building in a village: it was constructed with the best materials and attention which the villagers could muster. The 12th, 13th and 15th cen-turies were particularly notable for church building.

More generally the higher the social scale, the better was the quality of building and therefore the older it is likely to be. But the prosperity of the Tudor years also enabled humbler dwellings such as farmhouses to be rebuilt in stone sturdy enough to survive to the present day.

This period of 'the great rebuilding' as W.G. Hoskins called it, when the vernacular regional styles of architecture were established, came later to northern Britain. But the English village at least, with its farmhouses, cottages and possibly school and almshouses, was still shaped more by the 200 years from about 1550 than any other period in its long history. Hoskins writes: 'Before that time life had been hard and comfortless, with little or no margin to spare beyond the necessities of living: what little there was went to the adornment and beautification of the parish church. After that time we witness the break-up of the village community, the degradation of most of the rural population and the flight into the towns.'

The 'degradation' of the rural population in Ireland was more a consequence of famine than the Industrial Revolution. But the development of Irish villages was always somewhat apart from that of the rest of the British Isles, even compared to Scotland with which it shares a Celtic tradition. This tradition saw agriculture and rural settlement based on large farmsteads or small hamlets. Irish villages therefore grew more slowly than their English counterparts and indeed it was the great English 'plantation' movement beginning in the 17th century that saw the first sustained growth of farming villages – often built close to the gates of a local landlord's estate or demesne.

In Scotland rural development was also somewhat different to that of England. The dominant theme in the 19th century was not so much the inroads of the industrial revolution (which were largely confined to the central lowlands) but the 'clearances' in the highlands. Sometimes people were shipped overseas – the island of Rhum, for instance, was totally deserted to make way for sheep farming and the population transported to the Canadian prairies. Sometimes they were settled on the coast in new fishing villages such as Golspie or Kyleakin.

Generally, however, it was the industrial revolution that shook the foundations of rural life. But the process of change has continued into the 20th century. More mechanisation means that fewer people are required to work on the farm. Fishing has also declined.

Villages must therefore find new roles if they are to survive. Some are favoured by their location, becoming either tourist attractions (such as Clovelly and Polperro in Cornwall, or Bourton-on-the-Water in Gloucestershire) or commuter bases around major conurbations (such as Hathersage in the Peak District near Sheffield and Hutton Rudby at the foot of the Cleveland Hills near Teesside). Even then a price can be paid for survival in terms of the so-called 'gentrification' style of modernisation which can destroy traditional rural character.

Smaller or less favoured communities can simply die, however. Because there is insufficient work on the land, young people start drifting to towns or larger villages. Because the population is falling, shops close, bus routes are abandoned and the population falls still further. A parish council can no longer be maintained and a more distant local authority decides it can no longer main-

The 17th century market hall at Ledbury, Herefordshire

The 18th century 'model village' of Milton Abbas, Dorset

tain the village school or health clinic.

The scenario is a familiar one; Scotland, for instance, lost its parish councils as long ago as 1929. And so public services such as schools and health clinics are channelled increasingly into 'villages' of 5,000 people or more where they are economically 'viable'. Almost inevitably such communities become increasingly urban in character. The consequences of designating villages for growth thus can be as profound for the chosen villages as those which are not chosen.

Yet it is facile to imagine that nostalgia can turn back clocks as well as minds. Most villages were made by man for an agricultural role that is no longer necessary. But as caring communities villages can still have a living role in impersonal 20th century Britain. Their size and traditions encourage a spirit of communal activity whether it be focussed upon the church or pub, women's institute meetings or cricket on the village green. Villages can continue to offer this timeless sense of community, as well as the physical ambience of the past, if only man fights to save what his forebears once struggled to create.

Market towns: trade supplants defence as the factor for success

It is only since the middle of the last century that a majority of the British people has lived in towns. Even today many towns are rooted more in the countryside than the industrial revolution. Market towns are as integral a part of the rural scene as villages, with their very names embedded in the language – not just the Market Harboroughs and Market Draytons but the Chipping Nortons and Chipping Sodburys, for 'chipping' comes from the Anglo-Saxon 'cheapen' meaning to buy.

Towns have not always had this function, however. Protection was a greater motivating force initially, as in the creation of many hill-top settlements and walled towns. It was the Romans who established towns on the face of England and in many cases the urban roots went sufficiently deep to survive Rome's decline. Although the Saxons were once regarded as primarily farmers, it is now known that urban life continued in towns such as Lincoln and Canterbury through the Saxon centuries. Even the Scandinavian *burhs* or boroughs established during the 9th century invariably had Saxon foundations; Derby, Nottingham and Stamford, for instance, were all active

The 16th century carved market cross at Chichester, West Sussex: the finest in Britain

towns before Danish settlers arrived.

Many *burhs*, whether Scandinavian or Saxon, retained a defensive or military character but increasingly they developed as administrative and trading centres. The Scandinavian influence was evident in fostering trade particularly around the Irish Sea, but the commercial spirit also surfaced in the Wessex kingdom of southern England where in the early 10th century Edward the Elder, son of Alfred the Great ordered that buying and selling should only take place in the presence of a town 'reeve' or elder representing the crown. It was only a short step to the selling of charters through which most market towns established themselves.

Barnstaple in Devon claims the oldest charter – dating back to 930 – but it was during the 300 years after the Norman Conquest that the trade in charters was most brisk. Kings, and occasionally monasteries and noblemen, raised money by selling rights of self-government to boroughs in the form of charters. Among the most important of these rights was the permission to hold a market, usually on a weekly basis. And the ability of a town to trade successfully, rather than as previously to defend itself, then determined prosperity and even survival.

Charters could not guarantee success. Devon, for instance, had 69 medieval boroughs in addition to Barnstaple. Many foundered, with only an unusually wide street, as at South Zeal, remaining to indicate former glory as a market-place. Towns could not prosper in defi-

ance of geography. Yet often what was good for trade were the same factors that had assured military success: a position controlling a pass or estuary, a bridging or fording point of a river, a natural geographical crossroads. Many market towns thus developed around military strongholds, such as castles, to serve their needs and to shelter under their protection; Arundel, Barnard Castle, Launceston and Ludlow are good examples of such towns. Sometimes it was a monastery or abbey around which a town developed as at Abingdon, Bury St. Edmunds and Evesham.

Most of Britain's cathedral cities are in fact also market towns, their religious and commercial activities long intertwined. Quite small towns, such as Helmsley in North Yorkshire, have a church overlooking the market-place. Church bells used to be rung to summon people to market as well as to pray and market crosses were built to invoke God's blessing upon the trade of a town. The finest remaining examples of such crosses are at Chichester and Malmesbury.

Precisely why market-places took different forms nobody really knows. A location along a main road, as at Marlborough in Wiltshire, makes it more likely that the market takes place in a greatly-widened thoroughfare rather than a separate square. Market towns on the coast are almost inevitably centred upon the harbour, although they need a hinterland to have grown beyond fishing villages. The nature of goods to be traded was another factor, livestock needing more room than farm produce. In practice a number of factors usually coalesced but whatever these were it was invariably the market-place which shaped the town.

The location of market-places at the heart of towns has made them vulnerable in the 20th century. Market squares have become parking lots, market crosses roundabouts; medieval market halls, where they have survived redevelopment schemes, shudder as juggernauts manoeuvre around them. Yet many market towns still provide buildings of great architectural distinction and their general prosperity remains based on their traditional role as a centre for trade. Often, too, the centre of the town's activity is the market-place itself. Livestock markets may be fewer but for one day a week at least 20th century wares are sold beneath the shadow of, say, a 17th century market hall in a 11th century market square.

The village pond: the teeming life above and below — the still waters

For many rural communities the village pond has often been as much a part of the local scene as the church, pub and green. In many cases, as the original source of water, it was the very basis of a village's existence. Sadly, not all villages have preserved their ponds. Over the years, their usefulness outlived, many have been condemned through neglect to become the last, weed-choked resting places for unwanted bedsteads and rusty bicycle frames. But in the past two decades the village pond has undergone a modest renaissance. In a number of villages, volunteers have cleared old ponds and restored to them the rich aquatic life that thrives in still waters.

Living within this enclosed order are not only the instantly visible creatures, like the familiar mallard, the drake easily recognisable with its glossy, bottle green head, but also the teeming denizens of the secret world beneath the surface.

Forming the foliage of this underwater jungle are various kinds of pondweed – Canadian pondweed, curled pondweed, grasswrack pondweed – and other aquatic plants such as waterwort, autumnal starwort and occasional rarities such as the holly-leaved naiad.

Outwardly still and serene, the pond seethes with life down below. Fierce carnivorous dragonfly nymphs, water scorpions and great diving beetles prowl the green depths in search of freshwater shrimps (actually relatives of the sand-hopper) and tadpoles of the common frog. Ram's horn snails and great pond snails crawl among the submerged plant stems, browsing on algae with their rasping tongues, and are themselves preyed upon by the horse leech. Freshwater swan mussels rest on the bed of the pond.

The tadpoles hatch in May from the mass of jelly-like toad or frogs' spawn laid in early spring and, until they leave the pond in July as tiny, fully-formed toads or frogs, the tadpoles will share the water with another amphibian, the crested newt. This splendid jam-jar dinosaur with the polka-dotted orange belly can reach a length of 7in (18cm) or more, and is the largest of our three native newts. (The others are the smooth newt and the palmate newt.)

Not all fish can tolerate the torpid waters of a pond, but one that does is the diminutive three-spined stickleback. In spring the pugnacious male stickleback turns bright red and builds a nest in which the female lays her eggs. The male remains on guard at the nest until the fry are hatched.

The surface of the pond – the great divide separating the underwater life from that in the light and air above – is itself rapidly colonised by the flowers of yellow water-lily and water crowfoot, by floating carpets of duckweed made up of thousands of tiny individual plants, and insects such as the pond skater, a creature so light it can skim across the water without piercing the surface-film. The pond skater is a carnivorous bug, but it is

content with a diet of flies and other insects; whereas the water boatman, which lies on its back and rows with its hind legs, will also attack tadpoles and even small fish.

Village ponds are usually too small and too close to human habitation to make a suitable haunt for mammals, though the bank vole may build its grassy nest under the roots of a bankside tree. But a pond is ideal for water birds such as the coot and moorhen, which often become quite tame, and nest safely in the more inaccessible beds of reedmace – the plant with tall seed-heads like brown velvet sausages which most people call by their traditional country name of bulrushes.

Left: the surface tranquillity of the pond at Chiddingfold, Surrey

The coot and moorhen are easily identified: the coot by its bald white forehead; the moorhen by its sealing-wax beak and shrill, explosive 'prrk', uttered as it swims, head and tail jerking like a mechanical toy, among the water plants. Otherwise, both species have many characteristics in common; running fast on land, diving well, and flying low over the water trailing their feet behind them.

In late afternoon and early evening from May onwards, when mayflies are dancing over the water, the house martins which nest under the eaves of village buildings grace the pond with their acrobatic swooping flight and liquid silvery chatter. Britain's largest mayfly bears the scientific title of *Ephemera danica* – a lovely name for this ephemeral insect whose adult life lasts no more than three or four days. Anglers know it as green drake.

Mayflies and dragonflies all live through their larval stage under the water, when they are known as nymphs. But when the dragonfly nymph is fully grown it climbs from the water and clings to a reed stem while it sloughs off its larval skin. Some two hours later, its wings hardened and fully expanded, it takes to the air as a lustrous adult insect like the male emperor dragonfly in our illustration. The emperor belongs to the group of dragonflies known as hawkers. It has a wingspan of over 4in (10cm), may reach speeds of up to 30mph when pursuing insects or when alarmed, and can even fly backwards.

With its life cycle divided equally between the elements of air and water, the dragonfly is in many ways a symbol for the life of the village pond. And it is pleasing to think that these man-made

Key to illustration: 1 Emperor dragonfly 2 Green Drake Mayfly 3 House Martin 4 Coot 5 Moorhen 6 Reedmace 7 Bank Vole 8 Water Boatman 9 Pond Skater 10 Duckweed 11 Water Crowfoot 12 Yellow Waterlily 13 Male Three-spined Stickleback 14 Female Stickleback and Nest 15 Smoth Newt 16 Crested Newt 17 Common Frog 18 Tadpole 19 Frog's spawn 20 Swan Mussel 21 Great Pond Snail 22 Ram's Horn Snail 23 Freshwater Shrimp 24 Dragonfly Nymph 25 Great Diving Beetle 26 Holly-leaved Naiad 27 Waterwort 28 Autumnal Starwort 29 Canadian Pondwood 30 Curled Pondwood 31 Grasswrack Pondweed 32 Mallard Duck and Drake 33 Water Scorpion 34 Horse Leech 35 Arrowhead.

habitats can harbour an insect whose ancestors were flying 300 million years before man had even set foot in Britain

Country churches: the embodiment of rural life and rural pride

Look at any village, and almost certainly it will be dominated by the parish church, the centrepiece, perhaps, of village green, manor house and pub. It is also almost certain to be the oldest building, however drastically it may have been rebuilt or 'restored' through the centuries. Only in the 20th century has its pivotal role been eroded.

Traditionally the church was the forum of the parish to which all came for secular as well as for religious purposes. Markets were held beside the church and dramas within it. As in Victorian times, when elaborate town halls were built, so in earlier ages the church was the embodiment of community pride in addition to religious devotion. Thus churches can be far larger than necessary for the size of the parish, let alone the congregation. The great churches of Lavenham in Suffolk and Northleach or Chipping Campden in the Cotswolds were built and lavishly decorated from the profits of the wool trade, for instance.

Step inside a parish church and you immediately have an intimate view of a community's history. The feudal structure of the place is quickly assimilated; the aristocracy had comfortable private galleries or even private chapels, some-times with their own fireplaces and entrance; the squirearchy sat in comfortable family pews but often erected vast monuments to lives that cannot all have been as charitable and holy as the inscriptions would suggest; and the humbler people who sat on plain wooden pews have mere tombstones to mark their personal tragedies and triumphs.

The word parish comes originally from the Romans, to whom it signified a large region or province. The earliest evidence of Christian worship in England is to be found in excavated Roman villas. But many churches were built on ancient pagan sites; circular churches or churchyards are particularly associated

Left: a church sale at All Saints, Biddenden, Kent – still very much the centre of a thriving village
Above: St James's of Chipping Campden, one of the most magnificent of the Gloucestershire 'wool churches' built from the profits of the medieval cloth trade
Below: St Peter and St Paul, Lavenham, Suffolk, set in one of the most unspoilt medieval towns in England, and also a 'wool church' of the 15th century

with pagan origins.

Christianity returned to England, after the departure of the Romans, from the Celtic North and West. The oldest post-Roman christian sites are known to be in Scotland, Wales, Ireland and the south-west peninsula of England, yet hardly any buildings survive from those times. The buildings simply were neither strong enough to withstand the elements for so long nor remote enough to escape attack.

The great majority of the parish churches of England were built after the Norman Conquest, but many had Saxon foundations. And from the earliest times the church, and more particularly the church porch, played a key role in the community: marriages and baptisms of course, but also trade between farmers, was carried on there. The churchyard was the site for fairs and dances; the church bells the signal to prayer or an alert in case of danger.

In the less prosperous uplands of Britain parishes tend to be large and churches simple – the rectangular building with the simple open belfry, for instance. Since settlement is often scattered the church, too, often stands by itself.

All parts of the British Isles have experienced religious turbulence which has left its mark on the countryside: the ruined monasteries of England; the Scottish churches abandoned after the Calvinist reformation (although burial grounds were often still used); the proliferation of churches of different faiths in Wales and Ireland.

Whatever the faith the church played an important cultural role in a community. The priest was for many centuries the most educated man in a village and many village schools were run by the clergy. The church building itself is also a living testament to the outstanding crafts of its villagers – masons, wood carvers and painters – who contributed to the richness and individuality of the most dominant building of the area.

Nine hundred years of church architecture. *The traditional country church is usually an amalgam of styles: Victorian stained glass, a Norman font, medieval carvings in the choirstalls and seventeenth-century monuments in the chapel. This is part of its charm. It is also a record through the centuries of craftsmanship, and a repository of the history of style*

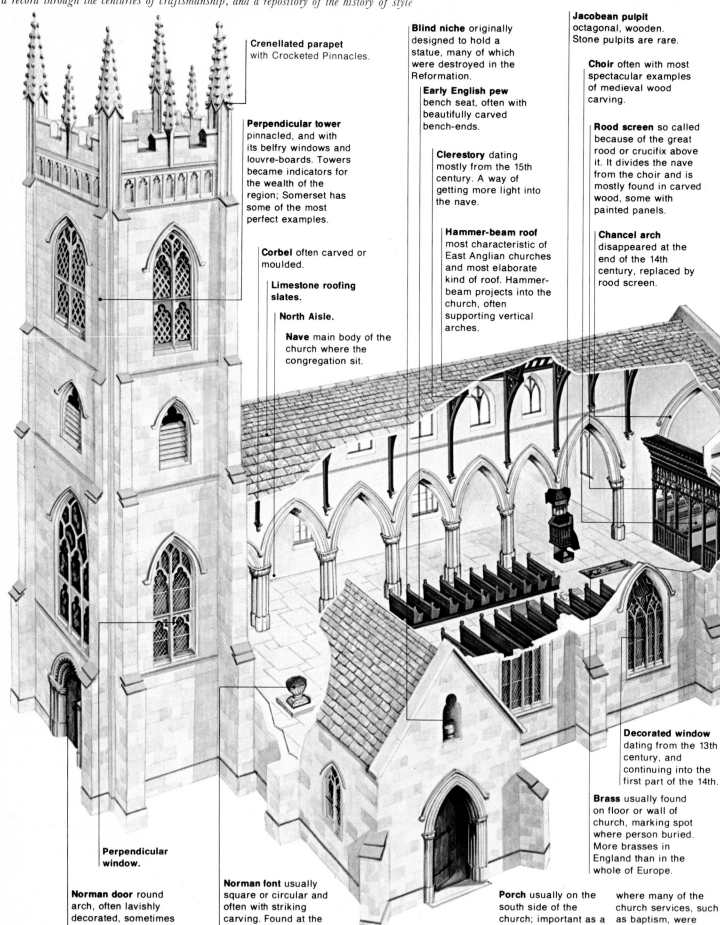

Crenellated parapet with Crocketed Pinnacles.

Perpendicular tower pinnacled, and with its belfry windows and louvre-boards. Towers became indicators for the wealth of the region; Somerset has some of the most perfect examples.

Corbel often carved or moulded.

Limestone roofing slates.

North Aisle.

Nave main body of the church where the congregation sit.

Blind niche originally designed to hold a statue, many of which were destroyed in the Reformation.

Early English pew bench seat, often with beautifully carved bench-ends.

Clerestory dating mostly from the 15th century. A way of getting more light into the nave.

Hammer-beam roof most characteristic of East Anglian churches and most elaborate kind of roof. Hammer-beam projects into the church, often supporting vertical arches.

Jacobean pulpit octagonal, wooden. Stone pulpits are rare.

Choir often with most spectacular examples of medieval wood carving.

Rood screen so called because of the great rood or crucifix above it. It divides the nave from the choir and is mostly found in carved wood, some with painted panels.

Chancel arch disappeared at the end of the 14th century, replaced by rood screen.

Decorated window dating from the 13th century, and continuing into the first part of the 14th.

Brass usually found on floor or wall of church, marking spot where person buried. More brasses in England than in the whole of Europe.

Perpendicular window.

Norman door round arch, often lavishly decorated, sometimes with the characteristic zig-zag pattern.

Norman font usually square or circular and often with striking carving. Found at the west end of the church.

Porch usually on the south side of the church; important as a protection for the door, and as a place where many of the church services, such as baptism, were performed.

Chapel often constructed by rich landowning families for their private use.

Tie-beam roof large horizontal main beam in timber roof.

Reredos a backing for the altar in painted wood or stone. Underneath the east window and shaped to take the figures of the twelve apostles.

Georgian memorial at the end of the 17th century marble took over from alabaster and the style was classical.

Right: the round knapped flint towers of East Anglia are one of its most characteristic features. There are still some 119 surviving examples in Norfolk and 41 in Suffolk. This charming one at Fritton in Suffolk has the added attraction of a thatched roof. Below right: the exquisitely vaulted rood-screen in the church of St Andrew, Bramfield, Suffolk is one of the best of its kind in the county

Chancel part of the nave which contains the altar.

Buttress support on an outside wall.

Altar focal point of the church. Before the Reformation altars were built in stone, afterwards in wood.

Altar rail introduced after the Reformation to protect the altar when screens were disappearing. Usually in wood, sometimes wrought iron in the 17th and 18th century.

Far right: detail from the rood-screen of St Helen's, Ranworth, Norfolk. Medieval craftsmanship in all its original colour and richness, with painted figures of saints and the twelve apostles. Right: the monument to Mrs Arthur Coke by Nicholas Stone at Bramfield, Suffolk is a piece of superb Renaissance sculpture

69

Architectural gems of country churches

Late Norman carving: seen at its most magnificent, c. 1170, at St. Mary, Iffley, Oxfordshire. The rounded doorway arch, with several recessed arches, sports the typical Norman zig-zag pattern or chevron

Beakhead decoration: St. Peter, Tickencote, Leics., has the most splendid and massive chancel arch in England. Dating from 1160–70, it has the characteristically repetitive Norman beakhead decoration

Door knocker: 12th century bronze door knocker or sanctuary ring from St. Peter, Dormington, Herefordshire. It was originally used by those claiming the ancient rite of sanctuary within the church. The ring is held in the mouth of a demon head

Two roofs from the Perpendicular period: top: sumptuous 16th century fan-vaulting from St. Andrew, Cullompton, Devon. Below: the double hammerbeam angel roof of the nave of St. Wendreda. March. Cambridgeshire. A speciality of East Anglian churches, this one has nearly 200 angels

Corbel: there are some 80 corbels on this perfectly-preserved Norman church, St. Mary and St. David at Kilpeck, Herefordshire. The mournful-looking dog and child's view of a rabbit have strong Celtic influences, but look extraordinarily modern

Misericords: the tip-up seats, usually in the choir stalls of a church which are frequently decorated on the underside with satirical carvings. The wood carvers had great freedom of choice and subjects in this church, St Laurence in Ludlow, Shropshire, range from animals and birds to feminine headdress. Dating from the 15th century

Murals: they could often transform a nave or chancel of a church, and in the case of this church, St. Peter and St. Paul at Chaldon, Surrey, the whole west wall. The subject, 17ft long and 11ft high, is the Ladder of Salvation, c. 1200, and is the only remaining mural on this subject in England. The painting, in dark reds and yellow ochres, is divided horizontally by a band of cloud, being the dividing line between the souls who are saved and those who are struggling below in the torments and fires of hell

Monuments: an elaborate post-Reformation one is the Fettiplace tomb (top) at St. Mary, Swinbrook, Oxfordshire. There are two monuments, 1613 and 1686, commemorating the Fettiplace family in tiers of three. The earlier one shows the figures reclining in a rather rigid pose; in the later one they are lolling in a much more realistic manner. Above: the church of St. Peter and St. Paul in Lingfield, Surrey, contains the Cobham family tombs, exotic and medieval monuments dedicated to the founder and his family. The feet in this picture are those of the effigy of the first lord Cobham, one of the original Knights of the Garter

English Gothick: the original Norman church of St. John the Evangelist at Shobdon, Herefordshire was transformed in 1753 into a delightful white and gold stage-set piece after the style of Horace Walpole's 'Strawberry Hill Gothick'. Lord Bateman, lord of the manor and friend of Walpole, commissioned an unknown architect to direct this rococo change. The Bateman family pew is complete with fireplace and has its own separate entrance

Arts and Crafts church: St. Andrew, Roker Park, Co. Durham, c. 1906, architected by E. S. Prior, has carpets by William Morris, tapestry by Burne-Jones and choir stalls, pulpit and lectern by Ernest Gimson

Font: this magnificent stone font at St. Mary Magdalene, Eardisley, Herefordshire, belongs in style to a local school of carving, c. 1150. The subject is the Harrowing of Hell. The plaited motif above and interlacing pattern below are typically Norman designs

Bench-ends: St. Margaret, Cley-next-the-Sea, Norfolk. The tops of these ends are called poppy-heads, probably derived from *puppis* meaning figurehead. This fierce primitive little figure represents the ancient rite of the sacrifice of the Grass King

The Country Pub: from alehouses for the locals to inns for travellers

The country pub is an integral part of rural life, rivalling the church as a focus of village activity. In the more mobile and secular 20th century it is rarely difficult to detect which institution is prospering more. The church may have retained a greater hold over its rural congregations than those in the towns, but it is to the pubs that people drive on Sundays. You do not see country inns appealing for funds to repair roofs.

Yet it was not always so. Inns have had a chequered life in the 2000 years since alehouses were recorded in the British Isles. The Romans introduced wine (and also inn-signs) but ale was the indigenous drink for most of Britain, as it has remained through to the present-day preoccupation with 'real ale'. Usually ale was brewed and consumed at home but by medieval times every community had at least one alehouse where ale was brewed from malted barley.

This was usually just a cottage which advertised its presence by hanging an evergreen branch or 'bush' from a pole above the doorway. Every year the court leet of the manor appointed an 'ale-connor' to test quality. Alehouses or taverns on well-used tracks might cater for the traveller, providing a meal or a bed, but mainly they were simply for drinking and met only local needs.

Wealthy travellers would seek out the manor house where there would always be a traditional welcome. The poorer travellers were mainly pilgrims or traders. By the 12th and 13th centuries thousands of pilgrims were setting out every year for Canterbury, Walsingham, St. David's or Iona; some even under-

took the arduous journey to Rome or Jerusalem. These pilgrims were helped by the monasteries whose 'Rule of Hospitality' laid down that all who asked should be given board and lodging. Simple hospices were provided, some of which still survive such as the *Pilgrim's Rest* outside Battle Abbey in Sussex and the 13th century *The Star* at Alfriston, Sussex. Monasteries also had their own brewhouses and made fine quality ales as well as some wine from home-grown grapes and mead from honey and water. In Ireland oats and malted barley were distilled to make usquebaugh which became a national drink.

The dissolution of the monasteries under Henry VIII meant that between 1536 and 1540 their hospices were also destroyed or acquired by noblemen. Alternative accommodation then had to be made for travellers and many new taverns and inns were built, sometimes on the site of the old hospice. *Ye Olde Bell* at Hurley in Berkshire is a good example. The *New Inn* at Gloucester is also on the site of an old hospice and is one of the few surviving examples of 16th century inn with a first-floor open gallery from which guests could watch performances by itinerant players in the courtyard below.

Elizabethan inns followed this pattern but the galleries, where they still exist, have now been enclosed to make draught-proof corridors – such galleries can still be traced in *The Bell* at Thetford, Norfolk, and *The White Horse* at Romsey, Hampshire. However, new building could not meet the increasing demand as people began to travel more. Many manor houses were therefore converted into inns, such as *The Oxenham Arms* at South Zeal in Devon and *The Lygon Arms* at Broadway in the Cotswolds (although

in the 17th and 18th centuries the latter was known as *The Whyte Hart*).

Horse traffic greatly increased in the 17th century and posthouses were needed where horses could be changed. After 1663 when the first Turnpike Act was passed, roads rapidly improved and stage coaches brought new custom to the inns. *The Haycock* at Wansford, Cambridgeshire on the Great North Road (see overleaf) was built to meet this need with an extensive courtyard and stabling for 150 horses. At this time strong ale was still brewed but to this was added a heavy 'double beer' and 'small beer' which was so light that it became a family drink. Wines and cognac were imported, mainly from France, for wealthier customers. And the Scots had now started to distil whisky, the equivalent of the Irish usquebaugh, for local consumption.

The new roads also led to a further increase in trade, particularly the flourishing wool trade. Packhorses carried fleeces to the weavers and took cloth to the towns for sale. It is not surprising to find that Kendal, which was a collecting centre for wool from the fell sheep of the Lake District, has two old inns called *The Fleece* and *The Woolpack*. The *Black Swan* at Helmsley, North Yorkshire, and *The Swan* at Lavenham, Suffolk, (see overleaf) also have packhorse origins.

Inn building and conversion were given further impetus early in the 18th century with the establishment of a postal service throughout Great Britain. With mail coaches as well as private post-chaises now on the road the heyday of the coaching inn had begun.

Many Tudor taverns were accordingly enlarged, refurbished and given an imposing Georgian frontage; examples include *The Bear* at Devizes, Wiltshire, *The White Horse* at Dorking, Surrey, and *The Royal George* at Knutsford, Cheshire. Georgian inns became social centres as well as resting places for travellers. Local people came to the inn to collect their correspondence and leave letters for the mail coach. Some inns added assembly rooms for concerts and dances. Many magistrates courts were held in inns.

It was a period of heavy drinking. Porter appeared – a drink made from a blend of beer and ale much favoured in Ireland. Stout was brewed using roasted barley as an ingredient. Gin was made in vast quantities, though mainly in towns. A duty on French wines and cognac led

Santon Bridge: the simple tavern, as here in the Lake District, is the most typical of inns

The traditional male world of the old-style pub: for some the taste for real ale was a 1970s fashion, for others it never went away

to importations from Portugal and port became a national favourite. The duty on cognac, however, led the English to bring in whisky from Scotland.

The coaching inns were used by everybody, although coachmen and servants naturally had their own humbler quarters. Even royalty patronised inns. In 1835 Princess Alexandrina Victoria, with her mother the Duchess of Kent, dined and slept at *The Haycock* in Wansford on their way to York.

But by the time Victoria had come to the throne two years later the railway boom was well under way and beginning to entice custom away from the roads. New inns were built alongside railway stations but the old coaching inns were hard hit. Within a few years many had fallen into disrepair and closed. Even *The Haycock* surrendered its licence. However, some inns in tourist areas of northern England, Scotland and Ireland flourished. Their owners sent horse-drawn carriages to the nearest railway stations to collect patrons and their luggage, often for a stay of some days. The travellers' inn became a holiday inn. *The Morritt Arms* at Greta Bridge in Teesdale, is a good example of such an inn.

The Industrial Revolution led to the rapid expansion of cities and some coun-try inns were engulfed in urban development. Who would think that *The Curlers* in Byers Road, Glasgow had once been a country inn on the road through the Vale of Partick? It now caters for city dwellers, few of whom realise that in 1665 Charles II and his retinue played a curling match on a nearby pond and afterwards enjoyed the hospitality of the inn so much that the king issued a special Charter allowing it seven-day opening.

In the 1880s cycling became popular and many inns such as *The Anchor* at Ripley, Surrey put up the sign of the Cyclists Touring Club. Then followed the motor car and slowly the demand for roadside refreshment and accommodation grew once more. Old stables were converted into garages or pulled down to make room for car parks.

Between the wars old inns expanded and became 'hotels'; private houses were converted. In Ireland even some of the old castles were rebuilt or reconditioned. Kilkea Castle, the oldest in Ireland, is now a luxury hotel. So is Ashford Castle, on Lough Corrib. The Bishop's Palace at Holywood has become the *Culloden Hotel*. More typical of Ireland, and the more sparsely-populated lands of the North are simple alehouses or taverns, however. Many Irish bars are not even housed in special buildings, being attached to other shops such as grocers, drapers and, in at least one case, an undertaker's.

The great growth of car ownership in the last 30 years has had mixed effects. It has meant that people living several miles away can regard a pub as their 'local' and thus the increasing popularity of country inns has encouraged major brewing and hotel chains to extend their network into rural areas. Buildings have been preserved from decay, but not always with the best of taste. Individuality has also suffered, both in the variety of beers brewed and the loss of the owner-landlord of a 'free house' who could provide an atmosphere sometimes lacking if an inn is merely a link in a chain.

Despite all the changes, the tradition of the alehouse serving a local community continues. A few free houses remain where landlords retain the skills of keeping 'real' ale in the wood that were jeopardised by the moves to managers and keg beers. Major breweries are also increasingly sensitive to their customers' tastes. Roadhouses, motels and posthouses may be necessary for motorists in a hurry but it is the nostalgic, unhurried and apparently unchanging atmosphere of country inns that most people seek given the chance.

The Packhorse Inn: The Swan, Lavenham, Suffolk. *In Tudor times the inn was an important centre in every village, not only for travellers but for traders transporting goods. The woollen trade was by then well established and the making of cloth had been stimulated by Flemish weavers who had settled in a number of East Anglian villages. Lavenham in Suffolk was an important centre where the industry was carried on by rich merchants who exported cloth to Europe. They built fine houses, a Guildhall and a Wool Hall and as the trade expanded found the need for a centre where weavers from the villages of Lindsay and Kersey could bring their cloth. In the 17th century four old half-timbered houses were united for this purpose and provided with stables for packhorses. Thus the Swan Inn was born, later to become a coaching inn. Now it is part of a hotel chain and patronised mainly by tourists. These are often attracted to Suffolk partly by the oustanding medieval architecture of Lavenham of which The Swan itself is such a fine example*

The Coaching Inn: The Haycock, Wansford-in-England, Cambridgeshires. *During the 17th century traffic on the roads began to increase rapidly. Long distance coaches carrying passengers and mail had to change their horses at definite stages on the journey and the need for post-houses increased. To meet this demand alehouses or farms were sometimes rebuilt as inns. The Haycock at Wansford-in-England on the old Great North Road was built round existing courtyards where the old brewhouse is still to be seen. One yard had an open gallery (now enclosed to form a passage) of a kind often associated with Elizabethan taverns in towns. The coming of the railway reduced the volume of horse traffic and by 1887 the decline was complete with the inn becoming a farm. However, the advent of the motor car enabled the owner, Lord Fitz-william, to reopen as an inn again after a break of over 40 years despite a legal battle to secure a licence. Now it is by-passed by the modern A1*

Inn signs and their meaning

The idea of indicating a tavern or inn's existence by a sign outside its doors has been dated back to Roman times, but it only became at all widespread in the British Isles from the Middle Ages. Many derive from five broad categories.

Religion. Many inns date from medieval times and took their names from those given to abbey hospices. 'The Angel' honoured St Michael; 'The Salutation', the Annunciation of the Virgin Mary; 'The Anchor' was hope, described by St Paul as 'the anchor of the soul'; 'The Cross Keys', the emblem of St Peter. 'The Lamb and Flag' was the symbol of the Knights Templar pledged to protect pilgrims to the Holy Land. 'The Swan' was the emblem of innocence and 'The Seven Stars' represented the celestial crown. 'The George and Dragon', often shortened to 'The George', was a symbol of the Christian fight against evil. When a hospice was destroyed at the Dissolution and an inn was built on the site it was often called 'The New Inn'; such inns are usually about 400 years old.

Country life. The names of village inns often reflect farm life. 'The Plough' in England, 'Coulter's' in the Border country and 'Cornkist' in Scotland are symbols of cultivation, 'Sheaf and Sickle' of the harvest, and 'The Fleece' of sheep-shearing. 'The Maypole' is a symbol of the dance.

Crafts. Symbols of the craft guilds were used as inn signs. For instance, 'The Axe and Compass' (Carpenters), 'The Ram' (Clothworkers), 'The Three Tuns' (Vintners), 'The Boot' (Cobblers), 'The Masons Arms', 'The Weavers Arms' and 'The Smith's Arms'. Sometimes the alehouse or inn would also sell meat or bread. 'The Shoulder of Mutton' signified the butcher, 'The Stone and Faggot' the baker.

Royalty. Many signs show respect for the monarchy. 'The Crown' is very common and royal badges often appear as 'The White Hart' (Richard II), 'The White Boar' (Richard III), 'The Blue Boar' (Henry VII). Also common are 'The Queen's Head', 'The King's Head' and 'The Feathers' (or 'Fleur-de-Lys'), badge of the Prince of Wales.

Sport. This has always been closely associated with British inns. 'The Bear' and 'The Bull' (bear-baiting and bull-baiting), 'The Bird in Hand' (falconry) plus some that speak for themselves – 'The Hare and Hounds', 'The Foxhound' and 'The Cricketer's Arms'.

The country cottage: architectural riches amid the humblest dwellings

When the poets of the 18th century created their ideal of rustic simplicity they also focussed the attention of artists, landscape gardeners and architects on the visual merits of country cottages. For those who did not have to live in them they represented a dream of peace and honest toil: a pastoral picture of cows, milk maids and scented roses round the door. It made a pleasant contrast to squalor and tension in the growing cities.

The poets have moved on to other founts of inspiration, but to the ordinary city dweller a country cottage remains an ideal, often the ultimate ideal for retirement. It is interesting that cottages, however dilapidated, without drainage or mains water, with low beams to catch the heads of a taller generation, with rising damp, awkward stairs and several kinds of rot will often reach higher prices at auction than a new dwelling complying with every byelaw. The old cottagers happily leave for a new dry council house, while the new owners eagerly prepare to spend a small fortune to make the old place habitable.

In carrying out the improvements they should remember Oscar Wilde's words 'Innocence is like a peach, touch it and the bloom is gone'. For alone among domestic designs, cottages are unpretentious direct expressions of the builder's art. Often the builder was the owner, with help from his neighbours, but even if built by farmers or landowners the same precepts were followed.

Local knowledge dictated the best places to build: cottages are usually on sites that have been used and tested many times before. The healthiness of the area, the quality of the soil, the micro-climate, protection from high winds or flooding and convenient supplies of fuel and water all had to be considered. A good view was not important unless livestock had to be watched. Since work was so much harder in the past, time was valuable so cottages were built simply and durably.

Today one should marvel that it was possible to build low-cost houses in the 15th century that would not only be standing 500 years later but be a much sought-after home for people with a completely different life style. There were simpler dwellings, similar to wigwams, for the very poor but examples of these have not survived – many early 'cottages' are in fact the former homes of small farmers. Although fuel was more plentiful in the past, it still took valuable time to gather so heat insulation was an important factor in cottage design. The traditional mud and thatch cottage with its small windows has a much better standard of heat insulation than a contemporary house.

Cottages built before 1800 had to use local materials; transporting heavy materials along roads which were poor at best would have been too expensive. In early times there was a plentiful supply of wood, cheap and easy to use but as it became scarcer local stone began to be used or brick where this was not available. Fire was always a hazard, especially with thatched roofs, so the increasing affluence of the 16th and 17th centuries would probably have led to the increased use of stone and brick in any case. The use of local materials led to the development of local vernaculars and the regional designs so much admired today.

The hard granites of Cornwall, the north of Wales and Ireland, Cumbria and Scotland cannot be carved easily like the limestones from Wiltshire and Oxfordshire. It was fortunate for Britain that the stone areas lie in the parts that get the worst weather – the western half. In the south-east, which has little or no stone, it was possible to develop light timber frame buildings (the timber often imported from Scandinavia) covered with plaster rendering which could then be moulded into decorative forms, called pargetting. Technology was another factor in determining local variations, usually following the broad ethnic divisions of the country. Before the 19th century the population was much more static than it is today. The railways blurred regional differences by transporting building materials as well as people more easily around the country.

The traditional cottage, built as the home for an unlettered man and his family represents his feelings for home as a simple, well-proportioned space, fitting the surrounding landscape: a warm, often dark interior in contrast to the dazzling light of the fields on a hot summers day or the blasting winds of the winter. The cottage garden, much admired and copied since William Robinson and Gertrude Jekyll wrote about it at the end of the 19th century is a functional extension of the cottage way of life.

The cottage orné, designed by architects and landscape gardeners during the eighteenth and nineteenth centuries, took the most decorative forms of the traditional cottage and put them together with up-to-date methods of construction. But designed on the drawing board, not in the field, they often miss the vital quality of simplicity.

Later, Voysey and Lutyens among others were much impressed by the cottage styles and used them as an inspiration for their own domestic designs. Their influence was huge and dictated the design of the semi-detached style that formed the basis of the inter-war period suburban development in Britain that was something unique in Europe. Today, the teaching of Le Corbusier and other leaders of the modern movement have made homeliness an uncomfortable word for architects to use and so the cottage style has little influence on them. But the popularity of the cottage ideal remains unabated.

Intricate pargetting – plasterwork mouldings – at Much Wenlock, Shropshire

Cob cottages in Minehead, Somerset, with walls made from loam, chopped straw and gravel protected by rendering. Cheap, warm and up to 300 years old, they could be built easily by their owner

Carefully restored thatched limestone cottage in Milton, Wiltshire, dating from the 17th century. The chimney stacks are in brick as they would be too difficult to make in stone. The porch is added

17th century limestone cottage near Banbury, Oxfordshire. Originally single storied, it now has upper windows with a later brick chimney and porch: a lesson in how to change without destroying

Rendered 'clay bat' cottages in Melbourn, Cambridgeshire, made from thin blocks of yellow clay and straw cast in moulds, air dried and used like lightweight concrete blocks. Early 18th century

A terrace of 17th century cottages at King's Lynn, Norfolk, built with Snettisham sandstone under a local pantile roof. There are six different dates of window: the surviving original has lead lights

Late 18th century stone cottages in Heskett Newmarket, Cumbria, painted in the manner traditional to the area. Two of the original horizontally sliding windows, first made in Yorkshire, remain

Box-frame timber cottages in Blackstone, Sussex, of a type widely built from the 14th to 17th centuries. The steeply pitched roof reveals it was once thatched. Originally the windows were leaded

These late 18th century weatherboarded timber frame cottages in Mitcham, Surrey, are of a type once common in the villages that now form South London – the originals for the US 'colonial-style'

19th century stone cabin in Murroogh, Co Clare, Eire. The small windows face away from the sea and are primarily for ventilation. Light is provided by opening the door, originally just a straw mat

A terrace of 17th century fishermen's cottages at Porlock Bay, Somerset, built from boulders collected on the beach, here in the foreground. Its fat, rounded shape follows the landscape

18th century brick and flint cottage in Peppard, Oxfordshire, with its traditional cottage garden. The windows are painted in the old way with the opening sections in white and the outer frames in colour

A 20th century return to simplicity: pleasantly coloured corrugated iron roof with black weatherboarding for a cottage by Orford Castle in Suffolk. The factory-made windows show today's need for light

Change in the countryside: new life for redundant rural buildings

As rural industries have withered, many village buildings have become redundant: mills, maltings, oasts, barns, not to mention once essential service buildings such as schools, churches and railway stations. Must these buildings simply be demolished or left to rot, or can a new use be found for them?

In many cases it can. They are often eminently suitable, once local planners make the mental adjustment, for conversion into offices, museums, craft centres and, perhaps most frequently of all, housing. Over the past decade or so much of the threatened fabric of British villages has been rescued as the conservation movement gathered momentum. Conversion of old buildings to new uses has been most common in southern England, where the demand for housing is greatest. But it is spreading throughout the British Isles, especially to Scotland where there is still a wealth of mills, barns and crofts.

The thousands of old buildings that have been converted mostly owe their continued life not to government finance, but to the enthusiasm and hard cash of private individuals. Two bodies, however, merit commendation. The Civic Trust has encouraged the conservation movement in general and sensitive restoration in particular, notably through its stewardship of European Architectural Heritage Year in 1975; and the Landmark Trust has 'rescued' some startlingly diverse and historic buildings such as castles, a railway station, martello tower, mills, a fort, medieval halls and, in Cornwall, even an entire hamlet.

For individuals restoration offers the possibility of living in unusual and often architecturally distinguished dwellings; for rural communities the buildings at least have been saved from decay or death. But conversion to alternative uses can compound the problems of village life. A maltings that has been turned into flats (as at Beccles, Suffolk) or a textile mill that is now an antiques gallery (as at Malmesbury, Wiltshire) is less likely than ever to revert to its original and essential role – providing employment.

A few attempts are being made to redress the balance: in Exmoor, for instance, there is a scheme called the Small Industries Group which aims to encourage one or two-man businesses to set up in derelict rural buildings. But such schemes are few and tentative, so the conundrum remains: how to save old buildings without damaging even further village life? Here, very briefly, are some of the main types of redundant buildings – other than cottages – now being given a new lease of life.

Barns

Increased mechanisation and farm mergers have made many storage buildings such as barns superfluous. Indeed, whole farms have sometimes been converted as at Wytham, Oxfordshire, for housing or Culzean, Ayrshire, for a country park headquarters. Barns are especially suited to conversion, despite problems of insulation and drainage. An 18th century barn and listed building near Seaford, Sussex, is also being used as an 'interpretive centre' for a country park. Many have been converted into private housing where the main aesthetic problem is where to put the windows necessary for human (as opposed to animal) habitation without destroying their character. For King's Barn, at East Hendred, Berkshire, a Grade II listed building, the problem was solved by keeping windows small and high under the eaves on the street side with larger windows on the garden side to let in more light.

Oast houses

Oast houses, once used for roasting hops, are thick on the ground in Kent and Sussex and scattered more thinly elsewhere. Most date from Victorian times and many have been converted into striking homes. But sadly many conversions have paid scant regard to the unique shape and working heritage of oasts. As with barns, roofs and windows pose the greatest difficulties; tall and narrow windows are generally the most aesthetically successful, dormer windows the most disastrous.

Mills and maltings

Three types of mill have attracted conversion: 19th century textile mills, which are common in Lancashire and Yorkshire; earlier watermills that had been used for grinding corn; and, perhaps most romantic of all, windmills. Maltings, which are characteristic of East Anglia, have also come in for their share of conversion – as with the now famous concert hall at Snape founded by Benjamin Britten for the Aldeburgh Festival in Suffolk.

Textile mills are invariably too large for conversion into a single home and most have been turned into warehouses, offices or flats – or a combination of both. A few have found new life as museums or art galleries, however. A museum is also housed in a National Trust owned watermill at Burwash, Sussex, and another Trust watermill is the City Mill in the heart of Winchester, which is also probably the most unusual youth hostel in the country.

The charm of watermills is their location on rivers or streams; their snag is often the lack of surrounding land. But several successful conversions have been made into houses as well as museums: that of Castle Mill, at Dorking in Surrey, won an Architectural Heritage Year award for a restoration accomplished, as the photograph shows, in a manner which respected its 19th century origins.

Preston Watermill, near Dunbar: working museum for the National Trust for Scotland

Castle Mill, near Dorking: 19th century watermill restored to be 20th century home

The restoration and conversion of the extraordinary 17th century Chesterton windmill in Warwickshire won an 'exceptional merit' Heritage Year award. The celebrated Jack and Jill windmills on the South Downs near Clayton, north of Brighton, are also now used as homes while that at Heage, Derbyshire, has become a working museum of the millwright's craft.

Schools

Most village schools that become redundant are Victorian, like the former school and meeting hall in Westbourne, near Emsworth, Sussex – a conversion which shows that a building can be adapted quite dramatically for its new function without destroying its character. School closures, as rural populations shrink, have brought many old school buildings onto the market, although none are probably older than the 1556 grammar school restored by the Landmark Trust at Kirby Hill, near Richmond, North Yorkshire. Schools were generally soundly-built and the internal space of classrooms and staff quarters often lends itself readily to conversion into village meeting halls, old people's day centres or private homes as at Westbourne.

Churches

Among other uses, churches and chapels have been converted into arts centres, bookshops, old people's day centres, concert halls, theatres, shops and museums as well as houses over the last 20 years. Acquiring a church for conversion can be a complicated process, however, since plans have to be approved by ecclesiastical authorities in addition to local government planners. Other problems commonly associated with churches are lack of drainage, electricity and insulation. Noncomformist churches tend to be sold with fewer reservations than Anglican ones, and some have even become factories.

Stations

Many railway stations were closed during the 1960s as a result of the decision to close uneconomical railway branch line services. Several stations have since been converted into private houses, usually as at Alton (a Landmark conversion) where the line is also closed but occasionally on lines where expresses still thunder past the bedroom windows. Larger stations that were closed in towns were generally redeveloped for their site value but where disused lines have been turned into paths or bridleways some former stations serve as information, refreshment or picnic areas.

Chesterton Windmill, near Warwick: a stylish 17th century folly as much as a mill

79

Country houses: shaping society in addition to the rural landscapes

In her novel *Night and Day* Virginia Woolf makes Ralph Denham comment with approval on the Lincolnshire countryside: 'Real country. No gentleman's seats.' This attitude may seem curious today when the cult of the country house is at its height. But it does underline the fact that the relationship of country houses to the countryside is more complex than that of farmhouses or cottages. The latter were built for people who earned their living by working the land. The essential common factor of the people who lived in country houses was not that they farmed the land, but that they owned it.

Most country houses had a home farm intended to supply fresh food to the house rather than to make a profit. A proportion of country-house owners (varying very much from century to century) went in for farming or forestry on a bigger scale, in order to make money. But the main basis of country houses was always rent – rent from tenant farms or house property, supplemented in recent centuries by income from shares and mineral royalties. Oddly enough it is in the past few decades, since changes in the law have made tenanted farms a doubtful asset, that large numbers of country-house owners have become working farmers on a very big scale.

The object of acquiring a country property was not just to enable its owners to live a comfortable life off their rents. Owning land was the only reliable and lasting way of getting into the ruling class. For many centuries the country was effectively ruled by, or through, its landowners. In early days their tenants, servants, and retainers fought for them; later on they voted for them. The important posts at court or in the government or in local administration were handed out by the Crown in return for their support. The landowning classes did everything they could to keep outsiders out – unless they joined the club by buying land themselves. The system only began to break down in the 19th century. It was then that the Industrial Revolution gradually began to shift power and money from the country to the towns.

So country houses were power bases as well as pleasure bases and family homes; they were more than homes, they were 'seats'. They were the outward and visible sign of a complex power structure based on property, service, protection, contacts, entertainment, tradition, and the mystique and affection which grow round anything that lasts many generations. A structure of this kind took time to build up, and its value was much more than a cash one. This was the main reason why landowning families held on to their houses from generation to generation.

The fact that they were a ruling class largely supported on unearned income meant that, unlike farmers in their farms or cottagers in their cottages, they were not tied to the country, and they were not tied to one kind of activity. Most country

Today Longleat is committed to the stately home business. In the 17th century (top right) it attracted visitors who were unaware of such future delights as safari parks, garden centres and charabancs

houses of any size were linked to a town house – in London, in the case of the richer families, and in York, Exeter, Norwich or wherever the county or local centre happened to be, in the case of the smaller ones. Both pleasure and power attracted country-house owners to the town – sometimes for very long periods. They went to London to attend Parliament or the court, to fill jobs in the government or to go to parties and

gamble at Crockford's and White's. They went to Bath or Buxton or Baden-Baden to recover from London. They travelled round England and many of them roamed round the world as well. In the Middle Ages they went on pilgrimages or crusades; in the 18th century they did the grand tour, and sent back crates of marbles and pictures; in the 19th century they went big-game hunting and brought back elephant trunks to make

umbrella stands and rhinoceros heads to decorate their front halls. Even when they stayed in the country they followed their own bent. Some hunted and shot; some built temples, others built churches; some developed coal mines; some bred race horses or prize pigs. Mr Fox Talbot, in Wiltshire, pioneered photography; General Pitt Rivers in Dorset dug up prehistoric sites; the Duke of Bridgewater built canals; the Earl of

Rosse built the world's biggest telescope on his front lawn.

As a result nearly all country houses had two aspects – a country aspect and an exotic aspect. On the one hand they were linked to their farms, woods and villages and the people who lived in them – and in a less immediate way to the whole neighbourhood. On the other hand they were linked to the outside world – and were often the main means

81

Holkham Hall, Norfolk: an 18th century Palladian-style mansion designed by William Kent

by which the local countryside kept in touch with what was going on in this wider world.

Most country houses were periodically shut up, sometimes for a few months, sometimes for years at a time. When the families came back to them, they brought every kind of novelty to astonish the neighbourhood – from a Negro page to a visiting Prime Minister, or a statue by Canova to a De Dion-Bouton, complete with French chauffeur. The first Palladian porticos, and the parks that went with them, must have seemed extraordinarily exotic to the locals; they certainly did not 'grow out of the countryside' but were sophisticated importations from Italy. But they grew *into* the countryside; their classical detail and clumps and belts of trees were copied in a modest way by lesser gentry, farmers and rectors, until what had been last century's novelty began to seem part of country life.

The more one knows about the background to country houses, the more one can look through their physical structure to the different varieties of family pride and ambition, hospitality, political calculation, private enjoyment, dynastic alliances, travel, fashion, class solidarity, individual taste, sense of responsibility and good stewardship which lie behind them. Any country house with a long history can be dissected into layers, like an archaeological dig. This kind of archaeology is social as well as architectural; country houses were built or adapted to fit a way of life.

The age of ceremony

Most people have some sort of picture of what life was like in country houses in their great days. Dinner is served at tables glittering with glass and silver, by silent footmen who melt imperceptibly into darkness beyond the candlelight. The squire walks home across the park in the evening light, his gun under his arm, his dogs behind him, and a brace of woodcock slung over his shoulder. Guests chat and lounge in the library, or play croquet on the lawn. Pretty maids in print aprons rustle up and down the backstairs. An apple-cheeked housekeeper sits amid her preserves, dealing out cakes and candies to the young ladies. The people in these vignettes are likely to be wearing 18th or 19th-century dress.

Everyone knows that country-house life in earlier centuries was somewhat different – but perhaps they don't realise how very different, and in what ways. For instance, not only were there no print aprons; there was no housekeeper and almost no maids. Medieval and Elizabethan households were almost exclusively male. In the 1520s the household of the Earl of Northumberland contained 166 men and nine women – his wife, his daughter, and five waiting-women and two nurses to look after them. Food was cooked, clothes repaired and the house kept clean (in so far as it was kept clean) entirely by men. This was standard practice; it was only in the 18th century that women servants began to approach the number of men servants in country houses, and only in the 19th century that they exceeded them.

The social reality which lay behind this was that early households were not all that far removed from a military garrison – even when they were not actually inside a castle. The power and status of a family were still ultimately based on the number of people who would fight for it. There were arms and armour hanging in the hall, and more in the armoury – at hand to turn the household into a fighting force. It was organised like an army, with the servants graded into the equivalent of officers, NCOs, and other ranks. The officer element in a big household were all gentlemen, often related to their employer. The household was constantly on parade. The colour and ceremony were different from that of a modern army, but there was an extraordinary amount of it. It all centred round the head of the household, who was treated as though he was an amalgamation of a high priest and a field-marshal. If he was sufficiently grand he ate seated beneath a canopy, and only talked to his social equals. A gentleman without a title would feel deeply honoured to be asked to sit at the same table as an earl, and would only speak to him if the earl spoke first. But usually he would eat at a separate table, and often in a separate room.

The popular picture of a medieval or Elizabethan great hall, filled with long tables of wassailing and carousing figures, bears only an approximate relation to reality. A rigid sense of hierarchy permeated every aspect of life. By the end of the Middle Ages the high table in big houses had been moved out of the hall into a room one storey above it, known as the great chamber. Serving dinner to the high table, whether in hall or great chamber, was a protracted ritual. It involved both the ceremonial preparations of the table and the bringing in of each course by a platoon of servants in livery, preceded by a household officer and accompanied by a fanfare of trumpets.

In smaller houses this kind of ceremonial was confined to great feasts, but in big houses it went on all the year round. The object of having large num-

Top right: billiard rooms became standard features of country houses from the 19th century. This one is at Newnham Park in Herts. Near right: the formality of the Great Hall at Blenheim Palace. Far right: the Hall as sitting room at Kinloch Castle, Isle of Rhum

To entertain Edward VII at a house party was the summit of social ambition. Here he sits by his host, the Duke of Marlborough, at Blenheim Palace

bers of servants and retainers constantly on view was partly to induce a spirit of *esprit de corps*, partly to bolster the image of the head of the household, and partly to display the number and spirit of his supporters to visitors.

In the later 16th and 17th centuries households gradually ceased to have a fighting function. The officer-and-gentlemen element disappeared and servants began to develop into the inconspicuous background figures of later centuries. But life in country houses was extremely formal. It was widely believed that a social hierarchy was not only useful but also divinely ordained and approved. A great man knew how and when to unbend, but even so, distinctions of rank were underlined by an elaborate system of ceremony and etiquette – and by the architecture and arrangement of the houses in which the action took place.

This arrangement was based on the apartment system. Every guest or member of the family had his or her own 'apartment' which varied from one room to five or six – like a grand hotel suite. An important visitor would expect a good apartment and be extremely disgruntled if he did not get it. Formal calls were paid from apartment to apartment, almost as though from house to house. A visit to a grand apartment was regulated according to the social rank of the visitor and the importance of his business. The higher he rated, the further into it he penetrated. The first room or rooms of an important person's apartment were used for his *levée*, at which he presented himself each morning to receive petitions or compliments, while his valet finished off his *toilette*. More privileged visitors would penetrate into his bedroom. Bedrooms were used for receiving calls as well as for sleeping in, and on certain occasions beds assumed an important ceremonial function – christening, for instance, normally took place in the bedroom, with a splendidly-dressed mother ensconced in a magnificently apparalled bed. Beyond the bedroom was a little room known as the closet or cabinet. To be allowed into a great man's closet was the greatest distinction of all.

The age of the house party

A fascinating account exists of how the King of Spain was entertained at Petworth in 1703 by its owner, the Duke of Somerset. The endless ceremony, the formal visits from apartment to apartment of the various people involved, the minute attention paid to who was received in what room and even to what grade of chair they were asked to sit in, gives a vivid picture of country-house life at its most formal.

A hundred years or so later numerous descriptions survive of life at Petworth under the Duke's descendant, the Earl of Egremont. the contrast is quite extraordinary. Formality had vanished entirely. As one guest put it: 'Everyone is left to take care of themselves, with all that opulence and generosity can place at their disposal entirely within their reach.' Guests were given the freedom of the great house, and the park and countryside around it; the library, the sculpture gallery, horses, guns and carriages were at their disposal. They often did not see their host except at breakfast and dinner; and one guest was treated exactly like another, regardless of rank.

The two hosts were admittedly extreme examples of their period. The Duke of Somerset was famous for pride and stiffness; he is said to have cut his daughter out of his will for daring to sit down in his presence. Lord Egremont was equally renowned for his hatred of any kind of ceremony; he could scarcely bring himself even to say 'Good morning'.

But the change did correspond to a general change. By the early 19th century a new pattern of country-house life had been established. With variations, it survived into this century; to a certain extent it still survives, however much eroded and altered by modern conditions. Country houses had become like little republics on the ancient Greek model – assemblies of more or less equal citizens, living a life of cultured elegance and ease made possible by a substratum of servants. Anyone admitted to the republic was admitted to all its amenities and treated like an equal – as in a small officers' mess, where the youngest subaltern calls the colonel by his Christian name.

The political and social reality which lay behind this was that the old model of the universe as a series of stratified and divinely ordained hierarchies, with kinds at the top of them, had collapsed in favour of government based on the ownership of property. England was ruled by her property owners, whose forum was the House of Commons – an organisation which only began to be democratic, in the modern sense, at the end of the 19th century.

It was the 'upper 10,000' who effectively ran the country. But they ran it as a result of constant bargaining and negotiation within the group. A big property-owner inevitably carried a great deal of weight, but he had only become really effective if he carried sufficient smaller property owners with him. Conscious of their independence and importance, the lesser gentry refused to be patronised, or to enter great households as superior servants as in earlier days. The house-parties which filled 18th and 19th-century country houses, and the balls, garden-parties and dinners at which they entertained the neighbours were partly just a pleasant way of passing the time. But they were also a useful way of striking up alliances and extending influence.

Of course, property owners had the good sense to realise that they had to look after their property – and the people who lived on it. The social and political side of country-house life shouldn't make one forget the other side – the running of the

estates, the interest in farming and fores-try, the care taken of retired servants, the visits made to the old and sick in the villages, the contact with local farmers on the hunting or cricket field. The relationship was a highly paternalistic one; but it was a real one.

Nonetheless, it was the needs of house-parties, friends and family that largely dictated the arrangement of country houses. It was true that most of them had a capacious hall, regularly used to give dinners or dances for the tenantry or the servants. But even these tended to fill up, in the intervals, with sofas, writing tables and games.

The pattern of social life produced a country-house pattern which also lasted, with modifications, right through the 19th century into the 20th. It was radically different from the earlier pattern. Apartments vanished. A bedroom, with a small dressing room next door for the husband, was the most that any except a royal couple could expect. Bedrooms on the ground floor, and grand reception rooms on the first floor – both regular features of earlier centuries – dis-appeared almost entirely. Instead, the ground floor was filled by a series of big living rooms designed for the recreation

of large house parties – a morning room for the ladies, a smoking room for the gentlemen, a hall as a communal sitting room for both sexes, a billiard room, a library, a dining room, a drawing room in which to assemble before and after dinner, a dining room and sometimes a music room and breakfast-room. These were all normally on the ground floor, so that they could have a comfortable rela-tionship with the garden, by means of low sills, French windows and conserv-atories. The garden tended to become a series of outdoor living rooms, used for afternoon tea, croquet, and tennis. Lawns and turf replaced formal par-terres and avenues. Servants, far from being on display, were kept as invisible as possible; dinner was conveyed from the kitchen to the dining room by backstairs and back passages, instead of being carried in a grand procession up the main staircase.

This kind of arrangement tended to produce a particular kind of house – rambling and irregular, with a long servants' wing discreetly tacked on to one side of the main block, where the gentry lived. New country houses assumed this shape automatically. Older houses were adapted to a greater or lesser degree.

Minley Manor, Hampshire: to cater for house parties a huge kitchen presided over by a chef was an essential feature of Victorian country houses

Chapter Four
Wildlife in the Countryside

One of the greatest glories of the British countryside is the wealth of wildlife
to be found in every corner of the landscape, from the windswept summits of the Highlands
and Islands to the soft, low-lying watermeadows of the southern counties.
There are so many wild plants and creatures that it is impossible to include them all
in a single chapter. Instead, the following pages are intended more as a celebration
of a wild heritage and a guide to the most important wildlife habitats.

In purely global terms the wildlife of the British Isles represents only a fraction of life on earth as a whole. There is, for instance, nothing to match the richness of the Brazilian rain forests, or the spectacle of the African savannah with its elephants, great carnivores and immense herds of plains game.

But then the wildlife of the British Isles is also infinitely less hostile. There are no dangerous wild animals; only one poisonous snake (none in Ireland), a couple of fish with poisonous spines, and a few deadly berries and fungi. Our jungles – marsh, moor, meadow and forest – are gentle ones compared with most other countries. This is what makes them so beautiful. This, and the fact that everything is on a much smaller, more intimate level, often enclosed within a habitat no bigger than a hedgerow or a village pond.

Nevertheless, the British Isles possess many wild plants and creatures of exceptional splendour. Among the mammals; red deer, wild cat, otter and grey seal. Among the birds, some of the world's most magnificent raptors; peregrine, osprey, red kite, golden eagle. The coasts are the stronghold of internationally important seabird colonies; the estuaries are major wintering grounds for huge populations of wildfowl and wading birds. The rivers are the home of the Atlantic salmon, king of fishes. The countryside is host to a year-long pageant of wild flowers; snowdrops, bluebells, foxgloves, orchids; and rare butterflies such as the swallowtail and purple emperor which are every bit as gorgeous as their tropical counterparts.

Furthermore, there is a great tradition of love and respect for wildlife in the British Isles, which manifests itself both in the form of protective legislation and in the abundance of nature reserves and organisations such as the Royal Society for the Protection of Birds, all of them

Close-ups in the wild. Above: Flourish of foxgloves, common flowers of the mid-summer countryside. Right: Face of the fox, a born survivor, still thriving in most parts of the British Isles despite a history of persecution

dedicated to the concept of nature conservation. This national passion for wildlife is essential in a countryside as small and heavily cultivated as that of the British Isles, and holds out the greatest hope for its survival.

Britain's share of the world's wildlife is also quite modest in terms of actual species. Countless plants and animals were lost in the Ice Age. Then, after a brief post-glacial period of recolonisation, the British Isles were marooned as the sea finally severed us from the wildlife of the European continent. As a result, most of the plants and animals are descendants of the species which existed when the British ark was finally set adrift.

Since then, of course, some animals like the wolf have been deliberately exterminated, and many other plants and wild creatures introduced, either deliberately, like the rabbit and the

walnut tree, or by accident, as in the case of the muntjac and Chinese water deer, alien species which escaped from captivity and are now well-established in the wild.

Another factor limiting the numbers of wildlife species is Britain's temperate climate, with its frosty autumn and winter seasons. To survive, wild life must be frostproof, or able to migrate like the swallow. Also, this time of short days and cold nights creates a season when plants cease to grow and life is dormant. This inevitably reduces the amount of food available, which in turn reduces the number and variety of creatures which the British Isles can support.

Even so, the array of wild plants and animals to be found in these small islands is quite astonishing. There are 70 different mammals, including seven kinds of deer and 14 kinds of bats; 38 freshwater fishes; six reptiles; eight different frogs, toads and newts; over 200 breeding birds and at least as many more which appear every year. There are more than 2000 wild flowers, 150 wild grasses, 600 mosses, at least 10,000 kinds of fungi and scores of trees (though only about 35 are regarded as true natives). And there are the insects; at least 20,000 in all, including some 250 different bees, nearly 50 ant species, 27 dragonflies, nearly 70 butterflies and over 2000 kinds of moths. Add the rich living world of the seashore and the overall picture is truly impressive.

Note: some of the illustrations in this chapter show wild plants, insects and other creatures which in real life would not necessarily appear together at the same time of year. For instance, spring and summer flowers are shown in bloom, irrespective of their proper seasons. But without this measure of artistic licence, it would not be possible to do justice to the immense variety and richness of the habitats portrayed.

The world's longest wildlife refuge

Key to illustration: 1 Oak 2 Scalloped Oak Moth Caterpillar 3 Honey-suckle 4 Wasp 5 Peacock Butterfly 6 Dog Rose 7 Chaffinches

8 Kestrel 9 Garden Spider 10 Cow Parsley 11 Ladybird 12 Flesh Fly 13 Hazel 14 Holly 15 Hawthorn 16 Hedge-brown Butterfly 17 Hedgehog 18 Whitethroat and Young 19 Hoverfly 20 Peacock Butterfly 21 Harts Tongue Fern 22 Ivy 23 Adder 24 Garlic Mustard 25 Cuckoo Pint

26 Bramble Flowers 27 Wall Pennywort 28 Bluebell 29 Stoat
30 Six-spot Burnet 31 Rabbit 32 Common Vole 33 Dragonfly 34 Rushes
35 Water Mint 36 Great Diving Beetle 37 Common Frog 38 Banded
Snail 39 Wood Mouse 40 Primrose 41 Early Purple Orchid

42 Bumble Bee 43 Common Vetch 44 Germander Speedwell
45 Wolf Spider 46 Dog Violet 47 Dandelion. Text begins overleaf

Hedgebank pageantry: bluebells, buttercups and red campion are three common wildflowers to be seen in hedgerows in May

Life of the hedgerow

The beauty of the British countryside owes much to its patchwork landscape of criss-cross hedgerows. The pattern was largely complete by the 18th century, though many hedges are much older than 200 years. Always they were planted for sound practical reasons: to mark boundaries, to contain footloose stock, to enclose. At any one time they were a windshield for crops, a shelter for animals and a handy timber-yard for the farmer. But in time they became something more. Every hedgerow is, in effect, a miniature wood, teased out in a thin green line. What has been created unintentionally is an unofficial nature reserve 600,000 miles (966,000km) long: a self-renewing lifeline for countless species of wild plants and animals.

The oldest hedges are often richest in wildlife terms. A rough yardstick used to estimate the age of a hedgerow is to count the number of different shrub species – hazel, hawthorn, elder, spindle, and so on – growing in each 30-yard (27.5m) length, allowing a hundred years for each species.

In reality you will not see at any one moment as much as we show within the few square yards or metres in our drawing. But you might if you watched long enough. There lies the first lesson: a plant or animal is playing a part in a chain of events, which you could not guess from a single sighting of it. Everything you see is part of a bigger, dynamic picture.

Let us take one simple example: the cow parsley at the hedge foot. This common umbellifer has many close relatives. Each one flowers in a different span of summer; each supplies food to different generations of flies and other insects.

The world of the hedge itself is divided into numerous micro-habitats, like chinese boxes, one within the other, all offering a niche to different species. A damp ditch for the frog at the base of the hedge; hawthorn for the chaffinch to nest in on top. No space is left unoccupied. Even the cracks between the stones of the wall on which this hedge is based provide a roothold for plants such as the wall pennywort and harts tongue fern.

One yard or metre of hedge may be very different to the next. Similarly, the sunny side offers a very different habitat to the shady side. The cuckoo pint grows on shady banks; the basking adder seeks the sun. Soil also plays a part in determining what grows. Lowland clays grow rich meadow grasses, clover and buttercups. Chalky soil has fescue grasses, orchids and other attractive flowering plants. And the constant fall of hedge debris – twigs, bark and leaf litter – create a rich humus for flowers like the bluebell and primrose.

Like all habitats, the hedgerow is a savage jungle in which life is a story of eating and being eaten. Plants obtain their food energy from non-living sources such as sunshine and salts in the soil. Some animals like voles and rabbits, eat plants, or parts of them. Other animals like the stoat eat the plant-eaters. But plants come first. Without them there would be no animals.

The cross-linking of each animal's food requirements builds up into a complicated food chain. On the bramble, the spider catches the fly, but is eaten by the foraging whitethroat, which in turn may fall victim to a marauding sparrowhawk.

The bramble is a stage upon which another strand in this complex plot is revealed. The wasp, the fly and the peacock butterfly all feed on blackberry. The wasps arrive first, cutting the fruit's firm skin with its strong jaws. When the skin is broken, flies are able to suck up the pulpy juices. But the butterfly has to wait until the juice is fermented and thin before it can feed through its delicate mouth tube.

Nothing is constant in the countryside, and hedgerows are no exception. At one time, during the 1950s and 1960s, Britain was losing on average about 4500 miles (7242km) of hedgerows every year. Even so, it has been estimated that today nearly half-a-million acres (202,300 hectares) of hedges remain, forming a total area twice the size of all our national nature reserves put together. End to end, it must add up to the longest wildlife refuge in the world.

But the hedgerow scene demonstrates its fragility. Yard for yard and metre for metre, it is a small and vulnerable world. If it were grubbed out, or regularly shorn with a heavy duty cutter, or accidentally sprayed with pesticide, how much of its wildlife would survive?

The alternative is a countryside of fences. But is that sound economics? Fences support no life, offer no shelter, grow no timber and need replacing every few years. But a hedge, cut-and-laid every five or ten years, lightly clipped every winter, may live – with all its wealth of wildlife intact – for the next 800 years.

The vanishing meadow

More than half of the entire land surface of the British Isles lies under grass. Much of it is permanent pasture, but naturalists are concerned by the speed at which old meadowland is disappearing. In many parts of dairyland Britain the traditional summer image of cows wallowing up to their udders in buttercups is fast becoming a childhood dream. Every old meadow that survives is a reservoir of wild flowers and grasses. A good site can hold a hundred or more different plant species, together with innumerable insects, birds and small mammals.

In the bad, old, inefficient days the grass was allowed to grow in its own sweet way, enriched by nothing more revolutionary than the cow-pat. It was a way of farming which made for harmony and tolerance between man and the land. But in the hard economic world of modern agri-business there is no room for the flowers of yesteryear. Increasingly the old turf is being ploughed under, primed with chemicals and re-seeded.

So meadows once bright with ox-eye daisies now sway with monotonous maxi-crops of cultivated grass or Italian rye. Not that you would notice the difference at first glance. But a closer inspection reveals a world of difference. Unlike a modern ley – a short-term sward which may consist of a single species of cultivated grass – an old meadow is a bewildering mixture of natural grasses and wild flowers.

The British Isles contain more than 150 species of wild grasses, and many can be found growing in our old meadows. Among them: crested dog's tail, meadow brome, the coarse cocksfoot with its distinctively clustered seedheads, the soft and hairy Yorkshire fog, and the common cat's-tail, also known as timothy grass, after Timothy Hanson, who introduced the species to the USA in the 18th century.

Grasses are generally pollinated by the wind, and by June most of our native species are at their best, their ripening spikes and nodding panicles adding rich glints of tawny, pink and purple to the fields. One exception which flowers earlier, in mid-April, is the sweet vernal grass. Locked in its plumes of spikelets is a secret smell of summer – an essential oil called coumarin that gives the meadows their fragrance.

Permanent pasture is frequently found on heavy soils or in low-lying, badly-drained spots too wet to plough. And here, especially in the wetter west of England, you are likely to find tussocks of the common soft rush growing among the pitted hoof-marks of grazing cattle.

Rushes are water-loving relatives of the grasses, with nearly 30 species growing wild in the British Isles. In former times their soft pithy core was soaked in kitchen fat and used to make rush-lights. Often growing in the company of rushes in the softer corners is the marsh horsetail, a primitive plant with a curious hollow jointed stem. Its ancestors were the giant horsetails which flourished when the coal measures were laid down 280–345 million years ago.

To be a real meadow sleuth you need to know the floral clues that reveal the presence of ancient pasture: cowslip, meadowsweet and yellow rattle are three of them. They are all flowers whose presence indicates undisturbed grassland. If you should also manage to track down uncommon plants such as the green-winged orchid and dyer's greenweed, then you know you have stumbled on a genuine antique plot. Other, more commonly encountered meadowland plants include the meadow buttercup, knapweed, ox-eye daisy, dandelion, bugle, red clover, creeping thistle, ribwort plantain, and the rusty spikes of the common sorrel, whose arrow-head leaves have a pleasant vinegary taste when chewed.

One of the prettiest meadow flowers of spring and early summer is the cuckoo flower, or lady's smock. It favours wet meadows and its delicate pale mauve flowers are an irresistible attraction for the orange-tip butterfly which is on the wing at that time of year. In midsummer clouds of butterflies start up at every step in the waist-high grasses; common blue, small copper, and most common of all our grassland butterflies, the meadow brown.

You may also disturb two common day-flying moths in the long grass: the weakly fluttering cinnabar, whose conspicuous black-and-yellow striped caterpillars feed on ragwort, and the fast, whirring silver Y moth, a migrant from southern Europe.

In summer the meadow teems with other insects. From July onwards there is the rasping song of common green grasshoppers (*Omocestus viridulus*), and in August the daddy long legs or crane-fly emerges. This gangly creature belongs to the family of two-winged flies, the diptera, and its larvae are the destructive leather-jackets which devour the roots of the meadow grasses.

Also on the wing is the common bumble bee (*Bombus terrestris*), largest of Britain's 16 bumble bee species, laden with pollen on its way back to its nest among tufts of meadow grass. At dusk the drowsy hum of the bees is echoed by the metallic blue-black dor beetle, droning through the warm summer air. The larvae of the dor beetle grow fat on the dung of the cow-pats which cover their earthen chambers. The sexton beetle (*Necrophorus humator*) has an even more unsavoury appetite. It is a carrion eater, feeding and laying its eggs on the bodies of dead animals. (In our illustration on the following pages, the corpse is a dead field mouse.)

The open meadows provide little cover for mammals, but small rodents, such as the short-tailed vole, tunnel among the grasses on which they feed. In the so-called 'vole years' their numbers can mushroom to plague proportions – a time of plenty for predators such as owls, stoats and foxes. That other common meadow mammal, the mole, spends almost all its life underground, only revealing its presence by the mole-hills pushed up as a result of tunnelling in search of the earthworms which are its favourite food.

The abundant insect life of the meadows makes the grasslands a rich source of food for birds. In spring and summer swallows skim the grass-heads, snapping up dipterous flies and other winged insects, while the lapwing, a typical bird of green pastures, both upland and lowland, runs and pauses to peck up a wireworm. And in autumn, when the swallows have gone, flocks of goldfinches descend on the thistle heads to hunt for seeds.

Sometimes you may flush a covey of common partridge. Though essentially ground birds, they are fast fliers, alternately whirring and gliding on downcurved pinions. The call of the partridge is a curious rusty creak, but the true voice of the meadow belongs to the elusive corncrake. The sound is similar to that made if you rub your thumb along the teeth of a comb. But alas, it is seldom heard nowadays except in Ireland and among the Scottish Highlands and islands. Like the old meadow itself, the rasp of the corncrake is fast becoming a part of yesterday's countryside.

Living world of the meadow
Key to illustration: 1 Bramble 2 Ragwort
3 Goldfinches 4 Creeping Thistle 5 Cinnabar
Moth 6 Cinnabar Caterpillars 7 Cowslip

8 Bugle 9 Dor Beetle 10 Mole 11 Dandelion
12 Sexton Beetle 13 Field Mouse 14 Ribwort
Plantain 15 Yellow Rattle 16 Corncrake
17 Orange Tip 18 Ladybird 19 Cuckoo

Flower 20 Common Green Grasshopper
21 Crane-fly 22 Common Blue 23 Red Fescue
24 Common Sorrel 25 Common Bumble Bee
26 Black Knapweed 27 Small Copper

28 Crested Dog's Tail 29 Meadow
Sweet 30 Marsh Horsetail 31 Soft Rush
32 Green-winged Orchid 33 Lapwing
34 Meadow Foxtail 35 Cocksfoot

36 Common Quaking Grass 37 Ox-eye Daisy
38 Dyer's Greenweed 39 Short-tailed Vole
40 Red Clover 41 Meadow Buttercup
42 Silver Y Moth 43 Common Partridges

44 Annual Meadow Grass 45 Yorkshire Fog
46 Meadow Brown 47 Timothy Grass
48 Common Rye Grass 49 Sweet Vernal Grass
50 Meadow Brome 51 Swallows

Fruit of the earth

From earliest childhood, fungi often exert a mysterious fascination. In part it originates from the pleasures of mushrooming, from folklore, fairy rings and nursery illustrations. But there is also something faintly sinister about them. Their pallid flesh and flaccid gills, earthy smells and strange other-worldly shapes arouse feelings of apprehension that cannot be entirely explained away by the knowledge that some species of fungi are poisonous.

In fact, of the 10,000 or so fungi which grow in the British Isles, no more than a score or so are dangerously poisonous, and of these only two or three, notably the death cap and destroying angel, are lethal. On the other hand there are at least 100 edible species in addition to the common field mushroom. Unfortunately many of them can be easily confused with similar species which are either inedible or positively poisonous. So the golden rule is: *never* eat a fungus unless it can be positively identified as edible.

All fungi, whether mushrooms, toadstools or puffballs, are non-flowering plants without chlorophyll. Unable to absorb carbon dioxide from the air and manufacture their own carbohydrates in the normal way, they must obtain their nourishment from other plants, either parasitically from living organic matter, or more usually, from newly decaying plant litter.

Fungi prosper therefore in habitats rich in humus, such as old-established woods and pastures, forming woolly webs of thread-like cells in the rotting underworld of manured meadows and forest floors. Then, when the mysterious alchemy of warmth and dampness create the right conditions, the fruiting bodies we commonly know as mushrooms and toadstools push up through the turf or leaf-mould and unfold their parasol caps to release their reproductive spores.

Fungi are divided into two main groups. The first group, the *Ascomycetes*, produce their spores inside sacs; these include the morels, truffles and cup fungi. The second group, the *Basidiomycetes*, contains the more familiar puffballs, bracket fungi, mushrooms and toadstools which produce their spores on the outside of radiating gills, or, in the case of the boletus family, in tubes which appear as sponge-like pores on the underside of the cap.

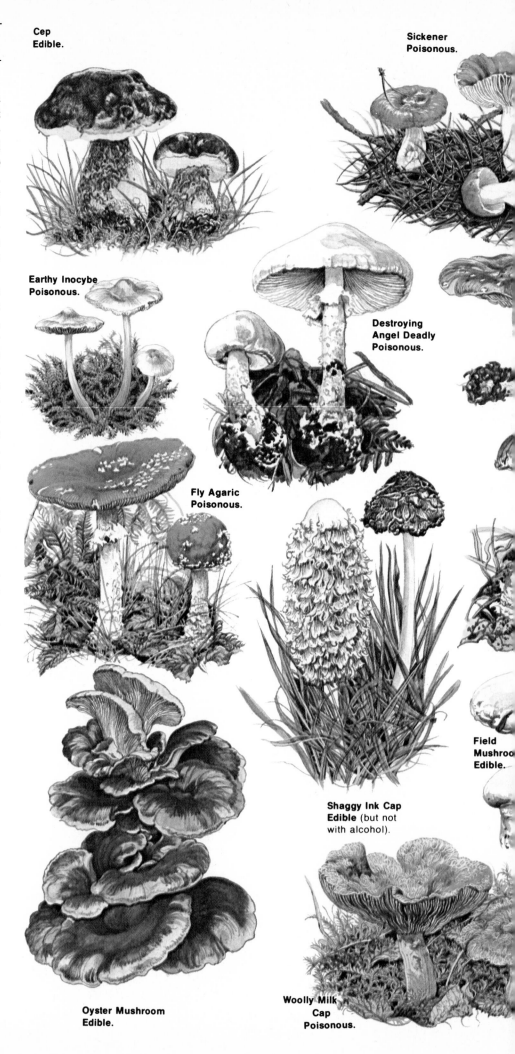

Cep
Edible.

Sickener
Poisonous.

Earthy Inocybe
Poisonous.

Destroying
Angel Deadly
Poisonous.

Fly Agaric
Poisonous.

Field
Mushroom
Edible.

Shaggy Ink Cap
Edible (but not
with alcohol).

Oyster Mushroom
Edible.

Woolly Milk
Cap
Poisonous.

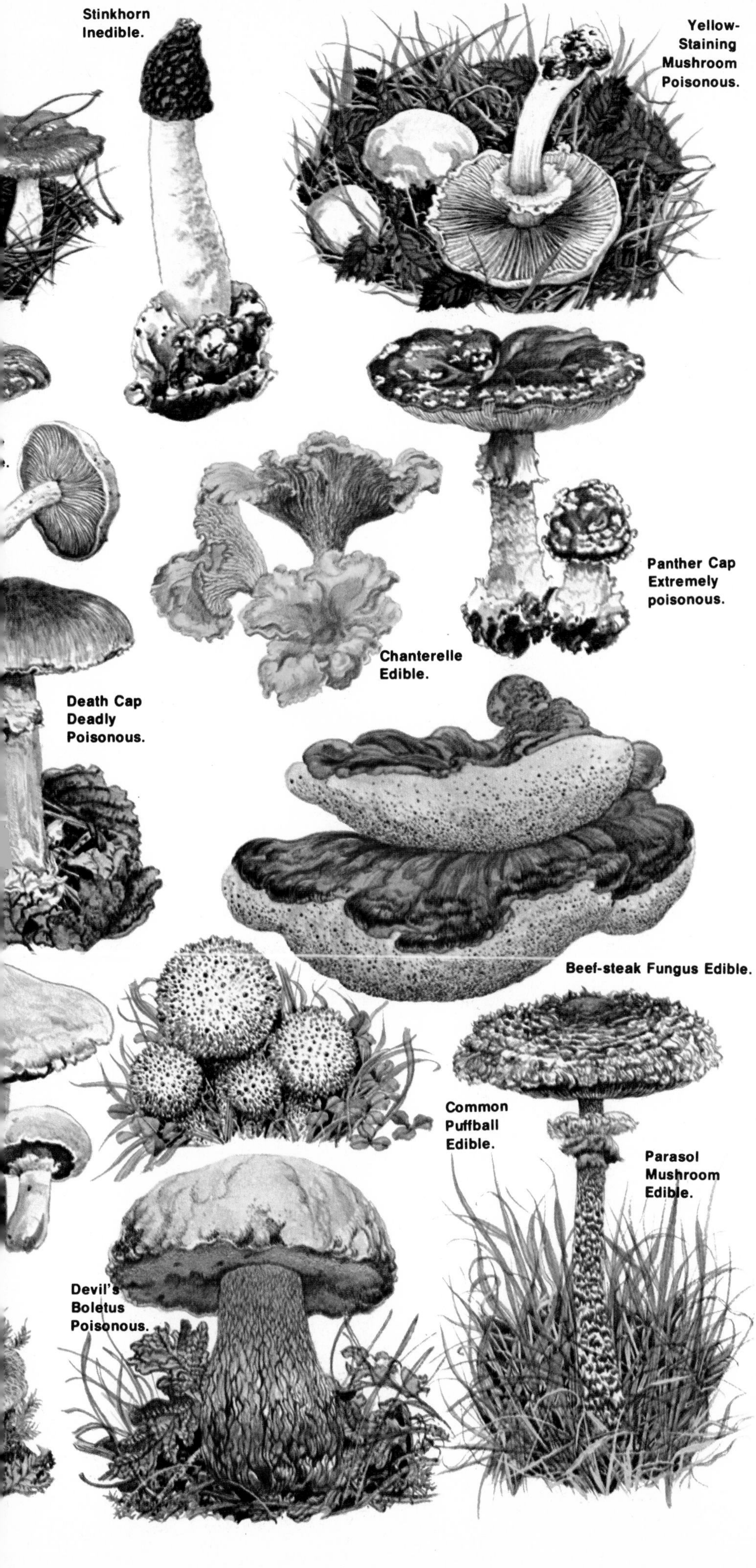

Stinkhorn
Inedible.

Yellow-
Staining
Mushroom
Poisonous.

Panther Cap
Extremely
poisonous.

Chanterelle
Edible.

Death Cap
Deadly
Poisonous.

Beef-steak Fungus Edible.

Common
Puffball
Edible.

Parasol
Mushroom
Edible.

Devil's
Boletus
Poisonous.

Life on the down

Chalk and limestone both give rise to very distinctive scenery. But just as landscapes reflect the composition of the rocks beneath, nature, too, has had to adapt to cope with the well-drained slopes and thin, calcium-rich soils of the chalk downs and limestone hills. More than that, it has had to learn to live with the cultivating hand of man and the nibbling teeth of sheep and rabbits. That process began over 5000 years ago when the first Neolithic farmers started to clear the wildwood from the southern chalklands. The resulting close-knit turf with its skylarks and butterflies and lime-loving flowers, is the oldest man-made habitat in the British Isles.

English chalklands are recognised by their curving skylines and plunging scarps, their combes, dry valleys and beechwood slopes. The Chilterns are chalk hills, and so are the Wolds of Lincolnshire, but the classic chalklands are the downs, the long green hills that rise in Kent and reach deep into Hardy's Wessex.

In Hardy's time a century ago the downs rose in huge grassy swells. Flocks of sheep shone like constellations of stars on their green flanks, keeping the turf in constant trim. In spring and summer every fold and combe was strewn with the wild flowers of the high chalk; harebells, bee orchids, carline thistles. Chalk-hill blue butterflies scattered at every step and skylarks sang over the burial mounds of the long-dead chieftains whose flocks were the first to graze these hills.

But modern farming technology and the pressing need to grow more food brought about a downland revolution. Arable farming has largely replaced the old sheep walks so that today, stripped of their thin green rug, vast acres of chalk down lie bare all winter long until the barley hides their flinty bones. The new landscape is not without a beauty of its own. But nothing can match the rich wildlife of the ancient pasture. And although much of it has gone under the plough, enough of the original living carpet remains to delight nature lovers each year with its chalkland flowers and summer butterflies.

One of the most prominent features of the downland turf is created by one of its smallest inhabitants. Long before the Romans came, Lasius flavus was busily

95

colonising the downs. *Lasius flavus* is the scientific name for the yellow field ant whose hillocks strew the slopes like grassy scatter-cushions. Each dome conceals a complex underground citadel honey-combed with passages and chambers. One colony may contain as many as 30,000 ants, and the hills they raise may last for decades – even centuries.

Among the downland flowers found among the anthills is the horseshoe vetch, foodplant of the chalkhill blue cater-pillar. Its sweet secretions are sought by the ants who cluster round to lick its body. In return, the ants protect the caterpillar from parasitic insects. The chalkhill blue is found south-east of a line from the Severn to the Wash, and the adult butterfly is on the wing in July and August. Other downland butterflies to be seen in summer are the marbled white, dark green fritillary and silver-spotted skipper. All three species are attracted to flowering thistles. Often they share the same flower head with the six-spot burnet, a common and lethargic day-flying moth.

Less conspicuous than the moths and butterflies but no less a part of the downland scene are the purseweb spider, which bushwacks its insect victims from a silken trap spun in the ground, innumer-able grasshoppers, including the rufous grasshopper, the bombardier beetle (so-called because of its ability to squirt a burning liquid from its rear), and an edible, chalk-loving gastropod, the Roman snail.

Larger forms of life are less common, though the brown hare is a typical mammal of the open downs. You can tell a hare from a rabbit by its larger size and

Beauty of the Burren.
Flowers in a Limestone Landscape
Unlike the gentleness of the chalk downs,
limestone country has a harder edge to it,
pushing through the skin of turf to form
grey cliffs and crags, or spreading in
fissured pavements and barrenlands
known as *karst*. Such a place is the
Barony of Burren, a lunar limestone
plateau filling 100 square miles of
County Clare, in the west of Ireland.

The Burren – its name means 'great
rock' – is a miraculous botanical crossroads, a giant natural rock garden in
which alpine, arctic and Mediterranean
flowers and rock plants thrive happily
side by side, sustained by the same, soft
cloudscapes of the Atlantic Ocean which
beats against Clare's western ramparts,
the colossal Cliffs of Moher. For the
botanist, the living treasures of the Burren are one of the glories of Ireland.

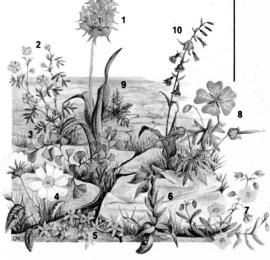

longer, black-tipped ears. Hares feed on
the sweet downland grasses; sheep's fescue and totter grass, or common quaking
grass, with its beautiful panicles that
shake in the slightest breeze.

Without the constant attention of
grazing animals the downs would soon
revert to a tangle of hawthorn scrub, and
eventually to woods of beech and yew.
Fortunately there are still generous
sweeps of open turf where the typical
downland flowers   harebell, round
headed rampion, salad burnet, common
centaury and bird's foot trefoil – still

bloom. But the most beautiful of all the
chalkland plants are the orchids. They
include the bee orchid, so-called because
its velvety flowers look remarkably like
bumble bees. The likeness is no accident.
Orchids rely on insects for pollination. A
male bee, mistaking the flower for a
female, alights on it and attempts to
mate. And in doing so is anointed with
pollen. Yet if orchids are among the most
marvellous sights of the downs, the most
evocative smell is surely the tang of herbs
crushed underfoot on a hot summer's
day: wild thyme and marjoram.

River banks and running waters

All living things are dependent on water. It is the land's lifeblood. And the streams and rivers are its veins and arteries. Wherever water flows – from the tumbling peat-stained upland burns to the slow spread of the widening estuaries – wildlife burgeons. Even the biggest river begins as no more than a trickle, sometimes along spring lines, sometimes in the clefts and hollows of the hills.

In their infancy, upland streams are lusty and fast-flowing, leaping over rocky ledges in their haste to reach the valleys below. As yet the current is too fast to offer a safe anchorage for flowering plants. But the dipper and grey wagtail bob on the midstream boulders, snapping up mayflies and other insects.

The clean, well-oxygenated waters suit pollution-prone fish such as the stone loach, and also the brown trout which flit like shadows through the rocky pools. To protect itself against these and other predators, the caddis fly larva builds a tubular shell of sand grains and bits of dead vegetation.

By the time the stream has reached the lowlands it has merged with other minor tributaries, growing in volume until it becomes a fully-fledged river. Here, salmon lie in the deep holding pools, bound for the spawning redds upstream, and the banks are lined with water-loving alder trees, though the elusive otter prefers to make its holt in the subterranean root-caverns of a riverside ash. Otters feed mostly on eels and other fish, but they will also take freshwater crayfish where they occur in chalk and limestone streams. These small crustaceans grow up to 4in (10cm) long and are mainly nocturnal, hiding beneath stones by day.

Much easier to see are the shoals of hungry minnow darting about in search of midge larvae. The minnow in turn is eaten by many predators, from the pike in the reeds to the kingfisher on its overhanging perch. The kingfisher may be Britain's most colourful bird, but it lays its eggs in a tunnel in the bank on a midden of stinking fish bones.

In May and June the chalk streams of southern England turn white, not with chalk but the flowering tresses of an aquatic buttercup: the lovely water crowfoot. Flitting above the surface on wings of gauze is a beautiful aquatic insect: the banded demoiselle, *Agrion Splendens*. Damsel flies and demoiselles are related to dragonflies, but unlike the dragonfly, they close their wings like butterflies when they settle.

As the year progresses the waterside vegetation becomes increasingly lush. Spires of purple loosestrife line the banks. The air is pungent with the smell of water mint. Ripening panicles of lofty reed grass rustle in the breeze. And the butterbur, having flowered in early spring, now covers the sides of the stream with giant heart-shaped leaves, like a kind of coarse wild rhubarb. Elsewhere the great willowherb flourishes, food-plant of the elephant hawk-moth caterpillar, which feeds at night on the soft hairy leaves. (The moth itself is on the wing in June.)

Farther downstream the widening waters flow still more slowly, meandering through flood plains where willows grow. The graceful foliage of the white willow is eaten by the fierce-looking but harmless puss-moth caterpillar, and the bark may harbour an elegant green musk beetle with long antennae and a distinctive musky smell.

Here the river is opaque with silt and suspended algae. There is less oxygen, and red-finned roach take the place of trout. The grey heron stalks through the shallows, spearing eels with its dagger bill. And soon after sunset, Daubenton's bat – also known as the water bat – may be seen hawking for gnats above the surface of the water.

A series of holes in a grassy bank may reveal the presence of the water vole. Often mistakenly called the water rat, it is the largest British vole, measuring about 1ft (30.5cm) from blunt, twitching nose to thin hairy tail. Water voles are extremely short-sighted and seldom stray more than a few feet from the river. They are completely vegetarian, nibbling the grass around the entrance to their burrows to form close-cropped patches known as water vole 'lawns'. Like the smaller, black and white water shrew, water voles are expert swimmers. With both species, air bubbles are trapped in their dense fur when they dive underwater, giving them a fish-like quicksilver sheen.

In its final stages, the river spreads in ever-widening coils until, far out in the salt-smelling world of sand bars, salt marsh and tidal mudflats, its brackish waters merge and finally become one with the sea.

☐ *See Chapter Six for seashore and estuary wildlife.*

Key to illustration: 1 Dipper 2 Grey Wagtail 3 Brown Trout 4 Mayfly 5 Alder 6 Otter 7 Ash 8 Banded Agrion Demoiselle 9 Reed Grass 10 Musk Beetle 11 White Willow

12 *Kingfisher* 13 *Puss Moth Caterpillar*
14 *Grey Heron* 15 *Butterbur* 16 *Daubenton's*
Bat 17 *Water Vole* 18 *Great Willowherb*
19 *Elephant Hawk-moth Caterpillar*

20 *Elephant Hawk-moth* 21 *Purple Loosestrife*
22 *Water Mint* 23 *Water Crowfoot*
24 *Minnow* 25 *Water Shrew* 26 *Roach*
27 *Pike* 28 *Damsel Fly (Pyrrhosoma nymphula)*

29 *Salmon* 30 *Freshwater Crayfish*
31 *Stone Loach* 32 *Caddis Fly Larva*

Freshwater fishes

The freshwater fishes of the British Isles are few in species. Fewer than 40 kinds are found here – a legacy of the Ice Age which literally froze the life out of most British lakes and rivers. But many of the individual species found today occur in large numbers – to the delight of anglers everywhere.

BULLHEAD
Small (3–4″) fish also known as miller's thumb because of its broad, flattened head. Hides under stones.

STONE LOACH
Streams that suit the stone loach are swift, clear, shallow, stony, and above all, clean. Maximum length: about 5″.

TENCH
Essentially a fish of still waters and weed beds, where it feeds on bottom-living insects, pond snails and water plants. Once called the 'doctor fish' because its slime-coated body was reputed to have curative properties that could heal sick or wounded fish.

THREE-SPINED STICKLEBACK
The jam-jar tiddler of juvenile anglers. Common everywhere except in mountain districts, swarming in shoals in ponds and streams. Average size: 2½–3″.

CHUB
Solidly built, blunt-headed river fish which can grow to between 8–10lbs or more. Widely distributed south of the Firth of Forth but absent from Ireland.

MINNOW
A fish of clear streams, common in Britain but more local in Ireland. Breeding males have a red belly. Maximum size about 4″.

EEL
Common all over the British Isles, even in polluted waters. Eels are believed to spawn in the Sargasso Sea. From there, the tiny leaf-like hatchlings drift to Britain on the currents, become finger-long elvers and wriggle up the rivers to mature. A full-grown female may measure 36″, a male seldom more than 20″.

BRONZE BREAM
Widespread in sluggish lowland waters throughout much of Britain and Ireland. A bottom-feeder living on worms, molluscs and insect larvae. Bronze colour identifies it from the smaller silver bream of

RIVER LAMPREY
The river lamprey, or lampern, belongs to the primitive class of jawless fishes. The adults live in the sea and are entirely parasitic, preying on other fish, to which they attach themselves with their rasping sucker mouths. But they return to breed in the Severn and other rivers, where they are quite common though seldom seen. Average length: about 15–20″.

GUDGEON
Small (6–8″) relative of the carp. Absent from Scotland but widespread elsewhere in rivers with sand or gravel bottom.

GRAYLING
Game fish related to salmon and trout but easily identified by its sail-like dorsal fin. Thrives best in fast-flowing streams with plenty of water and a stony bottom.

RUFFE
The ruffe, or pope, is a small member of the perch family, 6–7″ long. Found only in eastern England.

RUDD
A fish of weedy lakes, small ponds and sluggish rivers. Grows to a length of 14–18″. Easily confused with roach, but the rudd has redder fins and its dorsal fin is set farther back.

PERCH
Common all over the British Isles except the far north. (A 5lb fish is not uncommon)

CARP
Deep-bodied descendant of the fish bred in medieval monastic stew-ponds. Common and long-living, carp thrive best in still, weed-tangled waters, feeding mainly on water plants and occasionally weighing in at up to 40lbs.

DACE
Slender, dashing fish, smallish (about 10″) and silvery. Favours swift clear waters, where it is often seen shoaling close to the surface. Common in England, absent in Scotland.

ROACH
One of our commonest freshwater fishes, living in shoals in slow-moving lowland rivers, lakes and ponds. Seldom exceeds top weight of about 3lbs.

TWAITE SHAD
Uncommon member of the herring family. A plankton-feeder which only enters fresh water when it runs up the rivers – notably the Severn and Shannon – to spawn in the spring. Will grow up to 24″ but is smaller than its scarcer relative, the allis shad.

– the two pairs of sensitive feelers attached to its upper lip. Can exceed 3ft in length.

TORGOCH OR WELSH CHAR
Another fish related to the salmon. 'The torgoch – its Welsh name means 'red-belly' – is found only in the lakes of Snowdonia.

PIKE
Fierce freshwater predator which can attain a length of 36″ and weigh 30lbs or more. The torpedo body and backward set of the fins are designed for the sudden lunge at startled prey – fish, water voles, ducklings and moorhens. The gaping duck-billed jaws are armoured with sharp backward-curving teeth to make sure there is no escape.

BROWN TROUT
Found all over Britain in clean rivers and lakes, from rushing Highland burns to the classic Hampshire chalk streams. A length of 18″ is a good size, but trout twice as big have been taken.

SEA TROUT
Migratory trout which can grow to the size of a small salmon. Fresh run fish returning from the sea to spawn are a magnificent new-minted silver. In Wales and Ireland sea trout are known as sewin.

BLEAK
Active small surface-feeder found in many English rivers but absent from Scotland and Ireland. Feeds mainly on insects, often leaping for them like a trout. Maximum length: about 6″.

SALMON
The king of game fish. Breeds in freshwater but spends much of its life at sea. Spawning takes place from November to February, the female laying her eggs in 'redds' – hollows dug in clean gravel. The fry hatch in early spring. After one year they are called parr. After four years they become smolts and migrate to the sea.
Some return after little more than a year. These are called grilse. But the big fish may be away for four years, feeding and growing to a length of up to 5ft before running up the rivers to spawn. Big males acquire a hooked jaw, or kype. After spawning, the adults are called kelts. Many die, but some, the so-called mended kelts, reach the sea and return to spawn again.

Wildlife of the wetlands

Marsh, broad and fen are three of the most evocative words in the English language for any naturalist. They conjure up visions of flat horizons and huge skies filled with swirling flocks of wildfowl. A low-profile paradise of dykes and reed beds, alive in summer with the harsh chatter of reed and sedge warblers, and heady with the mingling of marshy smells; mud, reeds and water mint.

A thousand years ago that description would have fitted large tracts of lowland Britain. However today the half-drowned landscapes in which Alfred the Great and Hereward the Wake found refuge have been largely reclaimed. But in parts of Somerset and the Norfolk Broads, and in the nature reserves of Minsmere, Wicken and Woodwalton, a few precious pockets of the old Saxon fens survive. These relic wetlands are exceptionally rich in wildlife, and in many cases are the last stronghold of species found nowhere else in the British Isles.

Foremost among these is the largest British butterfly, the swallowtail, pride of the Norfolk Broads. Late May and June is the best time to see this beautiful insect. The caterpillar feeds mainly on milk parsley. Another rare butterfly, the large copper, is found only at Woodwalton Fen in Huntingdonshire, where it was introduced from the Netherlands in 1927 after the native British breed had been hunted to extinction.

The summer sun brings out numerous dragonflies; big hawker dragonflies with a 4in (10cm) wingspan, and broad-bodied darter dragonflies (so-called because of their darting flight) such as

Libellula depressa. Sitting watchfully on a floating leaf or rushing over the surface of the dykes in pursuit of insect prey is the raft spider, the biggest British spider. The female of the species has a body measuring 0.75in (1.9cm) long. Beneath the surface lives the water spider, unique among spiders in its sub-aqua lifestyle. It makes its home underwater by spinning a silken bathysphere and filling it with air bubbles, which it traps on the surface with its body hairs.

The banks of dykes are a good place to look for the grass snake, a non-poisonous reptile which loves to bask in the sun. Frogs form a large part of the grass snake's diet, but the marsh frog could prove too much of a mouthful since the female can grow to about 5in (12.7cm) long. This is the largest British frog, but is not a native, having been introduced from Europe in 1935, and it is found only in Romney Marsh.

Another wetland alien is the coypu, a Latin-American rodent the size of a cat. Brought to Britain in the 1930s for fur (nutria) farming, some coypu escaped and quickly established themselves in the Norfolk Broads where their destructive burrowing undermines the river banks.

Among the many interesting fenland plants are the marsh fern and rare marsh pea. Everywhere, vegetation fights for light and space. Lilies and pondweeds carpet the sluggish waterways, pierced in May and June by pink and white spikes of bogbean. The burnished gold flowers of the marsh marigold, or kingcup, are followed by a succession of other flowers; early marsh orchid, marsh helleborine and yellow iris.

But the most characteristic feature of the fens are the near-impenetrable reed-jungles; the vast beds of tasselled common reed (*Phragmites*) and fen sedge (*Cladium*) which provide a perfect refuge for the marshland birds. So dense are the reeds that the bittern is heard more often than seen; its strange, booming cry carries more than a mile. Equally elusive is the water rail, a furtive relative of the corncrake that squeals like a stuck pig as it runs through the reeds.

Many birds build their nests in the reeds. The great crested grebe, easily recognised by its slim, upright neck posture and prominent ear tufts, moors its floating nest of weeds to the edge of the reed beds. The bearded tit is altogether more secretive. It nests at the base of the tall *Phragmites* reeds; while the reed warbler weaves its nest among the stems.

Reed warblers are frequently chosen as the unwilling hosts of the cuckoo, whose parasitic nesting habits are as well-known as its springtime voice. It deposits its eggs in other birds' nests, leaving the young to be raised by the luckless foster-parents. In flight the cuckoo bears a fleeting resemblance to the kestrel, but there is no mistaking the marsh harrier as it quarters the fens on buoyant, leisurely flapping wings, looking for frogs and small mammals. Unlike the cuckoo, the marsh harrier is a true fenland bird, though its numbers are few. It is now possibly the rarest daylight-hunting bird of prey breeding in the British Isles.

Key to illustration: 1 Marsh Harrier 2 Cuckoo 3 Bearded Tit 4 Reed Warbler and Nest 5 Sedge Warbler 6 Fen Sedge 7 Bogbean 8 Raft Spider 9 Coypu 10 Marsh Frog 11 Grass Snake 12 Marsh Marigold 13 Marsh Helleborine 14 Early Marsh Orchid 15 Marsh Pea 16 Swallowtail Caterpillar 17 Milk Parsley 18 Swallowtail 19 Marsh Fern 20 Large Copper 21 Water Rail 22 Great Crested Grebe 23 Bittern 24 Yellow Iris 25 Common Reed (Phragmites) 26 Libellula depressa Dragonfly

The lowland heath

Heathland occurs on the sands and gravels of southern England. From Breckland to the Lizard, around the Hampshire and London basins, wherever the soil was too poor to bring into cultivation, the open commons glow with the rich colours of heather, gorse and bracken. Heaths are, in effect, lowland moors. And, like the moors, they support their own distinctive wild plants and creatures.

Centuries ago the heaths were covered by woodland. The woods were cleared long ago, but the acid sandy soils were of little value except as rough grazing. Even today, without constant grazing by all kinds of animals – cattle, deer, wild ponies – and the regular devastation caused by accidental fires, the open heaths would eventually revert to woodland. As it is, considerable areas of heathland have been colonised by trees, notably Scots pine and birch (*Betula pubescens*), which thrive on sandy soils.

But the dominant plant species are the head-high bracken, the golden flowering gorse (also known as furze and whin), and above all, the pink and purple heaths and heathers; wiry, shallow-rooted plants, well suited to their impoverished environment. There are five different species in Britain, including the bell heather of the drier heaths, and the cross-leaved heath of the boggier areas. The Cornish heath is a more local species, being found only on the Lizard peninsula in south Cornwall. The Dorset heath (*Erica ciliaris*) also grows in Cornwall but its main strongholds are the Purbeck heaths.

Numerous grasses also grow on the heaths, including the common bent and wavy hair grass. Here on dull summer days the small heath butterfly rests with wings closed among the grass stems. But when the sun shines it takes to the wing, together with that other typical heathland butterfly, the silver-studded blue. The grayling, on the other hand, is a butterfly which likes to settle on paths and bare patches where its subtle stony colours blend perfectly with its background.

Ants, bees, wasps and beetles are all numerous. Keep an eye open on sandy paths for the irridescent green tiger beetle. You may also disturb a devil's coach horse, a fierce black beetle which

runs with its tail arched over its head, scorpion fashion. Moths are also plentiful, in particular the fox moth, which flies in June, and the clouded buff. The fox moth caterpillar feeds on bell heather and is $2\frac{1}{2}$in (6.3cm) long when fully grown in autumn.

The presence of the pinewoods allows the hobby to breed on southern heaths. This beautiful sickle-winged falcon – like a miniature peregrine – usually chooses an old carrion crow's nest for its eyrie.

On hot days, above the murmur of

bees and the crack of gorse pods bursting in the sun, you may hear a sound like two pebbles being tapped together. The source is a small, rufous-chested bird perching in a very upright position on fence posts or gorse bushes: the stonechat. At first glance the resident stonechat is easily confused with its close relative, the whinchat, a summer migrant. But the males may be quickly identified; the stonechat by its all-black hood; the whinchat by its bold white eyestripe. Other birds of the lowland heath

are the linnet and the woodlark. And the rarest heathland bird? Undoubtedly, the Dartford warbler, now, alas, confined to a few pairs in the hinterland of Poole harbour, Dorset.

The Dorset heaths are also the stronghold of Britain's two rarest reptiles: the sand lizard and the harmless, 18in (46cm) long smooth snake. They share their native refuge with the common lizard and Britain's only poisonous snake, the adder. (For illustration, see p89.)

Like so many wildlife habitats, heathland is in rapid decline. Some areas have been reclaimed for agriculture; others planted with conifers or swallowed up by urban sprawl. Those areas that remain are desperately vulnerable to fire in dry summers. One carelessly tossed-away cigarette end can cause irreparable damage, immolating rare creatures such as the sand lizard and smooth snake, together with fledgling birds and other small creatures unable to escape from such a holocaust.

Key to illustration: 1 Woodlark 2 Bracken 3 Wavy Hair Grass 4 Clouded Buff 5 Sand Lizard 6 Common Lizard 7 Rabbit 8 Stonechat 9 Gorse 10 and 11 Silver-studded Blue 12 Cornish Heath 13 Fox Moth 14 Fox Moth Caterpillar 15 Ground Tiger Beetle 16 Grayling 17 Cross-leaved Heath 18 Devil's Coach Horse 19 Smooth Snake 20 Dorset Heath 21 Heath Potter Wasp 22 Whinchat 23 Small Heath Butterfly 24 Common Dodder 25 Heather 26 Dartford Warbler 27 Common Bent Grass 28 Linnets 29 Hobby 30 Silver Birch 31 Scots Pine

1 SCOTCH ARGUS

1 HEDGE BROWN OR GATEKEEPER

1 LARGE HEATH

3 COMMON BLUE

3 SMALL BLUE

1 RINGLET

1 MOUNTAIN RINGLET

1 SMALL HEATH

3 ADONIS BLUE

3 SILVER-STUDDED BLUE

3 CHALKHILL BLUE

1 MEADOW BROWN

1 SPECKLED WOOD

3 LARGE BLUE

3 BROWN HAIRSTREAK

3 BROWN ARGUS

3 HOLLY BLUE

3 WHITE-LETTERED HAIRSTREAK

1 MARBLED WHITE

1 WALL

5 DUKE OF BURGUNDY FRITILLARY

3 LONG-TAILED BLUE

3 BLACK HAIRSTREAK

1 GRAYLING

4 MONARCH OR MILKWEED

3 GREEN HAIRSTREAK

3 PURPLE HAIRSTREAK

2 CLOUDED YELLOW

3 SMALL COPPER

3 LARGE COPPER

2 SMALL WHITE

2 WOOD WHITE

2 LARGE WHITE

2 ORANGE TIP

2 GREEN-VEINED WHITE

2 BRIMSTONE

Butterflies of the British Isles   KEY M—MALE F—FEMALE U—UNDERWING

FAMILIES 1—SATYRIDAE (BROWNS)   2—PIERIDAE (WHITES AND YELLOWS)   3—LYCAENIDAE (BLU...

6 RED ADMIRAL

6 COMMA

6 PAINTED LADY

6 SMALL TORTOISESHELL

6 PURPLE EMPEROR

6 WHITE ADMIRAL

6 DARK GREEN FRITILLARY

6 SILVER-WASHED FRITILLARY

6 SMALL PEARL BORDERED FRITILLARY

6 LARGE TORTOISESHELL

6 PEACOCK

6 CAMBERWELL BEAUTY

6 PEARL BORDERED FRITILLARY

6 GLANVILLE FRITILLARY

6 HEATH FRITILLARY

6 HIGH BROWN FRITILLARY

6 QUEEN OF SPAIN
FRITILLARY

6 MARSH FRITILLARY

7 GRIZZLED SKIPPER

7 ESSEX SKIPPER

7 LARGE SKIPPER

7 CHEQUERED SKIPPER

7 SILVER SPOTTED
SKIPPER

7 LULWORTH SKIPPER

7 DINGY SKIPPER

7 SMALL SKIPPER

3 GREEN
HAIR-
STREAK

8 SWALLOWTAIL

CM

Butterflies: insects of beauty

Butterflies are the most beautiful of all insects – creatures of the sun, with names as gorgeous as their wings, such as purple emperor, red admiral and Camberwell beauty. About 70 different kinds of butterflies can be seen in the British Isles, and most of them are shown here.

British butterflies are divided into eight families, each with a scientific Latin name. The *Satyridae*, or browns, and the moth-like *Hesperidae*, or skippers are essentially grassland species. The *Lycaenidae* include the irridescent blues and coppers of downs and meadows, and the woodland-loving hairstreaks. The *Pieridae* include not only the familiar and destructive cabbage whites, but also the beautiful clouded yellow and delicate wood white. The largest family, the *Nymphalidae*, covers the fritillaries (a distinctive tribe of tawny-gold butterflies with black freckles and silver-splashed undersides), the purple emperor, the admirals (red and white), peacock and painted lady. The three remaining families are each represented in Britain by a single species: the *Papilionidae* by the swallowtail; the *Danaidae* by the monarch, or milkweed; and the *Riodinidae* by the Duke of Burgundy fritillary.

The brimstone – both the sulphur yellow male and its pale greenish mate – are usually the first butterflies to appear. Brimstones winter in Britain and emerge after hibernation during the first warm days of February or early March. Other species quickly follow, including the very common small tortoiseshell, and in May no country lane would be complete without an orange-tip flitting among the cow-parsley (though only the males flaunt those candescent wing-tips).

In high summer the downs and meadows are alive with blues, browns, skippers and small coppers. During good butterfly years, migrant species such as the painted lady and clouded yellow swarm in from the Mediterranean. Other species are confined to specific localities. The swallowtail, the largest native butterfly, occurs only in Wicken Fen and the Norfolk Broads. Sometimes rare vagrants turn up; a monarch from America, a Camberwell beauty from Scandinavia. These you are unlikely to see. But some of our loveliest butterflies – peacocks and red admirals – will grace any garden where buddleia, valerian and Michaelmas daisies grow.

The butterfly is the end process of a life of metamorphosis which begins with an egg, hatches to become a caterpillar, pupates as a chrysalis, and finally emerges as the imago – the adult insect. Most butterflies of the British Isles spend only two or three weeks in the chrysalis stage, though there are exceptions. The green hairstreak, for instance, hibernates right through the winter as a chrysalis.

The food plants of caterpillars vary from one species to another; buckthorn for the brimstone, garlic mustard for the orange tip, succulent oak buds for the purple hairstreak, dog violet for the pearl-bordered fritillary and stinging nettles for the peacock, small tortoiseshell and red admiral. Nettle eaters like the peacock form conspicuous colonies, festooning their host plant with gossamer marquees. Each cobweb purse contains a wriggling mass of black and bristly caterpillars, progeny of the gorgeous adults that will hatch in mid-July.

Butterflies themselves are attracted by sight and smell to the nectar of flowers, especially mauve flowers such as thistles and buddleia, while species such as the hedge brown and the white admiral are drawn irresistibly to bramble flowers. Some also feed on honeydew, sap, rotting fruit, and even – in the case of the purple emperor – on the putrefying juices of a dead animal. Butterflies can taste with their feet. As they light on a flower and detect its sweetness, the watchspring tongue uncoils to probe for nectar.

The colours of butterflies have a twofold purpose. They help the males to recognise the females (in some species colouration is strikingly different between the sexes), and they provide protection from predators. When a comma closes its ragged wings it looks exactly like a dead leaf – a perfect camouflage to avoid being eaten by birds. The bright 'eye' markings on the wings of many butterflies serve a similar protective purpose. They deflect attention away from the vital parts, often enabling the butterfly to escape with nothing worse than a tattered wing.

Today, inevitably, butterflies are fewer. Insecticides, climatic changes and loss of habitat have all taken their toll. The large blue, numbered in thousands only two decades ago, was pronounced 'probably extinct' only last year. The Queen of Spain fritillary has not been seen for over three decades. But county naturalists' trusts and the British Butterfly Conservation Society, aided by a growing general awareness of the need for conservation in all its forms, are fighting hard to make sure that the most important butterfly haunts survive.

Twilight world of hungry hunters

When evening comes, the woods and fields awaken as nature's night watch takes over, and a host of creatures seldom seen by day creep out under cover of darkness, to eat – and be eaten.

With the fading of the light, the sun's warmth evaporates. The air grows cooler, distilling itself as dew in the open meadows as the moisture level rises. With the chill onset of evening, many day-flowering plants close their petals to protect their delicate stamens. But some, like the night-flowering catchfly, remain closed by day and only unfurl at dusk to release a fragrant scent and attract the night-flying insects which pollinate them.

The most spectacular of the night-flying insects are the moths. More than 2000 species occur in the British Isles, ranging from the hordes of tiny micro-moths to the large and handsome hawk-moths with their fat furry bodies.

Most moths rest during the day, relying on disguise to escape detection. In the case of the lappet moth, its wings are the exact colour of withered bramble leaves. But when day is done, they whir through the dusk, hunting for favoured flowering food-plants such as honeysuckle, whose sweet odour they locate with their incredibly sensitive feathered antennae. Moths themselves emit scents to attract mating partners, and from June onwards the male ghost moth can be seen hovering over long grassy meadows as it attempts to entice a smoky gold female.

The twilight wealth of flying insects – midges, moths, dancing gnats – attracts larger winged creatures. In midsummer the swift flies late into the evening, screaming and racing over village rooftops. And in June and July, as the insect build-up reaches its peak, bats give birth to their young to coincide with this time of plenty. The commonest bat is also the smallest: the tiny, mouselike pipistrelle, or flittermouse. A pair of them scarcely weigh more than one ounce (28gm). At the other end of the scale is the noctule bat, with a 15in (38cm) wingspan.

The needle-thin cries of bats are so high-pitched that many people are unable to hear them, but there is no problem in hearing the nightingale, which arrives in late spring and sings by day and night until the young hatch in June.

The woodcock, its plumage patterned like dead oak leaves, is also hard to see, being mainly nocturnal in its feeding habits. But during the breeding season the male performs a curious display flight known as 'roding', in which it flits slowly down woodland rides at dusk, emitting a low croaking call.

On open heaths the midsummer dusk vibrates to the strange churring song of the male nightjar, a moth-eating migrant with a gaping mouth evolved for catching its prey on the wing. But not all the night noises are made by birds. In late summer, especially in southern coastal counties, the hedgebanks ring to the stridulations of the great green grasshopper. This is Britain's biggest grasshopper, with a length of over 2in (5cm).

The humid conditions of the advancing night favour creatures such as slugs and snails, which would lose moisture in the heat of the day. One of the prettiest of these gastropods is the white-lipped banded snail. But pretty is not the adjective most people would use to describe the great grey slug, which grows up to 8in (20cm) long and mates upside down on a cord of communal slime.

Slugs and snails are eaten by the voracious larvae of the glow-worm, which is not a worm but a beetle. Damp meadows are a favourite habitat, and on warm evenings in July you may see the bright greenish-yellow pinpoints of light which are the females shining in the grass. Damp nights also bring out the earthworm from its burrow. A single acre of meadowland may hold three million earthworms. As they search for leaves the worms are themselves sought by many creatures, and are devoured in large numbers by the shy nocturnal badger. This powerful, short-legged woodland dweller sleeps by day deep within the underground chambers of its sett, but emerges after dark to patrol its miles of well-trodden territorial paths.

Sometimes a fox will take over a disused badger sett to raise a family, and on warm summer evenings the vixen and cubs can sometimes be seen playing at the entrance to the earth.

If you hear a sharp, dog-like bark, it is more likely to be the alarm signal of a roe deer, another largely nocturnal mammal which lies up by day and emerges at dusk to browse at the edge of woods and clearings. The bark of a deer may be unfamiliar, but there is no mistaking the soft, quavering hoot of the tawny owl. This mournful cry, and its sharp 'ki-wik' – uttered as it flies on silent, rounded wings – is the sound of a true night hunter.

Even more eerie than the voice of the tawny owl is the screech of the barn owl, which prefers to hunt in more open

country, ghosting over the meadows like a huge, pale moth. Not quite so well-known are the yowling and yelping cries of the little owl, though the bird is now widespread in England and Wales, having successfully established itself since it was first introduced into the British Isles during the 19th century. Another British owl, the long-eared owl, is a bird of the conifer forests, and is much more nocturnal. The so-called 'ears' are simply feathered tufts whose sole purpose is for courtship display. The true ear orifices, as with all owls, lie hidden behind the facial disc.

When dusk has deepened into dead of night there is a lull in the activity of creatures such as owls and bats. But in the grey, misty hour towards first light there is another brief flurry of hunting and feeding before the dawn chorus announces the return of the day shift – and the prying eyes of man.

Birds of winter

In winter the woods fall silent, the fields lie dormant. Few birds sing. The battalions of summer migrants – warblers, swallows, cuckoos and turtle doves – have long since fled to sunnier haunts. Without them, the land seems strangely empty. But migration is a two-way traffic, and winter brings some exciting visitors to these shores. For bird-watchers, this is one of the most rewarding times of the year, especially around the coasts and estuaries of the British Isles where wintering wildfowl and waders gather in enormous numbers.

On the Dee estuary, for example, large mixed flocks of waders congregate, with perhaps as many as 40,000 dunlin, 40,000 knot and 20,000 oystercatchers. Large flocks of Greenland white-fronted geese winter on the marshes around Wexford harbour in Ireland, amongst other places, and in winter Essex becomes host to half the world population of dark-bellied Brent geese, which fly in from Siberia.

One of the commonest winter visitors is the fieldfare, a handsome, slate-headed Scandinavian thrush with a harsh chuckling cry. With the first real cold snap of the year they are joined by flocks of redwings, and they are often seen feeding together, either in open fields or stripping hawthorn berries from the hedgerows. The waxwing, a much scarcer visitor with a prominent chestnut crest, prefers rowan berries, but will also happily plunder rose hips, pyracantha and cotoneaster berries from gardens.

The brambling, a Scandinavian relative of the chaffinch, frequently appears in large numbers when beech mast is plentiful. Its plumage blends well with the winter beechwoods. The snow bunting nests in the Scottish mountains, but flocks move south in winter and may be seen feeding on seeds in coastal areas.

The great grey shrike is a loner, a bold pied bird with the hooked beak of a predator and a habit of impaling its victims – mice and small birds – on thorns or even barbed wire. Among the true birds of prey to be seen in winter are the rough-legged buzzard, whose plumage is paler than the resident common buzzard, and the short-eared owl, a daylight hunter with a moth-like flight and a taste for voles. The magnificent snowy owl is a true bird of the arctic, and seldom seen in Britain outside Orkney and Shetland, where it now breeds on Fetlar.

Like the snowy owl, the dumpy grey and white knot is a bird of the high arctic, but in winter these diminutive waders form compact flocks of up to 10,000 birds, and head south. In mid-winter there may be a quarter of a million of these arctic refugees feeding around our coasts. More solitary, much less common is the green sandpiper, an inland wader which prefers the cover of ponds, streams and riverbanks. When flushed, it zigzags skywards with a startled fluting cry.

On estuaries, reservoirs and other inland waters, huge flocks of wintering wildfowl gather. Some – mallard, teal, tufted duck – are permanent residents. But many are migrants escaping from harsher northern latitudes. Rafts of pintail bob on the waters. They use their elegant tails to balance as they up-end to feed. Flights of wigeon come whirling out of the sky, the drakes uttering their whistled exclamations of surprise. And on northern and eastern coasts broad chevrons of pink-footed geese fly in from their mudflat roosts to feed among the stubble. The jangling music of flighting pink-feet is one of the most thrilling sounds of the British countryside; the shrill nasal 'ang-ank' of the male easily distinguished from the yelp of the female, which is exactly one octave lower.

Another sound guaranteed to lift the hairs on the nape of a bird-watcher's neck is the melancholy bugling of wild winter swans – the whooper swan from Iceland and Lapland; Bewick's swan from arctic Russia. In the field they are hard to tell apart. Both species have buttercup bills with black tips, but the whooper is the bigger bird, with an $8\frac{1}{2}$ft (2.6m) wingspan. One of the best places in Britain to see Bewick's swans is the Wildfowl Trust's headquarters at Slimbridge, Gloucestershire.

Not all winter birds are true migrants. Some, like the lapwing, remain all year, but flock together in winter and move south during hard weather, where they become a familiar sight as they forage for worms in the fields and ploughlands. Other residents undergo a complete change of plumage to see the winter through. The most striking example is the ptarmigan, which loses its mottled summer coat and turns white to merge with the snows of the Highland summits. Survival is the name of the game, and a white ptarmigan in a winter landscape is more likely to evade the watchful eyes of hunting eagles.

Fieldfare: The grey rump and head are useful identifying features

Green Sandpiper: In flight this freshwater wader has a very black-and-white appearance, and a bold white rump

Ptarmigan: Highland resident that turns white in winter to hide from golden eagles

Wigeon: The drake (shown here) has bold white wing-flashes in flight

Redwing: Hawthorn
[ber]ries are a favourite food
[th]ey also feed in open fields

Waxwing: Exotic visitor from
Scandinavia with a taste
for garden berries

Great Grey Shrike:
Fierce fence-post
sentinel. Its victims
are impaled
on thorns

Brambling: Northern finch,
sometimes mistaken for the common
resident Chaffinch

Snow Bunting:
In flight its beautiful black
and white markings
are unmistakable

Snowy Owl: The remote
Shetland isle of Fetlar is
the only British breeding
site of this splendid
arctic bird

Short-eared Owl:
Daylight hunter of saltmarsh
coasts and open countryside

Rough-legged Buzzard:
Paler than the resident
Common Buzzard, this
rare but regular visitor
arrives in October

Bewick's Swan and (right)
Whooper Swan: Confusingly
similar, but smaller Bewick
usually swims with tail end
well above water

Pink-footed Goose:
Upward of 50,000 birds
winter in the British Isles

Lapwing:
Also known
as the Green Plover

Pintail: Long pointed tail
identifies the drake (shown here in
full winter plumage)

Knot: Migrates as far
south as West Africa, but
the British Isles are
its main winter stronghold

Great Spotted Woodpecker

Nuthatch

Sparrowhawk

Green Woodpecker

Jay

Grey Squirrel

Nut Weevil

Cockchafer Beetle

Oak Bark Beetle

Purple Hairstreak

Caterpillar

Marble Galls

Oak Apple Gall

Andricus kollari

Biorrhiza pallida

Young Leaves and Blossom

Common Oak Leaf and Acorn

Tree Creeper

BlueBell

Early Purple Orchid

Woodruff

Wood Sorrel

Wood Anemone

Primrose

Weasel

Polecat

Mistletoe

Lichens

Bracket Fungus

Ivy

Teeming tenants of the oak

The richest of all our greenwood habitats in wildlife terms is the oakwood: a nature reserve in its own right. Every oak is host to (see left) plants, insects, birds and animals from the oak bush crickets which browse on its crown to the roe and fallow deer which walk in its shade. Compare, for instance, the wealth of insect life in an oak (284 different kinds) with that of alien species such as the horse chestnut (five) or the plane tree (only one). There are bugs that feed on oak flowers, beetles that eat the bark, and caterpillars like those of the purple hairstreak butterfly that eat the young leaves.

The insects attract birds: tree-creeper, nuthatch, pied flycatcher, wood warbler. The great spotted woodpecker nests in holes drilled into the hollow heart of rotten branches. Acorns provide food for the jay and grey squirrel, and the abundance of wildlife attracts fierce predators such as the weasel, the sparrowhawk and the rare polecat.

Galls are caused by parasites. Most conspicuous are the hard marble galls and oak apples, caused by the larvae of the gall wasp. Galls are made by the tortured tissue of the host tree, not by the insects. In the light shade and rich loam of the oakwood floor many wild flowers thrive. Among them are bluebell, primrose and wood anemone.

As the tree grows older it may be invaded by ivy and rarely, by mistletoe, and in wetter, western districts, by mosses, lichens and ferns. As it approaches the end of its 250-year lifespan, the crown grows stag-headed. Death is hastened by fungi which invade the wood and feed on its cells, causing rot and decay.

How the woods were made

The British Isles are among the least wooded countries in Europe. The collective woodland canopy scarcely covers 15 per cent of the land. In the past 40 years, more than half our mixed native woodland has become open field or conifer plantations. It is an old story. Man has been hacking away at the greenwood since the Stone Age. In the process, our use and abuse of trees, both native and alien, has helped – perhaps more than

Cathedral columns of an English beechwood: few plants grow in its dense shade

any other single factor – to shape the countryside we live in today. When the Ice Age was ending Britain was a treeless tundra still joined to the Continent. As the climate improved, the time was ripe for arboreal invasion. Dwarf birch, juniper, willow and Scots pine formed the advance guard. Then, following still warmer weather, came oak, hazel, ash and elm. These trees gradually became the dominant species, usurping all others except in the far north where the Great Wood of Caledon clung to its fathomless forests of pine, forming the untamed wildwood which still covered most of Britain right up until Saxon times. In the wildwood the lime tree also flourished, especially in the east, and alder in the wetter places.

From the Stone Age onwards, man's impact upon the wildwood grew with every passing century. Even in those primitive times it has been estimated that three men with stone axes could fell 600 square yards of forest in four hours.

By the Norman Conquest the boundless no-man's land of the old wildwood was already a folk memory. Even the composition of the ancient broad-leaved canopy was changing. The Romans had introduced walnuts and sweet chestnuts. Many other species, including the ubiquitous sycamore and horse chestnut – the conker tree beloved by generations of schoolboys – would become established by the 16th century.

But by then even the traditional method of woodland management known as coppicing was in decline. A thousand years ago woods were crucial to the economy. They provided logs to burn, timber to build, and shelter for the deer whose venison filled many a royal paunch. So early Britons learned to live with their woods, not clear-felling them as if they were cornfields, as some modern foresters do, but using them wisely as a renewable resource.

In this they were assisted by the remarkable ability of most British broad-leaved trees to regenerate themselves by sending up vigorous new shoots from the stump or stool, after they have been cut down. Thus coppicing evolved, where favoured hardwoods – hazel, ash, hornbeam – were cut on rotation to provide a regular crop of staves and poles from the same parent stool.

A coppice needed to be well protected, otherwise deer and cattle would eagerly browse the tender young shoots. So an alternative cropping method known as pollarding developed. Pollards are a kind of up-in-the-air coppice, where the trees are cut above the reach of browsing animals, leaving a stump between six and 15ft (2–4.5m) high, called a bolling.

Willows were pollarded in the same way (and still are in Somerset) to produce slender withies for basket-weaving. But the best examples of ancient pollards are to be found in places like Burnham Beeches, in Buckinghamshire, and in the relic scraps of the medieval royal forests, such as the New Forest in Hampshire and Hatfield Forest in Essex.

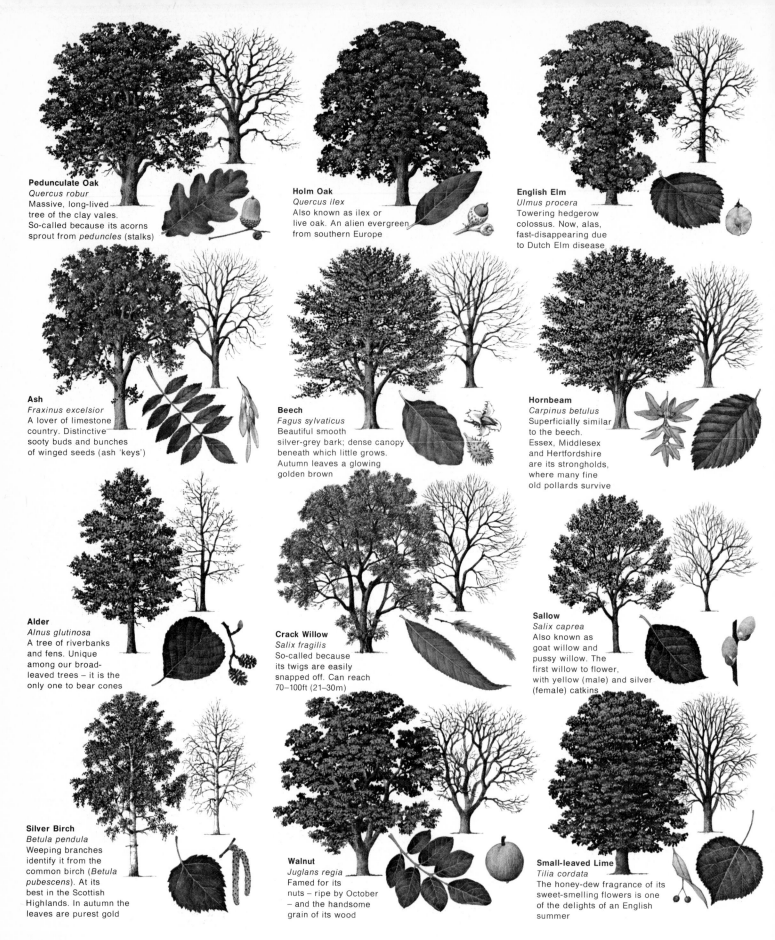

Pedunculate Oak
Quercus robur
Massive, long-lived
tree of the clay vales.
So-called because its acorns
sprout from *peduncles* (stalks)

Holm Oak
Quercus ilex
Also known as ilex or
live oak. An alien evergreen
from southern Europe

English Elm
Ulmus procera
Towering hedgerow
colossus. Now, alas,
fast-disappearing due
to Dutch Elm disease

Ash
Fraxinus excelsior
A lover of limestone
country. Distinctive
sooty buds and bunches
of winged seeds (ash 'keys')

Beech
Fagus sylvaticus
Beautiful smooth
silver-grey bark; dense canopy
beneath which little grows.
Autumn leaves a glowing
golden brown

Hornbeam
Carpinus betulus
Superficially similar
to the beech.
Essex, Middlesex
and Hertfordshire
are its strongholds,
where many fine
old pollards survive

Alder
Alnus glutinosa
A tree of riverbanks
and fens. Unique
among our broad-
leaved trees – it is the
only one to bear cones

Crack Willow
Salix fragilis
So-called because
its twigs are easily
snapped off. Can reach
70–100ft (21–30m)

Sallow
Salix caprea
Also known as
goat willow and
pussy willow. The
first willow to flower,
with yellow (male) and silver
(female) catkins

Silver Birch
Betula pendula
Weeping branches
identify it from the
common birch (*Betula
pubescens*). At its
best in the Scottish
Highlands. In autumn the
leaves are purest gold

Walnut
Juglans regia
Famed for its
nuts – ripe by October
– and the handsome
grain of its wood

Small-leaved Lime
Tilia cordata
The honey-dew fragrance of its
sweet-smelling flowers is one
of the delights of an English
summer

Among the coppices, some trees, especially oaks, were left and allowed to
reach maturity before being felled.
These, the standards or maidens (untouched trees) were grown for their
timber. The medieval woodman made a
clear distinction between wood and
timber. Wood was anything from brush-
wood and firewood to the poles obtained
by coppicing. Timber was a term reserved
for the heavy stuff.

After the Middle Ages, and after the
kings had relinquished many of their
hunting forests, the woods were plun-
dered by charcoal-burners to fuel the
furnaces of the iron-masters. They
shrank before the onslaught of expanding agriculture. The great oaks were laid
low to build Tudor towns and Georgian
battle fleets. Railways and the age of
cheap coal undercut the firewood trade.
Two world wars, the felling of timber to
pay death duties, the grubbing out of
hedgerows - and the ravages of Dutch

Sycamore
Acer pseudoplatanus
Hardy, grow-anywhere
alien introduced to
Scotland 400 years ago.
Spreads by means of its
whirling winged 'keys'

Grey Poplar
Populus canescens
Grows to height of
80–90ft (24–27m). Attractive
red catkins; leaves
with downy grey undersides

Black Poplar
Populus nigra
Rare, craggy 100-ft (30m)
giant. Grows fast,
loves damp. Not found
north of Trent

Field Maple
Acer campestre
Smallish tree
about 25ft (8m) high
Small leaves a
rich yellow-gold in
autumn

Hazel
Corylus avellana
Mostly seen as
hedge or coppice but will
form small tree if left.
Dusty yellow 'lamb's-tail'
catkins at winter's end;
sweet edible nuts
in autumn

Horse Chestnut
*Aesculus
hippocastanum*
Pride of parks and
avenues. Sticky buds,
huge waxy candle
flowers, shiny conkers

Sweet Chestnut
Castanea vulgaris
Can outlive the oak.
Massive trunk with fissured,
spiralling bark. Edible nuts
encased in prickly green
hedgehog shucks

Holly
Ilex aquifolium
Small evergreen
with glossy prickly
leaves and clustered
scarlet berries

Scots Pine
Pinus sylvestris
Scotland is its native
stronghold, but grows
just as happily in Hampshire's
New Forest

Mature
tree

Mature
cone

Young
tree

Young
cone

Larch
Larix decidua
Attractive conifer
which sheds its
needles in winter, replacing them
with delicate spring greenery

Mountain Ash
Sorbus aucuparia
Propagated by
birds – especially
the thrush family – which
strip the scarlet berries

Yew
Taxus baccata
The sombre
evergreen of country churchyards.
Grows to a great age

Elm disease have all conspired to reduce
our woodland heritage to a shadow of its
ancient glory.

Yet enough trees remain in our man-
made landscape of field and hedgerow to
create the illusion of wooded countryside, enclosing, shading, walling in
with cliffs of leaves. The wildwood is
gone for ever, to be replaced by something no less precious: a scattered mosaic
of clumps and copses, beech hangers and
pagan groves of yew, pocket woodlands
and thin green lines of waterside willows.
And sometimes, the welcoming depths of
a true forest – a Savernake or a Wyre –
preserved with all its living elements.

☐ Of the trees shown here, all but one
(the black poplar) are common, and all
but six (holm oak, walnut, larch, sycamore, horse chestnut and sweet chestnut) are true natives. Our guide shows
leaves, fruit, and appearance in summer
and winter. These clues will help you to
recognise different species.

The primeval pinewood

Even to Sassenach eyes, the Scots pine is a familiar sight. It thrives all over England, from wildest Lakeland to genteel Bournemouth. But only in the Scottish Highlands can it be seen in its true glory, growing as nature intended in majestic stands among the lochs and glens, where it provides both food and shelter for the wildlife of northern Britain.

In the shadow of the Cairngorms at Rothiemurchus, at Beinn Eighe on the west coast, in the Black Wood of Rannoch, Glen Affric and a few other places, are the last relics of the Great Wood of Caledon, the primeval northern pine forest. The Great Wood once covered more than three million acres. Wolves and wild boar roamed there, sharing the trackless deeps with brown bear, lynx and elk. Outlaws found refuge in its glens and hollows. For centuries the pines grew undisturbed. Far to the south, the Romans came and went. The Saxons carved out petty earldoms.

Then came the Vikings, and the war on the Great Wood began. In the west they fired the forests and felled the tall trees to carve as dragon prows for their longships. The wildlife of the forest began to go, too, as their stronghold diminished. The bears were gone by the tenth century; the last wolf was killed in Inverness-shire in 1743.

Further inroads were made by the impoverished clan chiefs who, forced to pay homage to Hanoverian overlords, sold off their timber to English ironmasters. Two world wars and the Forestry Commission in its bad old backwoods heyday finally brought the Great Wood to its knees, reducing it to railway sleepers and telegraph poles. Today the remaining 20,000 acres (8093 hectares) are mere remnants, with no more than about 4000 acres (1619 hectares) of true closed forest in which it is still possible to catch the illusion of a long-vanished Caledon.

The relic trees support forms of wildlife seldom seen outside the Highlands. The pine is host both to the fish-eating osprey, which builds its massive eyrie in the topmost clefts of the spreading crown, and to the crested tits which excavate their nests in the rotting stumps. Pine seeds provide food for the crossbill and the red squirrel. The squirrels in turn are hunted by the rare pine marten, the fierce tree weasel whose chief stronghold is in Beinn Eighe National Nature Reserve.

The fresh green shoots are eaten by the caterpillars of the pine beauty moth, and also by the capercaillie, the giant grouse of the Caledonian forest. During the 'lek' – the season of courtship and display – the woods echo to the popping and wheezing cries of the aggressive males as they perform their extraordinary antics, strutting and leaping with swollen necks and fully-fanned tails. The capercaillie was exterminated in Scotland during the 18th century but was reintroduced successfully from Sweden in 1837.

When the pine needles fall they are gathered up by the wood ant, the largest British ant, to form a mound sometimes several feet high covering the main subterranean nesting chambers and galleries. Here, too, on the forest floor, you may find two wild orchids seldom seen elsewhere: creeping lady's tresses and the coralroot orchid.

Unfortunately, man's tampering with the works has broken down the Scottish pine forest's system of natural regeneration. When squirrels and crossbills scatter the pine seeds there are no longer any boars, bears or elk to root in the undergrowth and open up the soil to aid germination. Worse, any seeds that do actually reach the seedling stage are speedily chewed up by the red deer.

The final blow could be the fickle British climate. Over the last few centuries the weather has been getting warmer and wetter. That process may now have been reversed but the damage has been done. As a result the forest floors

Left: Monarchs of the glens. Native Scots pines provide a rich habitat for Highland wildlife

are suffering a creeping invasion of spongy, soaking sphagnum moss, piling up in thick cushions among the trees. Tear up two handfuls and you can wring a cup of water from it. And that, to the Scots pine, is disaster. The accumulated wetness is steadily loosening the clenched roots until in the winter gales, even the strongest tree will lurch from its socket like a rotten molar.

Fortunately there is now a greater awareness of the pine's plight. The Nature Conservancy Council is involved in schemes to save the forest. Some areas have been declared national nature reserves or sites of special scientific interest, although that is no cast-iron guarantee against the forester's axe. The Govern-

ment has finally recognised the landscape value of Scots pine on its native ground and has greatly improved the grant available to private foresters who plant native pine. As for the Forestry Commission, it no longer regards the Scots pine simply as a cash crop. Its Glen Affric forest, for instance, is now managed as a Caledonian pine reserve.

Its value is twofold. Firstly, there is the beauty of the forest. The way the trees grow wide apart, almost in glades, in a way that lets in the light and creates magical depths of space and serenity. There is the way they grow in company with the beautiful weeping Highland birch (*Betula pendula*), and still retain a rich wildlife. And there is the beauty of

Key to illustration: 1 Scots Pine 2 Pine Beauty Moth 3 Pine Beauty Caterpillar 4 Crossbill 5 Coralroot Orchid 6 Creeping Lady's Tresses 7 Sphagnum Moss 8 Chickweed Wintergreen 9 Wood Ant Nest 10 Capercaillie 11 Heather 12 Hairy Wood Rush 13 Red Squirrel 14 Wood Ant 15 Crested Tit 16 Pine Marten 17 Osprey 18 Red Throated Diver

the individual tree itself; the flaky fissured bark, all silvery-grey and flaming salmon-pink; the blue-green canopy; the gnarled and craggy shape. Like the oak, it has a courageous quality that suits its wild surroundings. It is the Scots pine, not the red deer, that is the real monarch of the glen.

The last wilderness

The mountains and moorlands of the British Isles form our last great wilderness. Barren, desolate and at first glance empty, they support a spectacular variety of wild plants and creatures. Many of the rarest flowers and the most magnificent birds and animals find sanctuary in the fastness of these remote and beautiful rainswept uplands.

Moorland occurs on the uplands of the north and west of the British Isles where the old, hard rocks rise up and the moist Atlantic airstream creates a constantly waterlogged habitat which encourages the formation of peat and bogland. It takes a special breed of plants to cope with the harsh climate and thin soils.

Most characteristic of all moorland plants is heather, a close-knit evergreen undershrub with tough woody stems covering immense tracts of peaty uplands. There are five different species but the commonest is *Calluna vulgaris*, the true heather or ling. Its clustered spikes of tiny flowers are rich in nectar, and from July to September they transform the burnt cork hues of the drier moors with a glorious blaze of summer purple. From May to late July the flowers of the heath spotted-orchid are fairly widespread on the moors. One of the most interesting plants to look for on these acid peatlands is fir clubmoss, which is neither a fir nor a true moss, but a primitive, 6in (15cm) high relative of the ferns.

Heather is a valuable food plant for many creatures, including the caterpillars of the emperor moth, which feed on the leaves from June to August. When fully grown they are about 2in (5cm) long, and pupate in a spun silk cocoon. The adult male moths can be seen whirring over the heather on sunny days in April and May; the females have the same bold eye-spots but are a ghostly grey and fly by night.

On grouse moors large swathes of heather are regularly burned to encourage the growth of succulent new shoots for the red grouse. The guttural chuckling go-beck, go-beck of grouse is one of the most evocative sounds of the high moors. The heather feeds the grouse; the grouse, in turn, is eaten by the golden eagle, Britain's largest bird of prey. Something like 200 pairs of eagles breed in Scotland, nesting on remote crags or in old Scots pines. The eyrie is a huge pile of sticks sometimes measuring

Barren world of the Highland summits above Loch Inchad, near Rhiconich, Sutherland

Key to illustration: *1 Heather 2 Heath Spotted orchid 3 Fir Clubmoss 4 and 5 Emperor Moth and Caterpillar 6 Red Grouse 7 Golden Eagle 8 Merlin 9 Meadow Pipit 10 Bilberry 11 Bilberry Bumble Bee 12 Cotton Grass 13 Sphagnum Moss 14 Bog Asphodel 15 Round-leaved Sundew 16 Greenshank 17 Curlew 18 Sheep's Fescue 19 Mat-grass 20 Mountain Ringlet 21 Red Deer 22 Wild Cat 23 Mountain Hare 24 Ptarmigan 25 Moss Campion 26 Starry Saxifrage*

Where the peat thins out at around 2000ft (610m) the herbage becomes sweeter and more alpine in character, with grasses such as sheep's fescue and mat-grass, food plant of the mountain ringlet caterpillar. The mountain ringlet is Britain's only alpine butterfly, a glacial relic, found locally in Scotland above 1500ft (457m). The adult insect is on the wing during July and August, flying close to the ground on sunny days.

In summer the red deer move to the high corries to escape the irritation of biting flies. The red deer is Britain's largest living wild land mammal. A full-grown Highland stag can weigh over 200lbs (91kg) and stand 4ft (1.2m) high at the shoulder. The stags shed their antlers at the end of winter. By late August their new antlers are complete and clean of velvet. September and October is the time of the rut, when the stags roar and wallow and round up their harems of hinds. Outside the rut, the females and immature males live in separate herds from the mature stags. The calves are born in May and June.

Among the crags and summits of the mountains the wild cat finds refuge from persecution, making its lair among the boulders and slopes of shattered rock. Record length for this fierce predator with the flat head and ringed bottle-brush tail is 3ft 9in (1.14m). Its prey includes the mountain hare, the only true mountain mammal in Britain. In winter its thick coat turns white except for the black tips of its ears.

Another mountain resident which turns white in winter is the ptarmigan, seen here in summer plumage. It lives in the harsh world of the high tops, where the snow lies among the rocks for maybe eight months or more. Yet even here, spring and summer bring a delicate beauty to the wet rock ledges. Moss campion and starry saxifrage are among the hardy wild flowers which evolution has shaped for survival in the climate of Britain's highest mountains.

10ft (3m) across. Immature eagles retain distinctive white patches on wings and tail until they are five years old. Sharing the eagle's domain but at the opposite end of the scale is the diminutive merlin, the smallest falcon in Britain, scarcely bigger than a blackbird, but a fast, dashing flier with a taste for meadow-pipits. Look for merlins perched on fence posts or telegraph poles along lonely moorland roads.

Where the peat becomes deeper and wetter, and along the upper limits of the heather moors, bilberry often becomes the dominant ground cover. From April to June its flowers provide nectar for the bilberry bumble-bee. The sweet, edible berries appear from July onwards. Another familiar sight on wet moorland is cotton-grass, its seed heads adorned with cotton wool tufts in May and June.

In the hollows and on the wettest hillsides the spongy ground is carpeted with blanket bog. Here a different range of plants grow, cushions of sphagnum moss in varying colours from green to red, the beautiful bog asphodel which blooms in August, and a living fly-trap, the round-leaved sundew. Sundews supplement the poor nutrient levels they receive from the blanket bog by catching insects with their sticky red leaves. When an insect becomes trapped, the leaf folds up and digests its prey.

Birds which feed in the soft peat of the blanket bog include the greenshank, a rare Highland wader, and the curlew, a more common wader with a gull-like flight and the most beautiful call of all moorland birds, as it cries its own name with a mournful, broken liquid whistle. The greenshank's long bill is slightly upturned; that of the curlew curves downwards; but both are adapted for probing in soft mud in search of worms, grubs and small snails.

Chapter Five
Working in the Countryside

The countryside is a place of work and country life is often hard and rigorous. Yet for many the satisfactions of working in it are deeply felt. Shepherding high above Loch Katrine in Scotland demands special qualities of man, dog and sheep. This shepherd's flock of Scottish Blackfaces is bred to survive the meagre grazing and heavy weather of the hills. Even so without his care and stamina, many would die. For such a man shepherding is a way of life rather than just a form of employment. The uncompromising economics of hill farming underline this. This chapter explores his world and that of other farms and farming, presents detailed and personal profiles of rural craftsmen, recalls the working countryside of yesterday and identifies what there is left of it still to see

It is easy to overlook the countryside as a gigantic food factory in which harsh practicalities take priority over pretty views. In the last 50 years farming in the British Isles has created its own 20th century Agricultural Revolution. This has transformed it into a highly efficient, highly mechanised science-based industry, worth over £7,000 million a year in receipts; an industry in which more and more crops and livestock are being produced with less land and labour. In the process it has altered the appearance of wide areas of the countryside as dramatically as did the great enclosure movements of earlier centuries.

A drive through the countryside in 1930 would have revealed a farming landscape hardly changed for a century. Heavy horses – Shires, Clydesdales, Suffolk Punches and Percherons – over a million of them, worked the land pulling only slightly modified versions of the implements invented by the farm improvers of the 18th and 19th centuries.

The few primitive tractors in use had made little impact and men still sweated behind horse and plough, breaking the earth in a patchwork of small, thick-hedged fields. Rattling horse-drawn harrows crumbled the soil into a tilth fit for seed; and drills, which seemed all spring, sprocket, cog and wheel, metered seed into the soil down vibrating coiled-spring tubes.

Farmworkers scythed the edges of the fields, cutting a swathe through the grass and corn to make access for the mowing machine and reaper. There was a lot of grass, permanent pasture for the cattle, and mostly it contained species of grasses which had altered little since the pastoral farming of early man.

Cereals were grown from tall-strawed strains which the farmer's grandfather had sown. At least harvesting them was easier than haymaking. The reaper-binder, which both cut the corn and tied the sheaves, was a miracle of the 1880s for which farmers still gave thanks, although plenty of manual effort was required to stand the sheaves into stooks to dry before being carted to the stackyard to await the thresher in the autumn.

Large as a country bus and hauled by a hissing traction engine, its arrival brought a temporary interruption to rural tranquillity. The laboured beating of its engine, the whirr of the driving belts, the tinny percussion of the grain sieves and the cries of the men made it a time of great animation and prodigious thirst.

Amidst clouds of chaff and smoke the grain was flailed from the wheat ears, cleaned, graded and bagged. A mound of chaff grew beneath the belly of the machine; pummelled straw was cast out behind to be re-stacked for use as animal bedding and feed.

This was a climax to a year in a system of farming which was largely self-sufficient. In 1930 farmers grew both crops and kept livestock. Wheat, potatoes and some of the pea crop were sold but most of the other produce was consumed on the farm. The horses ate much of the oats and hay. The remainder, and a lot of barley, was eaten by the cows, which, with beef cattle and sheep, fed on swedes, turnips and kale too. Barley straw, chopped fine, provided bulk in the cattle's diet; bedding too. Straw, when mixed with dung and trodden down,

Power and productivity on the farm

Horse and ploughman 1930

Output: horse and man could plough one acre (0.4 hectares) a day

Numbers: a 350 acre (142 hectares) mixed farm had six horses and four horsemen. Work on arable land kept them busy most of the year

Cost: £50 to £60 for a heavy working horse, £25 for a set of harness and from £9 to £12 for a plough

Ploughman: worked longer hours. Implements had to be man-handled at end of each furrow. After work horses had to be watered, groomed, fed and bedded down

Food: a daily diet of 16lbs of oats and 16lbs of hay (7.25kg) and 10lbs (4.5kg) of roots or greens

The farm: yesterday and today

This shows the changes on a 350 acre (142 hectares) mixed farm in the last 50 years. Yesterday's farm occupies the half of the illustration to the left, the modern farm the half to the right. The major alterations, discussed in more detail in the main text, are in the size of the fields, larger with fewer hedges; the crops in them, more pasture then, more ploughed land now plus new crops like maize; and in the machinery working them which has taken the place of horses and a greater number of men.

Haystacks have given way to silos, milk churns to mobile tankers, animals and poultry in the fields to animals and poultry indoors. The harvest scene has changed enormously and helicopters were hardly heard of – let alone used to spray potatoes with fungicides.

The farm used to employ four stockmen, four horsemen and a shepherd; today a family runs it with two workers. It then cost £1,000 to equip the farm with machinery, including the horses; at 1980 prices the machinery – tractors, combine, ploughs, harrows, rollers, mower, forage harvester, muck spreader and so on – would come to well over £80,000. To run the machinery the farm uses 6,000 gallons (27,274 litres) of diesel a year and just over 140 tons of fertiliser for the fields instead of 64 tons.

Some of the 1930 fields used to grow hay and oats to support the farm's working horses. Now they grow hay and barley to feed livestock for meat and milk production.

Today the farm's dairy herd consists of 80 Friesians yielding over 60,000 gallons (272,700 litres) of milk a year which have replaced yesterday's 20 lower yielding Dairy Shorthorns. The arable land produces 500 tons of crops against just over 80 tons 50 years ago. In 1930 good agricultural land cost £20 an acre. Today it averages over £1,300 an acre.

Tractor and driver 1980

Output: modern 90hp tractor and driver can plough an average of 25 acres a day, more if necessary

Numbers: on a 350 acre mixed farm one 90hp and two 65hp tractors. One driver

Cost: 65hp £8,000, 90hp £11,000, 180hp £26,000 and the newest 400hp tractor £40,000

Driver: a skilled mechanic whose tractor has air-conditioning, all-weather, tinted glass cab and radio-cassette player. After day's work he switches off ignition and goes home

Fuel: a 90hp tractor working with a 3-furrow plough uses 3 gallons (13.6 litres) of diesel per hour

provided the main enrichment for the land.

By-products of the farm dairy – skimmed milk, buttermilk, whey – went to the pigs together with waste from crops and kitchen. Chickens were fed on tail corn (grains too small to sell) and what they scratched from the farmyard.

There was a great variety of animals: more breeds of dairy cows, beef cattle, sheep and pigs than there were counties. Farms in the wetter southern and western counties, where grass grew best, tended to specialise in dairying and cattle raising with sheep on the hills.

Ploughing featured less and less the farther west one travelled. The 1930s were characterised by steadily decreasing acreages under the plough throughout the whole of the British Isles. The emphasis was on permanent grass and livestock.

Hill farmers in the mountain areas and the Pennine, Dartmoor, Exmoor, Antrim and Wicklow uplands were heavily dependent on sheep. Lambs and older ewes from Herdwick, Cheviot, Blackface and other mountain breeds were sold to farmers in the lowlands for fattening or breeding. This produced healthy cross bred lowland flocks with the vigour of mountain sheep and the meat and wool growing ability of lowland ones.

Similarly hill cattle, Welsh Blacks, Galloways and long-haired West Highland breeds, sometimes crossed with beef Shorthorns, provided store cattle to be sold to lowland farmers for fattening.

The pace and the power of the horse, and the endurance of human muscle, determined the progress of work in the fields. Wooden waggons with wheels

Traditional farmscape near Nymphsfield, in the Cotswolds. The old farmhouse and its out-buildings, made of the beautiful local Cotswold stone, blend perfectly with the surrounding fields

This livestock farming, requiring fewer men, aggravated the problems of rural unemployment and by 1930 the British Government was moving towards a programme of State aid for farmers. Throughout the Thirties it was expressed in the form of subsidies for wheat, barley and oats and meat. There were import quotas on foreign food and central marketing boards were established to control sales of milk, bacon, hops and potatoes at guaranteed prices.

Government policy even put new crops into the fields. Before World War One sugar had been entirely imported but by the early 1930s substantial subsidies encouraged farmers to go in for sugar beet. The new home industry soon supplied a quarter of the country's sugar needs.

All these measures gave agriculture a slight lift but even so the drift from the land continued, and 1930 was half-way point in a twenty-year inter-wars period which saw many thousands of labourers leaving the countryside. At the end of World War One there were one million farmers, their families and workers on the land in Great Britain. By the end of World War Two their numbers had shrunk to 889,000. Today there are just over 500,000.

The year 1930, then, was marked by much rural hardship and deprivation but save for macadamised roads, growing numbers of National Grid electricity pylons and the city-dwellers out for a drive in their square-backed saloon the rural landscape still retained much that had enchanted painters like Constable a hundred or so years earlier.

Today many features of that landscape have vanished. Milk churns no longer await collection by the roadside; instead milk is pumped direct from the cow, through filters, to a stainless steel holding tank where it is chilled and stored until the tanker lorry comes. Cottage-loaf haystacks, thatched to keep out the rain, have been replaced with great blocks of machine-handled bales protected by black polythene sheeting. Fields are larger, hedgerows fewer, so that huge costly machines can be easily and profitably used. The power of the tractor has increased, in cases up to 300hp, as the labour force on the land has fallen. A heavy horse and a man working a field is a rarity (see p 136) and great hedgeless tracts where there is not a cow to be seen are commonplace in the eastern half of the country.

But in other areas modernisation of

six ft (1.8m) in diameter lurched through the farm loaded with dung. Hay and wheat were hauled home on large, flat carts, sometimes elaborately decorated.

Most farm buildings were made of local materials used in characteristic regional styles. Only the curved and arched corrugated iron roofs of the big open sided Dutch barns struck a mass produced note.

Farms were smaller than today's: 63 acres (25.5 hectares) for the average sized holding then against an average of 120 acres (48.5 hectares) now. And 75% of the farmers in the United Kingdom were tenants in contrast to the 60% who now own their farms. In Ireland by this time thousands of tenant farmers had – with the active assistance of the State

through the Irish Land Commission disabused themselves of landlords and were establishing themselves as peasant proprietors, setting a pattern of small, dispersed but compact family farms which persists over much of the country today. Nearly 70% of all holdings are less than 50 acres (20 hectares).

The economic climate of 1930 had much to do with the look of the farming landscape. In World War One the Government encouraged the ploughing of grassland to grow more cereals and won the co-operation of farmers by giving them guaranteed prices. But after the war agriculture slumped, the price of wheat halved, farmers were no longer bolstered by government aid, so they returned the ploughed land to pasture.

farming has been at a slower pace. In Ireland many farmers still take their milk to the creameries in churns, and herds of cows being driven to the milking byres are a common sight on the roads.

The changes in farming have thrown up new silhouettes on the skyline. It is puzzling to know what Constable would have made of the silver, cylindrical, space-age silos which stand in the old stackyards; or the long factory-farm sheds with their rows of roof-top air vents; or the huge, slowly revolving, cantilevered spray-irrigation systems in the fields.

The animals, often unseen, have changed. So, too, have the crops (see pp 129–135) and the greater use of fertilisers, insecticides and herbicides and the application of new scientific discoveries in animal and plant genetics have transformed farming.

Detailed understanding of how hereditary characteristics are transmitted from parents to offspring, and the way in which these can be controlled and exploited, has led to the introduction of new, disease-resistant, high-yield varieties of crops and improved breeds of animals.

Artificial insemination, introduced in the 1940s, has enabled the advances in animal breeding to be widely adopted. It means one outstanding bull can father calves in cows anywhere, 600 a year instead of the 60 he used to serve naturally on a few score farms within reach. Nowadays 80% of all dairy cows are inseminated artificially.

A further development is ovum transplant. Eggs shed by a high performance cow during ovulation (most of which are normally wasted) can be collected, fertilised artificially and the resulting embryos stored in deep freeze until planted in the womb of a foster cow who bears the calf in the normal way. Thus quite ordinary cows are able to bear outstanding calves.

Dairy herds are now dominated by one breed, the tall, black-and-white British Friesian which has eclipsed other well known breeds (see p 132) because it is a high milk yielder and its male calves make good beef, even better when the cows are crossed with beef breeds such as the stocky brown, white-faced Hereford. In beef farming success depends on the daily rate at which cattle increase in weight in relation to the amount of food they consume. This is why high meat yielding foreign breeds and their crosses can now be seen in the fields (see p 132).

Harvest, ancient and modern. Above: Machine-handled bales await collection in the wide fields of East Anglia. Top: Barley stooked in the old manner on a Scottish croft

The only pigs seen outdoors are likely to be pregnant sows whose owners feel that added exercise makes them fitter for motherhood. Most breeding sows, like their fattening piglets, are kept indoors all their lives. They are very different animals to the pigs which snuffled and grubbed in the mud patches of the past (see p 135); modern hybrids which have little resemblance to their individual parents but are uniform in looks and performance and, in any given batch, are all ready for market at the same time.

Most poultry are also hybrids, producing a predictable number of eggs or weight of meat when automatically fed on a uniform diet in battery house or broiler shed.

Precision feeding of animals, the daily ration to give a predicted weight increase, is pointless if the performance of the animals is very variable. To avoid this breeders use computers to make thousands of calculations in a technique known as progeny testing. Before a bull's semen is used to artificially inseminate cows on a large scale, farmers will want to know that the calves will prosper uniformly. Computer analysis of statistics from accumulated experimental inseminations enables breeders to give this assurance.

On some advanced dairy farms cows wear plastic necklaces which house radio transponders. These emit radio signals with different frequencies for individual cows. The cow's identifying signal, linked to a computer, enables her output to be recorded while she is being milked. And, as she lowers her head to the feeding trough, the signals also tell the computer whether she is getting the right amount of food to support her output.

Scientific measurement in the cowshed also extends to piggeries. Electronic sensors measure the thickness of the lean and fat on the animal's back and the pig farmer is able to tell precisely whether it is ready for butcher or bacon factory.

The great expansion of the area devoted to cereal crops, especially wheat and barley (the latter is now the single most important crop grown) has been at the cost of ploughing several millions of acres of permanent grass since World War Two. Areas such as the Chalk downlands and parts of Exmoor have increasingly come under the plough. In recent years this huge new cereal acreage, much of it is in eastern England, has been associated with new, improved strains which are much more compact than they used to be: larger heads carrying more and bigger grains are borne on shorter, tougher stems which are better for supporting heavy crops without collapsing in bad weather.

Such cereals have been created in the laboratory by 'engineering' the genetic materials in the sex cells of the plants. The increased yields resulting from this are startling. In 1930 16cwt per acre (2008 kilos per hectare) was thought good for winter wheat. One of today's improved strains can yield up to 5 tons (5.08 tonnes) per acre on good land in a good season.

Genetic engineering of this sort has also led to leafier cabbages which store better, vastly improved potato crops and more productive grass. It has also brought new strains of crops which previously did not do well in the British Isles. Maize is an example (see p 129).

The need for the continuing application of fertilisers and pesticides throughout the growing season has made its own impact on the fields. Rows are left unsown at specified intervals so that tractors can get through easily and apply nutrients and pesticides with greater precision. The tractor-wide stripes across the fields are called 'tramlines'.

Hills farms have been the least obviously touched by the farming revolution. This is not surprising since the flavour of the past is always more persistent where it is hardest to make the profits to finance change. Both the terrain and the nature of the farming make it difficult to use machines to replace men. But better longer-lasting sheep dips have helped the shepherd keep his flock free from parasites and some hill farms have managed to finance buildings in which sheep can shelter a few weeks before lambing which greatly reduces losses. And the occasional patch of emerald green on the hillside signifies at least one farmer who has found money to drain, lime and re-seed his pasture.

At first sight dairy and cattle farms have changed little; fields are still small for easy control of grazing, walls and hedges still provide shelter in bad weather, and their main crop is still grass. The grass may look the same as it did in the 1930s, but it isn't. The old grass sward had a dozen or more of grasses and other plants in it. The new pastures which have been sown have no more than four – and they are much more productive.

There is rye-grass which begins to grow earlier in the year, takes longer to reach the less digestible flowering stage and yields more hay or silage per acre. The clovers in the new mixtures are as pretty as the wild ones of old but are more robust and erect, with bigger leaves like solar panels trapping more of the sunlight.

Haymaking is wholly mechanised. Instead of being carted loose the hay is compressed by machine into bound bales, rectangular blocks of 30 to 40lbs (13.6 to 18kg) in weight. The large rolls seen in the fields – they weigh more than half-a-ton (508kg) – are mostly straw bales. Grass for silage is mown and left for several hours to wilt. Then it is gathered by a forage harvester, a spectacular machine which chops it into tiny pieces and blows it in a plume into an accompanying trailer.

The chopping helps it lose even more moisture and pack tightly into the silo. Tight packing excludes air and allows the right type of bacteria to develop. These produce the acid conditions which suspend further activity and preserve the grass green until required as winter feed. Grass has its highest food value when young so it is cut for silage several times a season. This gives more, higher quality fodder than if cropped for hay.

Some farmers believe that allowing animals to trample grass they are grazing is wasteful. So they keep them in covered yards using a mower and forage harvester to cut and carry the fresh grass to them daily. This is known as 'zero-grazing'.

Tractor mounted scrapers, lifting buckets and mechanical muck-spreaders make returning the dung to the fields much less of a burden than when it was horse-and-carted. Some yards have perforated floors through which the dung is trodden into a channel below. This is wide enough to allow the passage of a tractor-mounted scraper.

Liquid dung, or slurry, may be pumped into large storage lagoons where it is allowed to drain free of most of its surplus water so it can be spread as a solid. Sometimes it is pumped to the fields and spread, under pressure, as a coarse spray.

So the hand-forking of dung, a simple but back-breaking job, is another chore which has disappeared from the country scene. Some, no doubt, regret this and all the other changes on the farm. But those who work the farm may well feel that the new landscapes are better, less demanding than the old.

Yet, however the farming landscape looks and whatever the changes, the job of the farmer remains *fundamentally* the same. Soil is prepared; crops sown, harvested and sold; or fed to animals to be converted into meat, wool, hides, eggs and dairy produce. The farmer captures the sun's energy and uses it together with gasses in the atmosphere, minerals in the soil and moisture in the air to produce food.

Science and technology take him only so far. His success or failure is still very much determined by the weather and that indefinable quality, an amalgam of wisdom, wile and expertise, which marks the good farmer from the bad.

Hill farms. Their mainstay are sheep, supported by cattle. Land use varies with altitude and time of the year. The unfenced, open high country may be grazed with other farmers, each having a quota of grazing animals. Better pasture on the lower slopes may be walled or fenced off. This is privately owned and was originally reclaimed from rough pasture and improved. The best land is on the valley floor. This is the 'inland' or 'inby' where grass is rotated with roots and other crops to provide winter feed. Spring lambs born here are moved up the hill in late spring after they have been earmarked and the male lambs castrated. Later the flock is brought down to be sheared, then returned to the hills until late autumn. It is then brought pro-

Right: Pennine hill farm. The best land lies nearest the farm on the valley floor. The open moors above are fit only for rough grazing and may be covered in snow for much of the winter

Making 'hay' the modern way. Forage harvester gathering grass for silage in rural Warwickshire

gressively down the hillside to winter in the lower fields. Lambs and old ewes are sold in late summer to lowland farmers for fattening and breeding. Most hill cattle are cross-bred. Calves stay with their mothers on the hills for the summer and are sold to fatteners in the autumn.

Dairy farms. Modern dairy farms are sophisticated, highly mechanised factories for converting grass into milk. The average yield for a cow is 1000 gallons (4545 litres) a year. In summer the cow giving three gallons (13.6 litres) a day gets her daily food requirements by eating 167lbs (75 kilos) of fresh grass. On this she gives nearly 4% butter-fat milk and will be gaining weight. The lactation period, the time she gives milk after calving, is about 300 days. She produces a calf a year for five or six years. Most farmers have their cows calving in the autumn to take advantage of higher winter milk prices. In summer the cows are kept out in the fields; in winter they stay in a large covered shed where they can move freely. But each cow has a cubicle of its own where it can lie and chew the cud. Machine milking, twice a day, is a slick mechanical operation. Up to 20 or more cows can be milked simultaneously in a herring-bone milking parlour. This takes eight to 10 minutes.

Arable farms. The big specialist arable farms of eastern England which tend to specialise in barley, wheat, potatoes and sugar beet range in size from 400 to 1000 acres (162 to 405 hectares). They contrast sharply with the smaller farms of 50 years ago which produced comparatively small amounts of a wide variety of crops. Factors which favour large scale arable farming in the east are drier conditions which enables grain to ripen more easily, soils heavy enough to give cereals a good root base and light enough to allow reasonable drainage, and level land which facilitates minimum use of labour and maximum use of machines: up to 50 tractors and half-a-dozen combines on some farms. Some are operated with virtually no labour, all the work being put out to specialist contractors. Barley is the biggest single crop grown for animal feed and the higher quality varieties for malting. Crop rotation is less important now because pesticides and herbicides are efficient at cleaning the land and synthetic fertilisers boost the soil without having to rest it.

Fruit farms. Apples, pears and plums are the main orchard fruits grown. The character of the orchard, however, has changed. The tall trees of the past have been replaced with small, compact bushy trees which are easy to prune, spray and pick. Good orchard land is expensive, five times as much as arable land, so it must be intensively cultivated to get maximum yields of high quality fruit. Trees are planted close together in rows and the alleys between them are just wide enough for a tractor. Special narrow-width tractors have been designed so that even less land is taken up by the alleys. This type of orchard should produce six tons of apples an acre compared with three to four tons for orchards with larger, wider spaced trees. Pruning takes place from November to February. Spraying to control grass, weeds and pests and to apply foliar feeds and hormones to regulate fruit set and growth takes place up to a dozen times a season. Some picking takes place from tractor-drawn platforms instead of ladders. Early Worcesters and late picked Cox are still favourites. Newer varieties like Crispin and Spartan store well. In soft fruits the emphasis is on strawberries, raspberries and black and red currants. Many of these farms have gone over to Pick-Your-Own. This cuts out costly labour.

Market gardening. The deep-freeze has had a marked influence on the character of this. The traditional smallholding of a few acres has not the output to keep the freezer plants and canneries busy, so in areas like Norfolk and the Fens there has been a significant increase

Frostproof farming in Kent. Cloches protect the market gardener's tender young crops

Colourful crop of oilseed rape. Its oil goes into margarine and other uses in the food industry

in the growing of peas, beans and sprouts on a field scale. This requires investment in expensive machinery like pea-viners. But in traditional smallholding areas like the Vale of Evesham the produce is grown for direct supply to the big urban markets of the Midlands. Much is sold direct to motorists from roadside stalls. Here holdings vary from a few acres up to 50 (20 hectares). Many are fragmented and scattered, creating practical difficulties which do not arise on the Fenland farms. Growing lettuces, broccoli, cauliflowers and, under glass, tomatoes and cucumbers requires very intensive farming with a high investment in glasshouses, irrigation systems and fertilisers. The market gardener's most important asset is the soil itself which has to be kept in good heart. Over years of intensive working a market gardener sometimes virtually creates a new, improved soil. But in the early days 'gardens' tended to be located on light, easy to work soils which warmed up early. Nearness to large cities was also important but with rapid transport this is less so now. As with soft fruit, Pick-Your-Own is a developing trend.

Crofting and cottage farming. These are forms of subsistence farming found in the Highlands and Islands of Scotland and on the Atlantic coast of Ireland from west Cork northwards to Donegal. Scotland has seven designated crofting counties – Argyll, Inverness, Ross and Cromarty, Sutherland, Caithness, Orkney Islands and Shetland Islands. The living from this type of farming is meagre. Landholdings are small, often fragmented with some rough grazing held in

common. Crops are mainly confined to oats and potatoes for use on the farm. Sheep are the important livestock of the croft; cattle stand above sheep on the Irish cottage farm. Both are usually supplemented by other activities: fishing, tourism, home spinning and weaving. They are characterised by little capital, little machinery, rugged environment, windy and wet climate and the remoteness and isolation which make traditional farming methods extremely difficult to maintain. Various forms of Government aid – grants, loans etc – have been forthcoming both in Scotland and Ireland for this type of farming.

New crops in the fields

New and unfamiliar crops have been appearing in farm fields in recent years.

This is because plant breeders have been able to produce versions of crops like maize suited to British conditions and climate. Thousands of acres of this 'green giant' are grown annually, especially in the south. Mostly it is used for animal fodder; all the plant including the cob.

Fields of flaring yellow oilseed rape are becoming a much more obvious feature. This is grown to provide vegetable oil for the food industry. Much of it goes to the making of margarine.

In areas like Norfolk fields are being cropped with Chinese cabbage to meet a growing demand for a leaf vegetable which is dual purpose, eaten as salad or cooked as a green.

The next generation of new field crops are already on their way: lupins for high protein animal feed and enriching the soil; sunflowers for animal feed and oil; and Navy beans for the baked bean food canners who have had to rely until now on the United States for the crop.

The arrival of new, tall grass forage crops could have a dramatic impact on the farming landscape. One of these grasses is a cross between sorghum and Sudan grass and has been specially bred to give high yields of animal feed in the climatic conditions of southern Britain. The grass can grow to 7ft (2m) although ideally cattle would graze it when it was 3ft 6in to 5ft (1m to 1.5m) high. Its other advantages are that it yields in late summer when other grasses are at their weakest and after its first few weeks it is a very rapidly growing crop. The breeders who produced it believe it unlikely that any other summer forage crop currently grown in Britain can equal it for yield.

Subsistence farming. Cottage farmstead in the limestone landscape of the Burren, Co Clare

Anatomy of the barn

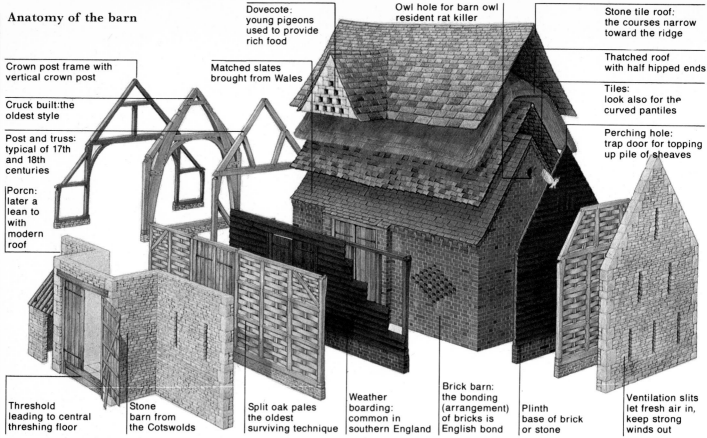

Dovecote: young pigeons used to provide rich food

Owl hole for barn owl resident rat killer

Stone tile roof: the courses narrow toward the ridge

Crown post frame with vertical crown post

Cruck built: the oldest style

Matched slates brought from Wales

Thatched roof with half hipped ends

Post and truss: typical of 17th and 18th centuries

Tiles: look also for the curved pantiles

Porch: later a lean to with modern roof

Perching hole: trap door for topping up pile of sheaves

Threshold leading to central threshing floor

Stone barn from the Cotswolds

Split oak pales the oldest surviving technique

Weather boarding: common in southern England

Brick barn: the bonding (arrangement) of bricks is English bond

Plinth base of brick or stone

Ventilation slits let fresh air in, keep strong winds out

The barn, as old and historic as the farmhouse itself, is a casualty of modern farming methods with no real function left for it. Some fine barns are literally falling to pieces because they are too costly to restore and it is cheaper to replace them with a modern building. Yet old barns reveal much about the working countryside of yesterday.

A barn is not a cowshed, a stable, a carthouse, a hayhouse, a granary or another of the innumerable buildings seen on farms. A barn is a barn, a special building, built in a certain way for a certain use.

The word 'barn' itself comes from Old English for barley store. Barley was the favourite grain of the Saxons, and probably they had barns, although the first written record of a barn is from some years after the Norman Conquest.

In those early centuries, farming was growing grain and grazing cattle. The building for grain became the barn; the cattle quarters became the yard, and together with the living hut, they set the style of the farmstead of today.

Barns were work places, not just store huts. The corn was cut by hand, bound into sheaves which were propped up to dry in the sun. They were then taken into the barn to be piled deep on one side of it. The central space of the barn, stretching between the facing pairs of doorways, was the threshing floor. Threshing was a winter job; the summer-cut sheaves were pulled on to the threshing floor and beaten with flails. The spent straw was then piled into the other side of the barn, for the cattle. The chaff was winnowed from the grain with the help of the breeze whistling through the wide central doorways. And the grain was usually stored in 'cornholes' next to the straw before being taken to the granary.

Barns remained essentially simple in plan for centuries, utility buildings, built of utility materials and from what was cheapest or closest to hand. Skills, or the lack of them, and local custom were handed down without question. The result was that the style of barns varied from parish to parish.

The illustration shows just a handful of types. The cruck style of construction is probably the oldest; today, examples are still found and they are commonest in the West and North. The crucks took the weight of the roof directly. But big trees were needed if the barn was to be of any size. The frame construction overcame this problem to some extent. The gaps between the timbers were traditionally filled with split oak pales, or weatherboards could be tacked up. Occasionally the wall was infilled with brick or stone.

Some of the ancient features which have been copied into more recent building are intriguing. Many stone barns have a pattern of ventilation slits on the end walls, allowing air to reach the stored straw and grain. But often these 'loopholes' are the same as the arrow slits of castles, wider inside than out. The design aerodynamically allows fresh air to seep through the slit while blocking sharp gusts of wind. Another advantage is that more light enters the barn.

By the beginning of the 19th century the threshing machine was replacing the old-fashioned flails. The first threshers were wooden contraptions powered by a horse walking round in a circle. Some northern areas have round sheds (called gin gangs) built alongside the barn, for the plodding horse.

At first, the steam engines were stationary, maybe thumping away on the floor of the barn. But later they became giant monsters, like road rollers, taking power out to the fields. The corn was threshed in the open, and the barn lost its use as a work place, becoming a storage place only. It meant the end of building new barns to old patterns. It also meant the beginning of the decline of existing barns. Large roofs were expensive to maintain, and British farming was in the doldrums – the result of imports of cheap foreign corn. Many barns were converted into cowsheds and other uses.

Unexpectedly, the farmyard barn was given a new lease of life this century. The new combine harvesters thresh the corn in the fields but bring the grain back wet. It had to be dried and the old, underused barn was an obvious place in which to put the grain drier.

Above: Farm cathedral. A fine example of a long tithe barn's timbered interior at Frindsbury, Kent. Below: Built to last. A well-preserved tithe barn with a magnificent tiled roof at Lenham, Kent. The tithes, a tenth of the farm produce of a parish given to support the clergy, were stored in such barns

Strangers on the pastures

A quiet revolution is taking place on the cattle pastures of the British Isles. In an effort to bring lean meat to beef production – and in the process improved profits for the farmer – unfamiliar breeds of cattle from the Continent, such as the Charolais from Burgundy and the Simmental from Switzerland, are being introduced.

As a result British herds are having the biggest injection of foreign blood in their history. This is why the appearance of beef cattle in the fields is very different to what it used to be.

Thus the traditional Sunday joint of beef is coming to owe more and more to these 'exotics', which is what farmers call the European breeds, than to native beef breeds alone.

Critics of the latter argue that while hardy and capable of thriving on poor pastures provided under extensive ranching systems abroad, they were not converting grass into meat at home as well as the 'exotics'. This was because home breeders, with an eye on the export market and the show ring, were producing animals which were too small and grew too slowly to make beef profitable.

Argentina, for example, was the biggest export market for Herefords, and her cattle raisers became the target for British breeders who knew the Argentinians favoured a smaller, more compact strain of Hereford than the animal which grazed the Herefordshire pastures at the turn of the century.

But the smaller animals and their crossbred calves matured earlier and at lower weights than their forebears. Attempts to feed them to greater weights led to accumulations of fat which butchers could not sell to housewives. The Hereford cows, or female crosses, produced less milk than their ancestors and since the mothers were less provident the calves' diet had to be supplemented with expensive concentrate feeds.

It was to overcome these defects that the first Charolais bulls were imported in 1961. The first results were dramatic: their crosses with Friesian cows grew faster than Hereford-Friesian crosses, were more efficient at converting food and the carcases had much less fat.

It takes a long time to judge whether the results will be sustained. Charolais and Simmental bulls now provide over 20% of all artificial inseminations in Britain but Hereford bulls are still the leaders at over 60%.

The success of the Charolais has prompted the introduction of other breeds. The Limousin, bred for survival in the hills of France's Massif Central, produces good lean beef from rough grazing. The Blonde d'Aquitaine capable of enormous growth, four lbs (1.8 kilos) or more a day, and the Maine Anjou, also capable of putting more size and a faster rate of growth into British crossbred beef, are both from France.

The robust Simmentals are natives of the Simme Valley in Switzerland's Bernese Oberland and quickly produce quantities of quality meat from grass and straw. The Chiananas are the largest and fastest growing cattle in Europe, frequently measuring up to 6ft 6in (2m) at the shoulder. They come from Italy.

The crosses resulting from putting these animals to British breeds clearly benefit from the characteristics fostered by Continental breeders in their animals. For instance, cattle there have long been used as draught animals for ploughing. When the farmer feeds his oxen he wants the food converted into lean muscle not layers of fat. For draught work he also wants large animals with massive loins and hindquarters – and these are the areas where the best cuts of meat are.

Continental breeds also tend to be dual purpose providing both milk and meat and this means they are good mothers with plenty of milk for their calves.

A characteristic of British beef production is that the bulk of it comes from the dairy herds: about 60% from calves born to dairy cows – and 80% of these cows are British Friesians. The calves are either pure Friesian or result from the cows being crossed with pure beef breeds.

In the dairy herds the pre-eminence of the Friesian is unchallengeable. For years the old favourite, the Dairy Shorthorn, has been losing popularity to the Friesian because its milk supply is lower, its calves are slower growing and its produces carcases which are over-fat.

By 1955 the Friesian accounted for just over 30% of the United Kingdom dairy herd. Now it stands at over 80%. In the Republic of Ireland the breed accounts for 68% of all dairy cows.

Beef cattle

Sussex. Has a reputation for thriving on poor pasture. Now a rare sight

South Devon. The largest British breed with bulls reaching 1 to 1.5 tons

Lincoln Red. Lincolnshire version of the Shorthorn. Numbers have dwindled

Galloway. These animals are tough enough to winter on the Galloway coast

Hereford. The most popular British beef breed, now spread all over the world

West Highland. A tough picturesque descendant of the original wild Scottish cattle

Beef Shorthorn. In the 1930s the commonest breed in Britain

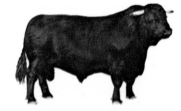

Welsh Black. Thrives in conditions many other breeds would find intolerable

Blonde d'Aquitaine. This heavyweight aristocrat from across the Channel is the most scientifically selected of all French breeds

Dairy cattle

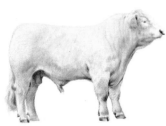   

Charolais. A native of the Charolais region of Burgundy. Introduced to Britain in 1961

Kerry. A small black breed indigenous to southern and western Ireland

British Friesian. Predominant breed in British Isles. First introduced from Holland

Jersey. Smallest and perhaps prettiest of the dairy breeds. It produces very rich milk

Aberdeen Angus. No other breed has its capacity to provide highest quality beef

Dairy Shorthorn. In Ireland still the most popular breed after the Friesian

Ayrshire. The only mainland native breed of pure dairy cattle to originate in the UK

Guernsey. A small animal, although slightly larger than the Jersey

133

Best of British sheep

The British Isles are the most important sheep farming area in Western Europe. This position is rooted in a long tradition of sheep raising which goes back to the Middle Ages. Then the emphasis was on wool which was exported to the Continent and made up into cloth. Later with the growing urban population of the Industrial Revolution the emphasis was switched to sheep for meat.

Today wool is still a major source of income for many farmers but the production of fat lambs for the table is increasingly important. Selective breeding and improved feeding now produce sheep which are larger and carry more meat than the animals of 200 years ago.

The main breeds are shown here, although there are many others which are often confined to a particular locality. The mountain breeds which are hardy, produce good mutton and wool are the most numerous, especially in those areas where sheep dominate the farming scene: the highlands and moorlands of Scotland, Wales, Ireland, the Pennines and the Lake District. Lowland areas such as Romney Marsh and the Downs are celebrated for their sheep. So are the lowland areas west of the Shannon where farmers combine sheep with cattle rearing. But the general trend has been for sheep to give way to the plough and more profitable types of lowland farming.

Lowland sheep

South Down. Smaller than many lowland sheep but produces the best carcase quality of any breed. It also produces high quality wool. Used in crossing with other breeds to improve their meat production

Border Leicester. The rams of this breed are much used to cross with Cheviot or Black Face mountain ewes to produce the ubiquitous Half-Bred and Mule (or Greyface) ewes. These are crossed with other lowland breed rams to provide lamb and wool

Dorset Horn. Unlike other British sheep this has flesh coloured lips. Its wool is fine and very white. Both sexes carry prominent, highly curled horns. It will breed earlier than other breeds sometimes

producing lambs in October. This makes it valuable in cross breeding for fat lambs for the early market

Hampshire Down. This developed as the ideal breed for grazing the chalk downlands of southern England. It tolerates being confined to arable field feeding areas. Its crossbred lambs grow well and put on meat quickly

Suffolk. Originated in East Anglia but is now seen in many other areas of the British Isles. It is also much used in cross breeding for meat production. It is prolific and popular

Romney Marsh. This is a heavy animal which produces high quality wool. It is the dominant breed in the densely sheep-stocked area of Kent, the name of which it bears

Hill sheep

Clun Forest. A hardy, thrifty breed used on mixed farms for consuming crops on arable land in winter. Both sexes are hornless. Common in the Midlands and Southern England

Kerry Hill. Originally from Kerry Hill, Montgomeryshire, this is a large breed popular in the Welsh borders. Its white face is broken by black markings on the muzzle. Neither sex has horns

Mountain sheep

Welsh Mountain. Small with a characteristic narrow shouldered, long necked appearance. The rams have strong horns; ewes are hornless. Kept for meat

Scottish Blackface. Small, shaggy with both ewes and

rams carrying small horns. Thrives well on high heather moors of Scotland and north of England. But now widespread, being reared mainly for meat

Cheviot. Strongest mountain rival of the Blackface. Hornless in both sexes. Tends to do best on coarse grass rather than heather. Has spread to Wales and even Exmoor. A good lamb producer

Herdwick. Predominant breed in the Lake District. It has the coarse, shaggy fleece of the Blackface but some of the rams are hornless. Lambs' face colour is black, later turning grey and white in old age. Kept for wool

Swaledale. Slightly larger than the Blackface but carries less wool at its fore end. It has a dark grey face with a mealy coloured nose. Hill farmers sell its lambs for lowland fattening

Pigs with a purpose

The changing face – and form – of the British pig is one of the least evident aspects of a changing countryside. Fifty years ago the leading breeds of pigs (illustrated here) could all be seen in the fields. Now pigs are rarely found out of doors. Instead they spend most of their lives in clinical (compared to the old farmyard sty) factory pig units.

The danger of rearing livestock intensively is fast-spreading disease. So build- ings are made from modern, easy to disinfect materials – plastic and weather- proofed compressed board on pre- stressed concrete or steel frames. Since infant mortality is one of the main scourges of the pig farmer some breeding stock are surgically removed from the mother's womb prior to birth and kept under hygienic conditions all their lives.

Some of the breeds which were once so popular occupy a much less important place in the pig herds now. Moreover they are losing their individual breed identity. Yet more pigs are being raised than ever. The United Kingdom herd has nearly trebled to 6.5 million since 1930. The Irish herd has remained much as it was at just over one million.

Today's most popular pig is a hybrid with all the good points of other breeds bred into him (see illustration). The Large White and Landrace have been dominant in these breeding pro- grammes.

Large White. High reputation as a producer of quality bacon. Boars have been used in cross breeding pro- grammes throughout the world

Landrace. Introduced from Scandinavia in 1949. Celebrated for the length of its back, providing a longer, leaner carcase for bacon production, and large litters

Welsh. Hardy pig which is excellent for grazing outdoors. Also a good bacon pig much used in breeding programmes

British Saddleback. Takes its name from the prominent white 'saddle' across its black back. Another good grazer. Renowned for its mothering qualities

Breeds better. Produces larger, stronger, faster growing litters

Good mother. Docile and easily managed

High quality meat. Little superfluous fat

Strong body ensuring longer life and lots of litters

Free from most endemic pig diseases

Efficient converter

The Super-pig. In recent years breeders have been attempting to combine the best qualities of all the formerly common breeds. Already 50% of the pig herd consists of these modern hybrids and the drive for a superior pig, aided by computer controlled breeding programmes, continues. All hybrids show what is known as 'hybrid vigour', an explosion of energy and performance capability which is released when pure strains of animal, or plant, are closely inbred for a number of generations – and are then crossed with other similarly inbred strains, A good example of the modern factory- produced pig is the Cotswold Hybrid which has Large White, Landrace, Welsh and British Saddleback in it.

Middle White. Smaller than the Large White. Too fat for bacon but widely used for crossing to produce good pork

Berkshire. One of the first to be improved by scientific breeding in the 19th century. It was raised for its high quality pork but is now rare

Large Black. One of the oldest breeds, favoured in the South West and East Anglia. Often used in crosses with Large White for bacon production

Rural craftsmen: Blacksmith

There is always admiration for those who create with their hands and a set of tools which seem as old as time. Yet few of us have other than the most perfunctory notion of the tried and tested expertise which is the skilled countryman's inheritance. Rural crafts and skills have always been part of the enduring continuum of country life but unhappily some are now long past their heyday. Others show surprising signs of life.

There are a few old time blacksmiths left, but not many. Mostly their forges are cold and silent. Twice a week, maybe, they coax a little life into the embers. Smokeless stuff fuels their fire these days, and it is mild steel they heat in it, for they can't get iron any more.

Only occasionally does a diehard farmer turn up with a broken plough or harrow; or a trawler skipper need a bit of new tackle; or a coal merchant want a new floor-plate for the cab of his lorry. Few of the jobs fall readily into the old workaday mould. Decorative stuff is now his mainstay.

By 'decorative' the true smith does not mean the lacy, light-weight wrought-iron gates of suburban gardens with their shallow scrolls and fishtails. These are cheap frills and look it: thin strips of metal 'cold-forged' (ie bent) to shape and spot-welded together. They have felt only the blacksmith's scorn, never the blush of his fire.

To see what a pair of proper, craftsman-forged gates looks like, take a trip to the municipal cemetery. Or Royal palace. Or the Falls Church National Memorial Park in Virginia. Its five pairs of particularly imposing gates all came from small blacksmith's shops in Devon.

One of these same five Devon smithies – it has been in business in Dartmouth since early in the 19th century – has also turned out railing scrolls and finials for London's Natural History Museum, and repaired cannon for the Tower of London, which is a far cry from the days when the local gas board regularly employed them as surgeons to fractured street lamps.

Door-knockers, fire-baskets and a whiff of nostalgia are, you might suppose, all that remains of the old days. Wrong,

Above: Old-fashioned horse-power on the farm. Right: Blacksmith in the heat of his forge

for three generations of the same family, the youngest aged but 11, are still rippling their biceps over the self-same forge.

Great-grandfather, the firm's founder who stares down yellowly from his dessicated photograph on the office wall, would recognise the pride in a job done permanently, and the gentle precision with which big men apply their enormous strength to tasks of small detail. An exquisite music stand, suffering no loss of strength or vitality through the delicacy of its design, permits a quiet satisfaction in its creator, but nothing more. They like to innovate and invent, and give their imaginations a bit of an airing. But so did great-grandfather. What kind of craftsman would he have been if he didn't?

A blacksmith does not so much mend things as recreate them. A broken bell-clapper from a church tower, demanding great particularity in weight, length and strength, is welded in the fire until only the brightness of the metal betrays the

repair. You would search for ever to find the weak spot: there isn't one. In another corner, a weather-vane is shaping up for a local bank; and next to it, a horse-head paper-knife for official presentation to a visiting dignitary at an agricultural show. From a gate-hinge to a gazebo: if you want it in metal, the blacksmith will make it. Plain or ornamental; everlasting or simply strong. But whatever it is, there is no way you will outlast it. Smithing is not like other trades, where a good job ensures a good customer. Here a job well done is a job never seen again.

Except, of course, in the matter of farriery. A good shoeing smith can not do much to prolong the life of a horse-shoe, though he can do a great deal to prolong the useful life of the horse. He is the archetypal rural craftsman, clothed in shiny hide apron, with rivulets of sweat carving pearly channels across his smoke-blackened skin. A bit of a character who might hobble and throw a kicking gypsy pony and shoe it upside down.

Give or take a bit of tail, there are 247 bones in a horse. Thirty-six of these are in the lower legs and depend for their trouble-free service on the skill of the farrier. The nine bones of each lower leg are powered, hinged and held together by a mass of tendons, ligaments, muscles and blood vessels, culminating in the horny outgrowth of the hoof itself. Simple it is not, and it can be cast into lame and limping disorder by any small disparity in a shoe. Nature can and does permit itself the luxury of a minor discrepancy here and there. Not so the smith. Not only must he avoid inexactitudes of his own; he must also compensate for nature's.

Few pairs of hooves are the same; yet the horse's comfort depends upon his heels riding at a uniform height and on each foot being level all round. It is a balance which can be achieved only by carefully cleaning and trimming each hoof, and by bespoke shoeing. Each shoe begins as a straight bar, gripped in the pincers and brought to white heat in the fire. The hammering at the anvil may look frantic, but it is merely rapid – and necessarily so. Mild steel cools quickly. The blows seem wild and impossibly massive for an operation which depends for its success on meticulous accuracy. But there is culture in the brawn. The farrier will check and recheck the fit, heat and reheat the shoe, until it is as personal as a fingerprint. It will roughly fit a great many horses; precisely fit only this one.

The final test, after the shoe has been burnt on with its alarming (to visitors) billows of sour acrid smoke, is the nailing, during which the unskilled operator (there are a few) has his greatest opportunity to cripple the horse. And himself, for that matter. Few animals are docile enough to suffer a puncture of living tissue without dealing out a retributive kick or two.

There is no telling where you might encounter a shoeing forge these days. On the M5 perhaps, or in a city high street. Most modern farriers have unshackled themselves from their Vulcan's caves and switched to portable, gas-fired forges mounted in the backs of Land Rovers or light vans. No shiny hide apron; no smoke-blackened skin; no drama. The horse stays where it is and the smith comes, like a hired servant, to the door.

The gamekeeper's year

A man in a green tweed hat is wading through a turbulent sea of maize. Wind whips the leaf-tips into brisk little ripples, and there is a forceful undercurrent – a gathering wash of sound that swells uphill, ahead of the man. And then the first wave breaks cover. The pheasants have been driven along the ground as far as their nervous dispositions will withstand. As they emerge from the maize they are confronted on the skyline by a rank of men and boys with flags. Up they go, standing on their tails with their bellies to the breeze, then wheeling away to ride the wind home. Straight over the man in the green tweed hat; straight across the line of guns.

For the guests with their fingers on the triggers, the day's sport is served on a plate. The birds come fast and hard, scrambling higher and higher into the sky as the danger declares itself. Tested to the limits, men and their gun-barrels grow hot with the effort.

For the head gamekeeper, the man in the green tweed hat, it is a confrontation that has taken a year's work to contrive. Nothing has been left to chance.

The gamekeeper is an expert at bending nature to his purpose. He does not want tame birds: there is no sporting challenge in a turkey shoot. But he does want wild ones whose instincts he can harness and whose behaviour he can predict. To such an end, there is no easy means.

First, the land must be right. Game birds need cover, to breed and to roost. Woods are handy – particularly if they are in the middle of the estate. On the boundary they are a mixed blessing: too many birds are liable to emerge on the wrong side. If there is not enough cover within the estate, then the gamekeeper must provide more. An island of kale, forlorn in an ocean of cereal fields, is a good indicator of a keeper at work. The kale provides both shelter and food for the birds, and its position will have been carefully plotted. The keeper's aim is to produce a good sporting flight, and his calculations will have been mapped out on paper, taking account of contours, existing boundaries and prevailing wind. He will have tried to *think* like a pheasant. How far would he run when flushed out? Where would he take to the air? In which direction would he turn in flight? If he is right, and his theory works in practice, then the cover becomes permanent. He will plant a thicket of bushy shrubs – lonicera, for instance – often with an adjacent 'garden' of kale or maize.

So here is another clue for the observer. Any patch of apparently uncleared scrub in the middle of well-kept farmland usually means game cover.

The keeper's year begins as soon as the last cartridge has been expended at season's end. He traps the surviving hen birds in coops (not all of them: just as many as he needs to produce eggs for next season), hobbles their wings with leather brails and releases them into laying pens. This is his investment for the future, and he treats it appropriately. Lavish feeds of wheat give way to a controlled diet of breeder's pellets and grit at around the beginning of March, and laying begins in early April. It is a period of anxiety, ceaseless hard work and unyielding routine. Four times a day until late June he goes to the pens and lifts off the glossy, grey-green eggs – up to 15 per bird. The eggs are bathed in a harmless disinfectant and placed in an incubator room at 60°F (16°C). Every day they must be turned to ensure that there is no settlement in the yolks.

At the same time each week – say 8am on Friday – the week's entire collection is moved into an incubator cabinet where it will be kept at a steady 100°F (38°C). After precisely three weeks, at the same time on Friday morning, the eggs are moved to a hatcher – still at the same temperature – within which the young birds will emerge after another three or four days. For three or four days more, the poults will gather strength in a warm room; then they will be carried to heated brooders in the wood, where they will slowly be introduced to the idea of freedom. Gradually they are released into larger and larger enclosures until, after six weeks, they are ready to move into a release pen.

Throughout the year – not only in the breeding season – a bloody battle wages. A pheasant's egg is a popular delicacy among nature's scavenging classes, and chicks and mature birds are ready meat for a whole catalogue of predators. Most persistent egg-stealer is the stoat. Whenever one of these razor-toothed bandits is seen, the gamekeeper must be resolved to kill.

A single stoat, loose in a laying pen, will clean up every egg it can find, and will keep on coming back for more. The risk simply cannot be taken. Next time the stoat passes, he will find a neat avenue of upright sticks leading into a fresh dry tunnel with a comfortable earth-strewn floor. The tunnel is a six-inch(15cm) drainpipe. Concealed in the earth is a humane trap from whose jaws, once triggered, there is no escape. Here perish not only stoats but the occasional weasel and a multitude of rats.

One invader the gamekeeper cannot skin – though he might like to – is the poacher. Game-stealing these days is carried out on almost an industrial scale, with commercial vehicles driving long distances to pick up loads worth hundreds of pounds on the London market. There are a number of simple electronic aids which can help a gamekeeper police his wood; but the main weapon in his armoury is still the same – vigilance. He is never off duty; seldom takes time off to visit a pub. It does not do, he says, for people to know where he is.

His dedication is total. His pheasants and his partridges – particularly his partridges, which are under great pressure from intensive farming techniques – are his treasure. He knows they will be shot; but nothing gives him more pleasure than the sight of a good strong bird beating the guns.

And nothing arouses his anger more than their theft. He will track down poachers with ruthless energy – even if the offenders are local men from neighbouring villages. It does not make him the most popular man in the rural working community. But then he never thought it would.

Logistics of a Suffolk shoot

The 1500 acre Suffolk estate shown in the illustration supports 17 organised shoots a year, including duck-flights. One gamekeeper works here with two guns (one shotgun; one rifle), five dogs, a dozen broody hens and a boy. The guns are for vermin. The dogs are for fetching and carrying. The broody hens are for hatching a few extra pheasants' eggs. The boy is for licking into shape.

The gamekeeper's equipment ranges from the money-gulping sophistication of the sporting catalogues (heated incubators, hatchers and brooders) to the age-old simplicity of the wire snare. Among the statistics of his trade, the one most difficult to calculate is his own working week. Nature never stands still; neither does the gamekeeper. In a good year he will successfully hatch 2,000 pheasants' eggs; 300 partridge; 50 mallard. These will cost him numberless hours of effort, and $21\frac{1}{2}$ tons of special feed for nesting mothers and chicks.

To protect the nests he will set 130 humane sprung traps in which he will expect to catch at least 1,500 head of vermin every year. In 15 years working the same estate, he has seen 29,000 assorted pests fall victim to trap, snare, gas and gun.

On a typical shooting day there will be nine guns. In the 1978/79 season, the total bag was: 461 cock pheasant and 373 hens; 3 young grey partridge and 19 old; 53 young French partridge and 104 old; 19 hares; 4 rabbits; 27 pigeons; 75 mallard; 8 teal; 8 gadwall; 46 moorhen; 1 jay; 2 Eastern collared doves; 1 coypu; 5 tufted duck; 2 woodcock; 11 pochard; 2 coot; 1 guinea fowl. That was not a good season: 500 head down on the year before. The pheasant season opens at the beginning of October and ends at the beginning of February; the partridge season is from the beginning of September to the beginning of February.

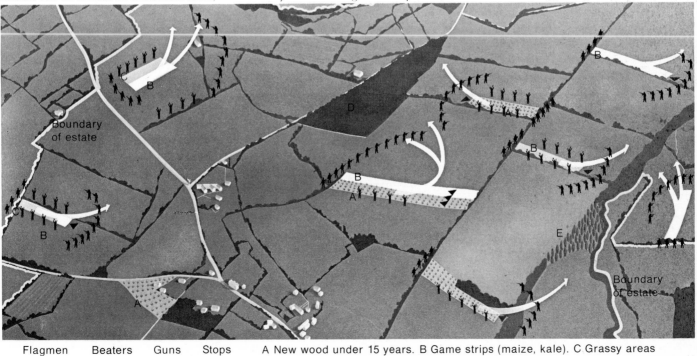

| Flagmen | Beaters | Guns | Stops | A New wood under 15 years. B Game strips (maize, kale). C Grassy areas and lonicera. D Established wood. E Poplars. |

The arrows show the expected direction of flight on each drive during a typical day's pheasant shooting on a Suffolk estate. Under the direction of the head gamekeeper, the birds are walked up through the cover by beaters. Flagmen prevent birds running out of the flank of the drive; other men and boys, called stops, are positioned to prevent their escape at the far end

Thorn hedge and dry-stone wall

Barbed wire was to the hedge-layer what the pneumatic tyre was to the wheelwright. Not quite the death-knell, but near enough. Anyone that remains is an anachronism to be remarked upon.

A few of the hedges that made up the 'typically English' enclosed field system were planted for shelter alone. Many were to keep in the livestock; others to make arable farming compact and efficient. None were provided for the exclusive benefit of wildlife. They were, in short, a convenience for the farmer. And it is a new sort of convenience that has persuaded him to grub so many of them up. Of those that remain, almost none are trimmed by hand. It is far too slow; far too expensive. But the mechanical flails are not a complete answer, even in a purely practical, non-conservationist sense. Over a long period, the top-chopping encourages the lower growth to thin out so that the hedge ceases to be stockproof. And when that happens the farmer has only two choices. He can put up a fence; or he can employ a hedge-layer to repair the damage.

Most stockproof hedges are hawthorn. And, although there are (or were) distinct regional variations in style, they all began in much the same way. Four-year-old thorn saplings were planted four inches apart along the line of the intended hedge: almost 16,000 to the mile. For their first few years they were kept weeded and trimmed, and often protected from the livestock by wattle hurdles or post-and-rail fencing. It was when they reached a height of seven feet (2m) or so that the hedge-layer demonstrated the nub of his craft.

He was always an individualist: a solitary worker whose bulky outfit (this was winter work) was completed by fingerless gloves of hard yellow horse-leather, and thick leather knee-protectors. Using a combination of billhook and long-handled slasher (whose precise patterns varied from region to region) he would cut away the rough, tangled

Hedges (top) are considered too slow and too costly to cut by hand nowadays. But wherever they remain, as in the hilly pastures of Somerset (centre), they help to perpetuate the typical chequered pattern of the English countryside. In the north and west of the British Isles, hedges give way to dry-stone walls (left), seen here at Ullswater, in the English Lake District, where there is an abundance of fieldstone. It is the very dryness of such walls which helps them withstand the worst of wind and frost

Jigsaw puzzle in stone. For a dry-stone wall to last, the pieces must be fitted with a craftsman's finely-judged precision

growth, taking care to leave a good number of strong upright stems. Always he cut *upwards*, with the grain, to leave a smooth clean cut. Ragged ends looked untidy, encouraged fungus growth and were the mark of a sloppy craftsman.

Some of the uprights were half-severed from the rootstock, with downward strokes of the billhook just above ground level. Others were simply topped at the intended level of the hedge. Then the hedger laid down the half-severed stems, called plashers or sears, and wove them into the uprights. Kept alive by their union with the roots, the plashers quickly threw out a thick infill of thorny branches. If the upright stems were too young and flimsy to bear the pressure, wooden stakes were driven into the ground to hold the plashers in place.

'Hedger' is not a universal term for such a craftsman. In Cornwall, a 'hedge'

is a stone-faced earth bank; while in Ireland a Cornish hedge is a 'ditch' – a word that also serves for a dry-stone wall. To add to the confusion, a dry-stone wall in Scotland is a 'dyke', a word which almost everywhere else means a ditch. It is not only etymologically that dry-stone walls have their regional peculiarities. Like hedges, they submit to local styles of construction and profile. But, also like hedges, there is a broad uniformity of method.

Dry-stone walls are basically a phenomenon of northern and western uplands of Britain, and parts of Ireland as well, where the poor growth-potential of hedging plants is balanced by an abundance of available fieldstone. Having collected his granite, or Cotswold stone, the waller (or dyker) begins by removing turf and topsoil along the line of the wall to provide a solid footing. The wall itself

rises in two converging 'skins', each tapering inwards at the rate of around one horizontal inch per vertical foot. The real hand-and-eye skill of the expert is in the selection and placing of each stone. The novice holds a rock in his hand, turns it and tries it in a variety of positions before he succeeds. The expert does it with the speed of a child who has learned a jigsaw by heart, pinning each stone with smaller ones to hold it firm and always making sure that each block is resting on two beneath, like brickwork. He spends his material economically, often splitting a stone with precisely-calculated hammer blows to make it do double duty.

But he is going the way of the hedger. To see a waller at work today is unusual. When the old boundaries begin to crumble, it's not craftsmanship that fills the gaps. It's barbed wire.

Thatching: one of the oldest crafts

Thatch belongs with green hills and valleys, nestling villages and church towers, and the art of it is probably the most ancient building craft in Britain.

In Norfolk, for good reason, there is much thatch and quite a lot of it is on the churches. The thatched naves of these flint-napped, field-corner cathedrals are a peculiarity of the region: a natural marriage of the two most abundant local materials.

Here is thatch in its warmest maturity. Here, too, is thatch in its earliest infancy. The native reed in the fens and marshes of Broadland is *Phragmites communis*: Norfolk reed, the finest in the world. If you imagine that this abundance of the thatcher's favourite material is a happy accident, you are half right. Happy it certainly is. Accidental it is not, save in the combination of natural conditions that enable it to thrive. Those feathery, nodding acres – the home of bittern, reed bunting and otter – which make up some of East Anglia's richest natural habitats, are all farmed. If they were not, they could not exist. Uncut and undrained, they would degenerate to a useless, impenetrable tangle of alder thicket.

The new year on the reed-marsh begins in early spring when the harvest is finished. Among the stubble of the old reed can be seen the first fleshy tips of the new growth, each no bigger than the nail of a little finger. When the cutting is finished, they get a generous soaking. The sluices are opened and the dykes flood across the fen in a single unbroken sheet. At the second high tide, the sluices are closed and the water locked in for a full two weeks before it is allowed to drain off again.

By July, the shoots will have raced away to make a solid green jungle, six feet (1.8m) tall. They will die and dry through autumn and winter, ready for harvesting the following spring.

The trouble is that demand for thatching reed, given the gentrification of the country cottage, now easily outstrips supply and the modern thatcher can ill afford to be choosy. Even the old-timer has learned to accept a proportion of old reed mixed in with the new – a compromise he would once have rejected out of hand.

In the drier eastern counties – given good maintenance and occasional repairs to the ridge – a reed roof will give good service for up to 80 years. Norfolk reed and Norfolk thatching skills are universally in demand: commissions for North Walsham men have come from as far away as the United States of America.

But – although no son of Norfolk will easily admit it – there is another thatching material: what in the West of England they call wheat reed. What in Norfolk they call, with the barest suspicion of a curl in the lip, straw.

However, not any old wheat yields a thatching reed. The modern, jug-eared varieties stand barely 18in ($\frac{1}{2}$m) tall. In terms of grain yield they have all the over-compensating vigour of the diminutive. For the thatcher, they are useless. He needs an old-fashioned variety, with stems a full three feet (1m) long. Not many farmers grow it and it is money rather than a sentimental attachment to the past that prompts those who do.

They get two cash crops in the space of one: thatching reed *and* grain.

Cutting and preparing the wheat is more of a performance than harvesting water reed. Most Norfolk marshmen these days use mechanical cutters and haul the reed from the fen on sleds behind load-spreading Snowcat-type tractors, which have solved the problem of driving heavy vehicles across the spongy peat. (In the old days the reed was all cut by hand and brought off the marsh by boat. A bristling lighter, loaded down like a floating haystack, was as slow as it was picturesque.) But the wheat-reed harvest is still firmly rooted in the pre-combine age. Cutting is by old-fashioned binder, and the grain is separated from the ear in an old-fashioned threshing machine, with a mechanical comber attached to keep the stems straight and unbroken. Such a machine requires eight men to operate it.

Wheat reed is sold to the thatcher in 14lb (6 kilo) bundles. After hand-combing to remove dead leaves and other debris, Norfolk reed is sold in 'standard bunches', each 24in (609mm) in circumference, measured one foot (304mm) above the butt-end. Six of these make one 'fathom'.

How do you tell a *Phragmites communis* roof from a wheat-reed roof? It is not easy for the layman, but largely a matter of habitat. On the steeply-pitched roofs of East Anglia, it will almost certainly be Norfolk reed; on the softer, more rounded roofs of the south and west of England, there is a better chance that it will be wheat. Before they are fixed to the roof, of course, the two materials are easy to distinguish. At six feet (1·8m) long, the average Norfolk reed is double the average wheat reed; and absolutely any townie can tell an empty wheat ear (which is left attached) from a *Phragmites* feather. In the far soggier West, the longevity of thatch is much reduced: 30 years would be considered not bad.

With both kinds of reed, the thatching method is essentially the same hard physical work. The reed is scratchy and sharp, damaging to clothing and flesh alike. Leather pads give a measure of protection to the knees, but hands and elbows have a hard time of it. The roof grows from the bottom upwards, with the first bundles laid cut ends downwards, projecting well out from the wall to form the eaves. Working upwards towards the ridge, each bundle overlaps the one below it to make a weatherproof seal.

Thatch in its warmest maturity – on the roof of a cottage – is the product of the oldest of crafts

New thatch for an old roof. Thatchers are in great demand. Each leaves his own distinctive mark

The thatch is pinned to the battens with horizontal hazel rods, usually called sways, and with twisted split-hazel pegs, usually called spars. For each 'square' of thatch (10ft × 10ft, the thatcher's standard unit of measurement), there are 300 spars. For all the thatcher's materials and tools, local names abound. To a Norfolk man, for instance, a spar is a broche. And to a Devonian, hazel is nuthalse.

Devon men use more blades for trimming their roofs than the Norfolk thatchers, but both use a legget to tap up and tighten the ends of the reed beneath the sways. There are individual variations on this, but it is typically a piece of elm plank on a short, angled handle, generously packed with horse-shoe nails. Pressed down by the sways, the packed reed is bent slightly upwards so that, in the finished roof, it is only the cut ends that are visible.

At the ridge, the joint between the two pitches is made watertight by a layer of pliable sedge or straw, extending a foot or two down each flank and clipped into varying patterns of scallops or chevrons, individually designed to suit each thatcher's personal taste. It is the way he adds his private signature to the landscape.

The spread of forests

It is a peculiarity of the English (as opposed to Scots and Americans who know better) to regard a forest as exclusively a thing of oak and ash, and a forester as a bulky tartan shirt with an axe. Industrialised conifer plantations are scoffed at as if the trees were in some way less real, less worthy of a place in the landscape. 'Outdoor pit-prop factories' is the way one acid-tipped critic described the Forestry Commission's woodlands.

In a sense that is exactly what they are: an astonishingly high proportion of the timber does still go to the pits. But they are much more besides. Take Thetford, on the sandy wastes of Breckland, on the Norfolk–Suffolk border: 80 square miles (20,720 hectares) of it, the largest lowland forest in England. Gone is the straight-line planter's geometry. Gone are the Keep Out notices. In their place are an energetic concern for environmental propriety, and an open-armed welcome to the public that is almost embarrassing in its effusiveness. There are picnic sites, camping and caravan grounds, nature trails and waymarked footpaths, all adding up to a pine-scented playground which attracts visitors in their thousands.

A great forest is like a great sea. Sense of time and direction are under siege from the sheer scale of it. Eighty square miles of trees growing 550 tonnes of new green wood a day is more than most English imaginations can take.

It all begins in a particularly unlikely way, in a particularly dog-eared potting shed. Here for a few days in March, and again in April, nimble fingers drop locally-collected seeds into biodegradable growing-containers. Immediately, the statistics gnaw at the edges of credibility. One man can sow 10,000 tree seeds a day; and the germination rate is nudging 100 per cent. What this means in terms of tree production can be better understood in the plastic cold-tunnels where the trays of seedlings are raised. A thick green carpet of infant trees translates in the imagination into mile after mile of unbroken leaf canopy: 140,000 trees in a single tunnel. Toughened by strictly-controlled temperature and watering, they will be ready to plant out in the forest within six months of sowing. Not long ago, before the growing-container came along, a seedling would need two or three years' growth before its roots would tolerate transplantation to the growing site.

All Thetford's new planting is on sites that have already produced their first crop. The methods are modern. There are no axes here (when the foresters needed one for an historical pageant, a special emissary had to be sent to the ironmongers!), but no forest worker need feel unmanned by the loss. His virility is handed back to him in the shape of a pulverising machine, armed with a catch-all assembly of whirling blades to smash the last relics of the original timber. It chews its way across the glade behind an armour-plated tractor. (It is not left-over army landmines that exercise the anxiety: it is left-over pinestumps, against which ordinary tractor bodywork offers no defence.)

The planting process itself is an almost surreal conjunction of ancient and modern. Behind the same armour-plated tractor lurches an enclosed orange planting machine whose tapering, backward-facing jaws give it the aspect of a praying mantis. At the front, a steel cutter slices open a planting furrow. At the back, a pair of angled wheels neatly earths it over again. It looks relentless, thoroughly automatic. But in the mantis's deeper recesses, suspended in mid-technology, is a man in a knitted woolly hat, manually placing the seedlings into the furrow, one every two metres. At no greater cost to himself than mild lumbago and a grain or two of compost beneath his fingernails, this man can plant a forest of 7,000 pine trees a day.

On the meagre soil of Breckland it is a Mediterranean immigrant, the Corsican pine, that adjusts most readily to the conditions. Superior yield and faster maturity (50 years) have underwritten

telegraph pole stage) will be well under way. It is not difficult to calculate the age of a growing Corsican or Scots pine. The branches climb the stem in easily discernible levels: for each level, count one year. A mature tree grows to more than 145ft (44m) with a trunk diameter of up to 5ft (1.5m).

In the nicest sense, pine trees are arboreal pigs: cut up and used, with hardly any waste. No remnant is too small, or too awkwardly shaped, to be ground up for chipboard or woodwool. Felling is by chainsaw, de-limbing is done by machines on the spot; and radio-controlled Commission vehicles are used to direct customers' lorries immediately to the felling site. Only 40 per cent of the output would satisfy the mind's eye impression of 'timber' – large logs for sawing into planks. A full 20 per cent still goes for pit props; 20 per cent makes pulpwood, principally for motor car lining panels; eight per cent makes chipboard; six per cent makes woodwool for packing and insulation. Then there is ground bark for gardener's soil-improver (or for horse-bedding: Newmarket is only a gallop away); and even charcoal. A private charcoal burner leases a pitch in the forest and turns out five tons a week. Which is an awful lot of barbecues.

Aesthetic objections to the 'unnatural' appearance of the plantations are being appeased by a mixed border of native hardwoods softening the outlines of the forest's edge. Among the forest wildlife perhaps the most significant new species is the naturalist. Human noses might once have been turned up at the man-made habitat, but the deer and red squirrels have had no such purist qualms.

All this calls for a lot of people. Thetford Forest employs 300: a head forester, 30 qualified foresters and specialist teams to handle every task from motor repairs to campsite management. But if you are a visitor remember that the foresters already have all the pests they need: pine shoot moth; pine shoot beetle; black pine beetle; pine weevil and conifer heart rot fungus. With modern pesticides and virulent fungi they can now hope to keep all these at bay. Against only two threats do they lack defence: freak gales (many acres were flattened in early 1976), and the idiot with the match.

Growing forests for the future

Thetford is the largest, man-made lowland forest in the British Isles. It is also the largest production forest, producing more timber than other forests which are bigger in area. The New Forest and the Forest of Dean make up the trio of big forests in the south of England.

Most of the major forests, established in mountainous or other open country, are designated as forest parks. These are open to the public for recreation although their prime purpose is growing timber commercially. They are the Snowdonia Forest Park in Wales and the Galloway, Queen Elizabeth, Argyll, Glen More forest parks in Scotland. The Border Forest Park, most of which is in England, is the largest man-made forest in Europe. Forest parks in both the Republic of Ireland and Northern Ireland – there are well over a dozen – are less extensive than those in Britain.

About 50 per cent of all productive woodland in Britain (4.2 million acres, 1.7 million hectares) is owned or managed by the Forestry Commission. The remainder is privately owned. British forests employ over 20,000 people and nine per cent of the land is devoted to forestry in the UK compared to 78 per cent to agriculture.

Above left: Forester David Hudson hauls logs by horse in a Northumbrian forest. Right: Wild wood anemones bloom in a man-made habitat. Encouraged by forest staff there is now rich plant and wildlife in the forests

its challenge to the more traditional Scots pine (65–70 years). It takes three or four years for a young Corsican to reach Christmas-tree size; after that it will make about 19 to 20in (0.5m) of new growth a year. The leaf canopy closes overhead after 20–25 years, by which time a programme of thinning (this is the

Chapter Six
The Sea and the Countryside

Nature's great divides are places of high drama and compelling interest. None more so than the margins of the British Isles where two worlds meet as here at Durdle Door, Dorset; where the towering cliffs of upland coasts and the crumbling clays of lowland ones display their strengths and expose their weaknesses to encircling seas. This chapter tells the story of the making – and unmaking – of the sea coasts and looks at the rich mix of shore life at the water's edge

Most people have some idea of the shape of the British Isles. The classic atlas 'picture' of these islands surrounded by sea, lying off the north-west coast of Europe, is an image etched upon the mind from early schooldays.

Their configuration is all the more distinct precisely because they are islands outlined against the traditional atlas-blue of the sea. It is the sea which sharpens our perception of the coastline's shape. And it is the same restless sea, with its waves, tides, currents and winds, which helps give the coastline shape.

In places the sea is bent upon destruction, cutting back the cliffs, wearing down the rocks, sometimes at a frightening, relentless pace when the loss of land is measured in yards from one week to the next. At other places where the rocks are

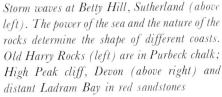

Storm waves at Betty Hill, Sutherland (above left). The power of the sea and the nature of the rocks determine the shape of different coasts. Old Harry Rocks (left) are in Purbeck chalk; High Peak cliff, Devon (above right) and distant Ladram Bay in red sandstones

hard and unyielding the process is slow, almost imperceptible, and a man will scarcely notice any change in his lifetime.

Yet, just as the sea destroys, so it builds, taking the detritus of its destruction and depositing it elsewhere, throwing up sand bars and shingle spits, and creating the tidal marsh from which reclaimed farmland comes.

The shore of the English Channel between Poole Harbour and Studland Bay is a cameo of the British coast – and an exhibit in the battle between these

two processes. From the dunes to the south of Poole Harbour, first look across Studland Bay to Foreland Point and Old Harry Rocks. Here the waves are cutting an ornamental edging to the coast, scalloping out the chalk cliffs.

Now turn and look in the opposite direction towards the sheltered creeks, mudbanks and salt marsh of Poole Harbour. Here the sea is returning what it is taking farther along the coast – as well as re-working silt carried down by rivers – to make the marshes grow. So, within a few square miles, two different views encapsulate the character and variety of the British coast.

The coastal variety is not solely the work of the sea. The land's abrupt and often awesome confrontation with the ocean is made with all manner of rocks,

and it is these which give different coasts such distinctive form, colour and texture.

The reefs and skerries of the Hebrides are a world away from the sea-sculpted red Devonian rocks seen from the train between Dawlish and Teignmouth. Just as is the Cornish granite which built the seamed and weathered headlands of Bosigran and Treen Cliff from the glittering mudflats and coarse grasses of the Essex marshes.

From Delabole to Bude black, knife-blade reefs of killas – the Cornish word for slate – tear at the incoming surf. On the other side of England a soft line of sand dunes at Horsey on the Norfolk coast holds back a sea intent on invading the Norfolk Broads.

In west Dorset foundering cliffs of gault clay, greensand, marl and lias 149

The Seven Sisters. Here the South Downs end – in magnificent chalk cliffs. The 'sisters' are truncated spurs at the cliff face

sometimes slip to the shore making strange, boggy 'weares' or undercliffs where wild orchids grow. Far to the north sea-lochs run deep into the coast of Scotland bringing salt water to what seems almost the heart of the land.

All this gives the British Isles coastal scenery second to none, a fretwork of bay and headland, sea stack and island, cliff and sand dune, shingle beach and marsh.

Sea cliffs

Sea cliffs provide some of the most spectacular scenery in the British Isles. The highest cliffs are found where the relentless Atlantic rollers have cut deeply into the seaward slopes of the western mountains, mountains already sharpened and steepened by former ice sheets.

On these exposed, windward coasts, open to the maximum fetch of the waves (the distance they are blown across the sea), wave energy is at its greatest. The sea battering Land's End, or any other great headland, in the fury of a gale is testimony to the prodigious force of the waves. Then, even the greatest of cliffs – and the British Isles are endowed with some of the most formidable in Europe – shudder from the assault.

Croaghaun cliff at 2192ft (668m), on Achill Island, Co Mayo, is western

Europe's highest. Ireland has three other high cliffs: Slieve League 1972ft (600m), Co Donegal; Sauce Creek 1400ft (426m) on Mt Brandon, Co Kerry; and Knockmore 1520ft (459m) on Clare Island, Co Mayo. In Scotland only the isolated island of St Kilda has anything of comparable stature in Conachair 1379ft (420m). Exmoor's Countisbury Hill at 990ft (302m) holds the record for southern Britain. Golden Cap 619ft (188m), near Seatown in Dorset, is the highest cliff on England's south coast.

It has been suggested that since most of these examples are not vertical they are not true sea cliffs; that the sea is responsible only for the relatively small active cliffs at the foot of the slopes. Vertical cliffs more than 1000ft (305m) in height are rare, but when they do occur they are an awesome sight, especially when viewed from below. One example is St John's Head, Hoy, which towers to 1140ft (347m) above the Orkney ferry boat as it creeps across the waters of the Pentland Firth.

Such steepness depends on a pattern of well-developed vertical joint-planes (cracks formed along planes of weakness) in the rock. Continuous weathering by wind and rain along these cracks causes

loosened blocks to fall directly into deep water instead of mantling and protecting the cliff foot from further wave erosion.

Other high vertical cliffs are those of Clo Mor 921ft (281m) near Cape Wrath; Dunvegan Head 1025ft (312m) and Waterstein Head 966ft (294m) on Skye; the Cliffs of Moher 668ft (203m) in County Clare; and Beachy Head 534ft (160m) in Sussex.

Beachy Head and the other chalk cliffs of southern England are remarkably vertical because the fallen masses of chalk are quickly destroyed by the waves, thus exposing the cliff foot to renewed undercutting.

Flamborough Head and The Needles, two of the most striking chalk coastal features in the British Isles, are very different in character. Flamborough Head, honeycombed with caves, is the northernmost nose at the end of the great chalk escarpment which runs from Devon to Yorkshire. Not far from the other end of the escarpment lie The Needles; more precisely they are part of a ridge of chalk which runs east-west across the Isle of Wight, and once continued to the Dorset mainland.

From the cliff above The Needles it is possible on a clear day to see how they

Sea cliffs and caves near Wick in the north of Scotland. Caves like these sometimes coalesce to form natural rock arches

fall in line with the chalk cliffs of Foreland Point and Old Harry Rocks across the water in the Isle of Purbeck. The Needles and Old Harry are remnants of the marine-eroded ridge. And, just as the sea detached The Needles from the Isle of Wight, so it detached the Isle of Wight – but over a much longer period – from the mainland (see illustration p. 153).

The chalk here and in Dorset has been up-ended by the folding and thrusting which occurred in the great earth movements which built the Alps. Indeed The Needles owe their resistance to the hardness imparted by these movements.

The hardest chalk is in the south face of the Needle nearest the shore. A slight broadening of this hard belt of chalk accounts for the increase in the size of the stacks seawards.

At Flamborough the chalk, unlike that of the south coast, lies in nearly horizontal beds which produce an impressive range of almost vertical cliffs. The headland itself is covered with thick boulder clay and the erosion of this above, and the chalk below, gives it a character not found elsewhere in chalk cliffs.

The different rates and magnitudes of cliff erosion depend not only on the hardness and the jointing pattern of the rocks but also on any structural weaknesses such as faults. Where these occur, or where relatively weak rock layers alternate with more resistant layers, waves will etch out a complex mosaic of caves, arches, stacks and geos. A marine cleft, or geo, may commence life as a sea cave, perhaps with a spectacular blow-hole at the inner end, like the Kettle Spout in North Uist, but roof collapse and a coalescence of geos will produce a variety of arches and stacks along the fretted shore-line (illustration next page).

All these features are displayed on one of the finest limestone coasts in the British Isles, the Stack Rocks area of the Pembrokeshire Coast National Park, near Flimston.

Here flat-topped, near-vertical cliffs of Carboniferous limestone are under constant attack from the sea, which has cut into the coast to produce the striking promontories of St Govan's Head and Stackpole Head. The plateau behind the cliffs was planed flat by the sea at a time when the sea level was higher.

This area has a wealth of stacks, arches, cauldrons and blow-holes, the result of marine erosion working on a mass of limestone already rich in caves, swallow-holes, faults and other lines of weakness in the rocks.

An outstanding feature is the Green Bridge of Wales, an arch formed of massive limestones. This was created when caves on opposite sides of a headland were cut back farther and farther by the sea until they coalesced. Nearby the twin Stack Rocks, pinnacles of limestone thick with colonies of sea birds, rise from shallow water close inshore. They are the remains of an old headland destroyed by the sea.

To the east of these is the Devil's Cauldron, a peninsula riddled with caves and passages formed by the sea eating away at lines of weakness in the rocks. The Cauldron itself is the result of a number of blow-hole caves coalescing and then collapsing.

Continuing erosion by the sea over a long period will transform this peninsula into a series of stacks and arches which are likely to be even more spectacular than the Green Bridge of Wales and the Stack Rocks.

Some of the most famous sea caves are found in the basalt lavas of the small Scottish island of Staffa where Fingal's Cave has basalt columns similar to those of the Giant's Causeway in Northern

At Fingal's Cave on the island of Staffa marked differences can be seen in the structure of the rocks. These differences tell the story of a mass of molten lava and the different rates at which it cooled as it was pushed up from within the Earth millions of years ago.

The very top layer of rock is a structureless, slaggy crust which now forms the roof of the cave. This cooled rapidly from above where it was losing most heat.

The middle section also cooled from above.

As the molten rock began to solidify it contracted to form a hexagonal pattern rather like cracks that form in mud as it dries. These cracks followed the solidification down through the molten rock, still cooling from above, but at a slower and more uniform rate. This led to the formation of the narrow columns of basalt.

The lavas at the base of the cliffs are massive, regularly spaced columns forming the 'causeway' into the cave. These cooled from below.

in such a way that it is possible to get excellent sectional views of a wide variety of rock patterns.

The folding and faulting has produced almost museum models of sharp anticlines (upfolds), synclines (downfolds), vertical strata, small faults and other interesting features.

This stretch also has some of the finest coastal waterfalls in England. Streams drain the land for only a few miles from the coast and in their short length they have carved deep wooded valleys which end with the streams falling over the cliffs. Normally the streams would cut down into the rock so that their mouths were at sea level. But here the coast, under attack from the waves, is being worn away more quickly than the streams can cut down. Thus their valleys are left 'hanging' with the water dropping over the cliffs.

Litter Water, nine miles (14km) south of Hartland Quay, ends in a sheer fall of over 70ft (21.3m). In other places the streams cascade over more irregular cliffs, especially where layers of rock of different hardness have caused 'steps' in the descent.

Ireland. How these columnar lavas are formed is clearly illustrated above. There are more of these to be seen in the cliffs of western Mull. There the lavas must have flowed into a forest, for trees have been found preserved in them.

Smoo Cave – from the Norse *smuga* meaning cleft – near Durness on the north coast of Scotland has the added attraction of a subterranean waterfall at the back of its limestone chamber. It has been created partly by the underground river which runs through it and partly by marine erosion. It is easy to imagine the sea-filled gorge outside the cave entrance once roofed by a layer of limestone, long since collapsed.

Examples of partly collapsed caves can be seen at the Bullers of Buchan, north of Aberdeen, and at the narrower Hunts-man's Leap near Tenby. Some of the more spectacular coastal arches in Scotland are the Brig o' Trams at Wick, the Devil's Bridge at Scrabster in Caithness and the Bow Fiddle at Portknockie, Banff.

Farther south the Green Bridge of Wales, already mentioned, Durdle Door and Stair Hole in Dorset are well known tourist attractions.

Of the sea stacks, Orkney's Old Man of Hoy is the best known; St Kilda's gigantic stacks are the highest, with Stac Lee 544ft (166m) and Stac an Armin 627ft (207m); and the Needles and Old Harry on England's south coast among the most photographed.

The Devon and Cornish coast between Hartland Point and Boscastle has magnificent cliffs which are being cut by the sea

Islands

Most people are fascinated by islands, none more so than the inhabitants of the British Isles who have no fewer than 1040 dotting the seas which surround them. Among these, differences in geology, topography, soils, vegetation and climate have created islands of contrasting shape, colour and land use. But whether the land use best suited to an island is still being achieved depends largely on its remoteness or accessibility.

Some islands are so remote that they are rarely visited. Rockall, about 200 miles (320km) to the west of North Uist, is the most extreme case. This island is no more than a 70ft (21m) pinnacle of granite washed over by the storm waves. It rises from a submarine platform of volcanic rocks.

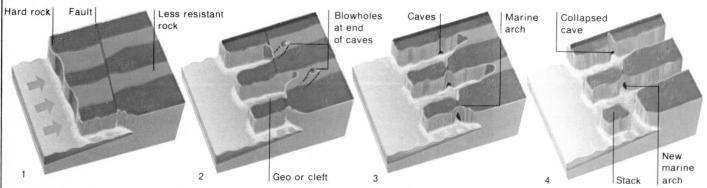

The cutting of a cliff coast. 1 Waves attack softer, less resistant rocks and 2 structural weaknesses such as faults, etching out geos or clefts. Blowholes form. 3 Caves begin to form on the fault line and a marine arch is produced by two caves coalescing. 4 Stacks remain as arches collapse

Some tiny specks such as Shetland's Muckle Flugga, the northernmost British landfall, Cornwall's Bishop's Rock and Ireland's Fastnet are occupied only by lightkeepers. Fair Isle, midway between Orkney and Shetland, is the most isolated inhabited island.

The rocky, windswept expanses of the Scottish Hebrides and Ireland's western isles support traditional fishing-crofting communities which are only now being touched by tourism. On these peat-covered, treeless margins of the 'Celtic Fringe' the magnificent scenery, booming surf and unforgettable sunsets are but one side of the coin; the islanders' precarious livelihoods are reflected in declining populations.

St Kilda, some 60 miles (96km) west of the Outer Hebrides, is renowned not only for its cliffs and stacks – homes of the world's largest colony of gannets – but also for the primitive life style of its former inhabitants, the last of whom were evacuated to the mainland in 1930 because of the harshness of life there.

Ireland's Blasket Isles, once a thriving community in the 'next parish to America', are now virtually deserted.

The neighbouring Skellig Rocks, seven miles offshore across the turbulent seas of St Finan's Bay, are even more remote. Their grey, splintery outlines rise out of the Atlantic to produce a series of fantastic spires and pinnacles.

They have long been abandoned but are famous as one of the strongholds of British Christianity during the Dark Ages, inhabited by a handful of Celtic monks. Perched on ledges in the cliffs are a number of drystone buildings which are a legacy of this remarkable monastic settlement.

The other well-known monastic islands of Lindisfarne (Northumberland), Caldey (Dyfed) and Iona (Scotland) have fared somewhat better, bolstered by recently developed tourism.

The Welsh isles of Skomer, Skokholm, Grassholm and Ramsey, once the haunts of Vikings, are now more celebrated for cliff scenery, seals and bird life than sporadic attempts to re-settle them.

In the Bristol Channel the inhabitants of Lundy's granite isle have maintained a successful farming community. Farther up-channel the conspicuous shapes of Flat Holm and Steep Holme are built of white Carboniferous limestone, the bedding planes of which – these are the surfaces which separate one layer of rock from another – provide ledges for countless seabirds.

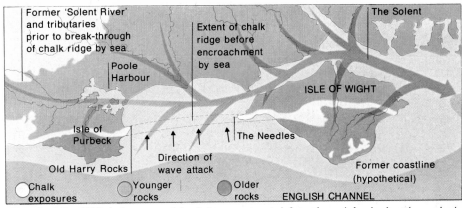

How the Isle of Wight became an island. It was separated from the mainland when the sea broke through the chalk ridge which once connected the two. The lower broken line marks the old cliff line of chalk. The sea breached it after marine erosion caused the coast to retreat from its former position farther out in the English Channel. The Needles and Old Harry Rocks are remnants of the ridge.

Limestone islands are often uninhabited because of water supply problems. This makes the Aran Isles of Ireland's Galway Bay all the more remarkable because of their thriving population in a limestone 'desert'.

Nearly every field has been made by the islanders artificially. Owing to a lack of soil on the bare limestone they have, over the centuries, carried thousands of tons of sand and seaweed from the low-lying north-eastern shores and piled it on the limestone 'pavements' near the village.

To preserve their new soil the joints in the limestone were first filled with rubble and the small plots surrounded with drystone walls, as protection against the wind. The islands are criss-crossed with miles of these walls within which cattle are grazed and potatoes grown.

The sea cliffs of Aran are constantly being eroded and undercut by Atlantic waves and consequently the horizontal layers of limestone often overhang the ocean. These have been used as fishing stances from time immemorial.

The islanders of Clew Bay, Co Mayo, are better blessed – geologically speaking! They gather rich hay harvests from their emerald green archipelago, for their islands are the well-watered remnants of boulder clay drumlins which were drowned by the sea.

The carefully manicured fields of the Scillonian islanders sit on the partially drowned tors of a granite massif which was reputedly inundated and isolated from Land's End when the intervening land of Lyonesse was submerged by a rise in sea level after the glaciers had melted.

The Isle of Man also was once part of the mainland. Submarine contours indicate that a broad ridge of less than 20 fathoms depth (120ft, 36.5m) joins the island to the English mainland.

Generally there is no simple and complete answer to the question: how are islands formed? In the previous section it has been shown how the sea, by cutting away softer rocks and attacking lines of weakness in them, can separate one land mass from another.

Sometimes, as a river cuts its valley down to sea level, a rise in sea level drowns the low lying land and leaves the higher parts as islands. This, plus continuous erosion by the sea, is how the Isle of Wight was cut off from the mainland. At one time its chalk ridge and those of Dorset were continuous and the Frome river valley extended along the present Solent and Spithead (illustration above).

How Anglesey, the lowest area in North Wales, came to be a plateau which rises to less than 300ft (91m) above sea level, is not so certain. One theory is that it is a platform which was shaped by waves when the sea advanced over the area, slicing across hard and soft rocks alike, flattening their structures. Across the Menai Straits, in a coastal strip several miles wide, plateau levels of a few hundred feet above sea level persist – and they are more comparable with Anglesey than the mainland about them.

An alternative theory is that Anglesey represents a land surface from which a former cover of New Red Sandstone has been stripped, just as the Torridonian sandstones are being stripped off the Lewisian gneiss in Scotland.

The 15 mile (24km) long channel of the Menai Straits which separates Anglesey from the mainland looks much like an enlarged river valley. It is probable that this was once cut by glacial meltwater. Later, like so many Cornish valleys, it was drowned by the post-glacial rise in sea level.

Straits

The Straits of Dover are one of the most celebrated stretches of sea round the British Isles: a narrow piece of water, 18 to 25 miles (29km to 40km) wide separating Britain from France.

This, however, was not always so. The affinity of the geological structures of Kent and Sussex with those of northern France suggests that a land link once existed. This was 250,000 years ago. How, then, was the connection with the Continent broken? How were the straits formed? In short, how did the British Isles become the British Isles. There are two theories.

A chalk dome, the remnants of which can be seen in the long ridges of the North and South Downs, formed the original isthmus, with rivers flowing on one side to the North Sea and on the other to the Channel, which then reached only to Beachy Head. Even when the crest of the chalk dome had been breached, to reveal the underlying Wealden rocks, the rivers maintained their courses across the ridges, just as the Medway cuts through the North Downs and the Cuckmere through the South Downs today.

While this was happening the sea was also cutting into the isthmus on both its flanks. This slow process of erosion was assisted by the gradually rising sea level which led to the isthmus being breached. This may have occurred more than once – the isthmus being reconnected and breached again.

The other, but less likely explanation is that during the Ice Age a huge glacial lake was impounded behind the land-bridge. As the ice sheets covering the North Sea melted the level of the lake rose until it overflowed the lowest part of the chalk ridge, perhaps cutting a gorge which was later widened by erosion. Following this the rising sea level would have submerged the remaining part of the ridge.

Again, since sea level fluctuated with the advance and retreat of the ice sheets it is likely that the straits alternated between land and water several times. If the Ice Age were to return it is possible that the straits might become land once again. At their deepest they are no more than 300ft (91m).

Estuaries and bays

The beauty of the coastline does not depend solely on cliffs and islands. They provide the *fortissimo* passages in the coastal symphony but the waters of the Dart, Helford River with its woods fall-

ing to the water's edge and the serene countryside of Constable's Suffolk drifting down to the Stour and Deben represent gentler *pianissimo* moods.

These three estuaries have in common the manner of their origin. They are former river valleys which were drowned by the rise in sea level of about 100ft (30.5m) which accompanied the melting of the ice sheets 10–20,000 years ago. When this happened in upland areas the mountainous divides were transformed into headlands like the Iveragh Peninsula in south-west Ireland. Simple, funnel-like bays like Bantry and Kenmare River contrast with the more tortuous drowned river channels in nearby Kinsale and Cobh. Here the coastal configuration closely resembles south-west Britain, an area in which tidal waters have burrowed deeply into flat, rocky plateaux.

The picturesque, tree-lined shores of Milford Haven in South Wales are echoed by Cornwall's Helford River, with its famous Frenchman's Creek, and by the submerged estuaries of the Fal and Fowey. Whether in Ireland or Cornwall they are all typical coastal features known as rias. Plymouth Sound, possibly England's best known ria, is the estuary of the Tamar. It can be seen to great effect from Brunel's famous Saltash railway bridge or the Tamar suspension bridge. The smaller, sheltered estuaries of the Yealm, the Dart and Salcombe are nearby. One of the finest views of the Salcombe estuary is from the National Trust gardens at Sharpitor.

Fjords, also the result of a submerged coastline, are valleys which have been greatly over-deepened by glaciers. They are typical of the coasts of North West Scotland and Donegal. They are most

weight caused considerable downsags in the Earth's crust. The localised coastal uplift which raised the beaches represents the slow recoil of the Earth's crust when relieved of this weight.

In the softer clays of lowland England the drowned estuaries are not cliff-bound but are stitched around with a maze of winding, shallow creeks, mud-flats and broad tracts of tidal marsh.

With some notable exceptions (see page 160) these are coasts of deposition where off-shore bars, sand spits and forelands help straighten out the many indentations caused by the submergence of the coast.

Thus, the marshy backwaters of Poole, Portsmouth and Chichester are almost closed off from the Channel but are kept open by tidal scour. Similar coastal scenery occurs round the Isle of Sheppey and the Medway in north Kent and in the great Essex marshlands of the Crouch, Blackwater and Colne. Farther north are the broad, drowned estuaries of Suffolk's Deben, Orwell and Stour.

Since waves attack any chink in the coastal armour, most of the largest bays in the British Isles are carved in rocks of relatively poor resistance. Belfast Lough, Solway Firth and Morecambe Bay occupy submerged basins of New Red Sandstone cradled between older, harder rocks. The Welsh bays of St

Celtic seascapes. The bones of a long-abandoned boat (left) near Dunvegan, Isle of Skye. Across the turbulent waters of St Finan's Bay, Co Kerry (below) lies the rock of Skellig Michael and its ancient monastic site

deeply cut where the glacier was constricted in its journey down valley. But near the valley mouth, where the glacier spreads out, downward erosion decreases. The deepening is not so marked and a rocky threshold bar occurs at the mouth of the valley. Sometimes this is amplified by a terminal moraine left by the glacier. This is why a fjord shallows at its mouth, unlike a ria which is at its deepest at its mouth. The characteristics of these two coastal features and the differences between them are shown in the illustration overleaf.

To complicate matters the rise in sea level which made the rias and fjords has been exceeded in places by an uplift of the land itself. This has created the so-called emergent coastlines of Ulster and Western Scotland which are seen in the raised beaches of those areas. Here the ice sheets were at their thickest and their

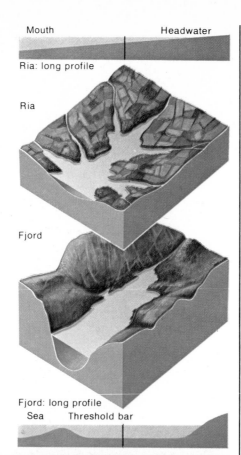

Mouth   Headwater

Ria: long profile

Ria

Fjord

Fjord: long profile
Sea   Threshold bar

A ria is formed when a river valley is drowned by a rise in sea level (above and top right). The Salcombe estuary shown here is a ria. Its deepest point, as the profile of its slope from source to sea shows, is at its mouth. A fjord also results from a drowned coastline but its valley was previously over-deepened by glaciers. Its shallowest point, as the lower profile shows, is at its mouth

The way a coastline is shaped when waves attack the cliffs depends on how resistant its rocks are. On the Dorset coast softer rocks adjacent to harder ones are being cut away more rapidly. This process has produced notable features such as Worbarrow Bay and (above) Lulworth Cove. At these places the sea has breached the Purbeck and Portland limestones and is cutting out the softer clays and sandstones

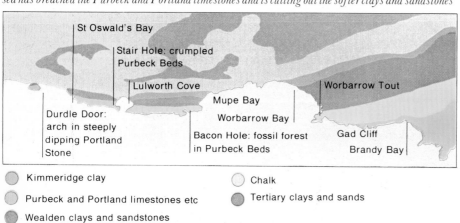

St Oswald's Bay

Stair Hole: crumpled
Purbeck Beds

Lulworth Cove   Worbarrow Tout

Mupe Bay
Durdle Door:
arch in steeply   Worbarrow Bay
dipping Portland
Stone   Bacon Hole: fossil forest   Gad Cliff
                   in Purbeck Beds   Brandy Bay

◯ Kimmeridge clay   ◯ Chalk

◯ Purbeck and Portland limestones etc   ◯ Tertiary clays and sands

◯ Wealden clays and sandstones

◯ Greensands and Gault clays

Brides, Carmarthen and Swansea were eroded largely in Carboniferous rocks. On a smaller scale the detailed differential etching of hard and soft rocks is well shown by Lulworth Cove and Worbarrow Bay in Dorset (illustration below) and by many of the North Devon coves between Lynmouth and Croyde.

Orkney's Scapa Flow and Shetland's deep-water voes, or inlets, are neither drowned estuaries nor simple bays. They are thought to have been formed in part by the post-glacial drowning of depressions formed by Earth movements.

Beaches and dunes

Camas Sgiotaig, a remote northern bay on the Hebridean Isle of Eigg, is the site of a rare and curious phenomenon. Here the sands of the beach 'sing' when walked upon. The Gaelic name means Bay of the Musical Sand.

In fact the song is not particularly musical but more of a squeaking note. Scientists have shown that the sound is something to do with (although no one knows exactly what) the uniform size and rounded form of the local sand grains which come from the weathering of a calcareous sandstone.

Other beaches have sands which do the same. Near Banff on Scotland's north-east coast the singing white sands come from the tough local quartzite and those at Porth Oer in the Lleyn Peninsula, Wales, are derived from similar rocks.

Not all beaches have sands, let alone singing or whistling ones. Whether a beach is sandy, pebbly or muddy depends partly on the character of the local bedrock.

If sandstones, or sand from glacial meltwaters predominate, then sandy beaches usually occur. Where chalk is exposed, flinty shingle beaches are common. Where rocks rich in clay are being eroded, or where muddy rivers debouch into estuaries, mudbanks abound. Sometimes beaches yield pebbles of great beauty (see page 171).

On the beach at Port na Churaich, the spot where St Columba landed on Iona more than 1400 years ago, it is possible to find beautiful Iona pebbles. These come from a submarine extension of Iona marble which the sea has eroded. This attractive green and white rock – a white metamorphosed limestone streaked by a green variety of serpentine – occurs in narrow veins among the Pre-Cambrian rocks of the seashore at the south end of the island.

It does not follow that a beach will be

Camel estuary, north Cornwall. Within a small compass this has every sort of coastline feature – cliffs, bays, dunes, mudflats and marshes

Maldon, Essex. A small, picturesque port at the head of the Blackwater estuary much concerned with sailing barges and the making of sea salt

made up of one type of material whether it be fine sand or pebbles. It is common to find within a single bay a beach which grades from the coarsest shingle through intermediate sands to the finest muds. This is because waves and currents are constantly sorting these different sized materials.

Not all beaches, whatever the publicity brochures claim, possess golden sands. Most are shades of yellow, red or brown but they can also range from purest white to dramatic black.

At Arisaig, south of the River Morar, the road passes through some of the most magnificent coastal scenery in Scotland. Here a narrow outcrop of psammite, a mica-spangled quartzite rock, has weathered into the glittering silvery sands which adorn a multitude of tiny bays. Yet at Glenbrittle on the Isle of Skye the beach sand is black, derived from the gabbro rock of the Cuillins. At Duntulm, Skye, where olivine minerals are common, the sands are dull green.

Many of the dazzling white beaches of Ireland's Connemara or the Hebridean 'machair' strands (illustration below) are due to the presence of myriads of broken shells.

A few localities boast coral beaches. At Claigan in northern Skye tiny pieces of attractive pinkish material have apparently been broken off growths which flourish just offshore in a few fathoms of water. But this Hebridean coral, like that in Connemara and at Tanera Beg in the Summer Isles near Ullapool, is the product not of coral polyps but of a seaweed called *Lithothamnion calcareum* which abstracts carbonate of lime from sea water.

Sand dunes occur on exposed coast-

Lack of harbours forces fishing boats to launch from the beach. These are at Hastings

lines where prevailing winds blow copious quantities of sand from the foreshore at low tide. Most large dune areas in the British Isles are found, therefore, on westerly coasts. Unspoiled stretches can be seen at Braunton Burrows, North Devon, and Perranporth, Cornwall. Wales has Harlech, Pendine and Swansea Bay. In north-west England there are the dunes of the Duddon estuary. Western Scotland boasts the Uists and Tiree while Dingle Bay and Donegal have Ireland's best examples.

Occasionally, the mobility of sand dunes has led to the burial of coastal settlements: 'lost' villages and churches occur at Kenfig Burrows, South Wales; St Piran, Cornwall; Forvie and Rattray, Aberdeenshire; and, most famous of all, at Skara Brae, Orkney, where an entire Stone Age village has been excavated.

Spits

Chesil Beach is a long, unbroken ridge of shingle which extends for over 15 miles (25km) on England's south coast from Bridport to the Isle of Portland. For eight miles south-east of Abbotsbury it is separated from the mainland by the tidal waters of a lagoon called the Fleet which is fed by the sea through a breach in a smaller, subsidiary bank of shingle running between Portland and Weymouth.

Chesil Beach is made up largely of rounded pebbles of flint. There are also some of quartzite and, at the Portland end, some local limestone pebbles. What is so extraordinary about the beach and its pebbles is the way in which they are systematically graded throughout its length. They increase in size from north-west to south-east, being about the size of a large pea near Bridport to fist-size and larger at Portland.

Experiments have shown that brick fragments thrown down on the beach move to the part of it where there are pebbles of similar size. Even more curious is the claim that the pebbles below water increase in size in the opposite direction!

It is this process of grading which makes Chesil Beach unique in the British Isles – and possibly in the world. Predictably this, and the sheer accumulation of material making the beach, has caused much controversy and speculation among geologists.

Various theories have been advanced as to how it was formed but it seems likely that it owes its origin to longshore drift (illustration opposite) which in this case cut off an existing body of water, leaving it as a lagoon. Another explanation is

Machair			Rough grazing		Bare rock
Beach	Dunes	Shell sand	Shell sand over peat	Peat over boulder clay	Peat stripped off boulder clay

W

Sea level

E

Lewisian Gneiss

The 'machair' is an unusual coastal landscape found in Scotland's Western Isles which has its origins in wind-blown sand.

The low, flat stretches of true machair lie to the landward of the beaches and dunes. It is a mixture of glacial sands and numerous marine organisms which have improved formerly barren tracts of land and made them capable of growing good crops.

Today, after hundreds of years of agricultural use the machair is a mature surface which has dark, rich, stoneless loams. It depends for its stability on nit-

rogen fixing plants. The key to its formation is the stabilizing of coastal dunes by marram grass. A later stage is the development of a dune pasture.

It is a vital ingredient in the economic and cultural life, and on an island like Uist it demonstrates how physical processes which shape the land surface, the growth of vegetation and land-use are interwoven into a delicately balanced system.

On these areas village settlement was arranged in strips, at right angles to the coast, so that each crofter had a share of each of the different soils.

that it was constructed by some form of off-shore bar being driven towards the land to form a bayhead bar, a shingle or sand bar which, as it names suggests, cuts off a bay. Those in Ireland west of Carnsore Point, Wexford, are similar but less impressive examples.

Off-shore bars are low, sandy, pebbly islands formed either by material combed down the beach by the back-wash of waves or more likely by material drifted by currents along the shore and deposited at the line where incoming waves first break. Off-shore bars can be seen at Culbin on the south shore of the Moray Firth, in the island of North Uist and at Scolt Head, Norfolk. Similar to Chesil Beach are Slapton Sands, Devon, and Loe Bar, Cornwall.

These different types of bars are classic features of what geologists call a constructive coastline. This is one being built up by marine deposition which produces smooth curving beaches of sand and shingle. The character of a constructive coastline, whether it consists of bars, spits or forelands (these will be explained below) depends on the nature of the original coastline, upon the energy of the constructive waves and tidal currents and on a continuing supply of sediment.

Where longshore drifting of material crosses river mouths it is unlikely that the estuary will be blocked because of continuing river action and tidal scour. Nevertheless, shingle spits have deflected rivers varying distances from their former mouths and away from the direction of dominant wave approach.

In East Anglia the rivers Alde and Butley have been deflected southwards by the pebbly extension of Orfordness. The Alde flows behind this for about nine miles parallel to the sea (see illustration). Yarmouth, Blakeney Point and Spurn Head (see page 162) are other well known East Coast spits. So are those on the south coast at Hurst Castle and Calshot in the Solent, the Sandbanks peninsula at the mouth of Poole Harbour, Dawlish Warren and Braunton Burrows in Devonshire and, in the same county, the splendid pebble ridge of Westward Ho!

Occasionally an extending spit will join an existing island to the shore creating a tombolo. By linking Portland Island to the mainland Chesil Beach created Britain's largest and best known tombolo, but on a smaller scale there are numerous examples in the Isles of Scilly, Orkney and Shetland including the picturesque St Ninian's Isle. In Ireland there are large tombolos at Rossguill,

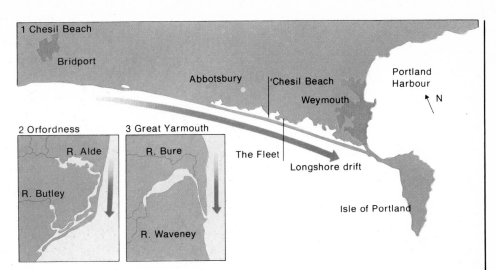

How spits are formed. 1 At Chesil Beach the longshore drift of material has cut off an existing body of water leaving it as a lagoon. 2 The spit at Orfordness has deflected rivers southwards so they flow parallel with the sea. 3 Much the same has happened, but on a smaller scale, at Great Yarmouth

Raised beaches, Dunure, Ayrshire. Signs that sea level was once higher

Donegal, and at Castlegregory, Kerry.

At certain places on the coast waves approach from more than one direction and because of this, complex shingle forelands accumulate. Here shingle spits coalesce and cut off the former coastline completely from the sea, leaving the intervening space to be converted into marsh. The best example of this is Dungeness in Kent with its abandoned shoreline and Romney Marsh behind (see page 163).

In post-glacial times during periods of higher sea level waves and currents fashioned other forelands which remain to-day as raised beach features. Selsey Bill, Sussex, is an example of one of these 'fossil' forelands. So is Magilligan Point, Co Londonderry. On the Moray Firth there are a pair of matching raised beaches at Chanonry Point. At Ardersier a whole suite of raised beaches occurs.

The extensive raised beaches of Northern Ireland and Scotland contain many other cases of old shorelines of deposition which are now high and dry above the waves.

Wind-blown waves play a powerful part in shaping the coast. As a wave approaches the shore its lower part is slowed by friction with the sea-bed. Its upper part continues moving but since it is unsupported from below it develops into a breaker which topples over and sends a mass of water foaming up the beach. This is called the swash. Its return is the backwash. The first pushes pebbles and sand towards the land, the latter carries them back towards the sea. Constructive waves 1 have a powerful swash and little backwash. Destructive waves 2 have a

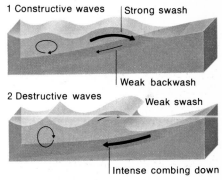

strong backwash which combs down the beach material. In calm conditions only limited amounts of beach material are moved; in storms quite the opposite. If the prevailing wind drives the waves ashore obliquely, then sands and pebbles are also pushed up the beach obliquely. The backwash then returns them straight down the beach. This continual zig-zag move-

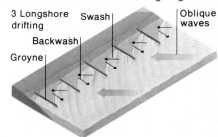

ment which transports material length-wise along the coast is known as long-shore drift. Groynes help arrest it and build up a beach.

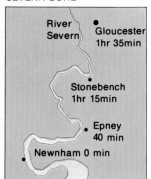

SEVERN BORE

WHIRLPOOL

PORTLAND EDDY

Left: The progress of the Severn Bore showing the time it takes to reach successive points up-river. Centre: Corrievreckan Whirlpool on Scotland's west coast is at its fiercest when the flood tide flows north through the Sound of Jura and then west into the strait between the island. Right: The Portland Tidal Eddy in the English Channel has built up a huge bank of shell fragments called the Shambles

Tides

The periodical rise and fall of large masses of water is a remarkable phenomenon of the coast. The tides can make as much as 40ft (12m) difference to the depth of water in places although the average tidal range in the British Isles is about 15ft (4.5m).

Most places get two low and two high tides every 24 hours. There are exceptions to this pattern: Southampton gets a double high tide, that is four high tides a day.

This is partly due to the existence of two entrances to the Solent. The tide of the Channel gives it its first high water by way of the West Solent, its second by way of Spithead two hours later. This unusual tidal regime has favoured the development of Southampton as a port.

The usual interval between the tides is 12hrs 25mins, roughly half the time the moon takes to circle the earth. The gravitational pull of moon, sun and earth combine to produce the tidal pattern; the tidal rise and fall is related to the relative positions of the moon and sun, with the tide reaching a maximum height a day or so after a new or full moon.

This is called a *spring* tide (nothing to do with the season) which rises higher and falls lower than usual. The minimum tides with small range are called *neap* tides. Both occur at intervals of about a fortnight.

About the time of the spring and autumn equinoxes in March and September, when the length of day is equal to night, the spring tides are generally the highest and lowest of the year.

A rising tide is known as a flood tide, a falling one an ebb tide. Slack water occurs between ebb and flood when the tide is almost at a standstill.

The configuration of an estuary or river mouth can turn a rising tide into a tidal wave called a bore. The Severn Bore is a wall of water 3ft to 9ft (0.9m to 2.7m) high which moves upstream during the period of spring tides.

The bore is most striking during the equinoxes. As the incoming tidal water is driven into the constricting estuary it rises in a high, abrupt front which overrides the slower river flow. It can pass from Sharpness to Gloucester at a rate which increases from $5\frac{1}{2}$ to 13 mph (8.8 to 20.9kph). It is best seen at Stonebench (see map) on the eastern bank of the river, three miles (4.8km) downstream from Gloucester.

There are places where the tide forms whirlpools. Corrievreckan Whirlpool on the west coast of Scotland is a 9-knot tidal race which produces a swirling pool of water of intense ferocity.

It is caused by rock pinnacles below water and develops most strongly when the flood tide sets north through the Sound of Jura (see map) and then drives west into the strait separating the northern tip of the island of Jura from neighbouring Scarba.

With a westerly wind blowing the roar of the whirlpool can be heard on the mainland coast five miles away at Craignish – and it can be seen from the hill above this point.

The Portland Tidal Eddy is another great circulating mass of water but larger than Corrievreckan. It develops in the English Channel in the lee of Portland Bill as the flood tide makes progress eastwards (see map). Within the slack water of the 'eye' a great bank of broken shell fragments, the Shambles, has been built up over the centuries. Although the Shambles is not visible from the shore it produces disturbed water and rips under certain conditions of wind and tide.

Coastal erosion

An unceasing battle between land and sea is being waged on the coasts of the British Isles. In places the sea is winning, eating into the land with dramatic results. Elsewhere the land is gaining from the sea.

The Holderness coast of Yorkshire is suffering the worst coastal erosion in Europe, possibly in the world, and now lies nearly a quarter-mile (402m) back from where it was 200 years ago. Farther south, off the Suffolk coast, the once thriving port of Dunwich is no more than a scattering of masonry on the sea-bed. Yet, in other places the valuable process of coastal accretion has resulted in the reclamation of substantial tracts of land, especially on the estuaries of the Humber and the Ribble, and around the shores of the Wash. A rough stocktaking suggests that the British Isles gain as much from the sea as they lose to it.

This is small consolation to owners of cliff-top properties on the Yorkshire and East Anglian coasts who have watched them destroyed by the North Sea's onslaught. Here it has been devouring land throughout recorded history. In the days of Julius Caesar the Holderness coast was, according to some estimates, two miles (3.2km) farther east than it is now. Such loss of land, however, would not be attributable to erosion alone. In those days the sea level was lower but after 1200 it rose again drowning the low lying land.

In recent times the parish church at Mappleton, south of Hornsea, has increasingly come under threat. In 1786 the church was 633yds (579m) from the sea; in 1835, 554yds (506.5m), and in 1912, 418yds (382m). In January 1979 it was only 170yds (155m) from the nearest point of the cliff top, and the sea is still advancing. In 1978 the owner of a shop and cafe at Skipsea reported losing 64ft (19.5m) of land to the sea in four years.

The stretch of coast between Bridlington and Spurn Head boasts more villages swallowed by the sea than anywhere else in Europe. About thirty have vanished from the map (see p. 162). Auburn, south of Bridlington, was the last to be lost. All that remains of the name is Auburn Farm which once had the village to the east of it. The farm itself has lost 17 acres (6 hectares) to the sea in the last 40 years.

Some experts see continued erosion producing catastrophic results. Towns such as Hornsea and Withernsea are protected by sea walls but as the coast between them is gnawed away they are

The crumbling coast of Holderness. At Skipsea cliff-top chalets are losing their gardens to the sea. Before long waves will destroy the chalets too

Derelict barn slipping into the sea at Waxholm and the end of the road at Tunstall. Both are on the vulnerable Holderness coast

Collapsing cliffs near Dunwich, Suffolk, and beach defences at West Runton, Norfolk. Groynes protecting one beach may starve another of sand

161

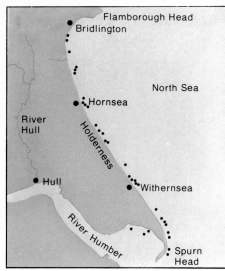

The lost villages of Yorkshire's Holderness coast. Each black dot represents a settlement claimed by the sea. Over 30 have vanished between Bridlington and Spurn Head

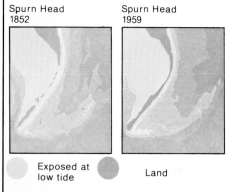

Spurn Head 1852   Spurn Head 1959

⬤ Exposed at low tide   ⬤ Land

The changing face of Spurn Head. In a little over 100 years the shape of this famous East Coast spit has altered dramatically. In 1852 it consisted of a chain of islets. By 1959 it was a continuous unbroken coastal feature, as it is today. Without man-made sea defences it would become a string of small islands again

gradually becoming 'capes'. If the sea were allowed to break through into the inland drainage system of Holderness they could become isolated at the end of peninsulas.

The sand and shingle spit of Spurn Head is the most vulnerable part of this coast. It used to lose land to the sea at a rate of a metre a year but this is now increasing. Although groynes have helped hold the spit, the cutting back of the coast farther north means that it too is forced to retreat. A north-westerly gale combined with abnormally high spring tides could wash the southern end of the point away.

There are two views as to what has happened and is happening to the spit. One is that over the centuries the spit has shown periods of growth and retreat with several changes in its position. The cycle of change is thought to take place over a period of about 300 years. Its present position has been held for 150 years.

An alternative view is that the present continuous feature is artificially maintained. If it were left to natural forces it would break down into a string of islets as it was in the first half of the last century.

Should the sea breach the spit, creating a tidal channel between it and the estuary, a new Spurn Head would appear, extending west of the present one, which would disappear.

Why is this coast so fragile? Holderness is a gift of the Ice Age which the sea is taking back. The coast consists of soft boulder clay deposited at the foot of the old line of chalk sea cliffs along the edge of the Wolds. If erosion worsens there is a possibility of Holderness disappearing and the sea washing against its former cliffs once more. This would take thousands of years and assumes no emergency coastal defence measures.

Obviously the soft cliffs of sand and clay which occur along much of England's east coast are particularly susceptible to erosion during winter storms. Steep-fronted waves breaking along the shoreline can, within a few hours, lower a beach by as much as 10ft (3.5m). Then the waves are able to launch a frontal assault on the cliffs.

This happened at Torcross in Devon in January 1979 when property was severely damaged by the sea. An earlier storm lowered the beach level which left little protection from the January storm.

Dunwich provides an exceptional record of coastal retreat over several centuries. Founded in the 7th century it became an important medieval town

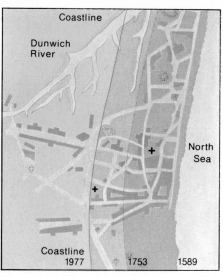

Town plan of Dunwich, Suffolk, in 1589. The broken lines show past coastlines and how much of the once-thriving town has been lost to the North Sea over nearly 400 years

and seat of a bishopric. Then it suffered almost total destruction by the sea. In Norman times its lands were already being eaten away and in 1326 a great storm caused severe flooding and destruction. A detailed town plan of 1589 shows how much of the town remained even then (see map) but the sea was paring back the cliffs at a rapid rate. By 1677 it had reached the market place and the inhabitants sold the market cross. Twenty-five years later the Town Hall was destroyed and the sea was washing at the doors of St Peter's Church. Between 1589 and 1753 a broad strip, 1000 feet (304m) wide, on the outer edge of the town was lost. The remains of All Saints, last of old Dunwich's churches, finally fell down the cliff in 1919.

Erosion has continued to the present day (although at a slightly slower rate) leaving only a vestige of town and port.

At Hallsands, South Devon, man himself has contributed to coastal erosion. Until 1897 this was a fishing hamlet of 16 cottages tucked beneath the cliffs and apparently safe behind a broad beach of shingle. Then a contractor was given permission to remove shingle from close inshore for construction work.

But he removed 500,000 tons from the beach itself which was lowered by about 12ft. Soon the cottages were under direct attack from the waves. The final blow came in 1917 when a severe storm from the east virtually destroyed the hamlet.

In the constant battle between land and sea the outcome is not always on the debit side. Today there are thousands of acres of valuable farmland which were once beneath the sea. The process of regaining it is often started by the sea itself and then completed by man.

In sheltered situations mud brought in by the tides accumulates to a great thickness. When the sea is excluded by throwing a bank round the area the land can be reclaimed. On the Norfolk shore of the Wash 8000 acres (3239 hectares) have been gained since Roman times and in the South Holland area of Lincolnshire 37,000 acres (14,980 hectares).

Reclamation has also taken place at the mouth of the River Parrett in Somerset, round Southampton Water and Poole Harbour, and in Morecambe Bay. In the last 100 years *Spartina townsendii*, a species of salt marsh grass with the ability to hold and bind silts and muds, has been an important aid in gaining land.

An outstanding example of the sea itself making land is provided by Romney Marsh. Here, long before there was

Romney Marsh today. Rich lowland sheep country which had its beginnings in sandbanks similar to the Goodwin Sands

any marsh, the sea threw up a barrier of sandbanks and from that point in pre-historic times the evolution of the present day Romney Marsh can be traced.

This, and the development of the Dungeness promontory, has taken place over thousands of years. The rise of sea level following the melting of the ice sheets led to the formation of a shallow bay enclosed by a low line of cliffs. This persisted for much of pre-historic time.

Elongated sandbanks which formed offshore were very much like the Good-win Sands of today. When the Romans landed and over-ran Kent these 'island' sandbanks, surrounded by accumulating marsh, formed the only suitable areas for settlement.

The area between these dry points and the old cliff line was damp and marshy. From about the 6th century the sea level began to drop and this marshy area became better drained and more suitable for settlement.

But in the 13th century violent storms and a period of rising sea level posed a serious threat. Only the building of Dymchurch Wall and the drainage schemes of Dutch experts prevented the marsh from returning to the sea.

The cost of fighting the sea is high. Sea-walls, which last 30–40 years, cost about £1.5 million a mile to build. Revetments, lines of boulders or large stones piled at weak points, are cheaper but have a shorter life. And a well-built groyne costs about £50,000.

Groynes which successfully prevent a beach from being stripped away rely on the longshore drift (see page 159) of sand and shingle. Most of the sand comes from

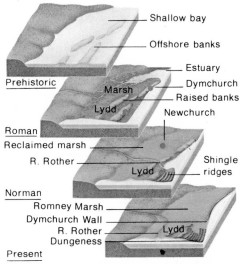

The four stages in the making of Romney Marsh from prehistoric times to the present day

cliffs which are being eroded; but if the cliffs are being protected successfully by sea defences the beaches down-coast are starved of sand.

Then the groynes cease to do their work effectively and what was a stable beach starts to be eroded. This can be seen at Clacton, Essex, where the beach is disappearing because its supply of sand has been reduced by sea defence work and dredging farther north.

It might, however, be restored by 'beach feeding'. Some engineers believe money spent on such schemes is better used than on building groynes and sea-walls. They argue that a good beach is the best defence against the sea.

Beach feeding involves either pumping sand ashore or dumping it on the beach by lorry and letting longshore drift transport it to where it is needed elsewhere. The technique is quite common in the United States and Holland and has been tried successfully at Portobello, near Edinburgh, and at Bournemouth and Teignmouth. Not only does it help protect coast and property. Popular sea-side resorts which depend for part of their prosperity on their sands may see it as a way of protecting their prime asset.

163

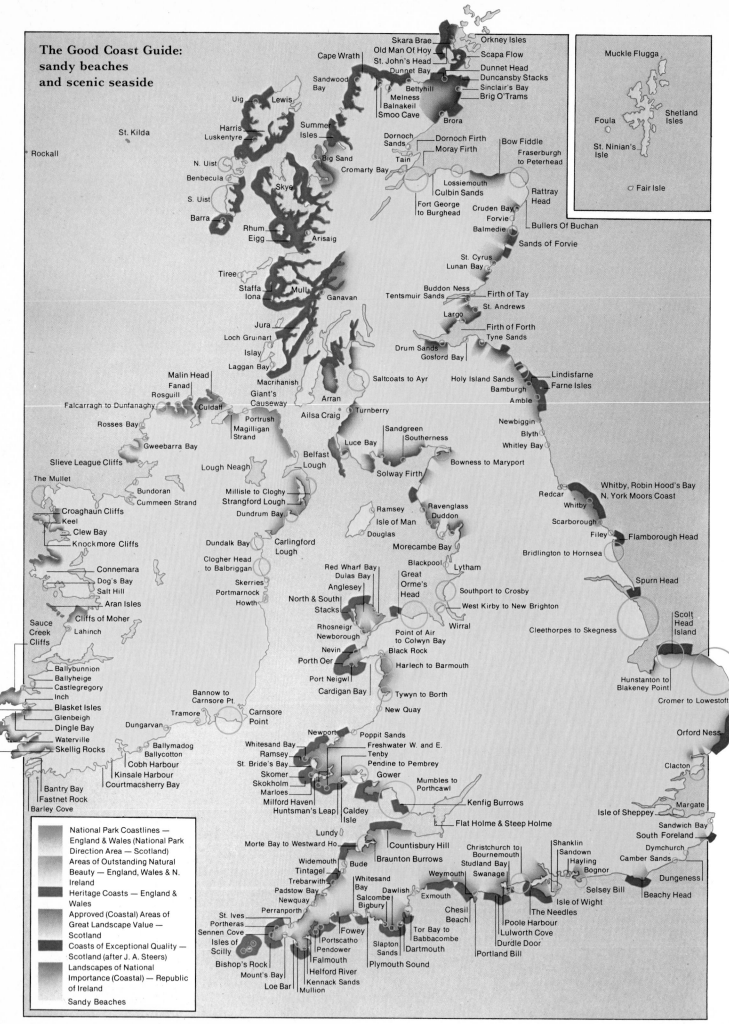

Major coastal features mentioned in this chapter are plotted on the map

The living world of the sea coast: its marvels and its mysteries

In the beginning the sea was life. Scientists believe that plants and animals of the land, ourselves included, originated in its salty, life-supporting waters. In the story of evolution the margin of sea and land was a great barrier which had to be crossed. It was a crossing which lasted millions of years. Yet much of the marvel of that great evolutionary progress, which took the creatures of the sea and made them into creatures of the land, is still to be seen upon the shore.

Changing conditions imposed by tidal regimes, the seasons and the terrain require of the plants and animals that live there a degree of adaptability and development near to miraculous. And, for all the hazards of pollution and development by man, it still provides a home for a wide variety of them.

It is not the easiest of environments, although parts of it are more felicitous to life than others. The problems of its inhabitants are those of coping with extremes: the alternate wetting and drying out of the shore with the flooding and ebbing of the tides; the mixing of salt water with fresh in river mouth and estuary; the violent turbulence and pounding of the waves one moment, the switch to a profound calm the next.

Yet, for all its harshness, it is beneficient, supplying the essential ingredients of life – light, water, oxygen and minerals. They are provided within the context of a remarkable tidal rhythm to which the pulse of seashore life is tuned.

Life at the top of the beach, where tides rarely reach, is moistened by spray. Life at the very bottom of the beach thrives in a world which is nearly always covered by salt water. And between the first, which marine biologists identify as the splash zone, and the latter which is the lower shore, other zones of life grade one into another. Each of these zones provides a different habitat to which seashore creatures and plants have adapted.

The variety of life also depends on whether the shore is one of rock, sand, shingle, mud or marsh. On rock beaches the signs of life are much more obvious, with animals and plants clinging to the rock surfaces; on sandy beaches, where animals burrow below the surface, less so. In the following pages some classic seashore habitats – cliffs, sand, shingle and saltmarsh, and rock pools – are described, and their mysteries and inhabitants revealed.

Seabirds soar at cliffs by making use of 1 eddies produced by off-shore winds and 2 up-draughts created by on-shore winds

The sea cliffs: precarious refuge for determined colonists

Sea cliffs are among the last true relics of wild Britain. Lashed by gales, battered by waves, the bare, steep cliffs present an inhospitable and barren face to man. But their narrow ledges and breezy tops provide a precious foothold for wild flowers and a near impregnable refuge where seabirds can find space to form colonies and breed.

For, among all the birds of the British Isles, it is the seabirds who most prefer living in colonies. Many of them return to the same cliff nesting site year after year. Some of the sites are enormous. St Kilda in the Outer Hebrides, famous for its fulmars and gannets, has colonies with tens of thousands of nests. The most crowded are usually those of gannets and guillemots. The reasons for living in colonies are related to various factors. The abundance of fish as a food supply and the security of living in large groups in a safe site are the most important.

One of the sights of the sea cliffs are the birds soaring about them. As the wind from the sea hits the cliffs, gulls and other birds ride the updraughts which are produced. If the wind is blowing in the opposite direction, from the land, it spills over the edge of the cliff and then curls upwards in eddies which the birds use to gain height (see illustration).

By harnessing the roller-coaster power of these invisible air currents, the cliff dwellers – gulls, kittiwakes, fulmars, ravens – are able to conserve precious energy.

A past master of the soaring technique is the herring gull. Of all the sounds of the sea cliffs, none is more evocative than its wailing cry as it glides about its business. The red spot on the beak stimulates the chick to beg for food. Its rapacious relative, the great black-backed gull has a deeper cry and is the largest of the native gulls, with a 65in (1.6m) wingspan.

The kittiwake which cries its own name, is a successful cliff ledge colonist. It cements its seaweed nest to the rock with guano. The guillemot and razorbill belong to the auk family, cliff-dwellers which spend much time swimming and diving for fish, and are therefore particularly vulnerable to oil spills. The puffin is another auk. It nests in clifftop burrows and is easily identified by its multi-coloured parrot bill.

The cormorant and its smaller, bottle-green cousin, the shag, prey on fish which they chase underwater. Afterwards, they perch on rocks to dry their outstretched wings. The gull-like bird boomeranging around the cliffs on stiff, straight wings is a fulmar. The curious tubular nostrils are an ornithological mystery; their function is still obscure.

Farther out to sea, the big snowy white bird with black wing-tips soaring and skimming the troughs and crests of the waves is the gannet, an ocean wanderer and spectacular crash-diver that breeds in large offshore colonies on rock stacks, from Scotland to the Skelligs.

Around the coasts of Wales and Ireland the chough may be recognised by its curved red bill. Impossible to confuse them or their shrill whistling with the

White sea campion on flower-covered cliff

Key to illustration: 1 Red Valerian   4 Puffins 5 Guillemot 6 Peregrine Falcon   9 Rock Dove 10 Herring Gull

2 Humming-bird Hawkmoth 3 Fulmar   7 Cream-spot Tiger moth 8 Golden Samphire   11 Kittiwakes 12 Herring Gull 13 Clouded

Yellow 14 Clover 15 Kittiwake 16 Raven 17 Black-backed Gull 18 Cormorant 19 Sea

Pinks 20 Gannet 21 Gannet 22 Basking Shark 23 Atlantic Seals 24 Slender Thistle

25 Painted Lady 26 Chough 27 Razorbill 28 Sea-Campion 29 Oak Eggar Caterpillar

guttural croaking of the raven, a bird of the rocky western coasts where it can often be seen twirling and tumbling in the up-draughts. Here, too, the peregrine breeds in remote eyries, dashing out to stoop at a luckless rock dove, ancestor of our town pigeons.

Other cliff-top fliers are the painted lady and clouded yellow. These butterflies are summer migrants from across the Channel. Thistles attract the former, clover the latter.

In June they are joined by another migrant, the day-flying hummingbird hawkmoth, seen here buzzing around red valerian. The cream-spot tiger is more nocturnal, and most commonly found in the southwest, where you may also see the finger-sized full-grown caterpillar of the oak eggar crawling over the cliffside turf in midsummer.

In summer the cliffs are bright with cushions of thrift or sea pink, together with sea campion, a flower which may have lived in Britain since *before* the Ice Age, and the fleshy-leaved golden samphire. Lichens add a deeper splash of yolk yellow to the rocks. Our illustration shows the common *Xanthoria parientina*. Like all lichens, it is a good indicator of clean air.

On the rocks below, the grey or Atlantic seal rests between fishing forays. An adult bull seal can reach a length of 12ft (3.6m). The basking shark is even bigger, but is harmless and feeds on plankton. In Atlantic waters basking sharks often cruise close inshore during warm weather.

Sand, shingle and saltmarsh: wildlife at the tide's edge

On low lying coasts the cliffs give way to shingle bars, sand dunes and salt marsh – three very different wildlife habitats, each with its own characteristic flora and fauna, and sometimes problems.

The pounding of the waves on a shingle beach can, as we have seen, strip it of several feet of material. Even in calmer conditions wave action constantly grinds the pebbles and sand grains against each other, crushing and destroying anything living. Anyone who has paddled on such a beach knows how painful it can be as each wave, charged with pebbles and shingle, swirls round the feet. A shingle beach is virtually a desert. Yet plants do survive.

One of the most spectacular flowers of a shingle coast is the frosty blue sea holly. The beautiful yellow horned poppy, with

long curved pods like curlews' bills, grows here too.

A familiar bird of the shingle ridges is the ringed plover with its harlequin head and liquid cry. The nest is a mere scrape among the stones, in which eggs and chicks are perfectly camouflaged.

Another bird which breeds on shingle spits is the little tern, smallest of the terns or 'sea swallows'. All terns have forked tails but the little tern may be identified by its yellow legs and black-tipped yellow bill as it hovers in search of sand eels or whitebait.

Sand dunes, where the spray is salt, the sun hot, the wind strong and the sand always on the move, often drifting in huge quantities, make a difficult environment. The plants which survive most successfully are those which sprout easily, send runners through the sand, can cope with drought and struggle back to the surface if they are buried.

The most distinctive is marram grass. Invaluable in the fight against erosion, its long, tough 2oft (6m) roots bind the shifting sands. Among the prettier plants is the sea bindweed with its pink and

white striped flowers. Growing along the drift line on the seaward side of the dunes, look for the succulent leaves and pale lilac flowers of sea rocket.

On the Lancashire coast near Southport, freshwater pools, or dune-slacks, appear among the sandhills, providing a breeding ground for one of Britain's rarest wild creatures, the endangered natterjack toad.

The richest of all coastal habitats are the estuaries, a magical mingling of mudflats, salt marsh and coiling tidal creeks which are usually sheltered from the ferocity of the sea. They are alive with the wild cries and flickering wings of wading birds like the redshank. The mudbanks harbour enormous populations of lugworm, ragworm, crustaceans and molluscs. The handsome shelduck, a common sight on many estuaries, feeds mainly on molluscs. It nests in old rabbit burrows.

In summer the saltings are bright with marsh flowers; sea aster and purple swathes of sea lavender. Here, too, grows the succulent marsh samphire, a great East Anglian delicacy which can be

Key to illustration: 1 Yellow Horned Poppy 2 Ringed Plover 3 Little Tern 4 Sea Rocket 5 Sea Holly 6 Marram Grass 7 Shelduck 8 Sea Aster 9 Redshank 10 Sea Lavender 11 Marsh Samphire 12 Spartina 13 Natterjack Toad 14 Sea Bindweed

boiled and served with melted butter.

The carpet of the sea marsh is composed of tough grasses that thrive on the salty inter-tidal mudflats. Among them, spartina, which binds the mud to form continuous stretches of turf, helps raise the level of the marsh.

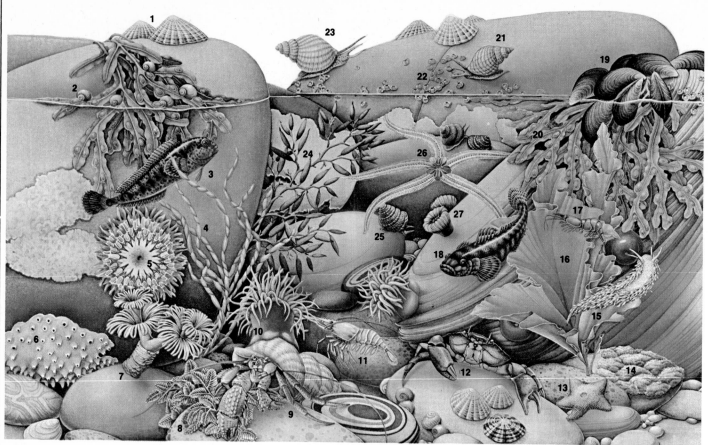

The rock pool: round-the-clock struggle for survival

The rock pool is a mysterious world: a complex habitat of vibrant colour and varied life-forms evolved for survival in the transitory no man's land between the tides.

Every rock pool is an ocean in microcosm. But whereas the ocean provides a relatively constant habitat, the rock pool is exposed to a daily cycle of extremes dictated by the tides, and the life that thrives within it has had to adapt to the perils and hardships of an inter-tidal existence – or perish.

An obvious hazard is the sheer weight and force of the crashing waves. To withstand them, the limpet clings fast to its rock with proverbial tenacity. But there are many other problems which marine life has to overcome before the rock pool can be colonised.

Hot sunny days cause rock pools to evaporate and become saltier; rainy days dilute the sea water. At night the water temperature in a rock pool may fall below that of the sea by several degrees. On a sunny summer's day it may become much warmer than the sea only to be rapidly cooled by the returning tide. (In winter, when the wind is colder than the sea, the effect is reversed and the incoming tide can actually warm the pool.)

The smaller or shallower the pool, and the farther it lies from low water level, the greater the extremes of temperature and salinity are likely to be. Indeed, some pools – those that lie in the so-called 'splash zone' above the high water mark – are replenished only by spray or by the waves of exceptionally high tides or rough seas. Their brackish waters are more hostile and lack the rich variety of life to be found in the true marine pools which are filled by the tide every day.

Photosynthesis – that miraculous alchemy which enables plants to harness the energy of sunlight with the aid of chlorophyll and manufacture food from carbon dioxide and water – also exerts a powerful influence on rock pool life.

By day the seaweeds are busily taking in carbon dioxide and liberating precious oxygen into the water. After dark, when photosynthesis ceases, the process is reversed, and all rock pool life – plants as well as animals – relies on the dissolved oxygen and releases carbon dioxide in exchange. In the open sea the effect is minimal, but in the miniature crowded world of the rock pool the build-up of carbon dioxide causes the water to become increasingly acid as the night goes on. These changes could render the rock pool uninhabitable, had not life adapted to withstand such extremes.

It is a tight-knit world, in which surprising relationships sometimes develop. The hermit crab and its anemone

are a well-known example; a symbiotic association between two different species for their mutual benefit. The anemone attaches itself to the discarded whelk shell in which the soft-bodied hermit crab has taken up residence, and its sting-armed tentacles provide additional protection for its host. In return the crab transports the anemone around the pool, providing it with more feeding opportunities.

Unless you approach a rock pool cautiously, you will miss half of what is there. Animals like the tube worm retract instantly at the slightest shadow; shrimps and small fish like the shanny, rock goby and (harmless) sea scorpion dart away.

The most rewarding pools to explore are those which provide plenty of cover – stones, crannies and clumps of seaweed – where animals can find refuge from the hungry prowlers of the tidelines.

Oystercatchers stab with bright orange bills at bivalve molluscs such as the glossy clusters of blue-black mussels. Turnstones use their slightly upturned bills to pry under stones – hence their name – in search of small crustaceans.

So camouflage plays an important part in the lives of the rock pool inhabitants who seek to avoid detection. Prawns and shrimps are hard to see because they are translucent. The chameleon shrimp, a small relative of the common shrimp or prawn, goes one step further and disguises itself by changing the size of its colour spots to merge with a red or green background. But it is a slow job, taking about a week to change.

The dog whelk changes colour with its diet. It is a flesh-eater, preying on barnacles and mussels (which cannot move away) or limpets (which can). The predatory whelk bores through their shells with its rasping tongue and sucks out the succulent innards. White or yellowish dog whelk shells mean a diet of barnacles; brown or mauve mean mussels.

Not all the animals move. Many sit tight and wait for the food to come to them. Sponges are primitive animals living in colonies, sifting the water which passes through their communal pores. Sea anemones, those exquisite flowers of the rock pool, are in fact animals, who wait for their prey with gently waving tentacles. A shrimp or small fish touching the tentacle is first dazed by the anemone's sting; other tentacles close round it, and stuff the living food into a central maw. The common beadlet anemone has a blue spot at the base of each tentacle, which marks a battery of stinging cells. The beadlet anemone retracts to a blob of jelly when struck or when the tide leaves it exposed. The larger dahlia anemone does the same, but is disguised to look like rock by the warts on its body.

Much of the pool life emerges at night, and just like the African plains, there are hunters and browsers. Among the latter are the limpets, which move around when the tide is in, grazing the rocks bare of algae.

Many animals cannot see red light so if you want to extend your exploration, go down to the beach with a red torch. But whether you investigate by night or day, remember that pool life, like any wild life, is finely in balance. If you disturb stones in your quest, replace them as they were, because animals which live on the bottom side of the stone cannot survive on the top. Such is the exact fit of rock pool life.

Pebbles. The sea coasts of the British Isles have an enormous variety of pebbles. The following selection describes some of the most distinctive and commonly found types.

1 Flint. The pebbles vary in shape from highly irregular to spherical. Being so hard they may have a high degree of polish. Flint pebbles can be picked up almost anywhere on the coast from Humberside to South Devon.

2 Quartzite. The pebbles are grey, yellow or liver-coloured. Hard, smooth and rounded discs, rollers and spheres occur by the million in the famous Budleigh Salterton bank in south Devon. Also Scottish, Yorkshire, Hampshire, Devon, Wirral and Lancashire coasts.

3 Granite. The rocks range widely in colour and texture. All are largely composed of the hard minerals quartz and feldspar. Their pink or yellow colours are due to tiny amounts of iron oxides; the dark specks are mica or tourmaline. The coast of east and south-west Scotland, north-west and north-east Ireland and south Cornwall have large granite pebble populations.

4 Jasper. These pebbles, distinctive and rare, occur in areas where the dominant materials are granite and basalt ores. Silica, in the form known as chalcedony, is the principal constituent of jasper. The blood-red colour is produced by submicroscopic iron oxide particles.

5 Limestone. This is so variable in composition and physical character that it is difficult to generalise. The pebbles can be any colour, soft or hard, full of calcite crystals or fossils. Some, such as marble, can be polished until they have a mirror-like quality. At the other extreme is the limestone pebble which has been bored by tiny organisms, penetrating the outer centimetre or so, until it resembles a sponge. How it happens is still uncertain, for every surface of the pebble seems to be covered uniformly. They are common along many coastlines.

6 Porphyry. This pebble is a trachyte in composition. This means it is made up of the minerals feldspar and amphiboles with their crystals characteristically set in a finer-grained homogenous matrix which gives the porphyritic texture. The white pieces are feldspar crystals, the much smaller greenish specks are crystals of amphiboles. Porphyries are hard volcanic or igneous rocks. They are very attractive and can be dressed or polished for building and ornamental purposes. The pebbles are found along the Cornish coast and, more easily, along the coasts of western Scotland, Northern Ireland, and south-east Ireland.

7 Milky Quartz. Quartz is the most indestructible and one of the most widespread of all common rock-forming materials. It occurs in virtually every kind of sedimentary and crystalline rock. Flint, chert, jasper, chalcedony, agate, smoky quartz, rose quartz, milky quartz are all varieties. Pebbles are common on the Celtic coastlines – south-west England, Wales, Scotland and Ireland. They are also abundant in glacial deposits along the northern and eastern coasts.

Chapter Seven
Leisure in the Countryside

It is only in the last 100 years that the countryside has become a playground for urban man. Before that it was simply where most people lived and worked. Now it is being used for recreations as diverse as the landscape itself. For some, like these ramblers in the Peak District, it is the rugged slopes of upland Britain that beckon. Others take to the hills on horseback or to climb precipitous rock crags. Then there are the gentler pursuits of angling, boating or merely enjoying a picnic and a simple drive or stroll through pleasant countryside. Even in these crowded islands it is possible to leave the bustle of city life far behind, especially if you know how to use a map. How to enhance your enjoyment of such diverse activities in the countryside is the theme of this chapter

Bed and Breakfast: a welcome sign for travellers found from farms to bungalows

1 Birds eggs
It is generally illegal to take or destroy the eggs of wild birds, exceptions sometimes being made for edible eggs of gulls, for example. Birds themselves may not be shot or harmed by members of the public or even, in the case of rare birds of prey, to be photographed at the nest in case this causes any disturbance

2 Rare plants, and those not so rare
It is now totally illegal to damage or even pick our 21 rarest flowers (see Ch. 10), except for 'good farming' or licensed research. It is also illegal to dig up any wild plant without the permission of the land-owner or occupier, mushrooms and their like excepted

3 Rare animals
It is illegal to kill, injure or capture (or attempt to) smooth snakes, sand lizards, natterjack toads, large blue butterfly, otter and two rare species of bats

4 Is it a footpath?
The definitive maps showing footpaths and bridle paths can be consulted in District and County Council offices; also some libraries. These maps show up-to-date changes. (However, Ordnance

Rambling: exploring 120,000 miles of public right of way

Rambling in the British Isles is more than a holiday and satisfying form of exercise. It is a close and natural contact with the land which provides a more intimate insight into the mysteries of the countryside and enables you to enjoy sights, sounds and scents denied to road or rail travellers. Moorland, coastal or pastoral scenes lie within easy reach of virtually every town or city and are often accessible only on foot.

Footpaths exist in Britain in greater number than anywhere in the world. But despite their supposed legal protection they are all too often overgrown, obstructed, vandalised or even ploughed up. The illustration shows ramblers their rights, the slight protection given to wild animals and plants – and what abuses walkers might find. The greatest hope for saving footpaths as public rights of way undoubtedly lies in the popularity of rambling itself.

Since 1935 the Ramblers Association has campaigned to secure legislation for the protection of natural beauty, the establishment of national parks, the preservation of footpaths and the right to walk on mountains, moors and shores. The result is a network of well over 120,000 miles (192,000km) of footpaths and bridleways where the public has the legal right to walk. There are also great tracts of common and access land which offer unrestricted walking and many nature or forest trails offering scenic routes through beautiful woodland

Nor is rambling limited to summer. Properly clothed and equipped, you can walk throughout the year. Only when you take to the hills is it vital to follow the rules. They are detailed overleaf, but the most important is never to allow enthusiasm to overtake ability and experience.

Where to walk
Any common or heath where the going is rough underfoot offers a good introduction to rambling. Failing that, try short evening strolls across the local parks. Aim to work up to five-mile (8km) Saturday afternoon hikes and then on to a 10-miler (16km) for which you should allow a day. Weekend and holiday rambling requires careful planning, even when following one of the waymarked long-distance footpaths (see overleaf).

You always need a map and guidebook. The 1:50,000 Ordnance Survey sheet of your chosen region will show the possibilities; a guidebook of the area will show specific details of different walks. Guidebooks range from the excellent long-distance footpath series published for the Countryside Commission by HMSO to the multi-paged loose-leafed AA-Readers Digest compendium of short walks called *No Through Road*. National Park authorities often publish their own 'walk sheets' and these, along with many other publications, are sold widely in the area concerned.

When you have chosen your route, make a route card detailing each leg of a day's trip, with 10–15 miles (16–24km) across country being good going at first. A rough rule of thumb calculation is that

Survey maps are a good guide.)

5 Signposting
Footpaths should be marked with a sign (County Council's job) where they leave a metalled road. Many councils have not done their job. Some volunteer organisations have always waymarked their local paths across country

6 Piles of litter
Litterers can be fined if caught (and prosecuted). In view of the deterioration caused by litter and rubbish, not many people can have doubts about reporting offenders – to District Council (or to police if there is urgency or danger resulting)

7 Up on the hills
Can you wander where you like? Generally walkers are tolerated, but only sometimes are there legal rights of access to some commons, or rights gained by agreements between councils and landowners

8 Path disappears
Walk on, in single file. If you edge round the field to protect the crop, you can be sued for trespass. Farmer should notify the County Council at least seven days before ploughing and make good the path

after; but few bother, and fewer councils take any notice if they don't

9 Other traffic
You can take a pet (within reason, no horses or elephants) on a footpath, but farmers can shoot uncontrolled dogs worrying animals. Horses are allowed on bridle paths, and cycles, but they have to put up with pedestrian-oriented surface. Cars and motorbikes can be driven on footpaths only with permission of landowner; otherwise they are limited to within 15 yards of the road (and landowner can still order those cars off)

10 Whose path?
Who owns the path? The surface 'belongs' to the County Council (which is the Highway Authority), but the soil under the surface belongs to the owner of the neighbouring land, and the landowner enjoys some rights, and obligations

11 Gates and stiles
In bad repair? The owner of the land must maintain them in good order, but can claim a quarter of the cost from County Council. It can do the work, and charge him with cost, if he fails to keep them in good repair

12 Bulls
Only a few counties allow bulls to be pastured in fields crossed by footpaths. If you are attacked, remember that they have difficulty in stopping or turning on a down slope; but there is no magic formula to get you away safely. You can try suing the farmer if you are hurt, but with no guarantee of success if bull is pastured legally. If illegal (if a by-law is disregarded) inform local police

13 Paths churned up, overgrown
Maintenance of surface is the job of County, District or (sometimes) local Parish Council. They can request landowner to trim back overhanging branches

14 Barbed wire, bungalows
And other obstructions; the landowner cannot close a path, so report any obstructions to the County Council. If you are a bona fide traveller, not just a troublemaker, you can lawfully continue on your way but causing as little damage as possible. You can bring a private prosecution alleging obstruction

15 Misleading notices
Report them to the highways department of the local council

you will walk at 2½mph (4kph) plus an extra half hour for every 700ft (210m) climbed. But this does not account for rests, extra weight carried, companions who prove unfit or delays caused by mist, wind and bad weather. High, remote and exposed ground can be risky at any time of year. At 500ft (150m) a mild valley breeze becomes an icy gale. Temperatures drop fast, rain becomes heavier. Always let experience govern ambition, always respect the elements.

How to walk

This is not the daft question it might seem. Nor is there a simple answer. Walking footpaths is different from walking city streets, walking off the beaten track altogether very different again. Long grass, loose stones, concealed holes, tree roots, heather clumps, matted bracken, greasy boulders and scree slopes require a knack which only comes with practice. And nowhere is this difference shown more than in ascending slopes where the urban walker tends to spring off the toes trying to lift the knees too high – a style ensuring strain.

Two general tips are always to begin slowly and allow your system to warm-up; and to know that it will warm-up very quickly so only wear waterproof clothing when it is either raining or bitterly cold. Too many walkers wear far too much clothing and become 'heat exhausted' without knowing why.

When to walk

Sunstroke (when your body temperature gets too high) and hypothermia (the opposite effect) are hazards to be avoided by leaving off or putting on layers of clothing as you travel. Such a system of 'climate control' mean it is possible to walk in any weather the whole year through – although winter rambling needs extra safeguards (see page 217). Climate control, however, does depend on carrying a full issue of bad weather clothing in your rucksack in the first place – an important safety precaution.

Where to stay

Lists of farms offering bed and breakfast can be obtained from National Park information centres, public libraries in walking areas and from the Ramblers Association. Youth hostels are a popular alternative. And while the by-laws of popular tourist regions require campers to tent together on official sites, there is still scope for anyone prepared to walk some way from the road and agricultural land on to upland slopes. In more remote areas you can pitch camp wherever a farmer gives permission.

A quiet lane lined by high drystone walls in the heart of the Lake District. Here walking can range from well-worn lakeside paths to the high open fells for which a compass is often essential

Backpacking

Backpackers, unlike ramblers, carry everything they need to survive at least a long weekend in the wilds. Properly kitted-out, and with enough food, drink and the right protective clothing, they can safely penetrate the most remote and wintery regions. Solitude is what they seek. And where better to find it than in darkest winter when the wild places are empty and brittle with ice? For many backpackers the season begins in October, just as the majority of Britain's fair weather walkers are starting their hibernation. The rewards in return for careful and prudent planning, and a little fortitude, can be spectacular.

Kit is carried by pack frame or anatomic-shaped rucksack with light flexible internal frame, a padded waist belt giving vital additional support from the pelvis. Tents are nylon and double-skinned which greatly reduces the condensation inside and from which rain-water is easily shaken – their weight down to as little as 3–4lbs (1½–2kg). Sleeping bags filled with man-made fibre like Fibrefill 2 and P3 are more efficient than duck down when wet. Synthetic fibres can be wrung out and still work. Insulation from ground chill is provided by close-cell foam mats which are light and non-absorbent. Meths storm cookers are becoming increasingly popular since the heat goes into the pan instead of dissipating into the wind.

The long-distance paths

Eight long-distance paths have been established across some of the most beautiful countryside of England and Wales. Their routes are shown on the map on page 251 of the Days Out section of this book. They can be followed in their entirety or in shorter stretches – several one-day walks along long-distance paths are included in the 1000 Days Out section.

Ramblers' groups have developed other long-distance routes, such as the Cotswolds Way and Cambrian Way. But the 'official' paths run by the Countryside Commission are:

Pennine Way: 250 miles (402km). The first of the long-distance paths and still the one regarded as the greatest challenge. It runs through three national parks. A high-level route along the backbone of England this is rugged walking that, more than any other long-distance path, requires close attention to weather and equipment.

Pembrokeshire Coast Path: 167 miles (269km). This runs along the entire coastline of Pembroke (now a part of Dyfed county), mostly on clifftops, and offers some of the finest scenery in Wales. The route is also rich in bird and plant life. Only the more industrial section around Milford Haven is outside the Pembrokeshire Coast National Park, although even here there are fine opportunities for bird watching.

South West Peninsula Coast Path: 515 miles (825km). Really a combination of five separate coastal paths stretching from Somerset to Dorset via Land's End. Its length inevitably means a great variety of scenery. It also means that it is more likely to be used in relatively short stretches by holidaymakers than by ramblers trying to complete it all at one time.

Offa's Dyke Path: 168 miles (271km). This mostly follows the remarkable 8th century earthwork described earlier in this book (page 43). The scenery varies from the wooded river valleys such as the Wye and Dee to the heathland of the Black Mountains with views into the heart of Wales. The dyke is only a remnant of its former size but still impressive for much of its length.

Cleveland Way: 93 miles (150km). This has two distinct parts – a coastal section along some of the most dramatic sea cliffs of the east coast and an inland section looping over and around the magnificent Cleveland Hills. It is signposted Coast Path and Moors Path respectively and the latter can be difficult going, especi-

TWELVE RULES FOR SAFE RAMBLING

DO check the weather forecast first. Leave word where you are going and when you expect to be back.

Keep to your planned route if possible. Let your route suffer rather than yourself and turn back when conditions worsen. Let those expecting you know when you are back.

Phone those expecting you (or the police) if you end up at some other point away from the original destination to avoid search parties setting out.

Do follow the rambler's code (below).

DON'T be over-ambitious in your routes.

Ignore the risks of crossing swollen streams (detour instead, even if it adds miles to your route).

Travel alone in hills.

Split your group instead of keeping together.

Walk in groups of less than four or more than six on mountains and moors (too many is risky in case of accident and difficult to keep together in bad weather).

WHAT TO WEAR AND CARRY

T-shirts, shorts and training shoes are fine for summer rambles, but reserve clothing must also be carried in case the weather changes. And for routes over any rough and remote terrain you need:

Boots. Flexible soles are best, thick enough to cushion feet from stones and with cleated rubber Vibram treads. Also check: one-piece uppers; bellows tongue; D-rings and hooks for laces; and interior padding. Most vital of all is comfort.

Clothing. Wear thin layers to trap air in between: string vest, wool shirt, one or two lightweight jerseys. A proofed nylon anorak or cagoule (smock-length anorak) will keep off most rain like a 'shell', though even good ones leak to some extent. A zip right down the front helps ventilate you and prevents too much condensation building up on the inside of the garment. Also needed: wool hat to prevent 25 per cent heat loss; pair of mitts; climber's type breeches or long warm woollen pants (*not* jeans); long

woollen socks; rainproof overtrousers; long zip-up snow gaiters.

Kendal mint cake and dried dates to be chewed throughout the day to give a steady source of energy and stave off any effects of hypothermia); flashlight (with spare bulb and battery); and whistle (for emergencies – six long blasts or torch flashes repeated after one minute).

Day sack. This small nylon rucksack with big top flap and padded shoulder straps is the ideal size for rambling – not too big. In it should be carried spare clothing and the following contents: Ordnance Survey map (1:50,000 is the most popular size); Silva Compass (see page 190); first-aid kit (bandage, lint, adhesive tape, dressings, safety pins, cotton wool, small tube of antiseptic ointment); Bivi Bag (500-gauge polythene survival bag which you can climb inside and sit out a blizzard or benightment); vacuum flask (hot drink); high-energy food (such as raisins, peanuts, chocolate,

THE RAMBLER'S COUNTRYSIDE CODE

Guard against starting a fire. Heaths, plantations, woodland and fell-side are highly inflammable.

Fasten all gates. Animals will always be drawn by an open gate, a risk to themselves, crops and traffic.

Keep dogs under proper control. Keep your dog on a lead wherever there is livestock about and on country roads.

Keep to paths across farmland. Recognised routes might be signposted 'public footpath' or 'bridleway'; with green/white metal pointers signifying the same; with the sign of a walking man; with painted coloured arrows; with splotches of coloured paint; with the acorn symbol of long-distance footpaths; or with cairns (heaps of stones). Always use gates and stiles even if your path detours to do so.

Leave no litter. Plastic bags can choke livestock – one example of how litter can be dangerous as well as unsightly.

Safeguard water supplies. Your path may cross a catchment area which supplies millions. Avoid polluting it. The same goes for cattle troughs.

Protect wild life, wild plants and trees. Wild life is best seen, not collected. To uproot flowers, carve trees and rocks or disturb birds and wild animals spoils other people's enjoyment and can be illegal as already explained.

Go carefully on country roads. High banks, blind bends, slow moving tractors or animals all offer risk. Walk facing oncoming traffic.

Respect the life of the countryside. Set a good example and try to fit in with the locality and locals of the countryside.

ally in poor weather.

South Downs Way: 80 miles (129km). The only long-distance path which is also a bridlepath throughout its length (apart from an optional section along the cliffs at Beachy Head). The route follows the relatively gentle grass-covered slopes along the ridge of the Downs – a route used since Neolithic times.

North Downs Way: 141 miles (227km). Another great chalk ridgeway but this time also incorporating the traditional Pilgrims Way to Canterbury. Good views into the Weald. The closest long-distance path to London.

Ridgeway: 85 miles (136km). This mostly follows the line of the most famous of ancient routeways – the Ridgeway, as it is known south of the Thames where it crosses the Berkshire Downs as a wide bridlepath, or the Icknield Way, as it is also known in the stretch across the Chilterns where it is mostly a footpath. Evidence of the route's importance in prehistoric times is abundant, especially near such places as Avebury and Uffington.

These official paths as yet have no equivalents in Scotland or Ireland. The difficulty of walking the paths varies. Paths through upland areas or along the coast are the most likely to suffer misty or foggy conditions, so care should be exercised and enough time allowed to seek overnight accommodation. In these conditions compasses are invaluable, particularly where paths strike out across empty moorland – see also page 190.

However, the paths are 'waymarked' with signposts or milestones to indicate directions where the route is not obvious or where it departs from another footpath. These signs are not always particularly conspicuous because the Countryside Commission is anxious to preserve the 'natural' state of the countryside that presumably also attracts walkers in the first place. But the acorn symbol is used on all signposts for long-distance paths, except on open moorland where cairns of stones have been constructed as landmarks.

Anyone tempted to pit their energies against the challenge of a long-distance path should remember the basic rule of never allowing their ambition to outrun their abilities. Clothes and equipment must also be chosen to match the route: what is sensible for a summer stroll along the South Downs Way would be madness at almost any time of the year for the higher reaches of the Pennine Way or Offa's Dyke Path, for instance.

Climbing: from roadside crags to the highest mountain peaks

Mountains offer to many people an experience which enriches their lives like no other recreation. There is the challenge of hard exercise, of obstacles met on the ascent and even on the descent when special care may be needed to avoid slipping on treacherous surfaces. There is also the satisfaction of seeing a new landscape or even of viewing a familiar landscape from a new angle. Those with special interest in geology, botany, indeed any field science, will see more than others, for mountains have forests and open moorlands as well as rock faces.

For the climber, as opposed to the fell-walker, mountains are all about facing problems: the better the problem, the more memorable the climb. Mountains pose such a variety of problems, however, that it takes time for the beginner to experience all the situations which threaten danger. And although you may show early promise as a rock climber on roadside crags, it is important to realise that hill walking, scrambling, route planning, navigation, bivouacking, scree running, river crossing, snow and ice climbing, traversing skylines and adapting to emergencies along the way are also part of climbing, too.

In all these situations the crux of the matter is the same: how, by knowing what you are about, can you exercise judgment and competence to tackle each new problem as it arises? To do so successfully and work your way to the top – and safely down again – is why climbers climb. The companionship involved, as partners on a climbing rope rely on each other completely during each ascent, is also an important element in climbing's appeal for many people.

Climbers tackle rock faces one at a time with the leader 'sharp-ending' routes which he knows from the appropriate climbing guidebook are within his capabilities. Paying out the nylon climbing rope around his back and through his 'burning gloves' – a friction brake to hold the leader if he falls – the second man is attached or 'belayed' to the crag wherever rock spikes, flakes and other anchorages accompany a suitable ledge or stance. To shorten any possible fall the leader clips his rope through 'running belays' as he progresses. These slings (rope loops) and karabiniers (metal clips) act as a safety pulley system if he did fall. On reaching the next available stance and belays the leader stops, ties

himself to the rock and takes in the rope. Then putting it round his back he brings the second man up to his ledge. And so it goes on to the top of the crag.

Where to climb

There are thousands of rock faces in Britain ranging from tiny outcrops near most towns and cities to the great cliffs of North Wales, the Lake District, Scotland and Ireland. There are also sea cliffs from Land's End to the Orkneys which can offer superb climbing too. London has Harrison Rocks and High Rocks near Tunbridge Wells; Plymouth has the Dewerstone; Bristol has Avon Gorge and Cheddar Gorge; Leicester has Beacon Hill at Woodhouse Eaves and outcrops in Charnwood Forest; Liverpool has Helsby Rocks, Cheshire; Sheffield has Stanage Edge, Hathersage; Leeds has Almscliff Crag; Newcastle has Crag Lough near Hexham; Glasgow has 'The Cobbler' at Loch Lomond; and Dublin has Dalkey Quarry. All are examples of popular outcrops, their climbing as technically exacting as the crags of Snowdon, Scafell or Ben Nevis.

And it is on such low-level climbing that first ascents are best made – with an experienced climber as a companion. Mountain rock climbs can come later.

How to start climbing

Climbing courses are the safe way to begin. Many are run at mountain centres by local authorities. Climbing is on the curriculum at an increasing number of schools, too. Excellent courses are run by national Sports Councils and others. There are also climbing schools advertising in magazines like *Mountain* and *Climber & Rambler*. Run by expert climbers they provide bunkhouse accommodation, meals and climbing instruction. And in many areas there are British Mountaineering Council (BMC)-registered guides who can be engaged by the day to take you on climbs of appropriate difficulty.

Many tyros go on from their introductory course to join a climbing club. This gives continued opportunity to climb with experienced company, and the BMC will send details of local climbing clubs on request. Public libraries are another source of information, as are local climbing shops.

When to climb

Climb rock in summer, walk in winter – that could be the beginner's credo. Rock is always accessible, the routes always

Climbers on a rockface in Snowdonia, one of Britain's most popular and challenging climbing and mountaineering areas

available, cleaned and tested by thousands who have gone before and documented in guidebooks. Rock climbs let you become used to exposure and climbing movement in relative safety. You learn to judge steepness and difficulty and learn rope handling proficiency the more crag routes you do.

Climbing steep snow and ice, however, is something else – the very stability of the stuff you are climbing is often uncertain at a time when you still lack the experience to tell good conditions from downright dangerous. Avalanches regularly take their toll on British mountains. So do poor snow and ice conditions when rock spikes or ice screw 'belays' used as anchorage points prove unsound and a falling climber can pull his companion bodily from the ice to which he was attached. Leave such winter routes until you have won experience on rock first, and also find experienced companions to partner you on snow and ice tremendously thrilling though they are. Even in Britain mountain climbs can pose problems which are alpine in scale, especially in bad weather and always in winter.

Safety in the mountains

Various rescue services are available in some major mountain areas, such as Snowdonia and the Lake District. Much of their brave enterprise should not be necessary. If conditions are bad, through mist or snow, it may be foolish to go forward. Some deaths are caused by hypothermia, probably through failure to carry an adequate supply of extra clothing. It is prudence, not weakness, to turn back, or even to have a walk in the valleys, if conditions are bad. In general it is wise to do most of the harder climbing early in the day, especially under warm conditions. An ascent of 1000ft (305m) or more in the late afternoon can be a severe test of stamina and in no circumstances should there be a long descent after dark.

Emphasis on 'solitude', so often given by those who write of mountains in romantic terms, is dangerous. Probably experienced people may safely go alone but only in areas where other people will be met. They should also tell someone where they are going and at what time they expect to return to their base, perhaps their car, hotel or camp site – some walkers in the Lake District leave such information in their cars. Good sense means recognition of dangers and provision for emergencies.

□ *Walking in winter: see page 217*

Angling: the most popular participant sport in Britain

Angling has been increasing in popularity steadily since the Second World War. Every week more people go fishing than watch soccer, the most popular spectator sport. They range from boys with their improvised rods and jam jars at the local canal to the lavishly-equipped syndicates who fish the salmon rivers of Scotland. Whoever they are, and wherever they fish, they are deemed to be 'anglers' if they go fishing at least six times a year.

There are broadly three types of angling – coarse fishing, game or fly fishing and sea fishing. The variety of angling is partly a consequence of the diversity of landscape since this is directly related to a diversity of waters; from fast-flowing upland streams to lowland meanders, the chalk streams of Hampshire to the land drains of the Fens. And, of course, there is the relatively small size of the British Isles and their location between the North Sea and the Atlantic Ocean.

Sea fishing is thus more readily available in Britain than most countries since few people live more than a half day's drive from the coast. Although coarse fishing is the most popular, largely because it is the most accessible, anglers are increasingly practising more than one type of fishing. As the close season for coarse fishing also roughly coincides with the open season for game fishing, angling is becoming a year-round activity.

In Great Britain especially angling is becoming big business, too, with a shoal of specialist magazines and books to cater for anglers of all types and abilities. There are national organisations, local clubs, angling classes and fishing holidays. Fishing tackle shops are a good starting point for would-be anglers, not only for the necessary equipment but as a source of information about fishing licences and day tickets. As with most sports it is possible to spend a small fortune on equipment but it is better to borrow or buy cheaply until satisfied that a particular form of angling really is for you. We describe here the basic characteristics of the three branches of angling – and what a beginner needs to know before embarking on any one of them. Fishing at sea involves particular risks. A 10-point safety code, covering equipment and boating lore, appears in the section on boating later in this chapter (see page 187). Tourists boards are good sources of information about angling.

Coarse Fishing

Coarse fishing is quite simply fishing for freshwater fish which are not members of the salmon family – that is to say, salmon and trout. It is carried out in rivers, lakes, ponds, reservoirs, gravel pits, canals and land drains all over the British Isles. Among the species which can be caught in these waters are the barbel, bleak, bream, carp, chub, dace, eel, gudgeon, perch, pike, roach, rudd, tench and zander. However, not every water is suitable for all these species. Some fish like fast-flowing waters while others prefer sluggish waters. Others favour gravel bottoms to muddy riverbeds.

Where to fish. Unfortunately you cannot just pick up a rod and line and fish anywhere you fancy. Coarse fisheries are controlled in one form or another so you have to have the appropriate permission. If you do not, then you could find yourself in trouble – possibly facing a fine from a magistrates' court.

Firstly, you require a rod licence in the same way that shotgun owners need gun licences. These licences are issued by the various Water Authorities but are generally most easily bought at local fishing tackle shops. These licences cost from £1 to £5 but they still do not entitle you to fish any of the waters within a water authority area; they simply mean you are allowed to use a rod. You still need permission to actually go out and fish.

Again this is quite easy to come by. The most popular way is to join a fishing club. Membership entitles you to fish any of the waters owned by the club. Furthermore it allows you to take part in matches organised by the club. If, however, you prefer to fish several waters then the best type to look for are day-ticket waters where you just pay a nominal fee for a day's fishing. Whatever your choice the best way of pursuing it is via a local tackle shop where they are normally only too pleased to advise on such matters.

When to fish. Fishing in most areas is not allowed while fish spawn. Any close season is decided by the Water Authorities but it is generally between March 15 and June 15.

What you will need. The basic tackle needed for a fishing trip is a rod and reel, line, floats, hooks, split-shot to weight your tackle, bait, a landing net and keep-net. Other accessories – rod rests, umbrella, holdall, etc – can be added later as you gain experience.

Rods. There are literally hundreds of various rods available for all types of

Fisherman at work: an angler casts his line in the River Kennet, Berkshire, amid idyllic surroundings on an early summer day

coarse fishing – float rods, leger rods, specialist rods for such fish as carp and pike. However, a beginner would be best off buying a 12 or 13ft (4m) float rod because much of his early fishing will most likely be float fishing.

This is just what it sounds like – a float is attached to the line and a bite is indicated by either the float sinking or lifting in the water. The float is 'cocked' by adding small weights (split-shot) to the line. Float fishing enables the angler to present his bait on the move at various depths at the same pace as the flow. The other type of fishing is 'legering'. Here special weights – the most common of which is the pear-shaped Arlesey bomb – are used to fish your bait still on the riverbed. Bite indication is shown by such tackle items as swingtips, quivertips, butt indicators or by simply watching the end of one's rod.

Reels. There are two main types – the fixed-spool and the centre-pin – but the former is the most popular, its major advantage over the centre-pin being that it allows long-distance casting.

Floats. To begin with you will need two types of float – one for still and slow moving waters and the other for medium to fast moving rivers. The antenna, with its long thin tip and bulbous bottom, is the one for the first category. For faster waters you will require a streamlined float which has the majority of its buoyancy near the tip.

Which bait to use. Maggots in various colours and sizes are still the most common fishing bait around. However, there are many other baits which can be just as tempting. Among them are bread, worms, stewed wheat, hempseed, berries, cheese, luncheon meat, sweetcorn and so on. The list is endless because fish have been caught on just about everything that can be put on a hook.

Game Fishing

Game or fly fishing is regarded by many anglers as the finest and most exciting type of fishing in the world. And the species that have built up this reputation are the salmon and the trout. Years ago most of our game fishing was done on rivers, particularly in Scotland, Wales and Ireland. However, with the sudden upsurge of new trout-stocked reservoirs all over the British Isles, more and more people are taking it up.

Most trout fisheries are 'fly only', which means that you can only fish with an artificial fly and a proper fly line.

'Flies' are hooks dressed with feathers, fur, wool, tinsel or the like which, when tied, imitate a natural fly at some stage in its development. They can also represent other waterlife like shrimps, fish fry and beetles. Flies fished on the surface are known as 'dry flies'; those fished beneath the surface are referred to as 'wet flies'.

Where to fish. Salmon fishing is an expensive pastime and charges for visits to the top waters can be very high – even on a day-ticket basis, let alone a season. Some trout fishing is also expensive, but as it becomes more readily available it is also becoming somewhat cheaper, particularly at the new water authority reservoirs and purpose-built stillwater trout fisheries which now provide plenty of choice all over the country.

Most of these waters can be fished on a day-ticket basis for a few pounds at a time, but a few have a waiting list even for season tickets. The trout fisheries are often more expensive than the reservoirs but at least for the beginner there is the consolation of knowing he cannot be too far from trout. A third type of trout fishing is in rivers – either the rain-fed rivers of the north and west of Britain or the chalk streams of the south where fishing rights can cost up to £1000 a season for rivers such as the Test.

Nearly all fisheries have what is known as a 'limit bag'. If the limit is six, you must stop fishing as soon as you have caught six fish – or buy another ticket. As with coarse fishing you also need a general rod licence and again the local tackle shops can provide licences and general information about day or season tickets for game fishing in their area.

When to fish. The season begins around April 1 and ends around September 30, depending on where you live.

What you need. The beauty of fly fishing is that you do not have to kit yourself out with a lot of tackle. You simply need a rod, reel, line and flies. (Special clothing, like waders and fishing jackets, can be added later.)

Rods. These are hardly ever longer than 10ft (3m), except of course those used for salmon fishing on big rivers. The hollow fibreglass types are the most commonly used although carbon fibre rods are becoming increasingly popular. Their only disadvantage to the beginner is the cost – considerably more than fibreglass. (See below, under *Lines*, for the importance of matching rod and line and a description of the rating system.)

Reels. These need to be light. The $3\frac{1}{2}$in (9cm) diameter type costs only a few pounds and is ideal for the novice. Always make sure that your tackle is nicely balanced. Therefore if you buy the reel first, make sure you take it to the shop with you when you buy your first rod.

Lines. Fly casting is totally different to any methods used in sea or coarse fishing because there is no attached weight – ie a float or lead weight – to assist with the cast. It is quite obvious that a 'fly' weighs very little and is hardly likely to pull line from a reel. Therefore the fly line has to act as the weight.

As a result fly lines are thick and heavy compared with their sea and coarse counterparts. They are usually 30yds ($27\frac{1}{2}$m) long, thickest in the middle and taper off towards the ends. The way they are cast is much the same as the old coachman's whip. In other words the rod has to be used as a spring lifting loose line off the water, carrying it back over the angler's head, pausing while the line straightens out behind and then throwing the rod forward to send the line in the direction of the water (see illustration).

Lines come in different sizes because they have to match the various types of rod available. However, they are easily recognisable by a standard AFTM (Association of Fishing Tackle Manufacturers) rating. The rating is marked on line spools – AFTM7, for instance: the figure is based on the weight in grains of the first 30ft (9.1m) of line. The AFTM number is marked on the rod so if you have a number 7 rod – a good buy for beginners – then you need to have a number 7 line. The heaviest in common use is a number 9 while the lightest is a number 4.

The three basic types of fly-line – those that float, sink or only partly sink – are designed for fish feeding at different levels in the water. The beginner would do well to start with a floater – but do not economise on the quality of the line. A good one will last longer, cast more easily and float better.

What fly to use. Flies come in different types and sizes. 'Big lures', for instance, are streamers used for fishing big reservoirs but never for river or small still-water fishing. Sizes are identified by numbers and there are often maximum sizes specified for different locations such as reservoirs, rivers or small trout fisheries. There is not space here to go much beyond the fundamental distinction made at the beginning of this section, namely that 'dry flies' are used for fishing on the surface and 'wet flies' for fishing beneath the surface. But many of the subtleties which give such appeal to this branch of angling stem from the intricacies of the flies themselves.

Sea fishing

Most novice sea anglers get their early experience of this form of fishing from the beach or from piers and jetties. Such fishing is relatively inexpensive. Apart from the advantage of plenty of beach space in which to learn to cast there is the added bonus of being able to dig or collect free bait from the beach itself.

Boat angling is the alternative form of sea fishing but this can prove fairly expensive with the angler having to pay for boat fees and bait charges. If you are beach fishing you can also keep all that you catch, while some boat skippers may only allow you to keep just a few fish. For the skippers it is their living and they often sell catches to local markets or shops.

What you can catch. One exciting aspect of sea fishing is that you never know what you are going to catch. The movement of the various species of fish around the coastline means that the sea angler can expect variety during the year. Nor is there a close season for sea fishing which is another reason for its increasing popularity.

Cod and whiting are to be had from most sandy beaches in winter, with flat-fish, bass and thornback ray in summer. Piers and jetties will yield the same. Boat fishing is different, however, especially if you can fish the wrecks in the South West off Plymouth or the Irish coast. Wrecks are natural food larders for the big fish such as conger eel, ling, coalfish, pollack and cod. Hundreds of charter boats offer their services and the best way of finding them is by reading the classified pages of the national angling press. Shark fishing is particularly big business in the South-West with Looe the major centre.

What you will need. Unlike coarse fishing, you do not need licences and tickets to be able to go sea fishing. You simply need your tackle and bait – and a

---

The ones that didn't get away: some all-time record angling catches

More than 140 species are included in the anglers' hall of fame: a list of record weights and the (lucky?) anglers who caught them on rod and line in United Kingdom waters. In the 1979 list these ranged from a 851lb (386 kg) tunny caught by L. Mitchell Henry off Whitby, Yorkshire, in 1933 to a 4 dram (007 grammes) sea stickleback caught by Master Kevin Pilley at Poole Harbour, Dorset, in 1978. Records for ten of the more renowned species, if not necessarily the most frequently caught species, in the 1979 list were as below.

The record list is updated annually so if you want to claim a record – or obtain a copy of the full list and other information – contact the British Record (Rod-caught) Fish Committee, 5 Cowgate, Peterborough, Cambridgeshire. Claims for fish caught in the Irish Republic should be made to the Irish Specimen Fish Committee, Baenagowan, Mobhi Boreen, Glasnevin, Dublin 9.
* Different records exist for sea fish caught from boats and the shore; those listed here are the heaviest from either source.

Freshwater Fish

Carp 44lb (20 kg)
Pike 40lb (18 kg)
Roach 4lb 1oz (1.8 kg)
Salmon 64lb (29 kg)
Rainbow Trout $19\frac{1}{2}$lb (8.9 kg)

Sea Fish*

Bass 18lb 6oz (8.3 kg)
Cod 53lb (24 kg)
Haddock 13lb 11oz (6.2 kg)
Halibut 212lb 4oz (96.2 kg)
Mako shark 500lb (227 kg)

little luck. You can even stay ashore.

Rods. Beach fishing requires long casting if you are to land lots of fish. Therefore a long and powerful rod, or beach-caster as it is known, is necessary; hollow fibreglass around the 11 to 13ft (3.3–4m) mark is best. A good tackle shop will advise and generally allow you to try one or two.

While you may have to cast your bait at least 80 yards (73m) from the beach to find the feeding fish, with boat fishing it is generally a question of simply dropping your bait over the side of the boat. Therefore you do not need a particularly long rod – one between 6–7ft (2m) is quite sufficient.

Reels. Either fixed spool or multiplier reels can be used for fishing from the shore, but multiplier reels are the best bet when boat fishing. Fixed spools are much easier to cast since the multiplier may take a little time to master. However when you have mastered the multiplier, you will find that the reel creates a much smoother cast and therefore gives you the extra distance that is often required for successful sea fishing.

Whatever the choice make certain that your reel is capable of carrying at least 200yd (182m) of 20lb (9kg) breaking strain line for beach fishing or 200yd of 35lb (16kg) for boat fishing. Again a local tackle dealer is the best person to consult for advice.

Lead weights. Once you have bought your rod and reel you will need line, hooks, some swivels and a selection of lead weights. For beach fishing you will need weights of between 2–6oz (56–170gm) with spikes for fishing over sand, gravel or mud. For boat fishing you will need the much heavier stuff – from 4oz to $1\frac{1}{2}$lb (113gm–0.7kg). The choice depends on where you are fishing, at what depths and in strong or slack tides.

Baits. Lugworm and ragworm, which can be easily dug from many beaches, are the most popular sea baits and will take most species of fish. However, other baits worth trying include the flesh of almost any fish but especially those with a high oil content such as mackerel and herring. Also used are shellfish, crab baits, squid and artificial lures; the latter range from small hooks dressed with coloured feathers which are intended to lure mackerel to large metal weights, known as pirks, which take specimen cod and ling. The angling press carry weekly guides to sea fishing telling you where the best areas or 'marks' are, what is being caught and which baits are proving deadly.

Riding: how to choose a riding school or pony trekking centre

Two million people ride regularly in the British Isles. Half of them are children. Most do not own horses but hire from riding stables. The horseback rush, which sprouted in the 1960s, has burst out in an epidemic of riding schools all over the country. Many suffer from economic problems and labour shortages which inevitably restrict individual attention to horses and clients. For the beginner, choosing the right school is the first crucial problem, as tough as buying a second-hand car if you are mechanically illiterate.

Do you really want to ride? The first question to ask yourself (or your child) is: do you really want to ride, and, if so, why? A summer day in open country might charm your great-aunt on to a horse; a sleeting winter one, necessary if you are to keep in practice, wouldn't. Ambitions such as foxhunting are inconvenient if you live in Central London.

The sport is physically demanding, time-consuming and fairly expensive. There is little point in taking up riding unless you have time for constant practice. Learning to ride takes time. Even once a week means slow progress, whereas once a fortnight – don't bother. Nor can you ride unless you are physically fit. Costs at riding schools vary according to whether or not lessons are shared and sometimes whether or not you have the chief instructor's attention. If subsequent enthusiasm impels you to buy a horse you will be in for £1000–£2000 a year, maybe even more, depending on where you keep the animal and what you want to use it for.

What to ask. While not guaranteeing a seat in the saddle of the gods, there are a number of ways of ensuring that you do not prostrate yourself before the riding boots of the local incompetent opportunist. Riding stables do exist – not many, but some – who will take you for the wrong sort of ride. Careful inquiry will provide a reasonable guarantee that a school, though not necessarily perfect, is at least worthy of your custom. First-class instruction in the early stages of riding is essential. If a school satisfies the following requirements it is likely to provide it:
1. Is it approved either by the British Horse Society or by the Association of British Riding Schools? It is well worth writing to these organisations – and its Irish equivalent – for their booklets of approved schools (addresses overleaf).

Neither the BHS nor the ABRS will sanction a riding school unless the school is licensed, has adequate insurance cover and has been examined for quality of instruction, condition of horses, and standards of safety, and both reserve the right to spot-check approved schools without prior warning to the proprietor. (It is possible that a perfectly good riding school may exist without being BHS or ABRS approved, but some non-approved stables have either failed to satisfy the inspectors or have not asked for approval because they know they will not get it.) Schools offering residential holidays or pony trekking should be approved (see overleaf). If they are not, clients may expect indifferent tuition, if any, and overworked and neglected mounts.

2. Can it produce evidence that it is licensed by the local authority? If not, it has failed to pass that authority's veterinary surgeon. This not only means that its horses are in inadequate condition but that it is probably not insured against accidents to its clients. A properly insured school will carry cover to a minimum of £250,000 per rider.

3. Does it require its clients to wear hard hats to protect their heads against falls? If not, it is not only irresponsible, since a fall on the head is the most dangerous of all riding accidents, but it is almost certainly uninsured because insurance companies like to safeguard themselves against claims for brain damage.

4. Has it got either an indoor school or a small, fenced paddock in which beginners can be taught to control their horses without being exposed to the dangers of traffic? Any responsible school will also try out new customers in these enclosed spaces before allowing them on the roads, no matter how great the client's claim to expertise.

5. Is the riding school convenient to your home? If not, getting there is going to be a nuisance. If several schools in your area fulfil these requirements, ask for personal opinions from people who use them – from other children as well as adults since they can be more honest in their judgments.

6. How many pupils in a class? More than eight riders in one class in a covered school or paddock is too many: how much of the instructor's attention could they receive? On the road the maximum string for *experienced* riders should not exceed a dozen, so beware of schools where 20 or so novices are exposed to the dangers of traffic.

Children have always ridden ponies for obvious reasons of size. But pony trekking, as a sport or holiday activity, is relatively recent. There are now hundreds of centres offering pony trekking in the British Isles, especially in the upland areas such as above in the Olchon Valley of the Black Mountains in Wales.

For many people it is also their introduction to riding since the trekking itself is quite leisurely. All the rider normally has to do is to sit on his animal; the ponies are well used to walking in line with inexpert riders on their backs. They are often equally accustomed to the bridlepaths or old drove trails chosen by the trek guide or leader. But the treks can still be tiring so they are not recommended for children under 12 years of age.

Most centres operate between Easter and October and although one-week inclusive holidays are the normal minimum period, one-day treks are becoming increasingly common. Always choose a centre which has been officially approved: the Riding Holiday and Trekking Association of England, Wales, Scotland and Ireland run comprehensive schemes, often in conjunction with local tourist boards, while Ponies of Britain vets the standard of care for the animals.

Pony trekkers are accompanied by a guide, often with an assistant bringing up the rear. Ideally there should be no more than 12 riders in the string. Beginners usually go on short treks initially to build up confidence, but the distance to be covered in a day will rarely exceed 20 miles (32km). Some centres offer experienced riders 'trail riding', 'post trekking' or 'camping treks' which involve staying away from the centre overnight. These treks are much more rigorous, covering anything up to 25 miles a day.

It is not necessary to dress elaborately to go trekking but make sure you take warm, weather-proof clothing and strong shoes with heels. Riding hats can be hired or borrowed from the centre. Costs of trekking holidays vary greatly, largely according to the quality of accommodation. Often this is pretty basic. You may have to share a room – not with your pony, although you may have to help muck out his room, too.

It is generally possible to use layman's common sense to buttress the answers to these specific questions. You should obviously be wary of schools where instuctors are remiss enough to ride *inside* the pupil on roads; where pupils wear plimsolls or block heels while riding; where instructors shout (which may upset horses as well as human customers); and where the stables seem dirty and uncared for.

Having satisfied yourself as much as you reasonably can, it is time for a riding lesson. During this trial lesson you can establish whether you respect (important) and like (though this is not essential) the person who will be teaching you. Do not sign up for a course of lessons until you have tried and enjoyed riding. Likewise do not lash out on expensive clothing for your first lesson – see below.

What to wear. Riding is a physically demanding sport. It can be dangerous. It can be uncomfortable. It can hurt. In the early stages it is painful because you are having to use long-neglected (at best) muscles. If, in addition, your clothes rub, pinch, are too bulky, too tight, too hot or too cold, then you are on a crash course to misery.

Short-term gear. Safety and comfort are all that matter for the first few trial lessons. Essentials are a hard hat to protect your head. The best of these is not the pretty black velvet-covered peaked cap worn by show jumpers – it has a hard lining, but unless it fits perfectly, which is rare, it will usually fall off when you do. Much better is the really protective, inexpensive crash helmet or skull cap worn by jockeys and event riders.

Shoes should be lace-ups with plain leather soles, or the kind of rubber, smooth-soled riding boots which do double duty as elegant wellingtons. Stacked or block heels, corrugated soles or plimsolls are extremely dangerous because they can jam in the stirrups if you fall and may lead to you being dragged by the foot behind a panicking horse. Riders have been killed through wearing block heels.

Clothes should be close-fitting (a polo-necked sweater and windcheater, for example), not flapping about as this will impede your movement and may also frighten the horse. For trousers, avoid jeans which are stiff and pinch your legs excruciatingly against the stirrup leathers. Try a pair of soft trousers, corduroy or the like, and fold them into long, thick socks with the fold of the trousers lying on the outside of the leg so that the inside of the knee is spared from the rub of the trouser crease. Under the trousers wear tights for warmth (not cissy – jockeys always do), and bandage your legs from the calf to above the knee to safeguard against pinching. On a cold day, gloves are mandatory. Woolly ones will do, provided that they fit closely enough to allow each finger to move independently.

Long-term gear. If you decide to go on with riding, properly-fitting clothes will make your work much easier. Choose either ankle-length jodhpurs with leather jodhpur boots that cover and protect your ankles, or calf-length riding breeches with leather riding boots. Rubber boots are all right – but are cold in winter unless big enough to take two pairs of socks. The riding jacket should really fit so that your movements are unencumbered, or you could wear a lightweight windcheater over a sweater. String riding gloves help you to grip the reins when they are wet with rain or the horse's sweat, and never forget tights, undervests, woollen knickers if the weather calls for it. Above all, though, never forget the crash helmet.

Further information

National tourist boards publish lists of centres offering riding or trekking holidays; see appendix for details of the addresses and telephone numbers of the head offices of the tourist boards. Other sources of information on riding schools or trekking holidays include:
British Horse Society and the English Riding Holiday and Trekking Association, both based at the British Equestrian Centre, Kenilworth, Warwickshire;
Association of British Riding Schools, Chesham House, 56 Green End Road, Chesham, Surrey;
Ponies of Britain, Brookside Farm, Ascot, Berkshire;
Irish Horse Board, St Maelruan's, Tallaght, Co Dublin.

Boating: the many different ways of messing about on the water

Nobody in the British Isles lives far from water. This accessibility allied to increased affluence has encouraged a great growth in the popularity of all forms of boating in the last 20 years.

For people with a boat small enough to trail behind the family car, the choice of boating locations is almost infinite. For people without any nautical skills at all, hire boat fleets have expanded into a major holiday industry based on the easier waters of rivers, broads and canals. Even watching other people in their boats is attraction enough to draw large numbers of people to marinas and estuaries all around Britain.

Whatever the form of boating, it is an activity which offers the possibility of greater intimacy with the countryside. Here we examine what a beginner needs to know about starting to learn the three main types of boating: sailing, motor cruising and canoeing.

Sailing
Since the war sailing has changed from being a rich man's sport to one available to anybody with a few hundred pounds. Improvements in materials and technology have had a lot to do with it and the result is a new breed of cheaper, smaller, lighter and more mobile boats that can be kept at home.

Sailing dinghies
The simplest sailing boats are dinghies and most people who start the sport, especially those who start young, begin with dinghy sailing. But there are about 150,000 dinghies sailing in the British

Isles from over 100 different classes so the beginner needs to learn something about the sport before rushing off to buy his or her first boat.

Dinghy sailing is almost invariably based on a club because most owners race rather than potter, and all racing is club organised. Many clubs also have dinghy parks where members can safely keep their boats. But many restrict membership to owners of specific classes, which is another reason for not buying a boat before you have found a club.

Where to learn. The best way is through a Royal Yachting Association (RYA) approved sailing school. This will entail spending a week to get the RYA Dayboat Certificate. A few clubs offer instruction to members and their families, but these are mostly confined to the cadet classes for children. After a week at a sailing school, and having found your club, you will be able to decide what type of dinghy to buy. From there on progress is up to you and, to some extent, on how you fit in with the traditions and tempo of your club. The RYA booklet *Recognised Teaching Establishments* gives details of sailing schools and other organisations which run courses, and its publication code number G13 gives a complete list of 1500 affiliated clubs and sailing organisations in the United Kingdom. For the address of the RYA and other boating organisations, see page 188.

What to buy. If you are not interested in competitive sailing, but just want to buy a little boat and potter about on your own learning by your mistakes, buy a stable and slow general-purpose dinghy instead of an out-and-out racing ma-

Sailing on the tranquil waters of Ullswater amid the mountain grandeur of the Lake District

chine. You might also be interested in joining the Dinghy Cruising Association, its title is self-explanatory. Whatever your choice of dinghy you will need a trailer to take it either to race meetings or on holiday, for instance. A wet suit is also essential in this country in the early and late season. And on all but the warmest days waterproof clothing is needed as protection against wind chill. A buoyancy aid when sailing in sheltered waters or a BSI-approved lifejacket in tidal or sea conditions is considered essential and is mandatory for all racing, and for children whenever and wherever they are on the water.

Sailing cruisers

Coastal and deep water cruising, to which most dinghy sailors eventually graduate as they get older and can afford the cost, is an altogether different game. Whereas the newcomer to dinghy sailing can think of getting afloat for as little as £500, the cruising enthusiast must start to think of at least £3000 for quite a small boat built and equipped to be suitable only for inshore cruising. Large boats now cost as much as small London houses, that is around £25,000 for a 30-footer suitable for long-distance cruising.

What to buy. Remember that the bigger a boat, the more crew will be needed to sail her. Remember, too, that it is not always easy to find enough compatible people who are all free at the same time to form a crew. On the other hand, the longer the waterline length of a boat the faster she will sail, and bigger boats tend to be more seaworthy than smaller boats. Size can also be equated with comfort when it comes to living on board. But if a boat is to be used largely for day sailing, the inconvenience of cramped accommodation never lasts long enough to spoil the fun. Other advantages of smaller boats are that they will go further inland to explore sheltered waters, can be sailed more easily single-handed and only need a small outboard instead of a more expensive inboard engine.

There are about 390 designs of sailing cruiser on the market ranging in size from 16ft (5m) 'Weekenders' (which are little more than day boats with a shelter) to 40ft (12m) ocean-going cruiser racers. Publications such as the practical Boat Owner *Buyer's Guide to Sailing Cruisers*, which is published each spring, give cross-referenced details and photographs of all the boats available. If you buy secondhand the boat should be subject to a survey, which may well call the seller's bluff and bring the price down consider-

ably. But it is often a better investment to spend more on a new boat; in the last decade new boats of quality have held their original price so that owners have at least got their capital back when trading in for a bigger boat. Boats can be bought as bare hulls for completion by the owner. But although this can save 50 per cent of the cost, the work will probably take much longer than you estimate.

Finally, however exciting the prospect of owning a boat, it is more economic to charter than to buy. That way you can sail better boats than you could afford to own, and you can choose a different cruising area every time. For details of charter yachts look in the classified advertisements of the yachting press, or write to the Yacht Charter Association.

Where to learn. It is better and quicker to invest in professional instruction than to rely on friends to teach you sailing. During the winter go to night school to learn navigation and then take a practical cruising course at an RYA-recognised school. At the end of a week, if you are fit and keen, you should achieve your Competent Crew Certificate. After a further week at sea on a practical course you can get your Day Skipper Certificate. You are then competent to take charge of a watch when cruising offshore, or to skipper a small cruiser on short coastal passages. During the next season spend at least one week, but preferably two, taking your turn as skipper on a charter yacht with a qualified instructor in charge. Then you should have enough knowledge and experience to command your own boat and crew. Schools with cruising courses and skippers who give instruction are advertised in the yachting press and are listed in the RYA publication *Practical Cruising Courses*.

Motor Cruising

Anybody who can drive a car can drive a motorboat – after a fashion. Unlike a sailing boat, a powered craft needs no special skills to get it moving. Nor, of course, are you so affected by tides and winds so that greater distances can generally be covered in less time. Another attraction to many people is that boats designed for inland waterways can be planned and furnished for comfort rather than speed or sea-keeping qualities. Sea-going motor cruisers, of course, must have sea-keeping capabilities.

But it does need a sound knowledge of pilotage and navigation, weather and sea conditions to go cruising at sea with any safety. It also requires more stamina to

cope with rough conditions in a motor cruiser, especially one with a high-speed planing hull, than it does in a sailing boat which rides the waves better and is steadied by its sails.

Personal clothing and safety gear are much the same as for sailing: good waterproofs, proper deck shoes, an ample supply of spare warm dry clothes, a BSI-approved lifejacket and safety harness.

The greatest motor boat activity is on the inland waterways. A recent survey estimated there were 44,000 motor vessels on the island waterways of the British Isles *excluding* the Broads, the Fens and the Shannon. On the Thames alone there were more than 1000 boats available for hire. Irish waters are generally less crowded than those of England and the Shannon in particular is an ideal cruising area served by several large hire fleets.

The cost of buying a boat as opposed to hiring one can be anything from £600 for a simple 15ft (4.5m) boat with a shelter (plus a further £600 for an outboard engine) to at least £15,000 for a 35ft (10.6m) canal cruiser equipped for living on board. Luxury cruising homes for inland waters and sleeping eight people can cost well over £50,000. One advantage of hiring a boat – other than avoiding this cost of purchase – is that hire boats are already licensed. All cruising on inland waterways has to be licensed – contact the British Waterways Board or the Irish Tourist Board for details about boat licensing, hiring etc. (addresses overleaf).

Canoeing

There are around 250,000 canoeists in the British Isles and, like other forms of boating, canoeing appeals to both the highly competitive or adventurous and those who enjoy being on the water for its own sake. For the former it is as skilled and energetic a sport as skiing. But for the majority, and probably for most beginners, the big attractions are canoe touring along inland waters and sea canoeing. Either way it is about the cheapest and most independently mobile way of getting afloat. When it is time to go home a canoe can be carried atop the smallest car.

There are canoeing waters in Great Britain and Ireland to suit all tastes and abilities. There is a legal right to navigate, and therefore to canoe, on nearly all tidal waters and a long-standing or statutory right on a number of rivers such as the Thames, Medway, Wye, Severn, the Stratford Avon, Trent, Great Ouse, Suffolk Stour and Spey. On other rivers licences are often granted to clubs by public and private owners. There are fewer restrictions on rivers in Ireland where the principal canoeing waters are the Erne, Shannon, Barrow, Blackwater, Suir, Nore and Slaney.

All canals and some canalised rivers require a licence before launching a canoe. Canals with their still water make an excellent nursery for beginners and can be used to link up with the Severn, Trent and Thames. On rivers where canoes are allowed it is possible to go where no boat can reach. The canoeist has a choice of probably thousands of miles of routes throughout the British Isles which can be explored by no other means, often not even on foot.

Canals are neither particularly wide nor deep, so they are reasonably safe for young teenagers even on their own. But beginners should always canoe in company, and sea canoeing should always be done in groups. At sea canoes can also go where boats dare not – among rocky islets, over shallows, and into caves. Sea kayaks are longer than touring canoes and have greater directional stability. They must be fitted with buoyancy –

30lb (13kg) at each end – and a lifejacket must always be worn.

Before going into any rough water or to sea in a canoe it is essential to have been taught how to handle the craft and particularly how to right it when it capsizes, which it surely will. The British and Irish Canoe Unions will supply lists of clubs to join and regional organisers who run their coaching scheme. Canoeing can also be learnt under the auspices of the Sports Councils which also runs sailing courses.

Safety on the water

Messing about in boats can be dangerous as well as fun. Every year people are drowned as a result of boating accidents. Every year people are rescued. Children are particularly vulnerable, of course, and in addition to equipping them with adequate safety aids (see below) their enthusiastic parents should remember that they will stand up to cold and wet less well than adults.

Boating takes so many different forms that it is difficult to devise one set of rules which embraces all types of water and types of craft from canoes to sea-going yachts. Nevertheless these 10 rules are always worth remembering:

1. In sheltered waters (canals, tideless reaches of rivers, small lakes and gravel pits) children must wear a BSI-standard buoyancy aid or life jacket at all times while on the water.

2. In tidal rivers, estuaries, inshore around the coast and on big lakes (eg, Lake Windermere) children must wear buoyancy aids or, preferably, life jackets at all times, and so should adults when underway.

3. Extra warm clothing should be carried even on warm days. If anybody gets wet and the sun goes in, wind chill can be dangerous.

4. All boats must have an alternative means of propulsion: oars for a small motor boat or dinghy, an outboard engine for a larger boat.

5. In coastal waters there must be sufficient lifejackets of a size to fit all members of the crew, and two lifebuoys available to throw overboard, one of which must have a water-activated light attached to it. Lifelines and safety harnesses should be available for crew working outside the cockpit in rough water.

6. Every boat must carry an adequate anchor.

7. Boats going to sea must have adequate means of communicating with other

Canoeing: not only the cheapest way of getting afloat but also the only way to explore some of the most remote and beautiful waters in Britain

vessels or the shore if in distress – basically flares and smoke signals. Any boat going offshore should carry at least a small inflatable boat as a lifeboat; if going out further than three miles (4.8km) it should be a liferaft equipped with a survival pack and a radio to receive weather and shipping forecasts.

8. Small boats in any water should have sufficient built-in or installed buoyancy to keep them afloat when capsized or waterlogged, and no one should leave a capsized boat and try to swim to safety. A small boat, even upside down, is more visible than a person's head in the water, and always remember that even the strongest swimmer can be defeated by an adverse tide.

9. Boats with engines and galleys must carry adequate fire extinguishers, and all butane gas installations must be professionally installed, and containers vented outside the boat.

10. Good seamanship is good safety. A well-found and well-equipped boat, careful handling, and attention to weather are better safeguards than a lot of expensive safety equipment.

If you do get into difficulty at sea – or you see a boat in distress – contact the coastguard; they coordinate rescue services and alert shipping. If you have informed coastguards of your intended route before departure – a sensible precaution – do not forget to tell them when you arrive or else a search might be launched. The coastguards, like the RYA, publish various booklets on safety at sea.

Further information

National tourist boards and sports councils are good sources of information about holidays or courses in all forms of boating – see appendices. Other specialist organisations, including those referred to in the text above, are: Royal Yachting Association, Victoria Way, Woking, Surrey; Irish Yachting Association, 87 Upper George Street, Dun Laoghaire, Co Dublin; Yacht Charter Association Ltd., 33 Highfield Road, Lymington, Hampshire; British Waterways Board, Melbury House, Melbury Terrace, London NW1; Inland Waterways Association, 114 Regents Park Road, London NW1; British Canoe Union, Flexel House, 45 High Street, Addlestone, Weybridge, Surrey; and the Irish Canoe Union, Great Outdoors, Chatham Street, Dublin.

Country and Forest Parks: planning for leisure in the countryside

Individual concepts of leisure are as varied as the countryside itself. Not everybody wants to spend their holidays or weekends so actively as the practitioners of the sports discussed in preceding pages. For most people it is enough simply to be in the country with enough room for a picnic, the children to play safely and a gentle stroll. Of course, there should be pretty views and it would be nice if somehow you could know something of the countryside you are seeing. It is to help fulfil these quite modest ambitions – and to help the countryside itself – that a quiet revolution has been taking place throughout the British Isles.

The prime function of the countryside is as it always has been: to produce food. But today's city dwellers, ever more mobile, blessed with greater affluence and more leisure time than previous generations, look increasingly to the green fields to produce more than milk and potatoes.

Nowadays the rural areas serve a dual purpose. They are a giant playground, a place where batteries run down by the noise and pace of the urban rat-race may be re-charged with a breath of fresh country air. The result is that every weekend and all summer long the national parks and celebrated beauty spots are besieged and in some instances worn out by the sheer weight of visitors who, in all innocence, are to some extent participating in the destruction of the very landscapes they have come to see.

Clearly something needed to be done to ease the pressure where it was hurting most and reduce the impact of the lethal foot that is literally kicking some of the most beautiful bits of the British Isles to death. Artificial grass has had to be sown on the Pennines and a stretch of rubber matting laid near where the Pennine Way begins north of Edale, Derbyshire. One of the most positive responses to this challenge has been the emergence of the country park.

Just over a decade ago the country park concept was nothing more than an idea floated in a British Government report called *Leisure in the Countryside*. Today there are well over a 150 country parks flourishing in nearly every corner of England and Wales, and more parks are in the pipeline.

Such places had never existed before in the countryside. But they have been introduced with such little fuss and such modest publicity that many people are unaware of what has been achieved. Country parks are not half so wild or so big as the national parks which will be featured in Chapter 10. Nor are they so small and tame as a municipal recreation ground. Instead they fit somewhere between the two, with the accent on leisure rather than conservation.

They were designed to serve three basic purposes. Country parks would make it easier for town dwellers to enjoy the open air without travelling too far and adding to traffic congestion. They would ease the pressure on the more remote and solitary places. And above all, perhaps, in the words of the Government report, they would 'reduce the risk of damage to the countryside – aesthetic as well as physical which often comes about when people simply settle down for an hour or a day, where it suits them, somewhere "in the country" – to the inconvenience and indeed the expense of the countryman who lives there.'

A good country park will certainly be readily accessible for cars and pedestrians and you may be able to reach it by public transport. It will cover at least 25 acres (10 hectares) and may contain woods, open parkland or a stretch of water. It may even be on the coast.

Some country parks provide refreshment facilities, picnic sites, information centres and a warden service. All of them have car parks and toilets. There may be an admission fee or a charge for parking your car, and a few parks close during the winter, so try to check before setting out.

In some parks you can swim, sail, fish, or go horse-riding. Others offer the quieter pleasures of nature trails, gardens, ancient monuments and scenic viewpoints. The commonest type of park is the traditional parkland of a bygone ancestral estate, sometimes with the great house or castle still intact within the grounds, as at Elvaston Castle, near Derby. But there is no truly typical country park.

In landscape terms their range is immense; downs, cliffs, woods, moors, heaths – even reclaimed mineral workings, old gravel pits and derelict railway lines transformed with financial aid from the Countryside Commission. A few private individuals and non-public bodies such as the National Trust have established country parks, but so far most have been set up by local authorities.

In addition to the country parks in England and Wales there are vast forest parks. These are run, like those in Scot-

Deer graze in a country park of the 18th century: the grounds of Petworth Manor, Sussex: one of the first parks to be landscaped by Capability Brown

land (see below), by the Forestry Commission. Some of the parks are huge with more than a dozen areas within them laid out by the Commission as picnic areas, walks, trails or even special 'scenic drives'. Snowdonia is one such park. But there are also many smaller parks in both lowland and upland areas of England and Wales, often with information centres providing exhibitions about the ecology of the forests and details about the trails, etc.

In Scotland there are only a few country parks as yet. This is primarily because the pressures which led to the creation of the English and Welsh country parks have not yet made themselves felt to the same extent. North of the border, and particularly in the Highlands, the wild landscapes remain much as they were centuries ago. This is Britain's empty quarter, where there are often more sheep and deer than people, where cities are fewer, and even the industrial sprawl of Glasgow offers in-

stant release into the surrounding hills and sea lochs.

Nevertheless there is still a need to conserve, and in Scotland this has brought about the creation of forest parks and nature reserves. The forest parks include the beautiful Argyll and Queen Elizabeth forest parks, both within easy reach of Glasgow; the 135,000-acre (54,656 hectares) Glen Trool forest park with its lochs and falls and scimitar-horned wild goats; and the magnificent national forest park of Glen More at the foot of the Cairngorm mountains.

Scotland's nature reserves range in size and character from Rhum – an entire Hebridean island – to the mountain, moorland and relic pinewood reserves of Ben Eighe, Inverpolly, Cairngorm and Rannoch Moor, each one a refuge for wild cats, eagles and other Highland fauna. Conservation is paramount in these reserves, but many, like the forest parks, provide public access in the form of forest walks and nature trails.

Northern Ireland has only a handful of country parks but they include two of the finest in the British Isles. In Ness country park, Co Londonderry, the Burntollet River emerges from a narrow gorge called Shane's Leap and tumbles in a double cascade for nearly 40ft (12m), forming the highest falls in Ulster. And in the Castle Archdale forest and country park, Co Fermanagh, the shores of Lower Lough Erne are starred with the white flowers of grass of Parnassus.

Ulster also has a number of nature reserves open to the public, and nearly fifty state forests in the care of Northern Ireland's Forest Service, including over a dozen forest parks with nature trails, picnic sites, caravan sites and scenic drives. Ulster's first forest park, Tollymore, at the foot of the Mourne mountains, opened in 1955. Today over a million visits are made to Northern Ireland's forest parks each year.

The Republic of Ireland, too, has superb forest parks where visitors may walk, picnic, fish, swim or watch wildlife. For several years it has been the policy of the Republic's Forest and Wildlife Service to encourage the use of the state forests for leisure and recreation. Among them are the forest parks of Killykeen and Dun-a-Ri in Co Cavan, Lough Key in Co Roscommon, Guagan Barra in Co Cork, the John F. Kennedy park in Co Wexford, the Ards forest park on Sheephaven Bay in Co Donegal, and the Portumna forest park with its deer herds and wildfowl ponds in Co Galway. These are the major forest parks, but Ireland has another 250 woods and forests, great and small, all of them open to the public, and as romantic as their names: Three Rock Mountains, Pigeon Hole Wood, Kelly's Cave Wood, Cooleydoody. . . . Some historic estates in the Republic, such as Powerscourt at Enniskerry, 12 miles (19km) south of Dublin, are also open to the public and in Killarney, Co Kerry, magnificent Bourne Vincent national park covers several square miles.

Whatever other changes may alter the face of the countryside in coming decades, the country parks and forest parks of the British Isles are a welcome addition whose permanence seems assured by their popularity. A survey carried out by the Countryside Commission showed that on one Sunday in July well over 200,000 people visited the country parks of England and Wales.

Where to find the parks

Most country parks will be listed on a regional basis in the 1000 Days Out section of this book. Many of the more numerous forest parks, as well as nature reserves and trails, will also be featured in their appropriate regional sections.

A booklet listing country parks in England and Wales recognised by the Countryside Commission together with brief descriptions is obtainable post free from The Countryside Commission, John Dower House, Crescent Place, Cheltenham, Glos. GL50 3RA.
Other sources of information about country or forest parks are:
Northern Ireland Tourist Board, River House, 48 High Street, Belfast BR1 2DS.
A booklet called *The Open Forest* listing the state forests and forest parks of Ire-Forest and Wildlife Service, 22 Upper Merrion Street, Dublin 2, Ireland.
Scottish Tourist Board, 23 Ravelston Terrace, Edinburgh EH4 3EU.
Forestry Commission, 231 Corstorphine Road, Edinburgh EH12 7QT

Reading the Countryside
1: By Compass

Most people will not need a compass for a day out in the countryside. But it is an essential travelling companion if you wish to penetrate the wilderness areas that remain in the British Isles. These are invariably upland areas of moors and mountains where landmarks are fewest and severe weather conditions most common. These two characteristics make the Silva compass in particular as much a 'must' for the outdoors adventurer as the slide rule is for a mathematician. It cuts out errors in compass work and gives rapid results. It consists of three basic parts: a magnetic needle; a revolvable compass housing, its rim marked, N, S, E, W and with degrees from 0 to 360; and a clear plastic base plate marked with a Direction of Travel (DOT) arrow. The illustrations (below) show how it should be used.

Stage one. It is misty. Your route lies from X to the church in a straight line. Lay the compass on the map so one edge of the base plate touches both where you are now – and where you want to go – the DOT arrow pointing to the church.
Stage two. Turn the compass housing

rim until the 'orienting arrow' (printed on the base of this housing) points north on the map: ie, lies exactly parallel with the nearest map grid line and its arrow points towards the top of the map.
Stage three. Finally, in order to find the compass bearing – the number of degrees on the compass at which you will walk – check which degree mark on the compass housing rim touches the DOT arrow. Then allow for the magnetic variation. It is given on each OS map among the key to the symbols – the number of degrees deflected by the magnetic north pole (which moves about inside the Arctic circle) from the true north pole to which your map is drawn.

Let us say your original bearing is 35 degrees and the local magnetic variation is 10 degrees west from true north. So turn the compass housing until 45 degrees nudges the DOT arrow. Hold the compass base plate, pointing the DOT arrow away from you. Turn your body until the red magnetic needle points to north (360 degrees). Keeping the red needle here, walk slowly following the DOT arrow. And that, done carefully, will lead you to the church in mist.

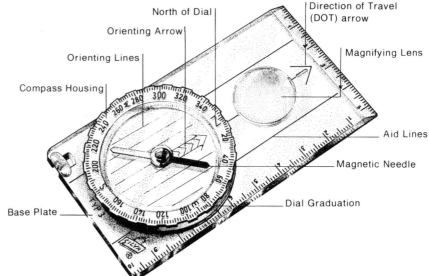

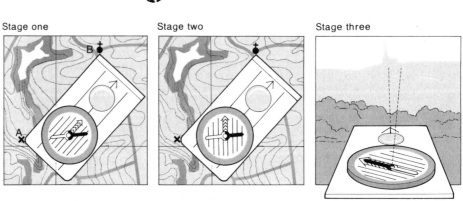

How to use a compass to travel accurately to a church – see text above for explanation of each stage. Good map readers will know from the Ordnance Survey symbol that the church has a spire

Walkers on the Long Mynd, Shropshire; an upland thoroughfare since sheep droving days

2: By Maps

The countryside can be used and appreciated in many different ways, as this chapter has demonstrated. But one common factor that will always enhance enjoyment is an understanding of maps. Once you have mastered the language of maps you cannot understand how you could have previously visited the countryside without them.

There are maps for all occasions and all interests. Some people will use maps to discover minor roads for a day out in the car; others will seek a footpath for a ramble. Some maps are designed for planning long-distance journeys, others for tracking down remnants of the past. For a few people maps can even provide interesting reading in themselves.

'There are Ordnance Survey maps which one can sit down and read like a book for an hour on end, with growing pleasure and enjoyment,' wrote W.G. Hoskins in *The Making of the English Landscape*. (This classic text has a fascinating section in which Professor Hoskins recreates the history of one small part of England simply by discerning the clues in a map.)

Although most people will have somewhat humbler ambitions (and capabilities), understanding a map remains essentially the same question of interpreting the clues. First, though, there is the question of which map to buy.

Which map to choose

The need to choose the 'right' map for your purpose is illustrated by the three maps of the same area of South Devon shown overleaf. But even these three scales, with their clearly visible differences, do not exhaust the possibilities. Generally the most comprehensive and best value maps of Great Britain are provided by the Ordnance Survey – for Ireland, see below. Most others are poor copies, with the important exception of the half-inch to the mile (or 1:127,620 in metric scale) maps produced by Bartholomew and filling a major gap in the Ordnance Survey (OS) series.

Most maps are now produced in metric scales. This means that a map in the 1:50,000 series is drawn so that one centimetre on the map represents 50,000 centimetres or half a kilometre on the ground. A map in the 1:25,000 series has one centimetre on the map representing 25,000 centimetres and therefore shows an area in larger scale or greater detail.

The larger the scale the smaller is the area covered so that closely related to a map's scale is its purpose. No map can show all features of the landscape so most concentrate on a single theme, or at most, a group of themes. This is illustrated by summarising the features of the main Ordnance Survey maps available in Britain. In order of scale, from smallest to largest, these are:

1. The 1:625,000 scale. A Route Planning Map (one sheet covering all of Britain) is revised annually and is useful for touring. A Geological map of Britain (two sheets) is suitable for observing major geological features and other special maps at this scale include Iron Age, Roman and Dark Age Britain.

2. The 1:250,000 scale. Routemaster Series (nine sheets). Primarily road maps although mountains and woodland areas are also shown. A better buy, second-hand, are the superseded Quarter-Inch series maps which showed the countryside in more detail until their withdrawal in the late 1970s.

3. The 1:63,360 scale. The old one-inch to the mile series has been superseded by the metric 1:50,000 but is still used in 'Tourist Maps' for Exmoor, Dartmoor, Peak District, Lake District, North York Moors, Loch Lomond and the Trossachs, Ben Nevis and Glencoe, and the Cairngorms. For historical interest there are also reprints of the 19th century first edition one-inch maps published by David and Charles.

4. The 1:50,000 scale. In 204 sheets at roughly $1\frac{1}{4}$ inches to the mile these are useful for local touring by foot or car but lack detail. The 1:25,000 map is better for walkers, but the 1:50,000 series maps have become established as the most widely available and most widely used of all current OS maps. The larger scale enables greater clarity and detail than was possible in the old one-inch to the mile maps which they have replaced.

5. The 1:25,000 scale. Over 1000 sheets. Some are rather out of date but these are gradually being replaced by the double-size and more colourful Second Series. This scale, which provides an effective compromise between detail and area coverage, can be purchased in two forms: the standard or the 'Outdoor Leisure Map' which includes such extra information as camp or caravan sites, parking places, picnic spots, viewpoints and places of interest like ancient monuments. Outdoor Leisure Maps are available for such places as the Three Peaks, the English Lakes, the Wye Valley, Malham, the Brecon Beacons, Snowdonia, the South Pennines, Cairngorms, the Cuillins, Brighton and the Downs, Purbeck, and South Devon.

6. The 1:10,000, 1:2,500 and 1:1250 scales. For specialist use only and not generally recommended.

Maps in Ireland

Both the Republic and Northern Ireland have their own Ordnance Survey organisations. For the Wicklow area, covering the fine mountains to the north of Dublin, there is an excellent layered map on the 1 inch to 1 mile scale (1:63,360). Elsewhere in the Republic the most useful map is the $\frac{1}{2}$inch to 1 mile (1:126,720) series, based on earlier editions but with some recent additions.

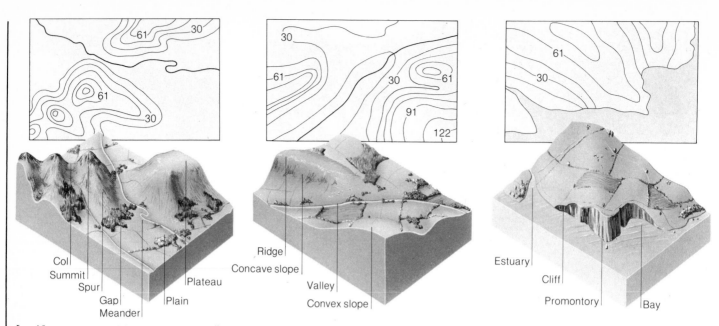

Landforms represented by map contours. The diagrams have been slightly realigned from contour equivalents to maintain symmetry of the illustration

The Irish Tourist Board issues a motoring map indicating distances between towns and villages, plus areas of special scenic beauty.

Northern Ireland has a more modern cover of maps, with a 1:50,000 map like those of the OS in Great Britain currently in production. This is intended to replace the 1:63,360 maps. Motorists may also find the ¼inch to 1 mile Bartholomew maps useful.

How to read a map
Firstly, the scale should be noted and fully understood. It takes only a little practice to judge distances simply by looking at a map – once you know the key. The next step is to examine the content of the map more closely. These are the most important features:

The key explains all the symbols used on OS maps. It is not necessary to memorise these details (although this is often easily done) since all OS maps have a clearly laid out key and some maps will incorporate features which others lack. Use the key to pick out points that interest you.

The National Grid is explained on the keys of most small-scale OS maps although the detail provided varies. The grid is a framework of artificial lines spaced at one or 10 kilometre intervals, according to the scale of the map. These not only enable distance to be judged more easily (remembering that one kilometre is roughly equal to 0.6 miles) but more important means that places can be located with complete precision by stating their coordinates or numbers on the national grid. This is how to do it.

First, study the key. Look for the two grid letters which cover the part of the map for which you want to give a reference. For the 1:25,000 series it is simply the two letters in the map's overall code number – SY in the example opposite. For smaller-scale maps there may be several sets of letters, each covering part of the map, so use the key to find out where these sets begin and end.

Second, take the west edge of the kilometre square in which the point lies and read the large figures printed opposite this line on north or south margins – 08 for Otterton church, opposite page. Then estimate its position in tenths eastwards – 0 in this case.

Third, take the south edge of the kilometre square in which the point lies and read the large figures opposite this line on the east or west margins – 85 for Otterton church. Then estimate in tenths its position northwards of this line – in this case, 2.

This gives the full reference of SY 080852 which is accurate to within 100 metres. No other place within Britain has this reference – *if* the grid letters are included. If the letters are omitted, the numbers will recur at intervals of 100 kilometres. Obviously the grid is seen most clearly and used most easily on the larger scale maps where the key is also invariably fuller, too.

Contours show places of equal height above sea level (in feet or the metric equivalent according to the key). If in doubt a good rule of thumb is to multiply metres by three to get the measurement in feet. Closely spaced contours indicate steep slopes while a lack of contours indicates a plain, river valley or hill-top plateau. A good eye for contour patterns will reveal promising viewpoints: where closely spaced contours give way to few contours, for instance, or where closely spaced contours jut out into a valley and thus allow panoramic views. (Somewhat confusingly the 1:50,000 OS maps show contour values to the nearest metre but the vertical interval between contour lines remain at 50 *feet*.)

Special features are included in all but the smaller scale route-planning maps so that the locations of, say, battlegrounds, burial mounds or Roman roads can be found. (As indicated earlier specialist maps also exist for interests such as history, geology and leisure pursuits.)

How to use a map
Once you understand the language of maps, as explained above, a map can easily be used in the field to read the countryside itself. The first task is to 'set the map' in the direction you want to look at or view. It is unlikely that the view will be directly to the north-south angle of all maps, so the map should be turned round until the view seen corresponds with the orientation of the map. It usually helps if this is done at a viewpoint. The next task is to look for landmarks, for example, prominent churches, lines of pylons, notable hills, woodland, river valleys, lakes or the coast. The map can then be used to fill in the gaps between these obvious landmarks and so complete the landscape jigsaw. A final job is to check for further access to the next stopping point, and the most interesting way of getting there. Remember, that the most direct route may not be the most rewarding route, either by road or footpath. The map may reveal many interesting spots, not apparent on the ground.

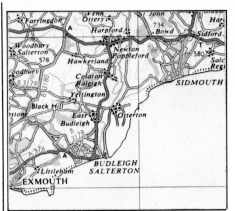

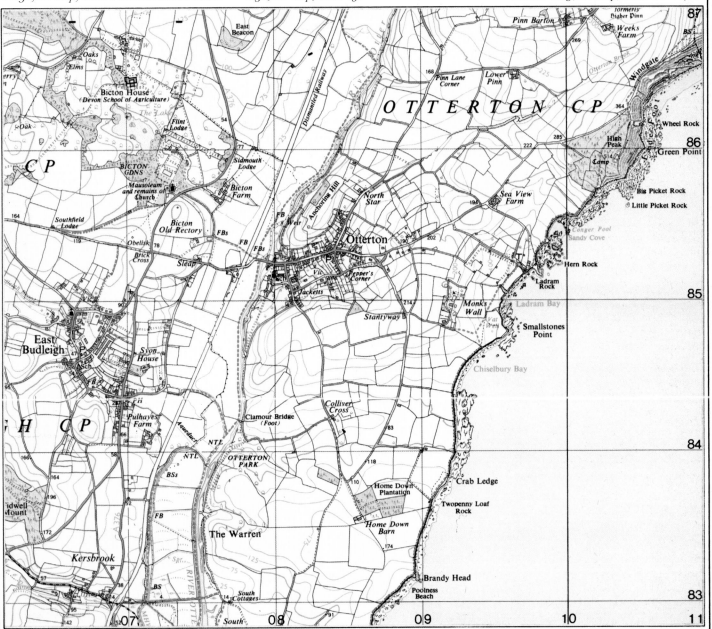

1:250,000 map; sheet 8 in Routemaster Series   1:50,000 map; sheet 192   Below: 1:25,000 map; sheet SY 08/18

The three Ordnance Survey maps reproduced above show the same area of South Devon and illustrate how the scale of a map determines how much or how little is revealed about an area. All three maps clearly indicate the valley of the River Otter but which map can best be used for further exploration? From the 1:250,000 map the lack of details suggest that access to the coast from Otterton is impossible. But the

1:50,000 map and to an even greater extent the 1:25,000 map show not only roads leading to the coast but also a good network of footpaths.

The larger-scale maps also illustrate most of the points made in the general text on these pages. For instance, the closely-spaced contours west of Otterton suggest good views over the Otter valley (if also a steep climb). Further places of interest revealed only by the larger-

scale maps include Bicton Gardens and the disused railway line. One common factor in all three maps, however, is the National Grid although it is read most easily and precisely on the 1:25,000 map. Otterton church is thus at SY080852 while the grid reference for Bicton House, north-west of Otterton, is SY071865 – see facing page for how to read the National Grid.

Chapter Eight

Gardens in the Countryside

There is no other area of the world where the garden is so enthusiastically worked, exhibited and celebrated as the British Isles. This passion has produced gardens which are unequalled anywhere such as the one shown here at Stourhead, Wiltshire. They have flourished because of a beneficial combination of climate and soils, a deep-seated compulsion to experiment and the wealth and resources of their creators. They reflect varying styles and great periods of history, and are open for all to see: some for only a few days a year, others virtually year round. In this chapter the evolution of the great country house garden, from the late Middle Ages to the present day, is described and its design and features explained. At the other end of the scale the origin and development of the cottage garden, for many the epitome of rural gardening, is unravelled

Sissinghurst Castle, Kent. A marriage of formality in design with informality of planting. In 1930 it was derelict. Now it is one of the great gardens

The great garden. It took history and talent to make it

To most people an English garden is a place of flowers. It may be a little lacking in design but makes amends with a rustic charm which is supposed to owe much to a long tradition of cottage gardening.

Yet experts have a totally different view of the great English contribution to the art of garden-making. For them it is the 18th century garden, wholly pictorial in conception and with a minimal requirement for flowers, which is supreme.

Fortunately, however, there are many different types of garden in the British Isles, for this is one art in which the British have proved to be unusually inventive. They have been encouraged to be so by an equable climate, a diverse geology, a love of travel and a fine independence of mind.

There is something else, too: the surprising fact that professionals have played a relatively small part in the story of garden-making. From quite early on the English seem to have concluded that however necessary it might be to employ master builders, surveyors and, as time went on, architects in the construction of their houses, anyone of average intelligence and good taste could design and plant a garden. Freed of the disciplines of a profession they were ready for any experiment that seemed promising. This passionate interest has produced some of the finest gardens in the world.

The British emerged rather late from the Middle Ages and by the time they were ready to start garden-making in earnest the Italians had already brought the architectural garden to a degree of perfection which precluded further improvement. Naturally ideas were borrowed freely from them, and also from the French and Dutch who had already adapted Italian garden-making principles to their own requirements. The resulting 16th and 17th century gardens were formal and (see illustration overleaf) sometimes elaborate. Examples of them are to be seen at Hampton Court, Chatsworth, Edzell Castle and Pitmedden (reconstructed in the 1950s), the two last in Scotland, as well as some excellent reproductions at Blenheim Castle and at Powerscourt, Co Wicklow, Ireland.

But unlike the French, who stayed at home because their king liked to keep them safely under his eye at court, and the Italians who saw little need to travel since they already possessed the best, the British considered their education complete only after a grand tour across Europe to see the wonders of Rome.

It was there that landscape, depicted by many artists, revealed itself to them in a new way. Not only was it beautiful, but it also afforded an alternative model for garden-making. It was from this that the English garden-makers invented a new style of their own where the natural beauty of the site was enhanced by planting. They were, in effect, contriving natural landscapes.

The conceptual leap from the formal, elaborate garden, acting as a buffer between house and wild countryside, to an 'improved' natural landscape sweeping right up to the house, still seems astonishing. Early in the 18th century Lord Burlington employed an artist, William Kent, to experiment in a more natural style of garden-making at Chiswick House; and in Yorkshire John Aislabie, in disgrace as a result of the South Sea Bubble financial crisis, consoled himself by making a formal water garden in an entirely informal setting at Studley Royal in the valley occupied by Fountains Abbey.

But the real revolutionary was Lord Carlisle at Castle Howard in north Yorkshire. Having engaged Sir John Vanbrugh to design a baroque palace, and the leading nursery firm of London and Wise to lay out an elaborate parterre to match it, he suddenly set off on an entirely different course. He began to dramatise the Yorkshire landscape with classical buildings, creating lakes and streams that appeared natural and building an elegant bridge, all for no reason other than they contributed to a picture that might have been devised by the landscape painter Claude Lorrain.

Very soon everyone who was anyone was doing much the same; Lord Cobham at Stowe, Colonel Dormer at Rousham, Henry Hoare at Stourhead and many more. By the middle of the century Lancelot (Capability) Brown, who had worked at Stowe, was setting up as a professional landscaper. In the next 35 years he made or altered about 200 gardens. Inevitably he had many imitators.

Classicism gave way to romanticism, with all the excesses of the gothic revival, plus a brief flirtation with Chinese art and architecture. Alton Towers in Staffordshire still shows this development at its maddest, although the immense growth of trees makes it difficult for visitors today to appreciate quite why J.C. Loudon, the Victorian garden writer and designer, should have described the emerging garden as 'in excessively bad taste, or rather, perhaps, as the work of a morbid imagination joined to a command of unlimited resources.'

In the great landscaped parks flowers were banished to the kitchen garden, and it was probably here that gardeners learned to mass them in long borders, as they still do on some old estates, particularly in Scotland at Williamston, Kincorth and Glen App Castle.

It was not until plant lovers at last revolted against this restriction, and declared that gardens should be designed for plants, that borders emerged from their exile among the vegetables and quickly became fashionable. So did terraces with multitudinous beds, the prime purpose of which was to display the vast numbers of half-hardy plants which gardeners were now able to raise in their greatly improved plant houses.

New plants were pouring into Europe from many parts of the world – pelargoniums from the Cape of Good Hope, fuchsias from South America and camellias from China and Japan – and there were no gardeners more eager to grow them than the British. The climate and geology of their islands combined to produce the varied conditions which made it possible to grow an astonishing range of these new introductions. In the mild coastal regions of the west, washed by the waters of the North Atlantic Drift, it was even possible to grow some of the more tender kinds out of doors. Magnificent collections were established in places as far apart as Tresco Abbey in the Isles of Scilly, Inverewe in north-west Scotland and Garinish Island in Bantry Bay, south-west Ireland.

Splendid conifers, many of them from America's north-west, inspired some landowners to plant collections in specially created pinetums; and when rhododendrons began to arrive from the Himalayas woodland gardens were created to give them the shade and shelter they enjoyed.

The interest in new species was so widespread that many garden owners subscribed to plant hunting expeditions, or even went to plant hunting themselves. They were so successful that they soon found themselves with more seedlings than they had room to accommodate. So gardens once again burst their boundaries and spread out into the countryside; not, this time, with the aim of creating idealised landscapes but of providing plants with conditions as much like those of their native habitats as possible.

The exuberant Victorians, having developed Switzerland as a winter playground, stayed on in summer to climb the mountains and were enraptured by the beauty of the alpine flora. Rock gardens, until then considered solely romantic features, took on a new role and were constructed to look like natural outcrops, and to provide the right conditions for the cultivation of rock plants.

The flowery English garden, with its supposed cottage ancestry, originated towards the close of the 19th century as part of the revolt against industrialisation and the return to traditional craftsmanship.

Although there was much talk about being guided by nature the new gardens were as highly organised as any which preceded them. Some were created by Edwin Lutyens assisted by Gertrude Jekyll, others by Harold Peto. One of the most beautiful and best preserved was made by an American amateur, Lawrence Johnston, at Hidcote Manor in the Cotswolds.

But the most popular of all came a little later and was the work of Vita Sackville-West and her husband, Sir Harold Nicolson. At Sissinghurst Castle in Kent they laid out a garden which might have been a text book illustration of the new ideals, summed up by its creator as being the maximum of formality in design combined with a high degree of informality in planting.

For possibly the first time flower-colour and leaf-texture received close attention and there was much discussion about the most felicitous associations of plants. Roses featured in many of these gardens, and although the old varieties were generally preferred, the public ignored these and took happily to the new races of perpetual flowering roses which were first produced in Britain towards the close of the 19th century. There is, as yet, little evidence that the spell of this kind of gardening has been broken.

Pitmedden Castle, Grampian, Scotland. An elegant reconstruction of a 17th century garden

Six ages of the country house garden

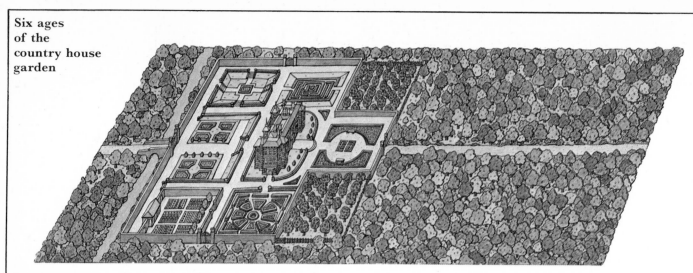

Early formal. The house was nearly always by water, the garden small and intimate, like a courtyard – a protection from the surrounding wild countryside. Gardens were often attached to abbeys. The design was formal geometrical. Plants were grown primarily for their medicinal value or for fruit. Gradually these functional requirements gave way to more aesthetic considerations until this category overlapped with the Baroque. Characteristics were: mazes, labyrinths, gazebos or pavilions; square fishponds; carved wooden statues, often brightly painted; topiary; terraced walks. Flowerbeds became more elaborate, culminating in the 'knot garden' – raised beds made from lines of clipped shrubs, box, thrift or herbs with infillings of coloured earth, gravel, ornamental flowers and shrubs. Plants included mulberry bushes, martagon lilies, hornbeam, rosemary, gillyflowers, lavender and primroses.
Examples: Ham House, Richmond, Surrey; Edzell Castle, Angus, Scotland.

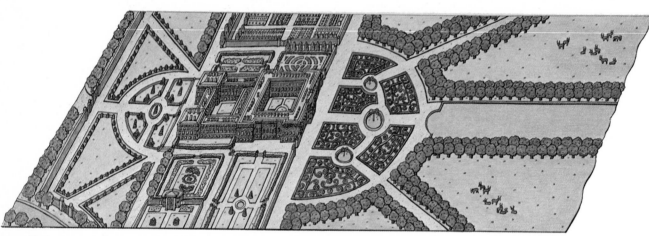

Baroque. Gardens were influenced by the flowering of the Renaissance in France and Italy. There was no longer the need for seclusion, gardens were more flamboyant, like a theatrical set, but still very rigid and formal and of an impressive size. Increased interest in horticulture popularised new species of trees and plants. The first botanic gardens were opened and also the first commercial nurseries. The main characteristics were avenues lined with hedges which fanned out, known as goose-feet or *pattes d'oie*. Beech hedges led the eye on to sculptures, temples and gently-playing fountains and long vistas. Topiary became commonplace but our native yew took the place of box which was very slow growing. Kitchen gardens were walled and separate from the main garden. Elaborate parterres – raised gardens, like embroidery, of plants, shrubs – took the place of knot gardens. There were geometric woods, grottoes and formal lakes.
Examples: Hampton Court, London; Cirencester Park, Gloucestershire.

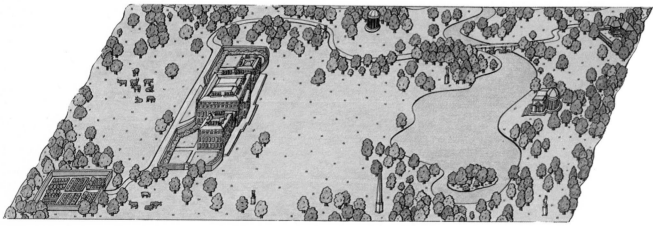

English landscape. This revolt against the preceding formality was influenced by the 'new thinking' of philosophers, writers and particularly the 17th-century landscape painters, Salvator Rosa, Claude Lorrain and Poussin. Two main elements were involved. One was the 'picturesque' which was wild, rugged and romantic, ornamented with garden buildings. The second was the larger 'idealised' natural landscape. In both cases contours were altered, hills raised, valleys excavated, streams dammed to form lakes, and estate villages moved where they would not impair the view. William Kent was the pioneer designer of the period, followed by 'Capability' Brown and Humphry Repton. Thousands of acres were reclaimed from bog and scrub and turned into parkland. The sense of immense space could be deceptive. Landowners planted trees at their boundaries so that it was difficult to tell where the estate ended.
Examples: Petworth, West Sussex; Stourhead, Wiltshire.

Victorian formal. This marked the return to classical and geometric layouts. It was an eclectic style, fond of mass-produced 'Italian-style' ornaments and reproduction works of art. This period saw the rise of the suburban garden as the mercantile classes became increasingly affluent. They were encouraged by a new breed of writers and designers, like John Loudon and his wife Jane who published endless, comprehensive books for the new garden owners. There were many new discoveries: David Douglas went to America and brought back conifers which became popular with Victorians (Douglas Fir). Robert Fortune brought back plants from Japan and China: anemone, winter jasmine, weigela, bleeding heart, forsythia, primulas. Greenhouses, conservatories, orchids and ferneries became popular. The flowerbeds were elaborate and full of dazzling bedding plants. Lawnmowers took the place of the scythe.
Examples: Ascott, Buckinghamshire; Cliveden, Buckinghamshire.

Robinson/Jekyll. A violent reaction to mid-Victorian formality. Both William Robinson and Gertrude Jekyll loved wild woodland gardens which worked particularly well in Surrey, hence the so-called 'Surrey School'. The movement coincided with the restoration and rehabilitation of long-neglected smaller country houses, farmhouses and cottages. Generally, elaborate geometrical beds full of half-hardy plants raised in greenhouses gave way to herbaceous plants in plain borders, creating the cottage garden effect. Robinson and Jekyll had great respect for country skills and village craftsmanship. There was a strong sense of colour, a back-to-nature effect, with flowers and foliage mixed together. Jekyll was famous for her grey-leaved plants. But there were a lot of other new plants for her disciples to take advantage of: camellias, magnolias and the old cottage garden plants which would flourish without further care or cost.
Examples: Barrington Court, Somerset; Wisley, Surrey.

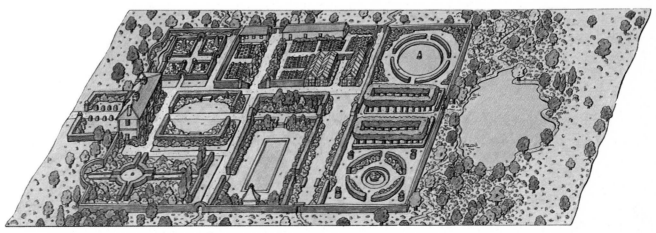

20th-century gardens. No one style has yet emerged as representative of our own age but among the large gardens of large houses two are generally reckoned to be pre-eminent – Hidcote and Sissinghurst. The garden at Hidcote, fashioned by architect Major Lawrence Johnston, forms 'rooms' in a variety of colours and styles, each one a perfect garden in itself, with maybe a pool, garden house or other firm feature. Sissinghurst, which follows a similar pattern, was planned by Vita Sackville-West who described it as 'profusion even extravagance and exuberance within the confines of the utmost linear severity'. Sissinghurst is particularly famous for the 'White Garden' which is full of either white or grey plants. The abundance of styles mean that the gardens feature everything from waterfalls to topiary, avenues of trees to miniature cottage gardens, rose gardens to a wilderness for shrubs, in a changing, orderly procession.
Examples: Hidcote Manor, Gloucestershire; Sissinghurst Castle, Kent.

The cottage garden. It isn't as old as you think

The cottage garden is one of the sweet contentments of the countryside, very personal to those who plant and work it, admired and enjoyed by those who don't. It is small and informal, a patchwork glory of flowers, beds and meandering paths. Ramblers and climbers clothe its walls; roses are well-nigh obligatory round the door.

Nothing quite like it exists outside the British Isles and the picturesque face it presents to the world is re-inforced by the world's expectation, as presented on calendars, jig-saw puzzles and the lids of toffee tins, of what it should be.

Its reality is that it works and looks right, making a good marriage with every style of cottage building – cob and thatch, slate and stone, timber-frame, cobble flint. Cottages and their gardens happily accommodate to each other's character. A haphazard confusion of flowers – lupin, poppy, petunia, violet, periwinkle, hollyhock, nasturtiums, shrub roses, pansies – work well when perspectives are foreshortened and views confined.

All these 'cottagey' ingredients make a heady mix and reassuringly suggest a sense of timelessness, hint at days when life was simpler, enhance a feeling of long tradition. Which is all very comforting, save for one thing: the cottage garden as we know it today has no long tradition. It is a comparatively recent phenomenon which owes much to the urban dream of a little place in the country.

Hardly any of the plants mentioned above were introduced in Britain before 1800. Many other characteristic cottage garden subjects had not arrived by then either. The fleshy-leaved sedums did not appear from Japan until 1868.

Climbing roses such as Zéphirine Douhin and Madame Plantier had not been bred. Although the rose was popular long before the 1800s it was transformed by the introduction of remontant forms (those with the ability to bloom more than once in a year) from China at the end of the 18th and beginning of the 19th centuries. Hybrid Tea roses started to appear in the 1860s; the Floribundas came much later – in the 1920s.

Even the blowzy, large fruited gooseberry bush, serving as the cottager's clothes drier on which household cloths sweetened in the sun, did not appear until the 1840s, although the native shrub had been cultivated in English gardens since Tudor times.

Much that grows in the kitchen garden of the cottage is of modern origin. The cabbage patch had no Brussels Sprouts in it prior to the 19th century. Many of its standbys today were the exotic vegetables of yesterday imported from the New World – potatoes, French beans, sweet peppers, tomatoes and cultivated strawberries.

In any case it was not until after the Industrial Revolution that cottage dwellers had either the leisure or means to indulge in anything more ambitious than gardening for the table.

A growing market for food among the new urban populations improved produce prices. Alternative employment in the towns, with factories and mills competing for rural labour, helped improve hours and wages on the land. For the first time cottage dwellers were able to obtain some aesthetic pleasure from the larger plots which they had gained the right to cultivate centuries earlier in the turmoil following the Black Death when there was a critical shortage of rural labour, aggravated by frequent wars.

No one is really sure what the medieval forerunner of the cottage garden looked like. The domestic affairs of peasants did not merit much attention or illustration in manuscripts, and it is unwise to deduce too much from those references which do exist, since artists in those days tended to glamorise.

The plants available to the cottager were limited. One manuscript of 1440 lists just 78. Many of these were herbs which were essential in disguising the off-flavours of badly preserved meat and fish in the winter months. Their other use was medicinal.

The main preoccupation of the cottager was subsistence. Onions, leeks, spinach, cabbage, broad beans, turnips, parsnips, radishes and beetroot were all grown in Britain then. So were native fruits – apples, pears, damsons and plums. Some plots, or part of them, were probably given over to livestock: geese, ducks, hens, a sow and her litter and possibly a cow. Flowers, if grown, were probably planted at random among the vegetables. There were wild flowers in the garden hedge and at the base of trees and it seems likely that they were encouraged for their colour.

Yet it is possible that by 1580 the cottage garden could have grown many of the plants common to cottage gardens today. These plants were either native to the British Isles, introduced by the Romans and later invaders, or arrived with returning crusaders. Some were spin-offs of Europe's trade with the East for silks and spices.

Two hundred years later a vastly greater range of plants was available to gardeners. These came in the wake of the great voyages of discovery, of European settlement in India, Africa and the Americas and a developing sea trade with China and the Far East.

Initially, as rarities, they first graced the gardens of the great houses. But the natural spread of seed and gardeners taking cuttings for themselves took them into the cottage garden. Many of these plants, so common in today's cottage gardens, had never been seen in the British Isles before 1780. Until then hollyhocks were merely the weeds beneath which Moghul princes lost their polo balls. Red hot pokers were still to arrive from South Africa, so were phlox from North America.

Today's typical cottage garden has most of its roots in the 19th century. It was probably the growing middle class, armed with intellectual awareness and possessed of romantic notions, who played a greater role in the development of the cottage garden than the traditional cottage dwellers.

They shared the gentry's enthusiasms for the new plants which collectors were bringing back from all corners of the world. Their desire to outshine each other in the glory of their displays was fuelled further by the hybridising activities of plant breeders as the understanding of plant genetics increased.

Much of this effort was directed towards annual plants and many have changed almost beyond recognition. Popular varieties like petunias and French marigolds grow larger, flower earlier and last longer than their ancestors of a century ago.

It is a process which continues although it is regretted by some who feel that in increasing their showiness, breeders have sacrificed much of their simple cottage garden charm.

Top: Cottage garden and gardeners in the hamlet of Three Cups Corner, East Sussex. The photograph was taken in August
Bottom right: Haphazard glory of a village garden at Castle Combe, Wiltshire
Middle left: Topiary about to jump the wall at Cranham, Gloucestershire
Bottom left: Running water and a riot of shrubs at Lee Bay, north Devon

Alcove. A recess in a wall or hedge, frequently semi-circular in plan, used to house statuary or protect a seat. Such features have existed in gardens since Roman times.

ALCOVE AND KNOT GARDEN

Arbour. A shelter from breeze, sun or drizzle placed so that a fine view of the garden could be admired and solitude preserved. In the Middle Ages arbours were built from trellis, or poles, and tent canvas. More elaborate brick arbours were created by the Tudors. Solid timber and complicated wrought-iron structures came later.

ARBOUR

Belvedere. An open sided lookout commanding an impressive view of both garden and surrounding landscape. This was frequently in the form of a turret raised from a wall or above the roof of the main building.

Bosket. A well defined block of solid woodland planted with similar and uniform trees or shrubs used to provide a background to some sections of the garden and to hide others. Alleys were sometimes cut through them to create vistas; or wider, cleared areas formed outdoor rooms, like natural theatres, in which seats, ponds with fountains and other features were placed.

Bridges. These usually had minimal function but high aesthetic appeal, forming a feature in an open landscape garden, or drawing attention to a section of it. Most architects favoured the Palladian style with the bridge walkway covered by a portico supported on columns.

Cisterns. These large rainwater collecting butts, usually made of lead, often had intricate and attractive surface designs.

GREENHOUSE AND CISTERN

Clair-Voyee. A break in a boundary wall or hedge which gave longer views into the landscape. Sometimes complete lengths of boundary were replaced by elegant, free-standing wrought-iron screens. Simpler forms consist of grills covering perforations in the wall, or 'window' holes cut in hedges.

Conceits. Imaginative or eccentric superfluities, such as bridges over dry land or ponds on hill tops.

Conservatories. These glass structures were used initially to house delicate plants from abroad and were built to provide maximum light. They were increasingly used from the late 18th century onwards.

Dovecote. One of the oldest garden features with its origins in the practicalities of rural self-sufficiency. In the Middle Ages the cotes housed pigeons – up to a thousand or more birds in large ones – whose flesh provided food at the end of winter

DOVECOTE

when other meat was scarce. It was a way of benefitting from the birds which were eating fields crops anyway. Later the dovecote became a decorative feature with Fantails and Tumblers adding to the charm of the country house.

Exedras. Fairly large, semi-circular spaces, created by a

TEMPLE AND EXEDRA

CLAIR-VOYEE, HA-HA, CONCEIT AND MAUSOLEUM

hedge backed by taller trees, usually housing an ornament or statue. Much less intimate than alcoves.

Fish or Stew Ponds. Originally stocked with carp for the kitchen in medieval monasteries and manors. Now they often harbour decorative fish and water lilies.

Follies. Eccentric buildings-towers, pagodas, tumbling ruins – placed to increase the interest of a landscape and satisfy personal whims.

Gazebo. A two-storied garden house with windows on all sides which provided extensive views. Its architecture was often frivolous.

Grottoes. These were built to resemble natural caverns and were either dug into earth banks, excavated into rock faces or constructed in stone and covered with a mound of earth. They were often lined with shells and came to house zoological and geological collections in the 18th and 19th century. In summer they provided a cool halt during a warm walk.

GROTTO

Ha-Ha. A division between open parkland and garden. It could not be seen from the garden and prevented game and cattle from entering the garden area. It consisted of a wide ditch with a vertical wall on the garden side and a gentle slope up to ground level on the park side. Thus viewed from afar the Ha-Ha appeared to be no more than a slight undulation in the ground.

Ice House. A building with a well drained, underground chamber which was packed with snow in winter and remained very cold throughout the summer, permitting iced sorbets and drinks to be served in hot weather. To improve insulation it was surrounded by trees or tall shrubs and remained in shadow all day.

FOLLY AND MOUND

Features of the grand garden Many of the architectural features of the grand English garden reflect the elegant and leisured style of 18th century country house social life. Making a circuit of the grounds, or an expedition to one part of them, either

Knot Garden. This consisted of small, low-level hedges of clipped shrubs, such as box or yew, planted in various patterns. Sometimes, by clever arrangement and plant choice, the designs appeared to be formed from ribbons of plants tied into knots. The ground between was filled with ornamental flowers, coloured earths, gravels and crushed rock or even coal dust. These rock infillings add to the intricacy of the design and remain decorative during winter months. Knot gardens were usually surrounded by walls or hedges and were quite small.

Mausoleum. An impressive family tomb, frequently in the form of a classical temple, housing bronze or stone sarcophagi, or memorials to ancestors, favourite horses or hounds. Like many features of the great gardens they became popular during the 18th century, and were ideas which were imported by the gentry after having seen them during the Grand Tour.

Maze or Labyrinth. This was a complex network of paths, divided by wall-like hedges to form a labyrinth. It often led to a central arbour. In a true labyrinth the hedges were arched over the path to form a tunnel.

MAZE

Mount. A relic of the watch tower in the form of an artificially created mound providing a prospect of the world both within and without the walls of the park.

Obelisks and Columns. A popular and spectacular way of commemorating victories or defeats.

Orangerie. This was the first form of shelter provided for exotic plants in winter months. Architectural style and masonry was much more prominent than in the later glasshouse. They have existed since Tudor times. The first plants they protected were pruned orange

ORANGERIE

trees grown in wooden tubs which were put out to line paths and form groves in summer. In winter they were heated and their windows were sometimes covered with wooden boards.

Parterres. In the 17th century the parterre replaced the more intimate 16th century knot garden. This was much larger, more formally arranged and open to view from one facade of the house. Clipped grass, flowers and sometimes even water basins, separated the uniform designs indicated by the low clipped hedges.

PARTERRE

Patte D'Oie. A series of paths radiating fanwise like the toes of a goose from a single point.

Pavilion. This was the largest of garden houses, designed to provide comfortable alternative accommodation during the day, and occasionally at night, for

PAVILION

householders seeking a change of surroundings in an epoch when the difficulties of travel kept people at home much more.

Pergola. A fanciful development of the arbour built as a support for vines, trained fruit trees and roses. Extended into covered, or partially covered, walkways they were simply constructed in wooden trellis work. But more sophisticated pergolas combined brick or stone columns and timbers.

PERGOLA AND SUNKEN GARDEN

Topiary. The pruning of trees and shrubs into various shapes has attracted gardeners since Roman times. Yew and box are favourite subjects for sculpting geometric cones, pyramids, cubes, balls, or free forms resembling animals, ogres, men and gods.

TOPIARY

Pleached Alley. A path lined with trees which have been pruned and trained to develop in a single direction to resemble a layered hedge.

PLEACHED ALLEY

Sunken Garden. An area at a lower level than the surrounding garden which gives a variety of contour. The sunken garden concentrated attention on the plants growing there, separating them from plantings in the rest of the garden. They were often sheltered so the blooms of favourite plants like roses kept longer.

Terrace. This was a level space skirting the house and acting as an open-air room to ease the transition from house to garden. Sometimes raised terraces created alongside boundary walls provided a change in perspective; and also gave a

TERRACE AND FISH POND

hanging garden effect, it being possible to walk at the level of the crowns of small trees planted alongside. Terraces were usually bordered by decorative balustrades of elegant masonry and ingenious and beautiful access stairways.

Temple. This was designed to be seen from afar, enhancing the classical aspects of the landscape. It was sometimes used as a mausoleum.

Trellis. Trellis was a simple interlaced diagonal or rectangular arrangement of thin wooden laths forming screens for climbing plants.

walking, riding or driving in a chaise, played a large part in the activities of the great houses. Walks and circuits were designed to include all manner of diversions: monuments and mausoleums, pavilions, arbours and gazebos, terraces and temples

Chapter Nine
Seasons in the Countryside

The British climate has an undeservedly bad reputation. It is hardly ever unbearably hot, seldom numbingly cold. Rain is distributed throughout the year and falls mostly gently with the characteristic lushness seen here near Newtown, Powys. Not for nothing did the Apollo 11 astronauts on their way to the moon in 1969 comment upon how green the British Isles seemed when viewed from space. It is the moderation of the British climate which has helped to give the countryside its distinctive qualities through the seasons

Forecast: a bright clear day as the cumulus and stratocumulus cloud begin to dissipate over the Lake District   *Forecast: a summer's c*

The origins and characteristics of the British Isles climate

The British Isles do not have a climate dominated by reliable or immutable seasons such as the Indian monsoon or Canadian winter. Instead the weather is so unpredictable that Midsummer's Day can be colder than Christmas Day. Almost every year new climatic records are set as the weather varies, apparently dramatically, from day to day and year to year; the drought of 1976 being followed barely two years later by the long hard winter of 1978–9.

Yet over a 20-year period it is still possible to make broad generalisations about the British climate and to that extent one must distinguish between the terms 'climate' and 'weather'. It is the actual day-to-day weather over a long period that establishes an overall climate – and paradoxically it is the moderation and limited variation which in world terms are its prime characteristics.

A few comparisons will serve to illustrate its moderation. First, temperatures. Annual averages are only part of the story. Illinois in the USA and Kazakhstan in southern USSR have similar average temperatures to England, but they have much colder winters and hotter summers. It is when *variations* in temperature are considered that the special features of the British climate become apparent.

In a typical year the lowest temperature recorded anywhere in Britain will be about −18 degrees Centigrade (0° Fahrenheit) and the highest around 30°C (85°F). Yet the overall range of a typical year in north-east Siberia would be 1½ times this maximum range for the whole of Britain. Throughout most of temperate Europe and North America the range of temperatures exceeds that of the British Isles.

Second, rain. The British climate is usually regarded as wet. Yet irrigation is often necessary for agricultural crops in the east and south-east of England, and London with 24in (61cm) of rain a year gets less than Rome or Nice. The average for England as a whole is 33in (84cm), is far less than New York's rainfall, while the average figure for Wales, Scotland and Ireland of about 50in (127cm) is roughly that of Sydney, Australia.

The catch, of course, is that rain in the British Isles falls comparatively lightly throughout the year. This means more wet weather and less sunshine. Nice, for example, has about 100 'rain days' (with a fall of a millimetre or more) in a year. Much of Britain has twice as many. But while the frequent cloudiness and rain may disappoint many holidaymakers it does not affect the gentleness of the British climate and the well-dispersed rainfall helps to make the countryside the glory that it is.

In one respect, however, the climate in many parts of Britain is not so moderate; its windiness. Around the coasts, particularly on the Atlantic seaboard, it is windy by any standards. One effect of the recurrent gales is obvious to the most casual observer even as far south as Cornwall. In places exposed to the full force of the winds from the sea, trees survive only in sheltered valleys or by cowering close to the ground, seeming to cringe at the memory of the wind on even the stillest day.

Friction with the ground always saps the strength of the wind so that inland Britain is not particularly windy. But on higher ground in Scotland and Northern England farmers have still found it necessary to counteract the wind by planting 'shelter belts' like the long strips of beech and pine that are such a feature of the Border landscape. And opposition to the destruction of so many hedges (see Chapter 10) is based partly on their value as wind breaks to protect crops and soil from wind erosion.

Latitude is a basic factor in shaping any climate since it largely determines the hours of sunshine and potential temperature range. But it is above all the Atlantic Ocean which gives the British climate its special characteristics. The temperature of the sea fluctuates with the seasons far less than that of the land, so that unless a major variation of the ocean currents were to occur – as has happened in colder centuries in the past – the sea is

Snowshill in the Cotswolds. Cumulus cloud sails across a blue sky with a chance of showers later in the day

a permanent force for moderation. Winds crossing water are affected by its temperature surprisingly quickly. A bitter wind from the Arctic may warm up 20 degrees (F) or so in a 24-hour journey from Iceland. Yet in summer air from the east, which is causing a heat wave in Germany, may arrive at the eastern coastline 10 degrees cooler as a result of its short passage across the North Sea.

Any large body of water has a moderating influence on climate, but in the North Atlantic there is the Gulf Stream as well. This derives its warmth from its origins as a westward moving current driven by the trade winds across the equatorial regions of the Atlantic Ocean. When it runs up against the land mass of South America this current splits into two parts, flowing north and south along the coast. The 'nose' of Brazil sends the greater part north where the waters pile up in the Gulf of Mexico. They emerge travelling north-east, again helped by the prevailing south-westerly winds towards Britain.

The warm waters of the North Atlantic Drift, as this part of the Gulf Stream is called, bring to the British Isles a climate that is remarkably mild for their latitude. Cornwall and County Kerry have average temperatures about 5.5°C (10°F) higher than the average for their latitudes, 50–52°N.

This is the reason why palm trees survive in parts of Scotland that are as far

north as Labrador, and the seas round Britain provide some of the warmest bathing in Europe north of the Mediterranean. The effects of the North Atlantic Drift are most marked in winter, when temperatures on the west coast of these islands are appreciably higher than those on the east coast.

A third great Atlantic influence on the British climate is the ocean's role as a prolific breeding ground for depressions. These depressions or cyclones are areas of low pressure which, with their cold and warm fronts, so dominate the weather charts which appear on television and in many newspapers. The weather associated with cyclones is broadly the opposite of that brought by anticyclones or areas of high pressure. In the simplest terms these are the characteristics and origins of these two systems:

Cyclones or depressions are areas of low pressure formed by the meeting of two or more air masses. When the warm air of one air mass meets the cold air of another their unequal characteristics lead to instability and the formation of cyclones with the original air masses over-running and undercutting each other at warm and cold fronts so that the lesser density of the warmer air brings this air mass to overlie the denser, colder air. These cyclones are in fact great circular storms, often a thousand miles or more across, which are driven by the prevailing westerly or south-westerly

wind in the upper air across the Atlantic to or near Britain. The actual weather caused by these cyclones varies even within the same cyclone, as illustrated overleaf. But it is these continually passing storms that are responsible for some of the prime characteristics of the British climate: the windiness of the coasts; the changeability of the weather from day to day; and the rain, since the winds are laden with moisture after travelling for thousands of miles over the Atlantic.

Anticyclones are areas of high pressure in which the air is stagnant or moving only slowly (in a clockwise direction). They are not the predominant feature of the British climate, but their influence is very strong since they 'steer' the depressions. There is also quite a high frequency of days in all seasons when anticyclones extend close to and partly over the British Isles. Whatever the season anticyclones bring settled weather for they are slow to develop, usually slow moving and slow to disperse. In summer this means high temperatures with usually minimal wind or clouds; in winter they can bring sharp frosts and persistent mists or fog. A strongly developing anticyclone will cause depressions either to break up or to change direction in order to avoid it.

The British climate is thus shaped by not only latitude but also this threefold effect of proximity to the Atlantic Ocean. But the weather in any one place within

Britain will be determined by other factors, notably height above sea level and longitude or, more specifically, distance from the continent.

Mountains have particularly important effects on local climate, notably on rainfall but also temperature. In parts of Snowdonia, the Lake District and Western Scotland the annual rainfall is around 200in (508cm), locally even more. Not much by world standards – at Cherrapunji, in the mountains of Assam, it can rain more than 1000in (2540cm) a year – but as much as ten times more than the driest parts of south-east England. Since most rain-bearing depressions arrive from the Atlantic, and most of Britain's mountains are in the west, this leads to a great drop in rainfall totals from west to east with inevitable consequences for agriculture.

There is also a natural decrease in temperatures as one goes further north. Coupled with the greater windiness of the north this accounts for the markedly more barren appearance of northern Scotland compared with, say, south-west England. More subtle, though, is the trend to greater 'continentality' from west to east. Continental climates are characterised by more extreme conditions, and one index of continentality is the difference between average temperatures in January and July. In south-east England, the part of the British Isles most

remote from oceanic influences, this is twice as great as in the Western Isles, where there may be little to choose between a mild day in the middle of winter and a bad one in high summer.

Ireland is the first landmass that many depressions encounter and rainfall is heavy on the western mountains. The number of rainy days varies from one in two in the east of Ireland to two in three in the west. In the inland districts sheltered by the mountains of Kerry, frosts are quite frequent though they seldom last as long as in England or Scotland. Snow is rare too, because of the warming influence of the North Atlantic Drift. Tree growth on exposed coasts is sparse but crops grow with luxuriance behind high walls and in the valleys, especially at Killarney, where there is rich and constant tree and plant growth.

Many factors, both global and local, thus combine to help shape the countryside – as explained alongside. They will continue to do so for the climate is continuously changing. There was, for instance, a Little Ice Age which was at its height in the 17th century when temperatures were on average a degree or so colder than today. There was a marked warming in the first 40 years of this century, although since about 1940 it has got a little colder.

Nobody really knows what will happen next. Climatic changes are imper-

ceptible in the short-term because of the much more prominent differences from one year to the next. Yet the implications of long-term changes are profound, particularly for agriculture if the growing season is curtailed, but also for the general water supply. There is now general agreement among climatologists that the climate over the last 30 years has got colder and that this 'cooling' is still continuing. Regions north of 50°N and especially the Arctic show the most significant changes. But the majority of climatologists are more worried by the possibility of a warming of the world climate which could shift crop belts and desert zones further north while raising sea levels with sometimes devastating effects as ice-caps melt.

One school of thought predicts as much as a 10 to 20°F warming over the next century simply as a result of the additional carbon dioxide man is adding to the atmosphere by burning fossil fuels. Others argue that this threat is unproven and claim that a one per cent increase in cloudiness would cancel out all the effects of extra carbon dioxide. It is an important but complex debate. And it is a fair bet that in the year 2000 climatologists will still be arguing about it, while as far as everyone else is concerned the British climate at least will be much the same as it always was: mild, damp and changeable.

Anatomy of a Depression

These illustrations (right) show how, and why, weather varies within an area covered by a depression, Air moves anticlockwise within a depression with 'fronts' forming between the masses of Tropical and Polar air of which the depression (or cyclone) is composed. At the warm front the Tropical air overrides Polar air whereas the cold front occurs where Polar air undercuts the Tropical air. An 'occluded' front occurs when a cold front 'overtakes' a warm front. Temperatures usually rise sharply at the warm front and fall at the cold front. Rainfall patterns are also different being more prolonged at the warm front although topographical features can cause considerable variation over land. Between the warm and cold fronts, particularly in the 'narrower' part of the warm sector, low clouds and drizzle are common. The weather associated with an occluded front is more or less a combination of the pre-warm frontal and post cold frontal weather, but sometimes heavy rain and thunderstorms.

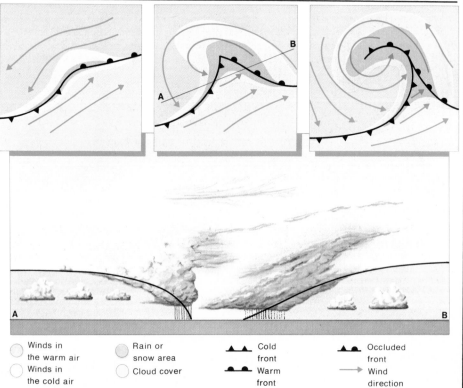

◯	Winds in the warm air	◯	Rain or snow area	▲▲ Cold front	▲▲ Occluded front
◯	Winds in the cold air	◯	Cloud cover	●● Warm front	→ Wind direction

Cold air from the north overlaps warmer air from the south (top left) to cause warm and cold fronts (top centre) and finally an occluded front (top right). The weather associated with these fronts on a line from A to B is shown above

Source: Climate: present, past and future by H. H. Lamb. NB: maps should be inverted for southern hemisphere where cold air comes from south

How climate shapes the landscape

The effects of climate upon the landscape are both superficial and profound. It is the rain, day after day, month after month, which gives so much of the British Isles the green colour that is so vivid to foreigners. And it was the climate along with geology which helped to shape patterns of agriculture and settlement. One yardstick of climatic differences within Britain is the 'growing season' for plants. This is affected by both the north-south and west-east differences described earlier in this chapter (see map below).

It is in the mountains that the most striking effects of climate on landscape can be seen. One is the 'tree line'. There has been so much interference by man that it is difficult to find a true natural tree line in Britain, but it can still be seen where the Rothiemurchus forest struggles up to about 2000ft (610m) near Aviemore in north-eastern Scotland. This is about the limit anywhere in Britain, and in many places trees find it difficult to survive above 1500ft (457m) because of the wind. Considering the mildness of the climate the natural tree line is surprisingly low. In central Norway, for example, where the climate is much more severe, it is some 1500ft (457m) higher. Paradoxically it is the moderation of our climate that is responsible. Winter temperatures may be

Cumulus cloud developing over the hills near Troutbeck, Cumbria – see diagrams below

higher than in Norway, but lower summer temperatures make the growing season shorter.

At a height of 1800ft (549m), with temperatures on average 3–4°C (6–7°F) lower than at sea level, the growing season is some months shorter than in the lowlands, and this sets a limit on the greatest single influence on the making of the British landscape: human cultivation. Above 1800ft (549m) there are no crops, only very limited pasture for grazing sheep. Altitude even determines the times at which lambs are born, since this is timed to coincide with the renewed growth of the grass in spring. On the highest farms there may be no lambs until May, lower down they appear months earlier.

In some parts of the country – Dartmoor is an example – rainfall as well as temperature helps to fix the upper limits for agriculture. The higher ground is only workable if it has good natural drainage, artificial drainage being uneconomic. Therefore it may be the better drained side of a valley rather than the one facing south which is farmed.

The high rainfall of the uplands also helps to determine their character beyond the limits of agriculture. Where the underlying rocks are impervious to water, as they are over much of upland Britain and Ireland, peat bogs form on which few plants can survive. Even heather, a typical moorland plant, can be ousted here. Cotton grass is one of the few species that thrives. Yet a few

miles from the desolate tundra-like peat bogs of the Pennines, in the lowlands where the climate is warmer, drier and less windy and the soil fertile, delicate exotics are cultivated by gardeners. Like the geological landscape of Britain the climate is on the whole gentle, but exceptionally varied, providing sharp contrasts in a comparatively small area.

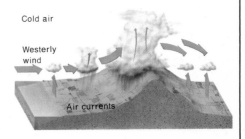
Cold air rises rapidly to cross hills or because of ground heating. Showers occur on upslopes. These can be heavy on the steeper slopes and near the tops of hills. Clouds disperse as descending air warms, though some local cloud can remain as a result of ground heating

Warm air also rises to cross hills but warm air masses aloft allow rising air currents less buoyancy. Only drizzle and fine rain fall, though this may be copious near the tops. Clouds disperse on lee side. See under 'Rain', p 211

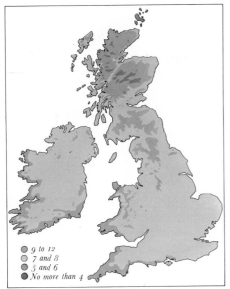

(Source: Accumulated temperature maps of the British Isles, S. Gregory, 1954)

- 9 to 12
- 7 and 8
- 5 and 6
- No more than 4

How the growing season for plants varies within the British Isles. The length of this season is defined by the number of months (above) with a mean temperature above 6°C (42·8°F). Even within these four broad categories the length of the season will differ not only from year to year but also in intensity or range of temperatures. Topographical conditions, such as frost hollows or hilltops, also cause marked local divergences

Red sky at night . . .

There are dozens of proverbs for predicting the weather – hours, days, and even months ahead. Are they the distilled wisdom of centuries of shrewd weather observation, or merely old wives' tales? Here and there the old sayings are undoubtedly sound metereological observations.

'When clouds appear like rocks and towers, the earth's refreshed by frequent showers', for example, contains an accurate description of typical shower clouds. 'A northern *haar* brings fine weather from afar' is also often true: a *haar* (a sea mist on the North Sea coast of Scotland and northern England) is frequently a result of anticyclonic conditions, and if the mist clears a lovely day can follow.

'Mackerel sky, not long dry' also has some scientific basis. A striped 'mackerel' sky is often caused by ripples in the high level cloud sheet associated with an advancing front. Still higher-level veils of cloud ahead of a warm front can produce the halo round the moon which is popularly supposed to mean that rain is on the way.

'Red sky in the morning, shepherd's warning, red sky at night, sailor's delight' is more doubtful. It might have some justification in the fact that a red sky can be a result of the haze produced by good weather, anticyclonic conditions. Most of our bad weather comes from the west, where the sun sets, so a red sky at night may be a sign that there is nothing nasty in the offing. A red sky in the morning – to the east – provides no such assurance, though there is no particular reason why it should be a warning.

There could also be a grain of truth in such sayings as 'If Candlemas day (February 2) be fair and bright winter will have another fight, if Candlemas day be clouds and rain winter be gone and will not come again'. A mild anticyclonic break early in February often does develop later in the month to give a spell of cold weather, often when the same anticyclone moves further north and brings easterly winds to Britain.

Similarly the belief that a fine St. Swithin's day (July 15) means that the rest of the summer will be fine, and vice versa, is supported by the fact that summers do tend to settle into a pattern around the middle of July. So the weather around St. Swithin's day, though not necessarily on it, can provide a hint of what is to come.

The idea behind 'For every fog in March there'll be a frost in May' has actually been investigated by the British Meteorological Office and found to have some foundation in fact. Some professional meteorologists also think there is a connection between the phase of the moon and the weather, as in the saying 'The moon and the weather change together'.

Traditional weather lore often uses the state of trees and other plants to predict whole seasons ahead. A good show of holly berries, for example, is supposed to indicate a hard winter on the way. In 'Oak before the ash, we shall have a splash; ash before the oak, we shall have a soak' the time the oak and ash come into leaf is meant to show what the coming summer will be like. Yet another is 'Onion skin very thin, mild winter coming in. Onion skin thick and tough, coming winter cold and rough'.

It is just possible that there is a connection between the weather at different times of year which would marginally save such sayings from being so many old wives' tales. The number of holly berries, for example, might be due to a wet spring and wet springs might tend to be followed by cold winters. But the numerous holly berries during the run of exceptionally mild winters in the mid-1970s did not inspire confidence in their value in weather prediction.

Country weather lore, in fact, often has something in it, but not much. It is a rash farmer who plans his harvest around the weather on St. Swithin's day, and a rash holidaymaker who sets out for the coast believing that 'rain before seven' really would mean 'fine before eleven'.

The differing climatic worlds of Dartmoor and Torbay

Climatic differences, and especially their relationship to altitude, play an integral part in shaping the scenic contrasts of the British Isles. This can be seen in microcosm in the contrast between Torbay – and Dartmoor in Devon: a journey of around 25 miles (40km) from lush subtropical vegetation on the coastal lowlands to sub-arctic species on the uplands.

At Torre Abbey gardens exotic species can be observed in both the open and the palm houses. Torbay is sheltered from all but the severest winters and so it can support a wide range of sub-tropical vegetation. The most popular exotics are Eucalyptus and Acacias as well as the well-known palms. An interesting local

tree is the Evergreen Oak. (Even in Torbay, however, cold spells can occur, and the winter of 1978–9 inflicted considerable damage.)

The road from Torbay to Dartmoor via Paignton and Totnes soon shows how vegetation deteriorates with rising altitude and distance from the sheltered coastline. An intermediate stage can be seen at Shinners Bridge. Looking north the mixed landscape of arable and pastoral farming, interspersed with a mixture of deciduous and coniferous woodland, reflects the normal progression of land use with increasing height from arable to pasture to woodland.

The road to New Bridge via Buckfastleigh and Ashburton travels upwards through first pasture and meadowland, and then woodland, before coming to the boundary of upland Dartmoor close to where it crosses the River Dart at New Bridge. Before the woodland gives way to the lower moorland vegetation of gorse and bracken it becomes poorer and thinner with the native birch, oak and hazel replacing the more luxuriant species found nearer the coast. But the decline is not solely due to altitude: the transition from the more fertile soil near the coast to the poor acid granites of Dartmoor is also a factor.

The drive from New Bridge to Princetown via Dartmeet and Two Bridges reveals not only the effect of altitude, but also the effect of local drainage conditions and man's attempt to modify the bleak Dartmoor climate. On the most exposed and wet sites only very poor vegetation can survive, but on the sheltered side of hills, or the lee side of shelter belts, or on freely drained sites, rich heather moorland or even cultivated fields can be seen.

Thus this short journey of such diverse vegetation illustrates very dramatically how patterns of agriculture and settlement can differ radically with very minor changes of climate. A slight deterioration would mean the elimination of all exotic species and much arable farming; a slight improvement could mean the reclamation of even upland tracts of Dartmoor to farmland.

□ The roads to follow in order to see these climatic differences for yourself are described in the Days Out section of this book under Devon. Also detailed in this section is the site of a settlement on Dartmoor which is believed to have been abandoned partly because of a deterioration in the climate.

Ten common phenomena of the climate in the British Isles

Cloud. The cooling of the air generally causes some of the water vapour in it to condense into a cloud of tiny droplets of water (or crystals of ice) which remain suspended in the air. Dust in the atmosphere plays a part in this process since the droplets of water tend to condense around a nucleus of solid matter. Clouds differ in appearance because they are formed in different ways – by rising air currents, cyclones or a combination of the two, for instance.

Dew. When the land cools at night this often causes condensation in the form of dew on soil or grass. When the point at which dew forms is below freezing point, the result is hoar frost.

Fog. Temperatures normally fall as altitude rises but the position is reversed on calm, clear nights. One consequence of this inversion of temperature, if the air is moist enough, is fog. Fog often forms first at valley bottoms where temperature inversion is most marked – see 'Frost hollows' below. Other places where fog forms first are over damp places such as marshes, wet fields and woodlands and where man adds moisture to the air, as in the exhausts of motor traffic. Occasionally, in still conditions, fog forms just along the roads or is thickest there. (See also: Sea Mists.)

Frost hollows. This is also a consequence of the inversion of temperature which occurs on calm, clear nights where hills surround substantial valleys. Cold air flows down the hillside during the night to accumulate at the valley bottom. As the air warms after dawn it rises and often mixes with cold air to form fog or low cloud. The effect of frost hollows on the landscape can be seen in areas like Kent and Worcestershire where orchards stick to valley sides where frost damage to the blossoms is less likely.

Rain. The droplets of water that make up clouds can unite to form larger drops which fall as rain (or, in the case of ice crystals, grow to form snowflakes). Rain can be caused in a number of ways. Cyclonic rain is produced by the low-pressure systems known as depressions described earlier; convection or convective rain is caused by warm moist air rising over hot ground; and relief rain occurs when damp air rises because of hills. Illustrations on page 209 show the different effects of warm and cold air passing over hills or mountains such as the Pennines.

As atmospheric pressure decreases with height, the air is rapidly cooled by expansion during its ascent. Whether the ascent of the air has been assisted by the wind being forced to rise over a ridge of hills or merely by the air coming over particularly hot land surfaces, the air can be cooled sufficiently by its ascent to produce a sharp, although usually short-lived, shower of rain or snow. Since temperatures of land surfaces rise during the day, showers are most likely to be frequent and heavy from midday onwards over strongly-heated plains and windward slopes or summits of hilly areas. In coastal areas they are likely to be much fewer, or not to occur at all, in the warm season. But in winter, when the sea is warmer than the land, shower activity is more frequent at sea or near the coast and rare inland.

Rainbow. This can be seen only when it is both sunny and wet. Rainbows are produced by the refraction and internal reflection of sunlight in minute droplets of water in the air.

Sea breezes. At sea level itself the sea is the major climatic influence: it is generally warmer than the land in the winter, and cooler in the summer. On warm summer days, therefore, as the land heats up and air begins to rise, cooler air from over the sea is sucked in to replace it, leading to sea breezes and often clear blue skies on the coast. Inland the moisture content of the sea breeze supplies the cloud development in the rising convection currents over the heated land, and sometimes plays an essential part in the thunderstorms that develop inland.

Sea mist. Fog can be caused by the mixing of warm and cold air and one instance of this breaks the general rule of warmth and sunshine at the seaside. The sea mist or haar is found most often on the east coast of England and Scotland in the early summer months when warm air from the continent travelling over the cold North Sea has been cooled so much that low cloud or fog is produced. As this air travels inland however, the warmer ground heats it up so that unbroken sunshine can then occur within 10 miles (16km) of the coast.

Thunderstorms. These are often violent over hills and mountains, but are probably most frequent and violent near rivers and lakes which ensure their moisture supply. Evaporation of moisture from the surface plays an important part in maintaining the essential moisture supply, the electrical charges being produced in the splitting of large raindrops in violently rising currents of air. Sometimes thunder and lightning are accompanied by hailstones, formed when raindrops are carried by a powerful updraught to levels where the air temperature is well below freezing point. Thunderstorms are a type of convection rainfall (see above) which occurs quite often in the British Isles, particularly in the summer, but which are more common in warmer climatic zones.

Winds. These have both global and local causes. Globally there are the great air masses and the depressions already described. Locally there are not only sea breezes but mountain and valley breezes which develop under much the same conditions. Cold mountain air descends into the valleys and plains during the night but in the daytime, since the mountains are first to be heated by the sun, warm air there rises causing a wind to blow from the valleys and plains towards the mountains.

Whatever the source or cause of a wind the recognised scale of measuring wind strength is the Beaufort Scale (below).

Beaufort Scale	Description	Speed metres per second	Observations
0	Calm	0–0.3	Smoke goes straight up
1	Light air	0.3–1.5	Drifting smoke; vanes still
2	Light breeze	1.6–3.3	Rustling leaves
3	Gentle breeze	3.4–5.4	Leaves and small twigs move
4	Moderate breeze	5.5–7.9	Small branches move; dust raised
5	Fresh breeze	8.0–10.7	Small trees sway
6	Strong breeze	10.8–13.8	Large branches move; singing telephone wires
7	Moderate gale	13.9–17.1	Whole trees in motion
8	Fresh gale	17.2–20.7	Walking difficult; whole trees sway
9	Strong gale	20.8–24.4	Chimney pots broken
10	Whole gale	24.5–28.4	Trees uprooted; much damage
11	Storm	28.5–33 5	Widespread damage
12	Hurricane*	over 33.5	Whole area laid waste

* Hurricanes are also known as typhoons, particularly in the Far East. They are both a consequence of cyclones which are more violent in tropical than temperate latitudes.

JANUARY

FEBRUARY

MAY

JUNE

SEPTEMBER

OCTOBER

This is one man's countryside, photographed each month for a year. It records not merely the passage of the seasons but less happily the march of electricity pylons across the landscape. The view looks north-west, from a height of about 800ft (244m) along the valley of the River Barle. At the very centre of the view, nestling between round-shouldered hills, is the Exmoor village of Dulverton, $3\frac{1}{2}$ miles (5.6km) away. The skyline, seven miles (11km) distant is Winsford Hill, maximum elevation

1275ft (389m) and true Exmoor.

If the man-made change to this particular view in the form of the pylons was the most enduring change that occurred in the 12 months, the changes wrought by the passage of the seasons were nonetheless dramatic. They were also unique for although every year people say that spring or summer is 'late' or 'early' there is never any fixed point when the four seasons begin or end.

They vary not only from year to year but also within Britain from area to area

in the same year. Although spring comes first to the south-west – because this is the area that benefits most from the warming effects of the North Atlantic Drift – the arrival of spring and the length of each season is closely related to the topographical features such as height above sea level, sheltered valleys and south-facing slopes. Even light sandy soils can make a local climate warmer.

If the seasons themselves are variable, so is the weather within each season. But here are the causes of the weather that is

MARCH

APRIL

JULY

AUGUST

NOVEMBER

DECEMBER

most characteristic of each season.

Spring. The land begins to get warmer than the surrounding sea so that rain starts to penetrate further inland to fall as April showers. Marked changes of temperature may occur with cold Polar airstreams dominant in some years giving late frosts and snow.

Summer. The best weather generally comes from a northwards extension of the Azores anticyclone. The combination of high pressure over the British Isles and light, warm and dry winds from the continent can produce a heatwave.

Autumn. From late August onwards the Azores 'high' becomes more variable in its behaviour and commonly sends offshoots over Britain and Europe in September and early October. Ultimately an anticyclone establishes itself over Siberia and starts to intensify. This, in simplified terms, tends to bring the track of Atlantic depressions further south to produce autumn gales.

Winter. Sometimes British winters are continuously mild with a strong anti-

cyclone near the Azores steering mild Atlantic air over the British Isles or an anticyclone over Eastern Europe steering southerly winds towards Britain. But the combination of high pressure over Scandinavia and a cyclone or low in the English Channel produces bitterly cold winds from the East. And where these meet moisture-laden air coming with a depression from the Atlantic, the result is snow. Similarly anticyclones over Greenland and Iceland send cold Arctic air towards the British Isles from the North.

Wildlife in the winter countryside

The inter-dependent worlds of nature are illustrated well by what can be observed – and not observed – during winter. It is a time of low sun and short days: in London the angle of the sun above the horizon at noon on December 21 is just 15° compared with 62° on June 21 and the day 7 hours 50 minutes long compared with 16 hours and 35 minutes.

The low sun and short days mean less energy for the plants and so less green leaf. Most woody plants shed their leaves while other plants die down to rootstock or underground tuber. Many survive the winter as seeds. And it is not only a matter of energy; drought can be a problem when water is locked up as ice in frozen soil. So the plants that retain their leaves tend to be those with thick, impervious skins such as pine, holly or ivy.

With leaves gone, the trees reveal their skeletons of trunk and branches. Each is distinctive. For instance, the ash, which is often the commonest field tree now that so many elms are dead, has the twigs of the bottom branches twisting upward at the end. Tree twigs with their late winter buds can also be as recognisable as leaves. Bark can be equally distinctive.

Without much plant life, insect life is also scarce. One exception is the winter moth which flies in December. The peacock butterfly and a few others hibernate, hidden in cracks in trees or in garden sheds; other butterflies pass the winter in the pupa stage. Many insects survive as eggs, aphids for example. Only the queen wasp survives, hibernating. Bees (Honey queen and workers) stay in the nest, living off honey stocks. Snails seal off their shells, and often congregate in groups. Communal winter dens of dormant, entwined adders have also sometimes been found. Frogs rest in the mud of the pond, while toads use holes in the soil. The danger to them all is a long, cold, snowless winter. Snow itself insulates – since it is mainly air (a foot of snow melts to an inch of water), and therefore protects the waiting life below.

Apart from the robin's sad little winter soliloquy, few birds sing. Natural food becomes scarce, and is even harder to find during a cold snap. This is the time for titbits of food. The greater the variety you put out, the more species you are likely to attract. The most regular visitors are robins, blue tits and great tits, starlings, blackbirds, song thrushes, hedge sparrows, chaffinches and greenfinches. But sometimes less common species such as siskins and marsh tits turn

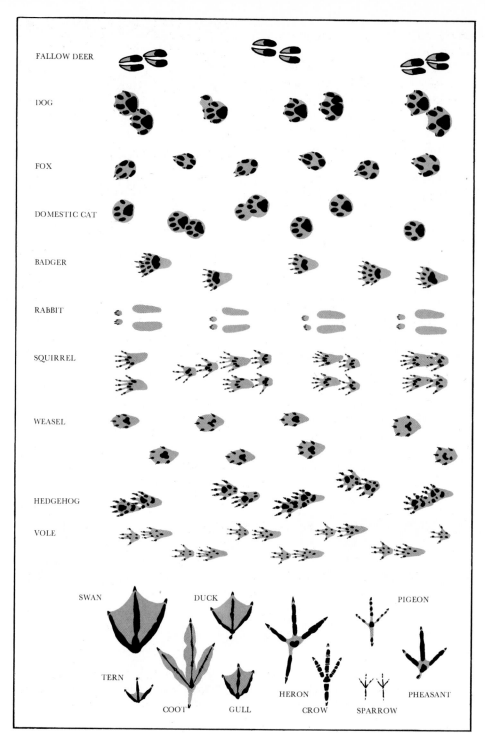

Animal and bird tracks in the snow: size and shape are the basis of identification

up, and in the extreme south and west of Britain you may even see a blackcap. This distinctive warbler is not rare but it is essentially a spring and summer visitor. However, some blackcaps have taken to over-wintering in the British Isles. Species such as starlings and hedge sparrows will peck happily at food put out on the lawn, but the acrobatic tits prefer hanging feeders topped up with nuts, while the robin and chaffinch are best served from a bird table.

Without plant or insect food, many birds leave Britain during the winter in search of warmer climates. But others, on the same quest, migrate to Britain – the

Greenland white-fronted geese that winter on the marshes around Wexford Harbour in Ireland and the dark-bellied Brent geese that fly into Essex from Siberia, for instance. Still more birds use Britain as a staging post in longer journeys while the behaviour of residents also changes, as described in Chapter Four.

Enough birds remain in the British Isles and enough large animals remain active to produce firm evidence of their existence in tracks across the snow. A thin layer of fine dry snow takes the best impression, though details fade and the tracks look larger as the edges melt. Tracks can also be found in the mud alongside a stream or on any soft ground where the minimal winter vegetation allows prints to be seen easily.

Even without a covering of snow the ploughed and bare fields can tell a story. Ploughing itself can bring to the surface scraps of tile, pottery and animal bone to indicate sites of former settlements. On pastureland lack of vegetation means that the ridge and furrow patterns of old strip farming can be seen more clearly, although snow also reveals these lines with great clarity. For those with the eyes to see the winter is alive with interest.

Walking in winter

Before you step out in winter remember that the landscape which has the beauty to entice also has the power to deceive and the power to kill. Even a gentle afternoon ramble can lead to a chilling shock. It can be made safe only by planning and applying some basic rules.

☐ Collect the right clothing and equipment (see Rambling, page 177) and break it in on short walks and rambles.

☐ Recruit some kindred spirits. In winter the balance favours the elements and companions help restore the odds.

☐ Plot your route – even for a stroll. Beside estimating your approximate speed, allow for fewer daylight hours. Start and finish than normal.

☐ Avoid steep grass above quarries, sea cliffs and other potential hazards. Proofed nylon waterproof clothing may be a hazard for its wearer and slide all too easily over the frozen grass as well as ice or snow; it is easy to slip and tumble out of control at high speed.

Snow and ice on mountains and wild moorland pose too much risk unless you have experience. You need to have learned the craft of climbing either from a course, or experience, or both. You need to know how to carry an ice axe, how to hold it, how to check a fall with it and how to cut steps. You must be able to navigate through mist so dense it merges with the snow to cause a 'white-out' and it is impossible to tell up from down without throwing snowballs ahead and spotting where they land. You need to be able to recognise the different types of snow and potential avalanche risks.

Pack your rucksack with care including food and a vacuum flask of hot soup or coffee. Fresh drinking water is difficult to find in winter; not only are pools and streams frozen solid, but taps and standpipes might be turned off in case they burst. Shops, cafes, pubs and hotels can be closed, too. Observe the 'Dos and

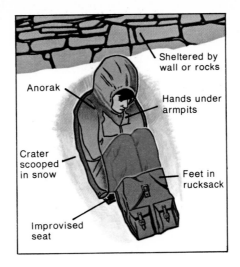

How to survive a blizzard in a 'snow hole'

Dont's' listed on page 177 and if unlucky enough to be caught in a blizzard in open country, dig a 'snow hole' and follow survival rules:

1 Get into the lee of any natural protection, like rocks or a wall.

2 Scoop a small cave or crater, depending on the firmness of the snow.

3 Put on all clothing except anorak.

4 Undo bootlaces, belts, cuffs and collars.

5 Make a seat from heather, maps, guidebook, towel, plastic food boxes, mug, water bottle, toilet paper and camera case.

6 Chew food from now on.

7 If no bivi bag (see page 177) sit on 'seat', put feet inside rucksack and put on anorak with arms inside (not in sleeves) and hold crotch or armpits; play pig-in-the-middle and huddle together.

8 If you have a bivi bag, climb into sleeping bag inside it. If no sleeping bag, sit in bivi bag on 'seat', feet inside rucksack and wear anorak as above. Pull bivi bag up over head and leave space for face.

9 Keep checking that your position is not restricting your circulation. Wriggle toes, move fingers and sing.

10 Wait until conditions improve (and probably daylight, too) and then move on without delay to notify anyone expecting you that you are alive and well.

The first signs of spring

There is a country saying: 'Spring has come when you can cover five daisies with your foot.' Each lengthening day of the new year weakens winter's grip as the earth tilts Britain closer to the sun. Soon, one by one, plants which have lain dormant through the dead mid-winter begin to grow again. Sap rises, buds swell; a miraculous built-in response to the lengthening daylight hours and rising temperatures.

In the south and west, where spring comes first, wild flowers begin to bloom: snowdrops from January onwards, followed by coltsfoot, lesser celandine, delicate wood anemones and dog violets, the leafless pink spikes of butterbur, and most welcome of all, the sight of hedgebank primroses. The deciduous trees are also stirring. On the bare ash branches, sooty buds are prominent; on the horse chestnuts, every twig bears large and handsomely varnished 'sticky buds' (the toffee-brown resin protects the embryo leaves within from insects).

The fat, furry silver and yellow catkins of the pussy willow and the dusty gold 'lambs' tail' hazel catkins are among the first flowers to brave the early spring frosts. They are followed by sprays of blackthorn – the so-called 'blackthorn winter' – when white blossom spreads in snowflake drifts along the hedgerows before the leaves are out.

By early March the first butterflies are on the wing. These adults are survivors of over-wintering species – brimstones and small tortoiseshells – emerging from hibernation during the first warm days to lay the eggs from which the summer broods will be produced. The hedgehog uncurls to root and snuffle for food in the leaf litter of the hedge bottoms. In the woods, badgers, though not true hibernators, become increasingly more active. Mating hares can be seen running through the open fields.

With the approach of spring the great bird migrations begin again. In Scotland the hills are still piebald with snow when the yelping skeins of wild geese fly north to their Arctic breeding grounds and the ospreys return from Africa to take up residence again in the Highlands.

In the south, the first migrants to make themselves heard are usually the chiffchaff and willow warbler, but everywhere birds are beginning to sing, announcing territorial sovereignty over nesting areas. One of the earliest resident songsters is the mistle thrush – also known as the stormcock because of its habit of singing on blustery days.

Elsewhere, other nest-builders are busy, and the raucous clamour of village rookeries is one of the most characteristic sounds of imminent spring. But one voice is more eagerly awaited than any other: the haunting call of the cuckoo. For the cuckoo's arrival in early April after its marathon migration from Africa is a sure sign of winter's end.

Chapter Ten
The Future of the Countryside

The surrealist domes of the Fylingdales Ballistic Missile Early Warning Station in the North York
Moors National Park symbolise the profound changes which modern technology is bringing
to the rural landscapes of the British Isles. In this final chapter, part requiem, part eulogy,
we look at the vanishing countryside and at what is being saved for posterity

The face of the countryside is changing as never before. Every year thousands of acres of open land are commandeered to meet the growing demands of urban man; new roads, new houses, factories, airports, reservoirs, power stations; swelling the lost countryside of the British Isles already buried under brick and tarmac.

Elsewhere, quarries, gravel pits and coal mines blight the land. Motorways and massive pylons march across the fields with scant regard for their impact on the scenery.

And everywhere, land is being farmed more intensively. Hedgerows are grubbed out, woods cleared, wetlands drained, old pasture ploughed, leaving less room for wildlife. Habitats that might have taken a thousand years to evolve can now be bulldozed, burnt and ploughed in a day.

There has always been change in the countryside, but never at the speed with which it has been gathering momentum over the past three decades. And it is precisely this, the sheer pace and volume of change, its impact on cherished landscapes and fragile eco-systems, that is the cause of so much concern.

The result, especially in the farming lowlands of England and Wales, has been dramatic. The Countryside Commission has stated that the changes taking place there are as substantial as those that resulted from the enclosure movement of the 17th and 18th centuries.

Many familiar traditional features of the countryside are disappearing as the pace of progress quickens. Old farm buildings – relics of the days when life moved no faster than the steady stride of a heavy horse – are crumbling away. Clifftops, downs and heaths are increasingly being taken into cultivation – a controversial practice in areas valued for amenity and a disastrous one for wildlife. A recent review of the effects of modern farming carried out by the Nature Conservancy Council has revealed a serious loss of habitats, leading to alarming reductions in native wild plant and animal populations.

Stitch by stitch, the old tapestry of woods and spinneys, streams, hedgerows, ponds and ditches, is being unravelled, and replaced by a new countryside, more open, less diverse, and with fewer of those rich local flavours which add so much spice to the landscapes of the British Isles.

Yet the very fact that the vast majority of people in these islands are now urban dwellers renders the surviving countryside even more precious, and not just as land set aside for food production, even if that remains its paramount function. Today the countryside also provides fresh air, open space for recreation and escape from the cities, as well as those quieter, deeper pleasures that have inspired generations of poets, painters, writers and musicians.

Concern for the future of the countryside is widespread, and grows with every threat, real or imagined. But at least the case for conservation is now broadly accepted. National parks and nature reserves seek to protect the finest landscapes and wildlife habitats. Long-distance footpaths enshrine the freedom to ramble over miles of clifftops and open countryside. Historic castles, houses and gardens are preserved for public enjoyment, and dying villages re-vitalised.

Nevertheless, much remains to be done. Woods and hedgerows, heaths and marshes should be identified and managed for their landscape value, especially if they have an ecological or historic value. Even individual trees and odd corners of rough or boggy pasture may be evaluated for the way in which they add perspective and enrich the texture of the local scene.

More trees are desperately needed to fill the gaps left by decades of disease and neglect. Fertile land need not be used; the food it will produce is too precious. But most landscapes have odd corners where the plough cannot reach, and where trees could once again enhance the view.

Fifty years ago the countryside was far richer in terms of beauty and the sights and sounds of nature than it is now. Today's countryside still offers those pleasures in good measure, credit for which is at least partly due to the system of development control which has evolved in the British Isles and which, though far from perfect, has made possible the saving of a civilised environment.

But what of tomorrow's countryside? Without even greater commitment to conservation, at national and local level, the outlook is bleak and the Countryside Commission has issued a stark warning to the people of Britain. 'If we try hard we might sustain what we can now experience,' it says, 'but that will mean substantially multiplying our efforts as a nation. If we do no more than we are doing, much of the lowland countryside of England and Wales will become very dull to look at 50 years from now.'

Vanishing Britain

Country greenery no longer always means what it did: slow pace and leafy shade, the hum of insects, of birds in the hedgerows, meadows in flower. They are, all of them, harder to find, and green today can signify a monoculture prairie, ecologically barren, though green none the less.

The landscapes of the British Isles have changed, out of all recognition in some places, especially in lowland Britain. And a great deal of the change has taken place in the third quarter of this century.

There is no better example of what has vanished from the country scene than the pond. In yesterday's countryside you might have found a pond between every two or three fields. Today it is often hard to find one anywhere, even in the heart of the country.

The field pond is obsolete, and as it no longer serves a useful purpose, there is no reason for keeping it. Nowadays, pipes bring water to the cattle, and often the spring feeding the natural pond has dried up – the result of increasingly heavy extraction of local ground water.

All too often the village pond has suffered a similar fate; reduced by neglect to a rubbish-filled eyesore, then filled in to provide a new car park for the re-modelled village pub.

In its turn the vanishing pond has brought about a decline in formerly abundant creatures – the Common Frog, the Crested Newt – which thrived in its placid waters.

A far more conspicuous change has been the loss of trees, especially large trees, over much of the British scene. In many places they have already gone, and none so sorely mourned as the English Elm. For centuries this under-rated monarch of the vegetable kingdom, soaring in cumulus clouds of summer leaf, has sustained the illusion of England as a woodland country. Just over a decade ago, 23 million elms flourished south of a line from Birmingham to the Wash. Today $15\frac{1}{2}$ million of them are gone, laid low by a small beetle, *Scolytus scolytus*, carrier of the deadly Dutch elm disease, which is still laying waste to the land, leaving millions of dead and dying trees in its wake – a ghastly vision of winter-in-summer that will remain to haunt the English countryside for years to come. The only hope is that a series of hard winters will kill off the beetles and allow the remaining elms to regenerate.

Not even the comparatively modern concept of protected countryside is proof against drastic change. Exmoor national park has only been in existence for three decades, yet already one third of its moorland has gone under the plough. The same fate has overtaken the ancient sheepwalks and hill pastures of the southern chalk downs. And every acre lost means fewer wild orchids, fewer chalkland butterflies. Nor is it only wildlife that suffers. Modern farming has destroyed much of Britain's prehistoric past, especially Bronze Age barrows. They may still appear on the older Ordnance Survey one-inch maps, but many have vanished from the fields.

As if all this was not enough, development is depleting Britain's precious farmland at the rate of 50,000 (20,200 hectares) acres a year: new houses, new factories, new roads to add to the 210,000 miles (336,000km) of existing highways. Some 30,000 acres (12,120 hectares) of Britain are now solid motorway – and there is more to come. Every additional mile of six-lane super highway devours another 30 acres (12 hectares) of green land, for which motorway kestrels and grassy banks are but small compensation. Furthermore, each new mile of motorway requires 100,000 tons of aggregate, which in turn enlarges the quarries, causing them to bite deeper into the Mendip Hills and the national parklands of the Derbyshire Peak District and Yorkshire Dales.

It is difficult to be sure exactly how much countryside is being lost nationally. One estimate is that Britain 'loses out of green' an area the size of Berkshire every five years.

Hand in hand with mineral extraction goes pollution: streams are throttled with slurry and sediment, lifeless lagoons created. Yet to balance the picture it must also be said that recent years have seen a considerable improvement in the overall quality of Britain's inland waters: salmon can again survive in the River Thames, and Great Crested Grebes are colonising the disused and flooded gravel pits.

Everywhere land is taken out of green, covered with concrete, deep-ploughed or drenched with farm chemicals, it creates an environment that is fundamentally hostile to wild plants and creatures. Drop by drop, the wildlife heritage of the British Isles is being squeezed out of existence. The old way of farming, slow to change and more tolerant of nature, is being replaced by a more demanding economic regime in which agriculturally unproductive habitats such as moors, hedges and wetlands are seen as burdensome luxuries.

Wildlife can no longer be taken for granted because there is just not enough land to go round. One of the reasons that Otters are so rare in England now is that they cannot tolerate human disturbance.

As always, the deadliest foe is habitat destruction. Cover the Lancashire dunes with holiday camps and the mating rattle of the already endangered Natterjack Toad could become a voice of the past. Demolish an old barn and the Barn Owl is denied an ancestral nesting site. Improve an old meadow and the Cowslips will go.

Ancient meadows and pastures are especially vulnerable to change. The centuries-old mixtures of wild grasses and flowering plants have been replaced by laboratory-bred hybrid grasses, and the soil itself ploughed, drained, re-sown and treated with chemical fertilisers. In such new meadows, flowers are few: even Buttercups are becoming rare in some areas. The beautiful Fritillary is another flower now severely limited in distribution as a result of these changes.

Diversity of habitat in nature gives overall stability and safety to large populations of plants and animals with their complex and interwoven food webs. Only in those relic patches of wild or semi-wild habitat protected as nature reserves, official and unofficial, is that diversity being conserved for the future.

Of course, in some places wildlife is still abundant, but to seek it you must look to the more remote corners of the British Isles, to the wilder coasts and uplands of the north and west. Here you can still see Atlantic Seals and Peregrine Falcons. The Red Kite, though it breeds at only a handful of secret sites, appears secure in Wales. The handsome Kentish Glory moth will never fly again in Kent but it still survives in Scotland. The delicate Irish Lady's Tresses Orchid (an inhabitant of marshy, marginal pasture land) still flowers at a number of sites in Ireland.

Yet nowhere in the British Isles is so remote that it is not threatened by progress. In 1979, one small oil spill at Sullom Voe in the Shetlands killed nearly 4,000 seabirds, including 146 rare Great Northern Divers, a species with only a small European population. It also killed 15 Otters – the equivalent of the entire population of Norfolk. A year earlier a disaster caused heavy loss of human life and pollution at the oil terminal on Whiddy Island, Bantry Bay, Ireland.

Elsewhere, estuaries are threatened by the insatiable demands of industry and agriculture. The salt marshes of the Ribble estuary in Lancashire, a wintering ground of international importance for huge populations of wildfowl and wading birds, were rescued from an agricultural reclamation scheme only through last-minute intervention by the Nature Conservancy Council and the Royal Society for the Protection of Birds.

Human life, too, has changed dramatically in the countryside in no more than a couple of generations. The farm has lost all pretensions to self-sufficiency; it is now part of a national food enterprise. New agricultural buildings, which do not need planning permission and so can be any size and shape, are put up alongside centuries-old barns, which are unrepaired and allowed to rot. The few remaining windmills function for weekend visitors, if at all. Most traditional country crafts have withered away, though thatching thrives and adds to property values. And the blacksmith (really a farrier) lives on, but with a mobile workshop, servicing local riding stables or making artistic ironware for residents who have settled in modernised country cottages.

The great country houses and gardens of the British Isles are no longer the exclusive domain of the gentry. Lucky the squire in his manor, the lord in his hall who can support the burden of maintaining a stately home from his own resources. Nowadays most country house owners depend upon the paying public – some 20 million visitors a year – to preserve what has been called Britain's most important contribution to European civilisation. Many of the finest homes and gardens are now preserved by the National Trust, but 40 stand derelict and others face a similar fate.

The country church, pride and glory of so many villages, is also facing an uncertain future. Empty and redundant churches are becoming an all too familiar feature of the country scene. Some small chapels have been successfully converted into private dwellings, but what alternative use is there for a medieval church, repository of 900 years of village history with its tombs and monuments, leaning headstones, bells, bench-ends and stained glass windows? The problem of the medieval church is all the more acute because, as buildings, they are all slowly falling to pieces, a reflection of the fact that they were largely built within the same brief span of centuries. Even without a congregation, the parish church cannot be allowed to moulder away, yet who will pay for the enormous upkeep of what is, after all, part of a nationwide architectural heritage?

Organisations such as the Society for the Protection of Ancient Buildings and the Civic Trust have done much to restore old country buildings of all kinds. But whatever miracles can be worked with brick and stone and tile, the old social fabric of the village is harder to replace.

Cottages are greatly sought-after by retired city-dwellers, second home-owners and affluent commuters. The dwindling indigenous workforce, unable to afford the new inflated house prices, are forced into peripheral council estates. All over the country, village schools of the kind immortalised by Laurie Lee in *Cider With Rosie*, are closing, the children being bussed to the nearest town. And as often as not, the village shop is now part of a chain, indistinguishable from one county to another.

As the older village inhabitants die, the age-old rites and customs of country lore die with them. Who today would hope to cure whooping cough by passing the afflicted child under the belly of a piebald horse? Or cure warts with nine bramble leaves dipped in spring water? Yet these are not medieval customs conned from books; they were current practice in Cornwall earlier this century.

Today, freed from such ignorance and superstition, there is no doubt that country people live a better life. Nostalgia for the past should not obscure the fact that yesterday's countryside offered nothing to many but a life of hardship and grinding poverty. No-one should mourn the loss of country cottages which, though possibly picturesque, were often comfortless and unsanitary hovels.

So there are two sides to the story of the vanishing countryside; gains as well as losses. Derelict canals are being restored to life by dedicated groups of weekend volunteers. The folk music revival has rescued a rich haul of long-forgotten songs and ballads. Everywhere, new life is being breathed into old buildings. Conservation is a word on everybody's lips. And there have been some outstanding success stories.

At the beginning of this century, the Osprey, one of the world's most spectacular birds of prey, was driven from its breeding haunts in the Scottish High-

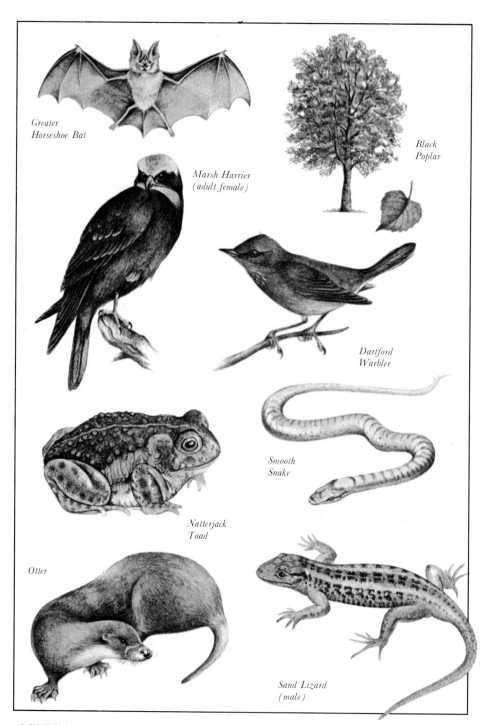

Wildlife in danger: all the species shown here are threatened with extinction

lands by human persecution. For fifty years the old eyries stood empty. It seemed as if the birds had gone for good, until one day the news came: the Ospreys were back. Protected by the Royal Society for the Protection of Birds, welcomed by a more enlightened public, the original home-coming pair and their offspring have now established a small but secure population of Scottish Ospreys which return every year to breed in the Highlands.

The return of the Osprey is a symbol of hope for the future of the countryside and its wildlife. Change in itself is not always harmful. The real task today is to recognise the speed of today's changes and take steps early enough to protect those things that are treasured most, so that the best of yesterday's countryside may also belong to tomorrow.

Going – bats, toads, snakes, lizards
It is easy to arouse public sympathy for a bird as attractive as the Osprey. Not so for bats, reptiles and amphibians, which are more likely to cause a shudder than a smile. Yet the wildlife of the British Isles would be infinitely poorer without these fascinating creatures, some so rare they are protected by the Conservation of Wild Plants and Wild Creatures Act in Britain. They include the Greater Horseshoe Bat, down from 7,000 in 1950 to a few hundred; the Natterjack Toad, more

Epitaph to the elm: one of the $15\frac{1}{2}$ million trees destroyed by Dutch elm disease

numerous than the Common Toad in Victorian times; the harmless Smooth Snake and the Sand Lizard – heathland species gravely endangered by loss of habitat and heath fires. Today even the Common Frog is not common any more.

Going – animals

The Otter is now so rare that it is protected in England, Wales and Ireland (though not in Scotland, where it is more numerous). Norfolk, one of its former strongholds, now has only about 15 Otters left. The decline began in the 1960s. A combination of hard winters, hunting, disease and the effects of pesticides have all helped to bring about the Otter's disappearance from many rivers.

Increasing human disturbance and the clearing of river banks makes a comeback more difficult. Otters are shy animals. They need plenty of cover to lie up in during the day, and bankside trees (ash trees are the favourites) whose roots make a secure holt or den. Now that otter hunting is illegal in England and Wales, the future looks brighter. Special 'otter havens' have been set up on some rivers to help the Otter recolonise its old haunts.

Going – birds

Watching birds is a major pastime in the British Isles, and most species are loved and protected. Nevertheless, many birds are rare and becoming rarer as wild

habitats are destroyed. There is concern for the Corncrake. In 1979 it was breeding in only a fifth of the sites logged a few years before. Hard winters and habitat loss have dealt the Dartford Warbler a double blow. A heathland species, it is now more or less confined to a few pairs in Hampshire and Dorset. Some common migrants are becoming scarcer. The Lesser Whitethroat has been hit by recent droughts in its sub-Saharan winter quarters. Many other migrants must run the gauntlet across Continental Europe, where millions of marksmen with shotguns lie in wait. But persecution has also left its mark in Britain, especially among birds of prey, and in particular upon the Marsh Harrier, now reduced to a handful of breeding pairs, and the even rarer Montagu's Harrier. Luckily, other species have been more fortunate. The Red Kite is holding its own in Wales. The Peregrine Falcon has recovered from the population crash of the late 1950s and early 1960s caused by pesticides. The Hen Harrier is steadily increasing its range and the Osprey is again breeding successfully in Scotland. Even the White-tailed Sea Eagle, absent from Britain since the First World War, could return. The Nature Conservancy Council is trying to re-introduce the species by raising and releasing birds from Norway on the Hebridean island reserve of Rhum.

Going – trees

Dutch elm disease has dealt the countryside a devastating blow from which it may never recover. To date, the plague has carried away at least $15\frac{1}{2}$ million of Britain's 23 million elms. Millions of other trees of all kinds suffered in the great drought of 1976. But while the elms perish in a blaze of national indignation, one of Britain's rarest native trees is passing away almost un-noticed. The Black Poplar (*Populus Nigra*), once a familiar sight in lowland Britain, is quietly dying for want of love. The last of these craggy giants are now so scattered they are simply too far apart to fertilise each other. Little more than a thousand remain, most of them already mature or beginning to die back. Unless the species is planted back into its natural flood plain habitat, the Black Poplar could die out within 50 years.

Oaks are also being lost. In some areas, half the oaks are over-mature and dying. The reasons here are more complex. Improved stream drainage can result in ground drought, which weakens the trees, which become vulnerable to disease and careless stubble burning. Sick, stag-headed oaks now abound in the scenery of some counties.

The loss of so many trees brings other problems in its wake. It is creating a new countryside, more open, more thread-bare, sometimes exposing unsightly modern development previously concealed by a screen of foliage.

That new treeless scene is here to stay, at least for the lifetime of anyone reading this book. To maintain any existing tree population requires six healthy saplings for each mature adult tree (disease and other hazards will claim the other five in time). Most areas have at best one sapling alive for each mature tree, and in some places the ratio is even worse.

The change brought about by the disappearance of these trees is all the more devastating in its impact upon the landscapes of lowland Britain because they were not clustered into dense woods. Most of them, the elms in particular, were strung out beside the lanes and along the hedgerows between the fields, or grouped in small clumps and spinneys, creating parkland vistas in all directions. Today many areas are losing not only their trees but their hedges too, as modern farming demands larger field units.

The Second World War is a good starting date to catalogue the decline, because at that time the British rural scene was in full maturity, a rich burgeoning based on centuries of slow change. Since then over half a million miles of hedgerows alive with flowers, butterflies and nesting birds have been lost – and are still being obliterated at the rate of 2,000 miles a year.

Nor can the remaining small woods and coppices be taken for granted. If they are not managed to provide timber, the land is more profitable when cleared of its broadleaved Oak and Hazel, and either ploughed or re-planted with fast-growing conifers.

In all, perhaps a third of the ancient hardwood woodlands have gone since the war, leaving less than nine per cent of the total land surface of Great Britain covered with trees. However, that does not mean new trees are not being planted. The Forestry Commission manages over 2 million acres (404,000 hectares) of productive forest – mainly conifers – and has begun to grant-aid the regeneration of the native Scots pine in the Scottish Highlands. The Countryside Commission is also helping amenity tree planting at the rate of around £1 million a year.

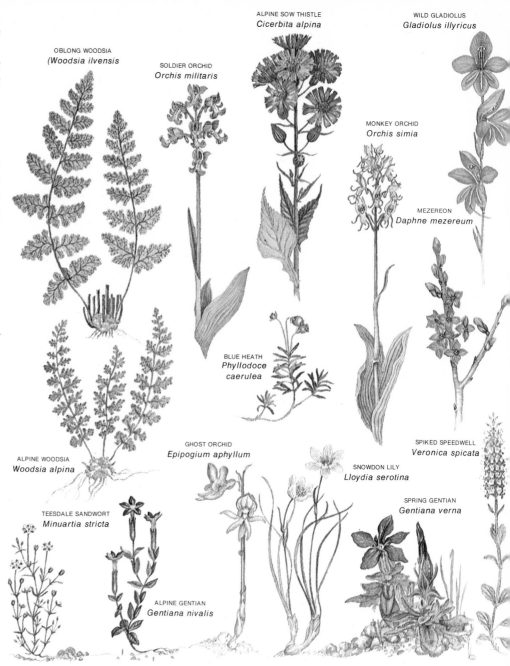

OBLONG WOODSIA
(Woodsia ilvensis

SOLDIER ORCHID
Orchis militaris

ALPINE SOW THISTLE
Cicerbita alpina

WILD GLADIOLUS
Gladiolus illyricus

MONKEY ORCHID
Orchis simia

MEZEREON
Daphne mezereum

BLUE HEATH
Phyllodoce caerulea

ALPINE WOODSIA
Woodsia alpina

GHOST ORCHID
Epipogium aphyllum

SNOWDON LILY
Lloydia serotina

SPIKED SPEEDWELL
Veronica spicata

SPRING GENTIAN
Gentiana verna

TEESDALE SANDWORT
Minuartia stricta

ALPINE GENTIAN
Gentiana nivalis

Of course the countryside changes. It cannot remain constant, a kind of giant open-air museum to preserve the past in perpetuity. That is generally accepted. After all, many of the hedges whose loss is mourned today were not growing 300 years ago, and it would be foolish to expect that every mile of hedgerow should be obstinately protected. What causes so much widespread public concern is the accelerating pace of change being imposed on the landscape by the new agriculture.

Going – prehistoric barrows
The practice of raising barrows, or burial mounds over the dead goes back to the Stone Age and continued into early Saxon times. Until recently there were at least 20,000 barrows in the British Isles, but most of them are concentrated on the chalk and limestone uplands where they are often vulnerable to ploughing. Many have been obliterated; others badly damaged. Of the 871 Bronze Age burial mounds recorded in South Dorset alone fewer than five per cent survive unscathed.

Going – cider orchards
Cider is the wine of the West Country, a golden, tipsy brew made from the fermented juice of sour apples. Sadly, the old cider orchards are following the heavy horse into oblivion. Relics of a bygone age when cider flowed freely in the harvest fields, most of them are long past their prime. Hoary with lichen, the oldest trees have stood since the reign of Edward VII. Every spring these octagenarian greybeards still glorify the landscape with pink and white blossom.

222

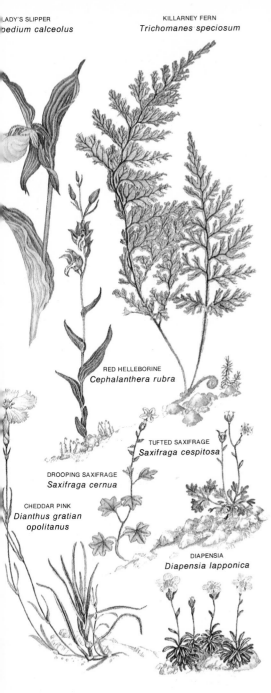

LADY'S SLIPPER
bedium calceolus

KILLARNEY FERN
Trichomanes speciosum

RED HELLEBORINE
Cephalanthera rubra

TUFTED SAXIFRAGE
Saxifraga cespitosa

DROOPING SAXIFRAGE
Saxifraga cernua

CHEDDAR PINK
Dianthus gratian opolitanus

DIAPENSIA
Diapensia lapponica

But in September when the apples ripen they are left to rot where they fall, and every winter when the gales come, more trees are swept away, and are not replaced. The traditional orchard, its standard trees widely spaced at no more than 40 per acre, is no longer economic. Somerset has lost 1,000 acres (404 hectares) of cider orchards over the past decade, though paradoxically it now has twice as many trees. But the replacements are diminutive modern heavy-cropping bush varieties. The big old standard trees, varieties with splendidly Bacchanalian names like Hangydown, Brown Snout and Slack-ma-Girdle, become fewer with every passing year.

Going – wild flowers

Thirty years ago there was not overmuch concern about wild plants. Today, flow-ers are vanishing at such a rate that it has now been made illegal to uproot any wild plant in Britain without the permission of the owner of land. And for 21 of the rarest plants (listed below), even stricter rules apply. Removing *any part* of these 21 plants is an offence under the Conservation of Wild Creatures and Wild Plants Act of 1975. Tomorrow, even flowers like the common Cowslip – still locally abundant but going fast as old pastures are improved – could find themselves added to the endangered list, along with the rare but as yet unprotected Fritillary, Pasque Flower and Alpine Catchfly.

The following plants are protected by law in the United Kingdom under the Conservation of Wild Creatures and Wild Plants Act of 1975.

Oblong Woodsia (*Woodsia ilvensis*). Confined to four localities.

Soldier Orchid (*Orchis militaris*). Two sites only, in Suffolk and Chilterns.

Blue Heath (*Phyllodoce caerulea*). Sow of Atholl, Perthshire only.

Alpine Sow Thistle (*Cicerbita alpina*). On inaccessible ledges in one area of the Scottish Highlands.

Monkey Orchid (*Orchis simia*). Trio of sites in Kent, Chilterns.

Spiked Speedwell (*Veronica spicata*). Breckland, East Anglia.

Alpine Woodsia (*Woodsia alpina*). Rock crevices in 15 upland localities.

Alpine Gentian (*Gentiana nivalis*). A few Highland mountains.

Spring Gentian (*Gentiana verna*). Upper Teesdale.

Teesdale Sandwort (*Minuartia stricta*). Teesdale.

Ghost Orchid (*Epipogium aphyllum*). Few shady woods, Southern England.

Snowdon Lily (*Lloydia serotina*). Remote sites in Snowdonia.

Wild Gladiolus (*Gladiolus illyricus*). Few sites on Hampshire and Dorset heaths.

Mezereon (*Daphne mezereum*). Few areas of lime and chalk woodland.

Cheddar Pink (*Dianthus gratianopolitanus*). Cheddar Gorge, Somerset.

Drooping Saxifrage (*Saxifraga cernua*). On three Highland mountains only.

Lady's Slipper (*Cypripedium calceolus*). One secret site in Yorkshire.

Red helleborine (*Cephalanthera rubra*). Cotswold beechwoods.

Killarney Fern (*Trichomanes speciosum*). Handful of plants in south-west and north-west Britain.

Tufted Saxifrage (*Saxifraga cespitosa*). Some Highland rocks.

Diapensia (*Diapensia lapponica*). One hill-top in Inverness-shire.

Protecting a threatened heritage

The scenery of nearly one fifth of England and Wales (18.6 per cent to be precise) is protected by designation either as a national park or an 'Area of Outstanding Natural Beauty (AONB).

Scotland has neither national parks nor AONBs, partly because the development pressures on fine scenery north of the border have never been as great as in England and Wales, and partly because, on any reasonable aesthetic judgement, so much of Scotland would qualify as to render such designation meaningless. Instead Scotland has five National Park Direction Area Orders covering Loch Lomond and the Trossachs (320 square miles; 512 sq km); Glen Affric, Glen Cannich and Strathfarrar (260 square miles; 416 sq km); Ben Nevis, Glen Coe and Black Mount (610 square miles; 976 sq km); the Cairngorms (180 square miles; 288 sq km) and Loch Torridon, Loch Maree and Little Loch Broom (500 square miles; 800 sq km). Together these areas comprise six per cent of Scotland.

In these areas all proposals for development must be submitted to the Countryside Commission for Scotland which advises the Secretary of State for Scotland on their desirability. The Commission aims to keep development to a minimum.

Northern Ireland has no national parks, but has seven AONBs covering some 1000 square miles (1600 sq km) of magnificent countryside. They are: the Antrim Coast and Glens, North Derry, Sperrin Mountains, Lagan Valley, Strangford Lough, Mourne Mountains and South Armagh. Two more – Lough Erne and the Slieve Croob area (to be added to the Mourne Mountains) – are proposed.

The Republic of Ireland has plans to establish three national parks: Killarney (22 square miles; 35 sq km); Connemara (just under four square miles; six sq km); and Glenbeagh in Donegal (39 square miles; 62 sq km). These parks will be wholly owned by the state, and they have been defined more for historical reasons than through any policy of distinguishing outstanding areas of scenery. For in Ireland, as in Scotland, there is so much countryside which is wild and beautiful that a visitor might be forgiven for thinking that the entire Republic had been given national park status.

The seven English and three Welsh national parks remain in mainly private ownership although public bodies such as the Forestry Commission, the regional water authorities and the Ministry of Defence are major landowners in them. More compatible with their purpose, so is the National Trust, which controls nearly a quarter of the Lake District National Park. There is no general right of public access to the parks and they are in no sense wilderness areas (as, for instance in much of the admirable American park system) since in the British Isles true wilderness vanished long ago.

It is an old jest but a true one that the national parks of England and Wales are neither national nor parks. Yet the campaign to establish them was long and hard fought. It was launched by the Council for the Preservation (now Protection) of Rural England in 1929 with a memorandum to the Prime Minister. Determined, knowledgeable visionaries, the park protagonists were drawn from every walk of life, welded by a love of the countryside and a belief that without its conservation there would be nothing of man's natural world left to provide those things of deep human satisfaction which are being obliterated at an alarming rate from daily life: tranquillity, nature, uncluttered horizons, clean air, clear rivers, and freedom to roam.

People went to prison for a nation's right to climb Kinder Scout and roam the neighbouring Pennine moors. They challenged a land-owning few for access rights, organised weekend trespass hikes over privately-owned shooting preserves and sheep-grazing moorlands which drew thousands of participants.

In 1943 John Dower drew up his seminal report calling for the establishment of national parks and gave them shape in a definition which, though never enacted in so many words, remains their *raison d'être*. A national park, he said, should be: 'An extensive area of beautiful and relatively wild country in which, for the nation's benefit, and by appropriate national decision and action; the characteristic landscape beauty is strictly preserved, access and facilities for public open-air enjoyment are amply provided, wildlife and buildings and places of architectural and historic interest are suitably protected, while established farming use is effectively maintained.'

But it was not until 1949 – after yet another consideration of the whole issue (the Hobhouse Committee) – that the National Parks and Access to the Countryside Act, providing for the designation of both parks and AONBs, went on the statute book. And here the legislation fell far short of what John Dower and the other campaigners for national parks had sought. It failed to place the parks under the guardianship of a powerful executive national body. Instead it left them – as they still are today – to be largely administered by committees or boards of the local county councils.

The Countryside Commission has little more than an advisory role and has never been armed with enough legislative teeth to be an effective watchdog.

Both Dower and Hobhouse saw that there were large areas of outstandingly beautiful countryside which could not meet the Dower definition of a national park, being neither big enough or wild enough. For such landscapes the cumbersome accolade of the AONB was devised. AONBs are considered no less beautiful than the parks and require the same degree of protection. But the 1949 statute places less emphasis on providing public open-air enjoyment and no special administrative machinery.

Cinderellas the AONBs may be, both financially and administratively, but they cover much of the best countryside, for the Dower definition of national parks excluded the less wild areas of lowland Britain – Dorset is a perfect example – which are most typical of the English scene.

There are now 33 AONBs, covering about 5,600 square miles (8960 sq km) of England and Wales. At one end of the scale are remote and little visited areas such as the Solway Coast and the Lincolnshire Wolds which scarcely seem to have enough problems to deserve special protection. At the other are national and regional playgrounds like the Cotswolds and the Cornish coast – subject to intense pressure from holiday crowds and highly vulnerable therefore to commercial development.

By statute the parks had twin purposes, to protect 'natural beauty' (though in fact it was never wholly natural), and to provide for suitable recreation. The two aims inevitably got in each other's way as the number of visitors to them rose with increasing car ownership, shorter working hours and longer holidays. Eventually, in 1976 the Government decreed that where conservation and recreation prove incompatible, the former should prevail.

The parks are far from being the Arcadian retreats from the modern world which their founders originally

Above: the heathery Culter Hills of Strathclyde, Scotl
of southern England.   Below right: the almost lu

North of the Border there are generally fewer pressures on fine scenery than in England. Below left: a new road cuts a broad swathe across the chalklands landscape of the china clay industry near St Austell, Cornwall. Locals call these white spoil tips the 'Cornish Alps'

Conserving countryside for posterity: National Parks and 'Areas of Outstanding Natural Beauty' (see map) confer a measure of protection to the finest landscapes of England and Wales, and also Northern Ireland (inset). But they are still vulnerable.

Brecon Beacons; 519 square miles (830 sq km). Flat-topped mountains rising to close on 3000ft (923m). Geographically the nearest national park to London, but largely unthreatened by development. The valley of the Usk divides the Black Mountains area in the east from the main massif of the Beacons in the middle of the park and (confusingly) the Black Mountain in the west. All three outcrops share the same precipitous sandstone scarps, their severity modified by the sweeping curves of ice-hewn amphitheatres. To the north there are fine views over the Wye Valley and the soft knuckles of the hills that lead down to it.

Dartmoor; 365 square miles (584 sq km). The last wilderness of southern England. Tors, clitters, cleaves and combes – Dartmoor names for the granite outcrops, rock litter, gorges and river valleys – add drama to the park and underline its wild aspect, as do the quaking mires and tussock bogs. Many remains of ancient man, notably Bronze Age Grimspound. Modern man threatens. Almost the whole of the northern moor is a military training area.
Reservoirs and afforestation are changing both uplands and valleys, though a major reservoir scheme at Swincombe was defeated. Farmers increasingly seek to enclose the moor. Tourist traffic clogs the lanes in summer.

National Park

Area of Outstanding Natural Beauty

North Derry — **Rathlin Island** — **Antrim Coast and Glens** — **Strangford Lough** — **Lagan Valley** — **Sperrin Mountains** — **Mourne** — **Lecale Coast** — **South Armagh**

Northumberland Coast — **NORTHUMBERLAND** — **Solway Coast** — **LAKE DISTRICT** — **NORTH YORK MOORS** — **Arnside and Silverdale** — **YORKSHIRE DALES** — **Forest of Bowland** — **Anglesey** — **Lincolnshire Wolds** — **SNOWDONIA** — **PEAK DISTRICT** — **Norfolk Coast** — **Lleyn** — **Cannock Chase** — **Shropshire Hills** — **Suffolk Coast and Heaths** — **Wye Valley** — **Malvern Hills** — **Dedham Vale** — **BRECON BEACONS** — **Cotswolds** — **PEMBROKESHIRE COAST** — **Chilterns** — **Gower** — **Kent Downs** — **Mendip Hills** — **Surrey Hills** — **EXMOOR** — **North Wessex Downs** — **North Devon** — **East Hampshire** — **Quantock Hills** — **DARTMOOR** — **Sussex Downs** — **Dorset** — **Chichester Harbour** — **Isles of Scilly** — **East Devon** — **Isle of Wight** — **Cornwall** — **South Devon** — **South Hampshire Coast**

Exmoor; 265 square miles (425 sq km). Bare moorland skylines, plunging combes, huge hog-backed hills tumbling into the Bristol Channel. A wild park of bog and bracken and brawling streams, but vulnerable to change. The superb heather moorland, for the sake of which the park was designated, has shrunk from 60,000 acres (24,240 hectares) just after the war to barely 40,000 acres (16,160 hectares) today, through conversion to more intensive agricultural use rather than traditional sheep grazing.

Lake District; 866 square miles (1385 sq km). The biggest park and one of the most famous landscapes in the British Isles, unique in its mingling of great fells and still waters. Here the Lake poets launched the romantic movement and the area has continued to attract writers ever since. Today the main threat to Lakeland's beauty is its own popularity – resulting in damage through sheer numbers of visitors. The water authorities continue to cast covetous eyes at the natural lakes.

Northumberland; 398 square miles (636 sq km). Fifty miles (80km) of lonely, surging hill country stretching from the most dramatic length of the Roman Wall to the Scottish border near Kirk Yetholm (terminus of the Pennine Way). Contains the heathery Simonside hills and the round-topped Cheviots, bleakly beautiful, deceptively benign, where there are more sheep than people. In the north the park is bisected by the Ministry of Defence Redesdale training area. Elsewhere afforestation is burying whole hills in conifers.

North York Moors; 553 square miles (888 sq km).
The biggest tract of heather in England. The main range, the Cleveland Hills, reaching 1490ft (458m) on wild Urra Moor, are flat-topped. The Cleveland Way path follows the northern scarp of these hills, leading eventually to a rugged coast of towering cliffs. For gentler views, the dales, notably Rosedale and Farndale are idyllic. Threats: potash mining near Whitby and loss of moorland to conifers and the plough.

Peak District; 542 square miles (867 sq km).
Britain's first national park and also the best run. Has its own financially independent planning board, internationally recognised for imaginative visitor management. Essential, this, because it is also the most visited park, wedged between the conurbations of Manchester and West Yorkshire. Geologically it is two areas, the gritstone moors and edges of the 'dark peak' and the romantic limestone dales of the 'white peak' in the south. Limestone and fluorspar extraction are the main threats.

Pembrokeshire Coast; 225 square miles (360 sq km).
The smallest park. No mountains here. Instead, one incomparable asset – 170 miles (272km) of majestic cliffscape rated among the finest coastlines in Europe – despite uncontrolled caravan sites and chalet developments. The cliffs are a paradise for birds – and bird-watchers. Skomer island (also in the park) is a national nature reserve open to the public, home of puffins, razorbills and

Manx shearwaters. And like all coasts, it is now prone to oil pollution, largely due to the oil terminal at Milford Haven.

Snowdonia; 845 square miles (1352 sq km).
The magnificent mountain fastness of North Wales, offering rock climbs whose challenge is out of all proportion to their height, lakes, woods, valleys, waterfalls and estuaries complete the picture. Quarries, power stations, afforestation and unsympathetic holiday developments mar parts of the park.

Yorkshire Dales; 680 square miles (1088 sq km).
Straddles England's spinal range, the Pennine Chain, offering visitors a choice of two worlds – the high and open striding fells, and the glorious dale bottoms with their sparkling becks and grey villages. The most spectacular countryside is the Three Peaks area (Whernside, Ingleborough and Pen-y-Ghent). Here quarrying has dug deep for limestone, and afforestation threatens.

envisaged. Perhaps that was always a vain hope in a nation as small and crowded as Britain. But the intrusions have been grievous and often, so conservationists believe, unnecessary.

After a long public enquiry in 1972 the British Government decided that the A66 dual carriageway linking the M6 motorway to the west Cumbria industrial belt should cross the Lake District National Park, skirting Skiddaw and spoiling the southern shore of Bassenthwaite. Yet an alternative route avoiding the park was available.

Seven years earlier there was a public inquiry into the proposal to turn the romantic and rocky chasm of the Meldon Gorge in north-west Dartmoor into a reservoir. Again there were alternatives available outside the park, but they failed to command official acceptance. On the other hand, farther south in the National Park, the shallow boggy basin of Swincombe has so far been saved from a similar fate.

In the North York Moors the amenity societies and the National Park Authority are resisting the establishment of a new potash mine on the edge of the park overlooking the ancient town of Whitby. There is one such mine already, but despite strong evidence of a world surplus of potash the industry seems determined to persuade the Secretary of State to make further inroads on the beauty of the area.

The Snowdonia National Park has a nuclear power station (Trawsfynydd) and the Central Electricity Generating Board secured legislation for a hydro-electric power station at Dinorwic in 1973, though plans for open-cast mining for copper and other non-ferrous metals on a massive scale have been thwarted for the time being.

Many of the most powerful presences in the parks are also the most controversial in their impact upon wild landscapes. The water authorities claim that their reservoirs create a public amenity for sailing or fishing. The Forestry Commission and the big private forestry companies present a similar case. In their forests are excellent camp sites, nature trails and scenic drives to serve visitors, but the wild land of the sheep walks is drowned under Sitka Spruce as deep as under water. Even the Ministry of Defence with extensive training grounds in the Dartmoor, Northumberland and Pembroke Coast parks and the Dorset AONB argues that by reducing or preventing public access it promotes nature conservation. Perhaps there is more than a grain of truth in this, but if so, what a despairing commentary upon the state of conservation in Britain, that it should take tanks and guns to protect wildlife from ourselves.

In some ways the preservation of wildlife habitats has fared better than the preservation of scenery. Nature conservationists have successfully concentrated their efforts on protecting specific sites typifying particular habitats or localities which are the strongholds of rare plants and creatures. But nobody would claim that the network of reserves is yet adequate in area or scope, or could ever be sufficient to allow the wildlife of the British Isles to flourish safely in its old abundance.

The Nature Conservancy Council (a Government body) now controls 164 national nature reserves totalling nearly 500 square miles throughout Great Britain. In addition there are 3356 'Sites of Special Scientific Interest' (SSSIs) designated on the Conservancy's advice and in which the Conservancy must be notified of proposed developments.

Many other reserves are run by the county naturalists' trusts, and the Royal Society for the Protection of Birds has 77 reserves in all, a total of 132 square miles (211 sq km), ranging from the marshes of Minsmere with their avocets and harriers to the lonely seabird cliffs of Scotland.

True wilderness parks like those of America and East Africa are a luxury that the British Isles – small, land-hungry and over-populated – cannot afford. There is just not enough space to go round. Instead the land, even the wildest and most precious havens, must be shared sometimes by different interests. When that happens, compromise is the only solution. But the balance has to be struck fairly. It is impossible to put a price on the value of national parks and nature reserves. They are – literally – beyond price. Yet all too often in the past they have been sacrificed for the sake of economic or political expediency.

What is needed if the parks are to survive is a reaffirmation of the original aims and ideals of those early campaigning conservationists. After all, the national parks, AONBs and nature reserves of the British Isles enshrine the finest landscapes, the richest wildlife. It is a magnificent inheritance. But every decision incompatible with wise conservation diminishes its value for all future generations.

Tomorrow's countryside

There is no countryside like the English countryside for those who have learned to love it . . . Other countrysides have their pleasant aspects, but none such variety, none that shine so steadfastly throughout the year.' H.G. Wells was right when he wrote these words, though the same could be said for Scotland, Wales and Ireland. Sadly, his declaration is less true today, and all the indications are that the most pervasive change the countryside faces in the remainder of this century is a steady erosion of its variety. Buildings, farms and trees are all being forced into a monotonous uniformity which contradicts the rural tradition.

The trend is nationwide, but one brief journey across Oxfordshire, starting where the M40 motorway from London to Oxford leaves Buckinghamshire on the escarpment of the Chiltern Hills and travelling as far as the Oxfordshire–Northamptonshire border in the vicinity of Banbury, is sufficient to show what is happening.

In the course of this short drive – only an hour in a car – the traveller will pass through three distinct and visually distinguishable regions.

At the beginning of the journey the traveller is some 800ft (242m) above sea level on the main ridge of the Chilterns. Behind, the hills break down gradually towards the Thames. Ahead, they drop sharply to the Midland plain. This is chalk country, where beechwoods and wild orchids grow. The beeches were originally grown for the furniture trade. Craftsmen called 'bodgers' thinned the woods and then rough-hewed the logs before they were sent for finishing in the factories at High Wycombe. Today the factories use imported timber and in many of the woods the beeches have been replaced by conifers, which grow faster and bring quicker profits than hardwoods.

But softwood plantations mean loss of variety. Wildlife in a wood of alien conifers is poorer than under trees that shed leaves.

The escarpment of the Chilterns – the series of hills which face the plain – used to be mainly downland turf kept short and sweet by grazing sheep. Now the sheep have mostly gone, as they have in other downland counties. Where the slopes are not too steep they have been ploughed. Elsewhere, scrub is invading or has taken over the grassland. Another variation in the scene is lost.

In the plain the traveller will notice one of the major changes which is occurring all over the landscapes once dominated by a pattern of small fields surrounded by stock-proof hedges – the landscape largely created by the enclosures. The modern trend is towards fewer hedges and bigger fields. In Oxfordshire this change is less pronounced than in the eastern and mainly arable parts of Britain where one can often look to the horizon and never see a hedge. But farmers everywhere want bigger fields for bigger contemporary agricultural machinery, less waste and greater efficiency. Even where fields are still used for free-ranging livestock it is reckoned cheaper to fence with posts and barbed wire than to employ a craftsman to lay a hedge.

In the villages of the Oxfordshire plain a particular building stone – limestone – predominates. It is reminiscent of the Cotswolds and contrasts with the brick and flint of the Chilterns, the flints being taken from the belt of clay which caps the ridge of the hills. A few miles farther north and the traditional local building material changes again, the pale limestone giving way to the ironstone of north Oxfordshire and south Northamptonshire. To find three different kinds of building stone within barely 40 miles (64km) of each other is typical of many parts of the British Isles. But with every new housing estate, each new example of Britain's obsession with bungalows, the regional differences become increasingly blurred. Ease of transportation, first by rail and then by road, paved the way for a flood of cheaper mass-produced building materials which are the same in Oxfordshire as in Cornwall, Humberside or Scotland.

Uniformity is the over-riding threat to the future of the countryside. It is a physical threat and also a social one. For just as the buildings of the villages and market towns are being debased by speculative development, the close-knit rural communities of the past are also changing out of all recognition. That was part of the price of the technological revolution on the farm. Modern farming using mass-produced machines, sprays and fertilisers can achieve heavier yields and greater efficiency with only a frac-

Right: In Dinas Forest, Dyfed, where this wild Welsh valley and its mossy oaks are preserved as a nature reserve by the Royal Society for the Protection of Birds.

tion of the old agricultural workforce. It is a rare discovery today to find a village where as many as a quarter of the population derive their income from the land. Nowadays the cottages are more likely to be inhabited by affluent incomers. The indigenous families whose names can be found on the headstones of the churchyard diminish every year. Such changes are inevitable – and not always for the worse. Many villages that were dying on their feet have been sympathetically renovated and the local communities revitalised. But the less fortunate villages – the smaller, more remote settlements – will almost certainly continue to wither away.

The countryside of the future will also have fewer wetlands, those areas of bog, marsh and fen beloved by naturalists, with their bitterns and reed beds and swallowtail butterflies. In Britain the acreage drained has multiplied six times since the early 1950's, from less than 50,000 acres (20,000 hectares) to more than a quarter of a million acres (101,000 hectares) a year. However, some of the best wet wild places should remain. The Ouse Washes in Bedfordshire, Hickling Broad and Horsey Mere in Norfolk, and the Dovey estuary and Borth Bog in Wales, Loch Druidibeg and Rannoch Moor in Scotland and Lough Neagh in Northern Ireland are among the wetlands designated for conservation.

Elsewhere, it is the plough that threatens the old-established rural landscapes. A quarter of the chalk downland of Dorset was ploughed in the 1950's and 1960's; half the pre-war total of downland in Wiltshire has now been ploughed; and three-quarters of the heathland in the Suffolk Coast and Heaths AONB has been converted into arable land or afforested since the 1920s.

Today there is some hope that these pressures are now being checked. The Ministry of Agriculture has begun to take a more critical line when considering the financial aid it gives to farmers for 'improvements'. In an outstanding case in 1978 grant aid for the draining of the 900 acres (363 hectares) of Amberley Wild Brooks in West Sussex was refused and a remarkable tract of near-fen at the foot of the South Downs saved. The Government is contemplating legislation which would enable national park authorities to make moorland conservation orders to stop the conversion of the remaining moors and compensate the affected farmer or landowner. This proposal was prompted by the catastrophic loss of moorland on Exmoor (see national parks, page 226). A report by Lord Porchester in 1977 said that the heartland of the moor should be preserved 'for all time'. The special significance of the proposed legislation is that it has the backing of the Ministry of Agriculture, whose traditional policy since the Second World War has been to encourage maximum food production regardless of its environmental effects, as well as that of the Department of the Environment.

However, there is little sign as yet that similar restraints will be applied to commercial forestry. It is true that the Forestry Commission (which runs the state-owned forests in Britain) and the bigger private forestry groups make commendable efforts to ensure that there is room for a varied wildlife in their forests, but the effect of mass afforestation on the open uplands – the only plantable land which does not eat too disastrously into the national agricultural estate – remains the same. The rate of afforestation in Britain has slowed somewhat in the last few years, but the Forestry Commission is still acquiring land at an average rate of over 50 square miles (80 sq km) a year.

So modern farming and forestry are mostly responsible for the future countryside being fashioned today, though urban sprawl, more strictly controlled in Britain, is still cited as the major threat to Ireland's rural acres.

Countryside conflicts which receive the most publicity often involve relatively small acreages, though their visual impact may be dramatic. The National Coal Board's controversial proposal to sink three new deep mines in the fertile Vale of Belvoir (mostly in Leicestershire) will be comparatively concentrated, though it will require pit-head installations and spoil tips. Perhaps more worrying to countryside conservation campaigners is the NCB's continued pressure – with Government backing – to expand open-cast coal production to 15 million tons a year from 10 million tons in 1975 when the target was set. This brings the spectre of strip-mining to hitherto unspoilt countryside far from the traditional coal-producing regions. Although the NCB has a good record for restoring worked out open-cast mines, the techniques are far less acceptable in agricultural areas which have not already been scarred and blackened by deep mining.

Another major consumer of open country if the British Isles opt for a nuclear future will be the rapid proliferation of associated power stations. For safety reasons they will need to be sited in remote locations, probably on the coast. Inevitably, such installations would reduce still further the dwindling miles of unspoilt coastline. They eat up land and are hard to hide. The Torness power station in East Lothian, for instance, will take more than 150 acres (60 hectares' of good farmland and require a network of giant pylon lines radiating from it.

On the other hand the roads programme has dwindled under a combination of economic stringency and effective criticism of the traffic forecasts on which it was based, though several major schemes are still under consideration.

Set against all these demands upon the countryside the forces for conservation seem puny by comparison. Yet they have their successes. Today wild life and wild places are cherished as never before. A new spirit of environmental awareness is in the air. Foul rivers are running clean again. Pioneers of conservation, among them the Nature Conservancy Council, the Countryside Commission and scores of voluntary amenity societies, are fighting to safeguard our finest landscapes, villages and wildlife habitats. The National Trust for England and Wales now owns and protects 628 square miles (1005 sq km) and has covenants safeguarding another 115 square miles (185 sq km). And whatever happens in the more fertile and heavily populated lowlands, huge expanses of peaceful and uncluttered landscape will remain inviolate for decades to come in the Welsh uplands, Scottish Highlands and the west of Ireland.

In the Scottish Highlands, especially in the west, many areas have lost almost all their population, and some have been taken over for forestry. Many of the crofts are deserted but some of the houses have been taken over as holiday cottages.

Although the west of Ireland resembles the west of Scotland, it has a far more numerous farming population, though even here, many old cottages have become holiday homes.

The sum total is a rich and heady mixture: osprey lochs and Cumbrian tarns; Dartmoor and the Brecon Beacons; Burren orchids, kingcup marsh; Norfolk flint and Skiddaw slate; Wicken Fen, Chesil Beach; scarp, swallet and gritstone edge, clint and cavern, drumlin, combe; tithe barn, henge, national park, heritage coast. . . . time has frayed the ancient fabric but the countryside of the British Isles still glitters with a green and irresistible magic.

1000 Days Out

What makes a good day out?

The answers will be as diverse as the countryside itself. They will reflect
not only varied interests but also different circumstances:
age, family commitments and geographical base can all restrict choice.
Yet the scope is still immense. We have suggested
1000 Days Out to enable readers to see and enjoy for themselves aspects of
the countryside described earlier in this book.
Nobody is normally more than an hour's drive from at least one such
'day out'; most people considerably closer to far more.

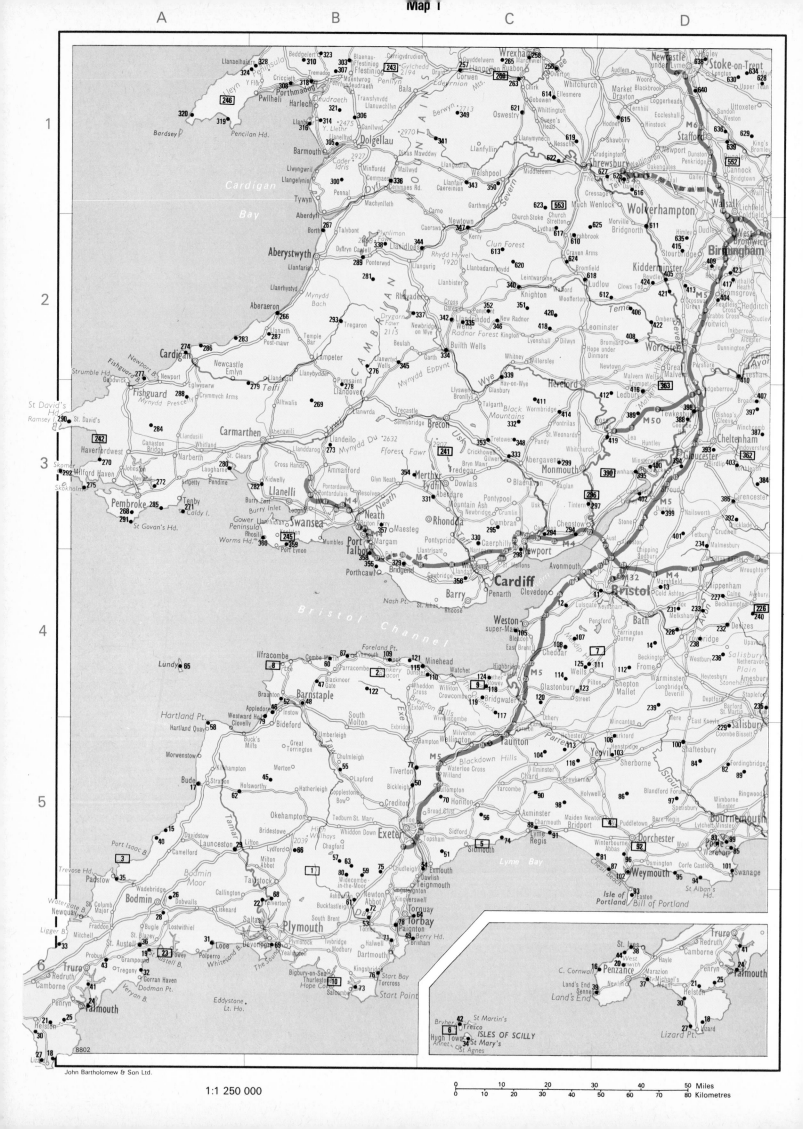

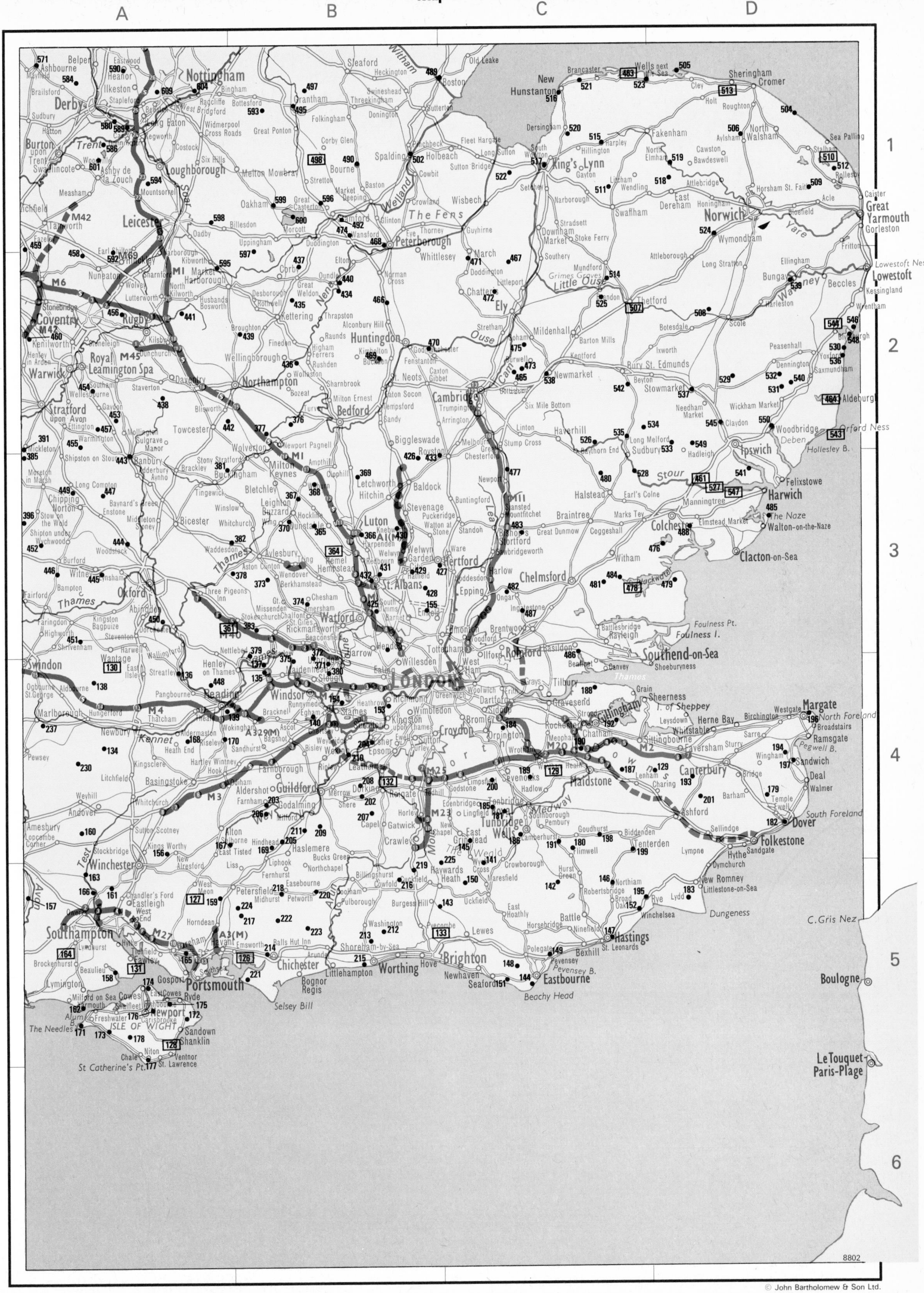

Map 2

1:1 250 000

© John Bartholomew & Son Ltd.

8802

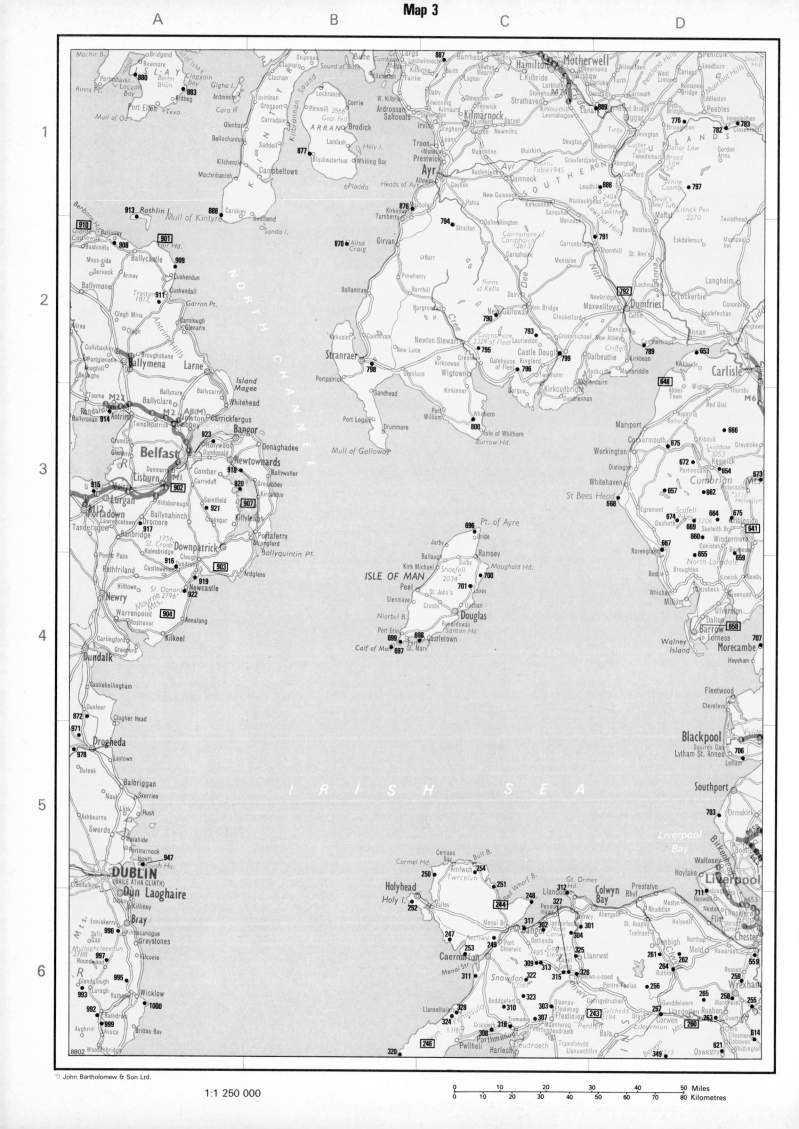

Map 3

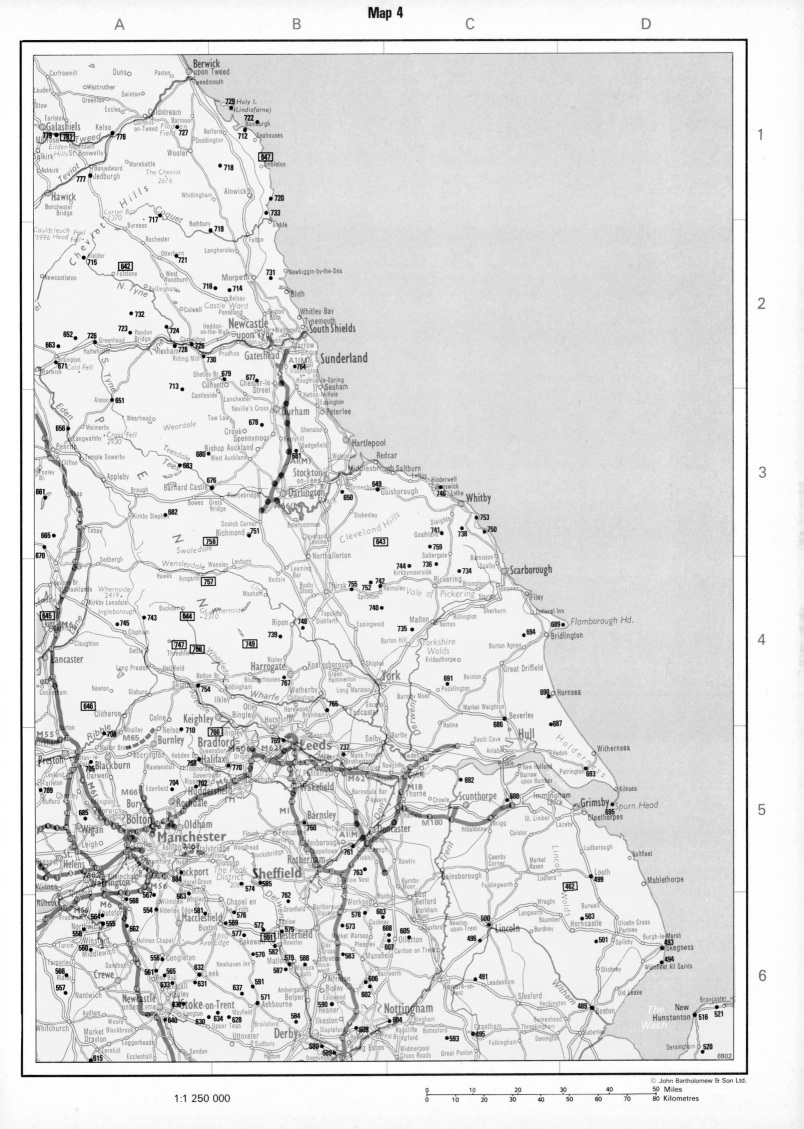

Map 4

1:1 250 000

© John Bartholomew & Son Ltd.

| 0 | 10 | 20 | 30 | 40 | 50 Miles |

| 0 | 10 | 20 | 30 | 40 | 50 | 60 | 70 | 80 Kilometres |

8802

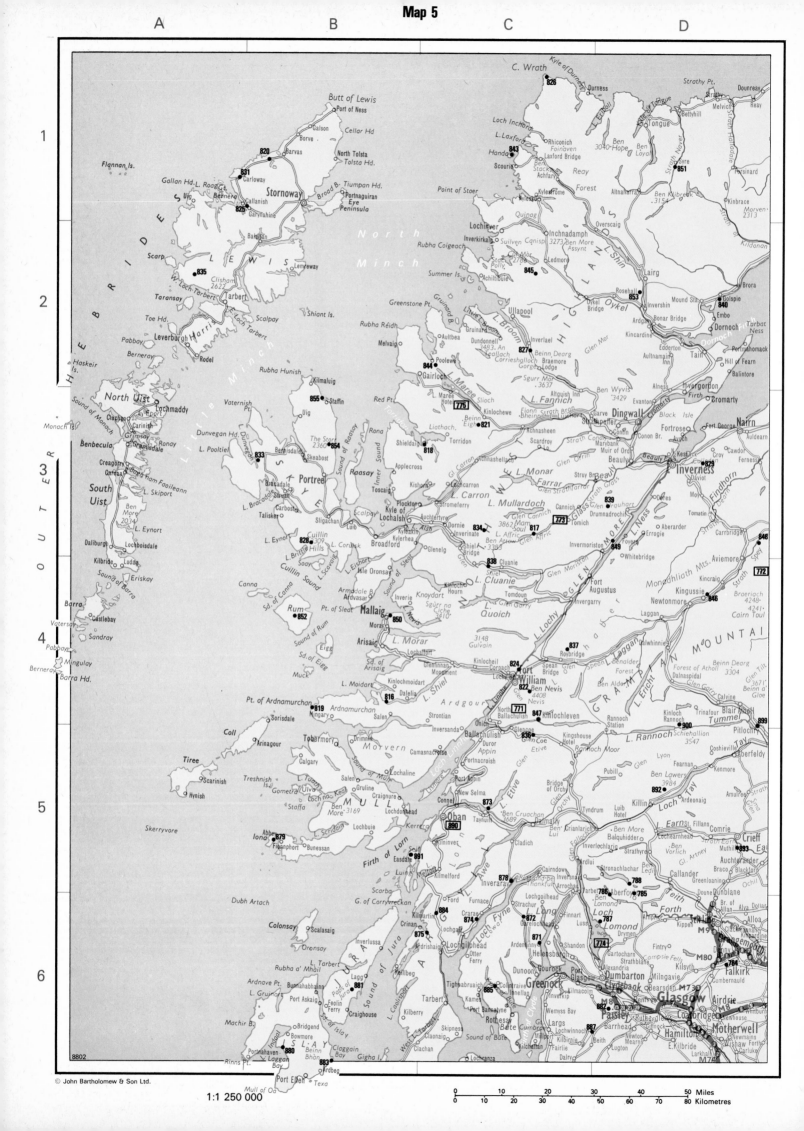

Map 5

© John Bartholomew & Son Ltd.

1:1 250 000

8802

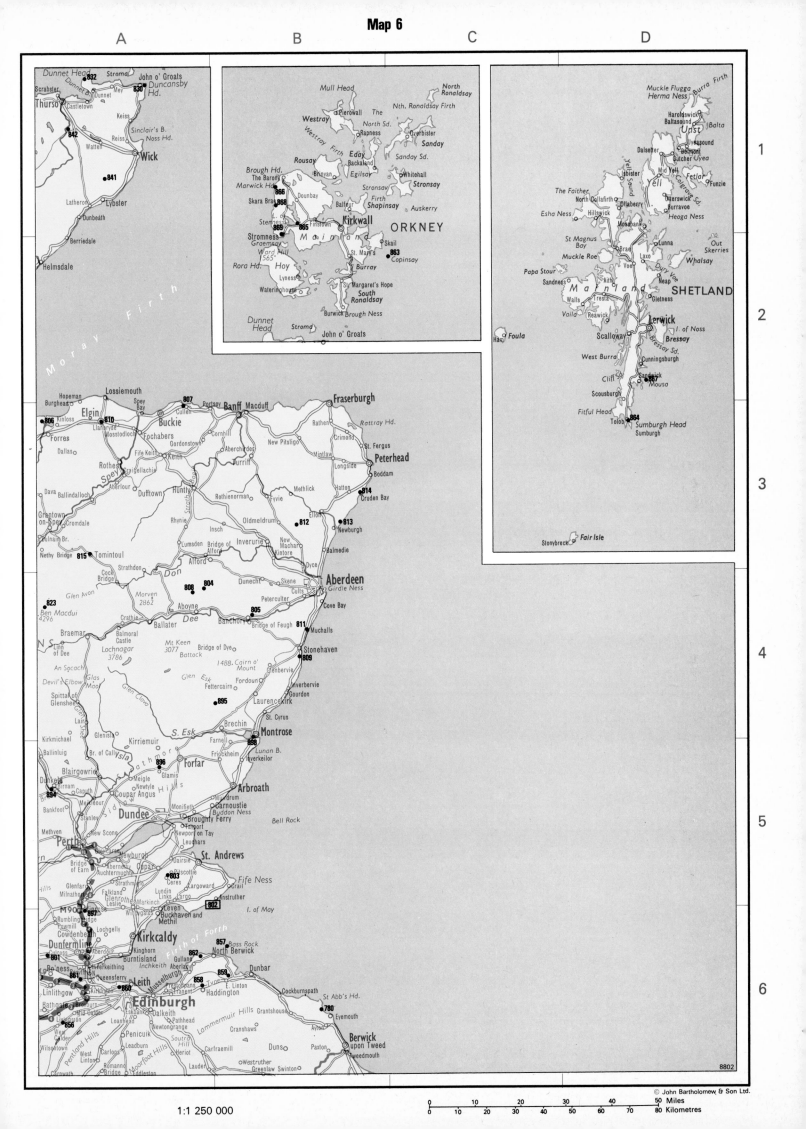

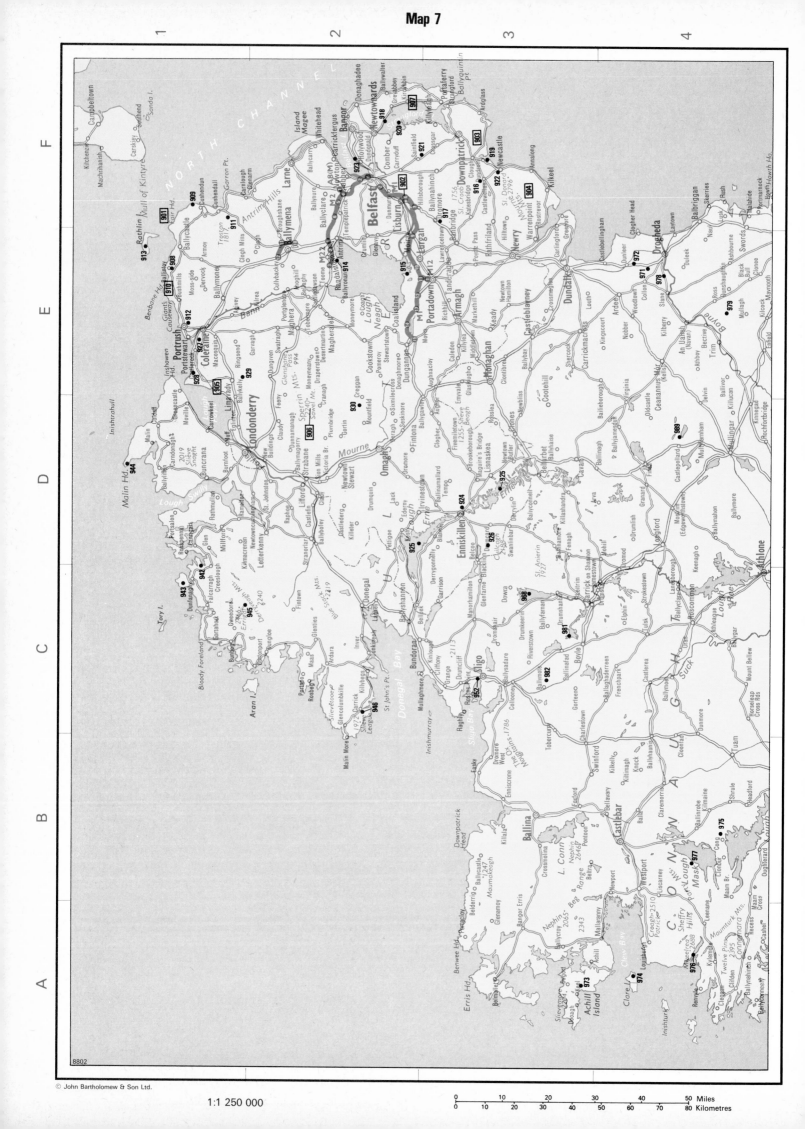

Map 7

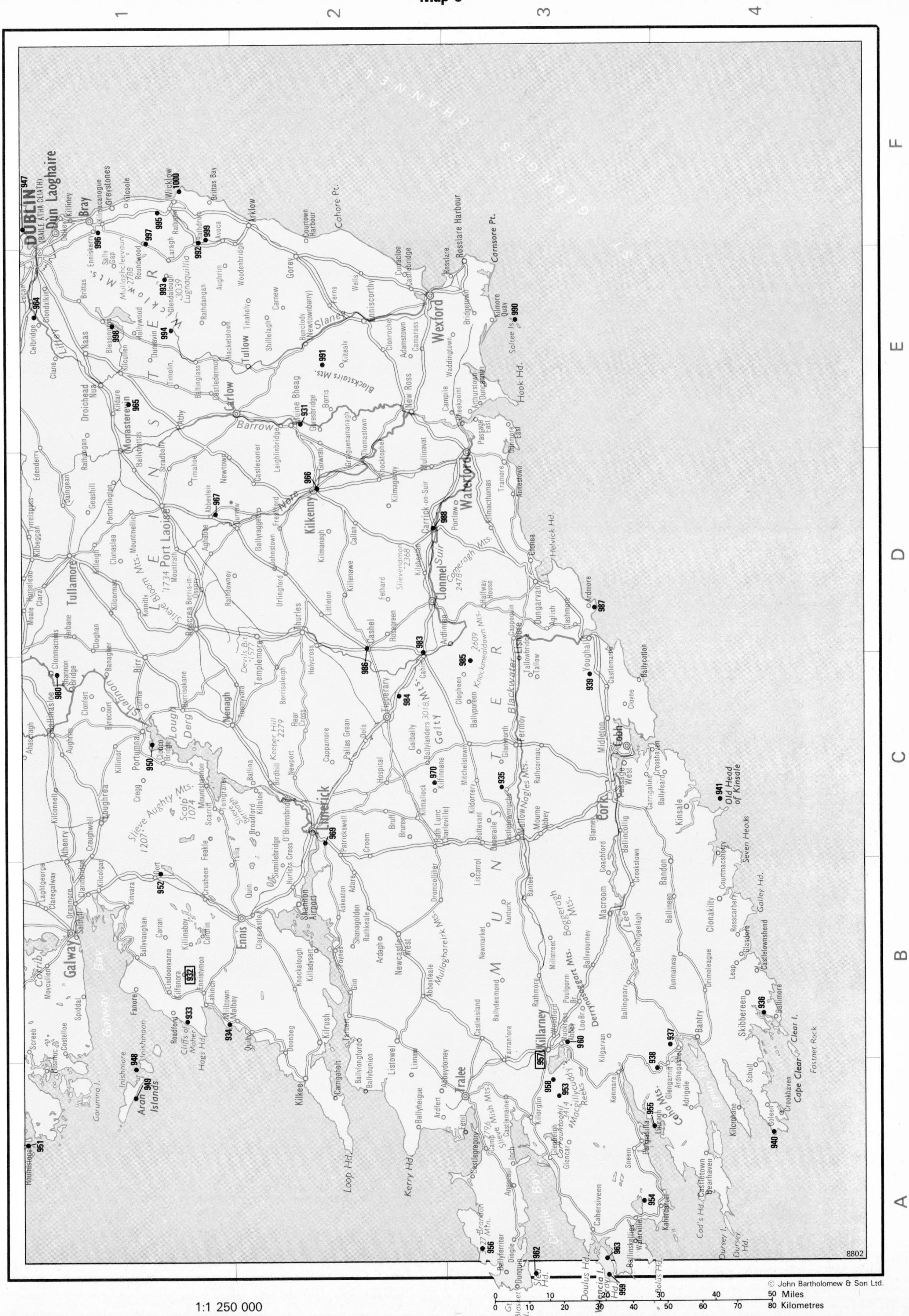

Map 8

DUBLIN (BAILE ÁTHA CLIATH)
Dún Laoghaire
Bray
Wicklow
Wexford
Rosslare Harbour
Carnsore Pt.
Waterford
Clonmel
Kilkenny
Port Laoise
Carlow
Tullamore
Galway
Ennis
Limerick
Tralee
Killarney
Cork
Cóbh
Youghal
Dungarvan
Tipperary
Nenagh

ST. GEORGE'S CHANNEL

LEINSTER
MUNSTER
Wicklow Mts.
Blackstairs Mts.
Slieve Bloom Mts.
Galty Mts.
Knockmealdown Mts.
Comeragh Mts.
Macgillycuddy's Reeks
Derrynasaggart Mts.
Slieve Aughty Mts.

Galway Bay
Aran Islands
Cliffs of Moher
Dingle Bay
Bantry Bay
Cape Clear I.
Fastnet Rock

© John Bartholomew & Son Ltd.

8802

1:1 250 000

0   10   20   30   40   50 Miles
0 10 20 30 40 50 60 70 80 Kilometres

How to use this section

Some of the suggestions will appear well known, especially if you live in the area. For this reason we have not always described in detail such cornerstones of the tourist industry as Warwick Castle or Stonehenge, Harewood House or Longleat. We have preferred to concentrate on additional locations or, as in places such as the Lake District, to suggest where crowds might be avoided – even on a Bank Holiday weekend in the height of summer.

The Days Out include less familiar, indeed virtually undiscovered, territory. Sometimes this is because places such as nature trails, farm museums or forest drives have only recently opened. However it is often because it has taken the eyes of our experts to appreciate the attraction or importance of what otherwise might be neglected. Little-known valleys in Snowdonia and Northumberland, for instance; the sites of deserted villages and failed medieval towns; and walks or drives along old drover's roads.

Generally towns have been included only where they remain rooted in the countryside or where they possess a building of particular importance. Villages are included where they, too, possess a feature of outstanding or unusual interest; mere 'prettiness' was not enough, if only because it would have resulted in more than 1000 Days Out suggestions for villages alone. Readers of this book may well find, possibly with some relief, that their 'favourite' village has thus been omitted.

This could also be a consequence of ensuring that each of the ten regions into which this section is divided has a comprehensive range of suggested Days Out. It cannot always be totally comprehensive: geology and history have not shaped the countryside that way. However we have tried to present the broadest possible range of suggestions for each region, even at the cost of excluding places from regions which are particularly rich in certain fields.

To take just one example of this – churches. Those which are suggested here in detail as churches worth visiting are not necessarily our nomination as the best churches in the British Isles nor even the best country churches. Areas such as Suffolk and the Cotswolds are so rich in churches that some have been excluded in order to accommodate interesting churches from other regions. We have also tried to select a variety of *types* of church. Much the same applies to categories as diverse as nature reserves and country inns, beaches and country houses.

The diversity which is a hallmark of the British countryside is reflected in these Days Out. Some are very detailed, with enough information for several days out. Some are broad descriptions of large areas, such as national parks or areas of outstanding natural beauty. Others are more limited in scale, possibly no more than a focal point of a day's drive.

One reason for such variety is the diversity of interests which can be pursued in the British countryside. Thus the naturalist will be able to use this section to devise the Days Out most likely to appeal to him while the garden-lover among others can compile a completely separate itinerary. A few of the larger entries are more catholic in their appeal.

How the Days Out are organised

The 1000 suggested Days Out are divided into 10 sections – six regions of England plus Wales, Scotland, Northern Ireland and the Republic of Ireland. Within each section the Days Out appear under their county heading, with both counties and the Days Out themselves presented in alphabetical order. Each county also begins with a short summary which includes the names of well-known attractions not described in detail as a Day Out and the details of the relevant regional or national tourist offices.

The only exceptions to this county-by-county presentation are National Parks and Areas of Outstanding Natural Beauty. These appear at the start of each regional section. Where such areas are so large that they extend into two regions, the main description will appear in the regional section where most of the area falls. Many features within National Parks and Areas of Outstanding Natural Beauty are also described in more detail as separate Days Out entries. A few panels of general interest also appear alongside the Days Out.

How to use the maps

Each Day Out is numbered and these numbers appear on the maps of the British Isles on the preceding pages. They are described in chronological sequence on the green pages which now follow. If you are starting from the Days Out text itself, you will find a map reference at the end of each Day Out entry. This will direct you to the page and the appropriate part of the relevant map to locate any particular Day Out.

Day Out numbers which appear in boxes either cover large areas such as national parks or are locations where the suggested Day Out is particularly detailed or varied. It is therefore always worth looking at such boxed numbers even if they appear to be some distance away from where you happen to be.

N.B. The final index to this book refers to Days Out by page number – not by number from one to 1000.

What about opening times

The standard DoE hours for many historic monuments are given below but the opening hours of many privately-run attractions, such as country houses, gardens and museums, vary from not only month to month but also year to year. Although we have omitted precise opening hours, we have indicated the days of the week and months of the year when places have been open in the past. Every effort has been made to ensure the accuracy of this information but because opening times do vary readers are advised to check times for themselves. This can usually be done through the telephone numbers given as part of the Days Out information. However a few telephone numbers are for offices which are only open weekdays. Other sources of information about opening times are tourist information offices and some of the publications mentioned below under Further Information. A particular problem which occasionally arises over churches is that they can be closed; if so, ask nicely for a key at the vicarage.

What the abbreviations mean

AM. Ancient Monument. This is often used to denote an ancient or historic monument which is open at any reasonable time rather than at the standard DoE hours described above.

AONB. Area of Outstanding Natural Beauty (see *How the Days Out are organised*, above).

Grid ref. The precise grid reference on an Ordnance Survey map, although in practice only the 1:50,000 or still larger scale maps can be used satisfactorily or precisely to identify particular grid references. See page 191 for how to use grid references.

Km. Kilometres.

Map ref. Map reference in order to locate a Day Out on the maps which begin overleaf.

NT. National Trust.

NTS. National Trust for Scotland.

OS map. Unless otherwise stated an OS map number refers to a particular map in the Ordnance Survey 1:50,000 series. These are often suggested for Days Out involving some walking across country.

RSPB. Royal Society for the Protection of Birds.

Tel no. Telephone numbers are given with the exchange but not the STD code.

□ The symbol is used at the end of each Day Out to denote the details required, in terms of distances and roads etc, in order to find any particular Day Out location.

Further Information

The tourist boards indicated for each county within the Days Out and the national tourist boards detailed in the Appendix on page 341 are invaluable sources of information. In the summer there are also many smaller tourist information offices throughout the country (some open summer only) which should have up-to-date details on opening hours of local attractions. Useful reference works include:

Historic Houses, Castles and Gardens: an annual publication from ABC Historic Publications (who also publish *Museums and Galleries*).

Properties Open: an annual publication by the National Trust.

Historic Monuments: a booklet published for the DoE by HMSO.

The Appendices on pages 337–341 details of other publications and organisations which offer considerable information in their specialist areas.

Road classification

The classification of roads in the Republic of Ireland is in the course of being changed. Some trunk and link roads have been re-classified and re-numbered as national roads. Where necessary both the old and new classification are given in the entries.

Standard DoE hours

The Department of the Environment is the body responsible for historic monuments. In Wales and Scotland the Secretaries of State take over these responsibilities. The term standard DoE hours is used in Days Out for historic monuments in England, Wales and Scotland where access is possible only at certain times and sometimes at a charge. These hours are detailed in the table below.

Many historic monuments are also open Sunday mornings during April to September. Where this is indicated it means they are open from 9.30am. Information about historic monuments in Northern Ireland and the Republic of Ireland can be obtained from the national tourist boards or their local information centres.

England and Wales	Weekdays	Sundays
Mar-Apr and Oct	9.30am-5.30pm	2-5.30pm
May-Sept	9.30am-7pm	2-7pm
Nov-Feb	9.30am-4pm	2-4pm
Scotland		
Apr-Sept	9.30am-7pm	2-7pm
Oct-Mar	9.30am-4pm	2-4pm

Exmoor pony. These shaggy, half-wild animals, a common sight in the Exmoor National Park, are descendants of wild horses first domesticated by the Celts of pre-Roman Britain.

South-West England

1. DARTMOOR
National Park

A short drive from Exeter, Plymouth and South Devon coast. M5 motorway reaches as far as Exeter; A30 from Exeter to Okehampton runs along the park's northern edge; A38 Exeter to Plymouth along the southern edge. The B3212 from Exeter cuts right across the roof of the moor via Postbridge and Two Bridges. Viewpoints (with or close to parking) include Haytor Rocks and Hound Tor, Whitchurch Common. Riverside beauty spots with parking include Fingle Bridge near Drewsteignton, Dartmeet and Huccaby on the West Dart. Lanes are heavily congested in summer and some are too narrow for caravans and wide vehicles. For walkers and pony trekkers there are about 180 square miles (228 sq km) of open moorland to explore. Chagford and Manaton are excellent walking centres. Viewpoints for walkers include Buckland Beacon, Chinkwell Tor and Kestor Rock. Guided walks are regular features during holiday season (details from any local tourist information centre or DNP office, tel: Bovey Tracey 832093. Some 40 square miles (64 sq km) of the northern moor are used as military firing range. Warning notices mark danger area and red flags fly on firing days. Details of firing times are displayed locally (post offices, hotels, newspapers). Sightseeing: Becka Falls, Widecombe-in-the-Moor and Grimspound prehistoric village, medieval

clapper bridge at Postbridge, Finch Foundry and Museum of Rural Industry at Sticklepath, and Lydford Gorge (NT).
□ Map ref 1B5.

2. EXMOOR
National Park

The M5 passes within 12 miles of the park as the crow flies. West-bound visitors turn off at Bridgwater (A39) or Taunton (A358), to enter at Dunster. The main information centre is at Dulverton. Tel: Dulverton 23665. Others (closed in winter) at Lynmouth, County Gate and Combe Martin. A spectacular drive is along the A39 from Minehead up Porlock Hill and then high above the sea to Lynton and Lynmouth. Viewpoints (with or near car parks) include Dunkery Beacon, at 1706ft (520m) the highest point on Exmoor, and Winsford Hill. In general there is freedom to walk anywhere on commons and open moorland. Also miles of well signposted walks (information centres have useful booklets on these). Watersmeet, Horner Woods, Badgworthy Water and the Chains are good walking areas, but best is long-distance footpath around the Southwest peninsula, which begins at Minehead and follows the park coastline of hogbacked cliffs and hanging woods to Combe Martin. Sightseeing: Selworthy, Allerford and Brendon (picturesque villages), Dunster Castle and Culbone (England's smallest church), the Lorna Doone country around Oare, the primitive stone footbridge of Tarr Steps spanning the Barle below

Winsford Hill, the twin coast resorts of Lynton and Lynmouth, and the Valley of Rocks.
□ Map ref 1B4.

3. CORNWALL
Area of Outstanding Natural Beauty

Not one area but a patchwork of isolated fragments which together represent the finest coast and countryside within the county. Apart from Bodmin Moor, they are all spread along the coast at different points. Most of West Penwith (the 'toe' of Cornwall) is included; so is the Lizard. Other areas include Morwenstow, the cliffs from Dizzard down to Pentire Point, Padstow to Watergate Bay, St Agnes, Portreath, and the estuaries and river valleys between Falmouth and Looe.
□ Map ref 1A5.

4. DORSET
Area Of Outstanding Natural Beauty

The Isle of Purbeck, the central downlands as far east as Blandford and the whole of West Dorset combine to form the third largest AONB in this, the least spoiled county in the whole of Southern England. This is the Wessex of Thomas Hardy's novels; heaths, chalk downs, combes and vales crossed by tunnelling country lanes and bounded by a splendid coast which includes Lulworth Cove, Durdle Door, the Chesil Beach and the fossil-studded cliffs of Charmouth and Lyme Regis. The Southwest Peninsula long-distance footpath follows the coast from end to end.
□ Map ref 1D5.

5. EAST DEVON
Area of Outstanding Natural Beauty

Takes in the Devon coast (with small gaps at Sidmouth and Seaton) between Exmouth and the Dorset border, and its hinterland as far north as Honiton. Its most outstanding features are cliffs of red sandstone and the high inland commons behind Budleigh Salterton, of which Woodbury Common is best for walks and views.
□ Map ref 1C5.

6. ISLES OF SCILLY
Area of Outstanding Natural Beauty

Smallest of all the AONBs, but also possibly the most beautiful. A cluster of tiny granite islands lying in the Atlantic some 28 miles (40km) off Land's End. Utterly peaceful, with bays and coves of dazzling sands and a mild climate which favours the cultivation of spring flowers. Tresco Abbey is famous for its sub-tropical gardens and 'Valhalla' of ships' figureheads from old wrecks. Boat trips to the out islands for picnics and bird-watching. Tourist information centre, Tel: Scillonia 22536. Day trips to the Scillies are operated by steamer and British Airways helicopter from Penzance.
□ Map ref 1C6.

7. MENDIP HILLS
Area of Outstanding Natural Beauty

A long swell of grey limestone hills rising abruptly above the dykes and watermeadows of the Somerset Levels.

South-West England

The limestone is riddled with stalactite-hung caverns, once the home of Stone Age man. Wookey Hole and Cheddar caves are the most famous. Map ref 1D4.

8. NORTH DEVON
Area of Outstanding Natural Beauty

Covers virtually the whole of Devon's Atlantic coast between Ilfracombe and Hartland point. Includes the sandhills of Braunton Burrows, the wooded cliffs around the show village of Clovelly, and the rugged headlands of Bull Point, Morte Point and Hartland. The Southwest Peninsula long-distance footpath provides continuous access.
□ Map ref 1B4.

9. QUANTOCKS
Area of Outstanding Natural Beauty

The Quantock Hills offer a foretaste of Exmoor, which lies to the west, but they have a character of their own: A 12-mile (19km) ridge of hills rising to a height of 1261ft (383m), comprised of red sandstone and covered with heather, bracken and tangled woodlands. Sea views, bracing walks, and the possibility of seeing red deer. Holford, just inside the AONB, is rich in memories of the poets, Wordsworth and Coleridge.
□ Map ref 1C4.

10. SOUTH DEVON
Area of Outstanding Natural Beauty

Includes the entire South Devon coast between Plymouth and Brixham, together with the valley of the River Dart as far as Totnes (river cruises ply in summer between Dartmouth and Totnes), and the fertile South Hams countryside beside the River Avon. Marvellous cliff walks from Thurlestone to Bolt Head, and from Prawle Point to Start Point (part of the South-west Peninsula long-distance footpath).
□ Map ref 1B6.

Avon

The heart of Avon is an urban complex composed of Bristol, Bath and the seaside resort of Weston-super-Mare. But there is also much of interest for country-lovers, especially in the limestone landscapes of the Cotswolds. The beautiful Georgian city of Bath is an ideal springboard for days out in Avon. West Country Tourist Board: Exeter 76351.

11. AVON GORGE
National Nature Reserve

This woodland reserve stretching along the west side of the Avon over Clifton Bridge is one of the most important reserves on lowland Carboniferous limestone. Oak predominates in association with ash, birch, small-leaved lime, beech and sycamore. Towards the north of the reserve yew and holly grow together and among the various species of whitebeam is the rare Bristol whitebeam, found nowhere else in the world except along the Avon Gorge. Woodland flowers and ferns thrive on the lime soils and autumn brings a good range of fungi, including poisonous fly agaric. The Iron Age hill fort of Stokeleigh Camp lies within the reserve.
□ Start at stone arch beside A369 to Portishead. Map ref 1D4.

12. BROCKLEY COMBE
Nature trail

This waymarked Nature Trail leads through Brockley Combe, a deep winding gorge cut through Carboniferous limestone. The woods are a mixture of oak, ash, beech and sycamore, sweet chestnut and yew. Other features include turkey oak and a handsome avenue of lime trees. Leaflet from Brockley Combe Fruit Stall.
Tel: Avon Wildlife Trust: Bristol 313396.
□ Near Brockley, three miles (5km) NW of Congresbury. Map ref 1C4.

13. CASTLE FARM MUSEUM
Folk museum

A rare and largely unrestored long house or farmhouse dating from the 16th century is the focal point of this museum which is also part of a working farm. Later buildings date from the 18th century and contain a dairy, cheese loft and granary. Old domestic and agricultural tools are also on show. Open three afternoons a week, mid-June to mid-Sept. Tel: Marshfield 469.
□ At Marshfield, eight miles (13km) W of Chippenham off A420. Map ref 1D4.

14. NORTON ST. PHILIP
Historic inn

The George is an excellent example of a country inn which started as an abbey hospice. The stone building of 1397 was partly burned down, however, and only the ground floor of the present inn survives from this 14th century structure. The half-timbered upper storeys were added about 1500, since when the inn has been used by, among others, Cromwell, the Duke of Monmouth and Judge Jeffreys.
□ Approx. five miles (8km) SE of Bath at junction of A366 and B3110 roads. Map ref 1D4.

Cornwall

The coast is Cornwall's glory. Wild and rugged where it faces the Atlantic, its savage cliffs of slate and granite interspersed with magnificent surf beaches. Softer and gentler on the south coast, with wooded creeks and sheltered fishing harbours. The Isles of Scilly, just over the horizon beyond Land's End, are an additional bonus of shell sand beaches and granite sea-

Clifftop monument to bygone industry: Botallack Tin Mine, St Just-in-Penwith, Cornwall

Quarries and kilns

A cliff is a natural vertical shaft giving easy access to minerals and stone, which can be transported immediately by boat.

Purbeck marble, granite, Lizard serpentine, alabaster, Portland stone, blue elvan and duller stuffs needed for cement and road building were quarried from sea cliffs and lowered or shot down to cargo carriers at cliff-bottom.

Coal, iron, oil shale and alum were reached from cliff entries and the mines drained by cliff face adits. Cornish tin was sought right out under the sea (as coal is now) and mine access shafts and ventilation chimneys went down and up from the last possible land point, a cliff top if need be.

All around the coast are remains of lime kilns which burnt sea-delivered limestone, using sea-coal, to produce agricultural lime. Also left are pits where kelp (seaweed) was burnt for potash; and evaporation pools where seawater was concentrated progressively until it could be boiled into salt crystals over a sea-coal fire. Industrial debris marked the coast too – Copperhouse at Hayle, Cornwall, has wharves of copper slag. Tipped coal, washed very clean, returns to the beaches of Druridge Bay, Northumberland, to be grubbed for.

Where to view: Tilly Whim quarries, Isle of Purbeck, Dorset; Botallack Mine, near St Just-in-Penwith, Cornwall; cliffs from Staithes to Whitby, Yorkshire; Beadnell lime kilns, Northumberland; Lymington salterns, Hampshire.

scapes. West Country Tourist Board: Exeter 76351.

15. BOSCASTLE
Coastal village

A village on the rugged coast of North Cornwall which matches the beauty of its surroundings. In effect it is almost two villages; one nestles on top of the cliffs, the other is clustered around a tiny but dramatic harbour in a twisting creek sheltered by the cliffs. A narrow street of white-washed cottages, Fore Street, runs steeply downhill to a ruined castle *motte* or mound that marked the founding of a town here early in the 12th century. The harbour – which prospered for more than a century after the building of a break-water in 1740 – is now owned by the National Trust.
□ On B3263, three miles (5km) N of Tintagel. Map ref 1A5.

16. BOTALLACK TIN MINE
Industrial archaeology

Cornwall has many relics of tin mining but few are more dramatically sited than this former mine on the very edge of the cliff. The workings – for copper as well as tin – extended far under the Atlantic Ocean and in places were 1200ft (366m) deep. The mine ceased to function during the 19th century after 100 years or so of dangerous productivity. The former manager's house is now a restaurant but otherwise the ruins, including engine house and stack are balanced precariously on a narrow platform just above the sea. Care should be taken when exploring.
□ Off B3306 one mile (1.6km) NW of St Just. Map ref 1D6.

17. BUDE
Sea coast and canal

Once a busy port, Bude is now prim-arily a beach resort renowned for surfing. Bude Canal was constructed between 1819–26 to carry beach sand inland for farmers to balance the acidic soil. Today it is used by pleasure boats, fishermen and towpath walkers. Ebbingford Manor, just by the canal, is a typical Cornish Manor dating from the 12th century with a walled garden. Open from June to Sept. Tel: Bude 2808. Nearby, Bude Historical and Folk Exhibition, housed in an old forge, gives a history of the canal. Open daily in summer.

The cliffs at Bude reveal spectacular contortions and folds in the rock strata. When the tide is out you can walk along the beach to the beautiful Coombe Valley, returning along the cliffs, a good seven mile (11km) walk. Several interesting nature trails start from the picnic site and car park in the valley.
□ On the A3073. Map ref 1A5.

18. CADGWITH
Coastal village

Cars are best left in the car park above this tiny village which is down a narrow valley and is crowded in summer. To the south-west of the village is the Devil's Frying Pan – reached via a steep cliff path which enables you to look down into this natural cauldron formed by the cave roof falling in.

The Poltesco Cadgwith Nature Trail starts from Ruan Minor taking

the walker along a circular trail of three miles (4.8km) through a wooded valley with a cascading stream, past caves and cliffs. You can see the remains of an 18th century serpentine rock factory.
□ On Lizard peninsula, reached by minor road off A3083 from Helston. Map ref 1D6.

19. CHARLESTOWN SHIPWRECK CENTRE
Maritime history

Charlestown is a small port which has hardly changed since it was built in 1791. The Shipwreck Centre, near the harbour, illustrates the history of Cornish shipwrecks. Open 10 days at Easter, then Thur and Sun; daily May to Sept, and Thur and Sun in Oct. Tel: St Austell 3332.

China clay has been mined in this area for about 200 years and is still loaded from the narrow harbour. Nearby at Carthew, two miles (3.2km) from St Austell, is the Wheal Martyn Museum in which you can see working waterwheels, a 220ft (67m) clay kiln and the trappings of clay works. Open summer only – Tel: St Austell 850362.
□ Charlestown is two miles (3.2km) E of St Austell, off A390. Map ref 1A6.

20. CHYSAUSTER
Prehistoric village

A 'village' of nine houses which were inhabited in Late Iron Age and Roman times. The houses, roughly oval in shape, have immensely thick walls with inner rooms opening on to a central courtyard. The rooms were originally roofed with stone or thatch but are now open to the sky. Archaeologists disagree over how Chysauster's first inhabitants lived, although they probably worked the tin deposits in the valley below. What is certain, however, is that the village is one of the most remarkable survivals of Iron Age settlement in the British Isles. Open standard DoE hours.
□ Three miles (4.8km) N of Penzance. Signposted off minor road between B3311 and the Penzance–Zennor road at New Mill. Grid ref SW 473340; OS map 203. Map ref 1D6.

21. CORNISH SEAL SANCTUARY
Wildlife

Do not be deterred by the approach through a new bungalow estate. The sanctuary itself has an idyllic setting overlooking the wooded banks of the tidal Helford River. Sick, injured and orphaned Atlantic seals are cared for in five spacious pools before being returned to the wild. An unrivalled opportunity to see these gentle wild mammals at close quarters. A splendid day out for all the family, but especially for children. Open daily, all year.
□ At Gweek, near Helston. Map ref 1D6.

22. COTEHELE
Historic house and garden

Romantic medieval house, now belonging to the NT, perched on the steep banks of the Tamar. House contains armour, furniture, tapestries. Beautiful terraced gardens lead down to ponds, quay and watermill with blacksmith's and wheelright's shops. Open daily,

except non-Bank Holiday Mons, Apr to Oct. Ring for winter opening times for garden and hall only. Tel: St Dominick 50434.
□ At Calstock, eight miles (12km) SW of Tavistock off A390. Map ref 1B6.

23. DAPHNE DU MAURIER'S CORNWALL

For many people the romance of Cornwall and its lawless seafaring history are indivisible from Daphne du Maurier's novels. Her stories – *Rebecca*, *Jamaica Inn*, *Frenchman's Creek* – are steeped in the magic of Cornwall, whose coves, creeks and lonely moors can still conjure up visions of the days when smuggling was the mainstay of many a Cornish community.

For a day out in du Maurier's Cornwall, where better to begin than the little port of *Fowey*? – where the authoress herself first fell in love with Cornwall at the age of five. She lived for a while at a house just below Bodinnick Ferry, and later moved to *Menabilly*, about one mile (2km) west of Fowey, where she lived for 26 years. Menabilly is thought to be the model for Manderley in 'Rebecca'. It is not open to visitors, but a splendid walk from Fowey along the Cornwall South Coast Path passes within half a mile (1km) of the house as it rounds Gribbin Head to Polkerris, setting for 'The House on the Strand'.

A narrow finger of the Helford River, called Frenchman's Pill, is nowadays better known as *Frenchman's Creek*, after du Maurier's novel of the same name. To visit this secluded creek, take the road from Gweek to Manaccan and turn off to the left where the sign says 'Kestle'. You will then have to leave your car and walk the last few hundred yards. Alternatively, there are regular boat trips to Frenchman's Creek and the lovely Helford River from Falmouth harbour during the holiday season. In the old days, contraband run ashore at spots like Frenchman's Creek was often smuggled further inland before being distributed to other parts of the country. A popular hiding place was the wild and empty expanse of Bodmin Moor, not far from the Devon border. This is the setting for *Jamaica Inn*, and at Bolventor the granite-built 18th-century Jamaica Inn still offers hospitality to travellers on the A30 road from Penzance to London. Nearby is the granite tor of Brown Willy, at 1375ft (418m), the highest point on the Moor, and *Dozmary Pool*, where King Arthur received his legendary sword Excalibur.
□ Map ref 1A6.

24. FAL ESTUARY
Cornish estuary

This beautiful mingling of blue tidal waters, secluded creeks and deep oak-wood valleys is best explored by boat from Falmouth or St Mawes. Details of sea and river trips from Falmouth Tourist Information Office. Tel: Falmouth 312300. The area is formed by the five main tributaries of the River Fal, which converge upon a four-mile (6.4km) long drowned valley, or ria, called Carrick Roads. There are passenger ferries from Falmouth to

Truro, St Mawes and Flushing, and a car ferry at King Harry Ferry. Pendennis Castle (AM) and St Mawes Castle (AM) face each other across the estuary. St Mawes has an exceptionally pretty harbour and waterfront and mild, sun-trap climate. Some two or three miles (4km) north of St Mawes is St Just in Roseland church, its church-yard a sub-tropical profusion of palm trees and exotic shrubs on the banks of a peaceful tidal creek.
□ Map ref 1D6.

25. GLENDURGAN GARDEN
Valley garden, spring flowers

Exotic trees and shrubs and a laurel maze planted in 1833. Many magnolias, tree ferns and good rhododendrons spreading down valley to idyllic NT hamlet of Durgan, on sheltered shores of Helford River. At its best with early spring flowers in bloom, probably the loveliest garden in Cornwall. Open Mar to Oct, on Mons, Weds and Fris. Tel: Mawnan Smith 250780.
□ Four miles (6.5km) SW of Falmouth on road to Helford Passage. Map ref 1D6.

26. KERNOW FOREST
Forest walks, industrial past

Cardinham Woods have picnic place, walks and trails. Picnic place is by a clear stream fringed with alder and slopes of the forest rising behind. Riverside walk is easy and follows stream; the Panorama trail is more strenuous with fine views down Glynn Valley; the Silvermine trail leads to Hurstocks lead mine worked in early 19th century. The path is steep in places. Old chimney and engine house ruins at mine are unsafe. All walks start from picnic place where leaflets are on sale from a dispenser. Distances vary from one mile (1.6km) to 3½ miles (5.6km).
□ Two miles (3.2km) NE of Bodmin on A38. Map ref 1A6.

27. KYNANCE COVE
Cliffs and caves

The Lizard is a flat, heathery plateau, ringed by dramatic cliffs, rock stacks, coves and caverns. Kynance Cove (NT) is popular with sightseers in summer. The cliffs are streaked with multi-coloured serpentine rock, made into ornaments by local craftsmen.

On the path down to the cove you can see jagged outcrops of rock caused by the diagonal jointing of the serpentine. The caves can only be seen at low tide. Exploration can be dangerous.

Following the Cornwall Coast Path to the Lizard you can see how the rock changes from serpentine to schist. The lighthouse is open to the public.
□ On Lizard peninsula, reached by toll road off A3801. Map ref 1D6.

28. LANHYDROCK HOUSE
Historic house and garden

A great Jacobean house two-thirds gutted by fire in the late 19th century, and rebuilt to cater for house-party life on the grand scale. All is now on show, from the kitchen to the billiard room, and the butler's pantry to the boudoir, A final bonus is the long gallery in the wing: one of the finest long galleries in England, with a barrel-vaulted ceiling.

The parkland extends to the River Fowey with fine formal gardens. House open daily, April to late Oct, gardens all year; Tel: Bodmin 3320.
□ 2½ miles (4km) SE of Bodmin off B3268 to Lostwithiel. Map ref 1A6.

29. LAUNCESTON
Market town

This market town grew like many others around the Norman castle which was both its protector and its customer. Its dominating site over the River Kensey had drawn earlier settlers, though; Celtic and Saxon settlements preceded the Norman castle. This castle still dominates the town which is built on a number of hills.

Its long history is reflected in a jumble of architectural styles, never more jumbled than in the *White Hart*, a former coaching inn with a front entrance formed by the Norman doorway of an old priory. There is also a gateway surviving from the old town walls; 16th century St Mary Magdalene Church carved out of the granite which is local to Cornwall but whose hardness makes it so rare in church buildings; and some fine Georgian houses in partly-cobbled Castle Street.

The castle is open standard DoE hours plus Sun mornings April–Sept.
□ 13 miles (21km) NW of Tavistock on A30/A388; Map ref 1A5.

30. LOE POOL
Lake and pebble bar

Between Porthleven and Gunwalloe stretches a great shingle bank thrown up by the sea. Behind it lies Loe Pool, the largest freshwater lake in Cornwall. The bar itself is composed mainly of rounded flints and is 600ft (182m) wide. The wooded Loe is encircled by footpaths, the round trip being six miles (9.6km) long. There are several access points where you can park and then walk to the pool. Among them, Penrose Hill car park, signposted off the B3304 as you approach Porthleven.
□ Near Porthleven. Map ref 1D6.

31. LOOE
Fishing port

Joined by a long stone bridge, the twin towns of East and West Looe share the same colourful river-mouth harbour and an international reputation as a shark fishing centre. All claims for world records in shark fishing must be channelled through the Shark Angling Club of Great Britain, whose HQ overlooks the quayside where the shark boats weigh their fearsome catch. Boats can be hired for shark fishing trips but it is advisable to book well in advance.
□ 16 miles (26km) W of Plymouth on A387. Map ref 1A6.

32. MEVAGISSEY
Fishing village

Fishing is still important here, though the old pilchard fleet has been replaced by shark-angling boats to attract the tourists. The village itself, and its sturdy inner and outer harbours, are as picturesque as any on this coast. The Folk Museum at East Quay occupies an 18th century boat building workshop and displays local crafts, fishing, seafaring, farming, china clay and copper mining. Open daily, Easter to Sept. Tel: Mevagissey 3568.
□ On B3273, about five miles (8km) S of St Austell. Map ref 1A6.

33. PERRANPORTH
Atlantic beach

Perran beach stretches for three miles (4.8km) to Ligger Point with its ancient wells, once believed to possess miraculous powers. Encroaching dunes, said to cover the lost city of Langarrow, lure surfers and caravan dwellers. The army uses the area north of Penhale Sands. St Piran's Oratory, one of the earliest known seats of Christianity was dug out of the sand in 1835. Now in need of maintenance, it is protected from the sand by a concrete shell. White stones mark the path to the church across the dunes. St Piran's Round, near Rose, one and a half miles (2.4km) E of Perranporth, is an ancient enclosure where, until quite recently, Cornish mystery plays were still performed.
□ Five miles (8km) S of Newquay off A3075. Map ref 1A6.

34. PORTH HELLICK DOWN
Prehistoric site

Around 50 chambered tombs from the Neolithic or Bronze Ages can be found in the Isles of Scilly – all on St Mary's, largest of the islands. The best preserved is probably one of a group of five on Porth Hellick Down in the southeast of the island. The tomb is still roofed and contained within a mound 40ft (12m) in diameter. The central chamber is reached through a curving passageway 14ft (4.3m) long. Access is available at any reasonable time.
□ Porth Hellick Down is reached by a footpath off A3110 and the tomb is at grid ref SV 929108; OS map 203. Map ref 1C6.

35. RIVER CAMEL
Cornish estuary

Camel is Cornish for 'crooked river'. The wide sandy estuary merges with

Built to last in slate and stone: the Old Post Office, Tintagel, Cornwall

the Atlantic between two noble headlands; Pentire Point (NT) to the east and Stepper Point to the west. Across the mouth lies a sand bar called the Doom Bar. The entire estuary is a splendid recreational playground. You can surf at Polzeath, swim safely at Daymer Bay, sail at Rock (dinghies on hire to competent sailors), fish for bass, or take a boat cruise from the picturesque fishing port of Padstow, one of the few havens on this wild Atlantic coast. There is a passenger ferry between Rock and Padstow, and parking at Padstow Quay, Rock, Daymer Bay and Polzeath. A pleasant walk along the sands will take you from Rock to Daymer Bay and on to Polzeath over the clifftop turf of the Greenaway, A slightly more strenuous walk runs from Polzeath out to Pentire Head and the Rumps, where Atlantic seals, ravens and sometimes basking sharks, may be seen. Until 1863 St Enodoc's church was buried but now it stands, re-excavated and functioning, amid the dunes and golf course on the east side of the Camel estuary.
□ Map ref 1A5.

36. ST AUSTELL
Industrial landscape

China clay has been quarried from open pits north of St Austell since the

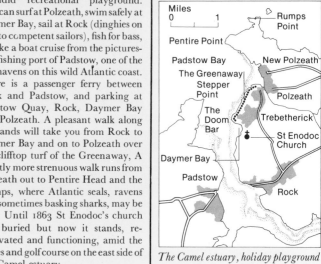

The Camel estuary, holiday playground on Cornwall's rugged Atlantic coast

mid 18th century. Two hundred years later great holes have been opened up and vast conical heaps of glistening white spoil built around them, often nicknamed the 'Cornish Alps'.
□ Main workings N of St Austell, around granite outcrop of Hensbarrow, along the A391. Map ref 1A6.

37. ST MICHAEL'S MOUNT
Causewayed isle

Fairytale fortress home of Lord St Levan, perched on a pyramidal granite island that dominates Mounts Bay from wherever you look at it. At low tide you can walk across the sandy causeway from Marazion in ten minutes. At high tide there is a ferry. The castle (NT) is 12th century, with later additions. For opening times, tel: Marazion 710507.
□ Marazion, three miles (4.8km) E of Penzance. Map ref 1D6.

38. SEAL ISLAND
Nature walk

Though not a designated nature trail, the four miles (6.4km) of the Cornwall Coast Path from St Ives westward towards Zennor provides a good chance of sighting wild Atlantic seals. In fact the nearer of the two rocky islets

The 'Cornish Alps': spoil heaps of the china clay industry near St Austell

just beyond Carn Naun Point is known locally as 'Seal Island'. This beautiful walk also offers magnificent scenery, seabirds and clifftop wild flowers.
□ Map ref 1D6.

39. SENNEN COVE
Sandy beach

At Sennen the granite cliffs give way to the pounding surf and finely-powdered white shell sands of Whitesand Bay. Sennen is the 'last village in England', only about one mile (1.6km) from Land's End. You can walk along the Cornwall Coast Path to Land's End and see the isolated Longships lighthouse and infamous Seven Stones Reef.
□ Near Land's End, reached by minor road off A30. Map ref 1D6.

40. TINTAGEL CASTLE
Sea castle

The sea-girt peninsula of Tintagel Head has been almost cut off from the mainland, so the ruins of King Arthur's Castle must now be reached by a dizzy footbridge. The Castle, which dates from the 12th century, some 600 years later than the legendary King Arthur, is open daily.
□ About 3½ miles (5.6km) SW of Boscastle on B3263. Map ref 1A5.

41. TRELISSICK GARDENS
Stately garden

Situated at the head of Falmouth harbour, this garden has glorious views and many exotic trees and shrubs, particularly a collection of over 100 species of hydrangea. Open Apr to Oct daily. Tel: Devoran 862090.
□ Near Truro, on B3289 overlooking King Harry Ferry. Map ref 1D6.

42. TRESCO ABBEY
Sub-tropical garden

No part of the British Isles has a milder climate than this, and so, ever since Augustus Smith started to make a garden here in the mid-19th century, the collection of rare plants from many parts of the world has grown in extent and interest. All types are grown, woody and herbaceous, but Tresco is particularly notable for its succulent plants and species from the southern hemisphere. Open daily throughout the year except Suns. Tel: Scillonia 22849.
□ On Tresco, Isles of Scilly. Reached by ferry from St Mary's. Map ref 1C6.

43. TREWITHEN
Spring garden

Magnificently landscaped garden containing camellias, magnolias and rhododendrons. Open daily, except Suns, Mar to Sept, afternoons only. Tel: Grampound Road 882764.
□ Probus, near Truro. Off A390 S of St Austell. Map ref 1A6.

44. ZENNOR
Moorland village, prehistoric tomb

A tiny Cornish hamlet with a moorland stream, wayside museum and church renowned for its carving of a mermaid. The surrounding pattern of tiny, stone-walled fields goes back to the Iron Age. Above, on the windswept granite moors, is Zennor Quoit, a chambered tomb dating from around 3000 BC.

Below the village, about two miles (3.2km) to the west along the Coast Path, is Gurnards Head, one of the wildest headlands in Cornwall. The Southwest Peninsular Coast Path provides continuous access along the cliffs.
□ On B3306 between St Ives and St Just. Zennor Quoit is off the B3306 at Grid ref SW 454385. Map ref 1D6.

Devon

Glorious Devon claims two splendid coastlines, North Devon has wild cliffs and Atlantic surf. South Devon offers sheltered estuaries and a mild climate. In between lie the heights of Dartmoor, idyllic river valleys, rolling farmlands, and Exeter, the county town. West Country Tourist Board: Exeter 76351.

45. ALSCOTT FARM MUSEUM
Farm museum

Old farm tractors, ploughs, barn machinery and a cider press. Also some dairying equipment. North Devon's agricultural past is recalled in a selection of photographs. Open daily, Easter to end Sept. Tel: Shebbear 206.
□ At Shebbear, 6 miles (9.6km) NE of Holsworthy. Access from A388 or A3702 via minor roads. Map ref 1B5.

46. APPLEDORE
Maritime history

Fascinating little town with long history of ship-building and glorious position overlooking the mouth of the sandy Taw and Torridge estuary. Hinks Yard specialises in building wooden working replicas of ships of old. Also in Appledore is the North Devon Maritime Museum. Open daily, Easter to Sept. Tel: Bideford 6042.
□ Three miles (5km) N of Bideford on B3236. Map ref 1B4.

47. ARLINGTON COURT
Nature trails and heronry

Handsomely furnished Regency House (NT), with extensive grounds containing nature trails, lake and heronry. Gardens open daily, throughout year. House open daily, Apr to Oct. Tel: Shirwell 296.
□ Seven miles (11km) NE of Barnstaple on A39. Map ref 1B4.

48. BARNSTAPLE
Ancient market town

Claims to be the oldest borough in the country with a charter granted in 930 by King Athelstan, giving Barnstaple the right to have a market. This still flourishes – now in the 19th century vaulted Pannier Market building – a commercial centre for North Devon. Interesting buildings include the colonnaded 17th century Queen Anne's Walk (once the trading place or exchange between merchants and shippers) and the bridge over the Taw which dates from the 12th century.
□ Nine miles (14km) NE of Bideford on A39. Map ref 1B4.

49. BERRY HEAD
Country park

Limestone headland east of Brixham with park and nature trails as well as coastal views.
□ Map ref 1B6.

50. BICKLEIGH MILL FARM
Rural life

A living example of farming and country life in Devon at the turn of the century, complete with horse-drawn equipment working the land and rare breeds of goats and cows being milked by hand. There is also an agricultural and crafts museum adjacent to the farm in an old watermill where you can see, among other things, a maker of corn dollies at work and observation bee hives. Open daily, afternoons only, Jan, Feb, Mar, and all day Easter to Christmas. Tel: Bickleigh 419.
□ Off A396 about four miles (6.4km) S of Tiverton. Map ref 1B5.

51. BICTON
Formal gardens and farm museum

Lots of family attractions at Bicton, including rides on miniature railway. For garden enthusiasts, the main attraction are the large formal gardens with terraces and pools made in the mid 18th century. Also a 19th century pinetum, conservatories, an 'American' garden and farming museum. Open daily, Apr to Oct. Tel: Colaton Raleigh 68465.
□ Colaton Raleigh, off A376 S of Newton Poppleford. Map ref 1C5.

52. BRAUNTON
Sand dunes and strip fields

This large North Devon village has two exceptional features in the vicinity: the rolling dunes of Braunton Burrows, and the Great Field between the village and the dunes. The Great Field is a relic of a medieval open field that covers some 350 acres (141 hectares) and is still shared by several farmers. The former strips of medieval farming, grouped together in blocks or furlongs, can be traced within the field. Braunton Burrows extends north from the Taw and Torridge estuary for three and a half miles (5.6km). Its rolling sandhills spread across over 2000 acres (809 hectares), making this one of the largest dune systems in the British Isles. There are two military training areas (watch for red warning flags) and a nature reserve at the southern end. Open Mar to Oct, restricted opening in winter. Tel: Croyde 890407.
□ Access from A361 and B3231. Map ref 1B4.

53. DARTINGTON HALL
Landscape garden

Peaceful stone-built 14th century hall with tiltyard around which a modern landscape and flower garden have been created since 1926. Many fine old trees and shrubs including rhododendrons and camellias. Open all year. Tel: Totnes 863291.
□ Two miles (3.2km) N of Totnes, off A384 S of Buckfastleigh. Map ref 1B6.

54. DAWLISH WARREN
South Devon estuary

A mile-long (1.6km) sand spit, almost blocking the mouth of the River Exe. Dunes swarm with holiday-makers in summer. The mudflats to the north are a National Wildfowl Reserve. To reach the beach of red sand you have to cross Brunel's railway.

□ Minor road off A379, 12 miles (20km) S of Exeter. Map ref 1C5.

55. EGGESFORD FOREST
Forest walk

Flashdown Woods picnic place is near site of the first trees planted by the Forestry Commission in Britain in 1919. Heywood forest walk is through Douglas fir plantations including landscaped felled areas giving good vistas.
□ On A377 midway between Exeter and Barnstaple. Map ref 1B5.

56. FARWAY COUNTRYSIDE PARK
Country park

Privately-run park on wooded heath and meadowland.
□ Four miles (6.5km) S of Honiton at Holnest Farm. Map ref 1C5.

57. GRIMSPOUND
Prehistoric village

Dartmoor is scarcely the most propitious location for farming even nowadays with all the aids of 20th century technology. How much more difficult it must have been in the Bronze Age when this settlement existed. Its size is clearly marked by a line of stone rubble from what were once the outer walls. Within the four acres (1.6 hectares) of this compound are the remains of some 20 huts and several cattle pens.
□ 7½ miles (12km) NW of Ashburton off minor road which leads S of B3212; grid ref SX700809; OS map 191. Map ref 1B5.

58. HARTLAND POINT
Coastal scenery

Here in this windswept, westernmost Devon parish the flat fields suddenly fall away to form the most savage coast in Southwest England. 'A sailor's grave by day and night', Hartland point has a lighthouse (open to the public; Tel: Hartland 328) to warn shipping of the jagged ribs and tusks of Carboniferous rock that tear the waves to ribbons at the base of these fearsome cliffs. The rock formations and contorted strata assume the most extraordinary shapes, and the force of the Atlantic can be gauged at Hartland Quay, three miles (4.8km) away along the North Devon Coast path. Here the old quay was swept away during a gale in 1896.
□ Minor road off A39, signposted to lighthouse. Map ref 1A5.

59. HAYTOR GRANITE RAILWAY
Industrial archaeology

In the 19th century, Dartmoor granite was used to build bridges, wharves and other heavy engineering works. One busy quarry lay on the eastern fringe of the Moor near Haytor Vale. To get the stone to the coast, a granite railway was built, with rails of stone. Parts of the old track still survive on the Moor northwest of Haytor Vale, below the popular viewpoint of Haytor Rocks.
□ W of minor road leading from Haytor Vale to B3344 near Manaton. Map ref 1B5.

60. HEDDON VALLEY
Nature trail

The National Trust owns nearly 1000 acres (405 hectares) of woodland,

moorland and meadow around Trentishoe in the Exmoor National Park. Here the Devon Trust for Nature Conservation has devised a beautiful and interesting nature trail which follows the little River Heddon down Heddons Mouth Cleave to the sea. The circular walk (two miles/3km) begins and ends near Hunters Inn Hotel.
□ Four miles (6km) W of Lynton (turn off A39 at Parracombe). Map ref 1B4.

61. HEMBURY WOODS
Woodland wildlife

These beautiful coppice woodlands (NT), lie in the valley of the River Dart. They once produced charcoal for the local copper mines but this practice ceased with the decay of the Devon mining industry. The wood is full of interesting flowers and mosses, including cow-wheat and yellow pimpernel. There are paths running through the wood down to the river. The wood is mainly oak but there is also willow, hazel, beech, sycamore and alder buckthorn, and several species of butterflies and dragonflies.
□ The wood lies N of Buckfast. Travel N along A38 past Buckfastleigh, and take left turn to Buckfast. Map ref 1B6.

62. HOLSWORTHY
Old market town

A market town still dominated by agriculture and especially on Thursdays with the weekly livestock market. A general market also takes place with stalls in the market square and adjoining streets on Wednesdays. There are some pleasant old cottages but essentially this is a place which has not outgrown its origins as a market centre.
□ Location: nine miles (14km) E of Bude at junction of A3072 and A388. Map ref 1A5.

63. HOUND TOR
Weathered rocks, abandoned dwellings

In the vicinity of this characteristically weatherbeaten granite outcrop are the remains of several rectangular buildings which have been laid bare by excavation. Situated at about 1100ft (335m) above sea level, these dwellings probably date from the early 12th century and could not survive a climatic deterioration which set in at a later date. The 1:50,000 and 1:25,000 OS maps for Dartmoor repay careful study since they show innumerable locations of cairns, hut circles and other ancient sites.
□ In Dartmoor National Park, off minor road between Widecombe-in-the-Moor and Manaton, four miles (6.4km) W of Bovey Tracey. Map ref 1B5.

64. KENT'S CAVERN
Lair of the cave bear

This vast limestone cave system is one of the oldest known dwelling places in the British Isles. Guided tours reveal a half-mile (0.8km) wonderland of floodlit stalactites and stalagmites and the skull of a former prehistoric resident – the Great Cave Bear. For opening times and admission charges, Tel: Torquay 24059.
□ Ilsham Road, Wellswood, near Torquay (off B3199 behind Anstey's Cove). Map ref 1B6.

65. LUNDY ISLAND
Wildlife haven

Lundy looms out to sea off the North Devon coast, a great granite mass, three miles (5km) long by half-a-mile (1km) wide, with high cliffs, bays and combes. The island was bought in 1969 by the NT in conjunction with the Landmark Trust. Some of the place-names – Kittiwake Gully, Seals' Rock, Gannet's Bay – give you an idea of the wildlife to be seen. Unfortunately, few of the puffins which gave Lundy its name have remained. (*Lunde* is Norse for puffin.) Boats from Ilfracombe throughout the year. Tel: The Landmark Trust, Barnstaple 73333.
□ 11 miles (18km) NW of Hartland Point. Map ref 1A4.

66. LYDFORD GORGE
Woods and waterfalls

On the western fringe of Dartmoor the leaping River Lyd plunges down a deep and narrow chasm (NT) to the leafy woods below. A mile-long (1.6km) footpath follows the river, with steep steps cut in the rock, past foaming falls to gentle trout pools set among banks of ferns and wild garlic.

Where the Great Cave Bear once roamed: Kent's Cavern, near Torquay, Devon

The gorge is open daily, Apr to Oct.
□ Just off A386, midway between Tavistock and Okehampton. Map ref 1B5.

67. LYNTON AND LYNMOUTH
Coast walk

The waters of the East and West Lyn, tumbling down from Exmoor through deep wooded valleys, merge at Watersmeet (NT), and enter the sea at Lynmouth. This picturesque little harbour resort has now recovered from the 1952 flood disaster which destroyed nearly 100 houses in the town. From Lynmouth an old-fashioned cliff railway, opened in the 1890's, rises sedately to the clifftop town of Lynton, starting-point for a spectacular stretch of the long-distance South-West Coast Peninsula footpath. The route passes through the Valley of the Rocks, with its rugged skyline and wild goats, and continues through hanging woods to Heddon's Mouth. Hunter's Inn at the head of Heddon's mouth Cleave is a convenient lunchtime stop. Total distance, Lynton to Hunter's Inn and back: about 12 miles (19km).
□ Lynton is on A39, midway between Barnstaple and Minehead. Map ref 1B4.

68. MORWELLHAM QUAY
Industrial archeology

In the last century these tiny docks leading off the Tamar were a thriving port, shipping copper ore from the mines up in the hills, notably the famous Devon Great Consols mine. The harbour decayed after the closure of the mines but it has now become the site for not only a fascinating outdoor museum of industrial archaeology but also a nature trail, open all year. Tel: Tavistock 832766.
□ Two miles (3.2km) off A390 between Tavistock and Gunnislake. Map ref 1B6.

69. PLYMOUTH
Sailing and boating

Plymouth Sound provides five square miles (1295 hectares) of sheltered waters. Even if it's blowing a gale outside the Sound, it is usually safe for sailing inside and the Hoe forms a natural grandstand for watching the club racing on summer evenings and at weekends. There are also plenty of slipways for launching boats and sailing boats can sometimes be hired from the Plymouth Sailing School.
□ Map ref 1B6.

70. PLYMTREE
Ancient church

Where else but in Devon could a village be with such a name as this? Built of the local brownish sandstone, this church is impeccably maintained, and harbours, as so often in this county, a

Cricket in the shadow of the Valley of Rocks, a celebrated beauty spot near the twin resorts of Lynton and Lynmouth on the North Devon coast.

spectacular screen, with its original colouring most delicately restored. The set of old benches is complete.
☐ 10 miles (16km) NE of Exeter off B3176 (nearest intersection on M5 motorway is junction 28). Map ref 1C5.

71. RIVER DART
Boat and rail trips

The best way to explore this beautiful wooded river valley is by boat. River trips from the historic port of Dartmouth to Totnes, 11 miles (17.7km) upstream take about 75 minutes and there are daily sailings each way during the holiday season. On the way you pass two pretty villages: Stoke Gabriel, which has a 1000-years-old yew tree in the churchyard, and Dittisham, famous for plums, salmon and thatched cottages.

Or you can take a journey into nostalgia by steam train along the old Buckfastleigh line for seven miles (11.2km) beside the Dart. Return trip from Buckfastleigh to Totnes by Dart Valley Railway takes about one hour. Tel: Buckfastleigh 2338.

Dartmouth itself is full of colour and maritime romance. The 15th century castle (AM) is open standard hours. The most picturesque part of the town is Bayard's Cove with its ruined stronghold and cobbled quay (AM).
☐ Map ref 1B6.

72. ROSEMOOR GARDEN
Woodland garden

Beautiful garden in wonderful woodland setting in the Torridge Valley. Famous for its ornamental shrubs and old-fashioned roses. Also rhododendrons, conifers, flowering trees. Unusual plants for sale. Open daily Apr to Oct. Tel: Torrington 2256.
☐ Great Torrington, one mile (1.6km) SE of Torrington on B3220 to Exeter. Map ref 1B5.

73. SALCOMBE
Scenic estuary

Salcombe is a yachting haven which has the distinction of being England's most southerly resort. It enjoys a very mild climate that is almost Mediterranean, and some of the loveliest views in the British Isles. No great rivers run down to the sea at Salcombe. The estuary, which broadens inland once past the hanging woods and sandy coves at its narrow entrance, is a drowned river valley. Its tidal creeks, splayed like the fingers of a hand, empty at low water, leaving narrow channels and miles of gleaming mudflats. There are fishing trips. cruises and boats for hire, both at Salcombe, and at the head of the estuary at Kingsbridge. A passenger ferry runs from Salcombe pier to East Portlemouth, and another runs in summer to South Sands and Kingsbridge. Best viewpoint is from Sharpitor (NT), a house high above the mouth of the estuary, with six acres (2.4 hectares) of luxuriant sub-tropical woodland gardens and a small museum. (Gardens always open; museum open Apr to Oct). Beyond Sharpitor the finest stretch of the South Devon Coast path

Tree pipit (below) and wood warbler, two of the birds to look for on a walk through Shaptor Woods in the Dartmoor National Park, Devon

leads to the mica-schist crags of Bolt Head, one mile (1.6km) farther on, and along the 400ft (120m) cliffs to Bolt Tail and Hope Cove. Total distance from Sharpitor, six miles (9.6km).

Another good walk is along the South Devon Coast path from East Portlemouth to Prawle Point and Lannacombe. Here there is a raised beach. The 'shelf' was once below high water. The original cliffs, up to 300ft (91m) high, can be seen half a mile (800m) inland, complete with caves.
☐ S of Kingsbridge on A381. Map ref 1B6.

74. SEATON
Pebbles and landslips

The beach here is mostly pebbles. Look out for semi-precious stones like beryls and agates. A narrow-gauge electric tramway runs along the west bank of the River Axe to Colyford and Colyton, daily in summer and limited service in winter. Tel: Seaton 21702. Bird-watching on Axe estuary (waders, wildfowl) is best in autumn and winter. There are good walks over the cliffs to Beer, where the chalk unexpectedly reappears to form Beer Head. Fishing and boat trips from Seaton and Beer. Axmouth, across the bridge on the B3174, was once a flourishing port but a major landslip on the east bank in the 12th century caused the river to silt up. From Axmouth you can follow the South Devon Coast path eastwards to Lyme Regis along Dowlands Cliff, scene of the grand landslip of 1839. This area is now a nature reserve. The walk is hard going, with no way off.
☐ On B3174, six miles (10km) SW of Axminster. Map ref 1C5.

75. SHAPTOR WOODS
Woodland walks and wildlife

Shaptor Woods is in one of Devon's most beautiful valleys, just within the Dartmoor National Park. It is owned and managed by the Woodland Trust who have added new public paths. The walk from Furzeleigh Cross takes you on a circular route through a variety of trees from mature beech to the twisted oak so characteristic of Dartmoor. Energetic walkers should try the climb to Shaptor Rock for panoramic views of the countryside. Birds include tree pipits and wood-warblers. Tel: The Woodland Trust, Grantham 74297.
☐ Near Bovey Tracey, five miles (9km) NW of Newton Abbot. Map ref 1B5.

76. SLAPTON LEY
Nature reserve

Here the road from Dartmouth to Torcross runs along the rim of a long pebble beach, with the sea on one side and a reed-rimmed freshwater lake called Slapton Ley on the other. This 460 acre (186 hectares) private nature reserve is rich in wildlife, particularly sea and marsh birds (reed warbler, water rail), dragonflies and rare plants. Open all year, with one and a half mile (2.4km) walk along the inner shore of the Ley, starting from Slapton village.
☐ On A379 between Dartmouth and Kingsbridge. Map ref 1B6.

77. TIVERTON MUSEUM
Farm museum

The Agricultural Hall in this museum is a mini-museum on its own, with a substantial collection of implements and tools, including rarities such as the 'Norwegian harrow', thought to be the only one of its kind in existence. There is a 17th century cider press, a variety of vermin and man-traps and an exhibition of wagons and carts. Open all year, except Suns, Bank holidays and Christmas week. Tel: Tiverton 2446.
☐ St Andrew's Street, Tiverton. On A396, N of Exeter. Map ref 1B5.

78. TORBAY
Scenic tour

This popular seaside area, stretching from Torquay to Brixham, is the starting point for a 25-mile (40km) drive into Dartmoor which dramatically illustrates how climate and altitude affect the landscape of the British Isles.

To see for yourself the features highlighted in this passage of Chapter Nine leave Torbay on the A385 to Totnes – an architecturally rich old town in itself and one well worth exploration. From Totnes follow the signs for Buckfastleigh where you join the A38 to Ashburton. Shortly before Ashburton, turn left on to the B3357 which climbs onto Dartmoor itself.

By the time you reach Two Bridges and Princetown you have not travelled much more than 25 miles (40km) since leaving the coast, but the countryside is radically different. Intermediate stages to observe these landscape changes are Skinner's Bridge between Totnes and Buckfastleigh and New Bridge (over the River Dart) on the B3357 west of Ashburton. In the Torbay area itself the Torre Abbey gardens feature exotic sub-tropical flowers and shrubs that

flourish in the bay's mild climate.
☐ Map ref 1B6.

79. WESTWARD HO!
Pebble ridge

This holiday resort was named in 1863 after the novel by Charles Kingsley. Its sandy beach, pounded by surf, is backed by a three-mile (4.8km) ridge of large grey pebbles. The ridge is two miles (3.2km) long, 50ft (15m) wide and 20ft (6m) high and it is moving inland at a rate of about a yard (1m) a year. Behind the ridge is the famous Royal North Devon Golf Course and Northam Burrow, some 650 acres (244 hectares) of flat common land. Across this common is Bideford Bar and the River Torridge estuary. The Somerset and North Devon Coast Path runs along the coast from the promenade of Westward Ho! The path climbs to Cornborough Cliff and Abbotsham Cliff with breathtaking views.
☐ By road via Northam or signposted footpath. Map ref 1B4.

80. WIDECOMBE-IN-THE-MOOR
Moorland village

Widecombe Fair, destination of Tom Cobleigh in the famous song, is on the second Tuesday of September. Tourists throng to this granite village deep in the heart of Dartmoor's most rugged moorlands. (Many of the finest tors – Haytor, Hound Tor, Chinkwell, Honeybag and Bowerman's Nose – are within a few miles of Widecombe.) The village church is known as the 'Cathedral of the Moor'.
☐ Off A38 or B3357, five miles (8km) NW of Ashburton. Map ref 1B5.

Dorset

Almost all of Dorset is still intensely rural. Behind its extraordinary coast of shingle banks and fossil-studded cliffs lie broad vales, quiet villages, rolling prehistoric chalklands, and a host of handsome old towns: Shaftesbury, Sherbourne, Blandford, and the county town of Dorchester. West Country Tourist Board: Exeter 76351.

81. ABBOTSBURY
Village and swannery

Mellow stone and thatched cottages line the long main street of this beautiful village near the Chesil Beach. Many of the cottages are listed buildings, recently restored with great sensitivity, together with the village pond, which provides an idyllic foreground to Abbotsbury's thatched monastic tithe barn. The barn is 276ft (84m) long, one of the largest in the country. Together with an old stone gateway, it is all that remains of the great 12th century Benedictine Abbey. It was the monks who built the prominent 15th century chapel on St Catherine's Hill, high above the village, to serve as a landmark for sailors. The hill itself is terraced with Bronze Age lynchets.

To the south of the village (follow the signs) is Abbotsbury Swannery, sanctuary for hundreds of mute swans, whose ancestors have nested here since Plantagenet times. Their home is the brackish western waters of the Fleet, the long lagoon behind the Chesil

Beach. Extensive reed beds provide an ideal habitat for marsh birds – and thatch for Abbotsbury's rooftops. Ringed plovers and little terns frequent the shingle beach. A fine example of a duck decoy can also be seen, together with a lofty pole commemorating the great storm of 1824 which drowned the swannery under 20ft (7m) of water. The Swannery is open daily, May to Sept (small admission charge).

☐ About seven miles (11km) NW of Weymouth on B3157. Map ref 1D5.

82. ACKLING DYKE
Roman road

This was the name given to the Roman road from Dorchester to Salisbury. It can be traced quite clearly in several places but never more easily than south-east of Handley (grid ref SU 015164) where it survives as a huge *agger* or bank some 40-50ft (12-15m) wide and 5-6ft (1.5-2m) high.

☐ 12 miles (19km) SW of Salisbury off A354. Map ref 1D5.

83. ARNE RESERVE
Bird-watching

Arne reserve covers 1000 acres (404 hectares) of land on the west shores of Poole Harbour. It is one of the last remnants of heathland once extensive in southern Britain. The three main types of heather: ling, cross-leaved heath and bell heather grow on the reserve and the less well-known Dorset heath is also found here. The rare Dartford warbler breeds on the heath as do many other bird species such as meadow pipits, stonechats and nightjars. A public footpath from Arne village leads to Shipstal Point where there is a nature trail (open May to

Sept). Access to the rest of the reserve is by permit, obtainable from the RSPB Warden, Syldata, Arne, Wareham.
☐ Near Wareham. Map ref 1D5.

84. ASHMORE
Hilltop village

A classic example of a nucleated village with all roads leading to a perfectly circular pond. Its hill-top location at 700ft (213m) above sea level in an area of early settlement – Cranborne Chase – prompted the celebrated interpreter of English landscape, W.G. Hoskins, to suggest that the village site has been inhabited continuously since prehistoric times. But the first certain evidence of its existence came in the Domesday Book of 1086 which recorded the village as *Aisemara* meaning 'ash-mere' – the pond where ash trees grow.

☐ Approximately eight miles (13km) SE of Shaftesbury off B3081 road. Map ref 1D5.

85. BROWNSEA ISLAND
Nature reserve

Brownsea, the largest island in Poole Harbour, is a haven of wild heathland, woodland and quiet beaches. A walk of about 1½ miles (2km) guides you through the southern part (excluding the Dorset Naturalists Trust Nature Reserve). Places of special interest are signalled by 26 posts along the way. At the start of the walk is a vantage point over the DNT Reserve lagoon with its wading birds, wildfowl and terns. There are red squirrels in the woods as well as pheasants and peacocks. Boats from Poole Quay or Sandbanks. Tel: Poole Tourist Information, Poole 5151.

Cerne Abbas, Dorset. On the downs nearby is the prehistoric 'Cerne Giant'

☐ In Poole Harbour, 1½ miles (2km) SE of Poole near Sandbanks. Map ref 1D5.

86. CERNE ABBAS
Prehistoric site

Nobody knows for certain how old he is and nobody knows why he is there at all, but the Cerne Abbas 'giant' is certainly a remarkable figure. For his size if nothing else: 180ft (55m) high and formed by a one foot (0.3m) trench cut into the chalk of the Dorset hills. But even more remarkable (and more puzzling) features should be apparent to even short-sighted non-archaeologists. Why is he wielding an enormous 120ft (37m) long club? And why are his sexual organs so explicit?

Most experts date the giant as 1800 years old and representing the god Hercules and many believe it became a fertility symbol; May Day celebrations, also associated with fertility rites, were certainly held on the hill until quite recently. But there are many other theories and legends surrounding the giant who is now in the care of the NT. In 1979 this care included the rejection of an idea canvassed locally that the giant should don a modesty loin-cloth. As with the Uffington White Horse and other chalk-cut figures, it is traditionally re-scoured every seven years. The giant in his full-sized glory is best seen from a distance: from the A352 road just north of Cerne Abbas, for instance. But footpaths lead to the giant himself from the village via the churchyard and the ruined abbey.

☐ Cerne Abbas is 5½ miles (9km) N of Dorchester on A352. Map ref 1D5.

87. CHESIL BEACH
Pebble beach

This unique beach stretches for about 16 miles (25.7km) from Burton Bradstock to Portland. No one knows why the huge sea wall of pebbles are so well graded: small pebbles to the west and larger ones to the east towards Portland. The pebble bank, mostly flint and chert, encloses a lagoon called The Fleet, which ends at Abbotsbury. The beach is excellent for beachcombing but swimming is dangerous.

☐ Best viewed from Abbotsbury Hill on B3157 from Bridport. Map ref 1D5.

88. CHARMOUTH
Historic inn

The Queen's Armes is housed in an unusually complete example of a medieval house with much original timbering. It was here that Charles II made plans to escape to France after the Battle of Worcester. After the Restoration the inn had a chapel where noncomformists could worship in safety. Most of the other houses in this small resort on the Dorset coast date from the Regency period but of greater interest to geologists are the nearby cliffs which contains numerous and important fossils.

☐ A little over one mile (1.6km) E of Lyme Regis on A35. Map ref 1C5.

89. CRANBORNE MANOR GARDENS
Romantic garden

Early Tudor house with framework

of early 17th century garden almost completely replanted in the 19th century and largely remodelled since 1950. Trees, shrubs, herb garden, herbaceous plants and a collection of old-fashioned roses. Open occasionally from spring to autumn. Tel: Cranborne 248.

☐ Near Cranborne village, on B3078, 18 miles (30km) N of Bournemouth. Map ref 1D5.

90. FORDE ABBEY
Historic house

A Cistercian abbey converted into a private house in the mid 17th century by Edmund Prideaux, Cromwell's attorney-general. The result is a rambling and fascinating mixture of monastic remains and 17th-century alterations, strung out along one side of an immense lawn. The highlights are the tower and great hall built by Abbot Chard shortly before the monastery was dissolved in 1539, and Prideaux's saloon, approached by a carved staircase of the same date and rich with panelling, plaster-work and tapestries. The house and garden are generally open on Suns, Weds and Bank Holiday afternoons from May to Sept.

☐ Four miles (6.4km) SE of Chard off B3167 or B3172. Map ref 1C5.

91. GOLDEN CAP
Fossil cliffs

This sandstone capped bluff (NT) is the highest cliff on the south coast at 625ft (190m), and is rich in fossils. There are also many fossils in the rock exposed by the massive landslip which took place in 1908 at Black Ven, west of Charmouth. Black Ven is a nature reserve, closed to the public. To see some of the spectacular prehistoric specimens found in this area visit Dorset County Museum, High West Street. Open weekdays and Sats. Tel: Dorchester 2735. Or The Philpot Museum, Bridge Street, Lyme Regis, which is a local history museum with local fossil finds. Open Easter-Sept, daily. Also Barney's Fossil Shop and Museum in Charmouth High Street.

☐ Near Lyme Regis. Approach along Dorset Coast Path from Charmouth, 3 miles (4.8km) or from Seatown, 1 mile (1.6km) or from behind at Morcombelake, on A35. Map ref 1C5.

92. HARDY'S DORSET
Literary landscape

Thomas Hardy was born in Dorset in 1840, lived there most of his life, and

Polished cross-section through an ammonite, fossil relic from Dorset's prehistoric past. The Dorset coast attracts fossil-hunters from all over the world. The County Museum in Dorchester has an excellent fossil collection

Birthplace of Thomas Hardy at Higher Bockhampton, near Dorchester, Dorset

The church at Bere Regis (the 'Kingsbere' of Hardy's novels), Dorset

The Hardy Country: Ten Hatches Weir on the River Frome near Dorchester

Thomas Hardy's 'Wellbridge Manor': Woolbridge Manor Hotel, Wool, Dorset

died at Max Gate, his home on the outskirts of Dorchester, in 1928. During his lifetime he established himself as one of the greatest writers of all time with his powerful 'Wessex' novels. To this day his home county is still talked of as 'Hardy's Wessex'.

Hardy took the name of Wessex from the ancient kingdom of the West Saxons and used it, like other place-names in his stories, as a thin disguise to blur the true identities of his Dorset locations. Part of the enjoyment of a

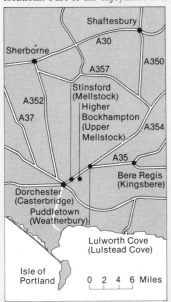

The heartland of Hardy's Dorset

literary pilgrimage to Hardy's Wessex lies in deciphering the fictional names and unearthing the real towns and villages. But the greatest pleasure is that today, though half a century has passed since Hardy died, much of Dorset has changed so little that keen readers will have little difficulty in recognising the rural scenes he immortalised in his novels.

The area covered by most of Hardy's works is about 50 miles by 35 miles (80km by 56km), with Dorchester, the county town and 'capital' of the Hardy Country, at its centre. From here you could spend several days exploring Hardy's world. The day out we have selected is based on a Hardy Trail devised jointly by the West Country Tourist Board and the Southern Tourist Board, whose special Hardy Trail leaflet is available at the Tourist Information Centre, Antelope Hotel, South St, Dorchester. Tel: Dorchester 67992. The names shown in brackets are those used by Hardy in his novels.

Dorchester (Casterbridge). The town is rich in its associations with Hardy and his novels. The County Museum in the High Street contains the finest Hardy source collection in the world, and a memorial room with a reconstruction of the author's Max Gate study. Hardy's statue stands at Top O' Town. The King's Arms Hotel and White Hart Hotel both feature in *Far From the Madding Crowd*. The Antelope Hotel, St Peter's Church, Maumbury Rings (a Roman amphitheatre) and Grey's Bridge over the

Frome all feature in *The Mayor of Casterbridge* – as also does nearby Maiden Castle.

Stinsford (Mellstock). Featured in *Under the Greenwood Tree*. Hardy's heart is buried in Stinsford churchyard, in the grave of his first wife.

☐ Two miles (3km) E of Dorchester. **Higher Bockhampton (Upper Mellstock).** Here stands Hardy's Cottage, the pretty thatched cottage in which Hardy was born and where he wrote *Under the Greenwood Tree* and *Far From the Madding Crowd*. Acquired by the NT in 1947. Exterior open March-Oct, 11.00-6.00; interior by arrangement with tenant (Tel: Dorchester 2366).

☐ Three miles (5km) S of Dorchester, ½-mile (1km) S of A35.

Puddletown (Weatherbury). Where Fanny Robin was buried in the churchyard and Troy spent a night in the porch in *Far From the Madding Crowd*. About one mile (1½km) northwest of Puddletown is Waterston Manor (Weatherbury Farm). Puddletown Heath (Egdon Heath) is part of the great heath, now much fragmented, which once stretched from Bockhampton to Poole Harbour. Hardy's cousin, Tryphena Sparks, was a student-teacher at Puddletown village school

☐ On A35 midway between Dorchester and Bere Regis.

Bere Regis (Kingsbere). Where Tess and her family set up their four-poster bed outside the church in *Tess of the d'Urbervilles*. Splendid church contains

tombs of the real Turbervilles.

☐ At junction of A35 and A31, between Dorchester and Bournemouth. **Wool** Woolbridge Manor Hotel (Wellbridge Manor) was the honeymoon home of Tess and Angel Clare in *Tess of the d'Urbervilles*.

☐ Five miles (8km) S of Bere Regis. **Lulworth Cove (Lulstead Cove).** Troy swam out from here in *Far From the Madding Crowd*. Today the beauty of the cove attracts madding crowds in summer.

☐ 4½ miles (7km) S of Wool on B3071. **West Stafford.** Tess and Angel Clare were apparently married in West Stafford Church in *Tess of the d'Urbervilles*. Nearby, in the lovely water-meadows of the Frome (Valley of the Great Dairies), is Stuart's Weir (Shadwater Weir), where Eustacia and Damon were drowned in *The Return of the Native*. West Stafford also has a pleasant village pub, the Wise Man, which provides excellent bar snacks.

☐ 2½ miles (4km) E of Dorchester. ■ Total distance of round trip from Dorchester: about 35 miles (56km). Map ref 1D5.

93. ISLE OF PORTLAND
Rocky peninsula

This bleak limestone peninsula, scarred by quarrying for Portland stone, is of great geological interest. Portland Bill has a large area of raised beach, rich in shells. The old lighthouse on Portland Bill is now a bird-watching station. Near the lighthouse is a large sea cave, inaccessible from land, called

Stair Hole, near Lulworth Cove, Dorset, where contorted strata and coastal erosion have created some of England's most spectacular cliff scenery. The cliffs on either side of Lulworth Cove can be seen from the Dorset Coast Path

Cave Hole. The tidal race off the Bill is one of the fiercest in Europe, caused by the tides meeting between here and the Shambles sandbank to the south-east. Portland Bill lighthouse is open to the public, most afternoons. Tel: Portland 820495.

□ Take A354 from Weymouth. Map ref 1D6.

94. KIMMERIDGE BAY
Fossils and marine life

A sheltered bay at the foot of green hills, backed by low cliffs of crumbling shale. The cliffs are full of fossils but there is constant danger from the falling rocks. The beach, also is an unattractive stretch of grey sand and shale. So why come here? Many reasons, one of the main ones being the clear, shallow water and its wealth of marine life – now protected as the Purbeck Marine Wildlife Reserve – which you can explore with mask and flippers. (Further details from Dorset Naturalists' Trust: Tel: Parkstone 24241.) The Romans had a thriving trade here, making jewellery from the wafery slabs of shale. Today the new industry is oil, with a 'nodding donkey' pumping on the clifftop to the west of the bay. On the opposite arm of the bay is a ruined 18th century watchtower built by the Clavell family, and a fine stretch of the Dorset Coast Path leading to Chapman's Pool. Coast walks to the west are restricted when the Army firing range is in use, but path is open for all but about six weekends a year as well as from late July to mid-Sept. Tel: Range Officer, Bindon Abbey 462621 ext 859 between 8am and 5pm.

□ Kimmeridge village is on a minor road off the Corfe Castle-Worbarrow

road. Toll road to bay; small charge for parking. Map ref 1D5.

95. LULWORTH COVE
Coast walk

A five mile (8km) walk along the finest stretch of the Dorset Coast Path from Ringstead Bay to Lulworth Cove takes you past Burning Cliff (NT), where in 1826 the oil shales of the Kimmeridge beds smouldered for several years, up White Nothe and past the Purbeck limestone arch of Durdle Door. Beside Lulworth Cove is Stair Hole where the sea has broken through the limestone to create another arch. Lulworth's natural harbour was formed when the sea breached the outer rock wall and eroded the softer clays and chalk of the cliffs behind. Parking on B3017.

□ Map ref 1D5.

96. MAIDEN CASTLE
Prehistoric hill fort

The most dramatic hill fort in England. The ramparts may seem deceptively simple when viewed from the main road but they are astonishingly steep and massive when approached on the ground. The triple ramparts and ditches are at their most complex at the two gates and protected a town rather than a mere fort. It was stormed by the Romans, probably in AD 45, and although later superseded by nearby Dorchester it was used in the 4th century as the site of a Romano-Celtic temple, the foundations of which can still be seen. Finds from extensive excavations on the site can be seen at Dorset County Museum in Dorchester. Open weekdays and Sats. Tel: Dorchester 2735.

The 45 acres (18 hectares) of the castle is open to the public at all times and its protected status means that it is rich in the natural wildlife of chalk downland. A footpath follows the highest rampart and a complete 1½ mile (2.5km) circuit of the fort can be completed in an easy 45 minutes. Many will prefer to linger, however. It is a spectacular spot for picnicking.

□ One mile (1.6km) S of Dorchester, signposted off A354 road to Weymouth. Map ref 1D5.

97. MILTON ABBAS
Planned village

An 18th century planned village of considerable charm. It was created when Joseph Damer, the first Earl of Dorchester, obliterated the original village in order to enlarge the park of his new mansion. The 'new' village was built a short distance away with identical four-square cob and thatch cottages facing onto a green. The country house itself, known as Milton Abbey and incorporating the hall of the original 15th century abbey, is now a school and stands next to a fragment of the abbey church, also 15th century.

□ Nine miles (14.5km) SW of Blandford Forum, off A354 road to Dorchester. Map ref 1D5.

98. PARNHAM HOUSE
Historic house and garden

Mellow mansion of Ham Hill stone dating from 16th century with ad-

ditions by John Nash. Now the home of distinguished craftsman John Makepeace, whose Furniture Workshops are also open to view. Extensive gardens in leafy valley beside the River Brit, with formal terraces, cascade, Italian Garden, pleasant riverside walks and picnic area. Open Suns, Weds and Bank holidays, Apr to Oct. Tel. Beaminster 862204.

□ On A3066, three quarters of a mile (1 km) S of Beaminster, five miles (8km) N of Bridport. Map ref 1C5.

99. POOLE HARBOUR
Natural harbour

The 95-mile (153km) coast of Poole Harbour, part of the drowned valley of the ancient Frome-Solent River, is one of the longest natural harbour shorelines in the world. Poole itself became prominent during the 15th century when the channel serving nearby Wareham silted up and is now a busy port. A vehicle and passenger ferry runs from Sandbanks to Shell Bay on the Isle of Purbeck. Also a passenger ferry to Brownsea Island within the Harbour.

Among Poole's many old buildings are the 16th century Scaplen's Court, High Street, which houses the local history museum. The Maritime Museum is in the old town cellars, Paradise Street. The Guildhall Museum is in Market Street. From the Guildhall there are guided tours round the historic precinct. Book in advance. For all these Tel: Poole 5151.

For good views of the Harbour and the Purbeck Hills visit Compton Acres gardens at Canford Cliffs on the B3065. Open daily, Apr to Oct. Tel: Canford Cliffs 708036.

□ Map ref 1D5.

100. SHAFTESBURY
Market town

Its old name was Shaston and as this it still lives in the novels of Thomas Hardy. The town stands on the edge of a 700ft (216m) plateau with outstanding views over the Blackmore Vale towards Somerset. The hill is dramatic within the town, too, with Gold Hill a picturesque echo of life in pre-motor car Britain; it is cobbled and lined by tiny cottages, some thatched and some tiled but virtually all stepped up or down on one another to adjust to the steep gradient.

□ 17 miles (27km) SW of Salisbury on A30. Map ref 1D5.

101. SWANAGE BAY
Sea coast

Swanage lies at the end of a valley of Wealden clay which the sea has carved away to form the bay. It is protected from further erosion by the hard limestone of Peveril Point, to the south. Swanage, formerly an Anglo-Saxon port, was used to ship marble quarried from the Purbeck hills. You can see working quarries south of the town, near Durlston Bay, where the whole Purbeck rock series is exposed. Many early prehistoric specimens were found here, including dinosaur tracks, now in the Natural History Museum, London. Following the Dorset Coast Path south you come to Dancing Ledge, a platform of rock with its own natural swimming pool. To the north

Quiet corner of Compton Acres Gardens at Canford Cliffs, near Poole, Dorset

are the chalk stacks of Old Harry Rocks. Studland Heath nature reserve has a mile-long (1.6km) woodland trail and another through the sand dunes, both starting from the car park, off Ferry road, in Studland village.
☐ Swanage, Isle of Purbeck, via A351 from Corfe Castle. Map ref 1D5.

102. WEYMOUTH
Coast path walk

This lively resort and cross-Channel port can also be the base for an unusual walk along one of the Countryside Commission's waymarked long-distance footpaths. The Dorset Coast Path forms a 72-mile (116km) stretch of the mammoth South-west Peninsula Coast Path. But whereas most long-distance paths are strictly linear, running from A to B, the Dorset path also includes an alternative inland section that offers the possibility of a circular walk based on Weymouth. Depending upon whether you wish to walk in a clockwise or anti-clockwise direction, you begin near the ruins of Sandsfoot Castle or the suburb of Overcombe (where the A353 turns away from the coast) respectively.

Assuming you are walking in a clockwise direction the path – waymarked by the official acorn symbol – takes you parallel with the extraordinary Chesil Beach to Abbotsbury and then West Bexington before turning inland. Then via Limekiln Hill, White Hill, the Hardy Monument, Upwey, Bincombe, Green Hill, East and West Hills, White Horse Hill, Osmington and Osmington Mills before rejoining the coastal path at Osmington Mills and turning back towards Weymouth.

The length of this walk is over 30 miles (48km) and so its entirety would be beyond a day's walk for most ramblers. But it can easily be broken up into smaller sections. A feature of the inland section is that it mostly follows the line of the prehistoric Dorset ridgeway and is accordingly rich in prehistoric remains such as tumuli and earthworks; it passes close to Maiden Castle, for instance. But for many people perhaps the greatest attraction of all is the peace and charm of the Dorset countryside.
☐ Map ref 1D5.

The official long-distance footpaths of England and Wales. The walk based on Weymouth (described above) is part of the longest path of all – the 515 mile (825km) South West Peninsula Coast Path

Dunster, Somerset, is renowned for its castle and 17th century Yarn Market

103. WORLDWIDE BUTTERFLIES, COMPTON HOUSE
Butterflies and moths

Stately home for butterfly enthusiasts. British and foreign species are bred in captivity, displayed and sold, dead or alive. In the grounds, dark muslin tents like a Bedouin encampment contain a host of caterpillars munching away at their favourite food plants. In the biggest tent, visitors may walk round, surrounded by adult insects on the wing, which may include, according to season, species rarely seen in the British Isles. Car park. Open daily, Apr to Oct. Tel: Yeovil 4608.
☐ Near Sherborne (on A30 Sherborne-Yeovil road). Map ref 1D5.

Somerset

The green hills of Somerset – Mendips, Quantocks, Poldens, Brendons and the lion's share of Exmoor – fill much of this cream and cider county of rich pastures. The low-lying 'Levels' add another dimension, as do their encircling towns: Taunton, Wells and Glastonbury. West Country Tourist Board: Exeter 76351.

104. BARRINGTON COURT
Historic house and garden

Mellow stone 16th century house (NT). Gardens by Gertrude Jekyll in 1920's. Aquatic plants in moat; formal iris garden; herbaceous borders. Open Weds only, all year. Tel: Ilminster 2242.
☐ Three miles (4.8km) NE of Ilminster off B3168. Map ref 1C5.

105. BREAN DOWN
Scenic viewpoint

This narrow limestone headland, jutting out into the Bristol Channel in a quiet and isolated corner of the Somerset coast, is a noted viewpoint (300ft; 91m) in a lowland landscape. A passenger ferry runs across the Axe estuary from Weston-super-Mare to Burnham-on-Sea. The Woodspring Museum, Burlington Street, Weston-super-Mare is housed in old workshops of the Edwardian Gaslight Company. There is a Victorian seaside holiday display plus local natural history and much more. Open all year, weekdays. Tel: Weston-super-Mare 21028.
☐ Minor road off B3140 to Brean, footpath to Head. Map ref 1C4.

106. CADBURY CASTLE
Archaeological site

This impressive prehistoric hillfort dominates the low-lying countryside for miles around. Iron Age ramparts ring the hilltop, strongest contender for the site of King Arthur's legendary Camelot. Excavations have proved that the fortifications were strengthened and a 'feasting hall' built at about the time of the historical Arthur, around 500 AD. But whether or not this was Camelot – if indeed Camelot ever existed – may never be known.
☐ At South Cadbury, off A303, seven miles (11km) NE of Yeovil. Map ref 1D5.

107. CHARTERHOUSE
Archaeological site

The area around this village on the open plateau top of the Mendips has been associated with lead mining since Roman times. The Romans had a small town here and a road led to Old Sarum but a small oval ampitheatre is all that survives of this Roman community. It was much later lead working that has given the landscape its present character with rumpled ground, spoil heaps and the remains of circular buddles or washing pits.
☐ Three miles (5km) N of Cheddar on minor roads off B3371 and B3134. Map ref 1C4.

108. CHEDDAR GORGE
Caves

The famous limestone cliffs of Cheddar Gorge tower 450ft (136m) above the winding road. Gough's Cave, open all year, plunges a quarter of a mile into the hills. Its stalactite chambers were once the home and burial place of Stone Age man. Cox's Cave and waterfalls is closed to the public in winter. Tel: Cheddar 742343 for details. Black Rock Nature Reserve has a one and a half mile (2.4km) circular walk from the B3135 at Black Rock Gate. Managed by the Somerset Trust for Nature Conservation, it winds through woodland, limestone scree and rough downland grazing.
☐ On S edge of Mendip Hills. Take B3135 out of Cheddar. Map ref 1C4.

109. CULBONE
Interesting church

Hidden in the woods not far from Porlock, the church at Culbone is said to be the smallest in England in regular use – just 33ft (10m) by 12ft 8in (3.8m). To reach it, the only way is to follow the North Somerset coast path from Porlock Weir – a pleasant and easy two-mile (3.2km) walk.
☐ Map ref 1B4.

110. DUNSTER
Historic village

This village is best known for its castle but contains much else of interest. The octagonal 17th century Yarn market in the wide main street is one of the most attractive market buildings in the country. The *Luttrell Arms* takes its name from the family which has owned the castle since the 14th century and was once the guest house of a Cistercian monastery at Cleeve. The core of the inn is a 15th century Gothic hall with a hammerbeam roof.

In Dunster there are also an old watermill, a packhorse bridge, a mainly perpendicular-style priory church, a 12th century dovecote and a Butter Cross, in addition to the castle, which although dating from the 13th century was extensively rebuilt in the last century. The castle is open during the summer but opening times vary according to season. Tel: Dunster 314.
☐ Two miles (3km) SE of Minehead near junction of A396 and A39; Os map 181. Map ref 1C4.

111. EBBOR GORGE
National Nature Reserve

Two waymarked walks lead through these beautiful Mendip valley woods. The short, half mile (1km) round trip route goes through lofty ash woods full of ferns, mosses, fungi and badger setts. Stout shoes are essential for the longer route which involves a strenuous climb up through the gorge itself, where scree slopes, crags and caverns of Carboniferous limestone are among geological features to be seen. Keep to paths and please do not enter caves. Display Centre at car park. Tel: Nature Conservancy Council, South East Region, Taunton 83211.
☐ Near Wookey Hole, three miles (4km) NW of Wells. Map ref 1C4.

112. LEIGH-UPON-MENDIP
Old church

The late-Gothic towers of some Somerset churches are among the great sights of England: at least a dozen are practically faultless. Leigh-upon-Mendip (pronounced 'lie') is specially moving, for it stands high, and you can feel how all the local effort went into the raising of this superb grey limestone tower. The attached church is tiny, but has old benches, tie-beam roofs and, happily, no Victorian glass.
☐ Located in a tangle of roads between Frome and Shepton Mallet, off A361 or 1367. Map ref 1D4.

113. MARTOCK
Country town with fine old church

In atmosphere more village than town. Almost every building, from the 15th century church to the humblest cottage, is built of the local honey-gold Ham Hill stone. The church contains one of the ecclesiastical glories of Somerset: a timber roof with 750 carved panels, supported by flying

angels also carved in wood.
☐ On B3165, signposted on A303 midway between Ilchester and Ilminster. Map ref 1C5.

114. MEARE LAKE VILLAGE
Archaeological site

The broken ground of these fields beside the River Brue may not appear particularly impressive at first sight, but it reveals the site of a village that flourished amid the protecting marshes in late Iron Age and Roman times. Excavation has revealed the foundations of scores of huts and the overgrowing peat has preserved dug-out canoes, baskets, wooden bowls and other relics now displayed in the Castle Museum, Taunton.
☐ Three miles (5km) NW of Glastonbury, beside the River Brue; (grid ref ST445422). OS map 182. Map ref 1C4.

115. MINEHEAD
Cottage architecture

This is almost two towns in one. One is the popular holiday resort with a vast holiday camp; the other is the old village or Higher Town which has probably the best examples of mud-built cottages anywhere in England. There is also a 17th century fishermen's chapel next to the harbour. Minehead is an excellent centre for Exmoor National Park. Steam railway enthusiasts (and others) will enjoy the reopened line between Minehead and Williton; Tel: Minehead 4996.
☐ Between Lynton and Bridgewater on A39. Map ref 1C4.

116. MONTACUTE HOUSE
Historic house and garden

One of the finest Elizabethan houses in England, built of golden stone from nearby Ham Hill (fine views). The house and its splendid formal garden, with topiary and gazebo, belong to the

NT. Open daily, afternoons Apr to Oct (except Tues). Also infrequently Oct to Nov. Tel: Martock 823289.
☐ At Montacute, on A3088 four miles (6.4km) W of Yeovil. Map ref 1C5.

117. NEROCHE FOREST
Forest walks

The Castle Neroche picnic place is 900ft (274m) up on the site of former earthworks and near the ruin of an 11th century castle. It has fine views of Taunton Vale, Bristol Channel and the Mendips. Forest walks cross many streams and pass through mixed woodland with over ten different tree species. Access via by-road off A303 W of Broadway. Prior's Park picnic place is six miles (9.6km) south of Taunton on B3170. It is in former parkland about 800ft (244m) above sea level set among oak, larch and beech.
☐ Near Taunton. Map ref 1C4.

118. NETHER STOWEY
Quantock village

An ideal centre for exploring the Quantock Hills. Numerous paths and trails, including the three-mile (4.8km) Quantock Forest Trail, starting two miles (3.2km) south-west of Nether Stowey. Wordsworth's former home is now a hotel but Coleridge's Cottage, owned by the NT, is open Apr to Sept (except Fri and Sat). Tel: Bridgwater 732662.
☐ Seven miles (11.3km) W of Bridgwater on A39. Map ref 1C4.

119. QUANTOCK INTERPRETATION CENTRE
Wildlife

The interpretation centre is housed in the restored stables of the 17th century manor house of this ancient hamlet on the eastern slopes of the Quantock Hills. There is a nature trail through the grounds with their woods and lake

which were landscaped in the 18th century but are now being returned to the kind of vegetation more characteristic of the Quantocks. Trail leaflets and a series of booklets describing the fauna and flora of the Quantocks are available at the Interpretation Centre. Tel: Somerset Naturalists' Trust, Taunton 45412.
☐ Fyne Court, Broomfield, four miles (7km) W of North Petherton. Map ref 1C4.

120. SEDGEMOOR
Reclaimed fen battlefield

The reed-choked wilderness which once hid the fugitive King Alfred from the Danes has been reclaimed and converted into lush pasturelands crossed by slow rivers and drainage ditches, known locally as 'rhines'. But much of this part of Lowland Somerset is still below sea level, and winter flooding drowns the fields, attracting large flocks of ducks and wild swans. The whole area is rich in marsh and meadow flora. Withies, or willow wands, are grown and woven by local craftsmen to make beautiful baskets. The Battle of Sedgemoor, the last major battle on English soil, was fought near Westonzoyland in 1685, crushing the Duke of Monmouth's rebellion against James II. After the battle, 500 rebel prisoners were locked up in Westonzoyland church tower. Among the most interesting of the surrounding towns and villages is Somerton, once the capital of the West Saxons, now a well-preserved market town.
☐ Map ref 1C4.

121. SELWORTHY BEACON
Scenic viewpoint

A magnificent viewpoint for Exmoor, the North Devon coast and Bristol Channel. This 1013ft (304m) moorland summit can be reached by coastal

footpath from Minehead via North Hill, three miles (4.8km), or more steeply from the village of Selworthy, (NT), one of the prettiest villages in England.
☐ On minor road off the A39, four miles (6.4km) W of Minehead. Map ref 1B4.

122. SIMONSBATH
Farming landscape

The Exmoor estate of the Knight family centred on Simonsbath is still very much a part of the contemporary landscape, yet it is well over 150 years since John Knight purchased 15,000 acres (6070 hectares) of desolate upland moor and within a generation transformed it into good agricultural land. A boundary wall 29 miles (46km) long fenced in the 15 Knight farms, and the wall, farms, shelter belts of conifers and high earth banks enclosing the rectangular-shaped fields are still there to emphasise Knight's success in taming the former upland wilderness.
☐ Around Simonsbath, at junction of B3223 and B3358. Map ref 1B4.

123. SOMERSET RURAL LIFE MUSEUM
Country life

Apart from craft tools relating specifically to Somerset trades such as cider-making, peat digging and the withy industry, this museum has given over two rooms to showing the life of one typical Victorian farmworker, who began work aged 12 and earned three shillings a week for a six-day week. Open Easter-end Sept, Mons-Fris; Sats; Sun afternoons. Shorter winter openings. Tel: Glastonbury 32903.
☐ Abbey Farm, Chilkwell Street, Glastonbury. On A361. Map ref 1C4.

124. STOGURSEY
Ancient village

Stogursey was one of many medieval new towns that failed. It was created after the Norman Conquest and given a castle and a fine priory. Of these, apart from the 12th century church, only a moat and a dovecote remain. However, Priory farm not only occupies the site of the old priory and bears its name but was largely built from the former monastic stone. The town had made little headway over the centuries when in the 19th century its fate as an urban centre was sealed by being by-passed by the railway. Today it remains a village with a wide main street that was once a market-place.
☐ Ten miles (16km) W of Bridgwater between the Quantocks and the sea, off the A39. Map ref 1C4.

125. WOOKEY HOLE
Limestone caverns

Subterranean birthplace of the River Axe, home of the legendary 'Witch of Wookey' and former refuge of Paleolithic Man, who sheltered in these caves during the closing phases of the Ice Age, when mammoth, woolly rhinoceros, wolf and bear roamed the Mendip Hills. Open daily. Tel: Wells 72243.
☐ Two miles (3.2km) NW of Wells on minor road between A371 and B3139. Map ref 1C4.

Somerset wagon: one of the exhibits to be seen at the Somerset Rural Life Museum at Abbey Farm, Glastonbury, Somerset

Enigma carved in chalk: the mysterious 'Long Man of Wilmington' on Windover Hill, near Eastbourne, East Sussex

Southern England

126. CHICHESTER HARBOUR
Area of Outstanding Natural Beauty

A peaceful expanse of creeks, saltings and tidal water centred on the picturesque and historic village of Bosham. The harbour includes about 50 miles (80km) of shoreline while the total area of the AONB covers 47 sq miles (75 sq km). Although Bosham is the largest village on the water's edge, there are several other attractive hamlets such as Emsworth, Dell Quay, Itchenor and Birdham. And nearby, of course, there is Chichester itself with its outstanding cathedral and market cross. This AONB can be the base for at least four distinct types of 'days out':

Sailing. The Harbour offers a well-sheltered stretch of water for a day's sail with a boatyard in almost every village and plenty of launching sites. Plenty of waterside pubs, too, for both sailors and those who want to watch the hundreds of craft going to and from their moorings.

Bird-watching. During the winter months many small wading birds come to these waters. They include sanderling, dunlin, large pied oystercatchers, ringed plovers and several different kinds of gull. On the mudflats huge flocks – maybe as much as a tenth of the world's population – of brent geese feed on the seaweed between November and March; on the saltings you should see curlew, redshank and shelduck. East Head, at the southern end of the harbour, is a particularly good place for bird-watching and can be reached by a nature trail from West Wittering (see under Selsey, West Sussex).

Walks. There are miles of footpaths around the harbour. These are detailed not only on OS map 197 but also in a Harbour Guide published by the Chichester Harbour Conservancy (Tel: Birdham 512301). Itchenor is a good starting point, particularly in summer months when a ferry operates to Bosham (weekends Apr to mid-July, then daily until Sept).

Angling. In addition to the tidal waters of the Harbour itself, the Chichester Canal is also popular with anglers. The canal joins the harbour at Birdham but is no longer used for commercial traffic.

☐ Chichester Harbour is SW of Chichester off A27 or A286. Map ref 2B5.

127. EAST HAMPSHIRE
Area of Outstanding Natural Beauty

Seemly spread of well-farmed countryside, spacious downs and beech-wooded hillsides extending eastwards from Winchester to join the Sussex Downs AONB. A village tour of the area could include Selborne, birthplace and home of the 18th century naturalist Gilbert White; Hambledon, the cradle of the game of cricket; and East Meon in the delightful Meon Valley. An alternative day out could be spent around Butser Hill, near Petersfield. The total area of the AONB is 243 sq miles (391 sq km).
☐ Map ref 2A5.

128. ISLE OF WIGHT
Area of Outstanding Natural Beauty

Covers almost all the coast and hinterland in the south and west of the island, from Shanklin to the Needles and along the Solent shore to Gurnard Bay near Cowes. It also includes a small pocket of coast between East Cowes and Ryde, and a large expanse of countryside reaching from Newport, the island 'capital', to the chalk downs which end at Culver Cliff. Fine views from Tennyson Down of passing ships and the distant Dorset coast. Good bathing at Totland Bay nearby. Total area: 147 sq miles. (235 sq km.)
☐ Map ref 2A5.

129. KENT DOWNS
Area of Outstanding Natural Beauty

This follows the North Downs from Westerham on the Surrey border to the Channel coast at Folkestone. It shares, with the Surrey Hills AONB, the North Downs Way long-distance footpath and has many pretty villages such as Charing and Chilham. The area includes two country parks, Trosley near Wrotham and Camer Park near Meopham, and is exceptionally rich in historic houses. Among them: Chartwell, Sir Winston Churchill's old home near Westerham; stately Knole and its 1000-acre deerpark near Sevenoaks; and Saltwood Castle, near Hythe. Its total area is 528 sq miles (845 sq km).
☐ Map ref 2C4.

130. NORTH WESSEX DOWNS
Area of Outstanding Natural Beauty

Largest of all the AONBs with a total area of 1086 sq miles (1738 sq km) spreading beyond Berkshire into Wiltshire, Oxfordshire and Hampshire. Southern chalk down scenery at its best: a rolling sea of smooth grassy hills scattered with tumuli and prehistoric hillforts. It contains probably the finest stretch of the Ridgeway long-distance footpath, from Streatley to Avebury and its famous prehistoric stone circle. Other sights and places of interest include the Uffington White Horse, Silbury Hill, Barbury Castle (Iron Age hillfort) and the West Kennet Long Barrow. Here, too, are the breezy summits of Inkpen Hill with its sinister gibbet, and Warbury Hill, 974ft (297m), the highest chalk down in England. Savernake Forest, easily explored from Marlborough, and the peaceful Kennet and Avon Canal offer a change of scene from the chalkhills.
☐ Map ref 2A4.

131. SOUTH HAMPSHIRE COAST
Area of Outstanding Natural Beauty

This consists of the Solent coast between Christchurch Bay and Southampton Water plus the hinterland of Beaulieu River. Places to visit include Buckler's Hard, Beaulieu, and the country park on the Lepe and Calshot foreshores. The latter covers 122 acres (49.5 hectares) of clifftops and beaches three miles (5km) south of Fawley with fine views and swimming. In all the AONB covers 48 sq miles (78 sq km).
☐ Map ref 2A5.

132. SURREY HILLS
Area of Outstanding Natural Beauty

London's weekend country playground. Suburbs lap against its northern edges but the beech groves, bluebell woods and chalkland slopes of the North Downs form a continuous *cordon sanitaire* of unbroken countryside

Southern England

from Kent to Guildford, which contains Leith Hill, Box Hill and the picturesque villages of Shere and Abinger. West of Guildford the Surrey Hills AONB is different in character, with sandy heaths and commons, wooded hills and many beauty spots, including Frensham Ponds, and The Devil's Punchbowl near Hindhead. Ideal countryside for gentle walks and picnics, much of it protected by the National Trust. The total area of the AONB is 258 sq miles (414 sq km).
☐ Map ref 2B4.

133. SUSSEX DOWNS
Area of Outstanding Natural Beauty

Superlative rolling chalk downland, from the Hampshire border through West Sussex to the sheer white cliffs of Beachy Head in East Sussex. Marvellous views from Ditchling Beacon, 813ft (250m), on the Downs behind Brighton. In addition to bracing walks over Seven Sisters there are many famous sights and places of interest; castles at Lewes and Arundel; stately homes and gardens such as Firle Place and Glynde Place (both near Lewes) and Petworth; the Saxon figure of the Long Man of Wilmington cut in the downland turf; and the smugglers' village of Alfriston with its 15th-century Star Inn. For horse-riders as well as walkers, the South Downs Way long-distance path provides a high-level route over the roof of the Downs from Beachy Head to the Hampshire border. The total area of the AONB is 623 sq miles (981 sq km), which provides the naturalist with some rare examples of flora and fauna (see page 96).
☐ Map ref 2B5/2C5.

Berkshire

A county bounded in the north by the River Thames and including part of the North Wessex Downs AONB – the largest in the country. Attractions include Windsor, with its castle and park, and the Thames itself from Maidenhead to the Goring Gap. Thames and Chilterns Tourist Board: Abingdon 22711.

134. COMBE HILL
Views/archaeology

At just under 1000ft (297m) this is the highest chalk hill in England. Almost inevitably, in an area rich in hill forts, it is therefore crowned by Iron Age fortifications. The hillfort is known as Walbury Hill and encloses a large area – 82 acres (33 hectares) – but otherwise is remarkable mainly for its views over the Kennet Valley. However the fort is crossed by a trackway, probably prehistoric, which can be followed southeast towards another hill-fort known as Beacon Hill (grid ref SU 457572) and the Seven Barrows burial mounds next to the A34 – a distance of just over six miles (9.6km) from Walbury Hill. On the same trackway barely ½-mile (800m) north-west from Walbury Hill is the extraordinary phenomenon of Combe Gibbet – a gallows first erected in the 17th century on a long barrow. OS map 174.
☐ Five miles (8km) SE of Hungerford on minor road to Inkpen. Map ref 2A4.

Heavy horse power: the animals and their history can be seen at the Courage Shire Horse Centre, near Maidenhead

135. COURAGE SHIRE HORSE CENTRE
Farm museum

Shire horses and their history are on display here, with harnesses, photographs, farrier's shop and agricultural implements. Open daily Mar-Oct, except non Bank Holiday Mons. Tel: Littlewick Green 3917.
☐ At Maidenhead Thicket three miles (4.8km) W of Maidenhead of A4. Map ref 2B4.

136. GORING GAP
River valley

The Thames cuts through the chalk escarpment at Goring in a beautiful wooded valley. Roads such as the A329 and B4009 offer glimpses of the river between Wallingford and Pangbourne, but it is seen more dramatically from viewpoints such as 500ft (150m) Streatley Hill, a prominent spur of chalk overlooking the meandering river. The 15 miles (24km) between Wallingford and Pangbourne offer recreations for most tastes: attractive villages, riverside walks, fishing, a wildlife park at Basildon, (for opening hours, tel: Upper Basildon 325); castle remains at Wallingford; Basildon Park (a Georgian house and grounds newly-opened by the NT: Tel: Pangbourne 3040) and, of course, boating.
☐ Goring is eight miles (13km) NW of Reading via A329. Map ref 2A4.

137. HURLEY
Riverside village/inn

The southern banks of the Thames here offer an attractive setting for picnicking and gentle strolls by the water's edge. The village itself was the site of a Benedictine Priory of which not only the church but the inn, *Ye Olde Bell*, can claim a connection. The Norman parish church was originally part of the priory while the inn was first founded in the 12th century as a hospice attached to the priory. A new half-timbered inn was built on the site of the earlier hospice towards the end of the 16th century and parts of this are still well-preserved.
☐ Four miles (6.4km) E of Henley off A423. Map ref 2B4.

138. LAMBOURN
Horse-racing village/antiquities

An attractive village, with a large Norman church and many Georgian houses, on the Berkshire Downs but now best known for racehorse training. Many famous stables are situated in Lambourn or neighbouring Upper Lambourn with the result that these villages and the surrounding Downland are some of the best places in the British Isles to see thoroughbred horses in action. The prehistoric Ridgeway path passes four miles (6.4km) to the north of Lambourn though an area which has many antiquities. The most famous are probably the Lambourn Seven Barrows, a group of round barrows about two miles (3.2km) north of the village (grid ref SU 328828). But there is also a long barrow (SU 326833) and a small Iron Age hill fort known as Alfred's Castle (SU 277827). The Uffington White Horse Hills is also not far away.
☐ Six miles (9.6km) N of Hungerford on B4000, near junction 14 on M4. Map ref 2A4.

139. MUSEUM OF ENGLISH RURAL LIFE
Agricultural museum

The museum is part of the Institute of Agricultural History at the University of Reading and has been open to the public since 1955. The permanent exhibition contains early agricultural tools from all over England, dating mainly from the 19th and early 20th centuries. Open throughout the year, Tues-Sat except Bank holidays. Tel: Reading 85123, ext 475.
☐ At Whiteknights, Reading, on A327. Map ref 2A4.

140. WINDSOR GREAT PARK
Parkland and gardens

The hunting territory of kings is now a picnicking ground for the masses. The park is vast: 4800 acres (1942 hectares) stretching from the river to Virginia Water. Tucked away in the south-eastern corner of the park, near Englefield Green, are two outstanding gardens within one mile (1.6km) of each other. The Savill Garden began as a bog garden and grew into a general ornamental garden with flowering shrubs, trees, herbaceous plants, roses and alpines. The Valley Gardens, located around Virginia Water, were developed in the 'natural' style with shrubs and a heather garden in attractive woodland. Both gardens are open daily Mar-Dec. Tel: Egham 35544.
☐ Off A30 between Egham and Virginia Water. Map ref 2B4.

East Sussex

The Sussex coast draws many visitors with a string of resorts of which the most famous are Brighton, Eastbourne and Hastings. Other attractions include the South Downs (with long-distance footpath), Rye, Lewes, Battle and the Bluebell Railway, South-East England Tourist Board: Tunbridge Wells 40766.

141. ASHDOWN FOREST
Forest

The Romans knew it as the Forest of *Anderida* and in those days it covered most of south-east England. It still extends over some 14,000 acres (5668 hectares) of sandy heathland and woodland between roughly East Grinstead, Uckfield and Crowborough. By the 16th century it was the centre of the British iron industry whose demand for charcoal denuded the forest of many more trees. Best explored on foot or the minor roads which cross the forest, e.g. around Nutley and Wych Cross off A22. Places of interest include The Beacon, a 792ft (238m) viewpoint west of Crowborough; a Forestry Commission picnic area and forest trail at Gravetye Manor, a Jacobean mansion (now a hotel) south of East Grinstead; and Nutley Mill (open afternoons on last Sun of month, Easter-Sept).
☐ SE of East Grinstead, N of Uckfield, W of Crowborough off A22 or A26. Map ref 2C5.

142. BURWASH
Jacobean mansion/watermill

A 'linear' village along a wide and tree-lined street. Among many lovely houses, the most renowned within the village is the 17th century Rampyndene with elaborate carving and a high roof. The most famous house, though, lies a short distance outside the village and this is Bateman's (NT) – a Jacobean stone mansion which became Rudyard's Kipling's home from 1902 to 1936 and now preserved as he left it. In the grounds of Bateman's is a restored 18th century watermill, itself a listed building. The house is open most days Mar-Oct but hours vary. Tel: Burwash 882302.
☐ Burwash is approximately half-way between Hastings and Tunbridge Wells on A265 with Bateman's half mile (0.8km) S of the village. Map ref 2C5.

143. DITCHLING COMMON
Country park

There are ponds, fishing and bridleways as well as the customary fare of picnic places and walks in the 183 acres (74 hectares) of the scrub-covered common land of this country park.
☐ Two miles (3.2km) N of Ditchling on B2112. Map ref 2B5.

144. EASTBOURNE
Downland walk

As 'with Weymouth this is a seaside resort which can serve as the base for an unusual circular walk along stretches of a long-distance footpath – in this case, the South Downs Way. An 18-mile (29km) circuit entirely on way-marked footpath can be achieved by using the alternative coastal and inland sections at the eastern end of the South Downs Way. The going over the chalk downlands is relatively easy and the views, over sea and Weald, are excellent. Roughly half way around the circuit is Alfriston, a pretty village in the Cuckmere valley with a fine 14th century church as well as the 15th century *Star Inn* described in Chapter Three. Also en route is the Seven Sisters Country Park (see below).

In a clockwise direction from East-bourne the route takes you over the Beachy Head clifftops to the Cuckmere valley; crosses the main coast road, the A259, at Exceat near the Country Park where there is a car park; continues through West Dean and Friston Forest to Alfriston; and returns along a brid-lepath over Windover Hill, Jevington and Eastbourne golf course. Smaller stretches, of course, can be undertaken and alternative starting points devised. OS map 199 details the footpaths.
☐ The South Downs Way begins (or ends) at the western end of Eastbourne, near where the sea front turns away from the coast to climb up to Beachy Head. Map ref 2C5.

145. FOREST WAY
Bridleway/country park

The old railway line between Groom-bridge and East Grinstead has been converted by East Sussex CC into a linear country park which is ideal for walkers or horse-riding.
☐ Map ref 2C4.

146. GREAT DIXTER
Romantic flower garden

The half-timbered 15th century manor house was reconstructed early this century by Sir Edwin Lutyens, who also laid out the gardens as a series of enclosures. This was densely planted in the style advocated by Gertrude Jekyll, who inspired Lutyens. Open daily, except non-Bank Holiday Mons, Apr-Oct. Tel: Northiam 3160.
☐ 12 miles (19km) N of Hastings at Northiam off A28. Map ref 2C5.

147. HASTINGS
Country park

A large and varied country park lies to the east of this seaside resort covering some 501 acres (203 hectares) and including woodland, heath, meadow-land, cliffs and the beach. Within this area there is a nature trail, bridleways, fishing and canoeing.
☐ E of Hastings on the coast. Map ref 2C5.

148. LULLINGTON HEATH
Wildlife

A national nature reserve for keen naturalists only. A steep walk (20 min) brings you to one of the best examples of chalk heath vegetation. It includes an unusually large variety of plants: not only chalk-loving species such as salad burnet and dropwort, but those usually associated with more acid soils, such as heather and tormentil. Left to itself, the grassland would quickly revert to scrub, so there is management in the form of grazing by New Forest ponies and sheep, and mowing. Where gorse and scrub has grown up, how-ever, this provides a good habitat for birds and insects. Visitors should keep strictly to the three public rights of way across the Reserve and keep dogs on a lead. A leaflet is available but no other public facilities. For further inform-ation, tel: Nature Conservancy Coun-cil, Lewes 6595.
☐ Off A2105 at Jevington, three miles (4.8km) N of East Dean. Map ref 2C5.

149. PEVENSEY
Roman and Norman fortress

Perhaps best remembered as the place where William the Conqueror landed in 1066. Pevensey was also the site of one of the Romans' Saxon Shore Forts and enough of those fortifications sur-vived for the site to be used again by the Normans who erected their own castle keep within the Roman walls. Now the remains of both castles stand guard over a harbour that has long since silted up with the result that they are one mile (1.6km) inland. The castle ruins are open standard DoE hours plus Sun mornings Apr-Sept.
☐ Four Miles (6.4km) NE of East-bourne near junction of A259 and A27. Map ref 2C5.

150. SHEFFIELD PARK GARDENS
Gardens/house/railway

More than 100 acres (40 hectares) of this large garden were landscaped by Capability Brown in the 18th century when the Tudor house which they surround was also extensively remodel-led. In the 19th century two more lakes, plus a considerable amount of tree and shrub planting, were added while the 20th century has seen an even greater influx of exotic plants. The gardens but not the house are owned by the NT. They are open daily, except non-Bank Holiday Mons, Apr-Sept but after-noons only Sun; tel: Dane Hill 790655 or 790338. The house is separately owned and open afternoons Wed, Thurs and Sun, Easter-Oct; tel: Dane Hill 790531. A short distance away from the house and gardens is a ter-minus for one of the best-known pri-vately-operated steam railways, the Bluebell Line, tel: Newick 2370. This operates from Sheffield Park to Hor-sted Keynes throughout the year, but daily only during June-Sept.
☐ Five miles (8km) NW of Uckfield on A275 between East Grinstead and Lewes. Map ref 2C5.

151. SEVEN SISTERS
Cliffs/estuary/forest

This is now the name not only of the famous line of chalk cliffs culminating in Beachy Head (532ft; 161m) but also of a country park. The cliffs are re-markable for their sheer vertical drops. Originally they extended further south, but over the years the sea has undercut the base of the cliffs. And because the chalk has vertical joints, chunks are broken off by the undercut-ting to leave the dry 'hanging' valleys and sheer cliffs which now form part of Britain's protected 'Heritage Coast'.

In addition to the downland adjoin-ing the cliffs (AONB) the country park contains the meandering valley of the River Cuckmere as it approaches the sea – one of the few remaining un-developed river estuaries in south-east England. The wide variety of habitats supports equally diverse wild life.

The park offers almost unlimited scope for picnicking and an inform-ation centre is housed in a splendid old barn. There is a nature trail, fishing, bridleways, footpaths (including a stretch of the South Downs Way, see under Eastbourne) and a forest walk. Magnificent views from the cliffs.
☐ Off A259 three miles (5km) E of Seaford. Map ref 2C5.

152. WINCHELSEA
Failed medieval 'new town'

The present sleepy town set on a hill above the marshes was created when an earlier town had been swallowed up by the sea. Edward I decided to lay out a new town in the 1280s and the inhabitants of Old Winchelsea were allowed burgess plots to recompense them for their loss. Today the grid-iron plan of the town still serves as a reminder of medieval planning. Some streets have vanished to become graz-ing ground for sheep, although their lines remain visible to the present day. A degraded sea cliff below Strand Gate shows how far the sea has retreated.
☐ Two miles (3.2km) SW of Rye on A259. Map ref 2C5.

The 16th century Star Inn at Alfriston, East Sussex

Arundel Castle, West Sussex, historic stronghold of the Duke of Norfolk

Southern England

Greater London

Innumerable tourist attractions with famous gardens at Kew, Hampton Court, Chiswick and in some of the royal parks. London Tourist Board: 01-730 0791.

153. HAM HOUSE
17th century house and garden

A fascinating example of an Elizabethan mansion converted and enlarged into a 'formal house' by Charles II's gross but able minister, the Duke of Lauderdale. One has the feeling that the clock stopped in 1700. Matching apartments for the Duke and Duchess on the ground floor, and a state apartment for a monarch above, all still containing an extraordinary amount of their original contents and decorations. None of the rooms is large; the house was designed for a few people to pass elaborate compliments to each other in a setting of intimate formality. The garden is being restored to its original 17th century form. Open daily except Mon; tel: 01 940 1950.
□ One mile (1.6km) SW of Richmond off A307 road to Kingston or by towpath walk through Petersham meadows. Map ref 2B4.

154. STAINES RESERVOIRS
Bird-watching

This is the best place in the London area for watching winter wildfowl. However, the birds themselves seem undisturbed either by birdwatchers or by the planes from Heathrow a few miles away. If you visit in October you stand a chance of seeing a black-necked grebe and in the later winter months there are usually wigeon, shoveler, goldeneye, tufted duck and pochard, with perhaps smew and goosander.
□ Immediately north of Staines, off A30 with access from a footpath off B378. Map ref 2B4.

155. TRENT PARK
Country park

The country park closest to north London with 680 acres (275 hectares) of wood and parkland including bridleways for horse-riding as well as footpaths, fishing and golf.
□ 1½ miles (2.4km) W of Enfield off A111. Map ref 2B3.

Hampshire

A large county stretching from the sea to London's commuter belt. Its attractions include river valleys such as the Test and Itchen; towns such as Winchester, Lymington and Portsmouth; stately homes at Beaulieu and Stratfield Saye. Southern Tourist Board: Eastleigh 616027.

156. AVINGTON
Village/fishing

A small village in the Itchen valley with a 17th century mansion once occupied by Charles II and Nell Gwynn and a stillwater fishery which has become famous for its development of fast-growing rainbow trout. The current British record – a 19lb 8oz (8.8kg) fish – came from this water.
□ Four miles (6.4km) NE of Winchester off B3047. Map ref 2A4.

157. BREAMORE COUNTRYSIDE MUSEUM
Farm museum

This exhibition in the grounds of an Elizabethan Manor House is arranged according to the year's farming calendar, from ploughing in the winter to root-crop harvesting in the autumn. As well as a collection of hand-tools, there are vintage tractors and several stationary engines used to work barn machinery. Indoor displays include a farm worker's cottage before electricity. There is also the Breamore Carriage Museum set in the 17th century stables of the house with a selection of 19th century carts, carriages and chaises. The museum (and house) are open daily, afternoons, except non-Bank Holiday Mons and Fris, Apr-Sept. Tel: Breamore 468.
□ At Breamore House, Breamore, nine miles (14km) S of Salisbury on A338. Map ref 2A5.

158. BUCKLER'S HARD
Riverside village/sailing

The sheltered waters of the Beaulieu river near Buckler's Hard offer fine sailing, with the river remaining navigable as far north as Palace House, the home of Lord Montagu at Beaulieu on the edge of the New Forest. One of Lord Montagu's predecessors had intended to turn Buckler's Hard itself into a port, but it never really developed that way. As a result it remains an attractive largely 18th century riverside village. The shipyard which once built ships for the Napoleonic wars has now been restored and houses a Maritime Museum, open throughout the year, tel: Buckler's Hard 203. Latter-day boats can be launched at the Marina adjacent to Buckler's Hard while non-sailors can either walk along the river banks or join one of the cruises which operate May-Sept.
□ Five miles (8km) NE of Lymington off B3054. Map ref 2A5.

159. BUTSER ANCIENT FARM
Iron Age agriculture

Within the 1400 acres (463 hectares) of open downland and forest which comprise the Queen Elizabeth country park, there is one section of special interest: Butser Ancient Farm Demonstration area, a unique project begun in 1972, to investigate the Iron Age, basing its researches on a reconstruction of a farm building dating from 300 BC. Its most impressive feature is probably Pimperne House, the largest reconstruction anywhere of an Iron Age structure. There are also crops and livestock appropriate to the period. On the lower slopes of 889ft (274m) Butser Hill, there are regular demonstrations of sheep management. Other features of the country park are forest walks, bridleways and views. The park is open daily all year; reception centre: daily Apr to Oct, closed Mon and Sat in Nov, and open Sun only, Dec to Feb. Demonstration area open May to Sept afternoons, Sun and Bank Holiday mornings. Tel: Horndean 595040.
□ Two miles (3.2km) S of Petersfield on A3 at Horndean. Map ref 2A5.

160. DANEBURY
Hill fort/nature trail

The Iron Age hill fort lies within relatively modest ramparts, but the site is an important one: excavations have shown a complex history dating back to the Bronze Age. Now its ramparts and central area of 13 acres (5.3 hectares) are dotted with trees – and 20th century picnickers. A nature trail winds round the fortifications.
□ 4½ miles (7km) S of Andover signposted off minor road between A343 and A30. Map ref 2A4.

161. HILLIER ARBORETUM
Trees and shrubs

The largest collection in the world of trees and shrubs from temperate regions. There are also dwarf bulbs, camellias, azaleas, magnolias and a bog garden in this arboretum which was founded by Harold Hillier. Open throughout the year Mon-Fri, plus weekend and Bank Holiday afternoons, Apr to Oct. Tel: Braishfield 68787.
□ At Ampfield three miles (4.8km) E of Romsey off A31. Map ref 2A5.

162. HURST CASTLE
Sea castle

This castle (AM) was built in the 16th century by Henry VIII to command the narrowest entrance to Southampton Water. It stands at the end of a shingle spit from the mainland barely half a mile (0.8km) away from the shores of the Isle of Wight. The castle can be reached either by walking along this 1½ mile (2.4km) long spit known at Hurst Beach or during the summer by ferry from Keyhaven. The castle is open standard DoE hours plus Sun mornings Apr-Sept.
□ Four miles (6.4km) of Lymington Off B3058. Map ref 2A5.

163. MOTTISFONT ABBEY
Priory garden

Originally a 12th century Augustinian priory, although the house itself underwent major changes in the 18th century. The grounds, which are bordered by the River Test, include old roses, a knot garden and a pleached avenue – a tree-lined walk where the branches are arched over and interlaced. Grounds are open afternoons Tues-Sat, Apr-Sept; the house Wed and Sat afternoons only, same months. NT. Tel: Lockerley 40757.
□ 4½ miles NW of Romsey off A3057. Map ref 2A5.

164. NEW FOREST
Old hunting forest

This is the largest expanse of unenclosed land in the south of England. Once a royal hunting forest, it covers 145 sq miles (37,555 hectares) the bulk of which is managed by the Forestry Commission. The FC provides over 140 car parks and picnic places, controlled camping areas and forest walks. Details of facilities and leaflets available from Lyndhurst Information Centre at public car park in village. Recommended guide book: *Explore the New Forest*. Ponies, cattle, pigs graze the open forest. Also four species of deer. Among forest highlights are the Bolderwood Woodland Walks from Bolderwood car park on by-road from Lyndhurst via Emery Down; Blackwater, Tall Trees and Brock Hill walks, all starting from Blackwater car park, two miles (3.2km) W of Lyndhurst off A35; Ober Water walks from Whitefield Moor car park on by-road two miles (3.2km) west of Brockenhurst, Wilverley Walk (2¾ miles, 4.4km) from Wilverley Plain car park on Brockenhurst-Holmsey road.
□ The forest is SW of Southampton and NE of Bournemouth. Map ref 2A5.

165. PORTCHESTER
Roman and Norman sea fort

The best preserved of the Roman sea forts, with its walls and gateways from about 300 AD the most perfectly intact in northern Europe. The site is an excellent example of the continuity of settlement within the British Isles. Even before the Romans, there is evidence of prehistoric occupation in the form of a rampart. And after the Romans came the Normans who used the Roman walls to enclose a splendid castle and church, both dating from the 12th century. The keep of the castle is open standard DoE hours plus Sun mornings Apr-Sept. Beyond its moat the grassy compound within the castle walls forms what must be one of the most richly historic settings for cricket anywhere in England.
□ Half a mile (0.8km) S of A27 between Portsmouth and Fareham. Map ref 2A5.

166. ROMSEY
Abbey/river valley

Romsey Abbey dates from the 10th century and although it was changed and enlarged by the Normans it contains some carving which is believed to have survived from Saxon times. The abbey dominates this little market town but it is not the only building of either distinction or antiquity. Near the abbey is King John's House, a 13th century house built possibly as a hunting lodge for exploring the New Forest.

Tufted duck (below), and wigeon, common winter visitors at Staines Reservoirs

Nowadays, the sportsmen who head towards Romsey are more likely to be anglers since the town stands on the banks of the River Test, generally recognised as the supreme trout fishing water in the country. Market days in Romsey are Friday and Saturday. Just south of the town is Broadlands, the home of Lord Palmerston and Lord Mountbatten. Open daily Apr to Oct except non-Bank Holiday Mons. Tel: Romsey 516878.
□ Six miles (9.6km) NW of Southampton A3057. Map ref 2A5.

167. SELBORNE
Village/literature

This village is firmly associated with the naturalist Gilbert White (1720–93) and Selborne Hanger or Hill, where he made many of the observations recorded in his most famous work, *The Natural History of Selborne*, is now protected and owned by the NT. White's former home, The Wakes, is a museum dedicated to the life and works of both White and Antarctic explorer Captain Oates; it is open Tues-Sun, Mar-Oct, tel: Selborne 275. Three miles (5km) up the road is an even more famous literary shrine: Chawton, one of the homes of novelist Jane Austen. Here, too, there is a museum in the former family home; tel: Alton 83262 for details.
□ Selborne is four miles (6.4km) SE of Alton on B3006; Selborne Hill is SW of B3006 between Selborne and Newton Valence. Map ref 2A4.

168. SILCHESTER
Abandoned Roman city

Calleva Atrebatum was a Roman regional capital in Hampshire and one of the few Roman towns of any size to remain deserted – the modern village of Silchester is smaller than its predecessor and on a separate site a short distance to the west. The Roman walls of flint bonded with blocks of chalk still exist, however, and enclose 120 acres (49 hectares) of farmland with a tiny medieval church standing close to the former eastern gate of the town. Outside the walls near the eastern gate (where a farm like the church incorporates some of the Roman wall) a hollow in the ground marks the site of the former amphitheatre. A small museum exists half a mile north of the modern village of Silchester.
□ Between Reading and Basingstoke in a tangle of lanes off A340 and A33. Map ref 2A4.

169. WAGGONERS' WELLS
Hammer ponds

The ponds are a reminder that this stretch of apparently unspoilt countryside was once part of a thriving iron industry. Wakeners' Wells, as they were originally called, were the site of an iron foundry as long ago as the 16th century with the water being stored in the ponds to power the wheels and hammers of the foundry. Now they are owned by the NT, along with large tracts of the surrounding land including Ludshott Common and Bramshott Chase. NT nature trails (plus leaflets).
□ 1½ miles (2.4km) SW of Hindhead between the A3 and B3002. Map ref 2B4.

170. WELLINGTON
Country park/dairy museum

A park covering nearly 600 acres (243 hectares) and what seems at first glance almost as many interests. The park is on the Duke of Wellington's estate and it contrives to offer both 'unspoilt' woodland and parkland (nature trails, bridleways, fishing etc.) and a 'developed' leisure area (crazy golf, adventure playground, model boats etc). A national dairy museum displays a collection of past dairy equipment and, like the park is open daily Mar-Oct, weekends Nov-Feb; tel: Heckfield 444. The Wellington stately home, Stratfield Saye House and its grounds are 2½ miles (4km) away and open Easter-Sept; tel: Turgis Green 602.
□ Seven miles (11km) S of Reading near junction of A33 and A32. Map ref 2A4.

Isle of Wight

Separated from the mainland by the Solent. Coastal resorts include Shanklin, Ryde and Ventnor. Isle of Wight Tourist Board: Newport 524343.

171. ALUM BAY
Cliffs

This bay, just north of the Needles, is famous for its sand cliffs which are striped vertically in 21 different colours ranging from chocolate brown to strawberry pink. Local shops sell souvenirs as it is dangerous for visitors to scramble up the cliffs to collect their own. A chair lift operates from the cliffs to the beach in summer. The Needles, a line of jagged chalk sea stacks with a lighthouse (not open to the public), are best seen from the Coastguard station on Tennyson's Down. The down was named after the poet who walked here regularly from his home in Freshwater.
□ Four miles (6.4km) SW of Yarmouth at end of B3322. Map ref 2A5.

172. BRADING
Roman villa

The fine mosaic pavements which have survived and which can be seen here indicate that it was something approaching a country house. But the manner in which the buildings are grouped around an open courtyard is a reminder that this, like most villas, was essentially the centre of a farm or estate with the 'courtyard' probably the equivalent of a superior farmyard. The villa is open daily in summer.
□ Four miles (6.4km) S of Ryde on A3055. Map ref 2A5.

173. BRIGHTSTONE
Forest walk

The Brightstone Jubilee Walk was laid out by the Forestry Commission to commemorate the 50th anniversary of the forest. The full walk is 2½ miles (4km), but waymarked short cuts reduce this to one or 1¾ miles (1.6 or 2.8km). The walk covers downland and woodland with some fine views. An FC leaflet describes the wildlife which might be seen. Details from tourist board, Tel: Newport 524343.
□ From NT car park on Brightstone Down, 1¼ miles (2km) N of Brightstone.

174. COWES
Yachting/Royal house

The yachting centre of the British Isles – some would say the world – with the headquarters of the Royal Yacht Squadron housed in Cowes Castle. Yachts of all shapes and sizes can be seen here throughout the year, but most especially during the eight days of Cowes Week beginning each year on the first Saturday in August. Unevenly numbered years – 1981, 1983 etc – are best of all, since in those years around 20 national teams from all over the world compete for the Admiral's Cup. Cowes itself is divided into two halves, east and west, by the Medina estuary. One mile south-east of East Cowes is Osborne House, said to have been Queen Victoria's favourite residence and open to the public Mon-Sat, Easter-early October; tel: Cowes 292511 for further information.
□ Cowes is at the northern tip of the Isle of Wight on the A3021 (to East Cowes) and A3020 (to West Cowes). Map ref 2A5.

175. FIRESTONE COPSE
Trails/picnics

Three waymarked paths lead through mainly conifers and some oak and beech to Blackridge Brook with fine views of Wootton Creek. Main walk is 1½ miles (2.4km). Other routes are shorter. Also picnicking in small glades in a young beechwood.
□ SE of Wootton Bridge ¾ mile (1.2km) along minor road to Havenstreet. Map ref 2A5.

176. ROBIN HILL
Country park

The woodland and fields on this chalk ridge form part of the Isle of Wight AONB. The country park covers 79 acres (32 hectares) and includes a nature trail and animal pens.
□ Three miles (4.8km) SW of Newport. Map ref 2A5.

177. ST CATHERINE'S POINT
'Riviera' vegetation

Running eastwards from this most southerly point of the island for some six miles (9.6km) to Ventnor is a remarkable ledge just above sea level. This ledge is composed of a series of landslips and is so sheltered that a variety of semi-tropical trees and shrubs have flourished to give the area an almost Riviera flavour. The landslip is featured (and explained) in the Geology Museum at Sandown Public Library; tel: Sandown 402748.
□ Six miles (9.6km) SW of Ventnor off A3055. Map ref 2A5.

178. YAFFORD MILL
Mill/museum

The present mill at Yafford dates from the 19th century, although the foundations suggest the possibility of medieval origins. It was fully working until 1970 and was principally a grist mill for grinding animal foodstuffs. It now contains a collection of agricultural tools in common use until the 1950s. There is also a collection of Isle of Wight waggons, in the process of being restored and repainted in traditional livery. One unique feature of

Yafford Mill is its Seal Pool, specially constructed below the millrace, as a centre for the Grey Seal. Open daily May-Oct, but afternoons only Sun. Tel: Brightstone 740610.
□ W of Shorwell on B3399 five miles (8km) SW of Newport. Map ref 2A5.

Kent

Known as 'The Garden of England' but landscapes range from the North Downs to Romney Marsh. Also long stretches of coastline. Attractions also include Canterbury Cathedral and the castles or country houses at Chartwell, Deal, Knole and Leeds. South-East England Tourist Board: Tunbridge Wells 40766.

179. BARFRESTON
Norman church

The small Church of St Nicholas was built partly of flint and partly of limestone imported from Caen, a vehicle for more delicate carving than the tougher sandstone of Kilpeck, but not so durable and therefore much more restored. Yet it is more authentic than Dalmeny and Leuchars, the two Scottish examples of this type. The principal pleasures are external: especially the very rich south door and the unusual wheel window at the east end, also profusely adorned.
□ Ten miles (16km) SE of Canterbury on minor roads off A2. Map ref 2D4.

180. BEDGEBURY PINETUM
Coniferous trees/village

Nearly 100 acres (40 hectares) of hill and valley planted by the Forestry Commission and the Royal Botanic Gardens, Kew, as a national collection of coniferous trees. It is beautifully landscaped with many broad-leaved trees to improve the pictorial effects and to increase autumn leaf colour. The Pinetum is open throughout the year; tel: Goudhurst 211392. The nearby village of Goudhurst is one of the most attractive in the county.
□ The Pinetum is at Bedgebury two miles (3.2km) S of Goudhurst on B2079; Goudhurst is 10 miles (16km) E of Tunbridge Wells. Map ref 2C4.

181. CHIDDINGSTONE
Half-timbered village

The church has 13th century origins and a fine Perpendicular tower, but the houses facing the church are the real glory of this village which is largely owned by the NT. A row of outstanding half-timbered buildings date from the 16th and 17th centuries. Chiddingstone Castle is an 18th century restoration of a much earlier manor house. Also nearby is Penshurst Place, a country house renowned for its medieval hall and Tudor garden; tel: Penshurst 870307.
□ Five miles (8km) NW of Tunbridge Wells off B2027 or B2176. Map ref 2C4.

182. DOVER
Castle/views

The castle high on the cliff tops to the east of the town dates from shortly after the Normal Conquest, though many additions and alterations were made in succeeding centuries. It is an impressive structure with walls 100ft (31m)

high and up to 21ft (7.5m) thick. The hill top site also shows evidence of occupation from even earlier times, most notably the 40ft (12m) high remains of a Roman lighthouse which stands beside a Saxon church within the castle. Dover was one of the Roman forts of the Saxon shore (*Dubris*) and the site continued to be important in controlling the biggest harbour on the shortest sea crossing to France. The castle is open standard DoE hours (plus Sun mornings Apr-Sept) and affords stunning views of the channel.

□ The castle is to the E of the town. Map ref 2D4.

183. DUNGENESS
Bird-watching/nature reserve

The RSPB has a 1190-acre (482 hectare) reserve on this vast and unique foreland of windswept shingle, which is on one of the main flight paths for migrating birds. Here, almost in the shadow of Dungeness Nuclear Power Station, 270 different species of bird have been recorded. Flooded gravel pits attract wintering ducks and waders. Breeding species include little tern, wheatear, ringed plover and great crested grebe. The area is also famed for its loudly croaking marsh frogs and typical flowers of the shingle shore. The reserve is open all year. Small charge for non-RSPB members. Visitors should report to warden's house at reserve entrance (Boulderwall Farmhouse, Dungeness Road, Lydd, Kent TN29 9PN). A leaflet is available.

□ Lydd is eight miles (13km) E of Rye on B2076. Map ref 2D5.

184. EYNSFORD
Village/Roman villa

An attractive forded village on the River Darent with the remains of a castle including a ditch and flint-rubble walls. Also nearby are Lullingstone Castle, largely rebuilt in the 18th century but with some Tudor elements, and Lullingstone Villa, the finest Roman villa within easy reach of London. The villa was discovered only in 1949 under the sludge and hill-wash of 15 centuries. Its history, well told in an imaginative museum on the site, reflects the experience of many villas whereby original farmhouses were re-built as grander country mansions. But the villa also contains the only Christian chapel to have been found in any Roman villa within Britain. For further information about the museum at Lullingstone Roman Villa, tel: Farningham 863467.

□ Midway between Sevenoaks and Dartford on A225. Map ref 2C4.

185. HEVER CASTLE
Gardens with statuary

This delightful little castle, dating from the 13th century and once the home of

Martello towers, built to repel Napoleon, still guard the Kent coast at Hythe

Martello towers

When an invasion by Napoleon seemed imminent in 1806 a new defence was introduced – the Martello Tower. Seventy-four were built, 30ft (9m) high, 25ft (7.5m) in diameter, with 6ft (1.8m) thick brick walls. The entrance was high above ground level with a gun platform mounting swivel guns and howitzers on top. The towers are concentrated between Seaford and Folkestone on the English coast; one at Dymchurch on Romney Marsh is open standard DoE hours. On Irish coasts a number of Martello towers were built following the landing of French republican soldiers in 1789.

Anne Boleyn, acquired its garden in the early years of this century when it was bought by William Waldorf Astor, 1st Viscount Astor of Hever. Part of it, in Italian style, was specially designed for the display of a large collection of Roman statues and antiquities. Other features are a grotto garden with many fountains, a rose garden, herbaceous borders, rock garden, water lilies in two moats, a set of chessman cut from yew, a maze and a vast landscaped lake overlooked by a colonnaded piazza. The castle and gardens are usually open afternoons on Tues, Wed, Fri (except Good Friday), Sun and Bank Holiday Mon; for further details, tel: Edenbridge 862205.

□ Three miles (5km) SE of Edenbridge off B2026. Map ref 2C4.

186. HIGH ROCKS
Picnics/climbing

To the west of the elegant spa town of Tunbridge Wells is an area of heathland rising to the impressive sandstone outcrop known as High Rocks. It is an ideal spot for walks and picnics or to watch rock climbers performing on the vertical crags. Similar rock faces occur at Harrison's Rocks in neighbouring Groombridge.

□ Two miles (3.2km) W of Tunbridge Wells S of A264. Map ref 2C4.

187. HOLLINGBOURNE
Downland walk

There are several interesting old buildings in the village of Hollingbourne but none so old as the Pilgrim's Way which traverses the nearby North Downs. In fact, this ancient trackway from Winchester to Canterbury was used long before Christianity established itself at Canterbury or anywhere else in the British Isles. Today it forms part of the long-distance North Downs Way and Hollingbourne can be the base for a short seven-mile (11km) circuit incorporating this and other footpaths. Follow first waymarked Greenway path to Harrietsham, turn left at Harrietsham Church and climb to where the waymarked Pilgrim's Way path crosses the road. Return along this to the Pilgrim's Rest Inn and Hollingborne. OS maps 188 and 189 details these and other paths.

□ Hollingbourne is on B2163, one mile (1.6km) NW of junction between M20 and A20 E of Maidstone. Map ref 2C4.

188. HOO PENINSULA
Roman field patterns/heronry

This peninsula between the Thames and the Medway can claim a survival of Roman land management known as 'centuriation'. This involved land being parcelled out in blocks measuring approximately 1500 by 750 yards (142m by 71m) and many academies believe the field patterns around the village of Cliffe in particular have remained unchanged in these dimensions since Roman times. The peninsula also has an RSPB reserve with the largest heronry in the United Kingdom. Over 200 pairs breed here in the reserve in mixed woodland and scrub on the edge of the North Kent marshes. A nature trail starts from

Northwood Avenue in High Halstow. For further information, tel: RSPB Reserves Dept, Sandy 80551.

□ Cliffe and High Halstow are both approx five miles (8km) N of Rochester on the B2000 and A228 respectively. Map ref 2C4.

189. IGHTHAM MOTE
Moated house

A medieval moat-encircled house hidden in the woods of the Kentish Weald. It grew round a courtyard from the early 14th till the early 16th century, starting with the great hall, and ending with the chapel. It was never at all grand; and the mellow and peaceful mixture of stone, brick and half-timbering that resulted is irresistible. Open throughout the year, on Fri afternoons only and Sun Apr-Sept. Tel: Sevenoaks 62235.

□ Six miles (9.6km) SE of Sevenoaks off A25 or A227. Map ref 2C4.

190. KNOLE
Country house and deer park

The house is one of the largest in England, with a series of fine state rooms containing rare furniture, rugs and tapestries dating largely from the 17th and 18th centuries. It is now owned by the NT and is open Wed to Sat plus Sun afternoons and Bank Holidays, from Apr to Nov. Tel: Sevenoaks 53006. The vast deer park which surrounds it is open daily.

□ One mile (1.6km) SE of Sevenoaks off A225. Map ref 2C4.

191. LAMBERHURST
Mill/abbey/garden

This village is on a busy road but amid some delightful Wealden scenery. It is an altogether unlikely place to have been an important industrial centre yet such it was during the 16th and 17th centuries. A faint echo of those times can be by following the little River Teise west of Lamberhurst to Furnace Mill, an 18th century corn mill (not open to the public) erected on the site of watermill that once served a major iron foundry. The mill is no longer on the river, however.

A little further west, however, the Teise was dammed to form a 'hammer pond' which now survives as a natural-looking lake close to the remains of Bayham Abbey. The ruins of the 12th century abbey are among the most notable in south-east England; they are open standard DoE hours plus Sun mornings Apr-Sept. Also close to Lamberhurst, and worth a visit, are the new reservoir at Bewl Bridge and Scotney Castle Garden, 1½ miles (2.4km) south-east of the village on A21.

Here a romantic garden has been set around a partly-ruined 14th century moated castle. In the 19th century the ruins were used to create a picturesque landscape with native and exotic trees and shrubs which are particularly memorable in autumn. An unusual ice-well, thatched with heather and used in the days before refrigerators, is a feature of the garden which is open daily except Mon and Tues Apr-Oct; tel: Lamberhurst 306.

□ Seven miles (11km) E of Tunbridge Wells on A21. Map ref 2C4.

The Straits of Dover are surprisingly shallow. Not even at their deepest would they drown St. Paul's Cathedral

Ightham Mote, a medieval moated house in the heart of the Kentish Weald

192. MEDWAY RIVER
River/boating

The river has a non-tidal part, with several locks, running deep into the heart of Kent. It is navigable to just beyond Tonbridge and is pleasant motor cruising country for those who are in no hurry. At Allington Castle, just north of Maidstone, the river becomes tidal to Sheerness off the Thames estuary. From a wiggling river close to green fields and villages it thus opens out into a wide delta of marshes, mud flats and creeks. This provides wonderful dinghy sailing water with all the room in the world at high tide, and a testing channel and twisting creeks to tack through at low water. The easiest access to the tidal reaches is the slipway at Upnor just north of Strood and Rochester. There is also a country park at Eastcourt Meadows bordering the estuary at Gillingham.
□ Map ref 2C4.

193. PARK WOOD
Woodland wildlife

One of the best examples of mixed woodland in East Kent, Park Wood nearly fell victim to the chain saw. Now, owned and managed by the Woodland Trust, visitors are welcome and its trees – hornbeam, oak, beech, and chestnut coppice – are secure. It is an ideal habitat for woodland songbirds such as blackcap, willow warbler and chiffchaff. There is also rich ground plant and insect life. For further information, tel: Grantham 74297.
□ On A252 SW of Chilham which is five miles (8km) SW of Canterbury. Map ref 2D4.

194. RICHBOROUGH
Roman fort and port

To the Romans it was *Portus Rutupis* and the main port of entry and departure between Britain and mainland Europe. The invading forces landed not far from Richborough where one of their sea forts was later built. It guarded the south-east entrance of the then navigable Wantsum Channel – the stretch of water which made the Isle of Thanet an island – while another fort and port, Reculver, near what is now Herne Bay, controlled the northern approach.

The Wantsum Channel has long since vanished – a combination of natural silting and monastic reclam-

ation that was complete by the 18th century. Richborough is now inland but it remains one of the greatest monuments to the Roman age with high flint walls dating from the 3rd century. The greatest mystery of Richborough is the huge mortar emplacement cross within the fort. Suggestions vary as to its function but it could be the foundations of a monument to mark the original invasion or a lighthouse.

There is a small museum on the site which, like the remains, is open standard DoE hours plus Sun morning Apr-Sept; tel: Sandwich 612013. Some Roman remains also exist at Reculver but they are less notable.
□ Two miles (3.2km) NW of Sandwich on minor roads off A257. Map ref 2D4.

195. RYE
Medieval town/walk

An ancient Norman Cinque Port which is now two miles (3.2km) inland. It is a highly picturesque town on a hill above Romney Marsh with steep, cobbled streets that still convey a medieval air. One of the old gates, the 14th century Landgate, survives to add to the general feeling of antiquity, much admired by 20th century visitors. Among many fine buildings the 15th century *Mermaid Inn* is deservedly one of the great attractions: a half-timbered building with tiled roof and dormer windows. Also of interest is Lamb House (NT), the home of Henry James for many years. Rye boasts a long tradition in pottery and tile making.

There is a fine walk along the dyke, keeping the sea at bay, from Rye Harbour to Winchelsea Beach. A nature reserve is run here by the Sussex Naturalists Trust with a good mix of sea and land birds, particularly little term. It is open to the public; for details, tel: Rye 3862. Return to Rye via Camber Castle. The walk is roughly seven miles (11km) long: OS map 189.
□ Rye is 10 miles (16km) NW of Hastings on A259 and A268. Map ref 2C5.

196. SALMESTONE GRANGE
Monastic remains

The word 'grange' was used to denote an outlying farm of a monastery. In this case it was a Benedictine grange of St Augustine's Priory at Canterbury which played an important role in

the reclamation of the Wantsum Channel (see also Richborough). It is open every afternoon May to Sept or by appointment; tel: Thanet 21136.
□ In Nash Road, Margate. Map ref 2D4.

197. SANDWICH
Medieval port/nature reserve

One of the Cinque ports, Sandwich survived the silting up of the Wantsum Channel (see also Richborough) but not for long. The River Stour which divides Pegwell Bay from Sandwich Bay also began to silt up from the 15th century, thus eroding Sandwich's importance as a commercial port. It still has a quay but today it serves only the occasional fishing vessel and pleasure craft.

Two miles (3.2km) north-east of the town to the south of the Stour is an NT nature reserve covering 193 acres (78 hectares) of coastal saltings and dunes. Access either via New Downs Farm or along the beach by toll roads from Prince's Golf Club; for details, leaflets etc, contact Kent Trust for Nature Conservation, 125 High Street, Rainham, Kent. Tel: Medway 362561.
□ Five miles (8km) NW of Deal. Map ref 2D4.

198. SISSINGHURST
Romantic garden

The Sissinghurst Castle Garden was made by Sir Harold Nicolson and his wife, Vita Sackville-West, between 1930 and her death in 1962, around the remnants of an Elizabethan house and two cottages. It consists of a series of enclosures, skilfully integrated, but each with its own distinctive design and planting. Plant associations have been studied with exceptional care. The garden's justified fame makes it vulnerable to serious overcrowding on Sundays and Bank Holidays. It is open daily except Mon, Apr-mid Oct. Tel: Sissinghurst 250.
□ The garden is one mile (1.6km) E of Sissinghurst off A262. Map ref 2C4.

199. TENTERDEN
Weather-boarded houses

A market town stretched out along a wide grass-verged main street typical of towns that once served as centres for large sheep markets (compare the high streets of Marlborough or Thame, for instance). But long before it was a main street or market-place it was a drove road for taking sheep to and fro between Romney Marsh and Thanet. Tenterden is also remarkable for the

Sissinghurst Castle, Kent, presides over one of England's finest gardens

large number of houses with exquisitely-maintained white timber weatherboarding.

☐ Tenterden is 10 miles (16km) SW of Ashford on A28. Map ref 2C4.

200. TOYS HILL
Viewpoint/woods

This is highest point in Kent with good views of the Weald. Woods are mainly beech, with oak, birch and pine. Many beeches are pollarded and are very old. Wood and heathland walks lead from the car park.

☐ 2½ miles (4km) S of A25 at Brasted. Map ref 2C4.

201. WYE
Nature reserve

The Wye and Crundale Downs National Nature Reserve forms one of the finest examples of grass and woodland habitat on the North Downs and is particularly rich in butterflies. Over 25 species occur in the reserve especially over the open grassy places with their show of chalkland flowers such as salad burnet, wild thyme and rockrose and several kinds of orchid. There are also some fine trees of the chalk: yew, whitebeam, and magnificent beech. There is a natural trail and information centre; tel: Wye 812791.

☐ Four miles (6.4km) NE of Ashford off minor road between Wye and Hastingleigh. Map ref 2D4.

Surrey

Commuter country for London but much beautiful countryside remains, notably around North Downs. Attractions include villages such as Chiddingfold and Shere; Guildford; viewpoints such as Box Hill and Leith Hill near Dorking; and Runnymede. South-East England Tourist Board: Tunbridge Wells 40766.

202. ABINGER HAMMER
Industrial archaeology/walks

Few places in the countryside of Kent or Surrey reveal their unexpected industrial past as explicitly as this attractive hamlet at the southern foot of the North Downs. The word 'hammer' comes from its days as a centre of the Wealden iron industry. Rivers were dammed to form ponds from which water was released with sufficient power to drive the wheels of watermills which operated the heavy hammers of local iron works. They are still known as hammer ponds (as at Abinger and the nearby Friday Street) or furnace ponds (as at Cowden in Kent). At Abinger Hammer another clue to its industrial past is an old clock in the main street depicting a blacksmith at his trade.

☐ Abinger Hammer is 4½ miles (7km) W of Dorking on A25; Friday Street is on minor roads south of Abinger Hammer. Map ref 2B4.

203. ALICE HOLT FOREST
Forest and wildlife trails

A former royal hunting forest straddling the Surrey–Hampshire border with associations going back through naval history to Roman times. Attractions include picnic places, forest and wildlife trails and coarse fishing. Ar-

boretum trail, starting at Lodge Enclosure picnic place is suitable for wheelchairs. Goose Green Trail leads into oak woodland planted in 1820 at Nelson's request to grow oaks to build ships for the British navy. Abinger Ranmore Forest Walk is on lip of North Downs escarpment with views to Dorking, Leith Hill and over the Weald. There is an information centre quarter mile (400m) SE of Bucks Horn Oak on Dockenfield Road off A325.

☐ Four miles (6.4km) S of Farnham. Map ref 2B4.

204. CLAREMONT
Landscaped garden

The earliest surviving English landscape garden, begun by Vanbrugh and Bridgeman before 1720 and extended and 'naturalised' by Kent. The National Trust completed the restoration of these lovely gardens in 1979. They now include a lake, island with a pavilion, a grotto, turf amphitheatre as well as viewpoints and avenues in true 18th century style. Open every day. Tel: Esher 62261. (Claremont House, not NT, is an 18th century Palladian mansion, now a school, open only on the afternoons of first weekend of the month Feb-Nov.)

☐ ½ mile (0.8km) SE of Esher, E of A307. Map ref 2B4.

205. DEVIL'S PUNCHBOWL
Viewpoint/nature trail

Below the magnificent viewpoint of Gibbet Hill, standing at 894ft (272m), the sandy heathlands of the Surrey 'Highlands' are trenched with deep combes such as the spectacular Devil's Punchbowl with its steep slopes covered in gorse and pine. Numerous footpaths criss-cross Hindhead Commons (NT) and there are opportunities to see four species of deer. The Punchbowl Nature Trail (NT) starts from the southern rim, marked by orange signposts, covering 2½ miles (4km). The Gibbet Hill Nature trail starts from the car park on the A3, marked by white signposts, and covers nearly two miles (3.2km). Note the contrast in the scenery between the sandstone ridge and its heathland with the neighbouring chalkland of the South and North Downs.

☐ Off A3 or A287 from Hindhead which is 13 miles (21km) SW of Guildford on A3. Map ref 2B4.

206. FRENSHAM COMMON
Antiquities/Country park

Prehistoric remains are rare in Surrey, partly because of the growth of many villages and towns as commuter bases for London. But on the crest of Frensham Common there is a line of barrows. The common is a large area of heathland, including Frensham Great Pond, and part of a country park which offers boating, fishing, bridleways and footpaths in 768 acres (311 hectares) of heath and common land.

☐ Four miles (6.4km) S of Farnham on either side of A287. Map ref 2B4.

207. LEITH HILL
Views/walks

This sandstone escarpment is the highest point in south-east England at 965ft (294m). The National Trust owns part

of the hill, including five acres (two hectares) near the summit where there is an 18th century tower open to the public in good weather. From the top of this tower there are panoramic views over the surrounding woods and farmland.

An Iron Age hill-fort Anstiebury Camp, can be seen on the eastern side of Leith Hill (grid ref. TQ 153440). The village of Coldharbour is an attractive base for the ascent of Leith Hill. Cars can also be parked one mile (1.6km) south-west of Coldharbour at Starveall Corner. More sprawling, and therefore usually less crowded than Box Hill.

☐ Four miles (6.4km) SW of Dorking on minor roads. Map ref 2B4.

208. POLESDEN LACEY
Edwardian garden

The 18th-century landscape garden was extended in 1906 with herbaceous borders, rose garden, hedges and beechwalks. The gardens (NT) are open daily throughout the year, but the house around which they stand only on certain days Mar-Nov. Tel: Bookham 52048.

☐ Three miles (5km) NW of Dorking off A246. Map ref 2B4.

209. WINKWORTH ARBORETUM
Trees/autumn colours

More than 100 acres (40 hectares) of trees and shrubs, begun in 1938. Spectacular autumn colours are best seen in mid-Oct, but the Arboretum is open throughout the year. NT. Tel: Bookham 53401.

☐ On E side of B2130, three miles (5km) SE of Godalming. Map ref 2B4.

210. WISLEY
Gardens

The Royal Horticultural Society's Garden covers 60 acres (24 hectares) and almost every style of gardening, from formal to informal. It is especially renowned for its rock garden, heather garden, woodland garden and collection of rhododendrons and azaleas. It also has magnificent mixed borders, two rose gardens, demonstration gardens, trial grounds and splendidly-stocked greenhouses. There are fruit and vegetable gardens in which new varieties are tested. Also lakes, a formal canal pool and a walled garden. Open daily throughout the year, except Christmas Day. Tel: Ripley 2163.

☐ NE of Ripley on A3. Map ref 2B4.

211. WITLEY COMMON
Heathland nature trails

These 377 acres (153 hectares) of west Surrey heathland have a wide range of wildlife, much of which can be seen from three trails. The blue route in the central part of the common passes through woods, glades and heathland. The red route takes you by wet and dry heath, and woods of pine and birch. A more specialized trail, the orange route, pays particular attention to the effects of management on neighbouring Milford Common (1hr). NT information centre is open Apr-Oct. Tel: Wormley 3207.

☐ Half mile (0.8km) SW of Milford between A3 and A286. Map ref 2B4.

West Sussex

The South Downs cross the county which also includes such well-known coastal resorts as Bognor and Worthing. Other attractions include Arundel Castle, Goodwood House and Chichester with its cathedral, harbour and Roman Palace at nearby Fishbourne. South-East England Tourist Board: Tunbridge Wells 40766.

212. BRAMBER
Norman settlement

A small country town on the River Adur, which still has the model plan of a Norman settlement with castle and church connected by the main street. The castle, now in ruins, was destroyed during the Civil War and the town has suffered unduly and unjustly through being located on a main road. But some fine timber-framed buildings remain.

☐ Five miles (8km) inland from Shoreham on A283. Map ref 2B5.

213. CISSBURY
Prehistoric fort/mines

On the highest point of a spur of the South Downs two miles (3.2km) inland from Worthing lies one of the largest Iron Age hill forts in the country (grid ref TU 139080). The huge single rampart and ditch encloses 60 acres (24 hectares) it is estimated that 60,000 tons of chalk rock went into the raising of the earthwork. At the western end of the fort and around the southern entrance the ground is heavily pocked with bumps and hollows – evidence of Neolithic (New Stone Age) flint mines second only in importance to those at Grimes Graves in Norfolk.

☐ ¾ mile (1.5km) E of Findon off A24. Map ref 2B5.

214. FISHBOURNE
Roman palace

Nearby Chichester was an important Roman town, *Noviomagus*, which still partly reflects its original grid layout. But even this does not explain why Fishbourne should be the site of a Roman villa of such magnificence that it is more aptly described as a palace. This is the largest Roman dwelling ever found in the British Isles, with around 100 rooms rich with mosaics and gaily painted friezes. The history of the palace, which was laid out about 75 AD, is excellently displayed in a fine museum on the site, open daily Mar-Nov; tel: Chichester 785859.

☐ One mile (1.6km) W of Chichester off A27. Map ref 2B5.

215. HIGHDOWN
Chalk garden

This garden was made in the first half of the 20th century in a disused chalk quarry, and on the rather barren chalk down in front of it. Thanks to the skill of its creator, the late Sir Frederick Stern, in choosing the right plants, the quarry is now almost completely covered with growth, and the down has been converted into a well-stocked garden which includes some very unusual plants and fine specimen trees. Open frequently throughout the year; tel: Worthing Borough Council for details, Worthing 37111, ext 96.

□ At Goring-by-Sea W of Worthing on A259. Map ref 2B5.

216. LEONARDSLEE
Woodland garden

A wonderful collection of rhododendrons, azaleas, magnolias, camellias, acers and other exotic shrubs and trees in a well-wooded valley with lakes. It is superbly landscaped and the autumn foliage colour is particularly good. Usually open Wed, Thurs, Sat, Sun and Bank Holiday Mons late April-early June, then weekends only in Oct. For details, tel: Lower Beeding 212.
□ In Lower Beeding $4\frac{1}{2}$ miles (7km) SE of Horsham on A281. Map ref 2B5.

217. MARDEN-STOUGHTON FOREST
Picnics/views

A beautifully secluded picnic place in the middle of the South Downs with tables set in beech woodland. There is a $1\frac{1}{2}$ mile (2.4km) walk through young beech and yew woods and a bridle road to viewpoint on Bowhill above Kingley Vale which is managed by Nature Conservancy Council. On a clear day there is a panoramic view of Chichester Cathedral and the south coast from Isle of Wight to Worthing.
□ Eight miles (13km) NW of Chichester off B2146. Map ref 2B5.

218. MIDHURST
Historic inn

The Spread Eagle inn was described by Hilaire Belloc as 'that old and most revered of all the prime inns of this world'. Whether or not everyone would go quite this far is doubtful, but it is certainly one of the most interesting inns in England let alone Sussex. The building consists of two parts: a half-timbered house with lattice windows dating from 1430, once used as an Elizabethan hunting lodge, and a stone and brick addition of 1650. In the 18th century it became a coaching inn.
□ 10 miles (16km) N of Chichester at junction of A272 and A286. Map ref 2B5.

219. NYMANS
Romantic garden

Rare plants from many parts of the world, including camellias, azaleas, magnolias, rhododendrons and eucryphias, are arranged here with great skill in a series of linked gardens in the manner advocated by Gertrude Jekyll and William Robinson in the early years of this century. There is also an exhibition on the history of the garden which is now owned by the NT. Open daily except Friday and non-Bank Holiday Mondays from Apr-Oct, although hours vary; tel. Handcross 400321.
□ At Handcross on B2114 six miles (9.6km) S of Crawley just off A23. Map ref 2B5.

220. PETWORTH
Country house/market town

A picturesque small town right next to a large house and, in fact, almost overshadowed by the large gateway to the house. Petworth House (NT) was rebuilt in the late 17th century with 19th century alterations. A great deal

Uppark, 17th century National Trust house near Petersfield, West Sussex

of rebuilding occurred in the town itself during the 17th century but some houses survive from even earlier times in the narrow streets set around a tiny market-place. Set around the house is a large deer park – one of the first to be landscaped by Capability Brown. The park is open all year but the house, which contains a fine collection of paintings, is open on afternoons only Apr-Oct except Fri and non-Bank Holiday Mon. Wed is 'connoisseur's day' with more rooms open and higher charges. Tel: Petworth 42207.
□ $5\frac{1}{2}$ miles E of Midhurst on A272 and A283. Map ref 2B5.

221. SELSEY
Beaches/nature trail

This peninsula was where the South Saxons first settled. For over 1000 years the area was a political and administrative unit known as the Hundreds of Manhood. Its historic past is best seen in the ancient farms which pepper the landscape of inland Selsey. Most visitors to the area, however, head for the miles of sandy beaches between Selsey Bill, the southernmost points, and West Wittering. A $1\frac{1}{2}$ mile (2.4km) nature trail starts from West Wittering around the beach and sand dunes to East Head, a spit of land jutting into Chichester Harbour which in the winter especially is the haunt of many birds.
□ The Selsey peninsula is S of Chichester via B2145; West Wittering is six miles (9.6km) SW of Chichester off B2179. Map ref 2B5.

222. SINGLETON
Open-air museum

A small village with a mainly Saxon church sheltering under the South Downs in general and 818ft (250m) Linch Down in particular. The village itself has strong racing connections with nearby Goodwood but is now probably best known as the site of the Weald and Downland Open-Air Museum. Among many historic buildings saved by being re-erected on this 40-acre (16 hectare) site are houses from the 14th–16th centuries, an Elizabethan treadwheel, a market hall, and a 19th century blacksmith's forge. The buildings and the setting are sufficiently attractive to mitigate the slight air of artificiality. There is also a short nature trail through the wood and parkland plus a reconstruction of a charcoal burner's settlement. Open most days Apr-Sept, three days a week during Oct and Sun only for the rest of the year; tel: Singleton 348.
□ Six miles (9.6km) N of Chichester on A286. Map ref 2B5.

223. SLINDON EARTHAM WOOD
Roman road/forest

Pleasant woodland setting with picnic tables among beech trees. FC forest walk of some two miles (3.2km) includes part of Stane Street, the Roman road which ran from Chichester to London Bridge.
□ Six miles (9.6km) NE of Chichester and one mile (1.6km) N of Eastham off A285. Map ref 2B5.

224. UPPARK
Country house

Lost on top of the Downs, and mellowed to a silvery pink by the sea breezes, this original 17th century brick house was redecorated and filled with beautiful things owned by the Fetherstonhaugh family in the 18th century. In Regency days Sir Henry Fetherstonhaugh, after a fling with Emma Hart (Nelson's Lady Hamilton), married his dairy-maid. She and her sister inherited the house and lived there for 50 years without touching it. Lovingly and conservatively-restored by recent owners (now NT), the gently-faded rooms have exquisite contents, including the best doll's house in England. Usually open three days a week Apr-Sept; tel: Harting 317.
□ Four miles (6.4km) SE of Petersfield off B2146. Map ref 2B5.

225. WAKEHURST PLACE
Exotic garden species

In 1965 this garden was leased from the NT by the Royal Botanic Gardens as an overflow garden, particularly for rhododendrons, pines and exotic species which do not thrive in the rather poor soil at Kew. A watercourse links several ponds and lakes in the picturesque way which makes Kew Gardens themselves attractive to people who know nothing of plants. Open daily throughout the year, Except Christmas Day New Year's Day and May Day holiday. Tel: Ardingly 892701.
□ $1\frac{1}{2}$ miles (2.4km) NW of Ardingley on B2028. Map ref 2B5/2C5.

Rural county with rolling chalk downs sporting several white horses. Rich in prehistoric remains, notably around Stonehenge and Avebury. Other attractions include Longleat House. Wilton House, Salisbury Cathedral and the market towns of Devizes and Marlborough. West Country Tourist Board: Exeter 76351.

226. AVEBURY
Prehistoric monuments

This small village is richer with prehistoric monuments than any other place in the country (see map). Yet although Avebury itself can become busy at summer weekends, it draws fewer visitors than the single monument of Stonehenge and the sites are sufficiently scattered to enable most visitors to avoid the crowds.

At the heart of the antiquities, and encompassed by the village, is a huge

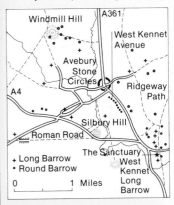

Avebury, Wiltshire, epicentre of an area rich in prehistoric monuments

ring-earthwork or henge covering $28\frac{1}{2}$ acres (11.5 hectares): a circular embankment with a deep ditch and standing stones which was a Bronze Age sanctuary. To the south runs The Avenue, 50ft (15m) wide and flanked by standing stones. Many of these stones survive, but by no means all. The Avenue originally ran for a mile (1.6km) to a smaller site, known as The Sanctuary, now next to the A4 opposite a transport cafe. Only the sites of the stones which once stood here can now be seen but there are several round barrows close by.

Also within a short distance and an easy walk of Avebury is West Kennet Long Barrow, the largest Neolithic chambered tomb in England and Wales; the mysterious Silbury Hill, the largest prehistoric mound in Western Europe at 130ft (40m) high; Windmill Hill, the site of a Neolithic settlement established around 3700 BC and topped by three concentric ditches; the route of the prehistoric Ridgeway track (now a long-distance footpath); a stretch of Roman road clearly visible as a grassy bank and many round barrows.

In Avebury itself there is a museum covering the antiquities of the area. This is open standard DoE hours plus Sun mornings Feb-Nov. Among other attractions of Avebury are a folk life museum in a converted 17th century thatched barn and a lovely Tudor-

Elizabethan manor house (open May-Sept). In short, a marvellous base for an extraordinary day's exploration of the past, with gentle walks and splendid views over the Downs OS map 173 covers the area.
□ 10 miles (16km) S of Swindon on A361. Map ref 1D4.

227. BOWOOD GARDENS
Landscaped gardens

Large 18th century landscape garden and lake by 'Capability' Brown with Italian style terraces added in the 19th century. Also fine rockwork and cascade with grottoes, daffodils naturalised in the park, aboretum, pinetum and rose garden. Open daily, except Mon, Easter-Sept; tel Calne 812102.
□ At Studley three miles (4.8km) SE of Chippenham on A4. Map ref 1D4.

228. BRADFORD-ON-AVON
'Wool' town/Saxon church

An attractive town which was a thriving centre of the Wiltshire wool trade until this began to decline in the last century. It is still dominated by the old Abbey Mill (now offices) but of greater antiquity are St Lawrence's, one of the most complete Saxon churches in the country, and a medieval bridge with an 18th century chapel on it. The town has many attractive little alleyways and cottages. Across the river to the south is Barton Farm Country Park with a spectacular 14th century tithe barn among several historic buildings alongside the River Avon.
□ Six miles (9.6km) SE of Bath on A363. Map ref 1D4.

229. CHISELBURY CAMP
Hill fort/medieval road

This hill fort is on an ancient routeway, possibly used in prehistoric times, certainly used up to coaching days and now the preserve of walkers and horse-riders. It is part of the old Exeter road south-west of Salisbury. But whereas the modern A30 runs along the valley of the River Nadder, the old road followed the chalk ridgetop – now a marvellous stretch of 'green road' lasting some 13 miles (21km) from Harnham, just south of Salisbury, until rejoining the modern road at the foot of Whitesheet Hill east of Shaftesbury. The route passes several tumuli as well as Chiselbury Camp, an almost perfectly circular hill-fort with a single embankment, grid ref. SU 018281.
□ Chiselbury Camp is eight miles (13km) SW of Salisbury off A30 or on the old medieval road as described above. Map ref 1D5.

230. CHUTE CAUSEWAY
Roman road

A classic example of a Roman road which was not straight. Just north of the village of Chute the Roman road from Winchester to Mildenhall in Wiltshire swings in a great arc to avoid not only the slopes of Haydown Hill but also the steep valley of Hippenscombe. A modern lane still follows this route but it is not quite the curve it appears to be on maps. The Romans built their uncharacteristic diversion through a series of nine short but separate alignments between $\frac{1}{4}$–$\frac{3}{4}$ mile (400m-1.2km) long. These alignments remain visible

Aerial view of Avebury, Wiltshire, showing its encircling prehistoric earthworks and stone rows

today. It is presumed that the diversion was made because the route was primarily a civilian one and therefore likely to carry heavy goods traffic. Where routes were essentially for military use they paid less respect to contours.
□ Seven miles (11km) NW of Andover on minor roads. Map ref 2A4.

231. GREAT CHALFIELD
Medieval manor

Church, farm buildings and manor add up to one of the most perfect medieval groups to survive in England. Great Chalfield Manor (NT) was built in about 1470–80, and its mellow but modest cluster of roofs and gables, all gathered round a central great hall, is still redolent of medieval hospitality. The house gently decayed into partial ruin, until lovingly restored at the beginning of this century. The house is usually open on Wed only from mid-Apr to late Sept; tel: NT regional office at Bourton (Dorset) 224 for details.
□ 2½ miles (4km) NE of Bradford-on-Avon off B3109. Map ref 1D4.

232. KENNET AND AVON
Canal/lock 'staircase'

One of the most scenic canals in England. This linked the River Avon with the River Thames at Reading, but it was no match commercially for the Great Western Railway and fell into decay earlier this century. In places the canal has completely dried up with broken-down locks, but over the last 20 years it has gradually been restored to life by painstaking volunteer effort. The most spectacular reclamation currently undertaken is the 'staircase' of 29 locks in a two-mile (3.2km) stretch of the canal west of Devizes, an attractive old market town with some fine houses and churches.

The lock 'staircase' is the longest range of locks in England and lifts the canal a total of 231ft (70m). East of Devizes the canal flows less dramatically through the Vale of Pewsey with every now and again old wharves and canal inns (as at Honey Street west of Pewsey) to provide reminders of a busier past. Popular now with fishermen, but there are also some boat trips; tel: Kennet DC public relations office, Devizes 4911 for details or inquire locally.
□ The 29-lock 'staircase' lies W of Devizes off A361. Map ref 1D4.

233. LACOCK
Village/'Abbey' house

A beautiful village now entirely owned by the NT – a state of affairs which can attract crowds during the summer and weekends (although less so than at nearby Castle Combe) but which safeguards its appearance. There are no intrusive urban features such as TV aerials or yellow traffic lines, for instance. Lacock has many claims to attention and preservation: hardly a building in the village is later than 18th century. The buildings reflect many styles, but blend together with a mellow charm. Particular buildings of note are a 14th century tithe barn, the 15th century half-timbered *Sign of the Angel*, the 14th century Church of St Cyriac, a packhorse bridge and, of course, Lacock Abbey.

This country house, on the edge of the village in meadows running down to the River Avon, is also owned by the NT. It was originally a medieval nun-

Lacock: scarcely a building is later than 18th century

nery but was turned into a house in the 16th century by Sir William Sharrington. He moved in on the first floor only and, apart from pulling down the church, left the ground floor as the nuns had lived in it. This part has scarcely been touched since, and the resulting contrast between the vaulted cloisters and convent rooms down below and the country house up above is quite extraordinary. The country-house part grew and altered over the centuries – a Renaissance tower, a Palladian dining room, a rococo Gothic hall, and final embellishments by W.H. Fox Talbot, who invented photography. The house is open most days from late Mar-Oct, but hours and days of admission can vary; tel: NT regional office at Bourton (Dorset) 224.

□ Three miles (4.8km) S of Chippenham, off A350. Map ref 1D4.

234. MALMESBURY
Market town

This town on the southern edge of the Cotswolds has benefitted from two sources and periods of prosperity. The first was the foundation of a Benedictine Abbey in the 12th century; a fragment of the abbey church remains today and, although partly in ruins, contains some elaborate and outstanding carving. The second period of prosperity came in the 17th and 18th centuries when it became established as a weaving centre. A late medieval octagonal market cross overlooks a small market square and, with its intricate carvings, the 40ft (12m) high cross is regarded as one of the best two such crosses in England – the other being at Chichester.

□ 10 miles (16km) N of Chippenham on A429. Map ref 1D3.

235. OLD SARUM
Abandoned city

This hill-top predecessor of modern Salisbury was first occupied by Iron Age man (who left the outer ramparts); taken over by the Romans as their city, *Sorviodonum*; and rebuilt by the Normans, who constructed the inner earthworks and the first great cathedral. But only the foundations of this cathedral and a Norman castle remain for the site was abandoned during the 13th century in favour of a new location with a better water supply in the Avon valley below. However it was not until the 19th century that Old Sarum ceased to return Members of Parliament to Westminster. The cathedral and castle ruins are open standard DoE hours plus Sun mornings Apr-Sept.

□ Two miles (3.2km) N of Salisbury, off A345. Map ref 1D4.

236. SALISBURY PLAIN
British prairie-land

Britain's prehistoric heartland has many places of interest other than world-famous Stonehenge. Follow the meandering waters of the Avon from Salisbury along narrow lanes among the water meadows and through sleepy villages like the Woodfords, Wilsford and Durnsford. The chalk streams of the Vale of the Wylye (north-west of Salisbury) and the River Bourne (north east of Salisbury) also offer quiet retreats for anglers or picnickers. The ancient Ridgeway offers miles of breezy walking with splendid views across the Vale of Pewsey. Army activity in several areas of Salisbury Plain can mean that access is often restricted, but warning notices indicate danger areas.

□ Salisbury Plain is N of Salisbury with Stonehenge two miles (3.2km) W of Amesbury and Imber eight miles (13km) S of Devizes. Map ref 1D4.

237. SAVERNAKE FOREST
Woodland walks/drives

An ancient forest that, although still large, is only a fraction of its former size. It is not quite as 'natural' as it looks since many fine avenues of beech were planted under the direction of 'Capability' Brown in the 18th century. The finest of these is the Grand Avenue, a three-mile (4.8km) drive through the heart of the forest; it is metalled but not in the best of conditions. Half way along its length is the junction known as Eight Walks where eight routes radiate in strict geometric fashion. Although there is only one statutory footpath through the forest (north from Cadley Church) walkers and horse-riders are in practice allowed general access to the forest. The Forestry Commission has provided a picnic site and nature trail at Postern Hill (off the A346 at the Marlborough end of the forest) but picnicking is also possible in the many glades accessible from the minor roads through the forest.

□ ½ mile (0.8km) SE of Marlborough, between A4 and A346. Map ref 2A4.

238. STEEPLE ASHTON
'Wool' church

The Church of St Mary the Virgin is one of a number of churches, characteristic also of the Cotswolds, which were entirely rebuilt in the 15th century through the generosity of rich clothiers and wool merchants. Spectacular exterior, with quite a regal tower, two big porches and an array of huge pinnacles and gargoyles. The very lofty interior is also sumptuous, with vaulted aisles and a nave roof of silvery oak in vault form, best seen with one's back to the east window.

□ Four miles (6.4km) E of Trowbridge on minor road off A350. Map ref 1D4.

239. STOURHEAD
Landscaped garden

A supremely beautiful example of 18th century landscape gardening with additional planting of exotic trees and shrubs in the following century. The main garden is around a large artificial lake, surrounded by temples, a rustic cottage, grotto, stone bridge and other eye-catching features. Even the little hamlet of Stourton, with its church, is incoporated in the design. The garden (NT) is open throughout the year. The Palladian house around which the garden was developed is open certain afternoons Apr-Oct, including afternoons daily May-Aug. Tel: Bourton (Dorset) 224.

□ In the village of Stourton three miles (4.8km) NW of Mere off B3092. Map ref 1D4.

240. WANSDYKE
Dark Age earthworks

This is the greatest of the English dykes and is believed to have stretched originally for some 50 miles (80km) from east of Marlborough to the Bristol Channel near Portishead. It is probably best preserved where it runs across the Marlborough Downs, roughly parallel with the A4 road two miles (3.2km) to the north. The dyke is a single bank with a ditch on the northern side, so that it was built to keep out invaders from the north. It originates from the early Dark Ages, around 500 AD, and thus pre-dates Offa's Dyke by nearly 300 years. Several tumuli, long barrows and other ancient earthworks are visible along this stretch of the dyke.

□ Off A361 three miles (5km) S of the A361/A4 junction near Avebury or off unclassified roads near the villages of Allington, Alton Barnes and East Kennet. OS map 173 clearly incidates the course of the dyke. Map ref 1D4.

Aerial view of Old Sarum, hill-top ancestor of modern Salisbury

Snow bound summits of Snowdonia; winter and summer, the Snowdonia National Park lures hill walkers and rock climbers from all over the British Isles

Wales

241. BRECON BEACONS
National Park

The nearest national park to London. At Newport the M4 motorway passes within a dozen miles of the southern boundary. The M50 to Ross-on-Wye (then A40 to Abergavenny and Brecon) speeds visitors from the Midlands and North. Some half-dozen south-north roads cut through the park. The A470 climbs 1440ft (443m) at Storey Arms, passing close to the

2906ft (886m) summit of Pen-y-Fan, highest of the Beacons. Storey Arms is one of several fine viewpoints with or near car parks. Others are Black Mountain, Sugar Loaf, Llangorse Common. Pony trekking is popular and most of the hill tops are common land, ideal country for ridge walkers. Offa's Dyke long-distance footpath follows the eastern boundary of this park in Powys. There is a country park at Craig-y-Nos north of Ystradgynlais and national park information centres at Brecon, Abergavenny and Llandovery, plus the excellent Brecon Beacons Mountain Centre near Libanus.

Sightseeing attractions: Brecon Cathedral; fortified manor house of Tretower; Llanthony Priory ruins; Carreg Cennen castle; and Llangorse lake.
□ Map ref 1C3.

242. PEMBROKESHIRE COAST
National Park

The motorway network now extends to Swansea and beyond (M4), then A48 to Carmarthen and A40 to Haverfordwest, from which lesser roads radiate to all points of the Pembrokeshire coast. A difficult park to see by car, since its prime attractions – cliffs, bays, head-

lands, estuaries – can only be fully appreciated on foot. However, there are numerous viewpoints with car parking, such as Newgale Sands and Wooltack Point. The B4329 from Haverfordwest to Cardigan crosses the Preseli Hills which are included in the park, as are the oakwood shores of the Cleddau estuary (best explored by boat). There are park information centres in Dyfed at Haverfordwest, Fishguard, Tenby, St David's, Pembroke, Milford Haven and Kilgetty. Also the information centre and countryside unit at Broad Haven, which organises talks and summer

walks with wildlife themes; tel: Broad Haven 412. Most of the park is private farmland with no public right of access, but the magnificent Pembrokeshire Coast long-distance footpath runs the entire length of the park from Amroth to St Dogmaels, 168 miles (269km).
☐ Map ref 1A3.

243. SNOWDONIA
National Park

To give an idea of Snowdonia's accessibility by road, Betws-y-Coed is 223 miles (357km) from London, 107 miles (171km) from Birmingham, 88 miles (141km) from Manchester. Main roads encircle all major upland areas and there are spectacular, though often crowded, scenic routes through the passes of Nant Ffrancon, Llanberis and Aberglaslyn, as well as gentler drives such as along the beautiful Mawddach estuary. Many viewpoints have car parks. A precipice-hugging rack and pinion railway runs from Llanberis to the top of Snowdon. For those who prefer climbing the hard way, the mountains of Snowdonia provide some of the most challenging rock faces in the British Isles. Not only on Snowdon itself – at 3560ft (1085m) the highest peak in Wales – but a host of other summits: Tryfan, Cnicht, Crib Goch, the Carneddau, the Glyders and more. The Central Council of Physical Recreation's Plas y Brenin mountaineering centre is at Capel Curig. In the southern half of the park there are several different routes to the 2927ft (892m) summit of Cader Idris. Bala, Betws-y-Coed, Llanberis, Capel Curig and Dolgellau are all favourite walking centres. Pony-trekking and angling are also popular. There are park information centres at Blaenau Ffestiniog, Aberdovey, Bala, Dolgellau, Harlech, Llanberis and Llanwrst.
☐ Map ref 3D6.

244. ANGLESEY
Area of Outstanding Natural Beauty

Apart from a few gaps – one of which is filled by the nuclear power station at Wylfa Head – this comprises the whole of the island's rich coastline of cliffs, rock stacks, dunes, shingle ridges, salt marsh, coves and gleaming sands. There are plenty of beaches, with safe bathing and sheltered spots for picnics, and the island, which forms part of the county of Gwynedd, is a paradise for bird-watchers with seabirds, waders and wildfowl much in evidence. The dunes of Newborough are a national nature reserve, and there are other bird sanctuaries at Cemlyn Bay (visitors may view from the road) and Puffin Island, near Penmon. Total area: 134 sq miles.
☐ Map ref 3C6.

245. GOWER PENINSULA
Area of Outstanding Natural Beauty

An unspoilt peninsula in West Glamorgan between Swansea and the Loughor estuary with beautiful bays and limestone cliffs on the south coast, culminating in the distinctive saurian profile of Worm's Head. There are cliff walks to Langland and Caswell Bays plus caves to explore. The north coast

has vast salt-marshes, cockle beds and tidal sands alive with oyster-catchers and other wading birds, and a National Nature Reserve, Whitford Burrows. Total area: 118 sq miles.
☐ Map ref 1B3.

246. LLYN
Area of Outstanding Natural Beauty

The Land's End of North Wales. A rugged peninsula in Gwynedd, largely treeless, its small green fields quartered by furzy hedgerows and dominated by the bare triple summits of Yr Eifl, 1850ft (500m). The peninsula is bounded by a succession of cliffs, headlands, coves, bays and sandy beaches, including the 'Whistling Sands' of Porth-oer. Nearly all the north coast lies within the AONB, and the south coast as far east as Llanbedrog, together with the offshore islands of Bardsey and St Tudwal's. Total area: 97 sq miles.
☐ Map ref 1A1/3C6.

Anglesey

Part of the county of Gwynedd. Anglesey is separated from the mainland by the Menai Strait. The island's coastline is an AONB while inland there are many fine prehistoric sites. Beaumaris has a fine medieval castle overlooking the Menai Strait which is crossed by bridges near Bangor. North Wales Tourism Council: Colwyn Bay 56881.

247. ABERFFRAW
Sand dunes/history

This quiet hamlet stands on the shallow tidal estuary of the River Ffraw which has an enormous warren of dunes at its mouth and a stark, single-arched bridge spanning the river. For over 400 years in the Dark Ages Aberffraw was the capital of North Wales but its buildings betray no clue to past glory or importance. One mile (1.6km) west of the village is a quiet rocky beach where you will find cowrie shells, curlews and the church of St Cwyfan on an islet in the bay. At low tide you can walk out to the church which was restored in 1893 on 7th century foundations.
☐ 12 miles (19km) W of Menai Bridge on A4080. Map ref 3C6.

Some common Welsh place-names and their English meanings

Modern form	Meaning
Aber	River mouth
Afon	River
Bettws	Chapel
Cwm	Corrie
Fach	Little
Hafod	Summer dwelling
Hendre	Winter dwelling
Llan	Church
Llyn	Lake
Nant	Valley

248. BLACK POINT
Headland/monastic remains

On this most easterly peninsula of Anglesey – curiously named since it is composed of greyish Carboniferous limestone – are the remains of Penmon Priory (AM), a 13th century Augustinian monastery. In addition to the monastic buildings themselves there is a gigantic stone dovecote dating from about 1600 and a Dark Age carved cross in the Deer Park. From Black Point, with its lighthouse and warning bell, there are fine views across the sweep of Lafan Sands and Conwy Bay towards Snowdonia. Half a mile (0.8km) off the shore is Puffin Island.
☐ Four miles (6.4km) NE of Beaumaris via B5109. Map ref 3C6.

249. BRYN CELLI DDU
Prehistoric tomb

This late Neolithic chambered tomb (AM) is one of the most impressive in the British Isles and certainly the best preserved in Wales. It dates from about 1600 BC and was raised over the relics of an earlier henge or circular embanked monument. The giant stones that form the burial chamber are covered by a grassy mound that is only a fraction of its former size. Inside the burial chamber is an upstanding monolith that rises almost to the roof. The chamber can be visited and is normally unlocked during standard DoE hours; if not, the key is available during those hours from the nearby farmhouse. Grid ref SH 508702.
☐ One mile (1.6km) E of Llanddaniel Fab church off a minor road between this church and the A4080. The tomb is 800 yards (700m) down a signposted lane that also leads to a farm; cars have to be left on the road. Map ref 3C6.

250. CHURCH BAY
Pebbles/islands

This remote sand and rock beach, sheltered by 100ft (30m) cliffs, is an excellent place to look for shells and pebbles. There is a footpath running along the cliffs to Carmel Head, a windswept headland covered with gorse and the occasional stunted pine. From here you can see The Skerries: a cluster of islets and reefs formed by a low tract of land which became submerged. Boats can sometimes also be hired from Holyhead or Cemaes Bay to see seals and sea birds which live on and around The Skerries.
☐ Five miles (8km) SW of Cemaes Bay, W off A5025 at Llanrhyddlad or Llanfaethlu. Map ref 3C5.

251. DIN LLIGWY
Ancient village

A thick enclosing wall here encloses substantial foundations of circular and rectangular stone houses to form one of the most impressive sites of early settlement in the British Isles (grid ref SH 497861). Some of the walls are still 6ft (1.8m) high. The fortified village, overlooking sandy Lligwy Bay, was occupied by native Britons during Roman times, certainly as late as the 4th century. Short walks from Din Lligwy are Capel Lligwy, a 12th-16th century chapel and Lligwy Cromlech, a Neolithic and Bronze Age tomb

topped by an enormous capstone weighing some 28 tons.
☐ ¾ mile (1.2km) N of Llanallgo along a minor road to Lligwy; Din Lligwy is a 500-yard (450m) signposted walk off this minor road. Map ref 3C5.

252. HOLYHEAD MOUNTAIN
Viewpoint/wildlife

Although only 720ft (222m) high this is one of the best viewpoints in Wales, embracing Snowdonia, the Lake District, Isle of Man, the mountains of Mourne and Wicklow in Ireland and Snowdonia. There are several paths to the summit. One starts from the road leading to South Stack Lighthouse. It is signposted to Hut Circles (AM), the remains of an Iron Age settlement which was occupied until the 3rd or 4th centuries AD. Further up the path is Caer y Twr, an Iron Age hill fort.

The South Stack headland forms part of an RSPB reserve which is not only prodigal in its birds and flowers, but in the beauty and variety of its surroundings. Access to the reserve is via public footpaths. Further information from resident summer RSPB warden or RSPB Wales Office, 18 High Street, Newtown, Powys. A leaflet for a nature trail along South Stack Steps is available locally or from NW Wales Naturalists' Trust, 154 High Street, Bangor, Gwynedd.
☐ W of Holyhead. Map ref 3B6.

253. NEWBOROUGH WARREN
Sand dunes/forest

A well-surfaced road through miles of coniferous trees leads to a sheltered car park and picnic spot behind the sandy shore of Llanddwyn Bay. To the west is the 'island' of Llanddwyn with its lighthouse and ruined 15th century church perched on an outcrop of rocks which are among the oldest in Wales. Eastwards is the miniature 'Sahara' of Newborough Warren with five sq miles (1295 hectares) of sand dunes, some rising to over 100ft (31m), now largely covered by conifers. The dunes are a national nature reserve and there is an information point and exhibition at the car park. This is also the starting point for a mile-long (1.6km) trail path through dunes to a medieval house exposed by blown sand.
☐ SW of Newborough nine miles (14km) SW of Menai Bridge on A4080. Map ref 3C6.

254. PARYS MOUNTAIN
Industrial landscape

In the 18th century it was the biggest copper mine in the world; in the 20th century it is an almost lunar landscape which, on a fine day, glistens with orange, brown and reddish hues. It is a copper mountain still, although the old workings scoured gigantic holes out of the mountain such as the 'Great Pit' on the south-western slopes (see overleaf). The feeling of devastation is intensified by the crumbling remains of old engine houses; the remnants of 'settling pits' where copper was extracted by precipitation from the metal-bearing waters draining the workings; disused mine shafts; and the stump of an old windmill on the mountain's 600ft (185m) crest. The massive quays and jetties of nearby Amlwch Port are another clue

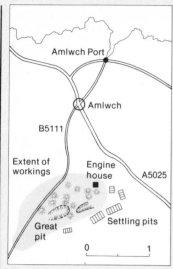

Extent of the Old Parys mountain copper mine workings near Amlwch, Anglesey

to the area's once equally massive commercial importance. NB: the old mountain workings should be explored with care and are not recommended for families with young children.
□ Two miles (3.2km) S of Amlwch off B5111. Map ref 3C5.

Clwyd

Largely mountainous county with holiday resorts such as Rhyl and Colwyn Bay in the north. Its many castles include Chirk, Denbigh, Ewloe, Flint, Hawarden and Ruthin. Rivers include Dee as well as the Clwyd. English architectural influence in east around Wrexham and Chester. North Wales Tourism Council: Colwyn Bay 56881.

255. BANGOR-IS-Y-COED
River meanders/angling

This ancient crossing point of the River Dee is a tiny piece of Wales lying on the English side of the river. Stand on its 14th century red sandstone bridge and watch the salmon fishermen at work in the gliding waters – fishing permits available in the village. Attractive walks along the meandering Dee.
□ Four miles (6.4km) SE of Wrexham on A525. Map ref 3D6.

256. CLOCAENOG FOREST
Walks/picnics

Bod Petrual visitor centre is a converted keeper's cottage with an exhibition presenting the forest in its ecological and historical setting. Near the visitor centre – open summer only – is a picnic area set among pine trees and beside a lake. The picnic area is the starting point for a series of waymarked walks from just ¼ mile to 2¾ miles (400m to 2.8km).
□ Seven miles (11km) SW of Ruthin off B5105 at Pont Petryal. Map ref 3D6.

257. CORWEN
Market town/inn

The Owain Glyndwr Hotel stands in the square of this small market town near the confluence of the Alwen and Dee. It was originally a monastery in the grounds of the church and later became a coaching inn on the route to

Holyhead. In 1789 an extension was built to house the first public Welsh Eisteddfod. North-east, on a hill overlooking Corwen is the town's predecessor: Caer Drewyn, an Iron Age hill fort, which still has some remains of its stone walls and houses (grid ref SH 088443). The modern Corwen caters for tourists – notably with fine angling in the Dee – but is also a centre for farmers. 'Town trail' leaflet.
□ 10 miles (16km) W of Llangollen on A5. Map ref 3D6.

258. ERDDIG
Country house/country park

A house cleverly shown by the National Trust as much from the servants' point of view as the masters'. The public enter by the back door, by way of the blacksmith's and joiner's workshops, stable yard, laundry, kitchen, servants' hall and butler's pantry. All retain many of their original contents and fittings, and the servants' hall and corridor are lined with portraits and photographs of generations of servants, commissioned by the Yorkes, their amiable but eccentric employers. The main house is remarkable less for its architecture than for its contents, which includes splendid furniture and mirrors commissioned for Erddig in the early 18th century. In the grounds is a country park with picnic sites, an industrial trail and an agricultural museum. Open daily (except Mon other than Bank Holidays) Apr-Oct. For information about the house, tel. NT office at Betwys-y-Coed 312.
□ One mile (1.6km) S of Wrexham off A483. Map ref 3D6.

259. GRESFORD
Stately parish church

It has to be admitted that what is acclaimed by architectural connoisseurs as the best parish church in Wales belongs both in style and in spirit to nearby Cheshire. Wholly Perpendicular, and of buff-coloured sandstone throughout. Stately west tower, a good deal of old glass, and original woodwork in fine profusion: stalls with misericords, screen with restored loft, and cambered tie-beam roofs everywhere, with angels and many carved bosses. A delight. (If locked, ask for the key at the vicarage.)
□ Three miles (4.8km) N of Wrexham off A483. Map ref 3D6.

260. LLANGOLLEN
Natural and man-made landscapes

This attractive town is often crowded with visitors and never more so than for the International Musical Eisteddfod. It stands on the Dee (which is crossed by a 14th century bridge) at the heart of some remarkable scenery where the works of man have complemented the natural beauty of the Dee Valley. A tourist information centre near the bridge will provide information about the features of the town.
River Dee. Some of Britain's finest incised meanders can be found near Llangollen. They were formed when the river continued to cut down its bed as the surrounding mountains were uplifted by crustal forces. The depths of the incisions can be appreciated from

viewpoints such as the Horseshoe Pass and Castell Dinas Brân (see below). In two places the river has broken through the neck of its meander to leave its former course high and dry. One such abandoned meander is south-east of Llangollen along the valley now followed by the minor road to Tan-y-Graig; the other is north of the town at Pentrefelin. There are attractive river (and canalside) walks.
Canal. Telford's Shropshire Union Canal flows into the town – see also under Pontcysyllte – and there is now a canal exhibition centre at the town's wharf. Open Easter-Sept, tel: Llangollen 860702. Also canal cruises.
Castell Dinas Brân. On a hill towering over the town from the northern banks of the Dee is the Hill of Brân, some 900ft (274m) high, and crowned by the ruins of a castle. This was a stronghold of Welsh princes before the English conquest making it one of the few Iron Age hill forts to have been occupied in medieval times. A steep climb but spectacular views over the Vale of Llangollen and the splendid white escarpment of Eglwyseg Mountain with its great apron of screes. See also under World's End, no. 265.
Valle Crucis Abbey. Founded in the late 12th century. These ruins to the north of Llangollen reflect an unusual mixture of traditional Cistercian styles with native Welsh craft tradition. The effect is diminished by some restoration work and an unsightly adjacent caravan site, but still worth seeing.
Eliseg's Pillar. Erected in the 9th century this is one of the most elaborate inscribed records of its kind surviving from pre-Norman Britain. It stands in a field close to the abbey ruins.
□ 10 miles (16km) SW of Wrexham on A5, A539 and A542. Map ref 3D6.

261. LLANRHAIADR
Church/stained glass

A charming church, not well known but full of interest. Excellent woodwork, including north porch and hammer-beam roof with angels. But the great treasure is the exceptionally well preserved Jesse window executed in 1533, with perhaps the most enjoyable late-Gothic stained glass in Britain – Fairford and King's College Cambridge not excepted. The rich colours are, principally, ruby, clear blue, green, yellow and white.
□ 2½ miles (4km) SE of Denbigh on A525. Map ref 3D6.

262. MOEL FAMAU
Country park

A vast area – 2374 acres (961 hectares) – of open moorland in the Clwydian Hills with a reservoir, a stretch of Offa's Dyke and a hill fort. Views and walks.
□ Six miles (9.6km) W of Mold. Map ref 3D6.

263. PONTCYSYLLTE
AQUEDUCT
Canal architecture/river valley

A masterpiece, even by Thomas Telford's standards. The engineering skill which carries the Llangollen arm of the Shropshire Union Canal over the River Dee 127ft (39m) below is complemented by its graceful execution and beautiful setting. It can be seen

from the A5 approaching Llangollen but perhaps better still from the small bridge carrying road traffic over the Dee between Froncysyllte and Trefor. To see a barge crossing the aqueduct high above you – or, indeed, to cross the 1007ft (301m) long aqueduct by boat – is an extraordinary sensation. Walkers with heads for heights can join the towpath from Trefor. See under Llangollen for more about the canal.
□ 4½ miles (7.2km) E of Llangollen off A5 or A539. Map ref 3D6.

264. RUTHIN
Half-timbered market town

There are more important market centres in North Wales – Denbigh and Mold, for instance – but Ruthin is architecturally the most interesting market town in the area. It grew around a castle (now a hotel) but it is the lesser buildings which now give Ruthin most of its appeal. Many are outstanding examples of half-timbering and, dating from the 15th-17th centuries, reflect the town's prosperity in the wool trade. The oldest buildings are mostly grouped around the market square which, set on top of a hill, still forms the heart of the town. 'Town trail' leaflet available.
□ Seven miles (11km) Se of Denbigh at junction of A525 and A494. Map ref 3D6.

265. WORLD'S END
Walk/valley

This is the exotic name given to the head of the steep and beautiful wooded valley of the River Eglwyseg north of Llangollen. A minor road leads there off A542 but it is best appreciated on foot. A section of the long-distance Offa's Dyke Path follows the valley and can be used as part of an 11-mile (17.6km) walk based at Llangollen. Follow the waymarked Offa's Dyke Path north of Llangollen, past Castell Dinas Brân under towering Eglwyseg Rocks to World's End – look out for a Tudor manor house in the valley. Return along the escarpment's crest to Pontcysyllte Aqueduct and back to Llangollen along the canal towpath. There is also a one-mile (1.6km) nature trail at World's End during the summer – details from North Wales Naturalists' Trust, tel: Bangor 51541, or inquire in Llangollen tourist information centre. OS map 117 details the paths in this area and see also under Llangollen and Pontcysyllte.
□ Five miles (8km) N of Llangollen. Map ref 3D6.

Dyfed

The largest Welsh county stretching from Mid Wales to the Pembrokeshire Coast National Park in the south-west. Tourist centres include Aberystwyth, Cardigan, Carmarthen, Haverfordwest, Pembroke, St David's, Tenby. Many castles. Mid Wales Tourism Council and South Wales Tourism Councils each cover parts of Dyfed.

266. ABERAERON
Regency-style village/harbour

Unusually for a Welsh village, this was laid out and built to a set plan – in the early 19th century. It not only reflects the prevailing Regency architecture of that time but does so with such style that it has been suggested that John Nash himself participated in their design. Certainly he was living in the area at the time and certainly the small two-storey houses in the squares and terraces around the harbour are like miniature versions of the Nash houses in London and elsewhere. The harbour is now almost totally devoted to yachting.

☐ 12 miles (19km) NW of Lampeter on A482 and A487. Map ref 1B2.

267. BORTH
Sand dunes/nature trails

Borth straggles for two miles (3.2km) along a sandy beach backed by a high bank of pebbles, ending in a spit of sand dunes at the mouth of the River Dovey. At low tide evidence of a submerged forest can be seen. Behind the village, which attracts many summer visitors, is Borth Bog (Cors Fochno). This contains many rare plants and can be dangerous to walkers who stray off the paths. The NCC Ynyslas Nature Trail runs through the sand dunes to the north which is part of the NCC Nature Reserve covering nearly 4000 acres (1619 hectares) of sandbanks and saltings in the estuary. These are important feeding grounds for thousands of waders, mallard and other wildfowl.

☐ Six miles (9.6km) N of Aberystwyth on B4572. Map ref 1B2.

268. BOSHERSTON
Lakes/walks

Sand dunes building up at nearby Broad Haven Bay cut off three streams from the sea to form the Bosherston Pools or Lakes: nearly three miles (4.8km) of water famed for their water-lilies (best seen in June) and their coarse fishing. The pools also attract a wide variety of birds including heron and kingfisher while east of the bay is a good example of a raised beach.

The village can also be the starting-point of a marvellous 10-mile (16km) walk along part of the long-distance Pembrokeshire Coastal Path. Head south to St Govan's Head – detouring to see the medieval cliff-side chapel (see p 269 under St Govan) and the Huntsman's Leap, 130ft (40m) above the sea. Then follow the coast path westwards via Elegug Stacks to the rock arch known as the Green Bridge of Wales. Return to Bosherston inland via Merrion and using the B4319 to fill the gap in the otherwise waymarked circuit. OS map 158 details the paths on this walk. NB: this walk is *not* possible when firing is taking place on the Castlemartin tank range. Check to see if red flags are flying, ask locally or tel: Castlemartin 321.

☐ Four miles (6.4km) S of Pembroke. Map ref 1A3.

269. BRECHFA FOREST
Walk/picnics

A 1¾ mile (2.8km) waymarked forest walk through an attractive wooded valley begins at a picnic area set among red oaks beside a stream on the east side of the village of Abergorlech.

☐ 16 Miles (26km) NE of Carmarthen on B4310. Map ref 1B3.

270. BROAD HAVEN
Cliffs/beach

Not the Broad Haven close to Bosherston (above) but a village and an extensive sandy beach backed by cliffs with evidence of the coal measures of the Pembrokeshire beds to be seen in the spectacular folding of the rocks. Both Broad Haven and neighbouring Little Haven were once coal mining centres. In the large car park is the Countryside Unit of the Pembrokeshire Coast National Park – tel: Broad Haven 412 – a focal point for a wide range of information on walks, excursions and lectures.

☐ Six miles (9.6km) W of Haverfordwest on B4347. Map ref 1A3.

271. CALDY ISLAND
Island/monastery

The limestone hill of Caldy was once part of the Coedrath Forest but the island, which is 1½ miles (2.4km) long, was severed from the mainland by the rising sea level. Celtic monks founded a monastery here as early as the 6th century. The Normans handed the island over to the Benedictines in the 12th century. Various ownerships followed the Dissolution of the Monasteries before it was taken over in 1929 by an order of Cistercian monks who farm the island today. The monks sell clotted cream and Caldy perfume from the scent of local flowers to visitors but allow only men in the Monastery. Non-sexist attractions on the island include its churches, the old Priory and the views from near the clifftop lighthouse (not open to the public). Seals and many sea birds have colonies on the island but are best seen by a boat trip around the island.

☐ About 20 minutes by boat from Tenby harbour. Frequent summer service. Map ref 1A3.

272. CAREW
Castle/tidal mill

This hamlet has two buildings of an outstanding interest: a castle dating from the 13th century and the last remaining tidal mill in Wales. There is a fine 11th century cross at the castle entrance but otherwise it is the setting as much as the building that gives Carew Castle much of its appeal. This same riverside setting increases the attraction of the Carew French Mill as it is known. The present building is 19th century but there has been a mill on this site since Elizabethan times. It is open daily Apr-Sept (but only afternoons on Sun) and there is a picnic site by the mill pond.

☐ Four miles (6.4km) E of Pembroke on A4075. Castle and mill on the S bank of the Carew River. Map ref 1A3.

273. CARREG CENNEN
Castle/views

In spite of its apparent isolation Carreg Cennen Castle was once of great strategic importance during the Norman advance into south-west Wales. The site is magnificent – there has been a castle here long before the present late 13th or early 14th century building – with a precipitous drop on one side down to the valley floor and overlooking the Black Mountain. It was largely demolished in the 15th century but its situation is so dramatic that the ruins retain a great romantic appeal that is enhanced by its links with caves in the rock beneath. Open standard DoE hours plus Sun morning, Apr-Sept.

☐ 4½ miles (7km) SE of Llandeilo. Map ref 1B3..

274. CEMAES HEAD
Cliff walks/estuary

Cemaes Head rises to 550ft (167m) with spectacular folding in the cliffs around the headland. It is the first (or last) highlight for walkers on the Pembrokeshire Coast long-distance path which has its northern terminus at nearby St Dogmael's. The headland can only be reached by foot along the clifftop path. Just south of the headland is an almost dry valley called Pwll Granant which runs into the Teifi estuary. This is an overflow valley formed by melt waters in the Ice Age. The Teifi estuary itself is a drowned valley almost closed by a sandbar. At St Dogmael's the ruins of a 12th century abbey (AM) can be seen in the grounds of the vicarage.

☐ Three miles (4.8km) NW of St Dogmael's via B4546 and paths. Map ref 1A2.

275. DALE PENINSULA
Walks/sailing

The peninsula is almost an island, separated from the mainland by a deep valley. The village of Dale itself has a sheltered muddy sand and shingle beach and is a popular sailing centre. The village is said to be the sunniest place in Wales and is noted for its early crops. It is a six-mile (9.6km) walk around the peninsula on part of the Pembrokeshire Coast Path; leaflets available locally, national park offices or the Countryside Unit at Broad Haven. The *Griffin Inn* at Dale is the starting point for the walk which passes Mill Bay, where Henry Tudor landed in 1485 to claim the English crown; an Iron Age promontory fort at Great Castle Head; Dale Point; St Anne's lighthouse (open to the public), tel: Dale 314; and magnificent views over the Milford Haven, a noted area for bird-watching.

☐ 12 miles (19km) SW of Haverfordwest on B4327. Map ref 1A3.

276. DINAS FOREST
Nature trail/birds

A beautiful oakwood valley with 1½ mile (2.4km) public nature trail managed by the RSPB. Plentiful woodland birds and flowers here, including buzzards, ravens, redstarts and pied flycatchers. A chance, too, of seeing the rare red kite. The trail starts from the warden's hut at Troedrhiwgelynen, Rhandirmwyn. A leaflet is available from RSPB Reserves Dept, tel: Sandy 80551.

☐ W of Rhandirmwyn about 11 miles (18km) N of Llandovery off minor road to Ystradffin. Map ref 1B2.

277. DINAS ISLAND
Wildlife/walks

Not an island but a small promontory on the North Pembrokeshire coast, Dinas offers some beautiful and exciting walks. It is about three miles (4.8km) right round the 'island' but shorter walks of just over a mile (1.6km) from Pwllgwaelod on the west or Cwm-yr-Eglwys to Dinas Point. Dolphins and porpoises may sometimes be seen from the point and there are always plenty of birds and flowers along the cliffs. Very good leaflet produced by the West Wales Naturalists' Trust, tel: Haverfordwest 5462.

☐ Four miles (6.4km) E of Fishguard off A487. Map ref 1A2.

278. DOLAUCOTHI
Roman gold mines/trails

Here, in the wooded Cothi valley, is one of the most remarkable yet least known survivals of Roman Britain: the Roman gold mines of Dolaucothi. The evidence of gold workings during the 19th and early 20th centuries are more evident, but two short waymarked trails explore surprisingly extensive remains of Roman mining. Perhaps the most interesting feature of all is the Roman aqueduct which can still be seen, as a channel running for seven miles (11km) along the valley to collecting basins on the hill slopes above the mine.

Here be treasure: Dolaucothi, Dyfed, where the Romans mined for gold

Dylan Thomas, doyen of Welsh poets. Laugharne in Dyfed was his home

An exhibition of the Roman mines can be seen in the museum at Abergwili, near Carmarthen, where a leaflet is also available. There is a picnic site close to the mines at Pumsaint and waymarked trails of one mile (1.6km) and ½ mile (0.8km) both start at Ogofau Lodge on the Cwrt y Cadno road. Visitors, especially those with young children are advised to stick to the waymarked paths.
□ Eight miles (13km) SE of Lampeter off A482 at Pumsaint. Map ref 1B3.

279. DRE-FACH FELINDRE
Wool museum/trail

This area was one of the most important centres of the Welsh woollen industry from 1860-1930. The Museum of the Woollen Industry was established in part of a working mill to show details of this rural trade with exhibitions of tools and machinery used in carding, spinning, weaving and finishing cloth. Open Mon-Sat Apr-Sept; Tel: Felindre 370453. A circular 'factory trail' showing other aspects of the woollen industry can be undertaken from here; details from the museum or Wales Tourist Board booklet, *A Glimpse of the Past*.
□ Four miles (6.4km) E of Newcastle Emlyn off A484. Map ref 1B3.

280. DYLAN THOMAS'S WALES
Laugharne village

He was born in Swansea in 1914 and lived there longer than anywhere else. But he is most identified with Laugharne in Dyfed where he lived for four years until his death in 1953 and where he is buried. Laugharne is an attractive village with a castle, quaint cottages and Georgian houses. Much of the atmosphere of the village is apparent in his greatest work, *Under Milk Wood*, even though the setting for the play – a 'cliff-perched town at the far end of Wales' – is more likely to have been New Quay on Cardigan Bay. Thomas is buried in the churchyard and his home, The Boathouse, is usually open daily Easter-Oct, but check; tel: Laugharne 420.
□ 12 miles (19km) SW of Carmarthen on A4066. Map ref 1A3.

281. HAFOD
Upland landscaping/trails

The mansion of Thomas Johnes is no more, but the idealism which surrounded his pioneering upland improvement scheme (see page 51) lives on in the landscape. The estate, now run by the Forestry Commission, still betrays features of his great experiment like the laid-out terraces, exotic trees and above all the estate church. There is also an arch erected over the road by Johnes as his tribute to the Golden Jubilee of George III. By the arch there is now an FC picnic place which is also the starting point for three forest trails between ½-1½ miles (0.8-2.4km) long. Leaflet available.
□ Two miles (3.2km) SE of Devil's Bridge on B4574 to Cwmystwyth. Map ref 1B2.

282. KIDWELLY
Castle/dunes/forest

Kidwelly stands at the confluence of Gwendraeth Fawr and Gwendraeth Fach. The estuary is crossed by a fine 14th century bridge but otherwise only the layout of the town's streets indicates its medieval origins. It grew up around the castle which still dominates the town, commanding marvellous views over the river estuary. The towers and gatehouse of the castle (AM) are particularly well-preserved; it is open standard DoE hours, plus Sun mornings Apr-Sept. South-west of the town is Pembrey Forest, a five mile (8km) expanse of sand backed by dunes and a pine forest. Good fishing, swimming and surfing are possible away from the estuaries; forest trails begin from a picnic place where the A484 crosses the railway near Pembrey.
□ Eight miles S of Carmarthen on A484. Map ref 1B3.

283. LLANGRANNOG
Village/cliffs

This tiny and picturesque village, nestling in a narrow coastal valley is sometimes called the Polperro of Wales. Its houses straggle down to a narrow sandy beach which is dominated by a bizarre 50ft (15m) sea stack. The cliffs rise steeply on either side and provide miles of coastal walks: northwards to the imposing 540ft (164m) headland of Ynys Lochtyn (NT) with two tiny sandy coves and prehistoric earthworks, or southwards to the sandy beaches of Penbryn.
□ 11 miles (18km) NE of Cardigan on B4334 or B4321 off A487. Map ref 1A2.

284. LLYS-Y-FRAN
Country park/boating

The Llys-y-fran Reservoir in a wooded valley in the foothills of the Preseli Mountains now forms a country park with scope for fishing, boating, a nature trail and picnicking. The park is run by Dyfed County Council which also operates another but much smaller country park called Scolton Manor, five miles (8km) NE of Haverfordwest.
□ 7½ miles (12km) NE of Haverfordwest off B4329. Map ref 1A3.

285. MANORBIER CASTLE
Norman castle/coast

A romantic moated Norman castle standing on the north slope of a valley, about ½ mile (0.8km) from the shore. The well-preserved remains give a good idea of life at the castle with a dovecote, fishpond, mill, park and orchard. Open Easter, Whitsun-Sept; tel: Manorbier 394. Below the castle, which is privately-owned, the valley falls into a small sand and shingle bay cut along a fault in the old red sandstone cliffs. Some of the cliffs have nearly vertical strata giving a striped effect when the different coloured beds are exposed. The cliffs (NT) can be approached via the A4139. On Priest's Nose, the headland on the east of Manorbier Bay is The King's Quoit, a ruined cromlech or burial chamber.
□ 5½ miles (9km) W of Tenby off B4585. Map ref 1A3.

286. MWNT
Sandy cove/cliffs

A remote cove with a delightful sandy beach and surrounded by steep shale cliffs. At the foot of the conical hill, rising 250ft (75m) to the north, is an ancient whitewashed church, one of the oldest in Wales. There are old lime kilns near the beach. Car parking at top of cliffs with a steep path down to the beach. NT.
□ Four miles (6.4km) N of Cardigan by minor road off A487. Map ref 1A2.

287. PLWMP
Rare farm animals

The West Wales Farm Park consists of some 60 acres (24 hectares) of parkland housing a large collection of rare and indigenous farm animals. Species of cattle alone include Belted Welsh, White Park and Gloucester. Open daily mid May-Sept, tel: Rhydlewis 317.
□ On A486 five miles (8km) S of New Quay. Map ref 1B2.

288. PRESELI HILLS
Prehistoric remains

Stone rocks from these hills were used at Stonehenge and started an as yet unresolved argument as to whether they were taken there by ice or by man. The hills bear their own traces of prehistoric man, notably the Gors Fawr stone circle (grid ref SN 135294 off A478) and the exposed stones of a former burial chamber known as Pentre Ifan cromlech (grid ref SH 099370 off A487).
A six-mile (9.6km) trail along a prehistoric routeway through the hills has been devised by the Pembrokeshire Coast National Park. It starts from Croesfihangel and passes many prehistoric remains as well as the site believed to have been used to quarry the materials for Stonehenge; leaflets available from national park offices.
□ The hills are a long range running roughly east-west to the south of Fishguard and Pembroke and crossed by the A478, B4329 and B4313. Map ref 1A3.

289. RHEIDOL FOREST
Trails/mountains

The Bwlch Nant-yr-Arian Forest Visitor Centre in sheltered heathery glades on western edge of Cambrian Mountains has an exhibition which interprets local landscape. Also here is a picnic area and the start of a trail which follows old lead mine paths along rim of the valley, crosses an open ridge and returns through larch and spruce woodlands by a small lake. Distance: 1½ miles (2.4km). Nearby, too, is the old Ponterwyd Silver Mine, open daily Easter-Oct.
□ 10 miles (16km) E of Aberystwyth on A44. Map ref 1B2.

290. ST DAVID'S
Cathedral city/cliffs/beaches

Britain's smallest cathedral city offers much to appeal to many different interests in the city itself and in the surrounding countryside of this most south-westerly tip of Wales. Among these attractions:
St David's. A medieval cathedral built on a site chosen by the patron saint of Wales in the 6th century. Next to it are the imposing ruins of the Bishop's Palace, open standard DoE hours plus Sun mornings Apr-Sept.
Beaches. Many small coves are tucked between the cliffs but the biggest beach is Whitesand Bay, a magnificent stretch of sandy beach enclosed by dramatic cliffs. Popular with fam-

ilies and also for surfing. Also known as Porth-mawr. Overlooked by summit and viewpoint of Carnllidi.

Cliffs. The waymarked long-distance footpath follows the clifftops. It can be used for circular all-day walks based on St David's but even short stretches are highly rewarding. Magnificent views with many sea birds to be seen on the islands and rocks offshore. A promontory fort at St David's Head is among several prehistoric sites. OS map 157 covers the area.

□ 13 miles (21km) NW of Haverfordwest on A487. Map ref 1A3.

291. ST GOVAN'S CHAPEL
Cliff-face chapel

This tiny stone-built chapel lies on the cliff face, in a cleft of the rocks, of the Castlemartin peninsula south of Pembroke. The building as it exists today is remarkable enough, given its position just above the high tide mark and its 13th century construction. But it also has a rude stone altar and rock-cut cell which tradition assigns to the 5th century saint of its name. Certainly the site and the well below the chapel are typical of early Celtic religious foundations. A footpath leads down to the chapel by 52 stone steps from the clifftop. NB: no access when the Castlemartin firing range is being used.

□ Five miles (8km) S of Pembroke off B4319 via Bosherston. Map ref 1A3.

292. SKOMER ISLANDS
Bird-watching/views

These are a group of islands just off the mainland between Milford Haven and St Bride's Bay. The name of Skomer is also given to the largest of the islands, a grey mass of igneous rock which is a national nature reserve with one of the finest seabird colonies in north-west Europe. There are fulmars, shags, kittiwakes, puffins, guillemots, gulls and Manx shearwaters. Grey seals can also be seen. Daily boat trips from Whitsun-Sept from Martin's Haven, near Marloes. A landing fee is payable to the warden. There are no visitor facilities on the island other than a 2¼ mile (3.6km) nature trail; a booklet published by the West Wales Naturalists' Trust is available from Lockley Lodge Information Centre at Martin's Haven, tel: Dale 234. Also worth visiting on the island is an Iron Age promontory fort.

Skókholm is an important bird observatory and has a lighthouse but it is not open to the public. Nor is there access to Grassholm, the smallest and most distant of the islands. In contrast Gateholm is so close to the mainland that it can be reached on foot at low tide from Marloes Sands – the starting point of another nature trail, details of which are available locally.

□ Martin's Haven is 15 miles (24km) SW of Haverfordwest via B4327. Map ref 1A3.

293. TREGARON
Drove roads/wildlife

Every other Tuesday cattle and sheep fill the market place and streets of this little town beneath the Cambrian mountains. Tregaron remains an important market town, although its fortunes have suffered along with those of the hill farmers whom it serves. It's past importance is illustrated by the number of old drover's roads that led through here over the mountains to England – see under Llanwrtyd Wells, Powys, for a motoring tour of some of these roads.

But some former drove roads remain in their traditional form and have recently encouraged a new growth industry: pony-trekking. Other interests which can be pursued here are angling in the upper Teifi (and its tributaries) and the wild life which exists north of the town in the great Bog of Tregaron, a four-mile wilderness which is now a national nature reserve.

Cors Tregaron, as the Bog is also known, is one of the oldest and most scientifically studied peat bogs in Britain. It contains in a semi-fossilized form a complete record of the vegetation of this remote Welsh valley from the Ice Age to the present day. Permits must be obtained to visit it to see the large variety of rare bog plants. This NCC reserve is also interesting to the birdwatcher since this is the largest overwintering station for Greenland's whitefronted goose. For further information, contact the NCC; tel: Bangor 4001.

□ 11 miles (18km) NE of Lampeter on A485 or B4343. Map ref 1B2.

Gwent

A hilly county in south-east Wales, its attractions include Chepstow, Tintern Abbey in the Wye Valley, Abergavenny. South Wales Tourism Council: Carmarthen 7557.

294. CAERWENT/CAERLEON
Roman remains

Caerwent was the site of the only walled civilian town in Roman Wales. The city of *Venta Silurum* was built to house – and civilise – the conquered natives. But the settlement did not retain its importance after the Romans' departure and it suffered badly at the hands of Irish raiders. Nevertheless there are substantial remains of the old Roman walls, in places up to 17ft (5m) high, and the village's main street still follows the old Roman lines. Rome's military settlement in this part of the Empire was nine miles (14km) west at Caerleon. Here there are some fine remains of a large Legionary Fortress, despite the suburban sprawl of modern Caerleon and neighbouring Newport. By far the most notable of these remains is a superb amphitheatre, excavated in 1928 on a site rich in Arthurian legend; it is open standard DoE hours plus Sun mornings Apr-Sept.

□ Caerwent is five miles (8km) SW of Chepstow off A48; Caerleon is one mile (1.6km) NE of Newport. Map ref 1C3.

295. CWMCARN
Forest drive

A seven-mile (11km) 'scenic drive' has been devised by the Forestry Commission and Countryside Commission in a side valley off Ebbw Vale. Picnic places, adventure play areas, forest or mountain walks and viewpoints are clearly marked along the route which is open Easter-Oct. There is an admission charge to the drive along twisting roads through mixed coniferous woodland with exceptional views of both the Bristol Channel and Brecon Beacons. Leaflet available from Forest Office at Abercarn, tel: Newbridge 244223.

□ Access from A467 S of Abercarn, approx six miles (9.6km) N of junction 27 on M4. Map ref 1C3.

296. LOWER WYE VALLEY
River gorge/woods

After leaving the Herefordshire plain the Wye finds its way to the sea barred by the limestone and coalbearing rocks of the Forest of Dean plateau. In its dramatic escape to the sea, the river has cut a deep gorge through the plateau. By swinging from one side of the valley to another and by eroding any softer rocks it may encounter, the Wye has created a series of loops and U-turns.

These loops and gorges are set against a frame of wooded hillsides and picturesque villages such as Tintern with its abbey and Goodrich with its castle. The result is some of the most spectacular – and accessible – scenery in lowland Britain.

There are many things to see in this popular touring area. Among them,

The extensive ruins of Chepstow Castle, Gwent. The Normans built this impressive strategic stronghold to command the lowest crossing of the River Wye

and including some less well-known spots are Goodrich Castle; Symonds Yat (car park nearest the rock is crowded at peak times, but alternative parking at Biblins picnic area and forest trail one mile or 1.6km to the south); the Kymin (National Trust hill east of Monmouth off A1436); Bargain or Whitestone Woods off A466 between Llandogo and Tintern; the extensive remains of the Cistercian abbey at Tintern and Chepstow Castle. OS map 162 in the 50,000 series and the Wye Valley and Forest of Dean 25,000 Outdoor Leisure Map detail minor roads, footpaths including the Offa's Dyke and Wye Valley Walks, nature trails and picnic sites. See also Tintern Forest (below).
☐ Between Chepstow and Ross-on-Wye. Map ref 1C3.

297. TINTERN FOREST
Trails/views/picnics

Priscau Bach. Picnic place and forest walks. Picnicking alongside Mounton Brook. Three walks climbing up steep wooded slopes with fine views over Tintern Forest. Longest is $1\frac{1}{2}$ miles (2.4km). On B4235 W of Chepstow.
Lower Wyndcliff. Picnic place with attractive view over horseshoe bend of River Wye. Alongside main Wye Valley road A466 about three miles (4.8km) from Chepstow. Also Lower Wyndcliff 365 Steps picnic place in woodland overlooking Severn Estuary.
Upper Wyndcliff. A viewpoint which is on a by-road off A466 $\frac{1}{2}$ mile (800m) N of St Arvans or reached by 365 steps from Lower Wyndcliff picnic place. A nature trail starts from Upper Wyndcliff car park and leads to Eagle's Nest viewpoint 700ft (213m) above Wye Gorge with fine view of confluence of Severn and Wye rivers.
Industrial history trail. Along the valley bottom to Pont-y-Saeson linking remains of sites which formed an industrial complex based on water power from 1556 to 1901. Trail starts from Tintern Sawmills car park. From Chepstow turn left immediately before Royal George Hotel in Tintern. Car park is about $\frac{1}{4}$ mile (400m) up on right in front of Forestry Commission workshops.
☐ Map ref 1C3.

298. TREDEGAR
House/park

Tredegar House is a 17th century building – with 18th century additions – which is widely regarded as the finest Restoration house in Wales. Two rooms are open to the public on afternoons other than Mon and Tues, Apr-Sept, and restoration work is continuing on other parts of the house. The park and woodland around the house now form a country park with a children's farm and fishing or boating in the lake. Tel: Newport (Wales) 62568.
☐ Three miles (4.8km) SW of Newport near junction of M4 and A48. Map ref 1C3/4.

299. WHITE CASTLE
Moated castle

The white plaster coating on the masonry which gave the castle its name has

Gloddfa Ganol Mountain Tourist Centre, slate quarry-turned-working museum at Blaenau Ffestiniog, Gwynedd

now virtually disappeared. But the inner bailey is still surrounded by a steep-sided moat which makes this quite small castle one of the more interesting of the castles which survive from the days when the Marcher lords were struggling to control the Welsh. It formed a triangle of defensive fortifications with Grosmont and Skenfrith castles. Grosmont and Skenrith are open any reasonable time, White Castle during standard DoE hours.
☐ Seven miles (11km) NE of Abergavenny off B4521 or B4233. Map ref 1C3.

Gwynedd

Dominated by Snowdonia National Park but also with Llyn Peninsula AONB. Tourist centres include Bala, Caernarfon, Conway and Harlech. Many castles but landscapes of mountains, rivers, lakes and sea are the main attractions. Other features: railways, slate mines and the Italianate village of Portmeirion near Porthmadog. North Wales Tourism Council: Colwyn Bay 56881.

300. ABERGYNOLWYN
Mountains/rivers

This small quarrying village on the Dysynni river, which flows from the ice-scoured Talyllyn Lake, three miles (4.8km) to the north-east, is a good base from which to explore the scenery around 2928ft (903m) Cader Idris. Two miles (3.2km) north-west of the village is Castel-y-Bere, the ruins of a 13th century castle built by Llewellyn the Great. This offers good views of the sharp crag of Bird Rock where cormorants and guillemots nest six miles (9.6km) inland. South-westwards (three miles; 4.8km) are the beautiful Dolgoch Falls (125ft; 37m) and the terminus of the Talyllyn narrow-gauge railway which runs seven miles (11km) to the coast and the railway museum at Tywyn. Tel: Tywyn 710472.
☐ 10 miles (16km) SW of Dolgellau on B4405. Map ref 1B2.

301. BODNANT GARDEN
Terraces and woodland

A very large garden (NT) overlooking the Conwy Valley with views of Snowdonia, terraces in the Italian style made in the early 20th century, an 18th century pavilion, water-lily pools and exotic planting. There is also an extensive woodland garden with a vast collection of rhododendrons, other shrubs and trees as well as rock gardens, herbaceous perennials and naturalised bulbs. Open daily mid Mar-Oct; tel: Ty'n-y-Groes 460.
☐ Eight miles (13km) S of Llandudno on A470. Map ref 3C6.

302. BONT NEWYDD
Nature trail/waterfall

The Coedydd Aber Nature Trail winds among the ancient woods and crags of the Aber valley to the Aber Falls or Rhaeadr Fawr, climbing gently from 150 to 700ft (46-216m) above sea level. On the higher slopes there is a mixture of oak, birch and hazel; in more sheltered places wych elm, ash, alder, blackthorn and sallow may also be seen with a good selection of spring flowers such as primroses, wood anemones, wood sorrel and bluebells. Watch for woodland birds such as woodpeckers, nuthatches, tree creepers and warblers, and by the riverside, dippers and grey wagtails. Ravens and buzzards can be seen near peaks. At the falls note the rich flora of mosses and liverworts, kept damp by the spray from the falls. Coedydd Aber is a National Nature Reserve. The distance from the car park at Bont Newydd to the falls is about two miles (3.2km). Sensible clothes and shoes are advised as the path may be wet and slippery. Further information from the Nature Conservancy Council; tel: Bangor 4001. OS map 115.
☐ $\frac{3}{4}$ mile (1.2km) Se of A55 on minor road from Aber between Bangor and Conwy. Map ref 3C6.

303. BLAENAU FFESTINIOG
Railways/quarrying

Quarrying for slate was centuries old in North Wales before it reached its peak during the 19th century. It neither did much for the health of its workers nor enhanced the natural beauty of the landscape. But, ironically, the narrow gauge railways and tramways that linked the quarries with the ports have outlived the quarries to become attractions in themselves taking tourists through the 'unspoilt' countryside.

The Festiniog railway is one of the most famous of the 'Great Little Trains' of Wales and currently hauls passenger services throughout the year from Porthmadog on the coast to Tanygrisiau just over a mile (2km) south of Blaenau Ffestiniog. One mile (1.6km) to the north of the town, off the A470, the Llechwedd Slate Caverns are taking visitors by train through old slate tunnels to vast subterranean caverns up to 200ft (62m) high.

There are also exhibitions devoted to the industry at both Llechwedd and another neighbouring quarry-turned-working museum now known as the Gloddfa Ganol Mountain Tourist Centre. Both open daily from roughly Easter-Oct, and both can be chilly underground. Tel: Porthmadog 2340

One of the 'Great Little Trains of Wales', the Festiniog railway, which runs down to the coast at Porthmadog

for details of Festiniog rail services and Tywyn 710472 for details of other 'Great Little Trains of Wales'. Tel: Blaenau Ffestiniog 306 for information about Llechwedd's opening hours. Tel: Blaenau Ffestiniog 664 about Gloddfa Ganol.

□ 10 miles (16km) SW of Betws-y-Coed on A470. Map ref 3C6/1B1.

304. CAERHUN
Roman forts/road

Here was the site of *Canovium*, a Roman fort commanding the Conwy river three miles (4.8km) further upstream than the site chosen 12 centuries later for the castle and 'new town' of Conwy. The outline of the Roman walls can still be seen in meadowland close to the river. Mountain walkers can experience a more arduous reminder of the Roman presence in North Wales by following the footpath that traces the route of the old Roman road west from Caerhun over the mountains to Aber. It is a route dotted with cairns and earthworks but also, and less evocatively, electricity pylons. The Roman road eventually led to *Segontium*, the Roman predecessor to another great 'new' medieval settlement – Caernarfon. *Segontium* was a large fort; a museum, and its remains to the east of the modern town, are open standard DoE hours. OS map 115 shows the route of the Roman road clearly.

□ Three miles (4.8km) S of Conwy off B5106. Map ref 3C6.

305. CLOGAU
Gold mine

Clogau mine provided the gold for the Queen's wedding ring, but the heyday of the mine was in the latter half of the 19th century. By a small car park is an interpretative display board which il-

lustrates a short walk along the banks of the river where prospectors used to pan for gold. There is also a summary of the history of the mine. Visitors wanting to find out more should go to the FC Maesgwm Visitor Centre – see below under Coed-y-Brenin.

□ At Bontddu four miles (6.4km) NE of Barmouth on A496. Map ref 1B1.

306. COED-Y-BRENIN FOREST
Mountains/rivers

A network of over 50 miles (80.5km) of attractive paths, tracks and forest roads taking walkers into the heart of the forest. Forest and mountain scenery, waterfalls and riversides. Best starting points are Dolgefeiliau and Tyn-y-Groes picnic places and the Arboretum car park. Maesgwm visitor centre (FC) has an exhibition on life and work in the forest, the extraordinary rich formations and the Clogau gold mines; open daily, Easter-Sept, tel: Canllwyd 226. Three miles (5km) to the south, in the NT estate of Dolmelynllyn, is Rhiadr Ddu or Black Waterfall, one of the most spectacular falls in Wales.

□ Maesgwm Forest Visitor Centre is eight miles (13km) N of Dolgellau off A470. Map ref 1B1.

307. COEDYDD MAENTWROG
Nature trail/lake

The Coed Llyn Mair nature trail may be followed either from Tan-y-Bwlch station (on the Festiniog Railway) or from the car park near Llyn Mair. It goes through oak woodlands and meadows with drystone walls. At one point there is a display of nest-boxes for different birds. Good view of lake. Length 1½ miles (2.4km), open Easter-Sept; a leaflet is available from kiosk at north point or 'honesty box' at south

car park. Further information from the Nature Conservancy Council, tel: Bangor 4001.

□ Off B4410 two miles (3.2km) W of Maentwrog. Map ref 1B1/3C6.

308. CRICCIETH
Castle/caves

Criccieth Castle was a native stronghold, later strengthened by Edward I. Its remains (AM) stand on a grassy headland overlooking Tremadog Bay with panoramic views of the sea and mountains. Beneath the castle – open standard DoE hours plus Sun mornings Apr-Sept – are sand and pebble beaches. About a mile (1.6km) east of the castle is Black Rock, pitted with caves which can be seen at low tide or reached by boat. 1½ miles (2.4km) west of Criccieth is Llanystumdwy where Lloyd George spent his early life. His grave is in the village and a memorial museum is open weekdays in summer.

□ Nine miles (14km) W of Porthmadog on A497. Map ref 1B1/3C6.

309. CWM IDWAL
Glacial landscape

For a chance to understand the workings of a former glacier, walk a rugged 1¼ mile (2km) nature trail (NCC) around Cwm Idwal. It starts at the western end of Llyn Ogwen, just south of Ogwen Cottage Mountain School on the A5, following a well worn track to the lake of Llyn Idwal. Cross the stepping stones to the right and climb to the ridge which gives a splendid view north of the glacial trough of Nant Ffrancon with the A5 running through it. Walk to the head of the lake, noting the hummocky ice-deposited moraines and the cliffs of the Devil's Kitchen with its waterfall. Pass the ice-smoothed climbing cliff of Idwal Slabs

and return over more moraines to the starting point. OS map 115 covers the area and a Trail leaflet is available; details Nature Conservancy Council, tel: Bangor 4001.

□ Four miles (6.4km) W of Capel Curig off A5. Map ref 3C6.

310. CWM PENNANT
Mountain pass

To see an unspoiled upland valley almost in the heart of Snowdonia's highest mountains visit the hidden Cwm Pennant. Travel along the picturesque River Dwyfor to the crag of Craig Isallt, a tough igneous intrusion which even the glaciers failed to breach. Behind the crag is lonely and beautiful Cwm Pennant with its scattered sheep farms encircled by a majestic sweep of frost-shattered summits and ice-eroded slopes. For the fit and energetic a scramble from the valley head one mile (1.6km) to the col offers an unusual view of Snowdon.

□ Four miles (6.4km) NE of A487 at Dolbenmaen. Map ref 3C6.

311. DINAS DINLLE
Hill fort/beach

This is a type of hill fort more common in Scotland and Ireland than Wales or England: perched on the very edge of the sea. Inland the twin ramparts of the 3½ acre (1.4 hectare) fort can still be seen, but on the western side they are heavily eroded by the sea. The fort has given its name to a three-mile (4.8km) stretch of sandy beach which it overlooks. In addition to offering good bathing and ample car-parking this beach is also a centre for sea angling, canoeing and surfing.

□ 4½ miles (7km) SW of Caernarfon off A499. Map ref 3C6.

312. GREAT ORME
Cliffs/nature trail

Great Orme's Head is the larger of two great masses of Carboniferous limestone on the North Wales Coast near the seaside resort of Llandudno, the other being Little Orme's Head to the east. The Great Orme has both a cable car and a tramway to take visitors towards its summit of nearly 700ft (213m) with its fine views. The headland can be explored either by car along Marine Drive (a toll road starting from Llandudno Pier) or via a nature trail (starting from the cafe in Happy Valley). The trail totals five miles (8km) and covers geology, wildlife, historical and archaeological sites. A leaflet is available from an information kiosk at the pier.

□ Immediately NW of Llandudno. Map ref 3C6.

313. HARLECH
Sea castle

Now a massive ruin, Harlech Castle (AM) was built by Edward I in 1283 on a rocky promontory overlooking the sands of Morfa Harlech and the Glaslyn estuary. Originally the castle was on a sea cliff but the sea has retreated leaving the castle stranded half a mile inland. Open standard DoE hours plus Sun mornings Apr-Sept.

□ Nine miles (14km) N of Barmouth on A496. Map ref 1B1.

Wales

314. LLANBEDR
Farm trail

The workings of a typical Welsh hill farm are explained by boards strategically sited along the two-mile (3.2km) Cefn Isaf Farm Trail within the Snowdonia National Park. Open all year. Trail starts near Salem Chapel in Llanbedr.
☐ Four miles (6.4km) SE of Harlech on A496. Map ref 1B1.

315. LLUGWY VALLEY
Mountain river/walk

To see a mountain river in all its moods follow the valley of the Llugwy between Capel Curig and Betws-y-Coed, a distance of just over 7 miles (11km). A good starting point is the attractive group of cottages at Pont Cyfyng, one mile (1.6km) south-east of Capel Curig, by crossing the bridge south of the A5 road. Here the river is terminating a stage of gorges, deep pools, rapids and 'white water'; follow the minor road eastwards where the river glides easily through alluvial meadows, swinging into meanders and leaving grassy gravel terraces above its floodplain, on one of which the Romans sited their fort of Caer Llugwy. Cross the A5 at the picturesque Tŷ-Hyll (Ugly House) and follow river by path or minor road on its northern bank to Betws-y-Coed. But detour along the A5 itself to see the magnificent drop of the river at the famous Swallow Falls, between Tŷ-Hyll and Betwys-y-Coed. OS map 115 details paths, etc.
☐ Capel Curig and Betws-y-Coed are on the main A5 road between Llangollen and Bangor. Map ref 3C6.

316. MOCHRAS
Shells/wild life

Also known as Shell Island since at least 100 varieties of shell and many unusual pebbles can be found here. The best time to hunt for shells is during the big tides in January, February, August and September. It is not a natural island but a man-made peninsula, created by the Earl of Winchelsea in the 19th century who diverted the river to reclaim the land. The channel silted up to form the high, grassy dunes which are now a haven for terns, oyster catchers, sand pipers and all kinds of gulls and even buzzards. Shel duck nest in the rabbit holes. There are many wildflowers, including orchids and wild dwarf roses. If you arrive early in the morning you can often see seals, particularly if the sea is calm. The 'island' is open to the public on payment of a toll and reached by a causeway which is covered at high tide.
☐ W of Llanbedr off A496 seven miles (11km) N of Barmouth. Map ref 1B1.

317. PENRHYN CASTLE
Neo-Norman castle

This is 19th century romanticism and social climbing at its most extravagant. Dawkins Pennant, whose fortune came from slate quarries and sugar plantations, established his family in the landed aristocracy by building an enormous neo-Norman castle on a splendid site looking along the North Wales coast below Snowdonia. Everything is elaborately Norman, down to the drawing-room sofas and dining-room wallpaper. A four-poster bed of solid slate advertises the family quarries. All designed with the utmost panache and obvious enjoyment by Thomas Hopper in 1824-34. Now owned by the NT it is open daily Apr-Oct, but opening times vary; tel: NT regional office for details, Betws-y-Coed 312.
☐ One mile (1.6km) E of Bangor at junction of A5 and A55. Map ref 3C6.

318. PORTHMADOG
Coastal villages/sailing

Once a great port for the slate industry this sheltered harbour at the foot of Snowdonia can be the centre for an unusual day out on water or land. The double estuary of the Afon Glaslyn and the Afon Dwyryd offers an intriguing day's sailing: when the tide is in, it is a sheltered lake, while, when the tide is out, you sail a winding channel through some 10 square miles of clean sands. These sands provide perfect beaches for children and family picnics. And for après sail, or simple landlubbers, there are the attractions of the picturesque Festiniog Railway (which has a terminus at Porthmadog but which was described on p. 270 under Blaenau Ffestiniog) and the Italianate village of Portmeirion, created here on a rocky headland by Welsh architect Clough Williams-Ellis. The village of Portmeirion, with its extraordinary collection of architectural styles and exotic gardens, is open to visitors daily Apr-Oct; Tel: Penrhyndeudraeth 453.
☐ Five miles (8km) E of Criccieth on A487 at western end of a toll road. Map ref 1B1/3C6.

319. PORTH NEIGWL
Beach/cliff viewpoint

This four-mile (6.4km) stretch of beach, backed by cliffs of boulder clay, is also known as Hell's Mouth and is virtually inaccessible except at either end. On a stormy day, when waves pound the shore, you can see the full force of Atlantic erosion. There are spectacular views from the headland of Trwyn y Ffosle (NT) at the south-eastern end of the beach. Note how the tiny River Soch turns away from the sea (its channel is blocked with blown sand) and instead follows a rocky gorge, cut by glacial meltwaters before reaching the sea at Abersoch. For the beach of Porth Neigwl itself there is an NT car park south-west of Llanengan.
☐ 1½ miles (2.4km) SW of Abersoch. Map ref 1A1.

320. PORTH OER
Whistling sand

This lovely beach is famous for its 'whistling sand': a strange phenomenon which is caused by the spherical shaped grains of sand rubbing together when you walk upon them. The beach is also good for bathing, with rock pools to explore at low tide, and sea angling.
☐ Two miles (3.2km) N of Aberdarm near Methlem. map ref 1A1/3B6.

321. ROMAN STEPS
Ancient trackway

More than 2000 slabs of rock or flagstones here mark out a route across a col in the mountains known as the Harlech Dome. Were they laid by the Romans as their name suggests? Certainly it lies near their inland fort at Tomen-y-Mur near Lake Trawsfynydd, so it is plausible to argue that the Romans used the route. But the stones themselves were more likely to have been laid in medieval times to provide a land supply route for Harlech Castle. Later it would have been used by packhorse teams. Now the Steps provide an interesting walk for ramblers.
☐ Four miles (6.4km) E of Harlech along minor road to Llyn Cwm Bychan where there is a car park. Map ref 1B2.

322. SNOWDONIA
1: The easiest way up Wales's highest mountain: 3561ft (1085m) Snowdon

The easiest way up Snowdon is by the Snowdon Mountain Railway from Llanberis. The second easiest way, however, is by foot and follows a very similar route. A broad and easy-angled track follows the same north-west ridge although there are boggy sections along the five miles (8km) and 3000ft (925m) of ascent. Stout shoes or boots are essential. Avoid the mountain if snowy conditions prevail and you lack the necessary experience.

Start from the Royal Victoria Hotel in Llanberis where signposts direct you along an initial 20 minutes stretch of tarmac road. Avoid this by taking the edge of the stream just past the cattlegrid to the viewpoint of the most spectacular Ceunant Mawr waterfalls before rejoining the tarmac. The Llanberis Track soon branches off left, and its route is rough, rocky and obvious.

The building of Halfway House (refreshments) can be seen well ahead, the path becoming barer and wider beyond. At 2521ft (775m) it passes beneath the rack-and-pinion railway to the edge of Cwm Glas Bach – with splendid views of mountainside and the Llanberis Pass below. About 600ft (185m) higher is Bwlch Glas ('the green col') just above path and railway and worth visiting to look down into Cwm Dyli. It is up here that the Llanberis Track meets two other paths: the Snowdon Ranger route on the right and the Pen-y-Gwryd path on the left. Another quarter of an hour's steep climbing alongside the railway completes the ascent which usually takes three hours or so. OS map 115.
☐ Llanberis is six miles (9.6km) SE of Caernarfon on A4086. Map ref 3C6.

323-327. SNOWDONIA
2: Five days out in the forest

Snowdonia Forest Park covers 23,400 acres (9473 hectares) of spectacular scenery within the larger Snowdonia National Park. The park embraces the forests of Gwydyr and Beddgelert amid the foothills of Snowdon. Its centre is at Betws-y-Coed and includes:

A dream of Italy: Portmeirion village, near Porthmadog, the creation of Welsh architect Clough Williams-Ellis

323 Beddgelert Forest

Trail on fairly level ground with views of Snowdon, ¾ mile (1.2km). Starts from camp site on west side of A4085 one mile (1.6km) north of village. Also forest walk with a steep climb through rhododendrons and young forest to viewpoint giving magnificent view of Gwynant Valley and lake, 1½ miles (2.4km). Starts from picnic place beside A498 between Beddgelert and Llyn Gwynant.
□ Map ref 3C6/1B1.

324 Tŷ Canol

Forest walk along short waymarked path with spectacular views across the coast to Caernarfon, ¼ mile (400m). Starts from car park one mile (1.6km) north of village of Lithfaen (Llyn). Bear north in centre of village which is on B4417 for minor road to car park.
□ Map ref 3C6/1B1.

325. Gwydyr Uchaf

Picnic place in Gwydyr forest at edge of meadow by 17th century chapel and Dower House overlooking Vale of Conwy. Visitor centre nearby. One mile (1.6km) west of Llanrwst on B5106 near Gwydir Castle. Also in Gwydyr Forest are 10 waymarked walks through varied landscape of woodlands, meadows, crags, stream sides and hidden lakes with spectacular views of Snowdonia. From ¾ mile (1.2km) to 5¼ miles (8.4km). These walks all start in vicinity of Betws-y-Coed.
□ Map ref 3C6.

326 Garth Falls walk

A smooth paved path with handrails which winds through mature open forest with ferns and shrubs alongside a stream. Designed for handicapped and elderly people the path ends by a waterfall where there are picnic tables and seats. There are descriptive texts in braille. 300 yards (274m) long. Walk starts at west end of Betws-y-Coed.
□ Map ref 3C6.

327 Cae'n y Coed

Picnic place on grassy slopes with scattered birches just below the forest edge. Off the A5 west of Swallow Falls, 1½ miles (2.4km) from Betws-y-Coed. Arboretum Walk, steep in places, starts from picnic place and climbs up through hillside arboretum with a collection of 48 exotic tree species. Fine mountain and valley views across the forest to Moel Siabod.
□ Map ref 3C6.

328. TRE'R CEIRI
Hill fort

This is one of the most exciting prehistoric sites in the British Isles: a fortified town on a narrow mountain top some 1800ft (549m) high with dramatic views over Snowdonia, the Llyn peninsula and across to Anglesey.

The five-acre (two hectare) site was protected not only by ramparts but was also completely walled. Some parts of this wall are still six feet (1.83m) high. The ruins of many huts can also be seen at Tre'r Ceiri which is on the most easterly summit of a mountain known as Yr Eifl. A footpath leads towards this mountain fortress from the B4417 road between Llanaelhaearn and Llithfaen. It is a steep and none-too-easy ascent which emphasises Tre'r Ceiri's strengths and weaknesses: easy to defend but impossible for peaceful agricultural settlement. Grid ref SH 374447; OS map 123.
□ Approx one mile (1.6m) W of Llanaelhaearn off B4417. Map ref 3C6.

Mid-Glamorgan

Small and largely industrial county with many mining valleys. Attractions: castles at Caerphilly and Bridgend. South Wales Tourism Council: Carmarthen 7557.

329. BRIDGEND
Castles/priory

More an industrial than a market centre these days but its position near three valleys – Ogmore, Garw and Llynfi – has left it with three nearby Norman castles. Coity Castle is two miles (3.2km) north-east of Bridgend off A4061; New Castle is near the town centre on 4063; and Ogmore Castle 2½ miles (4km) south-west on B4524. The latter is particularly interesting with its 13th century structure built on earlier earthworks and ditches. Ogmore also has some ancient stepping stones leading to its remains across the River Ewenny. A fourth ancient building near Bridgend is Ewenny Priory, a 12th century monastery which had military defences with walls and towers.

All four buildings are under the care of the DoE; Coity and Ogmore are open standard hours, Ewenny weekdays only, New Castle similar days but different times as standard DoE hours. The Wales Tourist Board say that if locked during recognised opening hours (detailed in the DoE booklet, *Historic Monuments*) the key for New Castle is available at Farm Cottage, 18 Llangewydd Road, Bridgend, while that for Ogmore is at the farmhouse opposite the castle.
□ 16 miles (26km) W of Cardiff on A48. Map ref 1B4.

330. CAERPHILLY
Moated castle

A town known for its cheese – although this is no longer made here – and its castle. The latter is partly in ruins but its design was one of the finest in Europe with particularly elaborate water defences: not one but two moats. Similarly there is an inner and outer ward within the central keep. The castle dates from the 13th century and just survived attempts by Cromwell to blow it up. However one tower is still leaning at a dizzy angle from that particular blast. Open standard DoE hours plus Sun mornings Apr-Sept.
□ Seven miles (11km) N of Cardiff on A469. Map ref 1C3.

331. DARE VALLEY
Country park/reclaimed land

More than 470 acres (193 hectares) of open moorland with a wooded valley have been largely reclaimed from derelict land which once contained six collieries. Now the landscaped country park offers ample scope for picnicking and walking. Leaflets available at the park detail several mountain or forest walks plus an industrial trail.
□ 1½ miles (2.4km) W of Aberdare off A4059 (via minor road to Cwmdare) or off B4277. Map ref 1C3.

Powys

The only landlocked county in Wales. The Severn, Usk and Wye all rise from its mountains. Brecon Beacons National Park is in the south. Many castles in the borderland of the Welsh Marshes, also the best stretches of Offa's Dyke. Other attractions include the city of Brecon with its outstanding cathedral. Mid Wales Tourism Council: Machynlleth 2401.

332. BLACK MOUNTAINS
Mountain drive/walks

A spectacular drive of about 17 miles (27km) through the Black Mountains is on the B4423 road from Llanfihangel to Hay-on-Wye – it becomes unclassified north of the ruins of the 11th century Augustinian priory of Llanthony. The priory was built on the site of a ruined chapel dedicated to St David and was originally consecrated as a hermitage. From these humble beginnings it grew into one of the finest priories in Wales and its still substantial remains are a fine reminder of its former splendour. The road climbs up the attractive Vale of Ewyas to a high pass (1778ft; 533m), known as the Gospel Pass on the road over Hay Bluff. The views northwards are glorious with wooded foothills, the great curve of the Wye near Hay-on-Wye, Radnor Forest and the Clee Hills. OS map 161 covers the area.
□ N of Abergavenny. Map ref 1C3.

333. BRECON AND
ABERGAVENNY CANAL
Canal walks/boating

One of the most beautiful canals in the British Isles. It was built between 1797 and 1812 along the Usk Valley from the outskirts of Brecon eastwards to Pontymoile one mile (1.6km) south of Pontypool where it joined the Monmouthshire canal. Thirty-three miles (53km) of the canal are still open to traffic, including the most attractive stretch of all – through the Brecon Beacons National Park between Brecon and Abergávenny.

The canal is no longer used commercially but is becoming increasingly popular with leisure craft. Boat trips operate during the summer from Goytre Wharf among other places (details from tourist information centres) and boats can be hired at Govilon, Gilwern, Llanfoist, Llanover and Pontypool. These places also provide access points for privately-owned boats, but prospective holidaymakers here should note that the canal is one of the shallowest in the country with a depth at places not much more than two feet (0.6m).

The canal often runs some distance away from villages through the wooded slopes of the valley and as such offers attractive walking along its towpath as well as boating along its waters. A typical walk might be from Llangattock. Take the towpath south-east to Llanellen via Gilwern, Govilon and Llanfoist to see the scenic glories and the industrial echoes of the canal. Cross Usk Bridge and walk two miles on the high road to Abergavenny, bussing

back to Crickhowell and the completion of a nine-mile (14km) walk.
□ Map ref 1C3.

334. BUILTH WELLS
Market town/farming

This town, near the confluence of the Wye with the Irfon, is famous not only for the medicinal waters suggested by its modern name but also for livestock. It is one of the great farming centres of Mid Wales with a weekly cattle and sheep market held on Mondays and the Royal Welsh Agricultural Society's annual show being staged here every July. Its position close to the mountains and several salmon rivers draws pony trekkers and anglers, but architecturally it is undistinguished.
□ Six miles (9.6km) S of Llandrindod Wells on A483 and A470. Map ref 1C2.

335. CEFNLLYS
Deserted town

Within an arm of the River Ithon faint hollows that were once streets and mounds that were the sites of medieval houses may still be discerned in a scrawny, rock-strewn pasture which was once a town. The town of Cefnllys grew up around a castle built in this exposed part of the Welsh Marches by the powerful and richly-endowed family of the Mortimers. Markets were held here in the 14th century and by 1360 Cefnllys is on record as a borough. Now even the castle has disappeared.
□ Two miles (3.2km) E of Llandrindod Wells, best approached via minor road SE off the A483 near Crossgates. Map ref 1C2.

336 CEMMAES
Angling

On the banks of the Dyfi – the best of the mid-Wales rivers known for their sea trout, known locally as sewin. Other rivers where sewin can also be caught are the Dysynni, Rheidol and Ystwyth. But for information about day or visitors' permits to fish in the Dyfi from south of Machynlleth to north of Cemmaes contact the New Dovey Fishery Association, tel: Machynlleth 2721.
□ Eight miles (13km) NE of Machynlleth on A470. Map ref 1B1.

337. ELAN VALLEY
Reservoirs and rapids – an
upland drive and walks

There are now four reservoirs adjacent to each other in the Elan Valley. The oldest, Craig Goch, was completed in 1904, but the landscapes created by these flooded valleys remain quite distinct from natural lakes. There has not been time for the banks to erode

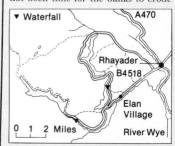

Elan Valley: the upland paths and roads along former drover's routes that reveal its man-made beauty

Stark memorials to a bygone industry: slate-slabbed fences quarried from the Snowdonian hillsides near Penrhyn, Gwynedd

into gentle curves and where there were once hillside depressions, the water now laps in long thin fingers.

For motorists the old drover's roads that made Rhayader a busy market town now provide an attractive drive around the reservoirs (see map) with rapids and waterfalls to be seen as well as the often spectacular dams of the reservoirs themselves. For walkers there are some attractive paths alongside some of the reservoirs. Rhayader has a livestock market on alternate Wednesdays and is a popular pony trekking centre. OS map 147.

☐ The Elan reservoirs begin three miles (5km) S of Rhayader off B4518. Map ref 1B2.

338. HAFREN FOREST
Headwaters of the Severn

The forest takes its name from Afon Hafren, Welsh for River Severn, which has its source here. A series of trails start from an FC picnic place at Rhyd-y-Benwch in the heart of the forest overlooking meadows and with a panoramic view stretching from the headwaters of the Severn to Plynlimon Mountains beyond. The shortest trail is known as the Cascades Trail and follows the tree-lined bank of the Severn for one mile (1.6km) passing several waterfalls. A leaflet available at the picnic place details this and other walks including one to the source of the Severn. Hafren walks are for the serious walker in remote and wild country which is often rough and wet.

☐ The picnic place is seven miles (11km) W of Llanidloes on minor roads following signs for Old Hall. Map ref 1B2.

339. HAY-ON-WYE
Market town/books

Its position in the Wye valley beneath the Black Mountains attracted first the Romans, who built a fort nearby, and then the Normans who built a castle. Nowadays it is best known for the second-hand bookshops which line the streets of Hay. Even what little remains of the castle has been partly adapted for second-hand books. For the local farming population, though, the town remains a market centre – market days are Mon and Thurs – while anglers are drawn to the salmon waters of the Wye itself.

☐ 18 miles W of Hereford on B4348. Map ref 1C2.

340. KNIGHTON
Offa's Dyke/walks

The Welsh name is much more revealing about the attractions of this small town on the River Teme. In Welsh it is Tref-y-Clawdd: 'the town on the dyke'. For around Knighton, especially to the north towards Newcastle, is one of the best preserved stretches of the Dyke with the bank as high as 30ft (9m) and the ditch as deep as 15ft (4.5m) in places. The Dyke is followed near here by a long-distance footpath.

☐ 15 miles (24km) W of Ludlow on A488. Map ref 1C2.

341. LAKE VYRNWY
Nature reserve/lake drive

Woods, meadows, heather moors rising to almost 2000ft (600m) and the lake itself are all contained within the 16,000 acres (6500 hectares) of this superb reserve on the catchment of the Upper Vyrnwy. Water birds include dippers, kingfishers, wagtails and sandpipers. Sparrowhawks, buzzards and ravens are common, and merlin breed on the moors. Mammals include the rare polecat and it is also a fine area for butterflies. Spectacular mountain drives to this man-made lake – a reservoir – Details and leaflets from Vyrnwy Visitor Centre, Llanwddyn, at SE corner of lake. Open Easter-Sept. Tel: Llanwddyn 246.

☐ Eight miles (13km) W of Llanfyllin. Map ref 1C1.

342. LLANDRINDOD WELLS
Spa town/fishing

Waters for fishing rather than for medicinal purposes are increasingly this town's prime attraction, although a legacy of its spa days are the elegant streets and hotels. Fishing is popular not only in the Ithon but also a 14-acre (5.7 hectares) lake which is stocked with several species, including carp.

☐ Six miles (9.6km) N of Builth Wells on A483. Map ref 1C2.

343. LLANFAIR CAEREINION
Railway/river valleys

An attractive little town at the western end of the narrow gauge Welshpool and Llanfair Light Railway. Just under six miles (9.6km) of the line has been reopened leaving the eastern terminus currently at Sylfaen, three miles (4.8km) from Welshpool, the ultimate destination for the enthusiasts who have brought the line back to life. Steam services operate daily from early June to early Sept and at weekend and Bank Holidays from Easter-early June and early Sept to early Oct; tel: Llanfair Caereinion 441. Around Llanfair are the attractive valleys of the Banwy and Vyrnwy.

☐ Eight miles (13km) W of Welshpool on A483. Map ref 1C1.

344. LLANIDLOES
Market town/lead mining

This somewhat remote town on the upper Severn – just 10 miles (16km) from its source – has had a long history as a market centre for the surrounding villages and hill-farmers. This is demonstrated by its early 17th century market hall, one of the finest in Wales. Markets are still an important feature of the town, with livestock markets being held on alternate Fridays and general markets every Saturday. But the town also had a period when it was the centre of lead-mining.

The biggest and most profitable mine was the Van Lead Mine, three miles (5km) north-west of Llanidloes off B4518. Now not much more than a lone chimney on the hilltop, the remains of an incline running down from the mine and the great heaps of grey spoil are left to indicate that Van was once a revered name in mining circles. The remains of the smaller Bryn Tail lead mine can be seen along the course of a 2½ mile (4km) 'scenic trail' around part of the lake formed by Clywedog Reservoir 3½ miles (5.6km) north-west

of Llanidloes off B4518.

☐ 15 miles (24km) SW of Newtown on A470. Map ref 1C2.

345. LLANWRTYD WELLS
Drove roads/pony trekking

This small town stands at the head of an old drove road over the Cambrian mountains to Tregaron. This follows the valley of the Irfon (a popular fishing river) with attractive Forestry Commission picnic areas and scenic walks signposted along the way. The road itself makes a dramatic drive and forms part of a tour by drover's roads of the Cambrian Mountains devised by the Wales Tourist Board (see map).

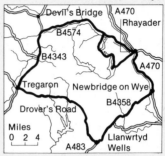

Cambrian Mountains: the scenic route which follows the old drove roads

These roads are suitable only for cars. Other drove roads remain in their original 'green' form and have helped to establish pony trekking here.

☐ 13 miles (21km) SW of Builth Wells on A483. Map ref 1B2.

346. NEW RADNOR
Failed medieval town

This was one of the scores of new towns that were founded in the two centuries after the Norman Conquest. It was established about the year 1250 to take over the functions of Old Radnor three miles (5km) to the south-east. A huge grassy castle *motte* or mound stands at the head of the main street to signify its intended importance. But the town never developed a full urban life, although it is possible to trace out in the hedges of adjacent fields the lines of streets that were never completed.

☐ Seven miles (11km) NW of Wington on A44. Map ref 1C2.

347. NEWTOWN
Market town/inn

This town's English name means what it says: it was developed as a new town by the English. Roger de Mortimer built it in the 13th century on the site of a small village called Llanfair Cedewain on a loop of the Severn. It was established to command an important route between the two countries after the defeat of Llywelyn, last of the Welsh princes, at Abermule, five miles (8km) to the north-east. Little remains of either Llywelyn's Dolforwyn Castle (AM) west of Abermule – or Newtown's medieval origins. But there are attractive riverside walks, a livestock market on Tuesdays and a fine former coaching inn, *The Bear*, with timbered gables and a wooden gallery supported by pillars at the first-floor level.

☐ Eight miles (13km) SW of Montgomery on A489 or A483. Map ref 1C2.

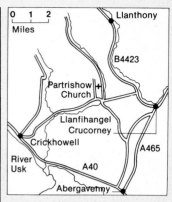

Partrishow church is well-hidden, but this map will help you locate it

348. PARTRISHOW
Tudor church

On a hillside, but embowered in trees, is one of the most secluded churches in Britain, serving no visible parish, yet alive. The great feature of this little Tudor church is its silvery oak screen, which, despite the Order in Council of October 1561 prohibiting them, preserved (with the aid of discreet restoration) its beautiful rood loft. Partrishow needs seeking out, but it is well worth the effort. If locked, the key is available from an adjacent farm.

☐ Six miles (9.6km) N of Abergavenny (see map). Map ref 1C3.

349. PISTYLL RHAEADR
Waterfall

Generally regarded as the finest waterfall in Wales because of its great height (240ft; 72m) and almost unbroken descent (the highest fall plummets vertically in a 100-foot leap, while the lower falls beneath a natural arch and a footbridge). On the border with Clwyd, the falls can be crowded in summer since the approach road is very narrow.

☐ Four miles (6.4km) NW of Llanrhaeadr-yn-Mochnant on minor road off B4580 W of Oswestry. Map ref 1C1.

350. POWIS CASTLE
Converted castle/terraced gardens

Perhaps the finest example of a fascinating type of British country house: the medieval castle, adapted and made increasingly comfortable over the centuries. Little survives of the original castle except its exterior, towering up from a spectacular hill-top site near Welshpool. Inside, the long gallery is Elizabethan, and the late 17th century staterooms include a frescoed staircase and a bedroom prepared and decorated for Charles II, with a bed in an alcove protected by a carved balustrade from the vulgar. The hill-side garden was laid out with terraces and topiary in about 1700, and also some modern planting both on the terraces and woodland. The garden and the castle, restored and part-redecorated with commendable taste in the 1890s, are usually open on afternoons other than Mon and Tues from Easter-Sept; tel: Betws-y-Coed 312 NT.

☐ One mile (1.6km) S of Welshpool – pedestrian access from High Street (A490), cars from A483 to Newtown. Map ref 1C1.

Powis Castle, near Welshpool, Powys. Medieval walls hide later restoration

351. PRESTEIGNE
Half-timbered buildings

The Radnorshire Arms is a fine timbered building, once a private residence, which dates from 1616. It became an inn in 1792 and was a posting house in the first half of the 19th century. *The Duke's Arms* is older but less distinguished architecturally. Despite its small size, Presteigne was the county town of the old county of Radnorshire and being near Herefordshire its architecture is typical of the borderland area known as The Marches with English styles such as half-timbering mixing with Welsh traditions. Market day is Wednesday. Three miles (5km) southwest of the town is Burfa Camp or Castle, an Iron Age hill fort incorporated into Offa's Dyke (SO 284610).
☐ 12 miles (19km) W of Leominster on B4362. Map ref 1C2.

352. RADNOR FOREST
Moorland/hill-walking

A remarkable mountain dome of Silurian grits and limestones, rising to breezy moorland summits with delightful names – the highest point at 2166ft (649m). The area provides invigorating but rugged walking off the beaten track with great panoramic views over the Welsh borderland. On the eastern side is the beautiful Harley Valley with its classic example of overlapping spurs incised by the river; to the south is the wonderfully named waterfall of 'Water-break-its-neck'. Since there are no roads fit for cars in this mountain massif it remains an unspoilt wilderness area – the ancient name 'forest' refers to the unenclosed moorland not to the new Forestry Commission plantations. OS map 148.
☐ Eight miles (13km) SW of Knighton between A488, A44 and B4372. Map ref 1C2.

353. TRETOWER
Fortified house

As the Welsh borderlands became more peaceful dwellings became less fortified. The gradual process of change can be seen at Tretower where a 13th century tower remains from a motte and bailey type castle. This was followed a century later and 200 yards away by Tretower Court, still retaining some of a fortified flavour but also beginning to show elements of a stately or country home. A stone gateway protects the house which overlooks an open courtyard. Both Court and Castle are open standard DoE hours.
☐ Three miles (4.8km) NW of Crickhowell on A479. Map ref 1C3.

354. YSTRADFELLTE
Waterfalls/walks

Narrow limestone gorges, thick with woodlands, have been formed where small rivers descend over hard ledges to the fault-guided and glacially over-deepened Vale of Neath. The best concentration of waterfalls is in the gorge of the Mellte south of Ystradfellte. Riverside walks lead south from a car park and picnic area about one mile (1.6km) south of the village. The paths can be slippery – so wear suitable shoes – but they are also spectacular. In little more than two miles (3.2km) you pass four falls: from north to south, Scwd Clyn-gwyn, Scwd Isaf Clyn-gwyn, Scwd y Pannwr and (on the sister river Hepste) Scwd yr Eira. Also approximately one mile (1.6km) south of Ystradfellte the Mellte disappears down a pothole to reappear a short distance away. Other potholes exist for experienced cavers.
☐ Six miles (9.6km) NE of Glyn-Neath on minor road to Defynnog. Map ref 1B3.

South Glamorgan

A mostly industrial county set around Cardiff. Attractions: Cardiff Castle, Llandaff Cathedral, Castell Coch. South Wales Tourism Council: Carmarthen 7557.

355. KENFIG BURROWS
Beach/nature trail

This is a wilderness of sand dunes behind a magnificent five mile (8km) stretch of sandy beaches which themselves make the area a great attraction. They are also recognised by the NCC as a Site of Special Scientific Interest for animals, flowers and coastal birds. A three-mile (4.8km) nature trail starts from Kenfig and a booklet is available from the Glamorgan County Naturalists' Trust, 104 Broadway, Cowbridge, South Glamorgan. Beside Kenfig Pool stands the ruins of Kenfig Castle – the medieval town of Kenfig was buried beneath the sand 600 years ago – and Sker House. The Burrows can be reached only on foot – from Margam Sands, Kenfig or Porthcawl. See also under Margam (West Glamorgan).
☐ NW of Porthcawl. Map ref 1B4.

356. ST FAGAN'S
Folk museum

St Fagan's Castle is an Elizabethan mansion within the walls of a medieval castle. What makes it even more interesting nowadays, however, is the Welsh Folk Museum housed within the 'castle' and its grounds. Many examples of typical Welsh vernacular architecture have been re-erected in the grounds, often saving them from destruction. They include a 15th century farmhouse, a 17th century thatched barn, medieval cottages, a toll house and even a cockpit. Woollen and corn mills are also there, in working order, and on weekdays and most Bank holidays craftsmen give demonstrations of their traditional skills. Open all day weekdays and Sun afternoons throughout the year except over Christmas, New Year and May Day Bank Holidays; tel: Cardiff 561357 or 569441 for details.
☐ Four miles (6.4km) W of Cardiff city centre off A48 or A4119. Map ref 1C4.

West Glamorgan

The Gower Peninsula (AONB) is the highlight of an otherwise largely industrial county. Also Pennard and Weobley Castles. South Wales Tourism Council: Carmarthen 7557.

357. AFAN ARGOED
Country park/woods

Five forest or nature trails run through forestry plantations in this valley; leaflets available from the park information centre. Other features of the park are bridleways, industrial archaeology and fishing as well as picnic areas.
☐ Five miles (8km) NE of Port Talbot on A4107. Map ref 1B3.

358. MARGAM
Country park/museum

A large country park near the Kenfig Burrows sand dunes (see under Mid Glamorgan) and appealing to a wide variety of interests. Within its 794 acres (322 hectares) of park and woodland are an outstanding 18th century Orangery; rhododendrons (particularly attractive in May); a herd of deer; waymarked walks and picnic areas; lakes; pony rides and monastic remains. The park is open daily Apr-Sept except Mon other than Bank Holidays and then Wed-Sun from Oct-Mar. Tel: Port Talbot 87626. Near Margam Church, part of a former Cistercian abbey, is a museum (AM) of inscribed early Christian stones; open all year on Wed, Sat and Sun afternoons.
☐ Two miles (3.2km) E of Port Talbot on A48. Map ref 1B3/4.

359. OXWICH
Nature trail/coastal scenery

Oxwich Sand Trail starts at the high tide mark and covers about half a mile (0.8km). A leaflet is available from the Oxwich Reserve Centre at car park. Tel: Gower 320. The dunes and marshes inland are a national nature reserve closed to the public. Oxwich Point offers a good view of the Bristol Channel. Other interesting places near Oxwich include two forest walks starting from the car park opposite the entrance to Penrice Castle, one mile (1.6km) north of Oxwich; Three Cliffs Bay, where faults in the rock have caused an impressive natural arch; and Pennard Castle.
☐ 10 miles (16km) W of Swansea off A4118. Map ref 1B3.

360. RHOSILI
Coastal walks/views

At the south-westernmost tip of the beautiful Gower peninsula the tiny village of Rhosili is an ideal centre for walks to explore the superb coastal scenery. A three-mile (4.8km) NCC nature trail starts from Rhosili car park and traverses cliffs with limestone flora. It is open all year and leaflets are available from the Oxwich Reserve Centre (see previous entry). To the north is the splendid curve of Rhosili Bay where smooth sands are backed by a three mile (4.8km) coastal hill walk to the hermit's cell of Burry Holms. To the west is the islet of Worms Head which can be reached at low tide. To the south is a four mile (6.4km) walk along 200ft (61m) high cliffs to the spectacular rock formations of Culver Hole, passing secluded Mewslade Bay and Paviland Cave, believed to have been a dwelling for prehistoric man; the cave can be entered at low tide. OS map 159.
☐ 15 miles (24km) W of Swansea at end of B4247. Map ref 1B3.

Canaletto's painting of Badminton House, Gloucestershire, Palladian home of the Duke of Beaufort and scene of the annual Badminton Horse Trials. Long before the Horse Trials Badminton was famous for its connection with sports. The game of badminton was first played there in 1851

Lower Middle England

361. THE CHILTERNS
Area of Outstanding Natural Beauty

Most of the AONB falls within Oxfordshire and Buckinghamshire, but in the east it extends into Hertfordshire with an outlying pocket in Bedfordshire, and in the west it joins up with the North Wessex Downs AONB, forming a long swathe of hilly countryside traversed by the Ridgeway long-distance footpath. The path, one of the most ancient trackways in the British Isles, can be followed from Ivinghoe Beacon, 800ft (244m) in Buckinghamshire all the way to Avebury in the North Wessex Downs AONB, a distance of 85 miles (137km). Beechwoods and bluebells, chalk hillslopes and downland scarps are among the chief glories of the Chiltern landscapes, with the additional delights of the upper Thames from Marlow to Henley, Pangbourne, Goring and Wallingford, where boats may be hired to explore these idyllic *Wind-in-the-Willows* riverscapes. Places of interest which are themselves a day out include Whipsnade Zoo near Dunstable, (open daily), and Hughenden Manor (NT), near High Wycombe, Disraeli's former home (open weekend afternoons, and Wed-Fri afternoons in summer).

☐ Oxfordshire and Buckinghamshire. Map ref 2B3.

362. THE COTSWOLDS
Area of Outstanding Natural Beauty

Gloucestershire contains the lion's share of the Cotswolds, but this second largest of AONBs also spreads into the adjoining counties of Avon, Wiltshire, Oxfordshire, Hereford and Worcester. A justly celebrated range of hills, rising in a green crest above the Severn Vale (glorious views from Birdlip Hill). Clear streams steal through the valleys, and beside them, mellow stone towns and villages built of Cotswold stone: Bibury, Bourton-on-the-Water, Burford and Upper and Lower Slaughter. There are noble churches endowed by rich medieval wool merchants (Northleach has one of the finest), stately Palladian houses at Badminton and Painswick, and historic Sudeley Castle at Winchcombe (open daily, March-Oct). Other places of interest include the show village of Broadway, with its long impressive main street, and the medieval wool town of Chipping Campden.

☐ Map ref 1D3.

363. MALVERN HILLS
Area of Outstanding Natural Beauty

This imposing miniature mountain range of ancient rocks provides one of the finest ridgewalks in England. The paths are good and access is easy with bus stops and car parks along the roads below. There are enormous views westward to Wales and eastward to the Cotswolds and chequerboard farmlands of the Vale of the Severn. Worcestershire Beacon 1394ft (425m), highest of the Malvern summits, can be reached from Great Malvern, past St Ann's Well on well marked paths, or from the car park at West Malvern. Many gently graded paths wind round the northern slopes. The southern hills (Herefordshire Beacon) are best climbed past the massive Iron Age hill fort of British Camp where the A449 crosses the range. The fort's ramparts wind round a ridge of the Malverns enclosing an area of 32 acres (13 hectares). A *motte*, or mound, at the very top was added in the 11th or 12th centuries. For the complete walk along the summit ridge start by climbing to North Hill from the North Malvern Road clock tower in Great Malvern, a beautifully situated spa town, continuing southwards by way of Worcestershire Beacon, Wyche Cutting, Ragged Stone Hill and Chase End Hill before descending for the last time to complete a nine mile (14.4km) walk. You will need OS Map 150.

☐ Great Malvern is seven miles (11km) SW of Worcester on A449. British Camp is three miles (5km) SW of Great Malvern on A449. Good but steep paths lead from a large roadside car park. Map ref 1D2.

The Malvern Hills, an Area of Outstanding Natural Beauty offering magnificent ridge walks and sweeping views across the surrounding counties

Lower Middle England

Bedfordshire

The rambling river Ouse drains much of the county's flat acres. In the south there are the breezy heights of Dunstable Downs and Whipsnade Zoo. Dunstable and Luton are industrial while Bedford, the county town, has miles of riverside walks, gardens and water meadows. Thames and Chilterns Tourist Board: Abingdon 22711.

364. DUNSTABLE DOWNS
Chalk hills

This largely open stretch of downland on the north-eastern fringes of the Chilterns takes its name from the nearby town sited at the junction of Roman Watling Street and the older Icknield Way. The town (now rapidly merging with neighbouring Luton) was the site of an important 12th century priory of which the nave and west front still survive. Part of the Downs are protected by the NT; part of them form a 'natural' setting for the animals of Whipsnade Zoo. There are good walks with fine views. Nearby Ivinghoe Beacon (NT) is reached by a narrow road just outside the village. From its summit, nearly 800ft (244m) high, there are good vistas of the Chilterns and the Downs. The Coombe at Ivinghoe is a classic feature of chalk country – a dry valley.
□ The Downs are two miles (3.2km) S of Dunstable off B4540 or B4541. Ivinghoe is on the B489 SW of Dunstable. Map ref 2B3.

365. EATON BRAY
Chalk-stone church

The Church of St Mary the Virgin is constructed of the local Totternhoe chalk-stone from the nearby Chilterns. The plain exterior gives no hint of the delights of the interior, entered through a door enriched with beautiful foliated ironwork over 700 years old. The north arcade of the nave, with its splendidly crisp stiff-leaf capitals, is one of the most exquisite examples of Early English architecture in a village church: a miniature Wells Cathedral.
□ Four miles (6.4km) SE of Leighton Buzzard off A4146. Map ref 2B3.

366. LUTON HOO
Stately home

Most people go to see the house with its unique collection of Russian Imperial family treasures and Fabergé jewels. Its setting is superb – in a park landscaped by 'Capability' Brown in the 1770s. There are two lakes, a rose garden and some fine cedars. The rock garden is a delight. There are fine views over the Lea Valley. Open from Apr-Oct daily, except Tues and Fri. Tel: Luton 22955.
□ Thirty miles (48km) N of London off M1 at junction 10. Lodge gates on A6129. Map ref 2B3.

367. STOCKGROVE PARK
Country park

Wood and parkland with lake and facilities for fishing.
□ Two-and-a-half miles (4km) N of Leighton Buzzard off A418. Map ref 2B3.

Woburn Abbey, Bedfordshire, stately home of the Duke of Bedford and now a major tourist attraction

368. WOBURN
Stately home

Few people need reminding that this is the home of the Dukes of Bedford whose 18th century abbey building was one of the first country mansions to become a stately home catering for 20th century tourists. The house has a magnificent collection of old masters and French and English furniture and silver. Among the outside attractions are one of the largest drive-through game reserves in Europe. In the deer park surrounding the house there are lakes which offer coarse fishing. Information and opening times. Tel: Woburn 666.
□ Eight-and-a-half miles (13.7km) NW of Dunstable on A50. Map ref 2B3.

369. WREST PARK
French-style garden

The oldest part of this garden was made at the beginning of the 18th century. A long canal pool has the mansion at one end and a handsome pavilion at the other. The vista was closed in by blocks of woodland crisscrossed by allees with statues and other ornaments at the intersections. Later 'Capability' Brown landscaped the surrounding park, and in the 19th century formal terraces were added. Open Sat, Sun and Bank Holiday Mon from Apr-Sept. Tel: Silsoe 60152.
□ On A6 at Silsoe between Bedford and Luton. Map ref 2B3.

Buckinghamshire

The Chilterns run across the south of the county. To the north lies the rich agricultural region of the Vale of Aylesbury. Aylesbury, where six routes meet, is the county town. Watling Street and the Icknield Way run through the county. Thames and Chilterns Tourist Board: Abingdon 22711.

370. ASCOTT
Garden of evergreens

Originally a hunting lodge. The gardens were planted with evergreens so that it would look its best when it was being used in winter. There is an unusual sundial garden set out in topiary, a large circular pool and an orchard of flowering cherries. The house (NT) is open regularly from Apr-Sept. Tel: Wing 242 for details.
□ At Wing SW of Leighton Buzzard on S side of A418. Map ref 2B3.

371. BLACK PARK
Country park

Woodland with bridleways and nature trail. It also has a lake for fishing, canoeing, swimming and sailing model power-boats.
□ Two miles (3.2km) NE of Slough off N side of A412. Map ref 2B4.

372. BURNHAM BEECHES
Forest walks and drives

This ancient wood with its gnarled and pollarded beech trees is owned and managed by the City of London Corporation. There are many delightful paths and six miles (9km) of forest drives. The woods are especially lovely in late autumn. From Lord Mayor's Drive, which runs south-west from Farnham Common, it is possible to see the remains of a prehistoric camp and the Druid Oak, estimated to be 400 years old.
□ Three miles (5km) N of Slough off A355 W of Farnham Common. Map ref 2B3.

373. CHEQUERS
A walk passing Chequers

Since 1917 this 16th century house in the Chilterns has been the country home of the Prime Minister of the day. The house is not open to the public, but a public footpath crosses part of the estate and can be used to form part of a rewarding nine-mile (14.6km) circular walk through the surrounding woods and hills. For part of the way, too, you follow the Ridgeway long-distance footpath which incorporates the prehistoric Ridgeway and Icknield Way routes between the Marlborough Downs and Ivinghoe Beacon. But for the purposes of this more modest outing make Wendover your base. From here you climb Bacombe hill and Coombe Hill – with spectacular views from the chalk escarpment – before descending through woods and crossing roads (including the Chequers drive) to where the Ellesborough footpath turns off. Follow this, then right again by the path from Ellesborough to the B4010 below Coombe Hill and back to Wendover.
□ Wendover is five miles (8km) SE of Aylesbury at the junction of A413 and A4011. Map ref 2B3.

374. CHESHAM BOIS
Woodland wildlife refuge

This area of woodland stretching along both sides of the road was bought in 1978 by the Woodland Trust, and is open to the public. It is a splendid refuge for the wildlife between the towns of Chesham and Amersham, and a fine example of the dense high forest of the Chiltern beechwoods. Tel: Woodland Trust, Grantham 74297 for details.

□ One mile (1.6km) S of Chesham on A416. Map ref 2B3.

375. CLIVEDEN
A view of the Thames

The present Cliveden House dates from the mid-19th century and is the third to have been built on this site overlooking one of the most famous and beautiful stretches of the Thames. There is a particularly fine view of the river from the boat house. The landscape gardens have terraces, wooded walks, lavish flower borders, rose garden, an open air theatre and an assortment of temples and statues in the fashion of earlier centuries. The water garden was designed by Lord Astor in the 1890s. Cliveden is now owned by the NT. The house and gardens are open regularly. Tel: Burnham 5069 for details and times.
□ Near Cookham three miles (5km) N of Maidenhead off B476. Map ref 2B4.

376. EMBERTON PARK
Country park

Created from restored gravel pits, this park features lakes, river, nature trail, fishing, boating, caravan camping and playground.
□ Four miles (6.5km) N of Newport Pagnell on A509. Map ref 2B2.

377. GAYHURST
Elegant estate church

The church's neighbour in this small hamlet on the River Ouse is the beautiful Elizabethan house which featured in the Gunpowder Plot. One of the conspirators was taken from here to the Tower of London. The church was built in 1728, generously, with no expense spared using fine ashlar masonry throughout. It has an elegant interior with beautiful plaster ceilings and good plain glazing, mostly original. The pulpit is a two-decker and the tester is a whopper, with marquetry on its underside. There are handsome wrought-iron communion rails, gilded reredos and one outstanding monument.
□ Three miles (5km) NW of Newport Pagnall on B526. Map ref 2B2.

378. HADDENHAM
Cottages of mud

Many of the houses and cottages in this small village are built of mud or, to be more precise, wichert-chalk marl compressed with straw. As such it is one of the best examples of this traditional form of cottage construction in this part of the country. The church is of 13th century origin with a Norman font and medieval glass in the north chapel.
□ Three miles (5km) NE of Thame off A418. Map ref 2B3.

379. HAMBLEDEN VALLEY
Chiltern valley

One of the most beautiful of the deep, wooded valleys which dissect the southern slopes of the Chilterns. Here the landscape of bluebells, cherry blossom and flint-built villages is rural England at its best. Starting at the Thames, at Mill End with its 14th century mill, the visitor can follow the tiny chalk stream up its valley past the pretty village of Hambleden to the hidden hamlet of Fingest. This is crad-led in chalk hills, overlooked by a splendid windmill and thick beech-woods, interspersed with the gorse commons of Turville Heath. Grey's Court (NT), an Elizabethan house which for generations obtained its water by donkey-power, is open to the public from Apr-Sept. It stands three miles (5km) west of Henley-on-Thames on a minor road to Rotherfield Peppard.
□ Three miles (4.8km) NE of Henley-on-Thames, off the A4155. Map ref 2B4.

380. LANGLEY PARK
Country park

Woodland and parkland with facilities for camping. There are also rhododendron gardens and bridleways.
□ Three miles (5km) W of Uxbridge off S side of A412. Map ref 2B4.

381. STOWE HOUSE
Classical landscape garden

Only the grounds and garden buildings are open to the public – and then only during the Easter and summer holidays of Stowe School – but they are among the wonders of Europe, providing an extraordinary and magical example of the 18th century English aristocracy's determination to model their parks on the landscape pictures of Claude and Poussin. The leading landscape designers of the day, 'Capability' Brown and William Kent, laid out the grounds, first as a semi-formal garden, but later in the new style with lakes, secret glades and turf-clad vistas, temples, statues, obelisks, a Palladian bridge and almost anything else you can think of. The great palace of the Dukes of Buckingham, in the centre of it all, became a public school in the 1920s. Tel: Buckingham 3650 for opening times.
□ Three miles (5km) NW of Buckingham off A422. Map ref 2A3.

382. WADDESDON MANOR
Park and garden

The house is built in the style of a French chateau. The extensive grounds have a collection of sculpture from Italy, the Netherlands and France. There are lawns, terraces, many rare trees, a herd of Japanese Sika deer and tropical birds in the aviary. Open frequently from late March to late Oct. Tel: Waddesdon 293 for details.
□ On A41 NW of Aylesbury. Map ref 2B3.

383. WEST WYCOMBE PARK
Palladian house and park

A Palladian house set in an 18th century landscape park with classical temples. Open frequently. Tel: High Wycombe 24411 for details.
□ On A40 W of High Wycombe. Map ref 2B3

Gloucestershire

The centre of the county is dominated by the Cotswolds, the west by the wide, fertile Vale of Severn beyond which lies the Forest of Dean. Gloucester with its cathedral is the county town. Cheltenham is stylish with Pump Room and Promenade. Vil-lages of warm Cotswold stone epitomise a tranquil rural England. Heart of England Tourist Board: Worcester 29511.

384. BIBURY
Trout water village

A small but notable Cotswold village on the River Coln. The river is a well-known trout water. A trout farm here is open to the public during late March-Oct afternoons. Arlington Row is a picturesque group of 17th century weavers' cottages and Arlington Mill, from the same period, is now a museum featuring mill machinery and old agricultural implements. This old corn mill is open daily March-Oct and weekends during the rest of the year. Tel: Bibury 368 for times and further information. The church has Saxon origins but reflects the additions and alterations of many different periods. The village, described by William Morris as the most beautiful in England, can be crowded in the summer months.
□ Seven miles (11km) NE of Cirencester on A433. Map ref 1D3.

385. CHIPPING CAMPDEN
Cotswold market town

The name begins to tell the story: 'Chipping' derives from the Anglo-Saxon *cheapen* meaning to buy and is now always associated with a marketplace. This market town thrived on the medieval wool trade and signs of the prosperity it brought are everywhere from the mostly 15th century church to the early 17th century almshouses. The stone-arched market hall also dates from the 17th century and stands in the centre of the town which, like other market towns such as nearby Moreton-in-Marsh and Broadway, is set around a wide main street. But unlike these Chipping Campden has been spared the rush of 20th century traffic using this street as a main trunk highway. It becomes quite busy with visitors during summer weekends, but they do not diminish the town's appeal. The age of its many excellent buildings gives the Cotswold stone a particularly mellow charm.
□ Five miles (8km) NE of Broadway on B4081 and B4035. Map ref 2A3.

386. CIRENCESTER
Capital of the Cotswolds

Self-styled 'Queen of the Cotswolds', it can claim a longer pedigree than most of its rivals to this title. As *Corinium Dobunorum* it was the largest Roman town outside London with a defended enclosure of 240 acres (97 hectares). It was also the meeting-point of the Fosse Way, Akeman Street and one of the two Ermine Streets. Hardly anything remains to be seen of the Roman city on the ground but finds from archaeological excavations are displayed in a local museum. Cirencester prospered again in the Middle Ages as one of the most important centres of the wool trade in Britain. The most remarkable legacy of this period, in a town which is generally built of the ever-attractive Cotswold stone, is the beautiful Church of St John the Baptist overlooking the market place. Particularly interesting is the three-storey porch which was added to the church around 1500 by the local guilds. It served not only as an entrance to the church but also provided rooms for the traders on its upper floors. This close link between secular and religious worlds at the marketplace is not unparalleled in Britain but rarely, if ever, has it been expressed so memorably.
□ Sixteen miles (26km) NW of Swindon. Map ref 1D3.

387. COTSWOLD FARM PARK
Rare breeds of farm animals

Cotswold Farm Park, created in 1970, contains the most comprehensive collection of Rare Breeds of British animals on display in the country. There are little Soay sheep, the last survivors of the prehistoric domestic sheep of Europe; the 'Seaweed Eater', a rare Orkney breed and a relic of Scottish croft sheep; striped 'Iron Age' pigs; fluffy Sebastopol geese and Wild White Park cattle thought to have been brought to Britain by the Romans. Open daily from end April-end Sept. Tel: Guiting Power 307 for times.
□ Near Guiting Power off B4077 about five miles (8km) W of Stow-on-the-Wold. Map ref 1D3.

388. DEERHURST
Saxon church and chapel

Here on the banks of the Severn between Tewkesbury and Gloucester are two outstanding Saxon buildings. The parish church of St Mary was certainly in existence by the beginning of the 9th century. Although it was extended in the 10th century, some of the building is thought to date from as early as the 7th century. But even this would not mark the first building on the site: recent archaeological investigations have suggested that it was first the site of a Roman villa. Barely a hundred yards from the church stands Odda's Chapel, a tiny Saxon chapel built in 1056 but only rediscovered towards the end of the last century since years earlier it had become part of a timber-framed farmhouse. It was only in the 1960s that the chapel was disentangled from the farmhouse and came under the care of the Department of the Environment. It is open standard DoE hours.
□ Two miles (3.2km) SW of Tewkesbury off B4213. Map ref 1D3.

389. DYMOCK
Poets' village

This village was the home of a group of poets who made their mark on the literature of the early 1900s. Robert Frost, Lascelles Abercrombie, Rupert Brooke, John Drinkwater, Wilfred Gibson and Edward Thomas lived here between 1911 and 1914. Some of their best known work first appeared in a quarterly which was published from the village. This included Brooke's sonnet The Soldier. . . . 'If I should die, think only this of me.' The First World War, in which Brooke and Thomas were to die, caused the break up of the Dymock Poets. Little Iddens, the cottage where Frost lived, and the Old Nail Shop where Gibson lived, can still be seen.
□ S of Ledbury on B4216. Map ref 1D3.

390. FOREST OF DEAN
Forest, rivers and industrial history

Few other British forests retain the character of the mysterious primeval forest which once covered the land better than the Forest of Dean, 50 sq miles (129 sq km) of broadleaved and coniferous woodlands and open country between the Severn and the Wye. This former royal hunting forest, managed by the Forestry Commission, is criss-crossed by hundreds of miles of lanes, paths and bridleways; dotted with dozens of car parks and picnic places; is rich in the relics of a long industrial history; endowed with some of the most spectacular river scenery in the British Isles (the Wye Valley is designated an AONB). It also reflects a powerful history in its great buildings and castles – Tintern Abbey, one of the most beautiful ruins in Britain; Goodrich Castle on its high spur above the Wye; and the massive Norman walls of Chepstow Castle which guards the mouth of the river.

Forest. Highlights include Abbotswood forest trail with superb views to the Black Mountains and over the Severn Valley to the Cotswolds; a circular scenic forest drive; and the Wilderness trails which identify different uses of land, passing through forest, fields, farm, former mine workings and two nature reserves. The latter start from Plumb Hill on A4136 two miles (3.2km) SW of Mitcheldean.

River. Symonds Yat with its dramatic view of the Wye Gorge is deservedly famous. Here the river loops round Yat rock in an enormous meander past grassy meadows before plunging through its steeply wooded valley to the sea. A less busy viewpoint can be reached by following a track south from Goodrich and walking along the crest of Coppet Hill for about two miles (3km). This vantage point looks across the Yat Rock to the Forest of Dean. The walk can be combined with a visit to Goodrich Castle (AM). Other good viewpoints are, on the Welsh side, Wynd Cliff, just above the main A466 at St Arvans; and, across the river, Wintour's Leap, an unexpected and easily missed spot where the B4228 passes close to the clifftop. Motorists may not realise this owing to a screen of vegetation.

□ Symonds Yat is three miles (5km) S of Goodrich on B4432. Map ref 1D3.

Industrial history. The Romans mined for iron here and there are many clues to the Forest's past importance as a centre for iron working in names such as Foundry Wood, south of Cinderford, and the presence of several hammer ponds. Two places with links with the industrial past, but where industry has long since vanished, are: The Scowles, just south-south-east of Bream, where iron was worked for almost 2000 years. It is thought the Romans pioneered the site but today it is a place of deep woodland and dark chasms.

Blackpool Bridge, north-west of Blakeney, has a stretch of exposed Roman road which used to connect the iron mines with the great smelting community at Ariconium (see Ross on Wye entry) and with the port of Lydney on the Severn.

Clearwell Caves, formerly the Old Ham iron mines, house a museum recording some of the history of mining in the forest. Paths and lighting have been installed so the caves can be easily explored. They are open daily Easter to Sept except Mon and Sat.

□ The caves are on B4321 NW of Lydney. Forestry Commission Offices, Bank St, Coleford, in the heart of the forest just off A4136, have full details on forest facilities. Map ref 1D3.

391. HIDCOTE MANOR GARDEN
Outdoor 'rooms'

No garden better exemplifies the 20th-century trend towards the division into numerous separate sections, intimately interwoven, yet each distinct in size, shape, character and planting. Hidcote owes something to medieval tradition, something to cottage gardening and a great deal to the skill of its creator, Lawrence Johnston, artist and plant lover. Open regularly from Apr-Oct. Tel: Mickleton 333.

□ At Hidcote Bartrim, off B4081 near Mickleton. Map ref 2A2.

392. KEYNES PARK
Country park

Restored gravel pits with facilities for fishing, bird watching and sailing.

□ Four miles S of Cirencester. Map ref 1D3.

393. LECKHAMPTON HILL
Scarp walk

The spa town of Cheltenham, with its splendid Regency terraces, can be the base for a 10 mile (16km) walk along part of the 100 mile (160km) Cotswold Way which runs along the limestone escarpment of the Cotswolds from Chipping Camden to Bath. Start from the foot of Leckhampton Hill. The fortress crowned summit can be reached by several steep paths, or by following a side road which leaves the B4070. Few of southern England's escarpments terminate in cliffs but the Cotswold scarp here is an exception, for creamy oolitic limestones outcrop in the artificially quarried cliffs of the hill, 967ft (294m). The most spectacular feature is the 50ft (15m) pinnacle known as the Devil's Chimney. The route is waymarked via Ullenwood, Crickley Hill country park and Air Balloon Inn to Barrow Wake viewpoint. The Peak, Birdlip, Witcombe Woods and Cooper's Hill (scene of Whit Sunday cheese rolling) lead to Prinknash Abbey and a bus stop for the return journey to Cheltenham. OS map 163 in 1:50,000 series is useful.

□ Cheltenham is six miles (9.6km) NE of Gloucester. Leckhampton Hill is S of Cheltenham on B4070. Map ref 1D3.

394. ROBINSWOOD HILL
Country park

Wooded hill with views, bridleways and nature trails.

□ On the southern edge of Gloucester. Map ref 1D3.

395. SEVERN BORE
Tidal wave

The Bore occurs twice a day on about 130 days a year (see Chapter 6) but those of any size only occur on about 25 days. A good viewing point is along the eastern edge of the Forest of Dean where the A48 from Lydney to Gloucester runs close to the river at several spots. Other viewpoints: in the car park at the north end of Newnham or from the churchyard; the car park next to the Bird in Hand inn at Minsterworth. Heart of England Tourist Board, PO Box 15, Worcester WR1 2JT, publishes a free information sheet giving dates on which better-than-usual bores can be expected.

□ Map ref 1D3.

396. THE SLAUGHTERS
Picture postcard villages

Two villages ½ mile (800m) apart which come close to fulfilling the picture postcard image of the Cotswolds. Both are on the River Windrush but this is most in evidence in Lower Slaughter where the river, having passed through a watermill, trickles through the village down the middle of the main street. It is like a smaller and less commercialised Bourton-on-the-Water, but even here crowds can become oppressive in midsummer and at weekends. Upper Slaughter is less obviously a showpiece village and perhaps the more appealing for that. It also has an outstanding Elizabethan manor house with extensive gardens and the remains of a 15th century priory. This is normally open on Fri afternoons only from May-Sept. Tel: Bourton-on-the-Water 20927 for details.

□ Three miles (5km) SW of Stow-on-the-Wold off A436 and A429. Map ref 2A3.

397. SNOWSHILL
Cotswold village

Cotswold stone village, less crowded with visitors than some, on the escarpment overlooking the Vale of Evesham. The quality of the cottages is generally high while Snowshill Manor (NT) is a fine Tudor building with a 17th century frontage and a terraced garden. This houses a collection of clocks, toys and musical instruments. It is open daily from May-Sept except Mon and Tues.

□ Three miles (5km) S of Broadway – home of the *Lygon Arms* – on unclassified roads running between A44 and B4077. Map ref 1D3.

398. TEWKESBURY
A town of beauty

Standing at the confluence of the Severn and Avon this is one of the finest half timbered towns in England with spectacular overhanging eaves, a labyrinth of medieval alleys, fascinating old inns and an ancient mill. The Bell was once a monastery guest house. The Hop Pole has a 14th century fireplace before which Dickens's Mr Pickwick warmed himself. From the tower of the magnificent Abbey Church, with its massive Norman architecture, there is a panoramic view of the Avon and Severn valleys and the Malvern Hills.

□ On A38 N of Gloucester. Map ref 1D3.

399. ULEY
Hillfort and long barrow

Two outstanding prehistoric monuments lie immediately north of this village. One can hardly be missed: Uleybury hillfort, the finest earthwork in the county. It has double ramparts and ditches enclosing an area of 32 acres (13 hectares). From it there are particularly fine views over the surrounding Cotswolds. Less dominating, but also hard to miss, is a chambered long barrow signposted as Uley Tumulus but sometimes known as Hetty Pegler's Tump. Mrs Pegler was apparently the wife of the 17th century owner of the field in which this grassy mound stands. Those particularly interested in archaeology can apply for a key to inspect its interior from Crawley Hill Farm in Uley itself.

□ Uley is five miles (8km) SW of Stroud. Both the village and the prehistoric sites are on or just off the B4066. Map ref 1D3.

400. WESBURY COURT GARDEN
Water garden

Seventeenth-century formal water garden. Earliest example remaining in England. Open Apr and Oct on Sat, Sun; from May-Sept daily, except Mon, Tues. Tel: Westbury-on-Severn 461.

□ At Westbury-on-Severn on A48 SW of Gloucester. Map ref 1D3.

401. WESTONBIRT ARBORETUM
Collection of trees and shrubs

This large arboretum owned by the Forestry Commission, contains a wide

A typical Cotswold stone manor house at Upper Slaughter, Gloucestershire

variety of coniferous and broadleaved trees. There is also a surprising amount of natural woodland with many woodland flowers. Numerous paths and rides and two recommended walks. Best visited in October when the autumn colours, especially those of the maples, are at their best. Open every day. Tel: Westonbirt 220 for times. Information Centre.

☐ Three miles (4.8km) S of Tetbury on A433. Map ref 1D3.

402. THE WILDFOWL TRUST
Wintering place for wildfowl

Slimbridge, the first Wildfowl Trust centre opened to the public, is on the east bank of the Severn estuary at a place which has always been a wintering ground for wildfowl. It consists of 73 acres (30 hectacres) of enclosures, lakes and paddocks where the most varied collection of wildfowl in the world is kept. In winter the graceful yellow and black billed wild Bewick's swans fly all the way from Arctic Russia. Many individual birds return year after year to Slimbridge. Beyond the collection area, hides and observation towers overlook the saltmarsh known as the Dumbles, where wild duck and wild geese congregate. Here is easy birdwatching with every facility provided. You can see the tame birds close to as you wander through the enclosures, or hire binoculars to observe the wild ones. There is a permanent exhibition, gift shop and restaurant and tea room overlooking a lake. Tel: Cambridge, Glos 333 for entrance fees, hours and membership information.

☐ At Slimbridge. Signposted off the A38, S of Gloucester. Map ref 1D3.

403. WITHINGTON
Village with Roman roots

An attractive village not far from the headwaters of the River Coln. Apart from its appealing domestic buildings in Cotswold stone, and the Roman villa at Chedworth in the next parish, the village is interesting because local historians believe the site to have been continuously occupied and farmed since Roman times.

☐ Six miles (9.6km) SE of Cheltenham, S of A40. Map ref 1D3.

Hereford and Worcs.

Here lowland England nudges the mountain land, and the Malverns are its first foothills. The country has the beautiful, fast-running Wye, the orchards of Evesham, the cathedral cities of Hereford and Worcester and Offas Dyke. Heart of England Tourist Board: Worcester 29511.

404. AVONCRAFT MUSEUM OF BUILDINGS
Buildings of the past

A splendid open-air museum which specialises in rescuing old buildings from destruction and completely restoring them. The buildings which most concern the museum are those which relate to local crafts, or those which modern farming methods have made redundant, for example, the late 18th century granary from Temple Broughton Farm. There is a small 19th

Cruck-framed barn at the Avoncroft Museum of Buildings, Bromsgrove

century Counting House which was originally in Bromsgrove's Cattle market and which was moved intact to Avoncraft. There is also a 17th century cruck-framed barn, a fully working windmill and nail and chain workshops. The manufacture of nails and chains was very much a cottage industry of the Black Country. Open daily from Mar 1-Dec 2. Tel: Bromsgrove 31363 for times.

☐ Redditch Road, Stoke Heath, Bromsgrove. Off M5 at junction 5, and three miles (4.8km) N on to the A4024, just S of Bromsgrove. Map ref 1D2.

405. BEWDLEY
River and railway valley

This town on the River Severn, near the eastern fringes of the Wyre Forest, is the headquarters of the Severn Valley Railway. Steam-hauled train rides of up to 12½ miles (20km) as far as Bridgnorth are operated daily during the summer and on weekends at other times. Much of this restored line closely follows the River Severn through one of the most beautiful stretches of its valley – and one which is not generally followed by any road. Riverside walks and picnic areas are available near all the intermediate stations. Tel: Bewdley 403816 or Bridgnorth 4361 for details.

☐ Three miles (5km) SW of Kidderminster on A456. Map ref 1D2.

406. BROADHEATH
Elgar's birthplace

Sir Edward Elgar was born here within sight of the Malvern Hills in 1857 in a cottage which was his family's summer home. The cottage in Crown East Lane has a collection of photographs, musical scores and objects associated with the composer. Open daily except Wed.

☐ On B4204 E of Tenbury Wells. Map ref 1D2.

407. BROADWAY TOWER
Country park

This consists of grassland and woods on the Cotswold scarp. It has fine views, a nature trail and Broadway Tower itself.

☐ Nearly two miles (3km) S of Broadway. Map ref 1D3.

408. BROCKHAMPTON
Walking and picnicking

Bringsty Common in the parish of Brockhampton is a hilly area of open heath with splendid views in every direction. Crossed by the main A44 it offers good walking and picnic spots. Lower Brockhampton (NT), two miles (3.2km) east of the old market town of Bromyard, is a small timber frame moated manor house dating from about 1400. It glories in a fine open-roof Great Hall and has a separate jewel of a gatehouse guarding the moat crossing. Open daily from Feb to Dec, except Tues and Thurs.

☐ Off A44 E of Bromyard. Map ref 1D2.

409. CLENT HILLS
Country park

Hilly grassland with views and bridleways.

☐ Eight miles (13km) W of Birmingham S of Halesowen W off A456 or A491. Map ref 1D2.

410. EVESHAM
Market town

Some market towns grew up around castles, some around abbeys. Evesham is an example of the latter and its role as the market centre for the Vale of Evesham has enabled it to outlive the abbey of which only a bell-tower and a gateway remain. Nonetheless, these are impressive and the abbey grounds which slope down to the River Avon also contain two churches. Evesham's position close to both the Cotswolds and the forests of Warwickshire with access to timber and stone has resulted in an appealing mixture of architectural styles. There are some old stone buildings but the most interesting tend to be half-timbered, such as the Almonry and Booth Hall, or Round House, both from the 14th or 15th centuries.

☐ Six miles (9.6km) NW of Broadway on A44. Map ref 1D2.

411. GOLDEN VALLEY
Remote and peaceful river valley

The placid valley of the River Dore is a place of small villages and farms, narrow country lanes, hills and meadows. A good road runs through it connecting the main villages of Dorstone, Peterchurch, Vowchurch and Abbey Dore. The latter lies at the gateway to Golden Valley and fine examples of Early English architecture can be seen in the great parish church, the red sandstone of its fabric contrasting with the rich green of its setting, which consists of the transepts and chancel of the Cistercian Dore Abbey, founded in 1147. The Abbey was even more richly endowed with estates than Tintern and its properties included 17 granges (outlying farms) of which nine were in the valley. The monks were diligent farmers and turned the forest chase into an agricultural estate, laying the foundation of the stock rearing and cultivation upon which Golden Valley depends to this day. The walled and river garden of Abbey Dore Court, specialising in ferns, is open daily. Arthur's Stone on Merbach Hill above Dorstone is a notable chambered tomb dating from Neolithic times.

☐ Valley starts 10 miles (16km) SW of Hereford off A465 on B4347. Map ref 1C3.

412. HAUGH WOOD
Woodland walk

Haugh Wood (FC) picnic place is tucked among the oaks and larches. The walk begins at the picnic place and leads through woods of oak and Douglas fir. There are views over Hereford and to the Welsh mountains. Walks 1½ miles (2.4km) and 1 mile (1.6km). Below Haugh Wood the village of Fownhope has an attractive black and white inn, the *Green Man*, and a church, the Norman tower of which has a broach spire constructed of 22,000 oak shingles. Tel: Head Forester, Gorsley 235 for details.

☐ Five miles (8km) SE of Hereford on the Mordiford to Woolhope by-road. Map ref 1D3.

413. HEREFORD AND WORCESTER COUNTY MUSEUM
Old farm waggons

The agricultural side of this museum is out of doors and consists of an interesting collection of farm waggons (including the Worcester waggon), gypsy caravans, bow-fronted Brougham and Hansom cab. There is also a complete cider press dating from about 1700. Open from Feb-end Nov daily except Fri. Tel: Hartlebury 416 for times.

☐ Hartlebury Castle, Hartlebury, near Kidderminster, on A449 from Worcester-Kidderminster road. Map ref 1D2.

414. KILPECK
Norman church

This small village in pleasant, hilly country between the Dore and the Wye possesses England's most perfect little Norman church which stands almost alone in a wholly rural area. It is a masterpiece of sculptural decoration, all in sandstone, marvellously well preserved. The chancel arch has religious figures of exquisite tenderness, but outside the mood is robustly secular, to the point of bawdiness: and none the worse for that! The gaps among the outside ring of corbels were caused, not by age, but by Victorians shocked at some of the subjects represented. The remains of a moated castle stand next to the church.

☐ Ten miles (16km) SW of Hereford off A465. Map ref 1C3.

The arcaded Market Hall at Ross-on-Wye, a popular Wye Valley touring centre

415. KINGSFORD
Country park

Wood and heathland with nature trail, bridleways and views.
□ At Kinver Edge three miles (5km) N of Kidderminster. Map ref 1D2.

416. LEDBURY
Market town

A market town to the west of the Malverns with outstanding black and white timbered buildings. These include houses, inns, and, from the 17th century, the finest half timbered market hall in the country. The church has Norman origins, but is mostly 13th to 14th century. In the 15th century Old Grammar School, a restored timber-framed building, a 'Heritage Centre' exhibition tells the story of Ledbury's growth from Anglo-Saxon village to market town (market on Tues). Open weekends from Easter-Spring Bank Holiday, then daily until Oct. A booklet detailing a 1½ hour tour of the town's most interesting buildings is available at the centre.
□ Twelve miles (19km) E of Hereford at junction of A438, A449 and A417. Map ref 1D3.

417. LICKEY HILLS
Country park

Wood, heath and meadowland with good views, bridleways and a bird sanctuary. Sports facilities include boating, golf and ski-ing and tobogganing when conditions are suitable.
□ Eight miles (13km) S of Birmingham. Map ref 1D2.

418. PEMBRIDGE
15th century inn

This village was on an old coaching road from London to South Wales but the timbered *New Inn* was already quite old by the time the first coaches called. This fine black-and-white building dates from the 15th century and was once used by wool traders. It also once contained a court room. Its old stables now form the dining room. Opposite the inn is an ancient covered market hall. The church is mainly 14th century and has a huge detached bell house of pyramidal design. There are also some attractive half-timbered houses in the village.
□ Seven miles (11km) W of Leominster on A44. Map ref 1C2.

419. ROSS ON WYE
Riverside market town

Set on a red sandstone cliff commanding a beautiful stretch of the River Wye, this delightful town attracts many visitors in summer. The parish church dominates the much photographed view of the town from the river. Beyond the church is the Prospect, a walled public garden, which gives fine views of the river's horseshoe bend, Wilton Castle, the town and the Black Mountains. Much of the character of Ross is due to the benefaction of one man, John Kyrle. Alexander Pope extolled the virtues of the Man of Ross in his 'Moral Essays'. John Kyrle's home, in the triangular Market Place, is now the office of the Ross Gazette and a chemist's. The Market Place is dominated by the massive, 14-arched Market Hall which forms the hub of the town. Penyard Woods lie to the south of Ross and nearby is the site of *Ariconium*, in Roman days an industrial settlement which made arms for the legions. It has been described as the Black Country of Roman Britain. There are good views of the river at Kerne Bridge to the west of Ross.
□ Access via A40 from Gloucester 16 miles (26km) or M50. Map ref 1D3.

420. SHOBDON
Rococo-Gothic church

The Church of St John the Evangelist is a delicious little ecclesiastical drawing room, created in 1752–6, and now admirably restored in the original colour scheme of white and grey-blue. Great play is made throughout the church with ogee curves, scrolls and pendants. It is marred only by the east window of 1907 and a primitive Norman font which should be moved elsewhere. Arches from an earlier Norman church – all that remains of a former 12th century priory – have been re-erected in the grounds of the former Shobdon Court.
□ Eight miles (13km) W of Leominster on B4362. Map ref 1C2.

421. STOURPORT
Canal town

The only town entirely created by the canal age. It grew from just a single ale-house at the point where the Staffordshire and Worcestershire Canal joined the River Severn and River Stour. Its 18th century origins have resulted in an appealing marriage between Georgian and canal architecture. Around the canal basin many of the old wharves, warehouses and cottages remain. The basin is used by pleasure craft.
□ Four miles (6.4km) SW of Kidderminster on A451 and A4025. Map ref 1D2.

422. TEME VALLEY
Day out drive

This 50 mile (80.5km) circuit covers some of the most attractive countryside and delightful towns and villages in the heart of England. It passes hopyards and orchards and is a picture in spring when the fruit blossom is out. The route is best followed in an anti-clockwise direction as this reduces the number of awkward right turns. It can, of course, be joined at any point on the circuit. Here we start at Bromyard, a market town with narrow winding streets, following the A44 over Brockhampton's Bringsty Common (see Brockhampton) before turning north on B4197 at Knightsford Bridge. From here the road towards Martley gives good views on both sides and, after Martley, especially from Woodbury Hill. After Great Witley, with its baroque church and ruined Witley Court, the A443 climbs over the Abberley Hills and drops down into the

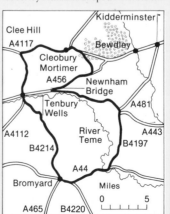

Teme Valley drive: a round trip for motorists, starting from Bromyard

valley of the Teme. At Newnham Bridge the route turns north-east and follows the A456 to the viewpoint of Clows Top, and then north on the B4202 along the edge of Wyre Forest (separate entry) joining the A4117 just before Cleobury Mortimer, a small market town below the Clee Hills. After the hills the route turns south on the B4214 crossing the Teme at Tenbury Wells (Burford House gardens are in a beautiful setting by the river) and returns to Bromyard.
□ Map ref 1D2.

423. WASELEY HILLS
Country park

Hilly grassland with bridleways and views of the Black Country and the Severn Valley.
□ At Rubery SW of Birmingham. Map ref 1D2.

424. WYRE FOREST
Remnant of primeval forest

Wyre Forest lies close to Bewdley and the Severn and, like the Forest of Dean, is a remnant of the primeval forest which once covered England. In the peaceful depths of the forest flora and fauna are relatively undisturbed. In places the Forestry Commission have planted new plantations, established car parks and picnic sites and a series of nature trails and walks. Green Walk, one of three which are waymarked, runs along an escarpment with views over the forest and Clee Hills. Walks start from picnic place by Callow Hill Visitor Centre which tells the story of Wyre Forest with displays of forest crafts, tools and a wildlife exhibit. Hawkbatch picnic place is in oak woodlands within ½ mile (800m) of viewpoint over River Severn and Trimpley reservoir.
□ Callow Hill Visitor Centre is on A456 three miles (4.8km) W of Bewdley. Hawkbatch picnic place is on B4194 two miles (3.2km) NW of Bewdley.
□ Map ref 1D2.

Hertfordshire

A county of leafy lanes and village greens with old Roman cities (Verulamium) and modern planned ones (Letchworth and Welwyn). The Icknield Way traverses the top of the county. The Chilterns lie in the west and the Lee Valley in the east. Hertford is the county town. Thames and Chilterns Tourist Board: Abingdon 22711.

425. ALDENHAM
Country park

The reservoir offers fishing and sailing in a meadowland setting.
□ NW of Elstree off A5. Map ref 2B3.

426. ASHWELL
Village since Roman times

A remarkably unspoilt village with some mud-and-timber cottages among a fine collection of domestic buildings from the Tudor period onwards. The village, though, has been occupied since at least Roman times and in the timber-framed early Tudor Town House (AM) there is a museum of village life from prehistoric times to present-day. The church is mainly

14th century and carved on a wall of its tower is a drawing of the old St Paul's Cathedral.

□ Four miles (6.4km) NE of Baldock, between the A1 (the site of the Roman Ermine Street) and the A505 (here following the route of the old Icknield Way). Map ref 2B3.

427. BENCROFT WOOD
Woodland walks

This small but interesting stretch of old coppice woodland has the traditional mix of hornbeam, oak and birch typical of southern Hertfordshire. There are picnic places within easy reach of the car parks and two forest walks. This and nearby Broxbourne Wood are managed by Hertfordshire County Council which publishes leaflets on both. Tel: Hertford County Planning Dept, Hertford 54242, Ext 253.

□ Four miles (6.4km) S of Hertford on White Stubbs Lane, off by-road forking off B158. Map ref 2C3.

428. NORTHAW GREAT WOOD
Country park

Woodland with bridleways and route-marked walks.

□ Five miles (8km) SE of Hatfield on B157. Map ref 2B3.

429. HATFIELD HOUSE
Garden history

Old and new styles of gardening combine here; an Elizabethan knot garden and modern herbaceous planting in which a parterre, previously used for bedding out plants, is now permanently planted. There are roses old and new, shrubs, trees, including some in fine avenues across the large park. There is a herb garden, a garden of scented plants and a maze. Open daily from Mar-Oct, except non-Bank Holiday Mons. Tel: Hatfield 62823.

□ Off A1 21 miles (33km) N of London. Map ref 2B3.

430. KNEBWORTH
Country park

Wooded parkland with bridleways and adventure playground. It also has deer herds and a narrow gauge railway. Knebworth House is open daily (except Mon) from March-Sept.

□ One-and-a-half miles (2.5km) SW of Stevenage off A1(M). Map ref 2B3.

431. ROYAL NATIONAL ROSE SOCIETY
Rose gardens

New roses are tested over a period of three years and established roses are grown in a well-designed display garden. There are also collections of shrub roses, rose species and roses of historic and botanical interest, as well as several model rose gardens. Open daily from mid-June to Sept. Tel: St Albans 50461.

□ Chiswell Green Lane, St Albans. Map ref 2B3.

432. ST ALBANS
Remains of a Roman city

Although there are some fine medieval and Georgian buildings in this city, ranging from the cathedral to the *Fighting Cocks* inn, from almshouses to a water-mill, its greatest days far preceded them. On its western outskirts are the remains of one of the largest Roman cities, *Verulamium*, where a Roman theatre, including a colonnaded stage, and a fine stretch of city wall can still be seen. There is also a museum with exhibits discovered during the excavations. Yet these are not the oldest surviving antiquities in the landscape. In Prae Wood, just above the Roman remains, are the banks and ditches of a prehistoric settlement that was a capital of the Belgae, one of the chief tribes of southern Britain in the Iron Age.

□ Verulamium is one mile (1.6km) W of St Albans' city centre off the A414.
□ Map ref 2B3.

433. THERFIELD HEATH
Barrows and burial mounds

Here, in a region somewhat barren of the relics of prehistory, is a Neolithic long barrow (about the only one in eastern England) and Five Knolls (not to be confused with the Five Knolls in Bedfordshire) a group of Bronze Age burial mounds. This concentration of antiquities is almost certainly related to the area's proximity to the prehistoric Icknield Way.

□ One mile (1.6km) W of Royston, a town at the junction of the Icknield Way and the Roman Ermine Street. Map ref 2C3.

Northamptonshire

An undulating countryside of farms and woods with the industrial towns of Corby, Kettering and Wellingborough in the north. Northampton is the county town. East Midlands Tourist Board: Lincoln 31521.

434. BARNWELL
Country park

These restored sand and gravel pits on east bank of the River Nene offer bird watching, angling facilities for disabled people and a riverside walk. There is a warden on site.

□ Just over ½ mile (1km) S of Oundle on Barnwell road A605 leading to Thrapston. Map ref 2B2.

435. BOUGHTON HOUSE
Great English house

One of the least known of great English houses and only recently opened to the public. Grew in layers from the Middle Ages until the early 18th century. The medieval and Elizabethan house rambled gently around a series of peaceful courtyards. In the 1690s the Francophile Duke of Montague, who had been ambassador in Paris, redecorated the medieval hall and turned one end of the house into a formal French chateau. Contents superb or fascinating throughout, from the very best French furniture to the only surviving country-house shovel board – on which upper servants used to play a grand version of shove-halfpenny. House and garden are usually open every afternoon from late July to end-Sept; also on limited days of the week up to late Oct and at Easter and Spring bank holidays. Tel: Kettering 82248 for details.

□ Three miles (5km) N of Kettering on A43. Map ref 2B2.

436. IRCHESTER
Country park

This is undulating reafforested land with a nature trail. Until 1940 the area was mined for ironstone and afterwards planted with pine and larch. The hill-and-dale topography of dry slopes and damp bottoms gives a good variety of habitats. There are goldcrests, blue tits, great tits, willow tits, long-tailed tits, squirrels and rabbits in the woodland. Guide from the warden's office. Tel: Wellingborough 76866 for details.

□ Nearly three miles (4km) SE of Wellingborough on road to E of A509. Map ref 2B2.

437. KIRBY HALL
Elizabethan house

One of the most evocative and beautiful of Elizabethan houses made all the more poignant by the fact that all except the great hall and one corner is a ruin. Originally built by Sir Humphrey Stafford in 1570-5, it was sold soon afterwards to Elizabeth's favourite, Sir Christopher Hatton. It has a courtyard surrounded by great windows and rich Renaissance carving, a long line of curved gables and chimney stacks surveying the restored Elizabethan garden and, round one corner, a pair of enormous bow windows, like the sterns of two Elizabethan galleons moored side by side. The entrance range was remodelled in the time of Inigo Jones, and shows his influence. The hall is open standard DoE hours.

□ Four miles (6.4km) NE of Corby off A43. Map ref 2B2.

438. KNIGHTLEY WAY
Country path walk

The section from Badby to Preston Capes covers the first four miles (6km) of the Knightley Way. This path passes through Badby Wood, a mixed woodland with wild cherry, ferns and rich bird life. Further on Fawsley Park has lakes, meadows and woods. Leaflet from Northamptonshire Leisure and Library Services. Tel: Northampton 34833.

□ Badby is two miles (3.2km) S of Daventry just off E side of A361. Map ref 2A2.

439. LAMPORT HALL
Historic house

This has been the home of the Isham family for over 400 years, although the present house dates mainly from the 17th and 18th centuries. Its south-west front is a rare example of the work of John Webb and was built in 1665 with wings added between 1732 and 1740. The house is set in attractive wooded gardens and parkland and has a fine collection of paintings, furniture and china. Open afternoons only from Easter to end-Sept on Sun. Also Thurs in June, July, Aug and Bank Holiday Mon and Tues.

□ Eight miles (12.8km) N of Northampton on A508. Map ref 2B2.

440. OUNDLE
County town

The finest among many old buildings in this small market town on the River Nene is an inn – *The Talbot*, built in 1626 on the site of a monastic hospice. It has three storeys with mullioned windows reaching from ground level to the gables. A central archway leads to the yard. The river has made Oundle into a popular boating centre. Cotterstock Hall, a stone manor house to the north of the town is where Dryden wrote the Fables. The house and gardens are not open to the public.

□ Eleven miles (18km) SW of Peterborough at junction of A605 and A427. Map ref 2B2.

441. STANFORD-ON-AVON
Coloured stone church

Easy of access yet very little known. A village church of singular charm, specially recommended to lovers of colour. The stonework is a blend of fawn, pink and grey; the interior unusually rich in mediaeval glass. Good monuments, and, what is unhappily rare in England, an organ which is a joy to behold.

□ Six miles (9.6km) NE of Rugby and four miles (6.4km) SE of intersection 20 on M1 motorway off B5414. Map ref 2A2.

442. STOKE BRUERNE
Canal centre

This small village on the Grand Union Canal has become something of a mecca for canal enthusiasts. In the village there is a typical canal bridge and lock, a fine example of a canal pub in the *Boat Inn*, and an excellent Waterways Museum in a former corn mill. Tel: Northampton 862229 for the opening times. There are also regular boat trips in season as far as the Blisworth tunnel, at 3000 yards (2775m) the second longest navigable canal tunnel in Britain.

Stoke Bruerne can also be the starting-point of a drive (with periodic towpath walks) to see several other examples of the scenery and architecture which canals brought to the relatively high and riverless plateau of the Midlands. Along the unclassified road north from Stoke Bruerne to Blisworth are the ventilation shafts of the canal tunnel below; at Braunston there are the old wharves which indicate its former commercial importance as the junction of the old Oxford canal and the Grand Union; at Little Braunston there is a beautiful old toll office and four locks, with Braunston tunnel a none-too-easy walk down the towpath. There are also several old canalside pubs in this area.

□ Stoke Bruerne is three miles (5km) E of Towcester off A508. Map ref 2A2.

Oxfordshire

The county has both the Chilterns and the Cotswolds. Oxford and its colleges are outstanding attractions and its rivers are the Thames and the Cherwell. Thames and Chilterns Tourist Board: Abingdon 22711.

443. BANBURY
Europe's biggest cattle market

The town has Saxon origins, but few buildings survive from before the 17th century. Even the Banbury Cross of nursery rhyme fame is a replica erected in the 19th century. The original was destroyed in 1602. Who the 'fine lady on the white horse' was is unclear, although she appears on the town's coat of arms. Banbury's Thursday market is the largest and most important cattle-market in Europe.

☐ Twenty-two miles (35km) N of Oxford. Map ref 2A3.

444. BLENHEIM PALACE
Home of the Marlboroughs

The birthplace of Sir Winston Churchill. The palace has an exhibition of Churchilliana. Designed by Sir John Vanbrugh in the classical style, the gardens and park were later landscaped by 'Capability' Brown made for the Duke of Marlborough in the 18th century. Open daily from Mid-Mar-Oct. Park open all year. Tel: Woodstock 811325.

☐ At Woodstock on A34 N of Oxford. Map ref 2A3.

445. COGGES MANOR FARM
Farm museum

A 13th century manor house and an Edwardian Farmhouse are part of this 11 acre (4.5 hectares) site where many traditional farm skills, such as hurdle-making and sheep-shearing, can be seen. Quantities of tools, waggons and horse-drawn vehicles show how, a century ago, farmers worked and raised their livestock. Visitors can follow an historic trail marking the moated manor, deserted village earthworks and field systems of medieval times. Open daily from Easter-Sept. Tel: Woodstock 811456 for details.

☐ Off A40, just S of Witney. Map ref 2A3.

446. COTSWOLD WILDLIFE PARK
Animals in 'natural' surroundings

The park is set out using ditches rather than fences so there is an overall sense of space rather than captivity. There are animals, birds, reptiles and exotic fish from all over the world. The Butterfly House has the largest butterfly flight cage in Britain. Open all year. Tel: Burford 3006.

☐ Two miles (3.2km) S of Burford on A361. Map ref 2A3.

447. GREAT TEW
Crumbling village

This Cotswold village is one of many acclaimed at one time or another as 'the prettiest in England'. It has become dilapidated now, sometimes

with total decay. But it is still possible to admire the 16th and 17th century thatched cottages set on the slopes of a wooded valley. Part of the charm of this village stems from landscaping of the estate carried out in the early 19th century. Its importance in the 1980s may be as a demonstration of what can happen to the most handsome of villages if people are not vigilant in their protection.

☐ Five miles (8km) E of Chipping Norton off B4022. Map ref 2A3.

448. MAPLEDURHAM
Country park

Part of a designated AONB with meadows giving a long frontage to the Thames. Mapledurham House is nearby. Between the house and river an old watermill is being brought back into working order. House open summer afternoons at weekends.

☐ Four miles (6.4km) NW of Reading off Caversham-Woodcote road A4074. Map ref 2A4.

449. ROLLRIGHT STONES
Prehistoric stone circle

A group of three prehistoric monuments all dating from the Bronze Age. A standing circle of nearly 70 somewhat gnarled stones is the largest of these monuments. Once it must have been more impressive but its state of preservation cannot have been helped by its site alongside on old drovers road following the route of the prehistoric Jurassic Way. Just across this now-metalled road is the solitary King Stone.

☐ Three miles (5km) NW of Chipping Norton on and just off an unclassified road running between A34 and A44. Map ref 2A3.

450. SINODUN HILLS
Thames valley viewpoint

Where the Thames meanders lazily through the clay vale south of Abingdon, a tree-crowned chalk knoll, sometimes called the Wittenham Clumps, provides a spectacular isolated viewpoint and a breezy escape from the sleepy river valley below. A gentle stroll, eastwards across Day's Lock and the river meadows brings you to the ancient Roman town of Dorchester with its massive Norman Abbey and ancient earthworks. Less than three miles (5km) north, past the attractive thatched villages of Little and Long Wittenham, is the Thames-side village of Clifton Hampden.

☐ Near Abingdon, Oxfordshire. A415 E out of Abingdon to Dorchester

(Oxon). Map ref 2A3.

451. UFFINGTON
Vale of the White Horse

A small town in the valley beneath the hill crowned by the Iron Age hill fort of Uffington Castle and the prehistoric outline of the Uffington White Horse. The latter is an extraordinary legacy from the Iron Age – the only prehistoric white horse of the many in the country – and can only really be appreciated from the valley below from the B4508 road or the modern village of Uffington. The church tower is one good vantage point. The fame of the White Horse and the marvellous views mean the hill can become crowded at weekends and the car park full. The crowds can usually be left behind, however, by following the route of the ancient Ridgeway trackway which passes Uffington Castle. About two miles (3.2km) south-west along this path is a chambered long barrow.

☐ Uffington is eight miles (13km) NE of Swindon off B4507. The White Horse and Uffington Castle lie one mile (1.6km) to the S and are reached by a clearly marked road also off B4507. Map ref 2A3.

452. THE WINDRUSH VALLEY
Rural river valley

The gently gliding waters of the Windrush burrow through the Cotswolds of North Oxfordshire, past picturesque villages of mellow grey and yellow limestone. Burford is an ancient market town, with an impressive sloping High Street, leading down to a stone bridge over the river. Upstream and down the water meadows, willows, and the surrounding stone-walled farmlands, evoke an atmosphere of agrarian England of the Middle Ages, virtually unchanged in centuries.

☐ Near Burford. Access via minor roads off the A40. Map ref 2A3.

Warwickshire

The Shakespeare country and Stratford-upon-Avon are set in a county of farmland and woods. The foothills of the Cotswolds spill over the northern boundary. There is industry at Rugby and a great castle at Warwick, which is also the county town. Heart of England Tourist Board: Worcester 29511.

453. BURTON DASSETT HILLS
Country park

Upland grass and agricultural land with views, bridleways and an ancient monument.

☐ Eight miles (13km) SE of Warwick off A41. Map ref 2A2.

454. CHESTERTON
Windmill of distinction

An unusual stone windmill stands here on high ground. It was built in 1632 with arches beneath a striking domed roof. Originally a viewing tower for a local nobleman, it is now a scheduled national monument. A superb restoration won a top award in the 1975 European Architectural Heritage Year. Not normally open to the public, but its exterior (which can always be seen) is in any case its chief glory.

Details of very occasional open days from Warwickshire County Council's Architects Dept. Tel: Warwick 43431.

☐ Five miles (8km) SE of Leamington Spa off A41. Map ref 2A2.

455. COMPTON WYNYATES
Tudor manor house

Both the site – in a hollow of the hills of the Cotswold Edge – and the house itself in its rich pink marlstone exercise a strong visual appeal. Work on the house (which replaced an earlier one on the same site) began in 1480 and it took 40 years to complete. A classic of early Tudor domestic architecture the house had not entirely forgotten the medieval conceptions of defence, as shown by the battlement-style turrents and the moat that once surrounded it. The moat was filled in after the Civil War of the 17th century, but two fishponds from that time remain. Another feature is the rich topiary work. The house and grounds owned and lived in by Lord Northampton are now only open by special arrangement. Tel: Tysoe 229 for details.

☐ Ten miles (16km) W of Banbury, off the B4035 Shipston road. Map ref 2A2.

456. COOMBE ABBEY
Country park

Facilities in this woodland park include lake boating and fishing, nature trail, bridleways and Abbey garden.

☐ Four miles (6.5km) E of Coventry on A4114. Map ref 2A2.

457. EDGE HILL
Historic viewpoint

If you are interested in the landscape of the English heartland where yeoman farmers tilled the red soils of the Midland Plain, few better viewpoints exist than Edge Hill (705ft, 211m) on the Cotswold escarpment, reached from the A422. You can look over the Civil War Battlefield of Edge Hill (1642) or visit the nearby village of Cropredy to the east, to recapture the atmosphere of another Civil War battle, when King Charles was almost captured as his army crossed the River Cherwell (1644). Nearby, is the village of Edgcote, the site of a battle in the Wars of the Roses (1469).

☐ About seven miles (11.3km) NW of Banbury, off the A422. Map ref 2A2.

458. HARTSHILL HAYES
Country park

A wood and grassland area adjacent to Forestry Commission plantations.

☐ Ten miles (16km) N of Coventry off A47. Map ref 2A2.

459. KINGSBURY
Country park

Restored gravel workings with facilities for fishing.

☐ Nearly 12 miles (19km) NE of Birmingham off A51. Map ref 2A1.

460. PACKWOOD HOUSE
Yew garden

Yew garden dating from the 17th century representing the Sermon on the Mount. Open frequently throughout the year. Tel: Lapworth 2024.

☐ At Hockley Heath off A34 and B4439 SE of Birmingham. Map ref 2A2.

Cotswold cottage architecture in the Oxfordshire village of Great Tew

Thatched church at Bramfield, near Southwold, Suffolk. In the background is one of the round towers, of flints and mortar, for which East Anglia is famous

East Anglia

461. DEDHAM VALE
Area of Outstanding Natural Beauty

Small but delectable tract of low-lying, leafy water-meadow country beside the River Stour immortalised by the paintings of John Constable (1776-1837) (see Constable Country entry on p 290).
☐ In both Suffolk and Essex. Map ref 2D3.

462. LINCOLNSHIRE WOLDS
Area of Outstanding Natural Beauty

Quietly beautiful expanse of low, rolling, sheep runs and farmland rising between Lincoln and the North Sea coast. A day out in the Wolds should also include a visit to Louth, a perfect Georgian market town on the eastern edge of the AONB.
☐ In Lincolnshire. Map ref 4D5.

463. NORFOLK COAST
Area of Outstanding Natural Beauty

The main area lies between Snettisham and Mundesley, a magical world of creeks and salt marsh, shingle spits, sea lavender and tidal flats that echo to the cries of gulls, terns, redshank and curlew. The AONB also includes two small outlying areas, one on the coast at Horsey, the other between Royal Sandringham and the Wash. Blakeney, built of brick-with-flint, is a popular yachting haven, as is Brancaster Staithe. Cley has a fine 18th-century windmill and Stiffkey is famous for its cockles. Other places of interest are Wells next the Sea and Holkham Hall.
☐ North Norfolk. Map ref 2C1.

464. SUFFOLK COAST AND HEATHS
Area of Outstanding Natural Beauty

Covers the coast and heaths from Kessingland down to the Deben estuary, which it follows inland as far as Woodbridge. Best explored from Walberswick, Southwold, Aldeburgh and Orford. Aldeburgh is renowned for its summer music festival, and Orford for its oysters and castle keep. At Dunwich the sea is eating away the crumbling cliffs. Elsewhere, there are lonely marshes and estuaries, and bird reserves at Minsmere and Havergate Island where rare avocets breed. Tel. RSPB, Sandy (Beds.) 80551.
☐ In Suffolk. Map ref 2D2.

Cambridgeshire

In the north and east are flat fenlands while the south has gently rolling chalk hills. Cambridge enriches the county with its old college buildings, standing in mellow and enduring perfection against water-meadow and stream. Ely Cathedral is a landmark in the flat landscapes. There is a castle at Kimbolton, the Cromwell Museum at Huntingdon and a famous Botanic Garden in Cambridge itself. East Anglia Tourist Board: Ipswich 214211.

465. ANGLESEY ABBEY
Herbaceous garden and house

Magnificent herbaceous garden and sweeping lawns, rare trees, avenues and vistas. In spring hyacinths, daffodils and cowslips in profusion. House is a mix of medieval, Elizabethan and early 20th century architecture, with works of art from all over the world. Open daily from Apr-Oct in afternoons but house closed Mon and Fri. Tel: Cambridge 811200 or 811175 for details.
☐ Off B1102, near village of Lode, six miles (9.6km) NE of Cambridge. Map ref 2C2.

466. AVERSLEY WOOD
Old established wood

The south part of this wood has recently been acquired by the Woodland Trust and opened to the public. Primary woodland (an area which has always been tree covered) is rare in East Anglia. Bluebells, wood anemones and dog's mercury carpet the ground and there are several examples of the beautiful wild service tree, now an uncommon species. This quiet attractive wood provides a good alternative to the over-visited Monkswood Reserve not far away. Tel: Woodland Trust, Grantham 74297 for further details.
☐ S of Sawtry off A1. Map ref 2B2.

467. BEDFORD LEVELS
Fen drains

The Romans began the process of reclamation in the Fens with the Car Dyke (see under Bourne, page 287) but the Bedford Levels represent the first large-scale attempt to tackle the problem of periodic flooding in this area of potentially rich farmland. The work was carried out at the request of the owner, the Duke of Bedford, by the Dutch engineer Cornelius Vermuyden in the first half of the 17th century. He constructed two artificial channels, the Old and New Bedford Levels, to run side by side for more than 20 miles (32km) from Delph to Denver. In between was a pastureland – the Wetlands (see Ouse Washes, page 286) to absorb more water in times of severe flooding. Unlike the Car Dyke the Bedford Levels remain a prominent feature of the Fenland landscape today.
☐ Good places to see the Levels are from the A1101 road between Wisbech and Ely near Welney, or the A142 road near Mepal between Ely and Chatteris. Map ref 2C1.

468. FERRY MEADOWS
Country park

A nature trail and bridleways through arable grassland alongside the River Nene which also offers sailing, rowing and fishing.
☐ Three miles (5km) W of Peterborough on A605 and A47. Map ref 2B1.

East Anglia

469. GRAFHAM WATER
Reservoir recreation

This man-made reservoir has facilities for fishing and sailing. It is also one of the best places to watch water-birds in England. The beautiful pintail, tufted duck, pochard and Bewick's swans frequent its 2½ sq miles (6.47 sq km). There are public footpaths running around much of the reserve and to places on the south bank (off the B661 at West Perry), north bank (east and west from Hill Farm and Grafham) round to the south-west corner where the path runs by the water's edge.
□ Five miles (8km) SW of Huntingdon off B661. Map ref 2B2.

470. HEMINGFORD
Twin villages

The twin villages of Hemingford Grey and Hemingford Abbots are situated on the River Ouse in a strikingly attractive setting. The former has a moated, stone-built manor house of 12th century origins, sometimes claimed to be the oldest inhabited house in England. It is not open to the public but remains a considerable attraction in twin riverside villages which also have a fine church on the bend of the river, a watermill, and several thatched roofs, brick and timber-framed cottages. Hemingford Abbots has a thatched inn, the *Axe and Compass*.
□ Three miles (5km) SE of Huntingdon between A604 and A1123. Map ref 2B2.

471. MARCH
Church of the angels

St Wendreda is not the parish church of March: it stands outside in comparative isolation. With its spire and, on the side facing the town, rich battlements, the exterior is a pleasure. The interior though, is a thrill! This is because of the double-hammer-beam roof, which is absolutely aflutter with angels: 78 of them on the wing, and another 40 at rest on the cornices.
□ St Wendreda is one mile (1.6km) S of March. Map ref 2C2.

472. OUSE WASH RESERVES
Water-meadows and wildfowl

The Ouse Washes are the water-meadows which lie between the Old and New Bedford Rivers. They are regularly flooded in winter providing lush summer grazing for cattle and an attractive breeding habitat for water fowl. Since the Washes are on the southward migration route from Russia and Scandinavia huge flocks of wildfowl winter on them. The Royal Society for the Protection of Birds, the Wildfowl Trust and other bodies have acquired properties extending along 9½ miles (15km) of the Washes. The RSPB reserve can be reached from the car park at Welches Dam. Public hides are open all year. The Wildfowl Trust's refuge is at Welney. It is important to follow signs and walk below the bank to minimise disturbance to the birds.
□ Welches Dam is E of Chatteris. Access via B1098 or B1093 and then minor road from Manea. Welney is 12 miles (19km) SE of Wisbech on A1101. Map ref 2C2.

473. SWAFFHAM PRIOR
Twin churches

There are some attractive thatched cottages here and 16th century half-timbered buildings, but the village is perhaps most unusual for its two churches sharing a single churchyard. This dates from the time when the village was divided into two parishes, although each parish shared the same burial ground. Both are 12th century but only one, St Mary's, is still used.
□ Eight miles (13km) NE of Cambridge on B1102. Map ref 2C2.

474. WANSFORD
Steam railway

The Great North Road crosses the River Nene here. It first did so by a 16th century bridge with 12 fine arches but the latterday A1 uses a more modern construction. The town's position on this prime coaching route north from London was important in the history of the *Haycock Inn* (see page 74). Wansford is now the headquarters of a partially-restored Nene Valley Steam Railway with some steam passenger services to and from Orton Mere during the summer. Tel: Stamford 782854 or 782021 for details.
□ Wansford is six miles (9.6km) W of Peterborough at junction of A1 and A47. Map ref 2B1.

475. WICKEN FEN
Relic fen

Few people realise what the true Fenland looked like before centuries of artificial draining and reclamation. Here is an opportunity to see a 730 acre (295 hectares) remnant of the former 2500 sq miles (6475 sq km) of marshes which once existed in this part of eastern England. Scientifically it is one of the most important 'wetland' nature reserves in western Europe with a range of insect, plant and bird life not found anywhere else. Carefully managed by the National Trust, who sell informative pamphlets on the great variety of wildlife, which includes such birds as the marsh and Montague harrier, bittern, heron, shoveller, smew and goosander. There is a 1½ mile (2.4km) nature trail open throughout the year except Thurs. It begins at the keeper's house (Grid ref TL 564705). Tel: Ely 720274 for further information. The windpump, which maintains the correct water level in the fen, has been restored as an old Fenland windmill. Rubber boots are advisable.
□ NW of Newmarket, off A1123 at Wicken village. Map ref 2C2.

Essex

Essex has three faces. In the south it is urban and industrial. In the east its ragged coast is made of sea-marsh and estuary while 'upland' Essex of the west and north is farm and orchard country. Chelmsford is the county town and Colchester is one of Britain's oldest towns. East Anglia Tourist Board: Ipswich 214211.

476. ABBERTON RESERVOIR
Easy birdwatching

Abberton's four sq miles (10.3 sq km) attracts large numbers of wildfowl.

Wigeon, pintail, shoveler, goldeneye, goosander, smew, Bewick's swan, gadwall, scaup, grebes and divers regularly visit the reservoir. Much can be seen from roads which cross it: B1026 and a minor road running south from Layer Breton.
□ Four miles (6.4km) S of Colchester between B1025 and B1026. Map ref 2D3.

477. AUDLEY END HOUSE
Jacobean mansion

It is hard to believe that this splendid house with its imposing facade is merely part of a house which originally existed. Vanbrugh demolished some of it when he was called in to remodel it in the 18th century. More disappeared later in the century. Robert Adam was responsible for some of its later decoration and 'Capability Brown' landscaped the park. Open daily Apr-Oct except Mon. Tel: Saffron Walden 22399.
□ One mile (1.6km) W of Saffron Walden on A11. Map ref 2C3.

478. BLACKWATER ESTUARY
Sea wall and marshes

Between Maldon and Mersea Island, on the north shore of the River Blackwater, there lies a sweep of country which has some of the loneliest, unspoiled landscapes in Essex. Tiny, unobtrusive lanes lead to expanses of sea marsh and sea walls which stretch to the horizon. It is a land of incredible skyscapes where skylarks sing in the shimmering heat hazes that hang over the marshes in summer. In winter when a wild north-easter is blowing the cold bites to the bone but the discomfort is forgotten at the spectacle of a sky filled with clouds of geese and other wildfowl. It is a unique part of England, an acquired taste perhaps, and it calls for solid sea wall walking to best appreciate it. Some of its highlights are:
Heybridge Basin. Here the Chelmer and Blackwater Navigation ends in a sea-lock. The canal basin is full of boats and can be unbelievably busy when the tide is high and the lock is functioning. There are two pubs within hailing distance of each other and a length of concrete wall on which to sit with a pint and watch the boaty world go by.
Goldhanger. The village high street ends at a farm gate and the local football field. Behind the far goalposts is Goldhanger Creek with miles of sea

wall snaking away to the east and open sea.
Salcott-cum-Virley. These twin hamlets used to lie on opposite sides of a tidal creek. The creek was blocked off long ago by a new sea wall and its old course is now covered with grass. The lane which runs the length of Salcott ends at a field gate. A short walk on the other side of it leads on to the great swathe of Old Hall marshes and a maze of creeks.
The Strood. This is the causeway on to Mersea Island. To the left the marshes stretch away to the River Colne. To the right they are the Blackwater's domain. The *Peldon Rose*, old, low-ceilinged, a cosy refuge on a wild night, stands on the 'mainland' nearby. Motorists should exercise caution as high tides sometimes cover the causeway.
West Mersea. Oyster fishery (you can eat them in a hut on the edge of the saltings if you have a mind to) and popular yachting centre, its coast road ends at Old City, a jumble of small weatherboard cottages.
□ All the places mentioned can be reached via B1026 from Maldon and the minor road off it which passes through Great Wigborough and Peldon to join the B1025 for West Mersea. Map ref 2C3.

479. BRADWELL-ON-SEA
Romans, Anglo-Saxons and seawalls

The village is not on the sea but Bradwell Waterside is. The creek here is full of moorings sheltered by marshy Pewet Island. The low-lying coast is dominated by the massive outline of the nuclear power station. This obtrusive monument to modern technology rears up in a landscape which has much older landmarks to show. Follow the sea wall from Bradwell Waterside eastwards for a couple of miles (3.2km) towards what looks, from a distance, like an old barn. In fact it is one of the oldest of all England's churches, St Peter's-on-the-Wall built on the wall of the old Roman fort of Othona by the Anglo-Saxon priest St Cedd in about 650 AD. Much of the brickwork from the old Roman fort was used in the building of the church. An alternative route to it is via the lane by the church in Bradwell-on-Sea. Follow it eastwards (it is on the line of the old Roman road) until you come to the farm buildings at the end. From here St

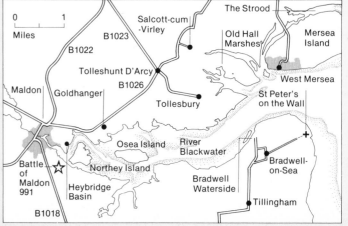

The Blackwater Estuary: a landscape of wide open skies and sea-marshes

Peter's is a short walk away. Southwards from St Peter's is one of the loneliest coasts in East Anglia, the sea wall running in almost a straight line past Dengie Flats and Tillingham Marshes, past outfalls and decoy ponds and the tidal flats of Ray Sands to Holliwell Point and the mouth of the River Crouch. From here it turns westwards to the popular sailing resort of Burnham-on-Crouch. It is a fair day's walk, 12-13 miles (19-21km), in which sea air and sea birds are dominant.

☐ Bradwell-on-Sea is reached via B1018 and unclassified roads from Maldon. Map ref 2D3.

480. CASTLE HEDINGHAM
Norman castle

The town is dominated by the castle keep built about 1140 and set high on a hill overlooking the River Colne. The keep is sufficiently intact to be one of the best preserved examples of an early Norman castle in England. Together with the slightly later Norman church, the castle provided the nucleus around which the medieval town grew but it lacked the economic base to develop into a fully fledged town and today it is more village than urban centre.

☐ Three miles (4.8km) NW of Halstead off A604 or B1058. Map ref 2C3.

481. DANBURY
Country park

Here there is a variety of interest – woodland walks, a string of lakes for coarse fishing, a walled garden and open parkland with picnic tables. Danbury, one of the highest villages in Essex, also has Danbury and Lingwood Commons (NT) with a mixture of woodland and heath.

☐ Danbury is five miles (8km) E of Chelmsford on A414. Map ref 2C3.

482. GREENSTED-JUXTA-ONGAR
Saxon church

In this small isolated hamlet is one of the most unusual churches in Britain. St Andrews has a nave wall consisting of vertical, split trunks of oak standing on a wooden sill. (The latter is a Victorian replacement.) It is the only surviving example of a Saxon wooden church and as such is a unique architectural treasure. The chancel was added at the beginning of the 16th century and the nave roof in the mid-19th century when the church was restored. The body of King Edmund rested here on its way from London to Bury St Edmunds.

☐ One mile (1.6km) W of Chipping Ongar off A128. Map ref 2C3.

483. HATFIELD FOREST
Remnant of a royal forest

This 1000 acres (405 hectares) of Essex woodland, is preserved almost as it was in the days of the Norman kings. It is a benign and open forest full of light and space, its coppices crossed by sunny rides. There are park-like tracts of magnificent pollarded hornbeams, acres of open pasture scattered with islands of hawthorn, and at the centre, a lake (boating and fishing) and a marsh (now a nature reserve) where wild orchids bloom. A nature trail of 1½

Village pond at Danbury, Essex. Nearby is a country park and attractive stretches of National Trust woods and heathlands.

miles (2.4km) begins at the Shell House nearby. Once much of England looked like Hatfield. The practice of combining pasture with woodland is very old and may go back to the Bronze Age and beyond. It is owned by the National Trust and is designated as a Country Park. Cars can be driven into the forest to the Shell House where an information room is open at weekends.

☐ Four miles (6.4km) E of Bishop's Stortford on minor road S of A120 leading to Bush End. Map ref 2C3.

484. MALDON
Ships and sea salt

Maldon, a salty picturesque little port at the head of the Blackwater estuary, is much taken up with the manufacture of sea salt, building boats and repairing and restoring old East Coast sailing barges. The Hythe Quay is full of them, berthed alongside each other, presenting the sort of spectacle which was commonplace in the little marshland ports of Essex in their trading heyday. There are two pubs where you can sit outside and watch the steady pace of waterside life – the *Jolly Sailor* and the *Queen's Head*. Further upstream are the sheds of the Maldon Crystal Salt Company and Fullbridge Quay where small coasters often lie alongside.

The site of the Battle of Maldon, subject of the epic English poem which tells of that fierce and bloody encounter with the Danes, is south of the town on a minor road east of B1018.

☐ Maldon is at the end of A414 E of Chelmsford. Map ref 2C3.

485. THE NAZE
Fossil hunting

The Naze is a promontory which juts out into the North Sea south of Harwich. There is a tower on the cliff top from which there are excellent views over the saltings and creeks of the Walton Backwaters and the Stour estuary. It is here that the usual London Clay which covers much of

Essex gives way to a shelly sand deposit called 'crag' which is rich in fossils – everything from shark's teeth to elephant bones. The beach and cliffs are the best places to search.

☐ N of Walton-on-the-Naze. Map ref 2D3.

486. ONE TREE HILL
Country park

This has nature trails and bridleways with fine views from the park and woodland areas.

☐ One mile (1.6km) W along unclassified road off A176 SE of Basildon. Map ref 2C3.

487. WEALD PARK
Country park

Wood, meadow and parkland with a lake for fishing. There are bridleways, walks and picnic spots.

☐ Two miles (3.2km) NW of Brentwood off A128. Map ref 2C3.

488. WIVENHOE
River village

This quayside town on the River Colne is still involved in boat-building as it has been for centuries. A walk along the river leads to Alresford Creek which winds some three miles (14.8km) inland. Look out for herons feeding. On the opposite side of the river, where thousands of Brent geese winter on the saltings, is one of three nature reserves on the estuary.

☐ Wivenhoe is SE of Colchester off A133 and B1027. Fingringhoe is S of Colchester off B1025. Map ref 2D3.

Lincolnshire

To the south-east lies the flat, fertile Fenland with Spalding and its bulb fields. Further north the gentle Wolds harbour fine houses such as Harrington Hall and towns such as Alford. Lincoln's hill top cathedral dominates the surrounding countryside. East Midlands Tourist Board: Lincoln 31521.

489. BOSTON
Old wool port

This was a great seaport of the medieval wool trade with Flanders and the prime reminder of its past importance is the 15th century Church of St Botolph, one of the largest parish churches in the British Isles. Its tower, known as the Boston Stump, is 272ft (85m) high and a landmark for many miles around. Like King's Lynn its great rival as a wool port on the further shore of the Wash, Boston is rich in old warehouses and enticing streets. Now the port, on the tidal River Witham, which not so long ago was in decline, is enjoying a new lease of life from trade with the Common Market.

☐ 15 miles (24km) NE of Spalding. Map ref 2C1.

490. BOURNE
Canal the Romans built

There are some good Georgian houses in this market town and a few Tudor cottages, but the historically-minded are drawn here by even earlier features. Half-a-mile (800m) to the east of the town (and running north, roughly parallel with the A15 and B1177) is one of the few traceable stretches of the Roman-built Car Dyke. This canal started the long process of reclamation in the Fens but for most of its length, from just north of Peterborough to the River Witham, it has disappeared from view on the ground. In Bourne itself the old castle, now no more than some mounds and a moat, is believed to have occupied the site of the home of Hereward the Wake, the last of the Saxon nobles to resist William the Conqueror.

☐ 10 miles (16km) NE of Stamford at junction of A15 and A151. Map ref 2B1.

491. BRANT BROUGHTON
Limestone church

The Church of St Helen in this village on the River Brant dates back to the 13th century. Built of the finest An-

caster limestone, the exterior is lavish. The grand parapeted tower is crowned by a lovely spire visible for miles. The interior is notable for something all too scarce: really sensitive Victorian restoration. But best of all is the cambered nave roof with angels.
□ 12 miles (19km) S of Lincoln or six miles (9.6km) E of Newark off A17. Map ref 4C6.

492. BURGHLEY HOUSE
Great English house

One of England's greatest Elizabethan houses. It was built by William Cecil, Treasurer to Queen Elizabeth I, between 1546 and 1587. The site he chose was originally a monastery which perished as a result of the Dissolution measures of Henry VIII. The grounds belong to a different period, being laid out by Capability Brown in the 18th century. The house is normally open April-Oct every day except Mon and Fri but afternoons only on Sun. It is sometimes closed during the Burghley Horse Trials which take place in the grounds in early Sept. Tel: Stamford 52451 for further details. Burghley stands on the south-eastern side of Stamford, one of the finest medieval towns in the country, and which also has particularly outstanding 17th and 18th century architecture. Part of its importance lay in its position on major routeways, first the Roman Ermine Street and later the Great North Road.
□ Burghley House is just over one mile (1.6km) SE of Stamford off B1443. Stamford is 10 miles (16km) NW of Peterborough. Map ref 2B1.

493. CHURCH FARM MUSEUM
Lincolnshire farm life

The house and farm buildings show aspects of farming in East Lincolnshire. Stables contain a blacksmith and wheelwright's workshop and displays of equipment used in connection with pigs and poultry, while the farmyard itself contains larger items of machinery. Other stables house a saddler's shop and veterinary equipment. The main part of the farmhouse was built about 1760, and added to at various times during the Victorian period. Visitors should see the wash-house with its original copper and an early example of a washing machine. Other interesting rooms include the scullery, living room, pantry, parlour and bedrooms. Open daily Apr to Oct. Tel: Skegness 66658. A few miles inland, on A158 at Burgh le Marsh, is the Windmill Museum. The mill, built in 1833, is working (free-wheeling) and open all year. Tel: Skegness 810281 for details.
□ Church Road South, Skegness. Off A52 Wainfleet Road, Skegness. Map ref 4D6.

494. GIBRALTAR POINT
Sand spit and bird reserve

This sand spit at the mouth of the River Steeping has a 1200 acre (486 hectares) nature reserve and field station. The terrain covers sand hills, marshes, rough grazing and beach. In spring there are thousands of larks singing over the dunes. Occasionally you can see kestrels and short-eared owls but its importance is as a key migration point for birds. Sea lavender grows here and seals can sometimes be seen basking off the sandbanks.
□ S of Skegness at end of minor road off A52. Map ref 4D6.

495. GRANTHAM
Coaching inn

The Angel and Royal Hotel dates from the 13th century, though the present frontage is mainly 15th century. The State Room, above the central archway, was used by Richard III in 1483. In the 18th century the hotel became an important coaching inn on the Great North Road. The modern A1 now bypasses the town which also has the fine cathedral-like church of St Wulfram's, with 14th century origins but with work from many periods.
□ 12 miles (19km) SE of Newark off the A1. Map ref 2B1.

496. HARTSHOLME
Country park

Wood and grassland with a lake offering a nature trail and fishing.
□ Three-and-a-half miles (5.5km) SW of Lincoln. Map ref 4C6.

497. HONINGTON
Lowland hill fort

Hill forts are almost non existent amid the flatness of Lincolnshire, and Honington Camp is only raised on a slight plateau. But 'hill' fort it technically is since the Camp has the ramparts and ditches characteristic of these Iron Age settlements. Its appearance is quite striking, however, because it is now marooned as an island of uncultivated land amidst farmland.
□ Honington is five miles (8km) N of Grantham between A607 and A153. The Camp is one mile (1.6km) SE of the village and is reached by a track or footpath leading off A153. Grid ref SK 954423; OS map 130. Map ref 2B1.

498. KESTEVEN
Woodland wildlife

Woodlands scattered in area between Stamford, Grantham and Bourne have Forestry Commission facilities including picnic places and woodland walks. **Morkery Wood** has picnic place in small abandoned limestone quarry. Short walk follows series of old fallow deer trails, used at dusk by badgers and foxes.
□ On Castle Bytham Road 10 miles (16km) N of Stamford.
Ropsley Rise Wood has picnic place and trail where badgers, foxes and long-eared owls may be seen.
□ One mile (1.6km) NE of Old Somerby off B1176.
Twyford Wood Walk is planted on World War Two airfield.
□ Half-a-mile (800m) E of junction with A1 at Colsterworth.
Clipsham Yew Tree Avenue picnic place adjoins magnificent avenue of clipped yews about 200 years old.
□ Eight miles (12.8km) N of Stamford on Stretton to Little Bytham road. Map ref 2B1.

499. LOUTH
Market town

There are a few remains of a 12th century Cistercian abbey in Louth Park but essentially it is an 18th century face which this market town presents to the world. Westgate Street probably has the best examples of houses from around this time with many featuring the red-brick and tiles characteristic of local buildings. But one building not so constructed is the Church of St James which is considered by some to be a masterpiece of the late medieval Gothic era and which is crowned by a magnificent 295ft (91m) spire. Louth is still a busy market centre with a cattle market on Fridays.
□ 26 miles (42km) NE of Lincoln on A157 and A16. Map ref 4D5.

500. MUSEUM OF LINCOLNSHIRE LIFE
Rural life museum

The agricultural, industrial and social history of Lincolnshire, with emphasis on agriculture as the most important factor. Extensive collection of large farm equipment. Open throughout the year (except Dec and Jan) daily Mon-Sat and Sun afternoons. Tel: Lincoln 28448.
□ Burton Road, Lincoln. Map ref 4C6.

501. OLD BOLINGBROKE
Henry IV's birthplace

This is one of a large number of failed towns which dot the English countryside. It is now no more than a single street village (albeit with a 14th century church and some 18th century houses) in a seemingly completely rural area, close to both the chalk wolds and the open marshland country. Yet at one end of this single street is a huge mound, the site of a former castle that obviously once gave hope of better things. It was here that Henry IV was born in 1367.
□ Six miles (9.6km) SE of Horncastle off A1115. Map ref 4D6.

502. SPALDING
Spring bulb field drives

A visit to the dazzling bulb fields of the Fens is a must in early April when the daffodils are out, or the last two weeks in April and first week in May when the tulips are normally in bloom. The local Tourist Information Office at Ayscoughfee Hall, Churchgate, Spalding supplies an excellent map containing signposted routes, called Rural Rides. These routes, up to 25 miles long (40km), are updated each year. The information office will tell you the best fields to visit. Tel: the Tourist Information Office at Spalding 5468 for details and the date of the local Flower Parade which takes place in May. Spring flowers can always be seen at their best at Springfields Gardens on the A151, near Whaplode on the outskirts of town. Open Apr-Sept. Tel: Spalding 4843.
□ Spalding is N of Peterborough at junction of A16, A151 and A1073. Map ref 2B1.

503. THE WOLDS
Escarpment journey

Escape to Tennyson's 'Calm and deep peace on this high wold' by following the lanes which run along the crestline of the chalk escarpment, especially the Bluestone Heath Road between Somersby, Tennyson's birthplace, north via Kelstern and over the county border to Wold Newton. The rolling hills with their vast flocks of sheep, the beechwoods in the hidden valleys, the tiny dreaming villages, belie the turmoil of the towns and main roads on the plains beneath..
□ Somersby is six miles (9.6km) NE of Horncastle off the A158. Map ref 4D6.

Common seals resting at low tide near Blakeney Point, a lonely stretch of the Norfolk coast renowned for its wildlife.

Norfolk

Norfolk has three distinctive landscape features: Broadland with its lakes and rivers, the forest and heaths of Breckland and the Cromer Ridge in the north-east. Reed-thatch and flint make appealing village architecture. Other attractions: Kings Lynn, Swaffham and Norwich with its castle and cathedral. East Anglia Tourist Board: 214211.

504. BACTON WOOD
Forest near the sea

Picnic tables set on a grassy area with scattered clumps of pine. Only 10 minutes drive from sandy beach at Bacton. Forest trail is gently undulating and winds through mainly pine woodland mixed with about 30 different tree species including oak, beech, maple and wild cherry.
☐ On by-road running S from B1150 2½ miles (4km) NE of North Walsham. Map ref 2D1.

505. BLAKENEY POINT
Sand spit for birds

The sand dunes and mudflats of Blakeney, and the six mile long (9.6km) shingle beach out to the point have long been famous for birds and flowers. Altogether 256 different species of bird have been recorded here. The 'swallows of the sea' – common terns and little terns – regularly breed on the point, and oystercatchers and other waders raise their young among the creeks and saltings. In late summer the flats are clothed in the pale lilac haze of flowering sea lavender and the silvergrey foliage of the other sea plants. The Point is reached by walking down the beach from Cley, or by boat from Morston and Blakeney. For further information Tel: NT Warden at Cley 740480.
☐ Access is from the A149 north Norfolk coast road. Map ref 2D1.

506. BLICKLING HALL
Country house and gardens

A large garden made over a period of more than three centuries with formal parterres, simplified in the 20th century, and herbaceous plants in place of bedding out. There is woodland intersected by allées in the French manner, a temple, an orangery, fine trees and shrubs and a large landscape lake.

The hall is a memorable building in mellow red brick (about 1620) and has much Jacobean work including the ornate Long Gallery ceiling. Open daily from June-Sept, regularly in Apr, May and Oct. Tel: Aylsham 3471.
☐ On B1354 NW of Aylsham on A140. Map ref 2D1.

507. BRECKLAND
History, heaths and forest

The barren heathlands of Breckland are one of the most arid areas in the country. Glacial sands left after the Ice Age have contributed to the making of a vast tract of poor, open country many acres of which have now been planted by the Forestry Commission to create England's largest lowland forest. During the Middle Ages 'sandblows' made the area even more desert-like and arid, with up to 30 villages being abandoned, although there is plenty of evidence of farming and settlement in Breckland long before this. Grimes Graves (see separate entry) are located here. But while farming was difficult in late medieval times the land did support rabbits. Parts of Breckland are still known as Warrens with fortified lodges where gamekeepers lived. The 15th century Thetford Warren Lodge, near the B1107 Thetford to Brandon road, is open standard DoE hours.

Thetford. This small, ancient market town was once the cathedral city of East Anglia and boasted 20 churches and several monasteries. Today only three churches remain although there are other fine buildings which reflect its past importance. Ancient House Museum exhibits Breckland life and history.

Thetford Forest. Picnic sites and forest walks are available at several locations – Bridgham Lane, Devil's Punchbowl, Hockham, Lynford, Two Mile Bottom. St Helen's picnic place, signposted from the road half-a-mile (800m) north of Santon Downham is by the bank of the Little Ouse. There is a church (13th century) and the site of a moated manor house nearby. A two-mile (3.3km) nature trail across woodland, heath and meres is open most days during summer at East Wretham Heath, north-east of Thetford.
☐ Thetford is on main Cambridge-Norwich road A11. Santon Downham forest information point, with details of all facilities, is on minor road running N from B1107 4¾ miles (7.6km) NW of Thetford. Open working hours weekdays. Map ref 2C2.

508. BRESSINGHAM
Gardens and steam museum

An unusual combination of colourful informal gardens, nurseries and one of the most comprehensive collections of steam engines, both road and rail, in the British Isles. There are over 40 of them and a steam driven roundabout too. Different railways take visitors on steam trips through the grounds. Open afternoons, Suns and Thurs May-Sept and Wed in August. Also Bank holiday Mons. Tel: Bressingham 386.
☐ Two-and-a-half miles (4km) W of Diss on A1066 Diss-Thetford road. Map ref 2D2.

509. BROADLAND CONSERVATION CENTRE
Floating exhibition

A nature trail of just over ¾ mile (1.2km) leads over paths and catwalks through marshy alder thicket to the Broadland Centre, a thatched building floating on pontoons between Malthouse and Ranworth Broads. The centre has an exhibition which shows the natural life of the Broads and demonstrates the urgent need for conservation. From the gallery upstairs, visitors have superb views over the surrounding Broadland. Cars should be left in the car park opposite the Maltsters public house at Ranworth. Tel: South Walsham 479.
☐ Ranworth Broad is 9 miles (14.5km) NE of Norwich along B1140 turning off at the village of South Walsham. Map ref 2D1.

510. THE BROADS
Unique waterways

There are more than 30 Broads, or lakes, and with the many rivers and inter-connecting channels in the area, they amount to over 200 miles (320km) of navigable water. The scale of the Broads long made people assume that they were natural features. During the 1950s scientific research revealed their man-made origins as old peat diggings which were flooded by a rise in sea level in the 13th century. The best way to see the Broads is by boat which can be hired in centres such as Wroxham and Horning, by the hour, day or week. There are organised boat trips too, but remember that the Broads are among the most congested waterways in the British Isles. In the summer especially boats may be booked up months in advance and visitors may have to content themselves *watching* other people messing about in boats. Many villages have fine churches and waterside pubs (although the latter, at least, get crowded) and places worth a detour include Broadlands Conservation Centre at Ranworth Broad (see separate entry), the ruins of St Benet's Abbey (south of Horning), and the windmills at Horsey Mere (a National Trust nature reserve) and Thurne. A water tour in association with the Naturalists' Trust operates daily

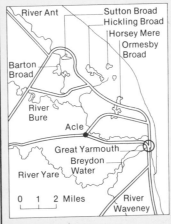

The Norfolk Broads: a scenic network of 200 miles (320km) of navigable waterways

throughout the summer from the dyke adjacent to the Pleasure Boat Inn, Hickling. Tel: Norwich 25540 for details.
☐ The Broads are contained in a roughly triangular area between Lowestoft, Norwich and Sea Palling. OS map 134 in the 1:50,000 series gives the best cover. Map ref 2D1.

511. CASTLE ACRE
Town on Peddars Way

Tucked away in the lanes north of Swaffham is one of the few towns on the line of the Peddars Way, a Roman and before that a prehistoric trackway which crosses the county. It is a small place now, but boasts military and monastic remains unlike anything else in East Anglia. At one end of Castle Acre is a massive Norman castle mound. Only fragments of the flint walls, a 13th century gateway and two towers remain but the size of the site – some 15 acres (6 hectares) – indicates its former importance. And at the other end of the town are impressive remains of an 11th century Cluniac priory (open standard DoE hours). Peddars Way itself is now mainly a 'green road' and as such it offers good walking, especially south past Great Palgrave and North Pickenham.
☐ Castle Acre is four miles (6.4km) N of Swaffham, off A1065. Map ref 2C1.

512. COUNTRYSIDE COLLECTION
Martham farm museum

Rural life of the late 19th century is portrayed here in the traditional Norfolk flint buildings of the area. Harnesses, historic agricultural equipment and tools of the local craftsmen are on show. Open daily throughout the year. Tel: Great Yarmouth 740223.
☐ Between Martham and Somerton about nine miles (14.4km) N of Great Yarmouth. Access via A49 and B1152 Map ref 2D1.

513. CROMER RIDGE
Norfolk's 'mountain' range

This stretch of high land, over 300ft (91m) in places, runs from near Cromer in a westerly direction behind Sheringham towards Holt and Salthouse and eastwards towards Mundesley. It is about five miles (8km) wide. In an area of gentle, undramatic topography its wooded slopes and heights produce unexpected and impressive scenery. It rises sharply from the lower country near the coast but its slopes are gentler on its landward side. Much of it is covered with heather and bracken which is a sure sign of its sandy, gravelly nature. It is also made up of much chalk and rocks from as far away as Scandinavia, Scotland and the north of England which were carried there by glaciers. The ridge itself is a moraine which was left by the glaciers. By its nature it provides interesting country for walks and many viewpoints – Franklin Hill, Roman Camp, the highest point in Norfolk, Pretty Corner, Upper Sheringham. Perhaps the most romantic way of enjoying this small, unusual piece of country is to ride a steam train from Sheringham's old station to Weybourne. Trains operate daily from Easter to Oct. Tel: Sheringham 822045 for details.

There are good cliff walks along the coast to Cromer. The cliffs between West Runton and Trimingham have peaty beds at their base which can sometimes be seen where not hidden by cliff falls. These are believed to have formed in a warm inter-glacial period under lake and estuary conditions. In these have been found the remains of elephant, rhinoceros, sabre-toothed tiger, bear and hippopotamus (first appearance in the country). Cromer Museum (open daily) exhibits the geology and natural history of the area.

Gastronomic note: for 20 miles (32km) along this coast clinker built boats launched from the beach (there are no harbours) fish for crabs. They put down creel pots in strings of 20-30 at a time, 100-200 pots per boat. Much of the catch is landed at Sheringham and Cromer where it is possible to buy direct from fishermen. The crab fishing

is at its best in May and June with lobsters mainly in July and Aug.
□ Cromer and Sheringham are main centres for area. Access via A149, A148 and B1159. Map ref 2D1.

514. GRIMES GRAVES
Prehistoric flint mines

The site of the largest and most important flint mines known to have existed in prehistoric Britain. In all more than 800 shafts have been identified with a labyrinth of galleries leading off the shafts which were up to 40ft (12m) deep. Here, 4000 years ago, Neolithic man hacked flints from the chalk, with primitive antler picks. Between here and Salisbury Plain a trade in flint tools was maintained along the chalk Ridgeway. The site of this axe-factory – for that is what it was – is now some 34 acres (12.5 hectares) of humps and hollows. The prehistoric miners themselves contributed to this landscape by filling in exhausted shafts with waste material from new ones. Natural subsidence over the last 2500 years has done the rest. It must rank as one of the earliest examples of industrial dereliction. The site is under the protection of the Department of the Environment and is open during normal DoE hours.
□ Four miles (6.4km) NW of Thetford off A134. Map ref 2C2.

515. HOUGHTON HALL
Palladian opulence

Like Boughton House (see page 283), this is a great English house that has been opened to the public comparatively recently. The quintessence of Palladian opulence, it was built in the 1720s for Sir Robert Walpole, for 20 years the most powerful man in Britain. The outside is mainly by Colin Campbell, the interiors superbly decorated by William Kent. The rooms are not as large as photographs suggest; like many great English houses, Houghton turns out to be more intimate than one expects. Splendid contents, and peacocks and milk-white deer in the surrounding parkland set off the architecture. Several breeds of shire horses on view in the stables. The house and grounds are normally open Thurs, Sun and Bank Holidays from Easter to mid-Oct. Tel: East Rudham 247 for details.
□ 13 miles (21km) E of King's Lynn, off A148. Map ref 2C1.

516. HUNSTANTON
Cliffs, boats and birds

This is East Anglia's only west-facing holiday resort. The long sandy beach is backed by cliffs which have been eroded to reveal horizontal stripes of red carstone and white chalk. The cliffs are excellent for autumn and winter bird watching and the cliff walk, past a ruined chapel and disused lighthouse, now a private house, to Holme next the Sea, is about 1½ miles (2.4km). There are boat trips from Hunstanton to Scoby Island and to the new lighthouse and cliffs. June-Sept daily.
□ On the A149. Map ref 2C1.

517. KING'S LYNN
Historic port and market town

An outstanding market town. Many fine buildings reflect its importance and prosperity from the 12th century

onwards. It was Bishop's Lynn before this particular ecclesiastical property passed to the crown in 1204. But by then the town had already acquired not one but two market places. Saturday Market, as it is known for the obvious reason, arrived first to be followed around 50 years later by Tuesday Market. Many of King's Lynn's oldest and most interesting buildings are grouped around these. Originally each had its own guildhall and church. The town's prosperity was based primarily on its dual role as market centre for the surrounding farmland and port on the Great Ouse. It was particularly noted as a wool port during the late Middle Ages but unlike places such as Lavenham, it did not remain ossified in the past when the wool trade declined. There are some excellent buildings from the 17th-19th centuries to testify to its continuing success as a port and market town. They represent a mixture of private, religious and public buildings located in ancient streets or by riverside quays. A tourist office is located in the Town Hall. Tel: King's Lynn 61241. A booklet details its historic buildings.
□ 13 miles (21km) NE of Wisbech on A47. Map ref 2C1.

518. NORFOLK RURAL LIFE MUSEUM
Norfolk's rural past

A new museum, housed in what is the only former workhouse open to the public in Norfolk, showing the history of the county for the past 200 years. There is a row of reconstructed craftsman's shops – saddler, basket-maker and wheelwright, and a fine collection of steam engines. Open June-end Sept, Tues-Sat daily, Sun afternoons. Tel: Dereham 820563.
□ Beach House, Gressenhall, East Dereham. Two miles (3.2km) NW of East Dereham on B1146. Map ref 2D1.

519. NORTH ELMHAM
Saxon cathedral

In the upper reaches of the Wensum valley is this little-known jewel in the quiet Norfolk countryside. It was not always quiet. Just north of the village church are the ruins of a Saxon cathedral, built early in the 11th century. A 14th century manor house was later built in the same moated enclosure but the Saxon elements are clearly recognisable since they were built from a distinctive local flint and deep brown carstone conglomerate. Elmham was the seat of the bishopric from 800 AD (or even earlier) before the latter moved first to Thetford and then to Norwich. The small cathedral survived largely because it was incorporated into the manor house.
□ Five miles (8km) N of East Dereham near junction of B1145 and B1110. Map ref 2D1.

520. SANDRINGHAM
Royal residence

Sandringham House is the country residence of the Royal Family. Here King George V and King George VI died. More happily it is where the Queen and her family spend their summer holidays. During the summer months, when no member of the Royal

Family is present, the house and grounds are often open to the public. Tel: King's Lynn 2675 for details or check with local tourist boards (see appendices). But a country park covering some 300 acres (121 hectares) of the Sandringham estate is open throughout the year. This includes a nature trail through wood and heathland.
□ Eight miles (13km) NE of King's Lynn off B1440. Map ref 2C1.

521. TITCHWELL RESERVE
Seashore and marsh birds

This RSPB Reserve covers reedmarsh, saltmarsh and sandy shore. The most delicate of terns, the little tern breeds here. So do oystercatchers and bearded tits. Winter wildfowl include Brent geese, goldeneye, wigeon and sometimes unusually high numbers of eider duck. Access from east sea wall from A149 between Titchwell and Brancaster; or west sea wall from A149 between Thornham and Titchwell. Car park. Information centre.
□ Five miles (8km) E of Hunstanton, Norfolk. Map ref 2C1.

522. WALPOLE ST PETER
Limestone church in flint country

Unlike most Norfolk churches, this mostly 14th century building is built not of flint but of limestone. It has a gorgeous exterior, with ornamental parapets, grand gargoyles and closely spaced ranges of windows, and a noble interior bathed in light, with raised east end. Much handsome woodwork; and six more chandeliers, all with attractive wrought-iron suspension rods, have been added to the fine original one of c.1700. Lovingly maintained in a churchyard worthy of it, this is among the most glorious of all village churches.
□ 10 miles (16km) W of King's Lynn between A17 and A47. Map ref 2C1.

523. WELLS-NEXT-THE-SEA
Old fashioned port

The delight of this small place is in its old houses, large town green and its creeks, sea marshes, sand dunes and pine woods. The Quay is dominated by a tall granary and has some fine houses and several old inns. Occasionally coasters trade here. Whelks and cockles are fished. Holkham Hall two miles (3.2km) west of the town was the home of Coke of Norfolk, otherwise Thomas William Coke, Earl of Leicester, one of the great farm improvers of the 18th century Agricultural Revolution. Here he transformed a sandy wasteland into fertile pastures and woodland. The hall is open May-Sept, Thurs and sometimes Mon. Tel: Fakenham 710227 for details.
□ Wells is on A149 north Norfolk coast road. Holkham is off A149. Map ref 2D1.

524. WYMONDHAM
Church of conflict

The great abbey church of this attractive market town was shared between monks and parishioners, who were constantly at loggerheads. The monks' part has mostly perished, apart from their tower of 1400, with its graceful octagonal top. Some 50 years later the

parish asserted its independence by building the grand west tower, seemingly to overpower the other. The lofty nave survives, crowned by a fine hammer-beam roof with enchanting floral bosses. There are many other fine buildings – from a 17th century market cross to the *Green Dragon* inn said to date from the 14th century.
□ Eight miles (13km) SW of Norwich on A11. Map ref 2D1.

Suffolk

Rich farmland, sandy heaths, sea-marshes and forests make England's easternmost county. Constable painted it, Gainsborough was born there – in Sudbury. It is a county of old houses, sleepy villages and towns of character such as Bury St Edmunds and Lavenham. Ipswich is the county town. East Anglia Tourist Board: Ipswich 214211.

525. BRANDON PARK
Country park

Nature trails and bridleways through landscaped grounds adjoining Brandon House and incorporating part of Thetford Forest.
□ One mile (1.6km) S of Brandon on B1106. Map ref 2C2.

526. CLARE CASTLE
Country park

A small park centred on a ruined castle (AM), its grounds and a disused railway station.
□ Between Clare and the River Stour off the A1092. Map ref 2C2.

527. CONSTABLE COUNTRY
Artist's landscapes

John Constable was one of the greatest of English landscape painters whose work will always be associated with the Stour Valley of Suffolk where he was born and mostly lived. Identifying the places Constable painted as they are today is a popular recreation, especially at the locations listed below. Sometimes, however, he removed a particular building to a different setting for artistic purposes. Dedham Church is the most notable example of this artistic licence. Several of the places become very crowded during summer months, notably Flatford Mill which is approached by a narrow lane.
Dedham. In addition to the much-painted church, with its 15th century tower, there are many superb timber-framed cottages, Georgian houses and old inns on and off the high street. Constable attended the local grammar school.
East Bergholt. Constable's birthplace and where he married the rector's daughter and painted many of his most famous paintings. Several houses in the village are Elizabethan.
Flatford Mill. This was one of the watermills owned by John Constable's father and is now owned and protected by the National Trust. Adjoining the mill, with its 15th century mill house, is **Willy Lott's Cottage,** the early 17th century subject of the 'Hay Wain' among other paintings.
Stoke-by-Nayland. Yet another village of the Stour valley – Stratford St Mary, Langham and Higham are others – much loved by Constable. The

Fishing boats on the beach at Dunwich, Suffolk. Most of the old town of Dunwich has long since vanished beneath the waves

perpendicular church, with its spire, features in many paintings.

There is no particular order in which these places should be visited. OS maps 155, 168 in the 1:50,000 series will enable you to find not only roads between these locations but also footpaths enabling you to leave the car behind at times. Among them will be paths used by Constable himself, such as that which took him to school at Dedham and which features in 'The Corn Field'.

□ Flatford Mill is on N bank of the River Stour one mile (1.6km) S of East Bergholt off the B1070. Map ref 2D3.

528. DAWS HALL
Wildfowl farm

The farm has a fine collection of waterfowl and pheasants in an extensive garden of rare trees. Tel: Twinstead 213 for details of opening.

□ Daws Hall is at Lamarsh two miles (3.2km) NW of Bures on minor road. Map ref 2C3.

529. DEBENHAM
Source of the Deben

A classic linear village stretched along not only the main road but also the River Deben. It has long been a centre of rush weaving and the church dates back to Saxon times. The Elizabethan Crows Hall (not open to public) is one of Suffolk's many moated manor or farm houses.

□ 10 miles (16km) N of Ipswich on B1077. Map ref 2D2.

530. DUNWICH
Lost to the sea

Dunwich has a long history but there is little left to show for it: a few ruins, some narrow leafy lanes which were once streets and now and then the bones of the long since dead revealed in the crumbling cliffs. The last church of the old town has long since fallen into the sea but its cliff-top graveyard is still being attacked by the sea. The Dunwich Museum (open from Spring bank holiday to end Sept, Sat, Sun, Tues, Thurs afternoons) tells the story of the town and its decline, from a flourishing port to what it is now, a handful of houses, an inn and a church. It is a strange place, splendid in its wild isolation (except on a fine summer weekend) with a great curve of stone and shingle beach stretching away northwards past Reedland and Corporation Marshes to Walberswick, a bracing three mile (4.8km) walk away. Take plenty of newspaper in the boot of your car to wrap the fresh cod and flounder you can buy from the fishermen's hut on the beach.

□ Reached by minor road off B1125. Map ref 2D2.

531. EASTON FARM PARK
Dairy farming past and present

This Victorian farm was built by the Duke of Hamilton in about 1870 as a model dairy farm. It now houses a museum of early farm equipment and tools. The Victorian dairy, octagonal in design, has many items which would have been in daily use: butter churns, cream settling pans, a cheese press and a butter worker. Contrasting with this is a modern milking parlour, a part of the working farm, where present day equipment is on show. Open daily Apr-Oct. Tel: Wickham Market 746475.

□ Off B1078 three miles (4.8km) NW of Wickham Market. Map ref 2D2.

532. FRAMLINGHAM
Castle town

A market town which, like many others, grew up around a castle. Both town and castle remain impressive. The castle dates from the late 12th century and although it was altered substantially four centuries later its outward appearance was largely unaffected: it is open standard DoE hours plus Sun mornings Apr-Sept. The parish church dates from the 15th century and many delightful cottages and other buildings from the 16th-19th centuries, notably on Market Hill, Castle Street and Church Street. The focal point is the Market Square, which is more of a triangle than a square. Markets are still held every Sat.

□ Seven miles (11km) W of Saxmundham at junction of B1119 and B1116. Map ref 2D2.

533. KERSEY
Cloth village

A beautiful village, set in a steep little valley, which is near Lavenham. Like Lavenham, Kersey owes its fine timber-framed houses to its former importance in the wool trade. Kersey cloth is said to have originated from here. Central to the village's charm is the ford where the River Brett crosses the main street. The view from the church on the hill overlooking the village is delightful.

□ One-and-a-half miles (2.5km) NW of Hadleigh off the A1141. Map ref 2D2.

534. LAVENHAM
Showpiece village

For about 150 years, from the beginning of the 15th century, Lavenham was one of the most prosperous towns in England – and it shows. It rose to riches on the back of the wool trade, the legacy of which is a stunning collection of timber-framed houses, colour-washed and with ornately decorated plasterwork, and a huge parish church with 141ft (43m) spire. Among the many superb buildings are *The Swan* (the pack-horse inn described on page 74) and the 16th century Guildhall overlooking the Market Square.

□ Six miles (9.6km) SE of Bury St Edmunds on the A1141. Map ref 2C3.

535. LONG MELFORD
Country town

A highly attractive small town with an impressively long main street and green. Around the green are a huge 15th century church, some 16th century almshouses and an Elizabethan mansion, Melford Hall, one of the best early Elizabethan houses in the British Isles. It is built in red brick and surrounded by a moat. For details of opening contact area office of the NT. Just north of the church is the moated Kentwell Hall, also 16th century and approached by a $\frac{3}{4}$ mile (1.2km) avenue of limes planted in 1678. Tel: Long Melford 207.

□ Three miles (5km) N of Sudbury on A134. Map ref 2C2.

536. MINSMERE
Bird reserve

Minsmere covers 1560 acres (631 hectares) of land with a wide variety of habitat: open water and reedbeds, woods, heathland and scrub. There is general access to part of the reserve from Minsmere Cliff and several public hides are located by the dunes overlooking the 'Scrape' where many wildfowl, wading birds (notably avocets) gulls and terns are seen. The splendid marsh harrier which breeds at Minsmere may often be spotted.

□ Minsmere Cliff is reached by minor road running eastwards off B1125 from Westleton which is E of A12 at Yoxford. Map ref 2D2.

537. MUSEUM OF EAST ANGLIAN LIFE
East Anglian crafts

Partly an open-air museum, with a collection of reconstructed buildings including a 14th-century farmhouse, a blacksmith's forge and an 18th-century watermill. Open daily from Apr-end Oct. Tel: Stowmarket 2229 for details.

□ Abbots Hall, Crowe Street, Stowmarket. Map ref 2D2.

538. NEWMARKET
Race horses and earthworks

The headquarters of English horse-racing with one of the most famous and oldest courses in the country on the south-western outskirts of the town on Newmarket Heath. The town is the home of the National Stud. The heath is also the best place to see what remains of Devil's Dyke, an impressive post-Roman earthwork probably erected in the 6th century AD by the East Anglians against their neighbours the Middle Angles. Devil's Dyke was one of a pair of such earthworks – the other was Fleam Dyke running roughly parallel with Devil's Dyke some 10 miles (16km) further south – that seem to have been built to bar access along the Icknield Way which runs through them.

□ Newmarket is 12 miles (19km) E of Cambridge; Devil's Dyke runs NW-SE across the Heath from just beyond the point where A45 and A11 meet. Map ref 2C2.

539. OTTER TRUST
Otter watching

On this 23 acre (9.3 hectares) riverside site at Earsham, broadcaster and conservationist Philip Wayre has set up a reserve principally for otters. The River Waveney runs along the boundary of the reserve and a small stream passes through the otter breeding enclosures. Otters were transferred to Earsham from the Norfolk Wildlife Park in 1975 and since then a number

of cubs have been successfully reared. There are not only British otters, but also European, North American and Asian short-clawed otters. Open Mar-end Nov daily. Tel: Bungay 3470.
□ Earsham is just SW of Bungay off A143. Map ref 2D2.

540. PARHAM
Moated manor

Parham Hall is an early 16th century manor house, timber-framed with high gables and still surrounded by a moat. It is one of 500 moated sites in Suffolk alone and probably replaced an earlier moated farmhouse from the 12th or 13th centuries which is when most such dwellings were constructed. The moat provided drainage (on heavy soils) and protection. Parham Hall is not open to the public, but still makes a picturesque sight when viewed from outside.
□ Eight miles (13km) N of Woodbridge on B1116 between Wickham Market and Framlingham. Map ref 2D2.

541. PIN MILL
Sailor's delight

This is an attractive tree-encircled hamlet on the south shore of the Orwell estuary. It has been completely taken over by yachtsmen and barge owners. At the top of the 'hard' is the *Butt and Oyster Inn*, which is sometimes itself awash at high spring tides. The Orwell is one of several East Coast rivers which are much favoured by the cruising yachtsmen in search of a day or two of calm water, good pubs and green grass.
□ SE of Ipswich off B1456 road to Shotley Gate. Map ref 2D3.

542. RAKE FACTORY
Craftsmen working in wood

Here, in a 70-year-old factory, near Sicklesmere, where belts turn and there's the smell of newly worked wood in the air, traditional country tools are still made: rakes, scythe handles, milking stools, platters and household ware. Everything is for sale. Factory is open Mon-Fri. Tel: Cockfield Green 630 for details.
□ Sicklesmere is on A134 S of Bury St Edmunds. Map ref 2C2.

543. RIVER ALDE
Estuary extraordinary

The Alde is the oddest of rivers. At the point where it could be expected to debouch into the sea it makes a sharp turn and flows parallel to the shore for about nine miles (14.5km). In places it is separated from the waves by no more than a few dozen yards of shingle, and it is of this that the long attenuated spit which stretches southwards from Aldeburgh to Orfordness and beyond is made. The spit, built by the drift of beach material along the coast, has deflected the course of the river. Eventually the Alde joins with Butley River to make the River Ore which flows into the sea at Orford Haven. These rivers and their marshes, the remarkable landform of the spit and the heathlands and forests which lie just behind the coast all combine to make a tract of country unlike any other in the British Isles. Some of its highlights are:
Rendlesham Forest. Here Staverton Park and The Thicks to the west of

Butley represent something rare: an area of untouched natural landscape where ancient oaks are descendants of the trees that grew in prehistoric times. There is a picnic place at Butley Corner (FC) and a 2½ mile (4km) forest walk through pinewoods starts from here.
Iken. Beautiful and tranquil, with heathland running down to the Alde, a little beach near Iken Cliff and Iken Church standing by itself on the edge of the estuary.
Orford. Dominated by the great tower which is all that remains of a castle which was once part of a substantial military complex. From the top of it there are fine views over Orford, its quay and the Suffolk coast. Open standard DoE hours.
□ B1084 from Woodbridge and B1078 from Wickham Market give access to this area. Map ref 2D2.

544. RIVER BLYTH
A river to sail or walk

The Blyth is a curious river and like the Alde behaves in its own unconventional way. Its narrow sea-entrance just south of Southwold is tricky but tow-boaters need not worry because there is easy launching on the Southwold bank. At first the river follows a reasonably straight course upstream – under the Bailey bridge, past Buss Creek (this runs round the back of Southwold virtually making the town into an island) with Tinker's Marshes on the left, Reydon Marshes on the right, and then suddenly opens out into a huge tidal lake much of which is uncovered at low water. At its western end is Blythburgh, its great church of Holy Trinity rising above the marshes. This is the sailor's way of coming upon the place. The size of the church belongs to a 15th century Blythburgh, a town with its own mint and jail and quays busy with shipping. But like so many East Coast ports the silting of its river put paid to its prosperity. Today all that is busy is the A12 which crosses the river here. The walker's way of coming upon Blythburgh is out from Southwold, crossing the Bailey bridge that others sail under, then following the track of the old Southwold Railway across Walberswick Common and on through the lovely countryside on the south bank of the estuary into Blythburgh itself.
□ Southwold is at the end of the A1095. Blythburgh is on the A12 NE of Saxmundham. Map ref 2D2

545. THE ROSARIUM
Roses, roses, roses

This garden at the Lime Kiln, Clayden, is dedicated to roses. Of the 500 different varieties growing many are very rare. All grow naturally and most of them are the old-fashioned scented roses. Open afternoons June to mid-July.
□ Claydon is on A45 just N of Ipswich. Map ref 2D2.

546. SOUTHWOLD
Limestone church

A small seaside town with a truly sumptuous church. Although the Church of St Edmund, King and Martyr, is not quite as magnificent as Long Melford's church externally, this

The tide-mill at Woodbridge, Suffolk, 800 years old and restored to working order

mainly flint building, with flush-work ornamentation in limestone, is of greater appeal within. The great feature of the interior – lofty and very light since the destruction of Victorian glass during the last war – is the screen with its charming, largely original, decoration. The roofs, well restored in 1867, also make a great show.
□ 10 miles (16km) S of Lowestoft on A1095 near the mouth of the River Blyth. Map ref 2D2.

547. STOUR
River estuary

The tidal waters of the rivers Stour and Orwell meet in busy Harwich Harbour before they join the sea. The Stour forms the boundary between Essex and Suffolk and flows in its upper reaches through Constable country. One of the best places to view the Stour is from the sea wall at Wrabness Point. This is reached by turning down a lane off the B1352. This latter road, running parallel with the Stour's south bank, offers attractive views of the estuary and of the countryside of Suffolk beyond it. Upstream from Wrabness there is one of the largest swanneries in England at Mistley.

At the mouth of the estuary, on the Felixstowe side, Landguard Point is a favourite spot for searching for semi-precious pebbles among the shingle. A ferry operates from Harwich to Felixstowe Dock and there are cruises on the two rivers from Harwich from Apr-Oct.
□ The two rivers occupy a triangular stretch of country with Manningtree, Harwich/Felixstowe and Ipswich at its three points. Map ref 2D3.

548. WALBERSWICK
Nature reserve

This village is the location of a national nature reserve which overlooks the estuary of the river Blyth to the north and to the south includes most of the reed beds of Westwood Marshes. There are mudflats, pools, brackish lagoons, rough grazing and heath, all of which attracts a large number and variety of birds. The hen harrier and the great grey shrike are regular winter visitors. So are snow buntings. The rare marsh harrier, short-eared owl, twite and a number of waders may also be seen.
□ Five miles (8km) E of Blythburgh on B1387. Map ref 2D2.

549. WOLVES WOOD
Nightingales singing

This RSPB reserve consists of 92 acres (37 hectares) of mixed woodland. Follow the signposted path from the large sign at the entrance. In early summer listen especially for warblers and nightingales. Open all year.
□ Two miles (3.2km) E of Hadleigh off A1071 to Ipswich. Map ref 2D2.

550. WOODBRIDGE
River port and market town

Woodbridge has always earned its living partly from the sea and partly from the land. There has been a tide mill here on the River Deben for 800 years and now, after a major restoration, hopefully it will last for another 800 years – and in working order too! The mill pond is now a miniature marina and the old ferry quay has become a yacht harbour. At the quayside dinghies and motor boats can be hired by the day. It's a popular place for yachting, and sailors and poets have always loved its wide river. Given an hour before and after high water it's possible to sail up river to Melton and Wilford Bridge. This is a romantic and appropriate way to arrive at the latter for the short walk to Sutton Hoo, site of the famous Anglo-Saxon ship burial, 100ft (30m) above the tides on the Deben's eastern shore. Unfortunately the site itself, now filled in, is not accessible, but the countryside here makes for good agreeable walking. And all about is rural, river estuary Suffolk at its best. The best view of Woodbridge is from a boat in the river but the dry land vista from Kyson Hill, a few acres of NT land on the west bank, will do the visitor very well. It was once said Woodbridge had not an ugly building in it, but it does have a mix of styles – 16th century with Georgian bits and bobs – all of which work together happily. The red brick Shire Hall dominates the market square. The *King's Head* and *Angel* are inns for looking at as well as drinking in. Outside the *Bell* is an old steelyard, or lever weighing machine, which measured Woodbridge's commerce in wool, hay and hides up until the 1880s.
□ Woodbridge is six miles (9.6km) E of Ipswich off A12. The Tide Mill is open daily from mid-July to mid-Sept. Map ref 2D2.

Quiet reflections at Matlock, Derbyshire, where the River Derwent flows through a deep valley of woods and high crags

weekends and some weekdays in winter. Tel: Bakewell 3227. Sightseeing: Arbor Low stone circle, the caverns at Castleton, Mam Tor – the 'Shivering Mountain', the historic houses of Chatsworth and Haddon Hall, and a choice of beautiful dales, of which Dovedale, with its stepping stones, hanging woods and limestone pinnacles mirrored in the crystal clear waters, is by far the most romantic.
☐ Map ref 4B6.

552. CANNOCK CHASE
Area of Outstanding Natural Beauty

Surprising oasis of wild upland heath and forest on the doorstep of the Black Country. Highest point is Castle Ring, 800ft (240m). Miles of quiet tracks and forest rides to explore. Foxes, badgers and wild fallow deer roam among the bracken slopes, relic oaks and dark stands of Forestry Commission pines.
☐ Map ref 1D1.

553. SHROPSHIRE HILLS
Area of Outstanding Natural Beauty

A wild cavalcade of empty hills and rolling ridges, haunted by the past and crowned by prehistoric hillforts such as Caer Caradoc. To the west the hills spill over the Welsh Border at Offa's Dyke to encompass the lonely uplands of Clun Forest. To the north a long arm of the AONB reaches out to include the unmistakable pyramidal silhouette of the Wrekin. Church Stretton is the best centre for walkers wishing to explore the Long Mynd and Stiperstones; historic Ludlow is a good base for the Clee Hills. Near Craven Arms is Stokesay Castle, the finest medieval fortified manor house in England, open daily, Mar to Oct, except Tues.
☐ Map ref 1C2.

Cheshire

Cheshire is where the landscape pauses for breath between the Pennine Hills and the uplands of North Wales: a low-lying plain of green fields, peaceful meres and magpie-patterned buildings as exemplified by Little Moreton Hall and the historic streets of Chester. North-West Tourist Board: Bolton 591511.

554. ALDERLEY EDGE
Village and scarp

On the south-eastern fringes of this commuter village for Manchester is a stretch of wooded sandstone escarpment, the scene of copper mining from possibly pre-Roman times to the last century. Now it is used strictly for leisure purposes with hardly any visible evidence of its industrial past. At nearby Nether Alderley a 15th century corn mill with wooden water-mill has been restored to full working order by the NT and is open daily, afternoons (except Mons) July to Sept and on Wed, Sun and Bank Holiday Mons from Apr to June and Oct. Tel: Wilmslow 528961.
☐ Alderley Edge village is five miles (8km) NW of Macclesfield on A34 and A535; Alderley Edge escarpment is one mile (1.6km) SE of the village astride B5087. Map ref 4A6.

Upper Middle England

551. PEAK DISTRICT
National Park

With motorways (M1, M6, M62) virtually hemming in the park on three sides there is fast access to the Peak from London, Midlands and the North. Sheffield and Manchester are almost on the Park's doorstep. Half a dozen main roads converge on Buxton and there is a choice of scenic routes across the 'Dark Peak' of the northern park. Favourite viewpoints (with or near car parks) include Monsal Head, the prehistoric hillfort of Carl Wark on Hathersage Moor, and Frogatt Edge, a dizzy gritstone crag above the Derwent Valley near Baslow. The Peak Park also operates a unique 'park and ride' scheme at weekends and Bank Holidays to keep the beautiful Goyt Valley near Buxton clear of traffic except for special coaches. For walkers there are wild walks over peaty moors and the gritstone 'edges' of the north, and gentle strolls through idyllic limestone dales in the south. The famous Pennine Way long-distance footpath begins at Edale. Main park information centre at Bakewell, open daily in summer,

555. ARLEY HALL GARDENS
Famous gardens

Vintage herbaceous borders, roses, topiary, walled gardens and remarkable avenues of pleached limes and clipped holm-oaks. Open Tues to Sat and Bank Holiday Mons, Mar to Oct. Tel: Arley 353 and 284.
□ Six miles (9km) W of Knutsford off M4. Junctions 19 or 20. Map ref 4A6.

556. ASTBURY
Old church

The Church of St Mary is sensational: the King's College Chapel of parish churches. It is mainly gritstone, a far tougher material than the Triassic sandstone that is general in Cheshire. The lofty, light interior is most distinguished, with glorious woodwork, in a county famous for its woodcarving: roofs and screen just before 1500; seating and pulpit Jacobean.
□ One mile (1.6km) SW of Congleton off A34. Map ref 4A6.

557. CHOLMONDELEY CASTLE GARDENS
Rare farm breeds

A farm with a collection of rare breeds of farm animals is one of the attractions in the grounds of the Marquess of Cholmondeley. The castle is not open to the public, but the farm and gardens with lakeside picnic area are open Apr to Sept, Suns and Bank holidays. Tel: Cholmondeley 203.
□ Six miles (9.6km) N of Whitchurch, off A49. Map ref 4A6.

558. DELAMERE FOREST
Forest walks

Forest walks. Waymarked through pine woods and linking with 14-mile (22.5km) Cheshire Sandstone Trail which passes through forest. Vary from half to three miles (800m to 4.8km). Also easy forest trail through Scots and Corsican pine woods with views of Blakemere Moss, 1½ miles (2.4km). All start from visitor centre half mile (800m) W of Delamere Station.
□ Access from B5152 near Delamere Station. Map ref 4A6.

559. ECCLESTON
Riverside hamlet

This hamlet grew up around the gates of Eaton Hall, a family home of the Dukes of Westminster, and adjoins a picturesque stretch of the River Dee. It is close to nearby Chester but visited by few tourists. You can drive there along the characteristically straight route of an old Roman road. Or better still, walk along the southern banks of the Dee through the meadowland that extends from Eccleston virtually into the city itself.
□ Two miles (3.2km) S of Chester on signposted minor road. Map ref 3D6.

560. LITTLE BUDWORTH COMMON
Country park

Wood, heath, moors and bridleways.
□ W of Winsford. Map ref 4A6.

561. LITTLE MORETON HALL
Historic house

The pinnacle of black-and-white timbered building. This 16th century moated manor house (NT) is built on three sides of a quadrangle with an open view on the fourth over a well laid-out garden. A feature of the house, as medieval Gothic merged with English Renaissance, is the intricately carved gables. Usually open every afternoon except Tues and Good Fri. Apr to Oct. Tel: Congleton 2018 for further details.
□ Four miles (6.4km) SW of Congleton off A34. Map ref 4A6.

562. LOWER PEOVER
Historic inn

This village has a 16th century timbered church but the inn, *The Bells of Peover*, is even older. Ironically, it was founded in 1369 for the priests of an earlier church. Mainly rebuilt, it later became the Warren de Tabley Arms and in 1895 was given its present name after a licensee named Bell whose grave is in the adjoining churchyard. During the Second World War the inn served as a billeting place for officers of the American Army who were based nearby.
□ Three miles (5km) S of Knutsford on B5081. Map ref 4A6.

563. LYME PARK
Country park and historic house

A large acreage of park, moorland and woodland surrounds Lyme Hall, a house of Elizabethan origin. There are red deer in the park, wildfowl and, in autumn, fungi. Trees are a mixture of conifer and broadleaved species. Open all year. 8am to sunset. Also beautiful gardens, orangery, stream, nature trail and playground.
□ On A6 at Disley. Map ref 4A5.

564. MARBURY PARK
Country park

Wood and pastureland setting with lake, canal water bus, arboreta.
□ Two miles (3km) N of Northwich. Map ref 4A6.

565. MOW COP
Moorland viewpoint

This straggling moorland village, perched on impossibly steep slopes of a gritstone crag, provides one of middle

The magpie architecture of Tudor England at its most exuberant: Little Moreton Hall, a moated and half-timbered manor house near Congleton, Cheshire

England's finest viewpoints. From its 1100ft (330m) summit, with its gritstone pinnacles and 18th century folly, the panorama includes the far-spreading Cheshire Plain, the Pennine moors and the headwaters of the Trent. Walk northwards along the narrow, rocky scarp of Congleton Edge, three miles (4.8km) or follow the steeply plunging lanes three miles W to Little Moreton Hall (see opposite page).
□ Near Biddulph, on Cheshire-Staffordshire border, W of Biddulph on minor road off A527 or A34. Map ref 4A6.

566. PECKFORTON HILLS
Scenic landscapes

Among the rich farmlands of the Cheshire plain, these steep sandstone ridges of heath and pine forest give a startling scenic contrast. Red cliffs, gorse and woodland glades abound. Black and white cottages crouch beneath prehistoric hillforts and a variety of castles, ancient and modern. At the northern end of the range of hills stand Beeston Castle ruins (AM), open daily, standard hours, and Sun, Apr to Sept. Good drive from Bulkeley on the A534 to Beeston, with paths up the hills at Peckforton.
□ At Peckforton, on minor road off A49, four miles (6km) S of Tarporley. Map ref 4A6.

567. STYAL
Industrial archeology

An unusual combination of natural beauty, industrial building and historic interest. Quarry Bank Cotton Mill was erected here by Samuel Greg in 1784, to be followed shortly after by some well-designed workers' cottages that together comprise an unusually complete industrial community. But there is also a fine half-timbered farmhouse and the setting of the wooded Bollin valley remains attractively rural despite bordering Manchester's Ringway airport. The disused mill, now housing a textile museum, is open to the public every day except Mons. Tel: Wilmslow 527468 for details.
□ Two miles (3.2km) N of Wilmslow. Map ref 4A6.

568. TATTON PARK
Country park and historic house

Garden-making has been continuing here for at least 200 years. In the late 18th century, Humphry Repton improved the park and lake. In the 19th century, Sir Joseph Paxton designed Italian-style terraces in front of the splendid Georgian mansion, and in the early 20th century, Japanese craftsmen made a Japanese garden beside one of the lakes. There is an orangery, a fern house and a great deal of modern flower planting. Other attractions include sailing, fishing, swimming, picnic site and medieval farm trail. Open daily, except Mons, throughout the year. Tel: Knutsford 3155.
□ Knutsford, off M6 at junction 19. Map ref 4A6.

569. TEGG'S NOSE
Country park

Wood, heath, moors, nature trail.
□ Two miles (3km) E of Macclesfield off A537. Map ref 4B6.

Derbyshire

The best of Derbyshire lies within the Peak District National Park, where the peat bogs and gritstone edges of the Pennine moors provide a striking contrast with the limestone scenery of the incomparable Derbyshire Dales. Buxton, Bakewell, Matlock and Castleton make good bases for days out. East Midlands Tourist Board: Lincoln 31521; North-West Tourist Board: Bolton 591511.

570. ARBOR LOW
Prehistoric monument

This is the greatest 'henge' monument of northern England. The ring bank encompassing the stones is still 6ft (1.85m) high and some 250ft (77m) in diameter. About 50 stones (or their fragments) now lie prone on the ground. Close by is Gib Hill, a large Bronze Age tumulus standing on an earlier Neolithic cairn.
□ 10 miles (16km) SE of Buxton, one mile (1.6km) E of A515 road, grid ref SK 161636; OS map 119. Map ref 4B6.

571. ASHBOURNE
Market town

This spacious market town on the edge of the Peak District has some fine buildings. St Oswald's Church, with its 212ft (65m) spire, was thought by novelist George Eliot to be the handsomest in all England. Another writer who knew the town well was Dr Johnson who, with James Boswell, stayed many times at The Green Man and Black's Head. This 17th century inn was enlarged in the following century to cater for coach traffic. Outside it a remarkable old gallows sign still spans the street.
□ 11 miles (18km) NW of Derby at junction of A52 and A515. Map ref 4B6.

572. BAKEWELL
Market town

Popular small touring centre for the Derbyshire Dales. The 13th century bridge over the River Wye is one of the oldest in England. Other notable buildings include the handsome parish church of All Saints with its lofty spire, and the 17th century Bath House, still fed by warm springs known in Roman times.
□ Midway between Buxton and Matlock on A6. Map ref 4B6.

573. BOLSOVER CASTLE
Historic building

In 1612, Sir Charles Cavendish, younger son of the formidable Bess of Hardwick, built himself a small mock-castle on the site of a genuine Norman one, on the brow of a steep escarpment above a valley. His son, the Duke of Newcastle, added a long range of state-rooms in which to entertain Charles I for an afternoon's visit, and a huge riding school in which to indulge his passion for Haute Ecole. The mysterious vaulted rooms and carved alabaster chimney pieces of the castle, the crazily eccentric façade of the ruined state rooms, the cavernous riding school complete with a little room, like a royal box at the opera, from which the Duke

looked down on his horses, combine with the surrounding coal mines to produce a group of buildings as memorable as it is strange. Now an historic monument, and open standard DoE hours plus Sun mornings, Apr to Sept.
□ Bolsover is six miles (9.6km) E of Chesterfield on A632. Map ref 4B6.

574. CASTLETON
Limestone caverns

This busy village is an excellent centre for a part of the Peak District National Park that is full of fascinating things to see and do. You could start with the ruins of Peveril Castle (AM), the Norman keep featured in Sir Walter Scott's Peveril of the Peak. It is open standard DoE hours, plus Sun mornings, Apr to Sept. The castle overlooks the entrance to the great labyrinth of the Peak Cavern, open daily, Easter to mid-Sept. Tel: Hope Valley 20285. The area has long been associated with lead mining and the extraction of Blue John, a beautiful translucent fluorspar which is made into jewellery and ornaments. Blue John Cavern is also open daily. Tel: Hope Valley 20638. Alternatively, you could take a mile-long (1.6km) boat trip –underground– in the Speedwell Cavern – to see the Bottomless Pit and its sinister water. Tel: Hope Valley 20512. Or visit Treak Cliff Cavern. Tel: Hope Valley 20571. Other places of interest are the Winnats Pass, a dramatic gorge through which the main road used to wind, and one and a half miles to the east, Mam Tor (2.4km), the 'Shivering Mountain',with its precipitous slopes of unstable shales.
□ 12 miles (19km) SW of Sheffield on A625. Map ref 4B5.

575. CHATSWORTH
Stately home and garden

One of the greatest English country houses, the so-called 'Palace of the Peak', built in 1707 for the 1st Duke of Devonshire and incorporating an earlier house. Every room filled with fabulous treasures. The very large and magnificent garden reveals the changing style of three centuries of garden-making. The huge water-staircase, or cascade, and fountains were made in the 17th century. There is an 18th century landscape by 'Capability' Brown, dramatic rockwork by Sir Joseph Paxton, an arboretum and pinetum planted in the 19th century, and the very latest in suspended glass-houses – complete 1971. Open daily April to Nov (house closed Mon). Tel: Baslow 2204. Nearby is the 'model' village of Edensor, constructed by the sixth Duke of Devonshire on a site where it could not be seen from Chatsworth House. The original Edensor was razed to the ground because it spoilt the view! Sir Gilbert Scott rebuilt the church, which contains Cavendish family monuments.
□ Four miles (6.4km) NE of Bakewell on B6012. Map ref 4B6.

576. CHEE DALE
Limestone landscape

Exceptionally fine scenic stretch of the valley of the River Wye overhung by limestone pinnacles and the cliffs of Chee Tor. Footpaths follow the river.

Farther downstream the Wye leads into Miller's Dale, then Monsal Dale and the pretty village of Ashford in the Water.
□ Five miles (8km) E of Buxton via A6 on B6049. Map ref 4B6.

577. CHELMORTON
Old field patterns

This street or linear village, comprised mainly of farmhouses, provides a striking illustration of field enclosure patterns in upland Britain. Close to the village, on either side of the street, the fields are narrow and rectangular. They look like the old strip farming, albeit enclosed within the drystone walls that form the field boundaries. And, indeed, they were laid out in the old open fields that once surrounded the village – fields still possibly being farmed in the traditional 'strip' manner as late as the mid 17th century. Higher up on the moors – the village itself is more than 1000ft (300m) above sea level – a different pattern of enclosure is revealed. Here the fields are square shaped: the result of parliamentary enclosure acts on former open common land.
□ Five miles (8km) SE of Buxton off A5270. Map ref 4B6.

578. CRESWELL CRAGS
Limestone caves

The grey cliffs of this narrow gorge contain caves which were once the home of Stone Age hunters. Many important paleolithic remains have been found here. There is now a picnic site, visitor centre and footpaths. Open Tues, Sat and Sun, May-Sept; Tues, Fri, Sat and Sun, Mar, Apr and Oct. Also Nov-Feb, Sun only. Tel: Worksop 720378.
□ Off A60 Worksop-Mansfield road. Map ref 4B6.

579. CROMFORD
Industrial archaeology

The small village on the River Derwent where in 1771 Richard Arkwright built not only his pioneering water-powered cotton mill but also a model village of workers' houses. There was also a chapel where Arkwright was buried. A fine 15th century bridge crosses the Derwent whose rushing waters – for a few decades before the steam revolution – turned this picturesque valley into a considerable industrial centre. Now nature has taken over again with, in many places, just a few millponds to serve as reminders of an industrial past. Horse-drawn canal boat offers trips on summer weekends to Lea Wood Pump House from Cromford Wharf.
□ Two miles (3.2km) S of Matlock on A6. Map ref 4B6.

580. ELVASTON CASTLE
Country park

Castle, wood and parkland with lake, bridleways, gardens, nature trail, playground.
□ Six miles (9km) SE of Derby off B5010. Map ref 4B6.

581. GOYT VALLEY
Pennine walks

A delightful wooded valley with a tumbling stream set among the wild

'Hardwick Hall, more glass than wall', the magnificent Elizabethan mansion built by Bess of Hardwick in 1590–97

Pennine moorlands of the Peak District National Park. Numerous contrasting walks and viewpoints have made this a popular picnic spot but no cars are allowed. A large car park allows visitors to stroll through the valley but a minibus service helps the less active to reach the remoter spots.
☐ Off A5002, three miles (5km) NW of Buxton. Map ref 4B6.

582. HADDON HALL
Historic house

Incredibly romantic medieval stone manor with beautiful terraced rose gardens in the valley of the Wye. Below the gardens the Wye is spanned by a pack-horse bridge. The Hall itself has splendid rooms, medieval banqueting hall, Mortlake tapestries and dark, rambling kitchens. Open daily (except Suns and Mons), Apr to Sept. Also Bank holidays. Tel: Bakewell 2855.
☐ Two miles 3.2km) SE of Bakewell on A6. Map ref 4B6.

583. HARDWICK HALL
Country park and historic house

'Hardwick Hall, more glass than wall' – the magnificent Elizabethan house (NT), built by Bess of Hardwick, the Countess of Shrewsbury. Gardens and park with lakes, fishing, canoeing, nature trail.
☐ Four miles (6.4km) NW of Mansfield E of M1 between junctions 28 and 29. Map ref 4B6.

584. KEDLESTON HALL
Stately home

Not open to the public very often, but worth every effort to see. A great Palladian house decorated and altered by Robert Adam at the height of his career. The huge hall lined with alabaster columns leads to a circular saloon modelled on the Roman Pantheon. Adam's state bed and drawing-room furniture have never been excelled. Usually open only Bank Holiday and Sun afternoons, Apr to Sept. Tel: Derby 840396.
☐ Four miles (6.4km) NW of Derby between A52 and B5023. Map ref 4B6.

585. LADYBOWER AND UPPER DERWENT VALLEY RESERVOIRS
Man-made lakes

This staircase of large reservoirs was created by damming the Derwent's headwaters to form the Howden Reservoir in 1912 and the Derwent Reservoir in 1916, and finally the Ashop Brook and lesser tributaries to form the vast Ladybower Reservoir (completed 1943), which helps to supply Sheffield, Derby, Nottingham and Leicester. Its construction drowned the two villages of Derwent and Ashopton, whose ruins are occasionally exposed during summer droughts. Much of the surrounding moorland is owned by the NT, and a maze of footpaths enables ramblers to obtain splendid views of these cradled lakes.
☐ Ten miles (15km) W of sheffield on A57. Map ref 4B5.

586. MELBOURNE HALL
Stately home and garden

Stately home of Queen Victoria's first Prime Minister, the great Lord Melbourne. The splendid formal garden has remained largely unaltered since it was laid out by Wise, in the style of Le Notre, at the end of the 17th century. There are allées, water basins, fountains, statues, urns and a wonderful wrought-iron pavilion, the 'Iron Arbour' or 'Birdcage', which was made by Robert Bakewell, the 18th century ironsmith. Open regularly, Easter to Oct. Tel: Melbourne 2502.
☐ Melbourne, on A514 S of Derby. Map ref 2A1.

587. MIDDLETON
Rail trail

One of the landmarks of the former Cromford and High Peak Railway has now become a focal point of an enjoyable day out. The railway, one of the first in Britain, opened in 1819 to carry minerals and owed more to the concepts of the canal age. A series of stationary engines hauled trucks up steep inclines which were linked by moving engines operating on the level stretches. The line reached a height greater than 1000ft (308m) over the Peak plateau, but travel was a slow business. When a passenger service was introduced in the mid 19th century a traveller could expect to take up to six hours to cover just 20 miles (32km). Yet the line only closed after the Second World War.

With the closure of the line, however, the track has been made into a fine upland footpath and bridleway known as the High Peak Trail. This runs from Cromford to Buxton linking with the Tissington Trail at Parsley Hay. It is readily accessible at Middleton Top where another attraction is one of the original stationary engines now restored and on public display in an 1825 engine house. Further information from countryside warden at Middleton Top. Tel: Wirksworth 3204.
☐ 1½ miles (2.4km) SW of Cromford. Map ref 4B6.

588. RIBER CASTLE FAUNA RESERVE AND WILD LIFE PARK
Rare farm breeds

Apart from its quota of zoo inmates, Riber Castle has been developing its collection of rare domestic breeds of livestock. Ten breeds of cattle and twenty breeds of sheep now jostle with the most comprehensive specialist collections of lynxes in the world. Open daily throughout the year. Tel: Matlock 2073.
☐ Riber Castle, Matlock, off B6014 on Matlock-Tansley road. Map ref 4B6.

589. SHARDLOW
Canal port

Shardlow was in existence before the Canal Age, but the town owed its greatest prosperity to the nearby junction between the Trent and Mersey canal with the River Trent. For a time Shardlow became an important inland port and many old wharves and warehouses remain from these years in the late 18th and early 19th centuries. Now its waterways are becoming busy again – primarily with leisure craft.
☐ Eight miles (12.8km) SE of Derby on A6. Map ref 4B6.

590. SHIPLEY
Country park

Meadow and woodland with bridleways, angling, nature trail, sailing.
☐ Access off A608 in Heanor, and A6007 Heanor-Ilkeston. Map ref 4B6.

591. TISSINGTON
Country trail

This village has given its name to a 13-mile (21km) stretch of disused railway line known as the Tissington Trail. It runs from Ashbourne to Parsley Hay where it joins a similar trail known as the High Peak Trail. The old rail route is now a fully-developed trail for walkers, horse-riders and cyclists, with car parking facilities at the former stations. Illustrated leaflet describing the route (and covering facilities such as bike hire) available from the Information Section, Peak National Park, Bakewell, Derbyshire.
☐ Tissington is four miles (6.4km) N of Ashbourne, off A515. Map ref 4B6.

Leicestershire

The countryside of Leicestershire is typical of the hunting shires of middle England: low undulating fieldscapes with quickthorn hedges, spinneys and beckoning church spires. Charnwood Forest adds a wilder dimension. Belvoir Castle imparts a fine flourish of feudal history. East Midlands Tourist Board: Lincoln 31521.

592. BATTLEFIELD OF BOSWORTH
Battlefield and country park

Where Richard III was defeated in final battle of the Wars of the Roses, in 1485. Now a country park set in farmland and woodland with visitor centre and battle trail.
☐ 11 miles (17km) W of Leicester between A444 and A447. Map ref 2A1.

593. BELVOIR CASTLE
Stately home

This large, romantic castle riding upon a lofty ridge overlooking the Vale of Belvoir has been the ancestral home of the Dukes of Rutland since the reign of Henry VIII, though most of the existing building was constructed in the 19th century. Paintings, tapestries, beautiful water garden. Open Apr to Oct, Weds, Thurs, weekends, Bank Holidays. Tel: Knipton 262.

☐ Six miles (9.6km) W of Grantham on minor roads between A52 and A607. Map ref 4C6.

594. CHARNWOOD FOREST
Scenic landscapes

The southern fringe of Charnwood Forest is reached through Anstey on the B5327 out of Leicester. Little is left of the ancient woods which once covered this landscape of heathlands, boulder-strewn hillocks and pre-Cambrian rocks rising above the rich farmlands of the plain, though new plantations flourish. Stand on Beacon Hill, 818ft (242m) across the road from Broombriggs Farm (with farm trail) at Woodhouse Eaves, off B591 – or Bardon Hill, 912ft (274m) off A50 – and you can see the curious rock formations of the surrounding hills, all carved from part of England's primeval floor uncovered from beneath the much newer rock strata. Neighbouring Bradgate Park, a medieval hunting park is a wilderness of moorland paths and lakes with fallow deer roaming by the ruins of a Tudor Mansion, once the home of Lady Jane Grey. Open all year; ruins open Apr to Oct. Tel: Leicester 871313.
☐ NW of Leicester. Map ref 2A1.

595. FOXTON
Canal architecture

A 'staircase' of 10 locks lifts the Grand Union Canal more than 75ft (23m) near this village with its church dating back to the 13th century. Set in a rural countryside between Leicester and Market Harborough, Foxton epitomises the engineering skills of the Canal Age. For in addition to the locks there are the overgrown remains of an inclined plane or lift that operated for about 10 years at the turn of the century. Now, with its shops, cafe and summer boat trips, Foxton has become a popular place to discover the non-industrial pleasure of canals.
☐ Three miles (5km) NW of Market Harborough off A6. Map ref 2A1.

596. GREAT CASTERTON
Archaeological site

This small village of pleasant stone-built houses on the old Great North Road was once a larger settlement. Here stood a Roman town on the line of Ermine Street which at this point the Great North Road (now known as the A1) follows. Remnants of the Roman defences can still be seen in the form of mounds, hollows and ditches. The village also has a large 13th century church with 15th century tower.
☐ Two miles (3.2km) NW of Stamford near junction of A1 and B1081. Map ref 2B1.

597. HALLATON
Folklore village

An attractive village with an unusual conical Buttercross standing on the small green. The green is surrounded by fine 17th–19th century stone built cottages and houses, some thatched. In a house off the High Street is a tiny museum with local farm implements. Open weekends, May to Oct. Tel: Hallaton 295 for details. On Easter Monday the village is the scene of the Hare Pie Scramble, a bizarre folk custom acted out each year.
☐ Six miles (9.6km) SW of Uppingham between A47 and B664. Map ref 2B2.

598. INGARSBY
Deserted village

One of 67 deserted medieval villages in Leicestershire and still visible in the form of grassy mounds (where houses stood), and faint green hollows which once were lanes or fish-ponds. The village was destroyed as a living community in 1469 when the owners of the manor, Ingarsby Abbey, decided to turn all the land (including that on which the village stood) into sheep pastures.
☐ Five miles (8km) E of Leicester off minor road, ¾ mile (1.2km) N of Houghton on the Hill on A47. Grid ref SK 687053. OS map 140. Map ref 2A1.

599. OAKHAM
Market town

Once the county town of Rutland, England's smallest county, which lost its struggle for survival in the local government reorganisation of 1974. It remains a busy market centre, with general markets on Weds and Sats, and cattle on Fris. In the market square is an old Buttercross, complete with stocks. Oakham Castle, in Market Street, has a lofty banqueting hall and famous collection of ornamental horseshoes. The castle is open throughout the year, but opening times vary. Tel: Oakham 3654 for details. The Rutland County Museum in Catmos Street contains a mixture of farm implements and craft tools and a display of Rutland wagons painted their original bright orange.
☐ On A606, SE of Melton Mowbray. Map ref 2B1.

600. RUTLAND WATER
Fishing and bird-watching

A reservoir created in 1970 of enormous dimensions: walk round it and you will have covered 24 miles (38km). It is many things for many people. For anglers it is the largest man-made fishing water in the country – stocked with half a million trout. (Fishing permits available from Whitwell Lodge – well signposted locally.) For naturalists there is an extensive nature reserve at its western end. Part of the reserve known as Lyndon Hill is open to the public on afternoons at weekends and bank holidays; other parts, with facilities for bird-watching etc, require special permits (see below). But even without a special hobby to pursue, the footpaths along the reservoir's landscaped shores make pleasant walking, with attractive villages such as Empingham and Exton either on or near the Water. For information about permits for the nature reserve or any other activity at Rutland Water, Tel: Empingham 321.
☐ Immediately SW of Oakham between A606 and A6003. Map ref 2B1.

601. STAUNTON HAROLD
Fine church

An estate church, with only the Georgian-fronted mansion for company. Not at all Puritan, yet all built, almost unbelievably, during the Commonwealth. Apart from the lovely setting, the special features are the finely proportioned tower, the pretty little organ high up in the west gallery, the wealth of 17th century woodwork and the magnificent wrought-iron screen c.1715, which is probably by Robert Bakewell, the greatest English smith.
☐ Four miles (6.4km) NE of Ashby-de-la-Zouch off B587. Map ref 2A1.

Nottinghamshire

Contains the relic oaks of Sherwood Forest, the spacious parklands of the Dukeries, and the broad vale of the Trent, which flows through Nottingham, the county town. Newark Castle, Southwell Minster and Newstead Abbey are important attractions. East Midlands Tourist Board: Lincoln 31521.

602. BURNTSTUMP
Country park

Park and woodland with nature trail.
☐ Seven miles (11km) N of Nottingham off A60. Map ref 4B6.

603. CLUMBER PARK
Country park

Large park landscaped out of the heathland bordering Sherwood Forest by 'Capability' Brown in the 18th century. The old mansion has gone but the park with its veteran oaks, magnificent avenues of limes and long serpentine lake offers good walks and a variety of wildlife, including great crested grebes. Open all year. Car park charge. Information Centre. Leaflet describes two walks. Tel: East Midlands National Trust, Worksop 86411.
☐ Four miles (6km) SE of Worksop. Map ref 4B6.

604. HOLME PIERREPONT
Country park

Restored gravel pits offering fishing, riverside walk, water sports.
☐ Five miles (8km) SE of Nottingham. Map ref 4C6.

605. LAXTON
Medieval field systems

A classic site in the evolution of the English landscape where a medieval open-field system has escaped the enclosure movement. Systems of farming have changed but one can still appreciate the spaciousness of the hedgeless arable land that once surrounded every medieval village. (Under the traditional system of open-field farming arable land was divided into three parts and farmed on a three-year cycle; one-third was left fallow and two-third farmed each year.)
☐ Four miles (6.4km) E of Ollerton, two miles (3.2km) S of A6075. Map ref 4C6.

606. NEWSTEAD ABBEY
Historic house and garden

Ancestral home of Lord Byron, containing many treasures of the Byron family. The original 12th century abbey was built by Henry II to atone for the murder of Thomas à Becket. Today it is owned by Nottingham City Council, together with its extensive gardens and lakes. Open every after-noon, Apr-Sept. Tel. Blidworth 3557.
☐ Near Linby, off A60, eight miles (12.8km) N of Nottingham. Map ref 4B6.

607. RUFFORD
Country park and historic house

Timbered medieval manor with wood and park, lake, mill.
☐ 15 miles (24km) N of Nottingham on A614 near Ollerton. Map ref 4C6.

608. SHERWOOD FOREST
Country park

Few English forests have such fame as that of Sherwood and its popular folk hero, Robin Hood. Most of the mighty oaks have been felled over the centuries, but enough survive here to give a flavour of the medieval forest. Edwinstowe Church is where Robin is said to have married Maid Marian, and the Major Oak (his hideout) is one mile (1.6km) N of the village. The Visitor Centre explains the economic and natural history of the Forest Park and Visitor Centre open all year. Tel: Mansfield 823202.
☐ Off B6034 near Edwinstowe, two miles (3.2km) W of Ollerton. Map ref 4C6.

609. WOLLATON HALL
Museum and nature trail

This fine Elizabethan hall houses the City of Nottingham Natural History Museum. It has collections of botany, zoology and geology and a new insect gallery. Outside are formal gardens, a deer park and lake. The Nature Trail leads around the lake. Fallow and red deer in the park. Open daily except Christmas Day. For opening times, Tel: Nottingham 281333.
☐ Three miles (5km) W of Nottingham city centre, off A609. Map ref 4B6.

Shropshire (Salop)

The River Severn divides this historic Border county, where ridge upon ridge of wild hills roll westward into Wales and Ludlow Castle still broods above the Teme. Shrewsbury, the county town, has many fine half-timbered buildings. Heart of England Tourist Board: Worcester 29511.

610. ACTON SCOTT WORKING FARM MUSEUM
Rural life

Life on a Shropshire upland farm before mechanisation, with many animals of the period rarely seen nowadays. Also demonstrates 19th-century arable techniques. Displays of butter making and other traditional crafts. Open daily Apr to Oct; afternoons only Mon to Sat in Apr, May, Sept and Oct. All day Sun, Bank Holidays. Tel: Marshbrook 306/307.
☐ Wenlock Lodge, Acton Scott, three miles (5km) S of Church Stretton. Off A49 between Ludlow and Church Stretton. Map ref 1C2.

611. BRIDGNORTH
Market town

An ancient market town by the River Severn. Low Town and High Town are linked by a bridge and the Castle Hill railway which has a 2 in 3 gradient. Only a tower remains of the Norman

castle which used to stand here but it is a memorable one since it is leaning at an angle of 17 degrees – three times greater than the leaning tower of Pisa. Other interesting and less precarious buildings include a 17th century half-timbered hall, the upper part of which served as a barn before being re-erected on the arches of the original structure; some 18th century houses in East Castle Street; and the Church of St Magdalene built by Thomas Telford.
□ 14 miles (22km) W of Wolverhampton. Map ref 1D2.

612. BURFORD HOUSE GARDENS
Riverside garden

Clever use of herbaceous perennials and shrubs in beautiful setting by the River Teme. Also interesting trees. Open afternoons, Apr to Oct. Also some days in Mar. Tel: Tenbury Wells 810777.
□ Tenbury Wells, off A456 Worcester-Ludlow road. Map ref 1D2.

613. CLEE CLUN RIDGEWAY
Drover's road drive

A prehistoric track running along the watershed crest separating the Clun and Teme valleys in the Welsh borderlands. The route was first used for trade with Ireland but later became a well-used drover's route. Today it can make a picturesque upland drive.
□ From Newtown head E on A489 to Kerry. Turn right via minor road to B4368 and follow this SE to climb onto the ridge beyond the Anchor Inn. Map ref 1C2.

614. ELLESMERE
Little lakeland

Locally termed Shropshire's 'Lake District', Ellesmere's nine meres or lakes, all accessible, are waterfilled hollows created when buried ice blocks melted at the close of the Ice Age. Today these placid lakes are the haunt of moorhen, heron, kingfisher, grebe and many other birds. They are also used for angling, sailing and swimming. Boats for hire throughout the summer months. Colemere Country Park is just over three miles (5km) south-east of Ellesmere and to the north of Colemere village.
□ Seven miles (11km) NE of Oswestry on the A495. Map ref 1C1.

615. HODNET HALL GARDENS
Lakeside gardens

Well-planted lakeside gardens which extend over 60 acres. Open Mar to Sept every afternoon. Tel: Hodnet 202.
□ Near Market Drayton, just off A442. Map ref 1D1.

616. IRONBRIDGE
Industrial archaeology

The very word is the epitome of the Industrial Revolution but the area around Ironbridge has an undeniable place in a book on the British countryside. Firstly, because the Severn Gorge and the valleys that join it, such as Coalbrookdale, have largely reverted to their natural form: steep, tree-lined and attractive. Secondly, because many of the developments which so altered the landscape were pioneered here and thirdly, because there are a

series of outstanding museums where this long-neglected area's past can be explored and celebrated.

The award-winning Ironbridge Gorge Museum Trust runs a series of

Where to find the Ironbridge Gorge Museum Trust sites in Coalbrookdale

museums on different sites (see map). The Blists Hill Open Air Museum, for instance, would provide a stimulating day out in itself. It has a stretch of canal, the Hay inclined plane linking canal and river, a Telford-designed toll house, mine works, mills, footpaths and even a special leaflet on the plants and wildlife to be seen.

Leaflets are available on each of the various museums. The Trust's shop,

Ironbridge: the commemorative plaque

next to the great iron bridge itself (erected 1779 and now pedestrianised), also sells pamphlets on walks in the area – both nature and industrial heritage trails. The museums can be visited in any order, but the Trust believes the best starting point is the Coalbrookdale Museum and Furnace Site where Abraham Darby first used coke to smelt iron in 1709. One ticket covers all museums. They are open throughout the year, but opening times vary. Tel: Ironbridge 3522 for details.
□ Four miles (6.4km) SW of Telford on A4169; OS map 127. Map ref 1D1.

617. LONG MYND
Scenic hills

Wild ridge of heathery uplands (NT) with marvellous walks and views. An ancient track, the Port Way, runs the entire length of the 10-mile (16km) long hill crest.
□ W of Church Stretton, 13 miles (23km) S of Shrewsbury. Map ref 1C2.

618. LUDLOW
Historic country town

A perfect example of the planned medieval castle-town – and one of the more successful of those established near the Welsh border. The castle, on a wooded bluff above the River Teme, was under construction by 1085 at much the same time as the Norman architects were laying out the streets of

the new town in a rectangular pattern that largely survives today. Notable features of the town are the 15th century church of St Lawrence, the extensive town wall and its streets of timber-framed and Georgian brick buildings.
□ Midway between Hereford and Shrewsbury on A49. Map ref 1C2.

619. MERRINGTON GREEN NATURE TRAIL
Wildlife

This trail shows the once-grazed common land of Merrington Green in the process of changing to scrubby woodland. It lies on heavy clay soil (take boots on wet days) and takes 1–2hr to walk. There are birds and plants of scrub, in plenty, damp parts with rushes and marsh thistle and splendid views. There are fish in a deep pool, once a marl pit (from which coarse lime-rich clay was extracted to improve the fertility of poor soils) and other swampy pools rich in aquatic life: water plantain, marsh horsetail, dragonflies and damsel-flies. Leaflet information from Shropshire Conservation Trust. Tel: Shrewsbury 56511.
□ Five miles (9km) N of Shrewsbury off B5067 (on by-road). Map ref 1C1.

620. OFFA'S DYKE
Historic earthwork

This linear earthwork can be seen as clearly as anywhere along its 120-mile (192km) length from the neighbouring Llanfair and Spoad Hills. The dyke was constructed in the last quarter of the 8th century to define the western limits of the Saxon kingdom of Mercia.
□ Llanfair and Spoad Hills are three miles (5km) W of Clun, S of B4368. Grid ref SO 254805; OS map 137. Map ref 1C2.

621. OLD OSWESTRY
Prehistoric hillfort

This is an outstanding hill fort from Iron Ages times built on a glacial mound just north of the modern town. Its elaborate ramparts and ditches were built at several different times; the western gateway is particularly intricate. The site covers some 68 acres (27 hectares) and, like most hill forts, is an interesting place for exploration and picnics with fine views over the surrounding countryside.
□ One mile (1.6km) N of Oswestry between B4579 and A483; grid ref SJ 295304; OS map 126. Map ref 1C1.

622. PRESTON MONTFORD NATURE TRAIL
Wildlife

Ferns, flowers and birdlife abound in this Shropshire Conservation Trust reserve on the banks of the Severn, in a wilderness known as Preston Rough. The trail is short (about 1km) but has ten stops (marked by alder leaf symbol) pointing out different habitats. Contact warden at Field Centre for permission to use trail and birdwatching hide. Booklet lists wildlife species (including sand martins, moisture-loving plants such as golden saxifrage, and goat willow – an important source of artists' charcoal). Tel: Preston Montford Field Centre: Montford Bridge 380.

□ Montford Bridge four miles (7km) NW of Shrewsbury. Map ref 1C1.

623. STIPERSTONES
Moorland hills

In the moorland hills of south Shropshire the 1700ft (510m) Stiperstones offer a contrasting scene to that of the more famous Long Mynd and Wrekin. Their long, bouldery ridge is punctuated by jagged tors of white quartzite rock. Approached easily on foot from the car park, these crags offer a delightful, breezy viewpoint and a jumbled frost-shattered wilderness of rocks and heather above the surrounding wooded valleys and farmlands where ancient Roman leadmines once flourished. The tiny village of Snailbeach is surrounded by the remains of a lead mine, once the richest in England. Derelict surface buildings still stand. Explore with care as there are a number of open shafts.
□ Minor road on E of A488 at Ploxgreen leads to The Bog. Car parking. Map ref 1C1.

624. STOKESAY CASTLE
Fortified manor house

Romantic, well-preserved manor house dating from the 13th century. Moated and fortified, with two stone towers, splendid gabled banqueting hall and picturesque half-timbered gatehouse. Open daily Mar to Oct, except Tues.
□ Approx three quarters of a mile (1km) S of Craven Arms on A49. Map ref 1C2.

625. WENLOCK EDGE
Limestone escarpment

This remarkably straight escarpment of ancient limestone is a well known landmark to the north-west of the attractive market town of Much Wenlock. Good viewpoints of Apedale and the Church Stretton hills can be found at intervals along its narrow wooded crest. Explore the peaceful villages of neighbouring Hope Dale or the lovely Elizabethan mansion of Wilderhope (NT), off the B4271, built from Wenlock limestone. Open Apr-Sept on Wed and Sat afternoons, Oct to Mar. Note the vertical limestone rock of Major's Leap, north of the B4371 about 2½ miles (4km) from Much Wenlock, with its legend of Civil War heroism. Much Wenlock Museum in the High Street has geological, social and local history exhibits. Open Apr to Sept. Tel: Much Wenlock 727773. Also visit the striking Guildhall in the Square, dating from 1577, which is open Apr to Sept and Wenlock Priory (AM) and abbey ruins, open standard DoE hours.
□ From Much Wenlock access is via the B4371 or B4378. Map ref 1C2.

626. THE WREKIN
Beacon hilltop

This isolated hill affords commanding views over the Vale of the Upper Severn so it is little wonder that it should be crowned with extensive ramparts that strengthened the position still further. It was an important hill fort of Iron Age Britain. Its height is 1334ft (411m), and so clearly does it

Regency Gothic at Ingestre Hall, Staffordshire. The fine church at Ingestre was also built in the 17th century, perhaps by Wren himself

stand above the surrounding land that in later generations it served as a beacon hill. Even today it is still crowned with a warning light to aircraft.

□ Two miles (3.2km) SW of Wellington off A5. Map ref 1D1.

627. WROXETER
Roman site

In the 2nd century AD this was the site of the fourth largest city of Roman Britain. But like Silchester *Viroconium* did not become the location of a major settlement in later times: the small present-day village of Wroxeter developed a little distance away from the Roman site. At least this means that some of the Roman remains are still visible on the ground, notably earthworks which were once the city ramparts and the stone foundations of the baths and a colonnade. In Wroxeter itself the Norman church probably

incorporates stone from the old Roman city. The Roman site and museum are open standard DoE hours plus Sun mornings, Apr to Sept.

□ Five miles (8km) SE of Shrewsbury off B4380; grid ref SJ 565087; OS map 126. Map ref 1D1.

Staffordshire

Staffordshire has some lovely countryside to compensate for the industrial areas of the Black Country and the Potteries. It offers the wild uplands of Cannock Chase and shares the beautiful limestone scenery of Dovedale with Derbyshire. Architectural splendours include triple-towered Lichfield Cathedral. Heart of England Tourist Board: Worcester 29511.

628. ALTON TOWERS
Landscape gardens

Do not be put off by the fact that Alton

Towers has become a fun-fair and amusement park for the Potteries. The enormous and mostly gutted house, partly designed by Pugin, provides a backcloth of towers and gables for one of England's most extraordinary and elaborate gardens. It was made early in the 19th century in a bare valley. It is now magnificently planted with trees and shrubs and ornamented with many strange buildings including a Chinese pagoda which is also a fountain, a Roman colonnade, a Gothic tower, a Druid stone circle and an elaborate conservatory. The Gothic mansion is now a ruin. Open daily, Easter to Oct. Tel: Oakamoor 702449.

□ At Alton, off B5032 four miles (6.5km) E of Cheadle. Map ref 4B6.

629. BLITHFIELD RESERVOIR
Bird-watching

One of the best places in this part of England to watch birds in winter.

Species likely to be seen include pintail, and goldeneye, Bewick's swan and jack snipe.

□ Eight miles (13km) E of Stafford, off B5013. Map ref 1D1.

630. CHEADLE
Market town

Old market town situated in moorland countryside within easy reach of the Weaver Hills and the Manifold Valley. The lofty spire of the red stone Roman Catholic church (a Pugin masterpiece, built in 1840) is a landmark for miles around. Brass lions at the west door guard a rich interior. Some two miles (3.2km) north-east of Cheadle is Hawksmoor Nature Reserve (NT), a stretch of curlew-haunted moorland, marsh and woodland planted with red oak and lodgepole pine.

□ Eight miles (12.8km) E of Stoke-on-Trent, on A521. Map ref 4A6.

631. CHEDDLETON
Watermills

Two watermills have been preserved here beside the Caldon Canal in the beautiful wooded valley of the River Churnet. Both contain much of the original machinery (including the two waterwheels) and are open on weekend afternoons throughout the year. One mill was formerly used to grind corn; the other stands as a memorial to the many which were once active in grinding flint for the local pottery industry.
□ Three miles (5km) S of Leek on A520. Map ref 4A6.

632. COOMBES VALLEY
Bird-watching

This RSPB reserve lies in a wooded valley and covers 261 acres (106 hectares). It provides a refuge for a large number of woodland birds including sparrowhawk and pied flycatcher. By the stream watch out for dipper and kingfisher. Report to the information centre on arrival. For car park charges and opening times. Tel: RSPB Reserves Dept, Sandy 80551.
□ Leek. Map ref 4A6.

633. GREENWAY BANK
Country park

Wooded valley at head of River Trent with lake, arboreta and sandstone outcrops.
□ Four miles (6.4km) N of Stoke-on-Trent off A527. Map ref 4A6.

634. HAWKSMOOR NATURE RESERVE TRAIL
Wildlife

Bracken and heather moorland and some woodland, this nature reserve and bird sanctuary slopes down to the river Churnet. Birds you may see include curlew and lapwing, redstarts, nightjars and warblers. Nature Trail and four recommended walks which also cover farmland, river, railway and disused canal. Open all year. Limited parking, six cars only.
□ Two miles (3km) NE of Cheadle (on B5417). Map ref 1D1.

635. HIGHGATE COMMON
Country park

Heath, wood, bridleways.
□ Two miles (3km) W of Kingswinford. Map ref 1D2.

636. INGESTRE
Parish church

The Church of St Mary is one of the best 17th century churches in England outside London, and probably by Wren himself in 1673–6. Interior notable for its fine proportions and admirable craftsmanship in wood and stucco. Look particularly at the pulpit, reredos and imposing screen bearing a splendid Royal Arms. This stately classical church has no need of stained glass, and that in the nave, at least, should be removed.
□ Five miles (8km) E of Stafford off A51. Map ref 1D1.

637. MANIFOLD VALLEY
Limestone dale

Start from the picturesque village of Ilam with its Saxon church and ancient field patterns, and stroll northwards along the beautiful wooded limestone gorge where the Manifold River, a tributary of the Dove disappears underground in dry weather. Ilam Nature Walk (NT) is set in the grounds of Ilam Hall, one and a half miles (2.4km) from car park. Alternatively, drive down the steep lane from Wetton, three miles (4.8km) further up the valley to Wetton Mill, or walk southwest from Wetton along the track of the old Manifold Valley Light Railway, now a footpath, to Beeston Tor.
□ Ilam is reached by minor road, four miles (6.4km) NW of Ashborne. Map ref 4B6.

638. PARKHALL
Country park

Sandstone heathland and coniferous woodland with nature trail, information centre, fishing, model air-flying, golf course, views and bridleways.
□ Weston Coyne, E of Stoke. Map ref 4A6.

639. STAFFORDSHIRE COUNTY MUSEUM
Farm museum

Agricultural history is on show in what was designed in the 19th century as a home farm to the estate, but in 1975 was taken over and turned into an agricultural museum. The farm is also a breeding centre for rare local livestock. A fine collection of horse-drawn vehicles, all with strong Staffordshire connections, are in the coach-house. Open end Mar-end Oct, Tues to Fris. Also weekend afternoons. Closed Mons except Bank holidays. Tel: Little Haywood 881388.
□ Shugborough, Stafford. On A513, five and a half miles SE of Stafford. Map ref 1D1.

640. TRENTHAM GARDENS
Stately garden

Neo-Italian terraces and a 'Capability' Brown landscape. Scented garden for the blind. Also demonstration plots showing a dozen back-garden layouts for the amateur. Open Easter to Sept daily. Tel: Stoke-on-Trent 657341.
□ At Trentham. On A34, three miles (4.8km) S of Stoke-on-Trent. Map ref 1D1.

Trentham Gardens, Staffordshire, provides acres of open space on the doorstep of the Potteries. Attractions include a scented garden for the blind and demonstration plots for amateur gardeners

The picturesque fishing village of Staithes, on the North Yorkshire coast, lies within the North Yorks Moors National Park and is surrounded by high cliffs

Northern England

641. LAKE DISTRICT
National Park

Easy access by road off M6 motorway, which skirts park's eastern edge. Within the park, roads run through the major dales and along the lake-shores to converge on Ambleside and also at Keswick. Here every road is a scenic drive – traffic jams permitting.

If you can leave your car and walk there are endless possibilities in this, the largest national park in England and Wales. Serious climbers head for spots such as Wasdale and the crags of Great Gable and Scafell Pike, whose 3206ft (997m) summit is England's highest. Yet these brooding fell tops can also be reached by walkers, provided you are reasonably fit, well shod and clad for the hills. Ambleside, Borrowdale, Coniston and Patterdale (for Helvellyn) are favourite walking centres. There are park information centres at Ambleside, Bowness, Coniston, Glenridding, Hawkshead, Pooley Bridge and Keswick.

One of the unique pleasures of this park are the leisurely scheduled services by steamer and motor launch on Windermere, Derwentwater and Ullswater. Sightseeing: the lakes, hills and dales steal most of the glory, but there is also a fine stretch of sea coast at Ravenglass. In the Cumbrian section we feature some Lakeland areas which remain relatively uncrowded on even the busiest Bank Holiday.
□ Map ref 3D3.

642. NORTHUMBERLAND
National Park

Few roads pierce this remote and splendid park, wedged between the Roman Wall and the Scottish Border, with the Border Forest Park on its western flanks. Indeed, there is only one main road, the A68, running through Redesdale on its lonely way from Otterburn to Carter Bar. Otherwise this is a walkers' park, offering superlative fell walks in the Simonside and Cheviot Hills. Finest is the Pennine Way long-distance footpath, which also takes in a spectacular length of the Roman Wall before swinging north towards High Cheviot, 2674ft (815m), the park's loftiest summit. Park information centres at Byrness, Ingram and Once Brewed.
□ Map ref 4A2.

643. NORTH YORK MOORS
National Park

One of the better parks for motorists. Viewpoints with or close to car parking include Sutton Bank on the scarp of the Hambleton Hills, Robin Hood's Bay on the Yorkshire coast, Danby Beacon and Newgate Bank. For walkers, a huge variety of cliff paths, forest trails and moorland treks beckon. Best-known are the 90-mile (144km) Cleveland Way long-distance footpath, the 40-mile (64km) Lyke Wake Walk over the moors, and Wade's Causeway, one of the best-preserved Roman roads in Britain. Information centres at Danby Lodge, Pickering and Sutton Bank.
□ Map ref 4B2.

644. YORKSHIRE DALES
National Park

Most roads follow the line of the dales, but sometimes climb over the fells to give glorious panoramic views. Notable viewpoints (with or near car parks) include Buttertubs, Dodd Fell and Newby Head. For walkers there are old Roman roads, a marvellous stretch of the Pennine Way long-distance footpath which takes in the dramatic limestone landscapes of Malham and the ascent of Pen-y-ghent, 2273ft (693m), as well as innumerable gentler walks in the dales from Kettlewell and other villages – a perfect counterpoint to the wild fell tops. Swaledale, Wensleydale, Wharfedale and Ribblesdale are the four major dales, but there are others, Dentdale and Littondale among them, which are every inch as delectable. There are park information centres at Aysgarth Falls, Clapham, Grassington, Hawes and Malham.
□ Map ref 4A4.

645. ARNSIDE AND SILVERDALE
Area of Outstanding Natural Beauty

A small but serene tract of coastline on the Lancashire–Cumbria border at the northern end of Morecambe Bay, beside the estuary of the River Kent. Much of it is owned by the NT, including Arnside Knott, 522ft (159m), a favourite viewpoint and the site of a nature trail featuring such characteristic limestone plants as rock-rose, columbine and burnet rose. Leaflet from local shops. Another attraction is 18th century Heron water-mill, at Beetham; tel: Carnforth 4858.
□ Arnside Knott is one mile (1.6km) SW of Arnside. Map ref 4A4.

646. FOREST OF BOWLAND
Area of Outstanding Natural Beauty

This wild collision of moorland fells on the Yorkshire border is Lancashire at its loneliest, a far cry from the industrial conurbations of Liverpool and Manchester. Highest points are Ward's Stone, 1836ft (560m), near the infant River Wyre, and Pendle Hill, 1831ft (558m), once the haunt of the notorious 'Lancashire Witches'. Minor roads penetrate the Hodder Valley and the wild pass known as the Trough of Bowland. There is a country park at Beacon Fell (north-west of Longridge) and several picnic sites in the northwest, including Weatheroak Hill, Birk Bank, Bull Beck and Crook o' Lune.
□ Map ref 4A4.

647. NORTHUMBERLAND COAST
Area of Outstanding Natural Beauty

A gloriously uncluttered Heritage Coast stretched between two classic salmon rivers, Tweed and Coquet. It keeps a low profile for the most part, but the Whin Sill breaches the bays and sandhills in places, forming dolerite crags surmounted by hoary sea-castles at Bamburgh and Dunstanburgh.

Northern England

Sturdy Northumbrian fishing cobles put out from village harbours such as Boulmer and Beadnell. Craster is renowned for oak-smoked kippers; Seahouses for boat trips to see the grey seals and seabird colonies of the Farne Islands (NT). Most romantic spot on the entire coast is Lindisfarne.
□ Map ref 4B1.

648. SOLWAY COAST
Area of Outstanding Natural Beauty

Apart from a small gap around Silloth, this includes the whole of the sandy southern shores of the Solway Firth between Maryport and the mouth of the River Lyne just below Gretna on the Scottish Border. Splendid views across the Firth to the hog-backed Scottish hill of Criffel.
□ Map ref 3D2.

Cleveland

A small county dominated by Teesside but including stretches of coast and the North York Moors. Northumbria Tourist Board: Newcastle 817744.

649. GUISBOROUGH
Monastic remains/views

An attractive little town in the shadow of the Cleveland Hills. It grew around a 12th century Augustinian priory parts of which can still be seen; the ruins, which include a gatehouse, dovecote and the priory's east end, are open standard DoE hours. Close to the ruins is a restored 15th century church. Guisborough is conveniently sited for exploring both sea and moors. One good view point just four miles (6.4km) to the south-west is 1057ft (321m) Roseberry Topping, overlooking the picturesque village of Great Ayton.
□ Seven miles (11km) SE of Middlesbrough on A171. Map ref 4B3.

650. NEWHAM GRANGE
Farm museum

An agricultural museum is incorporated into the running of a farm stocked with rare breeds of animals, especially pigs and poultry. There is also a 19th-century veterinary surgery, a late 19th-century saddler's shop, complete with tools and equipment of the period. Open daily during summer, Sun only during winter. Tel: Middlesbrough 245432 ext 3831.
□ S of Middlesbrough at Coulby Newham near junction of A174 and B1365. Map ref 4B3.

Cumbria

The county has a long coastline but it is the beauty of the Lake District which draws most visitors; Windermere is the largest lake in England. Northern fells and Pennine areas are less crowded, however. Other attractions include Carlisle, Kendal, Keswick and Penrith. Cumbria Tourist Board: Windermere 4444.

651. ALSTON
Market town/industrial landscape

Said to be England's highest market town at 1000ft (305m) above sea level. Market day is Saturday in this hilly little town where the old railway station now houses a tourist information office. The surrounding Alston Moor seems as 'unspoilt' as it is possible to be, yet it has been the scene of lead mining since Roman times. One of the most important developments was around Nenthead, five miles (8km) south-east of Alston on A689. Here, in the early 18th century, the London Lead Company launched a major development of the area's potential. Now only the cottages and chapels remain with the former lead works itself crying out for restoration as a monument of industrial archaeology.
□ 18 miles (29km) NE of Penrith on A686. Map ref 4A3.

652. BIRDOSWALD
Hadrian's Wall

Only a limited excavation has so far been undertaken at this fort (*Camboglanna*) but it is on one of the most dramatic stretches of Hadrian's Wall in Cumbria. Two well-preserved gates and a tower have been uncovered and the *vallum* can be seen on the edge of the escarpment. Access to these remains and this stretch of the wall is available at reasonable hours of the day via the nearby farmhouse.
□ Six miles (9.6km) NW of Haltwhistle off B6318. Map ref 4A2.

653. BOWNESS-ON-SOLWAY
Village/nature reserve

This little fishing village stands on the narrowest part of the Solway Firth with fine views over to Scotland just two miles (3.2km) away. It was the westerly end of Hadrian's Wall and the site of a Roman fort. Part of the road from Carlisle follows the line of the wall across a sometimes dangerous, boggy area but little remains of the wall or fort around Bowness other than the ditch of the old *vallum*. Bowness is an interesting village with a fortified farm to remind us of a more turbulent past and cottages whose charm has withstood sometimes excessively fussy 'restoration'. To the south is Glasson Moss, an NCC nature reserve with a public right of way available to anyone interested in rare mosses.
□ 12 miles (19km) W of Carlisle off B5307. Map ref 3D2.

654. CASTLERIGG
Stone circle

The finest stone circle in the Lake District, a region that has few spectacular prehistoric remains. Thirty-nine stones are still standing in a circle 100ft (30m) across which is also known as the Keswick Carles. It is a magnificent setting amid the surrounding mountains (grid ref NY 292237).
□ One mile (1.6km) E of Keswick via a lane off A591. Map ref 3D3.

655. DUDDON VALLEY
Uncrowded Lakeland

One of the least known Lake District valleys. Lacking in lakes but abounding with quiet, wooded tracts, flowing streams and tantalising views of the high fells. Take either the west bank or the east bank roads to the north from Duddon Bridge. There narrow and twisting lanes provide many picnic spots and viewpoints, especially the path to the stepping stones of the Low Crag gorge to the west. The valley has two 'hidden' lakes which can be approached only on foot: Seathwaite Tarn (two miles (3.2km) north-east of village) and Devoke Water (via the minor road which runs north-west off the main Duddon Valley road at Ulpha). OS map 96.
□ N from Duddon Bridge off A595. Map ref 3D3/4.

656. EDEN VALLEY
River valley

Not in the Lake District national park but an attractive and uncrowded river valley. Lush yet unexplored despite its proximity to the M6. Start at Armathwaite and work south taking in Nunnery Walks (a garden), Kirkoswald (castle), Long Meg and Her Daughters (stone circle), Milburn (village green) and end at Appleby. Or vice versa.
□ Armathwaite is nine miles (14km) SE of Carlisle off A6; Appleby is 12 miles (19km) SE of Penrith on A66. Map ref 4A3.

657. ENNERDALE
Uncrowded Lakeland/forests

Ennerdale Water is the most isolated lake without a road on either side. It is the only lake with this distinction and distinction it is now that parts of the Lake District are so often clogged with cars. The lake has been threatened by a controversial water authority scheme to raise the natural level of the lake. But still marvellous walking country here and in the valley beyond both for sturdy fell-walkers and the less ambitious attracted by FC trails and picnic areas in Ennerdale Forest.
□ Four miles (6.4km) E of Cleator Moor via minor roads to Ennerdale Bridge. Map ref 3D3.

658. FURNESS
Peninsula/abbey

The peninsula is what its name says it is – the 'fur-ness' or the far peninsula almost marooned by the sandy reaches of Morecambe Bay. There is still a sense of isolation as well as beauty here – two qualities associated with the Cistercian monks who took over a Sauvignac house here in 1147. The considerable remains of the monastery – only Fountains was wealthier – are in a sheltered wooded valley to the north of Barrow and are open standard DoE hours.

On Piel Island, three miles (4.8km) south of Barrow, are the ruins of a Norman motte and bailey castle which served as a defence and warehouse for the monks.

Other places worth a visit on – or near – Furness are the market town of Ulverston (market day is Thursday); the Millom Folk Museum, which recalls a century of prosperity which followed the discovery of the great iron ore deposits of the Hodbarrow Mine (open Easter-Sept); Dalton with its 14th century pele tower; Bardsea country park two miles (3.2km) south of Ulverston with views over the bay; and the village of Cartmel with its 12th century priory church and some delightful secular architecture.
□ Map ref 3D4.

659. GRIZEDALE
Forest trails

Millwood forest trail, one mile (1.6km), starts from a Forestry Commission visitor centre in the heart of Grizedale Forest. Also forestry exhibitions at the visitor centre (tel: Satterthwaite 273) and a theatre in the forest which stages musical and other performances.
□ The visitor centre is three miles (4.8km) S of Hawkshead on minor road to Satterthwaite. Map ref 3D3.

660. HARDKNOTT PASS
Roman fort

Near the summit of Hardknott Pass, nearly 1300ft (400m) above sea level, stands a stone wall and earth embankment of a Roman fort dating from the 2nd century. It is a magnificent position alongside the road that climbs out of Eskdale. Grid ref NY 218015.
□ 10 miles (16km) W of Ambleside on minor unclassified road via Eskdale to Ravenglass. Map ref 3D3.

661. HAWESWATER
Drive/walks

The eastern side of Lakeland has fewer large lakes than the west but that of Haweswater is well worthy of a visit, notwithstanding its artificiality and its major dam. The minor road climbs from Bampton village into the woodlands of Haweswater Beck before skirting the lakeshores for four miles (6.4km). There are many interesting views of the high fells to the west and if you are tempted to walk to the high corries there is a choice of paths where the road ends at the southern tip of the reservoir. OS map 90 covers the area.
□ Five miles (8km) by minor road W of Shap. Map ref 4A3.

662. JOHNNY'S WOOD
Nature trails

Some lovely walks over fell and forest with short diversions to see attractive waterfalls. There are superb views over Borrowdale, Seathwaite and the fells. The oak woodland is full of birdlife, flowers, mosses and ferns, excellently described in the Woodland Walk leaflet produced jointly by the NT and the Cumbria Naturalists Trust and available from NT information centres; tel: Ambleside 3003. Walks start from the car park at Seatoller on B5289. Stout footwear advisable.
□ Seven miles (11km) S of Keswick on B5289. Map ref 3D3.

663. LANERCOST PRIORY
Abbey church

A former Priory of Austin Canons, beautifully situated in the Irthing Valley. It is partly ruined, but the nave is now the parish church. It is pink sandstone without, grey limestone within: both taken from the Roman Wall less than a mile away to the north. The west front forms a singularly chaste composition in lancets, while the lofty interior is chiefly memorable for its gorgeous clerestory, with exceptionally bold ornamentation.
□ 12 miles (19km) NE of Carlisle off A69. Map ref 4A3.

Langdale landscape, Cumbria: one of the most beautiful parts of the Lake District National Park

664. LANGDALE PIKES
Mountains/archaeology

A characteristic example of the bare rugged landscapes of the highest parts of the Lake District. But what makes this area particularly interesting is that the apron of scree beneath the Pike of Stickle was the site of a prehistoric 'axe factory' (grid ref NY 275075) whose products were traded widely in Britain. The road from Ambleside follows the Great Langdale Beck. A path continues up the valley from where the road ends to beneath the axe factory – just over one mile (1.8km) – and beyond up the fells. OS map 90 for details of paths in the area.
□ Six miles (9.6km) W of Ambleside off B5343. Map ref 3D3.

665. LONGSLEDDALE
Uncrowded Lakeland

A dead-end valley which like Kentmere, its neighbour to the west, is often missed by people on the crowded route between Keswick and Windermere. Yet it is very accessible being near the southern gateway to the lakes, very attractive and very isolated.
□ Off A6 at Watchgate four miles (6.4km) N of Kendal. Map ref 4A3.

666. NORTHERN FELLS
Undiscovered Lakeland

A broad area located, as their name indicates, at the northern end of the Lake District. Much less crowded than the south with miles of unfenced roads heading across the fells where cars are rare, let alone traffic jams. Also, of course, great fell-walking and riding country – see OS map 90. Villages which are either attractive in themselves or good bases for exploring these fells are Caldbeck (birth and burial place of John Peel), Hesket Newmarket, Ireby, Mosedale, Mungrisdale, Orthwaite and Uldale.
□ S of B5299 and B5305 from 12 miles (19km) SW of Carlisle. Map ref 3D3.

667. RAVENGLASS
Castle/railway

Its position at the mouth of three rivers once made it a port but tourism is its main industry now. Access to the Ravenglass Nature Reserve, the largest breeding colony of black-headed gulls in Europe, is by permit only; apply County Land Agent and Valuer, 1 Alfred Street North, Carlisle. But there is both a nature trail and a tree trail in the grounds of Muncaster: a 13th century fortress with a 14th century pele tower built on the site of the Roman fort of *Glannaventa*. There are fine views from the castle over the Esk estuary and renowned rhododendron gardens among other attractions; the grounds are open daily Easter-Sept, the castle Tues, Wed, Thurs and Sun afternoons late Mar-Oct; tel: Ravenglass 614. Remains of Roman bathhouse can also be seen. Ravenglass is the western terminus of a narrow gauge railway which runs seven miles (11km) up to Dalegarth in Eskdale with daily steam services in summer and more limited operations in winter; tel: Ravenglass 226.
□ 12 miles (19km) NW of Millon on A595. Map ref 3D3.

668. ST BEES HEAD
Cliffs/walk

The red sandstone cliffs at this headland rise to over 300ft (91m) and are a breeding ground for guillemots and puffins. Magnificent views over Solway Firth from the clifftops where a lighthouse is open to the public; tel: Whitehaven 2635. A path leads down to the beach. The village of St Bees, which grew up around a priory, is the western terminus for an as yet unofficial long-distance footpath linking the Irish and North Seas. A fine circular seven-mile (11km) walk can use part of this route by heading west from St Bees seawall and then north over the cliffs via Fleswick Bay and past the lighthouse. At old quarry crater turn south by passing between two cottages into a red sandstone-flagged lane. Return by this lane and a private road (open to walkers) to St Bees via Sandwith. OS map 89.
□ Four miles (6.4km) SW of Whitehaven off B5345. Map ref 3D3.

669. SCAFELL PIKE
The easiest way up England's highest mountain: 3206ft (989m)
Scafell Pike

The ascent of Scafell Pike from any direction is serious hill walking. Its topography – along with that of neighbouring peak, 3162ft (975m) Scafell – is complex, and the crags plunging within range of its summit are among the biggest in Britain. In mist there is always danger here, and even the 'easy' route suggested here is only safe when fine weather is forecast and everyone is well prepared.

Wasdale Head offers the easiest approach – from the camp site at the head of Wastwater. Follow the path past Brackenclose climbing hut in the trees, and cross Lingmell Beck by the footbridge just beyond. Turn immediately right along the beckside until the left branch of Lingmell Ghyll is crossed by boulder-hopping. The path now climbs between the two streams via heavily eroded footsteps.

Keep to the track that carries on at the top rather than the one which veers to the right (the climber's path to Hollow Stones amphitheatre and the Scafell crags directly above it). The Scafell Pike route, however, swings off to the left and curves around the 'safe' side of the mountain and into the col between it and Lingmell. A well-blazoned track continues up right towards the summit: a huge stone dome with massive cairn. It is safest to return the same way. All the other descents hold one threat or another (as does most certainly the ascent of twin mountain, Scafell) to anyone save experienced hill walkers and mountaineers.
□ Wasdale Head is 10 miles (16km) NE of Ravenglass via A595 and minor roads to Wastwater. Map ref 3D3.

670. STAVELEY
Industrial landscape

The water resources of the Lake District were used to generate power from the 13th century onwards, but this exploitation was at its peak in the mid 19th century. The most concentrated area of industrial development – in what now seems a most unlikely region for any such history – was Kentdale on the south-eastern fringes of the Lake District. Here bobbin, textile, paper and snuff mills were once strung out along the River Kent and its tributaries like a string of beads, with Staveley the main centre of activity. Most mills have long since closed, but many relics remain of an unexpected past for a valley which now forms part of the Lake District national park.
□ Five miles (8km) NW of Kendal. Map ref 4A3.

671. TALKIN TARN
Country park

Wood and pastureland around the Tarn now form a country park with the accent on active leisure pursuits: rowing, sailing, fishing and swimming in and around the tarn plus bridleways for walking or riding.
□ 11 miles E of Carlisle off B6413 S of Brampton. Map ref 4A2.

672. THORNTHWAITE FOREST
Forest walks/views

A Forestry Commission visitor centre on Whinlatter Pass tells the story of man's impact on the Fells and also provides leaflets detailing a number of walks or trails. Comb trail starts from here with good views of Derwentwater and Bassenthwaite lake during its 1½ miles (2.4km) course. One mile (1.6km) east of the visitor centre is Noble Knott picnic place overlooking Bassenthwaite. Walks of varying length and steepness start from here through old oakwoods, young silver firs, Douglas fir, larch, spruce and sycamore.
□ Visitor Centre is two miles (3.2km) W of Braithwaite on B5292. map ref 3D3.

673. ULLSWATER
Uncrowded Lakeland

Uncrowded Ullswater can be found simply by driving down the minor road along its eastern shore. Most visitors stick to the busy A592 which runs along the western shore. Leave the A592 at the northern end of the lake, where the Dunmallet hill fort dominates the hamlet of Pooley Bridge, and follow the minor road south via Howtown to Martindale. You are away from the lake as well as the crowds by now and there is a choice of routes up into the Fells. Hallin Fell just north of Martindale village is an outstanding viewpoint over Ullswater. For the more ambitious a marvellous circular walk goes up Boardale over to Patterdale and back to Martindale along the roadless southern shore of Ullswater, approx seven miles (11km) in length

The deepest lake in England: Wast Water in the Lake District. Nature trails enable you to explore its peaceful shores

High Force waterfall in Upper Teesdale: one of the most dramatic in England

but often rugged walking with tremendous views over the lake towards Helvellyn's corries. Roads also lead from Martindale village some of the way up Boardale as well as to isolated Dale Head facing the cul de sac valleys of Bannerdale and Rampsgill.
□ Martindale is five miles (8km) SW of Pooley Bridge. Map ref 3D3.

674. WASTWATER
Uncrowded Lakeland/nature trail

Uncrowded because like Ennerdale you have to work your way around the west coast to get into it. A dramatic valley with deepest lake in England. The lake is followed by a minor road on its northern shore. It is popular with climbers since Wasdale Head provides a good, if arduous, way up to Gable and Scafell. Far less rigorous are two trails of about 1½ miles (2.4km) each laid out by the Cumbria Naturalists Trust. Walks vary to include lakeside, mixed woodland, rough fell, a small tarn and riverside, pasture, bog and magnificent views. Leaflet available from national park information offices. The trail starts at Nether Wasdale six miles (9.6km) east of Gosforth..
□ Five miles (8km) NE of A595. Map ref 3D3.

675. WORDSWORTH'S LAKES
Lakes/houses

There were other Lake poets such as Coleridge and Southey but nobody was more closely identified with the Lake District than William Wordsworth (1770-1850). Three of the houses in which he lived are open to the public. The house at Cockermouth, where he was born and which features in *The Prelude*, is open Apr-Oct, NT; tel: Cockermouth 824805. Dove Cottage at Grasmere, where he lived from 1799-1808, the house is open Mon-Sat, Mar-Oct; tel: Grasmere 418. And 2½ miles (4km) south of Dove Cottage at Rydal Mount, where he lived from 1813 until his death, the house is open Mar-Dec, tel: Ambleside 3002.

Rydal Mount and Dove Cottage each contain some of the poet's personal belongings and are particularly vulnerable to crowding at weekends.

The Lakes, of course, were a source of inspiration to Wordsworth as well as his home. **Aira Force** waterfall, the source of the legend in *The Somnambulist*, can be approached by a footpath from a car park close to the junction of A592 and A5091 on the northern shore of Ullswater. **Gowbarrow Park** close to Aira Force is where in 1804 the poet saw his 'host of golden daffodils'. They still grow wild there.
□ Dove Cottage is at Grasmere which is four miles (6.4km) NW of Ambleside; Wordsworth House at Cockermouth is in the main street of the town which is eight miles (13km) E of Workington. Map ref 3D3.

Durham

Coal mining and industry predominate in the east but to the west are the moors and valleys of the Pennines. Upper Teesdale and Weardale are scenic but the city of Durham, with its cathedral, castle and university, is prime attraction. Northumbria Tourist Board: Newcastle-upon-Tyne 817744.

676. BARNARD CASTLE
Market town/castles

A market town at a crossing point of the River Tees which not only grew around a castle but took its name from it: the present castle was built by one Bernard Balliol. But if the town is now dominated by anything it is not the ruined castle which takes the eye but the Bowes Museum. This was built on the edge of the town in the 19th century in French Renaissance style and houses one of the most important art collections in the country.

Other places worth a visit and only a short distance away include to the south-east the ruins of 12th century Egglestone Abbey and attractive Greta Bridge where the Greta joins the Tees; to the north-west, Bowes, with the village bisected by the line of a Roman road and a Norman castle set within the old Roman fort; to the north-east Staindrop with yet another medieval castle, Raby Castle; and to the north-west Upper Teesdale (see separate listing on page 305).
□ 16 miles (26km) W of Darlington on A688. Map ref 4B3.

677. BEAMISH
Farm and industrial museum

A home farm forms part of the 200-acre (494 hectare) North of England Open Air Museum, most of which is concerned with an excellent reconstruction of a northern colliery. Most of the farmstead is as it was in the 1790s with a few Victorian additions plus geese, cattle and chickens. Open daily Apr-Aug, Tue-Sun Sept-Mar. Tel: Stanley 31811.
□ Three miles (4.8km) W of Chester-le-Street on A693. Map ref 4B2.

678. BRANCEPETH
Church

The Church of St Brandon is situated in the park of the mainly 19th century castle, one of Britain's biggest white elephants. This church, Gothic of various dates, is memorable for a remarkably complete set of 17th century woodwork, partly 1638 and partly post-Restoration, but all associated with Bishop Cosin of Durham, who had been Rector here. So the interior is exceptionally harmonious.

☐ Four miles (6.4km) SW of Durham on A690. Map ref 4B3.

679. CONSETT
Nature trail

A nature trail through woods and parkland known as the Derwent Walk has been created along the former track of a disused railway line. In all the route from Blackhill to Swalwell covers some 10½ miles (17km). But it is accessible from many points along the route so shorter stretches can easily be walked. Good leaflet available from the planning departments of Durham County Council and also Tyne and Wear council. Picnic areas at some former stations.

☐ Blackhill is 1½ miles (2.4km) NW of Consett. Map ref 4B2.

680. HAMSTERLEY FOREST
Forest drive/walks

A forest drive (toll) leads through 4½ miles (7.2km) of mixed woodland beside the winding Bedburn Beck. There are several picnic places and six waymarked walks ranging from a gentle ½ mile (800m) along the riverside to an eight mile (13km) trek through the forest to High Acton Moor. A Forestry Commission information centre at Hamsterley has displays about the forestry and wildlife. Leaflets also available about the walks. Access from either Hamsterley west of A68 or Wolsingham on A689.

☐ 10 miles (16km) W of Bishop Auckland. Map ref 4B3.

681. HARDWICK HALL
Country Park

A lake is the centrepiece of this country park which also has nature trails leading through the woodland of its 39 acre (16 hectare) site.

☐ W of Sedgefield nar junction of A1(M) and A689. Map ref 4B3.

682. TAN HILL
Inn/moors

Tan Hill Inn is one of the loneliest and highest – at 1732ft (534m) – in the country. It stands at a junction of minor moorland roads which link the A66 following the old Roman route through the Stainmore Gap and to the south the B6270 along upper Swaledale. Yet it has survived in this bleak but spectacular setting for centuries. In this time it has served colliers, from the now-deserted mines south-east of the inn and the 'packmen' who used the inn as a staging post along drove roads such as the 'Jagger Lane' which goes east and west of Tan Hill. Now the inn caters for motorists touring the Dales or walkers along the Pennine Way.

☐ 3½ miles (5.6km) N of Keld off B6270. Map ref 4A3.

683. UPPER TEESDALE
Waterfalls/river valley

One of England's loveliest valleys. It can be enjoyed by car along the B6277 which heads up the valley from Middleton, once an important lead mining centre. But it can also be walked, following the Pennine Way for some of the route. Head west from Middleton on the southern bank of the Tees along the waymarked Pennine Way. The flat valley floor with its green fields, woods and swinging meanders is soon replaced by gorges and cataracts as the limestone valley walls close in. Three miles (4.8km) upstream is Low Force waterfall; another two miles (3.2km) on is High Force, 70ft (21m) and claimed by many to be England's finest waterfall. It is caused by a very hard band of igneous rock – The Whin Sill – which has invaded the limestone and withstood the river's down cutting. From here the Pennine Way continues steeply across dark moorlands for four miles (6.4km) to Caldron Snout, England's highest fall, cascading down 200 feet (60m) into a formidable gorge. Stout footwear and anoraks are essential for this walk.

For those disinclined to walk these long distances, Caldron Snout can be approached part of the way by car via the B6277 and a side road at Langdon Beck which leads to a picnic site at Cow Green Reservoir. Here a nature trail allows rare Alpine plants to be examined – but *not* picked; a path leads to Caldron Snout. OS map 91.

☐ Middleton is eight miles (13km) NW of Barnard Castle on B6267. Map ref 4A3.

Greater Manchester

An overwhelmingly urban county despite embracing fringes of the Pennines and Cheshire Plain. North-West Tourist Board: Bolton 591511.

684. ETHEROW
Country park

This park covers a wide variety of habitats: wood and marshland, river valley, reed beds and fish ponds. There is a nature reserve here and a nature trail plus canoeing and rowing.

☐ Three miles (5km) E of Stockport Map ref 4A5.

685. HAIGH HALL
Country park

The largest country park in the Greater Manchester area with 370 acres (150 hectares) of wood and heathland offering scope for a multitude of interests including a nature trail, fishing and an arboretum among the less active variety.

☐ Two miles (3.2km) NE of Wigan. Map ref 4A5.

Humberside

Divided into two by the Humber with the northern sector having the finest scenery – the Wolds. Other attractions include Burton Agnes Hall; Beverley Minster; the North Sea coastline; and Skipsea Castle. Hull is the major city. Yorkshire and Humberside Tourist Board: York 707961.

686. BEVERLEY
Market town/windmill

A lively market town which was formerly the county town of the old East Riding. Only one 15th century gateway survives from the original five. The 13th century Minster is the outstanding single building but there are many others from later periods. The 18th century for instance contributed the guildhall, an ornate market cross and many fine Georgian houses and shops. Market day is Saturday. Four miles (6.4km) south of the town a 19th century windmill now houses an agricultural museum. it is usually open May-Sept but details are available from Beverley council, tel: Hull 882255.

☐ Nine miles (14km) N of Hull on A1079. Map ref 4C4.

687. BURTON CONSTABLE
Country house/park

The grounds around an Elizabethan country house were landscaped by Capability Brown and now its 200 acres (81 hectares) of parkland and lake offer such diverse attractions as boating, fishing and a nature trail. The Yorkshire Farm Machinery Preservation Society also has an exhibition of farm machinery in the stables of the hall, although it is looking for a more permanent home of its own. The house and grounds are open weekends Easter to late May, then daily except Mon and Thurs until late Sept. But check opening hours and existence of farm museum; tel: Skirlaugh 62400.

☐ 7½ miles (12km) NE of Hull off B1238. Map ref 4C4.

688. ELSHAM HALL
Country Park/craft centre

A craft shop sometimes has craftsmen at work (pottery, copper, silver, etc) while outdoor attractions including pony trekking (by the hour), fishing, a bird sanctuary and on certain days guided nature trails. Open daily throughout the year but opening hours vary according to season or day; tel: Barnetby 738 or 698.

☐ Four miles (6.4km) NE of Brigg off A15. Map ref 4C5.

689. FLAMBOROUGH HEAD
Views/nature trail

Reputedly named from the flaming beacon which burned here prior to the construction of the lighthouse, the headland is a grass-covered plateau from which there are fine coastal views. The 150ft (46m) chalk cliffs, the termination of the Yorkshire Wolds at the coast, are riddled with caves and sea stacks such as the King and Queen, Adam and Eve and the outermost High Stacks. Arches can be seen near North Sea Landing and Kindle Scar. There are splendid cliff top walks northwards to Bempton Cliffs which have one of England's largest seabird colonies. This clifftop walk covers Danes' Dyke, a 2½ mile (4km) long Iron Age embankment constructed as a defence system to protect Flamborough Head from invasion. Where it meets the B1255 there is a short nature trail to explore the rich plant and bird life of the area. Leaflet from tourist office.

☐ Five miles (8km) NE of Bridlington on B1259. Map ref 4C4.

690. HORNSEA MERE
Inland lake

The largest freshwater lake in Yorkshire, Hornsea Mere lies ½ mile (800m) west of the town. It was left behind by melting glaciers at the end of the Ice Age. The lake, which is two miles (3.2km) long and about one mile (1.6km) wide, has good walks around the southern side. Although the public is not allowed access to the RSPB nature reserve it is still possible to see wildfowl and swans.

☐ E of Hornsea off B1244 or B1242. Map ref 4C4.

691. MILLINGTON
Wolds walk

This village, on the western edge of the Wolds, can be the base for an excellent day's walk of some 12 miles (19km) along stretches of an unofficial long-distance footpath known as the Wolds Way. The route is best started in an easterly direction from Millington towards Warren Farm.

Waymarks then lead north to the end of Greenwick Plantation. Return along track and path to Huggate via Glebe Farm, then along the road leading south. Walk westwards along a bridle road to Millington Pastures, a well-known local beauty spot. From here the Wolds Way can be retraced via Warren Farm to Millington. OS map 106.

☐ 14 miles (22km) E of York off B1246. Map ref 4C4.

692. NORMANBY HALL
Regency house/country park

The gardens and grounds around the house have been developed as a country park covering 168 acres (68 hectares) of wooded parkland. Part of this ground is a deer park and there are also a nature trail, museums and bridleways as well as facilities for sports such as fishing and archery. Open April-Oct daily except Tues, Nov-Mar daily except Sat. Tel: Scunthorpe 720215.

☐ Four miles (6.4km) N of Scunthorpe on B1430, E of Normanby village. Map ref 4C5.

693. PATRINGTON
Decorated church

Remote and little visited, Patrington has the finest Decorated village church in the country, although the spire, plunging aloft through an exquisite pinnacled diadem, was a perpendicular addition, as was the big east window. As well as the nave, the transepts also have aisles, allowing for some unusual cross-vistas. The profusion of carved detail is another delight.

☐ 15 miles (24km) SE of Hull on A1033. Map ref 4D5.

694. RUDSTON
Standing stone

The tallest standing stone in the country towers over the village church at a height of 25ft 9in (7.8m). It may once have been even larger – not only because its present top appears to be slightly damaged but because of the name it gave to the village which grew around it. *Rood* is an Old English word for 'cross' and *stan* means 'stone'. The monolith is believed to date from the Bronze Age and was probably some kind of pagan symbol. If so the site now represents an example of the quite common practice for Christian churches to adopt pagan holy sites and

thereby somehow sanctify them. The stone itself is composed of gritstone which does not occur here naturally; its nearest source is at least 10 miles (16km) away from Rudston.
☐ Five miles (8km) W of Bridlington on B1253. Map ref 4C4.

695. SPURN HEAD
Sand spit/nature reserve

A three-mile (4.8km) long sand spit in places only 150ft (45m) wide. Its shape has changed many times over the centuries as a result of coast erosion, sometimes being obliterated altogether and taking with it lost towns such as one called Ravenspur where Henry Bolingbroke landed in July 1399. A month later he forced Richard II to abdicate and thus founded the Lancastrian dynasty. Now artificial groynes help to preserve Spurn Head but it is still breached by exceptional seas. Its isolation has made it a good place for bird watching. The Yorkshire Naturalists' Trust has a nature reserve and bird sanctuary here, access and parking is limited; for details, tel: York 59570. No dogs.
☐ 25 miles (40km) SE of Hull on private road at end of B1445. Map ref 4D5.

Isle of Man

A partly independent holiday isle, with varied scenery and a mild climate. Attractions include Tynwald parliament at Douglas, Snaefell mountain railway and Peel Castle. Isle of Man Tourist Board: Douglas 4323.

696. THE AYRES
Beaches/lighthouses

A wilderness of flat heathland behind miles of deserted sandy beaches at the northern tip of the island. There are picnic sites and car parks at Ballaghennie and Point of Ayre where the old and new lighthouses are notable landmarks – the one in current use is open to the public, tel: Douglas 88238. There are miles of walks over the heather-covered shingle ridges of the ancient storm beaches, behind which is the bewildering hummocky terrain of a gigantic terminal moraine of a former ice-sheet – termed the Bride Moraine, from Bride village. To the north of the A3 Sulby to Ballaugh road is the Curraghs Wild Life Park, open Easter-Sept, tel: Sulby 7323.
☐ Seven miles (14km) N of Ramsey off A16. Map ref 3C3.

697. CALF OF MAN
Nature reserve/bird watching

This small island with its steep cliffs and pebbly beaches – off the south-west tip of the Isle of Man – is one of the most exciting spring and autumn migration points in the British Isles; 233 species of bird have been recorded here. Its 620 acres (250 hectares) is owned by the Manx National Trust and managed as a reserve. There are regular day-trips from Port Erin during summer – weather permitting.
☐ Off SW tip of Isle of Man. Map ref 3B4.

698. CASTLETOWN
Nature trail

Just outside this old capital of the island – with its fine 14th century fortress of Castle Rushen is a nature trail of geological as well as a natural history interest. Limestone (rare on this island of slate) and the only volcanic rocks on the Isle of Man are both magnificently exposed along the trail which in its shortest version is 1¼ miles (2km) long. There is also a wealth of plant and bird life. Details of this and other trails on the island from the Manx tourist centre in Douglas.

☐ The nature trail is ½ mile (0.8km) SW of Castletown. Map ref 3C4.

699. CREGNEASH
Coastal scenery/village

The village is sited on a peninsula at the extreme south-western tip of the island which offers coastal scenery as spectacular as anything in south-west England or Pembrokeshire. There are the dramatic cliffs and savage tidal currents of Calf Sound between the mainland and the islet of Calf of Man (see above). Coastal walks include the narrow gorges called The Chasms north-east of Spanish Head or the western cliffs which rise northwards beyond Port Erin to the 700ft (210m) precipices of Bradda Head. From the latter there can be excellent views as far as the mountains of Mourne and Snowdonia.

In Cregneash itself is the Manx Folk Museum with many examples of traditional crafts such as a smithy, weaver's shed and a crofter-fisherman's cottage. The cottages have been restored with great care and sensitivity. The thatching, for instance, has been redone in the comparatively rare Hebridean style. A small flock of the rare Manx Loghton sheep complete the picture of Cregneash as a 'living museum'. The village is worth visiting at any time but the folk museum as such is open only May-Sept. Tel: Douglas 5522.
☐ Five miles (8km) W of Castletown on A31. Map ref 3B4.

700. GLEN MONA
Mountain and coastal walks

A good centre from which to explore some of the island's most beautiful scenery. Footpaths lead to the foothills of 2036ft (621m) Snaefell or to the head of lonely Glen Cornaa. Seawards, there are walks down the beautiful wooded Glen Mona or Ballaglass Glen to the enchanting hidden bay of Port Cornaa. Two miles (3.2km) south is the picturesque Dhoon Glen with its waterfalls, rapids and hanging woodlands, whilst to the north are the rocky coastal cliffs of Maughold Head and its lighthouse (open every afternoon except Sunday). For the archaeologically-minded, just over ½ mile (800m) east of Glen Mona there is the excellent example of a Neolithic gallery grave or long cairn at Cashtal-yn-Ard, grid ref SC 462892.
☐ 4½ miles (7.2km) S of Ramsey on A2. Map ref 3C4.

701. LAXEY
Mountain railway/waterwheel

The A18 road passes close to the summit of 2036ft (621m) Snaefell, the island's highest (and only) mountain. The electric railway which starts from Laxey goes right to the top. Also here is picturesque Laxey Glen but the old harbour town is dominated by the world's largest surviving water wheel – the Lady Isabella. The huge wheel, see photograph on page 54 – is 72ft (22m) in diameter and was used to pump water out of lead mines here until 1919. It is open daily Easter-Sept; tel: Douglas 26262.
☐ Seven miles (11km) NW of Douglas off A11. Map ref 3C4.

Lighthouses

The Romans built two guiding lighthouses (one is still there) at Dover. For a thousand years after their Empire, candles and lanterns glimmered in coastal church towers and sea-edge chapels, maintained as a charitable religious duty.

All were extinguished when Henry VIII broke with Rome, and were only slowly replaced with free enterprise lights. The Crown granted patents to build and maintain lights, the patentees charging passing ships set dues, part of the revenue returning to the Crown.

Some private lights made fortunes, others went bust and their lights, usually inefficient coal fires in iron baskets, went out with them. These licensed lights began to be supervised by a charitable corporation, Trinity House at Deptford, which from the early 16th century had official approval. In 1836 it was empowered and financed by the Government to buy out the last light owners. In the 19th century lighthouses were enthusiastically built so that the whole coast was lit at about 20 mile (32km) intervals.

Trinity House still controls English lighthouses, lightships and navigation buoys. Scotland has the Northern Lighthouses Board and Ireland the Commissioners of Irish Lights. All are financed by Lighthouse Funds, held by specific Government Departments, made up of light dues paid by shipping, based on ship size.

Most lighthouses are now electrically powered. A few burn paraffin vapour, while unwatched lighthouses and buoys use acetylene gas from cylinders. Light from all these hits a great structure of prismatic glass – the optic – which collects every ray emitted and refracts it into one powerful horizontal beam.

Some optics revolve to give the light a rolling flash. This is used with on-off

The lighthouse at Flamborough Head, Humberside

rhythms and colour changes to give each light a distinctively patterned signature. When fog obscures the light warning signals are given, using compressed air or electricity to vibrate diaphragms and produce sounds through loudspeakers. A few lighthouses still use fog guns exploding a gas-air mix.

Where to view: St Nicholas' Chapel, Lantern Hill, Ilfracombe, Devon; Flamborough Head, Yorkshire; Ormes Head, near Llandudno; Hartland Point, north Devon and other coastal locations. Some – not all – allow public visiting in the afternoons.

Lancashire

A varied county with moors, plain and vast sandy beaches plus heavy industry in the south. Attractions include Lancaster and seaside resorts for all tastes. North-West Tourist Board: Bolton 591511.

702. BLACKSTONE EDGE
Roman road

The finest exposed piece of original Roman road in the country – so fine that a few experts have doubted that its paving stones and kerb stones may owe more to packhorse days than Roman. Most historians, however, are convinced of its Roman origins. It is on the line of the Roman road between the forts at Manchester (*Manucium*) and Ilkley (*Olicana*) and is exposed as it climbs the Pennines near Littleborough. The road surface is 16ft (5m) wide with a central channel and ditches on either side (see photograph on page 39) at grid ref SD 973470.
☐ One mile (1.6km) E of Littleborough on A58, then by signposted footpath. Map ref 4A5.

703. FORMBY HILLS
Sand dunes/nature trails

By 1910 the ancient fishing village of Formby was buried under the dunes and a new town has now grown up two miles (3.2km) from the coast. Dunes have been building up here for thousands of years from glacial deposits offshore. There is a 1¾ mile (2.8km) nature trail on Formby Point where you may see birds such as oyster catcher or sanderling and animals such as red squirrels or natterjack toads. A leaflet is available for the trail which is run by the Lancashire Naturalist Trust, Tel: Slaidburn 294. Always open. Three miles (4.8km) to the north near Ainsdale is an NCC reserve consisting of 1216 acres (492 hectares) of dunes, marshes and pinewoods. There is a three mile (4.8km) nature trail through an area which contains some 380 species of flowering plants and many species of birds and butterflies.
☐ W of Formby which is six miles SW of Southport on A565. Map ref 3D5.

704. HEALEY DELL
Walks

A beautiful Lancashire clough (deep valley) just two miles (3.2km) from Rochdale town centre with woods, waterfalls, a so-called 'Fairy Chapel' of curious waterworn rocks and a history going back to Saxon times. The nature trail reveals a disused railway, flourishing rookery, and a profusion of plants: rushes, ferns, mosses, orchids and moorland grasses. Comprehensive reserve booklet published by Lancashire Naturalists' Trust – tel: Slaidburn 294 – is available at reserve entrance.
☐ Two miles (3.2km) NW of Rochdale on A671 at junction of Market Street and Shawclough Road. Map ref 4A5.

705. HOGHTON TOWER
Elizabethan house/gardens

A fortified 16th century hilltop house, restored during the 19th century but containing 17th century panelling.

English lop-eared rabbit, on show at Sparrow Hill Museum, Rochdale

Inside is an exhibition of dolls' houses, outside are walled gardens and an old rose garden. Open Easter except Good Friday, Suns late April-Oct plus Sat July-Aug, afternoons only. Tel: Hoghton 2986.
☐ Five miles (8km) SE of Preston on A675. Map ref 4A5.

706. LYTHAM ST ANNES
Nature reserve

This reserve consists of sand dunes and damp dune slacks, all that remains of a much more extensive dune system. In the past this site suffered considerable human disturbance. Today the reserve shows recolonisation by characteristic dune plants such as marram grass and sea buckthorn. An excellent booklet produced by the Lancashire Naturalist Trust, and available at the reserve entrance, gives a guided walk through the reserve. Tel: Slaidburn 294.
☐ Lytham St Annes is six miles (9.6km) S of Blackpool on A584; the nature reserve is E of the turn off Clifton Drive North. Map ref 3D5.

707. MORECAMBE BAY
Bay/bird watching

At low tide almost 50 sq miles (38,850 hectares) of sand or mud are exposed in this vast bay which straddles the Lancashire-Cumbria boundary. But it can be treacherous – listen for siren warning that the tide is coming in and do not attempt to walk over the sands to Furness without a guide.

Good viewpoints over the bay are Arnside Knott (see page 301); Hampsfell Hospice, two miles (3.2km) north of Grange-over-Sands where there is also a woodland nature trail; and Humphrey head, south of Kent's Bank. The bay is an excellent area for birdwatching, especially in winter with large flocks of ducks, waders, geese and seabirds. At Leighton Moss between the villages of Silverdale and Yealand Redmayne is an important RSPB reserve. Further information from RSPB Reserves Dept. Tel: Sandy 80551.
☐ Map ref 3D4.

708. RIBCHESTER
Roman fort

Sited on the north bank of the River Ribble where the Roman road from Manchester to Carlisle crossed that from Ilkley to the Fylde. it was the headquarters for some of Rome's toughest soldiers – the Sarmatian heavy cavalry. Parts of the fort, *Bremetennacum*, building are visible and finds from the site are displayed in the adjoining museum. Open afternoons except Fri, Feb-Nov; Sat afternoons only, Dec-Jan. Tel: Ribchester 261.
☐ Nine miles (14km) NE of Preston on B6245. Map ref 4A5.

709. RUFFORD
Medieval Hall/Folk museum

The Old Hall, owned by the NT, is a medieval timber-framed manor house with an outstanding hammerbeam roof. The hall is late 15th century with wings added in the 17th and 19th centuries. One wing contains the Philip Ashcroft Folk Museum, a collection of ancient farm implements and domestic relics from Lancastrian life. Open afternoons daily except Mons other than Bank Holidays, Mar-Dec. Tel: Rufford 821254.
☐ Seven miles (11km) N of Ormskirk on A59. Map ref 4A5.

710. WYCOLLER
Country park

A large country park – 363 acres (147 hectares) of heath, grass and moorland – near a small village. In the village of Wycoller is a delightful 13th century packhorse bridge while in the country park there are picnic areas, nature walks and bridleways on the slopes of the Pennines.
☐ Four miles (6.4km) SE of Colne off A6068. Map ref 4A5.

Merseyside

Dominated by Liverpool – its top attraction – and the River Mersey. Also containing Southport. North-West Tourist Board: Bolton 591511.

711. THE WIRRAL
River estuary/country parks

The Wirral peninsula has become part of the Merseyside conurbation but it is also noted for its bird life, particularly in autumn. One of the small islets at the mouth of the estuary is a bird observatory. It can be reached at low tide from West Kirby or Hoylake but permits are required. From Thurstaston Hill there is a fine view of the estuary while at Thurstaston village on the Dee estuary there is a visitor centre for the Wirral Country Park – the first country park to be opened. It stretches between West Kirby and Parkgate, an interesting shrimping village, covering 43 acres (17 hectares) and including a disused railway line along the coast and three nature trails. On the Mersey side of the Wirral is another country park at Eastham Woods, six miles (9.6km) SE of Birkenhead, off the A41, with a nature trail and river views.
☐ Map ref 3D5/6.

Northumberland

England's most northernmost county and quintessential Border country – Roman Hadrian's Wall and many fine Norman castles. Towns include Berwick-on-Tweed and Alnwick. Outstanding scenery inland (Northumberland national park) and on the coast (AONB). Northumbria Tourist Board: Newcastle-upon-Tyne 817744.

712. BAMBURGH
Castle/coast

The village and dune-sheltered beach are dominated by a majestic castle – one of the most dramatic in England. The present building dates largely from the 19th century but even the original Norman castle (of which the keep remains) was not the first fortress to occupy this rocky crag of igneous basalt called the Whin Sill which runs the width of the Northumberland National Park. For 300 years before the Norman Conquest this was the capital of the kingdom of Northumbria. The castle is open afternoons daily, Easter to mid-Oct; tel: Bamburgh 208.
☐ 17 miles (27km) S of Berwick-on-Tweed on B1340. Map ref 4B1.

713. BLANCHLAND
Village/inn

This 'model' village in the Derwent Valley has been well restored in recent years; a ban on car parking in the village square helps as it would in many other traffic-congested villages and market towns. Blanchland, as it now stands, dates mainly from the 18th century, but it was built around the site of an abbey founded seven centuries earlier by an order known as the Premonstratensians. The 13th century church incorporates what remains of the old abbey church. Otherwise the village's most distinguished building is probably the inn, *The Lord Crewe Arms*. It was formerly a manor house and also includes some of the old abbey buildings, notably the Abbot's Lodging, the Guest House and the abbey kitchen and food store while the old cloisters now form the inn's garden.
☐ Nine miles (14.4km) S of Hexham on B6306. Map ref 4A3.

714. BOLAM LAKE
Country park

Over 90 acres (37 hectares) of lake and woodland here comprise a country park offering fishing, bird-watching

Thomas Bewick's engraving of the wild bull of Chillingham. The famous Chillingham herd of wild white cattle have roamed the castle grounds for over 700 years

and boating.

□ Eight miles (13km) SW of Morpeth N of Belsay. Map ref 4B2.

715. BORDER FOREST PARK
Forest drives/walks/views

The park extends over 145,000 acres (58,700 hectares) along the Cheviots and neighbouring hills. Between them and beyond the few main roads forest roads lead to hill tracks linking the dales. A Forestry Commission Visitor Centre is open late May-Sept at Kielder Castle which was built as a shooting lodge in the 18th century for the Duke of Northumberland. This is 17 miles (27km) north-west of Bellingham on the C200 road which runs for approx 25 miles (40km) from Bellingham on the B6320 to Saughtree on B6357. Opening hours of the visitor centre vary from weekdays to weekends, tel: Kielder 50209. Facilities in different parts of the park include a drive along 12 miles (19km) of forest roads starting from either Kielder Castle (see above) or Blakeshopeburnhaugh, two miles (3.2km) SE of Byrness on A68. Short walks and picnic places along the drive for which a toll is charged. Beyond Kielder Castle, along or off the C200 road described above, a number of picnic areas overlook the new Kielder reservoir – due to be completed in 1982 – and one at Ferry Knowe, near Falstone, has a visitor centre.

□ Map ref 4A2.

716. CAMBO
Village/country house

The village was part of a 13,000 acre (5263 hectares) estate which in 1942 was given along with 16 farms and 17th-18th century Wallington Hall to the NT. Much of the land on the Wallington estate lies beyond the 1000ft (305m) contour so that the farms represented a similar brand of pioneering to that introduced to Exmoor by the Knight family (see page 51). Wallington Hall itself is open afternoons except Tues, April-Sept, then Wed, Sat and Sun afternoons in Oct; its grounds, which include a lake and a walled flower garden are open all year. Tel: Scots Gap 283.

□ 12 miles (19km) W of Morpeth off B6342. Map ref 4B2.

717. CHEVIOT HILLS
Mountain drive/walk

For one of the loneliest roads in the Border country, drive into the uppermost reaches of Coquetdale by taking the lane which leads west from Alwinton. Follow the tortuous windings of the Coquet past lonely farmsteads deep into the hills, with nothing to break the solitude except the moorland sheep. Continue on the tarmac road steeply up to the last hill farm at Makendon and walk the remaining mile (1.6km) to what must have been one of the loneliest Roman fortresses in Britain or, for the more energetic, reach the highest of the Cheviot Hills – Windy Gyle (2036ft; 619m) – by taking a track which leaves the road going north-west towards the summit via Hindside Knowe. This follows the spur known as The Street and strikes the summit ridge near Mozie Law. A one mile (1.6km) walk eastward along the Pennine Way gives striking views of The Cheviot (2676ft; 810m) itself and glimpses into the deeply incised Scottish valleys beneath. Complete a memorable seven mile (11.2km) walk by returning southwards via Little Ward Law and the farm at Trows – but look out for the warning flags of the artillery ranges. OS map 80 covers this area.

□ Alwinton is 10 miles (16km) NW of Rothbury off B6341 on minor roads. Map ref 4A1.

718. CHILLINGHAM
Rare animals

The Chillingham Wild White Cattle is probably the last herd of horned white cattle which remains in Britain today. Cattle such as these, descendents of prehistoric wild oxen, have grazed the foothills of the Cheviots for over 700 years. They now roam the 300 acres of parkland which surrounds Chillingham Castle. Open April-Oct except Tues; tel: Chatton 213.

□ Four miles (6.4km) SE of Wooler off B6348. Map ref 4B1.

719. CRAGSIDE
Country house/park

Cragside was built between 1869 and 1896, mainly to the designs of Norman Shaw. The client was Lord Armstrong, millionaire inventor and manufacturer of hydraulic machinery and armaments. Hidden at the heart of 900 acres (364 hectares) of park is a romantic medley of towers, chimney stacks, and half-timbered gables which climb up a hillside so steep that the second floor is below ground level at the back of the house. Inside, inglenooks, stained glass, winding corridors and staircases, pre-Raphaelite pictures, boudoir, billiard-room and gun-room vividly recreate the mixture of fantasy and practicality that made up the habitat of a Victorian tycoon. The house (now NT) is open on afternoons (except Mon other than Bank Holidays) Apr-Sept and then on weekend and Wed afternoons in Oct; the grounds, which are noted for their rhododendrons, are open roughly the same days but also on Mon during Apr-Sept and in the mornings. Tel: Rothbury 20333.

□ Near Rothbury 13 miles (21km) SW of Alnwick on B6341. Map ref 4B2.

720. CRASTER
Coastal walks/castle

Famous for its kippers – the oak-curing kipper sheds can be visited – but

outstanding also for its scenery, part of the Northumberland Coast AONB. A coastal path leads north for 1½ miles (2.4km) to Dunstanburgh Castle, a ruined 14th century castle standing on cliffs 100ft (30m) above the sea. Beneath the walls of the castle – open standard DoE hours plus Sun mornings Apr–Sept – is a chasm called Egyn Cleugh and a derelict harbour. Another rewarding coastal walk from Craster is a three mile (4.8km) nature trail to Low Newton which passes a wide range of dune plants and colonies of kittiwake, fulmar and ringed plover.
□ Six miles (9.6km) NE of Alnwick off B1339. Map ref 4B1.

721. ELSDON
Border village

This has one of the biggest greens, some seven acres (2.8 hectares), among the many 'green' villages of Northumberland's 'Border Country'. In peaceful times its large green served as a market place for sheep driven across the Pennines through a complex network of drove roads; while in less peaceful times it offered security for the village livestock as the village defended itself by stockading all the gaps between the houses set around the green. Another reminder of its turbulent days as a frontier settlement is the 14th century 'pele' tower house, a fortified parsonage generally regarded as the finest of such buildings which survive in Northumberland. At the edge of the green is a stone cattle pound or pinfold.
□ 27 miles (43km) NW of Newcastle-upon-Tyne on B6341 off A696. Map ref 4A2.

722. FARNE ISLANDS
Nature reserve/trails

There are 28 outcrops in the sea but only three islands can be visited by the public: the Inner Farne, Staple Island and Longstone. Boat trips operate from Seahouses (weather permitting). The Inner Farne has a 14th century chapel and a pele or fortified tower, Longstone a famous lighthouse. But the islands are best-known as breeding grounds for seals and sea birds.

This NT reserve is one of the most important in the country and access may be restricted during the breeding season – mid-May to mid-July. Among the birds which breed here are puffin, guillemot, razorbill, shag, up to 1000 eider duck and three species of tern (arctic, common and roseate). There are nature trails on Inner Farne and Staple Island – leaflets and information about boat services from NT and tourist information office at Seahouses, tel: Seahouses 720424 or NT Northumberland regional office, tel: Scots Gap 234.
□ Off coast from Seahouses which is 15 miles (24km) N of Alnwick on B1339. Map ref 4B1.

723–726. HADRIAN'S WALL
Roman frontier wall

The most dramatic Roman monument in the landscape of Britain, originally stretching 73 miles (117km) from Wallsend-on-Tyne (Tyne and Wear) on the east through Northumberland to Bowness on the Solway Firth (Cumbria). It was built of stone up to 20ft

(6m) high in the east and turf 12ft (3.7m) high in the west.

An integral part of the defences was a system of ditches and earthworks – see illustration indicating their original dimensions. The road running between wall and *vallum* was known as the Military Way, but should not be confused with the Military Road built parallel with the wall after the Jacobite rebellion of 1745. Large sections of the wall can still be followed, particularly in its central sector, either on foot or by car. Roads leading to the forts can be crowded in high season, however, so there is a special bus service operated by the Northumberland national park authorities from their Once Brewed Information Centre on the Military Road (B6318) near Housesteads, tel: Barden Mill 396.

A number of forts, camps or milecastles along the wall have been excavated and can now be visited. Birdoswald is described under Cumbria. Listed below are some of the most interesting Northumberland sites – all of which, with their accompanying museums, are open standard DoE hours plus Sun mornings Apr–Sept.

723. Housesteads
A garrison fort (*Vercovicium*) covering three acres (1.2 hectares) of moorland and the only one to have been completely excavated. In fact, excavations are still under way and will probably reveal traces of the buildings that preceded the largely 4th century remains that are visible. The complex building history of this site is well explained on a site museum. An important element in the appeal of this fort is its position on a notably dramatic section of the wall. A little to the south of Housesteads is Chesterholm or *Vindolanda*, the site of another fort, where a turret and length of wall have been reconstructed in their original form and size. Considerable archaelogical finds have been made here recently.
□ 10 miles (16km) NW of Hexham off B6318. Map ref 4A2.

724 Chesters
Another fort (*Cilurnum*) in a spectacular position. It was the headquarters of a cavalry unit and visitors can see gateways, a barrack block and, among other remains, a complete bath house close to the River Tyne. It was here that the wall crossed the Tyne and the remains of the bridge are still visible.
□ Four miles (6.4km) N of Hexham off B6318. Map ref 4A2.

725 Corbridge
This is a short distance south of the wall but worth a detour for here was the great supply base of *Corstopitum* for the Roman soldiers manning the wall two or three miles (3–5km) to the north.

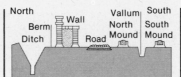

Cross-section of the Roman Wall in its heyday. The vallum was not always this close to the wall, since it ran on a straight course while the wall took advantage of the contours of the land

Workshops as well as temples have been found here. Good site museum.
□ Three miles (5km) E of Hexham on western edge of Corbridge off A68. Map ref 4A2.

726. A walk along the wall
Many walks can be done along the wall. This one also incorporates part of the Pennine Way and totals 20 miles (32km). Start from the village of Greenhead three miles (4.8km) northwest of Haltwhistle at the junction of A69 and the B6318 or 'Military Road'. Head for Cawfields Quarry (*Milecastle Inn* on the Military Road) and then on eastwards to Steel Riggs viewpoint and car park. Immediately south of Steel Riggs is the Once Brewed youth hostel and NP information centre. Follow the wall then as far as Housesteads and ascend Sewingshield summit before heading back to Greenhead. You can, of course, start from several other places en route and similarly return without completing the full 20-mile distance. OS map 86.
□ Map ref 4A2.

727. HEATHERSLAW MILL
Mill/farm museum

A water-driven corn mill has been partially restored here and houses an agricultural museum. Open daily Apr-Oct, tel: Crookham 338.
□ At Ford 11 miles (17.6km) SW of Berwick on B6353. Map ref 4A1.

728. HEXHAM
Market town/Saxon crypt

There was a Saxon bishopric established here in the 7th century and although the town, then known as Hagulstad, was largely destroyed by the Norsemen a Saxon crypt survives in the priory church. Although this otherwise mostly 13th century church is probably the most distinguished individual building in the town there are many others of note, including the 15th century Moot Hall and a 14th century prison known euphemistically as the Manor Office and now holding a museum devoted to Border history and a tourist information office. Market day: Tuesday.
□ 23 miles (37km) W of Newcastle-upon-Tyne on A69. Map ref 4A2.

729. LINDISFARNE
Priory/castle/nature reserve

The approach to the island is dramatic – across a causeway from Beal which is uncovered at low tides. You can save yourself a wasted journey by checking the tides in advance; telephone the Northumbria Tourist Board, Newcastle 817744.

The buildings include an 11th century priory (open standard DoE hours plus Sun mornings Apr-Sept), a 12th to 13th century church and Lindisfarne Castle, a small 16th century fort (NT) which earlier this century was turned into a holiday home for Edward Hudson, founder of *Country Life*. The Edwardian maestro Sir Edward Lutyens was responsible for the work which was romantic, inventive – and uncomfortable. Features are stone vaults, massive arches, winding stairs and superb views over the island with its limestone cliffs and sand dunes. Open daily except Fri Apr-Sept, weekend afternoons only in Oct; tel: NT regional office, Scots Gap 234.

The wildlife of the island is equally famous, although the national nature reserve is best seen out of season when there are fewer visitors and more birds, including huge numbers of geese, duck (up to 25,000 wigeon), arctic swans and flocks of waders. Lindisfarne is the only place where pale-bellied Brent geese from Spitzbergen winter regularly. Dunes, saltmarsh and mudflats combine to create a magical expanse of wild coast. Seals are often seen, and many interesting plants grow in the dune slacks including grass of Parnassus and northern marsh orchids. Telephone reserve office for information, Belford 386.
□ Five miles (8km) E of Beal. Map ref 4B1.

730. STOCKSFIELD
Farm museum

This farm museum is centred around its unique display of vintage tractors, although there are many other items depicting farm life and machinery over the centuries. These include a working water wheel, a 13th-century wishing well and an Edwardian dairy. There are plans to restore a water mill. Open daily all year; tel: Stocksfield 2553.
□ W of Corbridge on A69 near junction with A68 at Riding Mill. Map ref 4A2.

731. WANSBECK
Country park

The park takes its name from the river which runs through its 143 acres (58 hectares) of grass and woodland. Features of the park include boating and a picnic area.
□ ½ mile (0.8km) S of Ashington off A1068. Map ref 4B2.

732. WARK FOREST
Forest walks

Warksburn picnic place is by side of a stream in an open glade in tall spruce forest at Stonehaugh. Three waymarked forest walks start from here. Access from Chollerford on B6320 to Nunwick where there is a left turn signposted Stonehaugh.
□ NW of Hexham. Map ref 4A2.

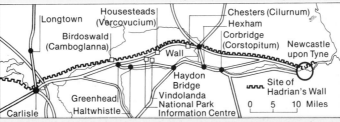

Hadrian's Wall, the northwest frontier of the Roman world, spanned the neck of England from coast to coast, a distance of 73 miles (117km). The map pinpoints the most interesting sites, such as Corbridge, Chesters and Housesteads

Northern England

733. WARKWORTH
Castle/coast

This small town within a loop of the River Coquet was laid out in the 12th century. It has all the features of a Norman planned settlement plus the characteristic of a border town – even the bridge across the river is fortified. Much of the medieval street layout remains and there are impressive remains of the castle – a setting for part of Shakespeare's *Henry IV* since it was the birthplace of Henry Percy (Hotspur). The castle is open standard DoE hours plus Sun mornings Apr-Sept.

Half a mile (0.8km) from the castle is a 14th century hermitage and chapel set into the cliff (AM); it is reached by boat and open standard DoE hours plus Sun Mornings Apr-Sept.
□ Seven miles (11km) SE of Alnwick on A1068. Map ref 4B1.

North Yorkshire

A large county containing two national parks covering the Dales and the North York Moors. Other attractions include York itself with its Minster, walls etc; Harrogate; Pickering; Ripon Cathedral; Whitby; and Settle. Yorkshire and Humberside Tourist Board: York 707961.

734. BRIDESTONES MOOR
Nature reserve/trail

The Bridestones Moor Nature Reserve is approached by a Forestry Commission drive through Dalby Forest. This 10-mile (16km) toll drive leads to walks and picnic places as well as the nature reserve; it starts either near Low Dalby on minor road to Whitby from Thornton Dale E of Pickering on A170 or from minor road from Hackness 3¾ miles (6km) W of Scarborough. The nature reserve, owned by the NT and managed jointly with the Yorkshire Naturalists' Trust, is within the North York Moors National Park on the edge of Dalby Forest. A four-mile (6.4km) circular walk leads through the typical habitat of the moors: oakwoods with a gill; paths through heather and lichen covered moor; and the Bridestones themselves. These are large and impressive weathered outcrops of sandstone known locally as millstone grit – a good view of the area can be seen from Low Bridestone, about ½ mile (0.8km) uphill from the reserve entrance. The nature trail continues down a steepsided valley to the marshy area of Dovedale Beck path. Leaflets about this and other trails available from FC visitor centre at Low Dalby; usually open daily Easter to Oct. Tel: Pickering 60295.
□ Seven miles NE of Pickering. Map ref 4C4.

735. CASTLE HOWARD
Country house/landscaped gardens

Not a castle but so named because it was erected for the Howard family on the site of an old castle called Henderskelfe. The house was designed by Sir John Vanbrugh and built at the beginning of the 18th century. It is surrounded by gardens to match the grandeur of the house: one of the most important and earliest landscaped gardens in the country (see chapter eight on gardens) with lakes, bridges and temples. A more formal garden and two rose gardens have been added in succeeding centuries. House and grounds are open daily Easter-Oct; tel: Coneysthorpe 333.
□ Six miles (9.6km) W of Malton on minor road to Coneysthorpe off A64. Map ref 4C4.

736. CROPTON FOREST
Forest walks

Three walks from one to six miles (1.6 to 9.6km) long and of corresponding toughness wind through a mixed coniferous forest in spectacular Newtondale. A drive through the forest has recently been closed so access to the valley is now by the North York Moors Railway which operates from Pickering to Grosmont, daily from mid-Apr to late Oct. Tel: Pickering 72508. A new halt called Newtondale has been built in the heart of the valley and all three walks begin here. The two shorter ones are circular, but the third goes to Levisham station to the south. A mapboard at Newtondale halt shows the routes of the walks; two ascend to Needle Point, a superb viewpoint. Leaflets are being prepared: see Day Out 734 for details of Low Dalby FC visitor centre.
□ N of Pickering. Map ref 4C4.

737. FAIRBURN INGS
Bird watching

A large flooded area created by coal-mining subsidence constitutes this RSPB reserve which is well-known for its wildfowl. In spring there are good numbers of garganey and summer brings a number of breeding duck. Late summer and autumn sees huge numbers of sandmartins and swallows. Both Bewick's and whooper swans come to the lakes in winter. Access all year from the public footpath from Fairburn village. Two public hides.
□ Two miles (3.2km) N of Ferrybridge off A1. Map ref 4B5.

738. FALLING FOSS
Waterfall/walks

Two walks, 3 miles and 1 mile (4.8 and 1.6km), start from picnic place near the waterfalls of Little Beck passing through mainly broad-leaved woodland to the Hermitage, a cell carved out of the rock in the 18th century, and to the waterfall viewpoint. The longer walk takes you on over farmland and moor. Leaflet available from Forestry Commission, tel: York 20221.
□ Five miles (8km) S of Whitby off B1416. map ref 4C3.

739. FOUNTAINS ABBEY
Monastic ruins/landscaped valley

The dramatic ruins of this large Cistercian Abbey, founded in 1133, provide a vivid picture of the impact of this order upon remote parts of the country. The monks contributed much to the taming of the landscape – but not everything for the abbey ruins now form part of the garden known as Studley Royal.

Here, in this wooded valley known as Skelldale, the history of the 18th-century landscape revolution can be traced from the first tentative steps in placing formal pools and classical temples in a completely informal setting, to the final romantic triumph which took in the ruins of Fountains Abbey as the garden's culminating feature, and provided them with a setting which appears completely natural.

The abbey and grounds are open all year. The abbey is floodlit during Aug-Sept, tel: Sawley 625.
□ Four miles (6.4km) SW of Ripon off B6265. Map ref 4B4.

740. GILLING CASTLE
Elizabethan house

This castle, beloved of Elizabethan enthusiasts, is in the village of Gilling East between the attractive Hambleton and Howardian Hills. It contains the most richly-decorated Elizabethan great chamber in England, a sumptuous concoction of pendentive-scattered plaster ceiling, painted frieze, elaborate panelling and armorial stained glass, all bought by Randolph Hearst, the American millionaire. He never looked at it, and the room spent several decades in packing cases before being reinstated in recent years. Approach by a handsome entrance front and baroque hall added on in the early 18th century, possibly to the designs of James Gibbs. Now a school, so there is little in the way of furniture. The hall and great chamber of the house are open throughout the year except Sun, the grounds June-Sept only. Tel: Ampleforth 238.
□ Four miles (6.4km) S of Helmsley on B1363. Map ref 4B4.

741. GOATHLAND
Moorland walks/glacial gorge

An attractive stone-built village straggling across a spur of the Esk valley below lovely stretches of the North York Moors. A good base for walking. South-west to the Roman road (see Wheeldale Moor, p. 312) past deep becks and foaming waters to Forestry Commission plantations; south-east to the high open moorlands of Goathland or Fylingdales where standing stones and earthworks testify to the area's importance 3000 years or so before the construction of the three globes of the early warning radar station (also visible from A169 Whitby-Pickering road). South of Goathland is the impressive gorge of Newtondale, followed by the railway but not by roads. The gorge was torn out largely by waters which overflowed from an ice-impounded lake complex which formed in the northern dales of the moors when the last major ice sheet invaded this area from the north.
□ Seven miles (11km) SW of Whitby off A169. Map ref 4C3.

742. HELMSLEY
Market town

As with many market towns Helmsley grew around a castle, a 12th century now largely in ruins but with some fine earth ramparts; open standard DoE hours plus Sun mornings Apr-Sept. The market square still forms the heart of the town – market day is Friday – for Helmsley was an important centre for

Lindisfarne Castle, built in the 16th century, dominates the low-lying island of Lindisfarne off the Northumberland coast

moorland sheep farmers. *The Black Swan* inn on the market square was originally a 16th century pack-horse inn for the sheep drovers. Helmsley is a starting-point for the long-distance Cleveland Way and for the less ambitious a three mile (4.8km) walk to Rievaulx abbey.

☐ 14 miles (22km) NW of Malton on A170 and B1257. Map ref 4B4.

743. HORTON-IN-RIBBLESDALE
Hill walking

This moorland village is on the route of the Pennine Way and can be used as the base for a seven mile (11km) circular walk incorporating part of this most famous of long-distance footpaths. Start in the village by taking the vicarage lane until it ends and becomes the Pennine Way path* to Hull Pot (one of many well-known pot-holes in the area). Then turn right to begin the steep climb up the Penyghent mountain (2273ft; 694m) that dominates the village below like a crouching lion. In fact, if you think of it as a lion you climb its flanks and mane by cart track and summit ridge and descend via its 'nose' (*keeping the wall on your right*) to Churn Milk Hole. You return to Horton via Long Lane, Dub Cote Farm path and Brackenbottom road.

*There are alternative routes of the Pennine Way around Horton-in-Ribblesdale, one of which does *not* ascend Penyghent. To be absolutely sure of following the correct route, buy OS map number 98.

☐ Five miles (8km) N of Settle on B6479. Map ref 4A4.

744. HUTTON-LE-HOLE
Village/museum/nature reserve

So pretty – with a beck running through the middle – that tourism is becoming its prime occupation. Some of its past is recalled in the Rydale Folk Museum which occupies 18th century farm buildings. Several crafts are displayed here as well as old farm implements and reconstructed buildings; open afternoons daily Easter-Sept, tel: Lastingham 367.

North of the village is Farndale, known as the dale of the daffodils. Here in a nature reserve wild daffodils can be seen each spring in an abundance once common in Britain. Short and long walks along the River Dove begin at Lowna, just over one mile (1.6km) north-west of the village, and Low Mill, four miles (6.4km) to the north. A leaflet is available from the national park offices, tel: Helmsley 70657.

☐ Nine miles (14km) NE of Helmsley off A170. Map ref 4C4.

745. INGLEBOROUGH
Cave/hill fort

Ingleborough Show Cave is almost $\frac{1}{3}$ mile (0.5km) long. It is reached either by a one mile (1.6km) nature trail from the Yorkshire Dales national park information centre at Clapham – open Apr-Sept, tel: Clapham 419 – or via Clapdale Lane north of Clapham. The cave is open daily Mar-Oct, weekends only for rest of year. tel: Clapham 242. A footpath continues past the cave through Trow Gill Gorge to Gaping Gill, the largest limestone cave in

Britain.

Ingleborough Cave is at the foot of Ingleborough Mountain, a 2373ft (712m) peak crowned by an Iron Age hill fort which is a superb viewpoint. The easiest way up the mountain is from Hill Inn, north-east of Ingleborough on B6225. For the geologically-minded note the water-eroded limestone terraces on the ascent up Ingleborough Mountain and the South Craven fault which, passing through Ingleton, Clapham and Settle, has created the great cliff of Giggleswick Scar alongside the A65 north-west of Settle.

☐ Just over one mile (1.6km) N of Clapham off A65/B6480. Map ref 4A4.

746. KETTLENESS
Lost village/headland

This headland at the east end of Runswick Bay was the site of a village at the foot of the cliffs which was carried into the sea by a landslide in 1829. You can still see walls belonging to the houses at the foot of the cliffs. Good views from the cliffs and the remains of a Roman Lighthouse. You can walk along the Cleveland Way footpath to Runswick Bay, down a steep hill. The old village of Runswick met a similar fate in 1682 when it too slipped into the sea. Nearby Staithes is an attractive old fishing village, also with fine cliffs.

☐ 16 miles (26km) SE of Redcar by footpath off A176. Map ref 4C3.

747. MALHAM
Limestone scenery/drove road

This hamlet is at the heart of some quite extraordinary scenery all of which is essentially the consequence of the effect of water on limestone. The results around Malham are so dramatic that the area can become very crowded, especially during summer weekends.

It is not therefore a place for the touring motorist at these times; indeed, the most remarkable features can be seen only on foot – see map. There is an information centre at Malham and here, too, is one of the few car parks in an area more notable for parking restrictions. In summer months it would be worth enquiring about the special railway excursion trains run at weekends to nearby Settle for ramblers; tel: Settle 3617 or Airton 363. Main attractions of the area are:

Malham Cove. An almost sheer cliff 300ft (92m) high. It was formed by massive faulting in the limestone blocks which here slipped vertically away from one another. The plateau above it is extremely porous, so any water that falls disappears into 'swallow holes' and does not see daylight again until it has travelled through many miles of

Map of Malham and its attractions, including Malham Tarn, Gordale Scar, Malham Cove and Mastiles Lane

underground caverns. In the Ice Age, however, the fissures became filled with ice and massive waterfalls created the horseshoe-shaped cove which at the time must have seemed as dramatic as Niagara does today.

Limestone Pavement. Between the Cove and Malham Tarn the limestone has been exposed at the surface and divided into a series of fissured blocks which the dissolving action of rainfall is continually widening. The fissures are known as 'grikes'.

Malham Tarn. An outcrop of impervious Silurian slates preserved by faulting has enabled the Tarn or lake to develop in a hollow. It is a renowned centre for the wildlife and landforms associated with limestone. Much of the area is now owned by the National Trust and the local Field Studies Centre has an information centre about the tarn and surrounding area. A small stream flows south from the Tarn but disappears into swallow holes.

Gordale Scar. Water still falls over this cliff (formed from the same vertical faulting as Malham Cove) because surface clays have clogged the fissures in the limestone along the route followed by the tumbling Gordale 'Beck' as streams in the Dales are often called.

Mastiles Lane. A man-made phenomenon after the natural ones. The 1300ft (400m) moors above Malham were the scene of a great autumn fair when thousands of cattle and sheep changed hands. The drovers converged on Malham along drove roads from all parts of the north. The most famous of these roads was Mastiles lane which was initially established in the 13th century as a monastic route from the sheep and cattle granges of Fountains Abbey near Ripon to the Lake District; bases of old monastic crosses survive in places. A three-mile (4.8km) stretch between Malham and Kilnsey remains restricted to walkers and horse-riders. This part of Mastiles Lane was walled in the mid-18th century when traffic was at its peak and is the longest stretch of the drove road to survive in anything like its original condition.

☐ Malham is four miles (6.4km) E of Settle; OS map no. 98 covers all the locations featured here, including the clearly-marked Mastiles Lane heading NE to Kilnsey. Map ref 4A4.

748. NEWBY HALL
Country house/gardens

Both house and grounds have been developed at different times over the last 300 years. In the 18th century Robert Adam added rooms to the original 17th century structure; in the 19th century a church was among the additions; and in the 20th century the grounds were laid out with 25 acres (10 hectares) of trees, shrubs and herbaceous perennials stretching down to the River Ure. Grounds open daily Easter-Sept; house Sun only Apr-May, daily except Mon afternoons July-Aug. Tel: Boroughbridge 2583.

☐ Three miles (4.8km) SE of Ripon on B6265. Map ref 4B4.

749. NIDDERDALE
River valley

The River Nidd falls from Great

Whernside (2310ft; 693m) through Gouthwaite Reservoir (one of the finest bird sanctuaries in the area), past Pateley Bridge and Knaresborough (a picturesque market town dominated by remains of a 14th century castle) to join the River Ouse at Nun Monckton. At the head of Nidderdale, on a minor road north of Lofthouse, is How Stean Gorge, a spectacular limestone valley sometimes known as Yorkshire's 'Little Switzerland'. Other things to see in or near Nidderdale are Foster Beck Mill, one mile (1.6km) north of Pateley Bridge; Stump Cross Caverns at Greenhow Hill five miles (8km) west of Pateley Bridge on B6265 (open daily Easter-Oct), and Brimham Rocks (NT), $2\frac{1}{4}$ miles (3.6km) east of Pateley Bridge. The latter are weird blocks of sandstone sculpted by wind and rain on heathery moorland. They now form the centrepiece of a country park. Leaflets and maps of paths are available from an information centre.

☐ Pateley Bridge is 10 miles (16km) SW of Ripon on B6265. Map ref 4B4.

750. RAVENSCAR
Geological trail

The waymarked Ravenscar Geological Trail is divided into two sections, the first covers nearly $2\frac{1}{2}$ miles (4km) inland to the Quarry, the second follows the path to the shore covering a further two miles (3.2km) with a steep climb. The rocks exposed in the quarry and on the coast belong to the Jurassic period, the grey shale contains alum, important in leather curing, hence the quarries. There is a major geological fault in the rocks at this point which has helped expose its geological history. Many museums throughout the country have fossils which were found in Ravenscar. Excellent explanatory booklet available from the North York Moors National Park information offices, tel: Helmsley 657.

☐ Trail starts outside Wildlife Centre on minor road off A171 into Ravenscar eight miles (13km) N of Scarborough. Map ref 4C3.

751. RICHMOND
Market town/castle

One of the most attractive market towns in the north of England. It grew around a castle set on a bluff of rock high over a loop of the beautiful River Swale. The importance of this position commanding the entrance to Swaledale was soon recognised by the Normans: their castle was built soon after the Norman Conquest and as such it is one of the earliest in England. The keep in particular has survived splendidly. It can be visited during standard DoE hours plus Sun mornings Apr-Sept. Also recommended is a walk around the outside of the 11th century walls.

The town of Richmond grew on the hill which sloped down from the castle and it developed around a huge cobbled market-place. Markets are held there on Saturdays. One particularly attractive and easy walk is along the banks of the Swale to the ruins of Easby Abbey one mile (1.6km) to the south-east.

☐ 13 miles (21km) SW of Darlington on A6108. Map ref 4B3.

Northern England

752. RIEVAULX ABBEY
Monastic ruins/terraces

Architecturally this is England's finest ecclesiastical ruin. Fountains is better preserved, but Rievaulx is much more poetic. The choir is Early English at its most exquisite, and comparable with Lincoln Cathedral. The church is very unusual in running north-south, because of the narrowness of the valley. No one should fail to visit the Rievaulx Terrace on the hill above, laid out in the 1750s. Abbey open standard DoE hours plus Sun mornings Apr-Sept; Terrace open daily Apr-Oct except Good Friday.
□ Three miles (4.8km) NW of Helmsley off B1257. Map ref 4B4.

753. ROBIN HOOD'S BAY
Cliffs/coastal walk

An attractive fishing village set between cliffs which are important to geologists (since a fault has revealed their history dating back 300,000 years) or simply dramatic to laymen. The cliffs overlook a bay which has a rocky reef running in strange concentric patterns which are the result of constant coast erosion. Boggle Hole is a pebble cove at the mouth of Mill Beck and on the shore itself are boulders which are the remains of glacial deposits.

The paths around the bay are waymarked since they form part of the long-distance Cleveland Way. From here to Scarborough is a 16-mile (26km) walk along beautiful coastal scenery. Start out along the shore and ascend from Boggle Hole and continue south via Ravenscar (where a hotel on the site of a Roman lighthouse is prominent); Hayburn Wyke (a dell with a waterfall on the beach); and Cloughton Wyke four miles or 6.4km north of Scarborough. OS maps 94 and 101.
□ Five miles (8km) SE of Whitby off A171. Map ref 4C3.

754. SKIPTON
Castle/canal

Skipton is surrounded by moors near the head of Airedale. Its strategic position was marked in the 11th century by the construction of a castle (although most of the present building dates from the 13th and 14th centuries) and in the 19th century by a canal. The 130-mile (208km) Leeds-Liverpool canal reaches its most northerly point near Skipton. Even many stretches of the canal in Lower Airedale, near the Leeds conurbation, offer surprisingly tranquil cruising and towpath walking while its technical accomplishments include not only the crossing of the Pennines themselves but the staircase of locks known as the Bingley 5-rise just north of Bingley. Boats can be hired at Skipton and other places in Airedale for cruises on the canal – details from the Yorkshire and Humberside Tourist Board. Other attractions of Skipton include the Craven Museum, with its exhibitions on local geology and natural history and the castle itself, tel: Skipton 2442.
□ Eight miles (13km) NW of Keighley on A6. Map ref 4A4.

755. SUTTON BANK
Walks/views

The highest point reached by the A170 as it climbs from Thirsk over the Hambleton Hills on the western fringes of the North York Moors. Many people park their cars and simply admire the view. But the car park with its national park information centre – tel: Thirsk 597426 – can also be the starting point for several different walks with outstanding views. These include the Garbutt Wood Nature Trail, 2½ miles (4km), north of A170, and White Horse Walk, 1½ miles, south of A170.
□ Four miles (6.4km) E of Thirsk on A170. Map ref 4B4.

756. SWALEDALE
River valley

Less well known than Wensleydale to the south, heather-covered Swaledale is perhaps less crowded and the more charming because of this. Richmond Castle (see entry, page 311) guards the eastern entrance to the valley which is followed at first by the A6108 and then the B6270. But explore, too, the side valleys and minor roads which follow them such as Arkengarthdale northwest of Reeth; the old 'high road' from Reeth to Richmond; West Stone Dale north of Keld and leading to Tan Hill Inn (see listing under Co Durham); and the roads south towards Wensleydale. For walkers the Pennine Way crosses Swaledale near Keld and heads north up West Stone Dale. Shorter walks can be made to several waterfalls (called Force in the Dales). Less obvious, but still visible, are the relics of the lead mining which was once an important industry here. Villages to see include Keld and Muker but Reeth is probably the best centre for exploring upper Swaledale; there is also a folk museum in the village. The valley of the Swale becomes progressively more wooded as it heads towards Richmond while to the west the B6270 heads over the Pennines towards the Lakes and Penrith. No one map covers Swaledale neatly; the best OS coverage comes from maps 92 and 98.
□ W of Richmond. Map ref 4A3/4B3.

757. WENSLEYDALE
River valley/villages

The beautiful River Ure, having left the wild moors of the high Pennines, flows eastwards along a valley known as Wensleydale which is popular with both walkers and motorists. OS map 98 covers most of Wensleydale. There are national park information centres at Aysgarth Falls, Hawes and Askrigg (Tel: Wensleydale 50441).

Drives. The A684 runs the length of Wensleydale from Leyburn in the east to Moorcock Inn west of Hawes where it divides with the B6259 following the Eden Valley to the north and the A684 running down Garsdale towards Kendal and the Lake District. But don't miss some of the smaller valleys such as Coverdale and Walden Beck or the minor roads heading over the moors to Swaledale or Wharfedale for dramatic upland drives.

Walking. The Pennine Way crosses Wensleydale at Hawes and is the prime route for serious ramblers or hill-

The romantic ruins of Whitby Abbey, founded in AD657, in North Yorkshire

walkers. But shorter walks can be undertaken such as the one-mile (1.6km) stretch of the Pennine Way from Hawes to Hardrow Force (see below); the wooded walks along a disused railway line from Aysgarth to the falls of Aysgarth Force, and two miles (3.2km) along the River Bain from Bainbridge to the lake of Semer Water. There is also a stretch of Roman road running south-west from Bainbridge where the site of their fort, *Virosidium* on Brough Hill, still dominates the village.

Waterfalls. Hardrow Force one mile (1.6km) north of Hawes is the highest waterfall in Yorkshire; Aysgarth Force is an attractive series of waterfalls and rapids near the village of Aysgarth where the Ure plunges through a wooded gorge. Other smaller waterfalls can be seen along the side of the valley where becks and streams pour off the moors.

Villages. Askrigg, Aysgarth and Bainbridge are all attractive villages but Hawes is the only one which approaches the status of a town. Markets are still held in its cobbled streets and market square on Tues (livestock) and Wed. Other features of Hawes are the Upper Dales Folk Museum and demonstrations of Wensleydale cheese-making – details of both from the national park information centre in Hawes, open daily Apr-Sept, tel: Hawes 450 or tourist offices.

Buildings. Near Leyburn, and guarding the eastern entrance to Wensleydale, is Middleham Castle. This still

has an excellent 12th century keep and was said to have been the favourite fortress of Richard III if that can be a recommendation; open standard DoE hours. Bolton Castle, a 14th century fortress near Redmire, which once held Mary Queen of Scots captive; open daily all year; tel: Leyburn 23408. Jervaulx Abbey, a ruined Cistercian abbey, near Middleham; open all year.
□ Map ref 4A4.

758. WHARFEDALE
Moors/rivers/villages

Whereas Swaledale and Wensleydale head east-west, Wharfedale runs from north to south and offers perhaps a greater variety of scenery than its more northerly neighbours. Upper Wharfedale is bare and lonely country with tiny hamlets such as Hubberholme that are not much more than pub and church. Lower down the scenery is lusher and villages become larger – Grassington is almost a town with its neat cobbled square. Most of Wharfedale forms part of the Dales National Park and offers magnificent upland walking. It is also easily accessible to motorists since the B6160 follows the valley from just north of Ilkley until it heads over the moors into Wensleydale. Heading off this main valley and its sometimes crowded road are some unspoilt and less well-known smaller dales of great charm, notably Littondale (with its lovely village of Arncliffe) and Langstrothdale at the very head of Wharfedale. Places to see include 12th century Bolton Priory at Bolton Abbey; the narrow gorge of the Strid, reached by riverside walks of about two miles (3.2km) north of Bolton Abbey; the nature reserve of Grass Wood and also Bastow Wood near Grassington; and Ilkley itself at the southern end of Wharfedale, with its brooding Cow and Calf Rocks as well as its much sung-about moors. OS map 98 covers the northern stretches of Wharfedale; no 104 the southern half.

☐ Map ref 4A4.

759. WHEELDALE MOOR
Roman road

One of the best stretches of Roman road still visible. The surface stones have eroded away – or been taken away for other uses – but the 16ft (5m) wide foundations and occasional kerbstones and culverts remain for up to 1½ miles (2.4km) across the North York Moors (grid ref SE 805975). This was part of a Roman road from Malton to Whitby that is also known, for reasons unknown, as Wade's Causeway. Roman camp sites are visible (more clearly in winter when vegetation is less) along the route of the road south of Stape at Crawthorn. OS map 94.

☐ Three miles (5km) SW of Goathland. Follow the narrow minor road to the hamlet of Hunt House from where a signposted path leads to the uncovered Roman road. Map ref 4C3.

South Yorkshire

A Metropolitan county covering a little of the Pennines but mostly industrial areas around Sheffield where Abbeydale Industrial Hamlet is a major attraction. Yorkshire and Humberside Tourist Board: York 707961.

760. BARNSLEY
Country parks/mill

Known for its coal mining and beer rather than any rural delights, but two country parks are close by. One at Worsbrough, two miles (3.2km) to the south on A61, is set around a water-powered corn mill but there is also a nature trail and fishing in a reservoir in nearly 100 acres (38.5 hectares) of wood and farmland. Cannon Hall Park, 4½ miles (7km) north-west of Barnsley, also has fishing plus gardens in parkland surrounding a 17th to 18th century mansion.

☐ Two miles (3.2km) E of junction 37 on M1. Map ref 4B5.

761. CONISBROUGH
Castle

There is some Norman work in the church of this small town on the Don but nothing so impressive as in the castle which boasts the earliest circular keep in England. It dates from the mid 12th century and is still 90ft (27m) high. A chapel within the keep, some walls and earthworks also survive. Open standard DoE hours plus Sun Mornings Apr-Sept.

☐ Five miles (8km) SW of Doncaster on A630. Map ref 4B5.

762. RINGINGLOW
Moors/views

Barely five miles (8km) from Sheffield city centre yet wild and apparently remote moorland within the Peak District National Park. Ringinglow is not much more than a bog, a pub and some cottages, but it has given its name to a road which offers a stunning drive across the Hallam Moors. Plenty of places to stop for views, picnics or walks. Rock climbers will head for Stanage Edge, a rocky outcrop revered among climbers. Among good routes for walkers is one along the top of Stanage and then via the line of an old Roman road, known as the Long Causeway, to the Redmires Reservoirs. Other paths lead towards the Ladybower Reservoir, in the Derwent Valley. OS map 110.

☐ The Ringinglow road runs north of A625 between Hathersage and Bamford in the W and Sheffield in the E. Map ref 4B5.

763. ROCHE ABBEY
Monastic remains

The most southerly of the great Cistercian houses of Yorkshire. The valley of the River Ryton in which it stands now seems less remote than it may have been in the 12th century when the abbey was founded, but it is still a beautiful setting. The gothic transepts and gateway to the old abbey church are the prime remains, although the outline of other buildings is clearly visible. Open during standard DoE hours plus Sun Mornings Apr-Sept.

☐ Two miles (3.2km) SE of Maltby off A634. OS map 111. Map ref 4B5.

Tyne and Wear

Metropolitan county revolving around Newcastle and Sunderland. Northumbria Tourist Board: Newcastle 817744.

764. WASHINGTON
Waterfowl/house

Washington Waterfowl Park on the eastern outskirts of the new town is managed by the Wildfowl Trust and the Washington Development Corporation, consists of 110 acres (45 hectares) of land, pools and pens on the north bank of the River Wear. The wildfowl enclosures are landscaped into the hillsides while in the valley lies the Wild Refuge which includes a wader lake and several ponds where visitors can watch wild birds from screened hides. In the Hawthorn Wood, which borders the refuge, there is a nature trail and bird feeding stations overlooked by a large hide. Migrant birds are to be seen in early spring or autumn. Later on the wintering wildfowl gather for the coldest months. The breeding season for the wildfowl is at its height between April and June. Open daily, tel: Washington 465454.

There is a special emphasis on American birds in the Park since the town has taken its name from what was the ancestral home of George Washington. Washington Old Hall, the family home from 1183 to 1613, is open afternoons daily, except Tues Mar-Oct and weekends Nov-Feb. Tel: Washington 466879.

☐ Five miles (8km) W of Sunderland. Map ref 4B2.

West Yorkshire

Metropolitan county with some moorland but more industry around Leeds and Bradford. Harewood House is top attraction. Yorkshire and Humberside Tourist Board: York 707961.

765. BRAMHAM PARK
French-style gardens

Large garden in the style of Versailles with allées through dense woodland, formal pools, statues, urns, temples and other decoration. New planting of exotic trees and shrubs has been introduced in the gardens and grounds around a Queen Anne mansion. Complicated opening arrangements but usually open several days a week late Apr-Sept. Tel: Boston Spa 844265.

☐ Five miles (8km) S of Wetherby on A1. Map ref 4B4.

766. BRONTË COUNTRY
Moors/village

The Brontës will always be associated primarily with this somewhat bleak village on the Yorkshire moors. And Emily's *Wuthering Heights* will always be the quintessential novel of these moors. Old cottages are set around a cobbled main street that climbs steeply from the valley to the church (and parsonage) at the top of the hill. A bypass has siphoned off the traffic to leave this street free for pedestrians and not even the crowds and souvenir shops can totally dispel the atmosphere of Haworth as it must have been when the Brontë family lived here in the first half of the 19th century. This is due as much to the proximity of the moors as to the survival of so many old buildings. The moors still begin close to the parsonage where the sisters lived and wrote.

This house is now a Brontë museum and, along with the adjacent church, the most obvious attraction for visitors. But even the pub, the *Black Bull*, claims its link with the legend by reminding visitors that it was there that Branwell Brontë spent so much of his time. The museum is open daily except the last three weeks of Dec, tel: Haworth 42323.

The sisters' favourite walk was reputedly the two miles (3.2km) to a small waterfall now known as Brontë Falls – the route is signposted from West Lane at the top of the village. Literary pilgrims may wish to walk one mile (1.6km) further to a ruined farmhouse called High or Top Withens, allegedly the setting for *Wuthering Heights* itself. Other buildings claimed by Brontë devotees to be models for places featured in the novels are Ponden Hall, a 17th century farmhouse near the neighbouring hamlet of Stanbury (Thrushcross Grange of *Wuthering Heights*) and slightly further afield, Wycoller Hall (Ferndean Manor of *Jane Eyre*). Both High Withens and Ponden Hall are near the route of the long-distance Pennine Way.

The final evocation of the 19th century can be attained through the steam railway which runs through Haworth from Keighley and Oxenhope; services at weekends and Bank Holidays all year, daily July-early Sept; tel: Haworth 43629.

☐ Four miles (6.4km) SW of Keighley on A6033. Map ref 4B5.

767. HARLOW CAR GARDENS
Gardening in a cool climate

The 60 acres (24 hectares) of Harlow Car Gardens has been laid out by the Northern Horticultural Society to demonstrate the possibilities, and to discover the limitations, of gardening in the north of England. Features include a rose garden, herbaceous borders, rock gardens, water gardens, a woodland garden, an arboretum and extensive trial grounds. Open all year, Tel: Harrogate 65418.

☐ 1½ miles (2.4km) from centre of Harrogate off B6162 to Otley. Map ref 4B4.

768. HEPTONSTALL
Village/nature trail

Up a steep lane from Hebden Bridge is the lovely hilltop village of Heptonstall with its ancient weavers cottages. Slurring Rock Nature Trail starts from the car park at The Lodge at Horse Bridge (NT). The walk, which takes about 1½ hours descends to the banks of Hebden Water then climbs to the escarpment above the woods – a favourite haunt of woodland birds and a number of red squirrels. A booklet is available from an Information Centre in Hebden Bridge.

☐ One mile (1.6km) N from Hebden Bridge. Map ref 4A5.

769. KIRKSTALL ABBEY
Monastic ruins/folk museum

The Cistercians are generally renowned for their agricultural impact upon the remote landscapes in which their monasteries were sited. But here, alongside the River Aire, they also pioneered the exploitation of iron ore in an area now dominated by industry. The abbey was built in 1152 by monks from Fountains Abbey and, although nowhere near on the same scale as its forebear, extensive remains of the abbey, particularly its walls, can still be seen. The monks here were also noted for craft skills such as spinning, weaving and pottery so it is quite appropriate that the former gatehouse is now a folk and craft museum; tel: Leeds 755821 for details.

☐ Three miles (5km) NW of Leeds off A65. Map ref 4B5.

770. SHIBDEN HALL
Hill farming and cottage industry

The Pennine hills were traditionally the home of hill farmers and later, with the Industrial Revolution, textile workers, the two occupations becoming inextricably intertwined. The West Yorkshire Folk Museum, which is housed in a half-timbered 15th-century hall, with a fine 17th-century barn and other farm buildings around it, shows something of this very distinctive local culture. Most of its farm tools are housed in the barn, including an early threshing machine with horse-wheel and many hand tools from the Pennine area. Open daily Mar to Oct, although afternoons only on Sun. In Feb open only Sun afternoons. Tel: Halifax 54823.

☐ ¼ mile (400m) SE of Halifax on A58. Map ref 4B5.

Scotland

Crofter's cottage on the Isle of Skye. Note the ropes weighted down with stones to secure the thatch when the wild winter gales are blowing

Scotland

771. BEN NEVIS, GLEN COE AND BLACK MOUNT
National Park Direction Area

Covers Scotland's highest mountain and most famous glen. The summit of Ben Nevis, 4406ft (1343m) can be reached by a rough five-mile (8km) track from Glen Nevis, but great care should be taken. The brooding pass of Glen Coe, the 'Glen of Weeping', where Campbells murdered Mac-Donalds in the notorious clan massacre of 1692, attracts large numbers of visitors but is still enormously impressive, as are the surrounding peaks of Bidean nam Bian and Clach Liathad. Total area: 610 sq miles (976 sq km).
□ Map ref 5C4.

772. CAIRNGORMS
National Park Direction Area

Magnificent mountain wilderness dominated by sub-arctic summits of Braeriach, Ben Macdui, Cairn Toul and Cairn Gorm itself, all over 4000ft (1218m). Below the peaks lie the resinous pinewoods of Rothiemurchus and the Glenmore National Forest Park, idyllic Loch Morlich and the Spey Valley. The Aviemore Centre, a Spey Valley sport and leisure complex, offers ski-ing in the winter; walking, pony-

trekking, canoeing and fishing in the summer. Cairn Gorm, summit – 4084ft (1260m) – can be reached, summer and winter, by a chairlift. The chairlift ends a little way below the summit at the Ptarmigan Restaurant. At this height the weather can change dramatically – so adequate footwear and clothing is essential at all times. Climate and vegetation is arctic-alpine, and the area, part of which is a national nature reserve, is rich in wildlife such as golden eagle, ptarmigan, capercaillie, dotterel, red deer and wild cat. Total area: 180 sq miles (288 sq km).
□ Map ref 5D4.

773. GLEN AFFRIC, GLEN CANNICH AND STRATHFARRAR
National Park Direction Area

A trio of wild glens thrusting deep into the Northwest Highlands. Cannich and Struy are the gateways. To make a scenic circular drive from Inverness, take the A82 beside Loch Ness, then A831 through Glen Urquhart, returning by the A9 along the Beauly Firth. Glorious loch scenery in Glen Affric, where relic pines of the ancient Caledonian Forest survive. Golden eagles patrol the surrounding hills, and red deer are common. Total area: 260 sq miles (416 sq km).
□ Map ref 5C3.

774. LOCH LOMOND AND THE TROSSACHS
National Park Direction Area

Romantic mingling of lochs, birchwoods, glens and mountains with the tourist village of Aberfoyle as its main centre. Loch Lomond is the largest loch, 23 miles (37km) long, and studded with 30 islets. The Rob Roy country of the Trossachs surrounds the even lovelier lochs of Katrine (for pleasure steamer cruises), Achray and Venachar. Several majestic peaks dominate the area: highest is Ben Lomond, 3192ft (972m); most dramatic is The Cobbler, 2891ft (880m) to the west of Loch Lomond. Total area: 320 sq miles (512 sq km).
□ Map ref 5D6.

775. LOCHS TORRIDON, MAREE AND LITTLE LOCH BROOM
National Park Direction Area

Wild and remote tangle of glens and sea lochs in the Northwest Highlands, lorded over by the red sandstone walls of the Torridon mountains and the looming peaks of Slioch and An Tealach, all well over 3000ft (914m). The whole area is a stronghold for Highland wildlife (pine marten, wild cat, golden eagle). The Beinn Eighe National Nature Reserve protects more than 10,000 acres of mountain

and pine forest, as well as providing picnic sites and nature trails starting from Loch Maree. NTS Visitor Centre at junction of A896 and Diabaig Road. Total area: 500 sq miles (800 sq km).
□ Map ref 5C3.

Borders

The salmon rivers of the Tweed and Teviot cross this region of rolling hills and ruined abbeys. Melrose, Selkirk, Jedburgh, Kelso and Peebles are among its main towns and attractions. Border Tourism Division: St Boswells 3301.

776. DAWYCK GARDENS
Riverside forest garden

Forest garden with exotic trees and shrubs by River Tweed. Arboretum. Open daily, Good Friday to Sept. Tel: Edinburgh 552 7171.
□ At Stobo, six miles (9.6km) SW of Peebles on B712. Map ref 3D1.

777. JEDBURGH
Border abbey/Roman road

Extensive ruins of what is perhaps the noblest of the four great 12th century Border abbeys founded by David I. The town of Jedburgh is an ancient Royal Burgh. Queen Mary's House, where Mary, Queen of Scots once stayed, is now a museum. Walkers can follow the line of Dere Street – the

Some common Scottish place-names and their English meanings

Modern form	Meaning
Blair	Plain
Clach	Stone
Craig	Cliff
Drum	Ridge
Eccles	Church
Eilean	Island
Gart	Enclosure
Howe	Hollow
Inch	Island
Kyle	Strait
Mains	Home Farm
Mull	Headland
Strath	Wide Valley

Roman road built by Agricola. What is now the broad green highway of this route is particularly well-preserved in a stretch south from Jedfoot, where the A698 crosses Jed Water some two miles (3.2km) N of Jedburgh. OS map 80.
□ 10 miles (16km) SW of Kelso. Map ref 4A1.

778. KELSO
Old market town

A charming market town still centred on its wide cobbled square and 18th-century Court House. Little remains of the once great 12th-century abbey, but John Rennie's graceful bridge over the Tweed still stands, giving excellent view of Floors Castle, the splendid Borders mansion built by William Adam in 1721 (but much altered a century later). The castle is open on afternoons, May to Sept; tel: Kelso 3333.

Other places of interest within easy reach of Kelso include the 16th-century Smailholm Tower, seven miles (11km) west, off B6404, in a romantic setting on a rocky outcrop above Eden Water. It is open standard DoE hours, but if locked, apply for the key at nearby Sandyknowe Farm.
□ Kelso is 20 miles (32km) SW of Berwick-on-Tweed, on A698. Map ref 4A1.

779. MELROSE
Border abbey

The site of the fourth great Border abbey – the others are Dryburgh, Jedburgh and Kelso. Like the remains at Dryburgh these are set on the green pastures of the Tweed Valley. It was founded as a Cistercian monastery in 1136. Under its patronage the nearby village of Fordel blossomed into the present market town of Melrose. The abbey suffered severely during the Border wars but considerable restoration work was commenced in the 19th century. Much of this work was inspired by Sir Walter Scott whose house at Abbotsford is nearby (see entry No. 781). The abbey is open standard DoE hours.
□ Four miles (6.4km) SE of Galashiels on A6091. OS map 73. Map ref 4A1.

780. ST ABB'S
Fishing village

This small village attracts some tourists, but it remains largely the fishing community it has always been. The cottages are grouped around the tiny harbour which is formed here in an otherwise inhospitably rugged coast. The cliffs to the north of the village rise to a height of more than 300ft (92m).
□ 12 miles (19km) NW of Berwick off A1107. Map ref 6B6.

781. SCOTT'S COUNTRY

Sir Walter Scott was born in Edinburgh in 1771. He continued to maintain close links with the capital and his use of the Trossachs in general and Loch Katrine in particular as settings for *The Lady of the Lake* and *Rob Roy* helped enormously to establish the popularity of these places. However, he is mostly associated with the Borders. It was in the rolling hills drained by the Tweed that Scott lived most of his later years and where he died. Few Border towns of any size do not have some link with Scott – local tourist information offices can provide details of his association with such places as Kelso, Melrose and Selkirk. Other places to see must begin with the home which he built and where he lived for 20 years until his death there in 1832.

Abbotsford. This was the highly personal off-shoot of the fortune he made from his novels. The outside (mostly designed by William Atkinson in 1822-4) is of interest to historians as a pioneer of the 'Scottish Baronial' style, but it is the inside which really makes the house worth a visit. Dark brown woodwork, stained glass, Gothic fireplaces, books, armour, antlers, and curiosities of all kinds, are crowded together to epitomize all Scott's enthusiasm for the past. His own study is still much as he left it, and personal relics and portraits of his many beloved dogs abound. The house is off A7 three miles (5km) west of Melrose and is open daily, late Mar to Oct and on Sun afternoons.

Scott's View. This name has been given to a dramatic viewpoint on Bemersyde Hill overlooking a tight meander of the Tweed and beyond to the Eildon Hills. Legend has it that Scott so loved this view that the horses taking his hearse to Dryburgh Abbey stopped here out of habit. Three miles (5km) south of Earlston on B6356 and clearly indicated by parking lay-bys etc.

Dryburgh Abbey. Scott's burial place and one of the great Border abbeys. Here the beauty of the ruins is enhanced by their setting in a loop of the Tweed. Three miles (5km) SE of Melrose off B6356.
□ Map ref 4A1.

782. TRAQUAIR HOUSE
Historic house

Few houses are more sympathetically redolent of lost causes. The Stuarts of Traquair were the leading Jacobite and Catholic family in the Scottish Lowlands, and political and religious persecution left them without the means to spoil their house in the 19th century. The old castle grew gradually upwards as well as outwards and the result is like something in a fairy story. Charming panelled and painted rooms inside, with Stuart and Jacobite relics of all varieties. Absolutely unlike any-

Bust of Sir Walter Scott, whose novels immortalised the Scottish Border Country

Abbotsford House, near Melrose, Scott's home for the last 20 years of his life

Loch Katrine and the Trossachs, setting for Scott's poem: 'The Lady of the Lake'

Scotland

thing in England. Open afternoons, mid Apr and early Oct, also mornings, July and Aug. Tel: Innerleithen 830323 for details.

□ Near Innerleithen, six miles (9.6km) SE of Peebles near junction of B709 and B7062. Map ref 3D1.

783. WALKERBURN
Museum of rural life

The Scottish Museum of Wool Textiles at Walkerburn tells a story which has its origins in the time when textiles were very much a cottage industry and when a man would raise and shear his own sheep leaving his wife to take the raw wool and do the rest. Visitors can see her spinning wheel, the plants she might have used to get her dyes and the finished article such as the Shepherd's Plaid of 1875. Other displays show the tools of the trade and the processes of textile manufacture. Open daily and weekends by arrangement, Easter to end Sept. Tel: Walkerburn 281.

□ Tweedvale Mill, Walkerburn on A72 E of Innerleithen. Map ref 3D1.

Central

This small region covers part of Loch Lomond and the Trossachs. Other attractions include Stirling Castle. Regional Council: Stirling 3111.

784. ANTONINE WALL
Roman Britain

Little now remains of a wall that for a time marked the northern frontier of not only Roman Britain but the Roman Empire itself. But it is still the most important Roman work to survive in any form in Scotland. It was built around AD 142 with the intention of superseding Hadrian's Wall but was finally abandoned.

By far the best preserved fragment is at **Rough Castle** near Bonnybridge where ditch, rampart, military way and a former Roman fort can be seen. This site can be visited at any reasonable time without charge.

□ The route of the Antonine Wall is shown on the map of Roman Britain on page 39. Rough Castle is at grid ref NS 843799 which is one mile (1.6km) E of Bonnybridge. Map ref 5D6.

785-6. QUEEN ELIZABETH FOREST
Forest park

Covers 65 sq miles (16,835 hectares) of one of the most scenic areas in Central Scotland. It extends from the Trossachs, 26 miles (41.9km) north of Glasgow, westwards to Loch Lomond, along the southern fringe of the Highlands. Included are the summits of Ben Lomond and Ben Venue, and six beautiful lochs: Lomond, Chon, Ard, Vennacher, Achray and Drunkie. There are 170 miles (273.5km) of forest roads open to the public on foot. Facilities in the separate forests of the park include: **785. Achray Forest.** David Marshall Lodge picnic and information centre open daily mid-Mar to mid-Oct. Off A821 one mile (1.6km) north of Aberfoyle. Waterfall trail starts from lodge car park. Achray forest drive is a seven mile (11.2km) long Forestry Commission road, open summer, except Tues.

Stained glass window in the Galloway Deer Museum, Clatteringshaws Loch

Starts off A821 1½ miles (3.2km) north of lodge. Many other forest walks and trails.

□ Map ref 5D6.

786. Loch Ard Forest. Silver Ring scenic walk through forest and by lochan and riverside. Six miles (9.6km). Starts from Aberfoyle. Loch Chon picnic place at forest edge beside loch. Access via B829 seven miles (11.2km) west of Aberfoyle.

□ Map ref 5D5.

787. ROWARDENNAN
Lochside walk

The hamlet of Rowardennan is a popular base for the ascent of Ben Lomond, 3192ft (984m). It is also the starting-point for a splendid walk along the eastern shores of Loch Lomond. The route is part of the West Highland Way, which runs for 92 miles (148km) from Milngavie to Fort William. From Rowardennan pier head north to Ptarmigan Lodge, then via forestry road to footpath alongside Loch Lomond by Rowchoish and Inversnaid Hotel to Rob Roy's Cave. Total distance to the cave and back is about 10 miles (16km).

Rowardennan can be reached by road or by ferries which operate on Loch Lomond from Balloch and Inverberg.

□ 10 miles (16km) NW of Drymen at end of road (at first B837, then unclassified) on E shore of Loch Lomond. Map ref 5D6.

788. THE TROSSACHS
Mountains/loch

The wooded hills of the Trossachs and in particular Loch Katrine were used by Scott as the setting for *The Lady of the Lake*. Ellen's Isle in the loch is named after Ellen Douglas, the actual Lady of the Lake but the 'Silver Strand' of the poem is now submerged. The loch also figured in another of Scott's works, *Rob Roy*, since Rob Roy MacGregor was born at Glengyle at the head of Loch Katrine or Loch Cateran as Scott called it. Scott's descriptions of The Trossachs – Gaelic for 'Thorny Place' and referring to the narrow pass between Lochs Katrine and Achray – did much to open up this previously little-known area to tourism. The debt is acknowledged in the name of the steamer which in the summer plies up and down Loch Katrine. It is called the 'Sir Walter Scott' and, since no road follows the shores of this steep-sided loch, is the best way of enjoying its beauty other than, perhaps, by foot or pony-trekking. Boats operate mid-May to Sept; details from Callander tourist office, tel: Callander 30624. The area, with Loch Lomond, forms one of Scotland's five 'National Park Direction Areas' and also contains part of Queen Elizabeth Forest Park (see entry No. 785).

□ Map ref 5D5.

Dumfries and Galloway

Attractions include the coast of the Solway Firth, towns such as Dumfries and Kircudbright and several castles. Dumfries and Galloway Tourist Association: Newton Stewart 2549.

789. CAERLAVEROCK
Winter wildfowl refuge

A large nature reserve extends along six miles (9.6km) of coastline here between the River Nith and the Lochar Water on the Scottish shore of the Solway Firth. The saltmarsh (called merse locally) is a great attraction for winter wildfowl. In particular it is one of the principle haunts of barnacle geese in Britain. In October they begin to arrive, building up to a winter peak over 8000. Pinkfeet and greylag geese also winter on the reserve and peregrine, hen harrier, merlin and sparrowhawk may be seen. Contact the warden of the Nature Conservancy Council (tel: Glencaple 275) first if you wish to explore the mudflats. For easy bird-watching make your way to East Park to enjoy the facilities of the Wildfowl Refuge, including an observatory and decoy pond. Tel:Refuge Manager, Glencaple 200, for admission times and charges.

□ Seven miles (11km) SE of Dumfries off B725. Map ref 3D2.

790. CLATTERINGSHAW
Deer Museum

The Galloway Deer Museum is situated beside Clatteringshaws Loch with a picnic place and car park nearby. It has many wildlife exhibits, including a collection of antlers. Book here for observation hides in the Red Deer Range where red deer can be seen in their natural surroundings. The Red Deer Range is further down the A712 (about eight miles (12km) NE of Newton Stewart).

□ Seven miles (11km) W of New Galloway on A712. Map ref 3C2.

791. DRUMLANRIG CASTLE
Turrets and trails

The first Duke of Queensberry, who rebuilt Drumlanrig from 1679 onwards, was a feudal chieftain by inheritance, and a powerful contemporary statesman by achievement. His house is semi-baronial, semi-baroque, a sensational mixture of turreted towers and lush Baroque carving, built on a ducal scale in glowing pink stone, and splendidly sited at the centre of a surrounding amphitheatre of hills. An operatic horseshoe staircase leads to the entrance, which is in a tower capped by a dome carved in the form of an enormous ducal coronet. Inside are carved and panelled rooms, and superb pictures, furniture and contents of many dates. There are nature trails and a children's 'adventure' play area in the grounds. House open afternoons, late Apr to Aug. Also over Easter. Tel: Thornhill 30248 for details.

□ Three miles (5km) N of Thornhill off A76. Map ref 3D2.

792. ELLISLAND
Robert Burns/farm

Robert Burns (1759-1796) is generally most associated with the old county of Ayrshire where he was born. The Scottish Tourist Board (STB) has established a detailed Burns Heritage Trail to take visitors to such places as Alloway, Tarbolton and Kirkoswald. However the Heritage Trail has a second segment – in Galloway. Again the STB can supply full details but particular, and less well-known places of interest include the farm of the 'ploughman-poet' at Ellisland.

He took over a farm at Ellisland in 1788 and built a new farmhouse. He also tried to introduce new farming methods, but they were not a success. Here he also began to work as an

Exciseman but, more lastingly, wrote *Tam O'Shanter*, *Auld Lang Syne* and other poems. Ellisland is seven miles (11km) north of Dumfries on A76; an exhibition in the Granary explains his agricultural innovations while plaques around the farm indicate inspirations of various poems.

In 1791 he moved to Dumfries after the failure of his farm at Ellisland to work full-time as an Exciseman. He lived first in a flat in the Wee Vennel (now Bank Street) and finally in a house in Mill Vennel. Both the house and the street of this latter home now bear his name. There is a museum in the house and some scratched verses and other mementoes can also be seen in the *Globe Inn* which he described as his 'favourite howff'. He died in 1796 and was buried in St Michael's churchyard. In 1815, however, his remains were moved to a mausoleum erected to his memory.
□ Map ref 3D2.

793–795. GALLOWAY FOREST PARK
Forest walks/drives

Covers 240 sq miles (62,160 hectares) of scenic forests and hills. It contains 16 lochs, and much of the Rhinns of Kells. The A712 scenic tourist route (The Queen's Way) from New Galloway to Newton Stewart passes through the park. Forest facilities include:
793. Bennan Forest. Raiders Road forest drive (7 miles; 11km) winds from Stroan Loch along picturesque Blackwater of Dee. Forest walks from Stroan Loch car park, ¾ mile (1.2km) and 1¾ miles (2km). Toll drive entered from A762 four miles (6.4km) south of New Galloway.
□ Map ref 3C2.

794. Carrick Forest. Cornish Hill walk on high craggy country with long distance views, three to four miles (4.8-6.4km). Stinchar Falls walk. Six miles (9.6km) along banks of river and forest roads. Panoramic views. Waterfalls recommended after rain. Both walks start from Stinchar car park eight miles (12.8km) south of B741 on Straiton to Glentrool unclassified road. Fly fishing for brown trout in some lochs and for trout and salmon in River Stinchar east of Pinvalley. Permits and bookings from Forest Office at Barr.
□ Map ref 3C2.

795. Kirroughtree Forest. Forest garden with over 60 different species of broadleaved and coniferous trees. Signposted on A75 ½ mile (800m) south of Palnure. Wild goat park in which feral goats can be seen in their natural habitat on A712 seven miles (11.2km) NE of Newton Stewart.
□ Map ref 3C2.

796. GATEHOUSE OF FLEET
Planned burgh

The symmetry of the pleasant stone-built houses set along and off the main road through Galloway to Stranraer is a clue to this burgh's planned origins. It was laid out in the late 18th century as a cotton milling town beside the Water of Fleet. The mill has gone but a slight urban air remains. The main road, of which the wide main street of Gatehouse forms a part, is one of the most attractive in Scotland with fine views both to the sea and inland. Near Gatehouse – 'Kippletringan' in Scott's *Guy Mannering* – are two ruined 15th

Anstruther, Fife, ancient Royal Burgh with a long seafaring tradition

century castles – Ruso and Cardoness.
□ 12 miles (19km) SW of Castle Douglas on A75. Map ref 3C2.

797. GREY MARE'S TAIL
Waterfall

High in the wild grassy fells north-east of Moffat, this spectacular 200ft (60m) waterfall is formed by the Tail Burn plunging from Loch Skeen. Visitors are advised to keep to the paths. A ranger/naturalist service runs guided tours from the car park information point between July and Aug. For details, tel: Chief Ranger, NTS Edinburgh 8212.
□ 10 miles (16km) NE of Moffat on A708. Map ref 3D1.

798. LOCHINCH AND CASTLE KENNEDY GARDENS
Trees and rhododendrons

In the early 17th century a formal garden with grassed terraces was created between two large natural lakes and around the ruined Castle Kennedy. More than a hundred years later a collection of exotic trees and shrubs, including araucarias and rhododendrons, were planted in this settings. It has grown to great size and beauty. Open daily, except Sats, Apr to Sept. Tel: Stranraer 2024.
□ On A75 three miles (5km) E of Stranraer. Map ref 3B2.

799. THREAVE
School of gardening

Island beds, woodland gardens, rock gardens and greenhouses make up the National Trust's school of gardening. Open daily. Tel: Castle Douglas 2575.
□ Off A75, one mile (1.6km) W of Castle Douglas. Map ref 3C2.

800. WHITHORN PRIORY
Early Christian site/walks

Here in the 4th century St Ninian founded the first Christian church in Scotland. No trace of the original building remains. The present priory ruins date from the 12th century, but the adjoining museum (open standard DoE hours) contains much older crosses and tombstones, including Scotland's oldest Christian memorial – the 5th century Latinus Stone. Two moorland walks, each one a round trip of about eight miles (13km), lead to St Ninian's Cave, at Port Castle Bay on the west coast, and the Isle of Whithorn to the south-east, with its 13th century ruined chapel.
□ 10 miles (16km) S of Wigtown on A746. Map ref 3C3.

Fife

The peninsula between the Firths of Tay and Forth. Attractions include Falkland Palace, St Andrews, Dunfermline Abbey. Fife Tourist Authority: Glenrothes: 75441.

801. CULROSS
Town and palace

This remarkable small town of steep cobbled streets and picturesque houses with white, crow-stepped gables and red pantiled roofs, has been superbly restored and cared-for by the NTS. It is a perfect example of an almost unaltered burgh town of the 16th and

17th centuries. Culross 'Palace' and its beautiful painted ceilings was the home of Sir George Bruce, who developed the sea-going trade in salt and coal from Culross at the beginning of the 17th century. The palace is open standard DoE hours.
□ Six miles (9.6km) W of Dunfermline on B9037 off A985. Map ref 6A6.

802. EAST NEUK
Village architecture

On the northern shore of this peninsula is St Andrews – the home of golf. On the southern shore are a string of small villages whose status as royal burghs reflects the area's importance as trade expanded to Scandinavia and the Low Countries during the 16th and 17th centuries. These villages contain some of the most attractive examples of traditional cottage styles from these centuries to be found in Scotland.
Dysart. Not technically on the peninsula and now almost swallowed up by the mostly industrial Kirkcaldy but still with enough fine old houses to make it worth a stop.
Pittenweem. Here the 'little houses' are grouped around a harbour. Five miles (8km) offshore is the Isle of May, a national nature reserve. Enquire locally about trips to the island.
Anstruther. Anstruther Easter and Anstruther Wester are two Royal Burghs on either side of the harbour. The village was an important herring port and a fisheries museum is housed in a group of buildings from various periods which enclose a courtyard adjoining the harbour.
Crail. Oldest of the royal burghs, with crow-stepped, red-tiled houses clustered around the fishing harbour.
□ East Neuk lies between the firths of Forth and Tay. The distance is approx 25 miles (40km) between Dysart and Crail. Map ref 6A5.

803. FIFE FOLK MUSEUM
Rural bygones

Situated in a restored 17th-century Weigh House and some adjoining cottages of a later date, this collection of tools is associated with a variety of regional trades. It includes those of stone mason, saddler, cartwright, reed-thatcher and claypipe maker. Special to this part of Scotland are the exhibits connected with hand-weaving and spinning of flax. Open daily (except Tues), afternoons only, Apr to Oct. Tel: Glenrothes 75441.
□ Ceres, off A916, three miles (4.8km) S of Cupar. Map ref 6A5.

Grampian

A large region with Aberdeen as its principal city. Exceptionally rich in castles of which the most notable are Balmoral (near Ballater) and Braemar. The mountains attract climbers while the salmon rivers of the Dee, Findhorn and Spey draw anglers. Grampian Regional Council: Aberdeen 23401.

804. CRAIGIEVAR CASTLE
Romantic castle

The castles built in and around Aberdeenshire in the late 16th and early 17th centuries are amongst the most

317

romantic and unusual buildings in the British Isles. Craigievar is possibly even more exciting than its neighbours at Crathes and Castle Fraser. From a small ground plan it shoots up seven floors, and at the top swells out into a frenzied skyline of towers and turrets, all built in pink granite. Inside, winding stone stairs and a great hall with rich Elizabethan-style plasterwork. Now owned by the NTS, the castle is open from May to Sept, 2 to 7 daily (not Fri). Grounds open all year. Tel: Lumphanan 635 for details.

□ Six miles (9.6km) S of Alford on A980. Map ref 6A4.

805. CRATHES CASTLE
Castle garden

Ancient Scottish mansion with old yew hedges and a modern garden made in a series of enclosures, each with a distinctive decorative treatment. Fine collection of herbaceous plants and shrubs, many of them rare. Castle contains unique painted ceiling and 16th-century relics. Open all year. Tel: Crathes 525.

□ Three miles (5km) E of Banchory off A93. Map ref 6B4.

806. CULBIN FOREST
Pines and dunes

This vast coniferous forest on the shores of the Moray Firth has been planted to stabilise the shifting dunes of the Culbin Sands. The Forestry Commission started reclaiming this Scottish Sahara in the 1920s, and Culbin Forest is proof of their success. Today it runs conducted tours through the forest and sands from Elgin and Nairn during the summer season. Various stages of reclamation can be seen including thatching the sand with birch wood so trees can be planted on stable ground. The forest is the home of nightjars, crested tits and capercaillies. Further details from FC Conservancy Office, tel: Inverness 32811. The Falconer Museum at Forres has archaeological and geological exhibits relating to the Culbin Sands. Open May to Sept. Tel: Forres 2938. Also to be seen in Forres is Sheno's Stone, thought to commemorate a Viking victory. Across Findhorn Bay – a good place for bird-watching in winter and sailing in summer – is the fishing village of Findhorn. It is the third such village to be founded on this site, its predecessors having been destroyed first by a sandstorm and secondly by a flood.

□ Off A96 to Dyke or forest road from Nairn to Kintessack. Map ref 6A3.

807. CULLEN BAY
Sands and crags

Nearly two miles (3.2km) of white sands, cradled between the craggy headlands of Scar Nose and Logie Head. This lovely bay, overlooked by Cullen, has a series of isolated rocks: The Three Kings, The Bow Fiddle, Boar Crag and Red Crag. The sands here are known to sing or whistle but not as well as the sands at Sunnyside, east of Logie Head. Good clifftop walk to Sunnyside from Cullen along a clifftop path, and on to the 15th century ruins of Findlater Castle perched high above the sea.

□ 13 miles (21km) W of Banff off A98. Map ref 6A3.

808. CULSH
Prehistoric site

Probably the only 'day out' in this book for which you will need a torch. At Culsh is one of the best preserved and most accessible of several 'earth houses' in Scotland. And unlike most other Scottish examples the roof of the Culsh earth house is still intact. You can walk several yards along a curving pitch-black passageway.

Its original function is unclear. It could have been a dwelling but it might also have been a hiding place or simply storage room. Open to visitors at all reasonable times, but if locked apply for key at adjoining Culsh Farm.

□ One and a half miles (2.5km) NE of Tarland beside B9119; grid ref NJ 505055; OS map 37. Map ref 6A4.

809. DUNOTTAR CASTLE
Historic sea castle/walks

Spectacular ruined clifftop fortress approached down a cleft in the rock called St Ninian's Den, where the headland has split from the main cliff. The castle stands on a rocky promontory surrounded on three sides by the sea, 160ft (48m) below. The oldest surviving part of the castle is the 14th century keep. Other outstanding features of this remarkable castle are the gatehouse, the large well and the horrific Whig's Vault, used as a prison in 1685 where many people died. Open to the public all year except Sat in winter. Tel: Stonehaven 62173.

There is a clifftop path to Crawton, three miles (4.8km) to the south, where the sandstone cliffs are breeding grounds for fulmars, razorbills, guillemots and kittiwakes. Catterline, a little further south is a picturesque village, loved by artists, clinging to almost vertical cliffs. There is an RSPB reserve here.

□ Two miles (3.2km) S of Stonehaven off A92. Map ref 6B4.

810. ELGIN
Market town

This market town and Royal Burgh stands beside the River Lossie six miles (9.6km) from the sea. Little remains of the castle but despite substantial plundering the ruined 13th century cathedral is still considered to be one of the finest church buildings in Scotland. Also ruined but still impressive is Duffus Castle, three miles (5km) northwest of Elgin. A 14th century tower crowns the Norman *motte* but what makes the ruin particularly striking is that the keep is still surrounded by a water-filled moat.

□ 22 miles (35km) E of Nairn on A96; Map ref 6A3.

811. MUCHALLS
Cliffs/village

To the north of the castle and village of Muchalls is a fine stretch of cliff scenery. Between the Burn of Elsick and Burn of Muchalls are two great rock arches, called Grim Brigs. The nearby village of Stanathro was entirely rebuilt in the 19th century as a 'model village' for fishermen but the growth of Aberdeen's fishing industry lured away many of the fishermen.

□ Four miles (6.4km) N of Stonehaven off A92. Map ref 6B4.

812. PITMEDDEN HOUSE
Historic garden

The 'Great Garden of Pitmedden' was first made about 1675 and reconstructed in the 1950s. It is a large rectangular parterre, enclosed by a high stone wall and terraces. It has many beds, elaborately patterned with clipped box and filled in summer with annuals, many of which would not have been available in the 17th century. Open all year. Tel: Udny 445.

□ 14 miles (22km) N of Aberdeen near junction of A920 and B999. Map ref 6B3.

813. SANDS OF FORVIE
Dunes and birds

The Sands of Forvie are the least disturbed dune system in Scotland. The NCC has a reserve here with the largest breeding colony of eider ducks in Britain, as well as waders and duck in winter, and four species of tern. The area around Newburgh Bar is closed to the public during the breeding season (Apr to July). Huge parabolic dunes, some rising to 200ft (60m) cover what was once fertile land and villages. The remains of Forvie Church can still be seen and there is evidence of Iron Age settlements. Please keep to the footpaths when visiting this reserve.

□ 14 miles (22km) N of Aberdeen N of Ythan estuary, stretching some four miles (6.4km) N to Collieston. Map ref 6B3.

814. SLAINS CASTLE
Sea castle/cliffs

Extensive 17th century ruins sprawl over the clifftop, north of Cruden Bay. This is the second Slains Castle – the old one, with only a ruined tower still standing, is on a promontory, six miles (9.6km) south, near Collieston. Open to the public at all reasonable times. To the north of the Castle is the Bullers of Buchan, an awesome natural amphitheatre in the cliffs. Dr Johnson, who was rowed into the chasm, called it a 'monstrous cauldron', as the sea rushes through a natural arch in rough weather.

□ Seven miles (11km) S of Peterhead, on A975. Map ref 6B3.

815. TOMINTOUL
Highland village

An altitude of 1160ft (358m) makes this the highest village in the Highlands, although not, surprisingly, in Scotland (see Leadhills). Its foundation in such an apparently hostile environment was the work of the 4th Duke of Gordon who was anxious to try his hand at settlement planning. The village thus established in the late 18th century is very much alive today – as a holiday centre for anglers or coach parties touring the Highlands. Some fine mountain roads radiate from here.

□ 13 miles (21km) SE of Grantown-on-Spey. Map ref 6A3.

Highland

Vast in area but small in population. This region covers not only the mountainous mainland of northern Scotland but also islands such as Skye and Lewis plus many smaller ones. Inverness is largest town. Highlands and Islands

Tourism Council: Grantown-on-Spey 2650 or 2773.

816. ACHARACLE
Walk/loch cruise

A little town on a little road to the Western Isles situated at the southwestern tip of Loch Shiel. Acharacle is popular with anglers and in the summer operates boat trips along the loch which can enable ramblers to combine a day's walk of some 20 miles (32km) with a restful cruise.

Start near Acharacle's *Loch Shiel Hotel* along a track heading east across the base of the mountain slopes to Achnanellen and Pollock, then along a forestry road running on Loch Shiel's eastern shore. Callop river bridge at the loch head leads to A830 – The Road to the Isles between Fort William and Mallaig – and Glenfinnan for the boat journey back down the loch.

□ Acharacle is between 35-40 miles (56-64km) SW of Fort William via either A830/A861 or A82/A861; OS map 40. Map ref 5B4.

817. AFFRIC FOREST
Historic pine forest

This is a classical highland glen: fine mountain, loch and forest scenery, with important remnant of old Caledonian pine forest and good chance of seeing golden eagles. There are four car parks and picnic places by loch and river. Four waymarked forest walks varying from ¾ mile (400m) to a 2½ mile (4km) circuit. Several longer walks round Loch Affric and Loch Benevean through pine reserve and to Dornie, Glen Cannich and Guisachan.

□ Access via A831 from Beauly or Drumnadrochit to Cannich and follow road to Fasnakyle power station. Map ref 5C3.

818. APPLECROSS PENINSULA
Highland seascapes

It is now possible to drive round this remote peninsula on a recently opened road, which has opened up spectacular seascapes formerly seen by very few. Start at the pretty village of Shieldaig on its sea loch and turn west for the coastal village of Kenmore. The coast road runs across trackless moorland past abandoned crofts, always with magnificent views across the sea to the islands of Raasay and Skye. The road from Applecross village to Kishorn is said to be one of the most spectacular in Britain, climbing to the 2054ft (616m) Bealach-nam-Bo – the Pass of the Cattle – before zig-zagging steeply down to Loch Kishorn and the Rassal Nature Reserve, the most northerly ash forest in Britain.

□ Shieldaig is 28 miles (45km) N of Kyle of Lychalsh on A896. Map ref 5C3.

819. ARDNAMURCHAN LIGHTHOUSE
Scotland's Land's End

If you want to stand on the westernmost point of the British mainland don't go to Land's End – the tip of Ardnamurchan is 23 miles (37km) further west. A twisting road follows the south coast of the Ardnamurchan peninsula across barren moorlands which cover the worn down wreck of an

The Cairngorms, Scotland's arctic-alpine rooftop. Snow lies on these bleak high tops for much of the year

Eighe Reserve is the natural pinewood which extends along the shore of Loch Maree, one of the few remaining fragments of the great Caledonian forest. The Glas Leitre Nature Trail starts at the Loch Maree picnic site and takes a circular route of about one mile (1.6km). With binoculars you may see golden eagles, and red or roe deer. The trail is at times steep and rough. Tel: Nature Conservancy Council, Inverness 39431.
☐ The nature trail is on the S side of Loch Maree on A832, but the nature reserve itself also extends W of A896 at junction with A832 at Kinlochewe. Map ref 5C3.

822. BEN NEVIS
The easiest way up Scotland's highest mountain: 4406ft (1343m)

Even its easiest path is a serious affair – especially as the same 'Tourist Route' lures many up it unprepared. It was after all a pony track made for the former Observatory (1883–1904) on the summit.

Yet cloud can cap the mountain when the rest of the sky is clear and it averages only two hours of bright sunshine a day. There is an annual rainfall of nearly 160 inches. Snow may fall up here at any time of year. And it is on the summit and easy slopes where many have died because of sudden changes in weather.

The Tourist Route begins from Glen Nevis, that tremendous glen around the mountain's western and southern flanks. Cross the River Nevis by bridge and follow the road to Achintee Farm on the east bank 2½ miles (4km) from Fort William. The well-worn pony track starts here and rises diagonally round the steep flanks of Meall an Suidhe until it reaches the ruins of Halfway House. To continue up in rocky zig-zags to the lip of Coire na Ciste before turning right for the summit. This ascent of five miles (8km) takes four to five hours plus another three for descent. Fine weather is vital. And be careful on the summit plateau where lingering snow forms huge cornices overhanging space at the edges of the mountain.
☐ Map ref 5C4.

823. CAIRNGORMS
Mountain walks

Glenmore Forest Park on the lower slopes of the Cairngorm mountain range (access via A951 from Aviemore) covers 4000 acres (1620 hectares) of pine forest surrounding Loch Morlich. There are facilities for sailing, canoeing, fishing, car parks and picnic areas, and Glenmore Forest treks for energetic walkers, three to six miles (4.8 to 9.6km) long. Information centre on access road.

But for an even more rugged walk, an exhilarating high-level five-mile (8km) circuit known as the Northern Corries of Cairn Gorm is popular among experienced hill-walkers. *Good weather, hill-walking equipment, including stout footwear and experience are necessary for this walk.*

From the summit of Cairn Gorm descend to the right to the Fiacall Ridge summit (no marked footpath on

enormous volcano, active here 60 million years ago. The lighthouse provides excellent views of the islands of Coll, Tiree, Rhum, Eigg and Muck and is open to the public at the discretion of the keeper, tel: Kilchoan 210. At Sanna Bay, to the north are magnificent white sands and dunes.
☐ Off B8007, five miles (8km) NW of Kilchoan. Map ref 5B4.

820. ARNOL, ISLE OF LEWIS
Crofting village

It would have surprised the original residents of house No 42 that it is now scheduled as an historic monument. It has been preserved as an excellent example of a traditional Hebridean 'black house'. The latter name correctly implies the bleak existence which must have been led by those first inhabitants. Built without mortar and roofed with thatch on a timber framework this 'black house' also has the typical central peat fire in the centre of the kitchen but no chimney. Other black houses even lacked windows and were sometimes shared with the

family's livestock. These low hovels were still being built in the 19th century. Ruined examples can be seen in many parts of the Hebrides but the house at Arnol retains many of its original furnishings, such as they were. Open standard DoE hours except Sun.
☐ Arnol is 15 miles (24km) NW of Stornoway; OS map 8. Map ref 5B1.

821. BEINN EIGHE NATIONAL NATURE RESERVE
Highland wildlife

The principal feature of the Beinn

Scotland

this stretch). Then follow a track along the edge, marked with cairns or stones, and dropping slightly for half-a-mile (0.8km). Ascend Coire an t-Sneachda, staying along the edge before descending into a col. Climb 500ft (154m) to the Cairn Lochan summit. Continue around corrie edge and down to flat grassy area, then more steeply to corrie base. Now follow cairned footpath via Jean's Hut back to Coire Cas car park above Aviemore. OS map in the 1:50,000 series is necessary for this walk, and OS map 36 in the 1:25,000 desirable.
□ Aviemore is on the A9 to Inverness. Map ref 6A4.

824. CALEDONIAN CANAL
Highland canal

There are 60 miles (96km) of waterway but only 22 miles (35km) of canal, as the remaining sections run through natural lochs in the Great Glen. Great problems were encountered during its construction so that although the route was surveyed by Telford in 1801 and building begun under him two years later, the canal was not completed until 1847. The most impressive section is Telford's series of eight locks near Banavie, known as Neptune's Staircase. An exciting inland waterway for the inexperienced, with motor cruisers for hire, although they get booked months in advance for high season. The lochs are also popular with yachtsmen who trail their craft behind their cars.
□ Banavie – the site of Neptune's Staircase – is three miles (5km) north of Fort William and close to the south-western end of the canal. It then flows through Lochs Lochy, Oich and Ness between other canalised sections before reaching the North Sea near Inverness. Map ref 5C4.

825. CALLANISH, ISLE OF LEWIS
Prehistoric monument

The 'Stonehenge' of northern Britain. This magnificent and complex prehistoric monument has a central burial chamber and tall thin monoliths up to 16ft (5m) high. There is also an avenue of standing stones which points to the distant skyline of the mountains of Harris. The scale of the monument, with its stone circle nearly 40ft (12m) in diameter, has been known for fewer than 100 years: the stones were buried beneath layers of peat when excavations began towards the end of the 19th century. This, and its isolated situation, enabled the monument to avoid destruction as well as erosion.
□ 13 miles (21km) W of Stornoway, well sign-posted from the village of Callanish on A858; grid ref NB 213331. Map ref 5B1.

826. CAPE WRATH
Giant sea cliffs

Cape Wrath is the north-westernmost corner of the Scottish mainland. A wild, desolate and forbidding reach of empty hills and boggy moors which end abruptly in dramatic cliffs. The cliffs of Clo Mor, three miles (4.8km) south-east of Cape Wrath are the highest sea cliffs on the mainland of Britain, towering 921ft (280km) above the waves. To visit this remote coast

you must follow the A838 to Durness, cross the Kyle of Durness by ferry and continue by Minibus for the last 11 miles (18km) to Cape Wrath lighthouse (open to the public).Tel: Durness 244 for details. Ferry and bus operate only between May and Sept.
About 1½ miles (2.4km) east of Durness at Leirinmore, is Smoo Cave, a giant cavern at the end of a deep cleft in the limestone cliffs, which visitors can enter on foot.
□ Map ref 5C1.

827. CORRIESHALLOCH GORGE
Gorge and waterfall

Here the thunderous Falls of Measach crash 200ft (60m) into the long wooded gorge of Corrieshalloch four miles (6.4km) south of Loch Broom. Parking by the A835, and a path leading to spectacular suspension bridge viewpoint.
□ On A835 about 12 miles (19km) SE of Ullapool. Map ref 5C2.

828. THE CUILLINS, ISLE OF SKYE
Mountain scenery

The so-called 'Black Cuillins' of Skye are a range of savage rocky peaks. The highest is Sgurr Alasdair, at 3309ft (1099m), but the mountains possess a majesty far greater than their height. The Cuillins are a rock-climber's paradise, but the beauty of their wild skylines can also be enjoyed by motorists and walkers. There are marvellous views from Elgol, Sligachan and Glen Brittle. There are paths from Sligachan into Glen Sligachan, and boat trips operate from Elgol to Loch Coruisk. Details from Isle of Skye Tourist Organisation; Tel: Portree 2137 or Broadford 361 or 463.
□ W of Broadford. Map ref 5B3.

829. CULLODEN
Highland battlefield

The best-preserved crofting farmhouse in Scotland is probably Old Leanach, around which the Battle of Culloden raged on April 16, 1746. It not only survived the battle (the last on British soil), but has been restored to its original thatched form. The farmhouse stands near a huge memorial cairn to the dead and a visitor centre which explains the story of Culloden and the defeat of Bonnie Prince Charlie's Highlanders. The moorland site of the battle (now partly forested) and its clan gravestones can be visited throughout the year. The visitor centre and museum are open daily from mid-Mar to mid-Oct.
A Battlefield Trail follows the battle line of Jacobite and Hanoverian armies past clan and regimental cairns. There is also a Culloden Forest trail running for 2½ miles (4km) through mixed woods and felled areas. Access off B9006 about ½-mile (1800m) west of Culloden Visitor Centre.
One mile (1.6km) to the south-east across the River Nairn are the Stones of Clava, an impressive group of Bronze Age standing stones and cairns.
□ Five miles (8km) E of Inverness on B9006. Map ref 5D3.

830. DUNCANSBY HEAD
Geos/sea stacks

These majestic sandstone cliffs, rising to 210ft (63m) have been ravaged by pounding seas to form caves, chasms (known as geos) arches and huge sea stacks. To the west of the lighthouse is Long Geo, a ravine with 200ft (60m) vertical walls running inland from the sea. Further west is the natural bridge known as The Glupe. The lighthouse commands a fine view of Orkney and the Pentland Skerries. Open to visitors,

but check first; tel: John O'Groats 202. There is an easy walk along the cliffs to the south with grand views of the sea stacks and famous tidal race called The Rispies. A steep path leads down to an empty shingle beach where the cliff has been cut into an arch, called Thirle Door. The beach in the Bay of Sannick to the south-west is known for its cowrie-like shells called 'Groatie Buckies', believed to be lucky.
□ Minor road or cliff path from John O'Groats leads to the lighthouse. Map ref 6A1.

831. DUN CARLOWAY, ISLE OF LEWIS
Archaeological site

A type of building found quite widely in northern Scotland, but nowhere else in the British Isles, are brochs. These are circular buildings dating from late Roman or early Christian times which in effect were highly defensive manor houses or fortified homes. Usually the circular towers had inner and outer walls. One of the best preserved of such brochs is Dun Carloway with walls 11ft (3.4m) thick containing a spiral passageway and still standing up to 30ft (9.25m) high. Standard DoE hours.
□ 15 miles (24km) NW of Stornaway off A858; grid ref NB 190413. Map ref 5A1.

832. DUNNET HEAD
Wild seascape

The road to Dunnet Head and its lighthouse is the most northerly on the British mainland. Although the lighthouse is perched on the cliffs more than 300ft (90m) up, the windows are still sometimes broken by stones hurled up by winter gales. Open to visitors, tel: Thurso 85 272. On a clear day you can see Orkney, the Old Man of Hoy and much of the north coast of Caithness, including Cape Wrath, 60 miles

Curtains of rock fall from Aonach Eagach Ridge to enclose the Pass of Glencoe, scene of the notorious 1692 Massacre

(96km) away. Dunnet Head itself is a great sandstone promontory rising over 400ft (120m) and covered with heather and rare plants, peat bogs and pools. An excellent spot to enjoy the celebrated Caithness sunsets. The cliffs are alive with sea birds. To the south is Dunnet Bay with high white sand dunes offering a complete contrast to the huge cliffs. Access from Dunnet village.

□ From Dunnet on B855. Map ref 6A1.

833. DUNVEGAN CASTLE, ISLE OF SKYE
Historic sea castle

Splendidly hoary castle on a sea-washed rock at the edge of Dunvegan Loch, looking across the water to the curious flat-topped mountains known as Macleod's Tables. Stronghold of the chiefs of the clan Macleod for at least seven centuries. Open afternoons, Easter to mid-Oct (all day June to mid-Sept). Closed Suns.

□ On A863 and A850 at head of Loch Dunvegan. Map ref 5B3.

834. FALLS OF GLOMACH
Waterfall

An arduous 1½-hour climb brings you to the Falls of Glomach, hidden in the hills above wild Glen Elchaig. The falls are among the highest in the British Isles, plunging 370ft (113m) into a deep pool. Stout footwear and suitable clothing essential.

□ Access from unclassified road off A87 at Ardelve, 18 miles (28km) E of Kyle of Lochalsh. or by a 7 mile (11km) long-distance walkers' path through the hills from Croe Bridge on Loch Duich via Dorusdain. Map ref 5C3.

835. FOREST OF HARRIS, ISLE OF HARRIS
Hebridean wilderness

Here the term 'forest' simply means an unenclosed deer moorland. There are no trees in this trackless wilderness. Only hidden lochs, golden eagles, staggeringly beautiful coastlines and magnificent views. Climb the slopes of Clisham, 2622ft (781m), to the north of Tarbert, to see remote St Kilda far to the west. Take the passenger ferry to the Isle of Scarp, off the west coast of the island; arrange a sea-angling trip from Tarbert; watch the spinning of Harris tweed at Ardhasig, on the A959; or tackle the rugged walk through the lonely valley north of Amhuinnsuidhe, off the B887, to see the most magnificent glacially truncated spur in Britain – the overhanging 1400ft (420m) precipice of Sron Ulladale.

□ Off B887. Map ref 5A2.

836. GLENCOE
Wild Highland glen

A main road, the A82, runs through the brooding Pass of Glencoe, the most famous and perhaps also the finest of all the Highland glens. This is Scotland at its most awe-inspiring, with glowering peaks towering above the winding road. Leave the main road and walk along the old road to a rock platform called The Study for magnificent views of the precipices of Bidean nam Bian, 3766ft (1128m). The NTS Visitors Centre at Clachaig explains the area's

geology and the story of the notorious Glencoe Massacre of 1692. Also guided tours run by the Ranger/Naturalist service Centre open Apr to Oct. Tel: Ballachulish 307. Near the centre is the start of the Signal Rock Trail, a short (1½ miles; 2.4km) historic trail through woodland and mountain scenery above the site of the Massacre.

□ SE of Fort William near Ballachulish. The A82 runs out of Ballachulish through the Pass of Glencoe. Map ref 5C5.

837. GLEN SHIEL
Scenic drive

One of the most beautiful roads in Scotland is the A87, which runs the length of wild Glen Shiel to the salty tidal waters of Loch Duich and the romantic Eilean Donan Castle on its rocky islet, with the Cuillins of Skye on the western horizon. Soaring above Glen Shiel are the majestic summits known as the Five Sisters of Kintail. The dominant peak, Sgurr Fhuaran, is 3505ft (1052m) above sea level. One of the best viewpoints for the Five Sisters is the Ratagan Pass, reached from Shiel Bridge at the head of Loch Duich by a narrow zigzag road running over the hills to Glenelg, on the Sound of Sleat.

□ W of Fort Augustus on A87. Map ref 5C4.

838. GLEN ROY
Long gone lake

High on the mountain side of Glen Roy three grassy terraces stand out against the darker heather. These are the 'Parallel Roads' of Glen Roy. They look artificial, so much so that local legends claim them to be hunting roads built by kings of old. In fact they are the signatures of a long vanished Ice Age lake, the old strand lines which show the lake's different levels as it slowly drained. It was impounded by ice, not only in Glen Roy, but also in neighbouring Glens Gloy and Spean. In Glen Roy the lake stood at a maximum height of about 1150ft (350m). As the ice retreated the water level dropped, first to about 1075ft (320m), then to 850ft (260m). Similar lake beach lines have been found at only one other place in Scotland – Rannoch Moor.

□ Glen Roy is off A86 at Roybridge E of Spean Bridge. Map ref 5C4.

839. GLENURQUHART FOREST
Forest waterfall

Falls of Divach walk. Half-a-mile (800m) through oakwoods to falls impressive in spate. Access via Drumnadrochit, turning first right in Lewiston. Reeling Glen picnic place and trails. Woodland setting in miniature glen. Trails 1¼ miles (2km) and 2½ miles (4km) to head of Glen. From A9 Inverness to Beauly turn left to Moniack, left over bridge and left again.

□ Access via A82 from Inverness. Map ref 5D3.

840. GOLSPIE
Old coaching inn/castle

The Sutherland Arms was built in 1808 by the Duke of Sutherland as the first coaching inn in the county on the main post-chaise route from Glasgow and Edinburgh to John o'Groats. This

fishing and holiday town was the administrative centre for the old county of Sutherland.

Just north-east of the town is Dunrobin Castle, the home of the Dukes of Sutherland for 500 years. The castle (much restored in the 1920s) is surrounded by a great park which includes a fine formal garden. Open May-Sept, weekdays and Sun afternoons; tel: Golspie 377.

□ Five miles (8km) SW of Brora on A9. Map ref 5D2.

841. GREY CAIRNS OF CAMSTER
Prehistoric burial chambers

One round cairn and one long cairn have been restored here, both dating from Neolithic times. The round stone-covered chamber is particularly impressive with a diameter of 59ft (18m). The burial chamber within this mound can be reached only by those willing to crawl on hands and knees since the passage is only 3ft (1m) high on average. Access is possible at any reasonable time, as is also the case at 'The Hill o' Many Stones' – around 200 small stones in 22 apparently parallel rows four miles (6.4km) north-east of Lybster off A9.

□ The Grey Cairns are four miles (6.4km) N of Lybster off minor road to Watten. Map ref 6A1.

842. HALKIRK
Planned village

Massive walls remain from the 14th century Brawl Castle on the opposite bank of the River Thurso but this village has its origins in the late 18th century. It was one of the planned settlements created by Sir John Sinclair as part of his scheme to improve the lot of tenant farmers, many of whom had been displaced in favour of vast sheep estates. With its grid-iron street plan the village has a somewhat formal appearance.

□ Six miles (9.6km) S of Thurso off A882. Map ref 6A1.

843. HANDA
Seabird island

This small island with its sandy bays and 400ft (121m) cliffs has been an RSPB reserve since 1962. No permits are needed and boats to Handa are run by local fishermen from Tarbet. Among the main attractions are the Arctic skua and great skua or bonxie, both of which breed here, but the island is also internationally important for its colonies of guillemot, kittiwake, razorbill, fulmar, puffin and shag.

□ Off the Sutherland coast about one mile (1½km) from Tarbet, three miles (5km) NW of Scourie. Map ref 5C1.

844. INVEREWE
Sub-tropical Highland garden

What was once a barren and windswept peninsula has been converted into a marvellous collection of mainly exotic and sub-tropical plants from many parts of the world. The secret is the windbreak of evergreen trees painstakingly nursed to maturity from 1862 when Osgood Mackenzie decided to make a garden in this damp, stormy, but nearly frost-free place. Open all year. NTS. Tel: Poolewe 200.

□ At Poolewe A832 between Lochs

Maree and Ewe. Map ref 5C2.

845. INVERPOLLY NATIONAL NATURE RESERVE
Highland wildlife

The Knockan Cliff Nature Trail explores the east end of this second largest reserve in Britain. Start at the NCC Information Centre at Knockan Cliff (pamphlets on local geology, fauna and flora). This is a marvellous viewpoint for the red sandstone monolithic peaks of Stac Polly, Cul Beag and Cul Mor. The variety of wild habitats – cliff, mountain, loch and woodland – provides a refuge for pine martens, wild cats and golden eagles. Wild flowers to be seen include mountain avens and autumn gentian. You can drive through the Inverpolly reserve by following the A837 beside Loch Assynt to the picturesque fishing village of Lochinver, then heading south on a narrow, tortuous road with stupendous views of Suilven and Stac Polly before meeting the A835.

□ Eight miles (12km) S of Inchnadamph on A835. Map ref 5C2.

846. KINGUSSIE
Highland life

The position of this little 'capital of Badenoch' in the Spey Valley between the Monadhliath Mountains and the Cairngorms has made it an ideal centre for outdoor recreation; ski-ing, angling, pony-trekking, canoeing, sailing (on nearby Loch Insh) and hill-walking. Well worth a visit is the Highland Folk Museum in Duke Street. The farming section has extensive displays illustrating the old-time way of life in the Highlands. A special feature is a tinker encampment. Open daily, Apr to Oct, and weekdays, Nov to March. Tel: Kingussie 307 for details.

□ On A9, 12 miles (19km) S of Aviemore. Map ref 5D4.

847. KINLOCHLEVEN
Military road walk

In the 18th century many so-called 'military roads' were built through the Highlands to link Army garrisons and help control the clans. One such road is known as Major Caulfield's Military Road and part of it can be followed today to make a stirring 15-mile (24km) walk over the hills from Kinlochleven to Fort William. Only the final five miles (8km) of this walk are along a metalled surface. Otherwise the 'road' begun in 1724 is a 'green road' ideal for sturdy walking. It zig-zags up the north-facing hillside above Kinlochleven, strikes west above the Allt Nathrach, cuts through a pass and descends the Allt na Lairige Moire by Lairigmor to Blarmfoldach and Fort William. OS map 41.

□ Kinlochleven is 23 miles (37km) SE of Fort William on A82. Map ref 5C4.

848. LOCH GARTEN STATUTORY BIRD SANCTUARY
Osprey eyrie

This small loch in the Abernethy Forest is famous as the Scottish home of the osprey. Responsive to the intense public interest in these spectacular fish hawks, the RSPB thoughtfully provided a hide from which the breeding ospreys may be viewed at the eyrie. The observation post is open from about mid-Apr to mid-Aug. It is important to keep strictly to signposted path. In this pine forest, loch and moorland habitat you may also see capercaillie, crested tits and crossbills.

□ At Strathspey off B970, four miles (6km) E of Boat of Garten. Map ref 5D3.

849. LOCH NESS
Scenic drive

From Inverness to Fort Augustus the A82 follows the western shores of this immense loch lying in the fault-guided Great Glen. The ruins of Castle Urquhart, midway along the loch, is a good viewpoint. There are deeper and more spectacular lochs in Scotland, but none so famous as Loch Ness, home of the legendary Loch Ness 'Monster'. Controversy still rages over the existence of what some people believe to be a creature akin to the prehistoric plesiosaurs of Jurassic times. There are boat trips and cruises in summer, mostly from Inverness but also from Fort Augustus. For details contact the Tourist Information Office, tel: Inverness 34353.

□ Map ref 5D3.

850. MALLAIG
Island excursions/sailing

A little herring port with a glorious setting on the Sound of Sleat, looking over the sea to Skye. Mallaig is the western end of the 'Road to the Isles' and a major departure point for car ferries and passenger steamers bound for Skye and other islands of the Hebrides. Armadale, barely six miles (9.6km) away, is the nearest point on Skye served by ferry services. Other ferries call at the smaller islands of Rhum, Eigg, Muck and Canna – the round trip itself is a magnificent voyage on a fine day. For information about ferry services, tel: Caledonian MacBrayne, Mallaig 2403. Places of interest within easy reach of Mallaig include the silver sands of Arisaig, and Loch Morar, whose waters – the deepest in Britain – are said to harbour a monster similar to that of Loch Ness.

□ Mallaig is 38 miles (61km) W of Fort William on A830. Map ref 5B4.

851. NAVER FOREST
Forest walks/village

Two areas have been opened up to visitors in this most northerly of FC forests. At Syre the Rossal Trail offers an interpretative walk around Rossal, a pre-clearance village. This starts on a forest road off B873 just over Naver Bridge at Syre (south-east of Tongue). Also in Naver Forest but almost 15 miles (24km) away to the north are the Borgie Walks – short sheltered walks in the north coast's only large woodland area. These are located off A836 at Borgie Bridge five miles (8km) east of Tongue.

□ Map ref 5D1.

852. RHUM
National nature reserve

The mountain summits and cliffs have a specialised alpine flora with plants such as purple saxifrage, moss campion and the rare pennycress. Guillemots, razorbills and fulmars nest on the cliffs and thousands of Manx Shearwaters breed in mountain-top burrows. Golden eagles (3 or 4 pairs) breed regularly on Rhum and an attempt is being made to reintroduce the sea eagle. The dunes, marsh, moor, lochans and sea coast support a large range of wildlife, including seals and otters. Highland cattle, red deer, wild goats and Rhum ponies graze the hill ranges. Tel: Chief Warden, Rhum 26.

□ Access by boat from Mallaig and Arisaig during summer months. Map ref 5B4.

853. SHIN FOREST
Forest waterfalls

Forest walks on either side of Kyle of Sutherland. Shin Falls walk 1½ miles (2.4km) starts at falls car park off A836 Lairg to Bonar Bridge road. Drumliah walk through sheltered larch woods, 1¾ miles (2.8km) starts on A836 north of Bonar Bridge. Carbisdale Castle walk starts from castle grounds, then through woodland to small loch, 2¼ miles (3.6km). From A9 at Ardgay take Culrain road. Keep right to castle gates. Park inside. Raven rock walk is an exciting 1½ miles (2.4km) through precipitous river gorge. From A837 Rosehall to Invershin take first left and first left again.

□ S of Lairg. Access via A837 and A836. Map ref 5D2.

854. STORR FOREST, ISLE OF SKYE
Forest walks

Storr forest walk gives rewarding views of the island of Raasay and the Sound of Raasay. The path continues to a black rock steeple called Old Man of Storr via a 2 mile (3.2km) walk.

□ Seven miles (11km) N of Portree on A855. Map ref 5B3.

855. TROTTERNISH, ISLE OF SKYE
Skye drive

The wild and lonely Trotternish peninsula makes a marvellous circular drive from Portree around this north-eastern corner of the Isle of Skye. Splendid views of Hebridean seascapes at Kilmaluag and Uig, and many remarkable sights, including the Quiraing. This extraordinary mass of rocky towers and pinnacles stands above the A855 at Digg, overlooking Staffin Bay. A rough zigzag path climbs to the natural 120ft (36m) obelisk called the Needle.

□ N of Portree. Map ref 5B3.

Lothian

Edinburgh is overwhelmingly the chief attraction of this busy commercial county. Others include Hopetown House. Lothian Regional Council: Edinburgh 229 9292.

856. ALMONDELL COUNTRY PARK
Country park

Network of paths and bridges constructed by young people from all over the world. Nature trails link with old drove roads over the Pentland Hills.

□ Off A71 at East Calder, 12 miles (19km) SW of Edinburgh. Map ref. 6A6.

857. BASS ROCK
Island gannetry

Bass Rock is a great sea-washed crag, the neck of an old volcano. It is about a mile in circumference and rises to 350ft (107m) a conspicuous landmark off the East Lothian coast. The most famous summer residents are the 7500 pairs of gannets. Shags, fulmars, puffins, kittiwakes and guillemots also breed here. The best views of the seabird colonies may be had from boating around the island and boats run every day in summer from North Berwick – weather permitting. Tel: North Berwick 2373.

□ Near North Berwick. Map ref 6B6.

858. HADDINGTON
Historic country town

An historic and attractive town, with 129 buildings scheduled as of Special Architectural or Historic Interest. This old county town of East Lothian is still largely contained within the triangular medieval pattern laid down in the 12th century. A town trail takes in the most interesting buildings (details available locally) but garden enthusiasts should make for Haddington House where the gardens have been restored in 17th century style. Three miles (5km) north of Haddington is an Iron Age hill-fort known as 'The Chesters' which offers fine views over the Firth of Forth.

□ 17 miles (27km) E of Edinburgh on A1. Map ref 6A6.

859. PRESTON MILL
Working watermill

Preston Mill on the River Tyne is a rare example of a watermill in working order – yet once there were 14 on the Tyne alone. The present building dates from the 17th century, though there has been a mill on this site since the 12th century. Surrounding it are an attractive group of pantiled buildings: a picturesque kiln and former granary and stable out-buildings now used to house an exhibition centre about the mill. The mill is owned by the NTS and is open all year, Sun afternoons; also weekdays, Apr to Sept. Tel: East Linton 426 for details. Nearby, and also owned by the NTS, is Phantassie Doocot – a medieval dovecote with nesting places for 500 birds.

□ At East Linton, 5½ miles (9km) W of Dunbar off A1. Map ref 6B6.

860. THE ROYAL BOTANIC GARDEN
Rare plants

The largest and best-stocked rock garden in the British Isles. Also has many exotic trees, shrubs and herbaceous plants both outdoors and under glass. The main rhododendron collection is now grown at Benmore, near Dunoon, Strathclyde, and tender plants from the southern hemisphere including tree ferns and cabbage palms at Logan Botanic Gardens on the Mull of Galloway. Open all year. Tel: Edinburgh 552-7171.

□ Inverleith Row and Arboretum Road, Edinburgh. Map ref 6A6.

861. SOUTH QUEENSFERRY
Forth bridges

A breezy little Royal Burgh on the shore of the Forth, formerly the port for ancient ferry crossing. Offers magnificent views of the two great bridges now spanning the water – the 1½ mile (2.4km) railway bridge of 1890 is one of the engineering wonders of the world. The road bridge was, when completed in 1964, the longest in Europe. Pier, yachts, seaside walks. Buildings include chapel of Carmelite friary (1440), and Hawes Inn of Kidnapped fame.

□ Nine miles (14.5km) NW of Edinburgh. Map ref 6A6.

862. YELLOW CRAIG NATURE TRAIL
Wood and seashore

The trail begins at the car park attendant's hut. It passes through mature and recent plantations of mixed woodland up to the Yellow Craig itself (part of the core of an ancient volcano) then down to the seashore. The rocks and rock pools have an interesting flora and a number of different seaweeds may be seen when the tide is out. There are also dunes and dune pasture. A nature trail booklet with details of geology, birds and plants, is available.

□ At North Berwick. Access road leads from B1345 towards sea. Map ref 6A6.

Orkney and Shetland

Two groups of islands off the north coast of Scotland. Both are rich in prehistoric sites. Lerwick is main town of Shetland; for tourist information, tel: Lerwick 3434. Kirkwall, with its superb cathedral, is main town of Orkney; tel Kirkwall 2856, for tourist information.

863. COPINSAY, ORKNEY
Bird reserve

This island reserve of 200 acres (80 hectares) is a memorial to the distinguished naturalist James Fisher. The cliffs of Old Red Sandstone give shelter to colonies of breeding seabirds, with especially large numbers of kittiwakes and guillemots. Day visits to the island can be arranged from Newark Bay. Tel: Deerness 245.

□ Off Deerness, Mainland, two miles (3km) SE of the Point of Ayre. Map ref 6C2.

864. JARLSHOF, SHETLAND
Ancient settlement

Continuity of settlement can rarely be demonstrated more vividly than at this site close to Sumburgh airport. The remains of a complex succession of settlements are visible alongside each other here: from the early second millenium BC through the Bronze Age and Iron Age on into the late Dark Ages with a Viking settlement and ending with a farmhouse and manorhouse dating from the 13th and 16th centuries respectively.

Some of the site has been eroded away by the sea, but an extraordinary amount remains to be seen, including houses similar to those at Skara Brae (opp.), a Pictish broch (see page 320, under Dun Carloway) and circular 'wheel houses' from the second and third centuries AD. This remarkable site is open at standard DoE hours.

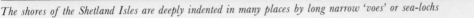

The shores of the Shetland Isles are deeply indented in many places by long narrow 'voes' or sea-lochs

Rugged cliffs of Orkney's Mainland

□ 22 miles (35km) S of Lerwick on Mainland, clearly signposted off A970 at grid ref HU 398096. Map ref 6D3.

865. MAES HOWE, ORKNEY
Prehistoric site

Rarely can the works of prehistoric man be classed as 'architecture' but Maes Howe is the exception: an enormous green mound, 24ft (7.3m) high and 115ft (35m) in diameter, containing a long passage leading to a central chamber 15ft (4.6m) high. The quality of the workmanship is remarkable. The largest stones weigh four tons (4000 kilos) but the great slabs are so accurately levelled and plumbed and so skilfully laid – without mortar – that a knife cannot be inserted between them. Maes Howe was built more than 4000 years ago.

Nearby are further notable works of prehistoric man: the Standing Stones of Stenness; the henge and stone circle of the Ring of Brodgar; and the chambered cairn of the Onston Burial Chamber. Maes Howe itself is open during standard DoE hours. If locked, apply for key at nearby farmhouse.
□ Maes Howe is five miles (8km) E of Stromness on Mainland, Orkney, just off A965 at grid ref HY 318128; OS map 6. The Stones of Stenness are at grid ref HY 306126; Ring of Brodgar at HY 294134; and Onston Burial Chamber is at HY 283117. Map ref 6B1.

866. MARWICK HEAD, ORKNEY
Seabird cliffs

Between May and July these sandstone cliffs are alive with the cries of thousands of seabirds. On these beautiful, flower-covered heights you can find a comfortable spot from which to observe closely the razorbills, guillemots, gulls and kittiwakes. There is access along the shore and on the cliff-top from the south. Open at all times. Tel: RSPB Reserves Dept., Sandy 80551.
□ On Mainland. Access from path N from Marwick Bay (W from B9056). Map ref 6B1.

867. MOUSA BROCH, SHETLAND
Iron Age site

Not the most accessible of locations but this is the best preserved example of the Iron Age brochs in Scotland (see page 320 under Dun Carloway). It still stands over 40ft (12m) high and is open to visitors standard DoE hours (page 240). Visitors will have experienced something of a 'day out' before reaching the broch. It is on an island off Sandwick. Boats can be hired at Sandwick on Sat and Sun mornings throughout year (weather permitting) and on afternoons, May to Sept.
□ Sandwick is seven miles (11km) S of Lerwick off A970. Map ref 6D2.

868. SKARA BRAE, ORKNEY
Prehistoric site

An Atlantic storm in the 19th century uncovered the stone huts of this Neolithic settlement which had been buried by sand dunes for almost 3000 years. The sandstorm which had destroyed Skara Brae must have been almost as dramatic as the gales and rain that uncovered it. In the rooms of the village's seven houses the cupboards, 'dressers' and beds recall life in Neolithic times.
□ Seven miles (11km) N of Stromness, along signposted footpath for 700 yards (640m) off B9056; grid ref HY 231188. Map ref 6B1.

869. STROMNESS, ORKNEY
Orcadian harbour

One of the two main towns of Mainland, largest of the Orkney Islands. Although it has no one building which can compare with Kirkwall's Cathedral, the narrow winding streets of Stromness exert great charm. The life of Stromness revolves around its harbour overlooking Hoy Sound and beyond it, Scapa Flow. Stromness has been used as a harbour since Viking days and is the main port for Orkney. Orkney Natural History Museum in Stromness opens Wed and Thur mornings.

□ 18 miles (29km) W of Kirkwall on A964; OS map 6. Map ref 6B1.

The most densely populated region since it covers the Glasgow conurbation but still containing attractive countryside – the coast and sea lochs from the Clyde to Oban, and islands such as Arran and Mull. Other attractions include Fingal's Cave and the Burns Country of Ayrshire. Strathclyde Regional Council: Glasgow 221 6136/7.

870. AILSA CRAIG
Island gannetry

This granite island, two miles (3.2km) in circumference is the home of a large seabird colony with a considerable gannetry. These magnificent seabirds breed only at 16 sites around Britain. Also razorbills, guillemots, kittiwakes, puffins. Tel: Girvan Tourist Information, Girvan 2056.
□ 10 miles (16km) offshore W of Girvan. Map ref 3B2.

871–2. ARGYLL FOREST PARK
Forest drives/walks

Covers 100 sq miles (25,900 hectares) of rugged West Highlands broken by sea lochs. Over 165 miles (265km) of forest roads open to public on foot. Facilities include:

871. Benmore Forest. Picnic places: Finart Bay, sandy beach on Loch Long at forest edge. Off A880 one mile (1.6km) N of Ardentinny; Rubha Garbh on wooded shore of Loch Eck. Off A815 11 miles (17.7km) N of Dunoon. Black Gates to Puck's Glen or Gairletter walk. Path up gorge to Puck's Glen doubles back to start or to car park. Main route continues over Creag Mhor 1500ft (457m) to Gairletter. View of Loch Long and Firth of Clyde. Starts off A815 six miles (9.6km) north of Dunoon. Ardentinny to Carrick Castle walk. Forest road and open hill giving views of Loch Goil and Loch Long. Starts from Finart Bay picnic place.
□ Map ref 5C6.

872. Glenbranter Forest. Dornoch Bay picnic place on shore of Loch Eck off A815 12 miles (19.3km) north of Dunoon. Two waymarked hill walks of about eight miles (12.8km) from Starchurmore and Coire Ealt to Lettermay on Loch Goil. Routes start off A815 17 and

Inverary Castle, seat of the chiefs of Clan Campbell since the 15th century

13 miles (27.3 and 20.9km) north of Dunoon.
□ Map ref 5C6.

873. BONAWE
Industrial archaeology

Despite the existence of granite quarries the mountainous shores of Loch Etive around Bonawe seem remote from an industrial development. Yet here for a time in the 18th century was Scotland's only source of natively-produced iron. Using the abundant local timber for making charcoal, Richard Ford built a furnace and forge to smelt iron brought in by sea from his native Furness. The quality of the product (and the low wages paid to Scottish workers) enabled the works to continue in use until 1873, in spite of increased competition from coke-fired smelting introduced in better-sited lowland areas. After many years of decay the Bonawe works, including the furnace, storage sheds and workmen's cottages, have been restored by the Scottish Office as a memorial to the first industrial settlement in Argyllshire.
□ Nine miles (14km) E of Oban on B845 off A85; OS map 49. Map ref 5C5.

874. CRARAE WOODLAND GARDEN
Woodland garden

Exotic trees and shrubs in a glen and ravine. Rich autumn colours. Open daily, Mar to Oct. Tel: Furnace 286.
□ One mile (1.6km) NE from Minard on A83. Map ref 5C6.

875. CRINAN CANAL
Scenic waterway

The canal is only nine miles (14km) long but it saves the long boat trip round the often stormy Mull of Kintyre. When constructed at the end of the 18th century it was scarcely envisaged that the principal users of the canal would be yachtsmen heading for the Western Isles. This short cut between Loch Fyne and the Atlantic waters makes an interesting day trip. Nearby, on the northern shores of Crinan Loch, is Duntroon Castle, one of the oldest inhabited castles in Scotland.
□ The canal runs from Ardrishaig on Loch Fyne at E end to Crinan on the Sound of Jura at W end. Map ref. 5C6.

876. CULZEAN
Castle and country park

Culzean Castle (NTS) is a magnificent mock-Gothic stronghold begun by Robert Adam in 1777 around an older castle of the Kennedys. The castle is open daily, Apr to Sept.

The spacious grounds of Culzean are the site of Scotland's first country park, established in 1969. Attractions include a walled garden, swan pond, camellia house and orangery, deer park, beach and cliff walks with panoramic views of Bute, Arran, Ailsa Craig and Kintyre. The red sandstone farm buildings designed by Robert Adam now contain an Interpretation Centre with exhibition, shop and Ranger/Naturalist service. Grounds always open; Exhibition Centre open Mar to Oct.
□ Near Maybole, on A719, 12 miles (19km) S of Ayr. Map ref 3B1.

877. DRUMADOON BAY, ISLE OF ARRAN
Semi-precious stones

In an island of geological treasures, the intrusive igneous sill at Drumadoon Point, near Blackwaterfoot on the A841 on the western side of the island, is a major highlight. Here columnar cliffs mark the intruded layer of hard quartz porphyry which was forced in molten form between horizontal, bedded sandstones, some 60 million years ago. Occasional pebbles of amethyst, topaz, or agate may be found on beaches.

Two miles (3km) north is the King's Cave and its legendary associations with Robert the Bruce. For a magnificent walk into the mountainous granite heart of northern Arran, follow lonely Glen Iorsa from Dougrie, north of Machrie Bay. The steep-sided, U-shaped glacial trough, though not as spectacular as the more famous Glen Rosa, is wilder and more open and takes you into an imposing amphitheatre of high peaks.
□ On W coast of Isle of Arran off A841. Map ref 3B1.

878. INVERARAY
Castle/planned town

Most visitors come to see the castle – home of the Dukes of Argyll and hereditary seat of the chiefs of the Clan Campbell since the 15th century. But the attractive white-walled town of Inveraray itself is interesting as a fine example of a new or estate town. The original village was burnt down in 1644 and built in present form as a Royal Burgh during the second half of the 18th century when the castle was also rebuilt. The castle is usually open to visitors daily, Apr to Oct, but is closed on Fri, Apr to June. Tel: Inveraray 2203 for details.
□ Inveraray stands on the N shore of Loch Fyne mid-way between Glasgow and Oban. Map ref 5C5.

879. ISLE OF IONA
Monastic remains

This tiny island was the most important centre of Christianity in northern Britain. Only three miles (5km) long and 1½ miles (2.4km) wide it is a grey spine of rock separated from Mull by the translucent green waters of the Sound of Iona. It was to Iona that St Columba came from Ireland in 563 AD to bring Christianity to Scotland and a 13th century abbey now stands on the site where Columba founded his monastery. Iona quickly became a place of pilgrimage and a burial ground of chiefs and kings. Both Duncan and his alleged murderer, Macbeth, are among the 48 Scottish kings buried at St Oran's Cemetery on the island.
□ Iona lies off the SW coast of Mull and is reached by two ferries. A car ferry runs between Oban and Craignure on Mull. A passenger ferry runs from Fionnphort to Iona. Also day trips in summer from Oban which pass Fingal's Cave on Staffa and stop at Iona. Map ref 5B5.

880. ISLAY
Hebridean isle/bird-watching

The most southerly of the Inner Hebrides. The island is 25 miles (40km) long by 20 miles (32km) wide with a great variety of landscapes – woods, peat bogs, moors, lochs, rivers, dunes, cliffs and beaches. Some of the beaches are magnificent – Laggan Bay has six miles (9.6km) of sand but there are also tiny sandy creeks dotted around the coast such as Kilchiaran Bay west of Port Charlotte. The variety of habitats allied to its position has made it a haven for birds – and bird-watchers. The island is the principal wintering resort in the world of barnacle geese but 96 other species were spotted in just two days during one recent winter. Good spots to see birds are on lochs Gruinart and Indaac and off the cliffs of the Mull of Oa in the south of Islay. Other attractions of the island include its many whisky distilleries.
□ Port Ellen and Port Askaig are the ports of access to Islay from the Mull of Kintyre. Map ref 5B6.

881. JURA
Hebridean island

The Paps of Jura, three conical quartzite peaks all over 2400ft (731m) high, dominate this ruggedly beautiful island. Jura means 'Deer Island', and there are 20 times more red deer than people on this, one of the most sparsely populated islands of the Inner Hebrides. There is only one road, the A846, which runs from Feolin Ferry up the east coast to Ardlussa. Raised beaches, formed towards the end of the Ice Age, can be seen on the deserted west coast, while to the north, the notorious Corrievreckan Whirlpool can be seen – and heard – seething and rumbling in the narrow strait between Jura and Scarba. This dangerous tide-race is at its fiercest during the spring tides of early autumn.
□ Jura can be reached by ferry from Kennacraig on A83 south of Tarbert to Port Askaig on Islay, where another ferry crosses the narrow Sound of Islay to Feolin. Map ref 5B6.

882. KILBARCHAN
Weaver's cottage

Weaving was the original cottage industry. Only with the coming of water and steam power did production of cotton and woollen goods begin to move to the new factories from their old cottage base. Here, in Kilbarchan, a 1723 weaver's cottage has been preserved as a museum of the old days complete with the final two hand looms used in a village that once had nearly 400 such looms.
□ 10 miles (16km) W of Glasgow off A737 or A761. Map ref 5D6.

883. KILDALTON, ISLE OF ISLAY
Celtic crosses

Two of the finest sculptured Celtic crosses in Scotland are located in an isolated churchyard at the south-eastern tip of Islay. It is a wonderfully peaceful setting reached by a drive along a narrow unclassified road from Ardbeg. Shortly north of the Kildalton churchyard the road peters out altogether but it is worth continuing in this direction for splendid views over the Sound of Jura.
□ 7½ miles (12km) NE of Port Ellen at grid ref NR 458509; OS map 60. Map ref 5B6.

884. KILMARTIN
Prehistoric remains

One of the few areas of Scotland to rival Orkney or the other northern isles of Scotland in the richness of prehistoric remains. The valley which widens westward to the shore of Loch Crinan has several impressive monuments from Neolithic and Bronze Age times. Outstanding – and more easily accessible than some – are Temple Wood stone circle; five cairns that form a linear cemetery from the Bronze Age; and the Dunchraigaig cairn. Kilmartin church also contains a fine collection of medieval crosses.
□ Kilmartin is eight miles (13km) N of Lochgilphead on A816 with the monuments mentioned above shown on the map. OS map 55. Map ref 5C5.

885. KYLES OF BUTE
Scenic seaway

The Kyles of Bute are the beautiful narrow channels separating the Isle of Bute from the Cowal peninsula. It is a seaway much loved by yachtsmen and also by generations of Scots who grew up with the tradition of going down the Clyde on the old paddle-steamers of yesteryear. Ferries ply between Wemyss Bay on the Scottish mainland and Rothesay, Bute's chief resort and steamer port, and ferries from Colintraive cross the Kyles themselves. In summer, excursions through the Kyles are a popular attraction.
□ Map ref 5C6.

886. LEADHILLS
Ancient village

As its name suggests, this area on the northern edge of the Lowther Hills has had a long history of mining, probably going back to Roman times and for not just lead but silver and possibly gold as well. The present scattered village is typical of mining communities, even though lead mining ceased a century ago. It lies at a height of 1350ft (416m) – only neighbouring Wanlockhead at 1380ft (425m) is higher in Scotland. Clearly it was only the prospect of a rich find which encouraged miners and their families to endure such a hostile environment. However this setting has become an asset: the village is now a ski resort.
□ 25 miles (40km) S of Lanark on B797 off A74; OS map 72. Map ref 3D1.

Iona: last resting-place for Macbeth and 47 other kings of Scotland

887. LOCHWINNOCH RESERVE
Wildfowl reserve

This shallow loch and the surrounding marsh provide a perfect wildfowl habitat as well as some interesting marshland and woodland plants. There are birds to see here in most seasons. In summer, good numbers of breeding duck, black-headed gulls and great crested grebes (rare in this part of Scotland). In autumn many waders, and excellent winter wildfowl. Nature Centre. Limited opening. Tel: RSPB Reserves Dept., Sandy 80551 for information.
□ Lochwinnoch, 12 miles (19km) SW of Paisley. Map ref 5C6.

888. MULL OF KINTYRE
Remote peninsula

The lonely lighthouse at South Point on this long and narrow peninsula can be reached by a steep and twisting narrow road from the Bridge at Carskey to the west of Southend off B842. The lighthouse is open to the public, tel: Campbeltown 83234. The southernmost point on the rocky coastal cliffs entails several miles walk across wild moorland with fine views to the island of Sanda, and further off, the coastline of Co Antrim. To the east are beautiful sandy bays on either flank of the rocky headland of Keil Point. Here is the traditional first landfall on Scottish soil of St Columba, en route from Ireland to Iona.
□ Take A83 to Campbeltown, then B842. Map ref 3A1.

889. NEW LANARK
Historic village

This cotton-milling village was built on the wooded slopes to the south of Lanark to exploit the potential of water power. It is popularly associated with the social reforms of Robert Owen, but was created in 1784 by Owen's father-in-law David Dale in conjunction with Richard Arkwright of Cromford (see page 295). Dale himself was an enlightened employer, taking on many dispossessed crofters and housing them in cottages which he built to remarkably high standards for that time. The original mill building survives as do many of the houses which are slowly being restored to a condition suitable for their place in British industrial history.
□ One mile (1.6km) SW of Lanark off A72. Map ref 3D1.

890. OBAN
Hebridean springboard

Life here revolves around the harbour which serves as the mainland port for many ferry services to islands of the Inner and Outer Hebrides. In the summer there are also regular day excursion trips by steamers to places such as Iona and Staffa. A few small sailing boats can be hired in Oban to those with experience.

But Oban is also a good base for a car drive exploring the sea lochs of Scotland which are among the impressive results of the Ice Age in the British Isles. The main characteristics of sea and fresh water lochs are their depth and length.

To get the best out of a drive in this area you need not only a good map (as you do anywhere) but sometimes patience since the most dramatic roads can be narrow with passing places and plagued by caravans. The rewards are astonishing. A round trip from Oban via Connel, Gleann Soloch, Barcaldine, Ballachulish, Port Appin, Ballachulish Bridge, Kinlochleven and back to Oban again involves around 110 miles (176km) past 3500ft (1080m) mountains, forests, beaches and three sea lochs – Etive, Creran and Leven – all of which open into Loch Linnhe, the biggest sea loch of them all.

Particular points of interest along the way include Dunstaffnage Castle (off the A85 at Dunbeg); the National Trust gardens at Ardchattan Priory; Port Appin peninsula with a sailing school and ferry to the island of Lismore (good for sea birds); several forest trails signposted by the Forestry Commission; Lettershuna for horse riding or boat trips to the tiny island of Shuna; wildlife from buzzards to seals.

The OS Tourist map, Ben Nevis and Glencoe, one inch to the mile (1:63,360) covers the entire area of the car drive suggested above and for this it is the best value. The tourist office at Oban, tel: Oban 3122 or 3551 is the best source of information about the area, including ferry services.
□ Map ref 5C5.

891. SEIL ISLAND
Atlantic bridge

The only Hebridean island linked by a bridge to the Scottish mainland. This hump-backed stone bridge at Clachan designed by Thomas Telford in 1792, is amusingly ·described as the 'Bridge over the Atlantic'. Follow the road fringed with montbretia ,as far as the tiny port of Easdale, on the west of the island. This former slate quarrying village and its brightly painted cottages stand below a prominent hill which gives excellent views of Mull, Jura and the smaller isles of the Firth of Lorn. A good centre for sea-angling and boat trips, with a car ferry to Luing from the south of the island on B8003.
□ On B844 from Kilniver, 15˙miles SW of Oban. Map ref 5B5.

Tayside

A county set around Scotland's longest river – the Tay – and rich in farming land. Attractions include Perth, Blair Castle, Huntingtower Castle. Tayside Regional Council: Dundee 23281.

892. BEN LAWERS VISITOR CENTRE
Arctic-alpine wild flowers

The lime-rich slops of lofty Ben Lawers, 3984ft (1196m), are renowned as a last refuge for rare arctic-alpine flora. The NTS has established a Visitor Centre here, which tells the story of the Ben, from the Ice Age to the present day. Nature trails start from adjoining car park, and there are guided tours with ranger/naturalists during the holiday season (open daily, May to Sept). Please do not pick or uproot any plants.
□ Off A827 midway between Aberdeen and Crianlarich. Minor road turns off near W end of Loch Tay to Visitor Centre near Loch Na Lairige. Map ref 5D5.

893. DRUMMOND CASTLE GARDENS
Castle and gardens

A 13-acre parterre laid out in the form of an elaborately decorated St Andrews's Cross on the floor of a valley below the steep escarpment off which stand the dwelling house and the keep of an old castle. In the middle is a multiple sundial with about 50 separate dials and bearing the date 1632. Open regularly, Apr to Oct. Tel: Muthill 321.
□ Three miles (5km) S of Crieff on A822. Map ref 5D5.

894. DUNKELD
Market town

The charm of this small town is partly its setting in the wooded valley of the Tay. But it also stems from excellent buildings representing several periods of history. The cathedral dates back to the 9th century but although the parish church is formed by the restored 14th century choir it is largely in ruins. However the pattern of streets still reflects the town plan laid down in the Middle Ages.

The 'little houses' of the town (in Cathedral Street and High Street, for instance) were built in the years of the late 17th and early 18th centuries when Dunkeld was awarded burgh status for merchants to trade between Lowland ports and Highland markets. One further building of note is the bridge built by Telford in 1809 across the Tay. Pony trekking, angling, nature and forest trails nearby.
□ 15 miles (24km) NW of Perth on A9. Map ref 6A5.

895. EDZELL CASTLE AND GARDENS
Early 17th century castle garden

A small parterre completely enclosed by walls and the ruins of an old castle. The walls are elaborately carved and further ornamented with niches arranged in a chequer pattern, and intended to be filled with plants. This unique and beautiful Renaissance garden was completed in 1604. Open all year. Tel: Edzell 631.
□ Six miles (9.6km) N of Brechin off B966. Map ref 6B4.

896. GLAMIS
Castle/rural museum

The original 14th century Glamis Castle was rebuilt in the 17th century in the romantic, conical-turreted style of a French château. It is reputedly haunted, and has strong royal connections, having been the childhood home of Queen Elizabeth the Queen Mother and the birthplace in 1930 of Princess Margaret. The castle is open afternoons only, May to Sept. Glamis itself is a picturesque village on the edge of the Vale of Strathmore with the Sidlaw Hills in the background. Some old cottages in the village have been restored to house the Angus Folk Museum. The museum contains agricultural exhibits from the largely self-supporting community of Angus over the past 200 years.
□ Four miles (6.4km) S of Kirriemuir at junction of A94 and A928. Map ref 6A5.

897. LOCH LEVEN NATURE CENTRE
Lochside wildlife

This lochside reserve consists of 298 acres (120 hectares) of shoreland, farmland, birch-wood and heather. Visitors are asked to keep to the Nature Trail and picnic area. The nature Centre is a converted farm building which has exhibition, sales and observation facilities. There is a wide range of birds to be seen including terns and many wading birds. In winter there may be as many as 70 different species, with spectacular flocks of geese, swans and duck. No dogs allowed. Open most days (except Fri). Tel: Warden, Kinross 2355.
□ Eight miles (15km) SW of Kinross on shores of Loch Leven (on B9097). Map ref 6A6.

898. MONTROSE
Tidal basin

With its gable-ended houses and narrow winding closes, Montrose is an old town full of character and seafaring atmosphere. Indeed, the town is almost surrounded by water, standing on the mouth of the River Esk with the huge tidal lagoon of Montrose Basin at its back. The harbour provides a haven for yachtsmen and a back-up service for North Sea oil exploration, and the basin itself is a favourite haunt for birds, especially wintering geese.
□ Map ref 6B4.

899. PITLOCHRY FISH PASS
Salmon-watching

From May to mid-November, visitors can watch salmon going through the 'fish pass' on their way upstream to their spawning grounds. Windows set in an underground chamber provide a good viewing point. There is also a permanent exhibition with aquaria, working models of fish passes and an audio-visual display. The Linn of Tummel Nature Trail guides you up-river to the Linn. This was known as the Falls of Tummel before the water level was raised by the Pitlochry Dam to form Faskcally Reservoir. Trail booklet.
□ The Dam is at S end of Loch Faskcally, signposted on A9. Map ref 5D5.

900. ROAD TO THE ISLES
Scenic drive

Though famed in song this well-known Scottish road, past Loch Tummel and Loch Rannoch now goes no further than the railway station on Rannoch Moor. The NTS have a visitor centre at Killiecrankie, open Easter to mid-Oct in the wooded gorge where the Jacobites routed the English troops in 1686. Four miles (6.4km) from here on B8019 is the Loch Tummel Visitor Centre at Queen's View (FC), open daily. Queen's View is where Queen Victoria enthused about the view over Loch Tummel to stately Schiehallion's brooding summit, 3547ft (1064m). The road continues to Tummel Bridge and the thick birch and pine woods along the shores of Loch Rannoch to the lonely peat bogs of Rannoch Moor.
□ B8019 from Pass of Killiecrankie then B846. Map ref 5D5.

Ireland

Thatched cottage at Articlave, Co Londonderry

Northern Ireland

901. ANTRIM COAST AND GLENS
Area of Outstanding Natural Beauty

The 68 miles (110km) of coastline between Larne and Portrush is one of the most beautiful in the British Isles and is of exceptional interest to geologists. Its scenic highlights include Rathlin Island, the 37,000 basalt columns of the Giant's Causeway, the Carrick-a-Rede rope bridge near Ballycastle, the lovely White Park Bay owned by the National Trust, and the spectacular limestone cliffs and caverns of the White Rocks near Portrush (see individual entries). The Antrim Coast Road is one of the most scenic corniche routes in Europe, though there is always the temptation to turn inland and explore the famous Glens of Antrim, nine green fingers thrusting deep into the lonely moorlands of the Antrim Mountains, all of which are included within this glorious AONB. Glenariff (see separate entry), with its gorges and waterfalls, Ossian's Cave and the Stone Age 'axe factory' on Tievebulliagh Mountain are other places of interest.
□ Map ref 7F1.

902. LAGAN VALLEY
Area of Outstanding Natural Beauty

Small area beside the River Lagan between South Belfast and Lisburn. You can follow the river for seven miles (12km) on a gentle towpath walk from Molly Ward Locks, on the Stranmillis Embankment, to Shaw's Bridge and Minnowburn Park, passing locks, rapids, woods and marshes.
□ Co Down. Map ref 7F2.

903. LECALE COAST
Area of Outstanding Natural Beauty

The Lecale Peninsula, between Newcastle and the narrows of Strangford Lough, is renowned for its immense sandy beaches. At Tyrella Strand on Dundrum Bay you can actually drive along the 3½ mile (6km) beach. Centre of this dune-scaped coast is the little port of Ardglass, renowned for its prawns. Now no more than a pleasant fishing village it was a far more important settlement in the early days of the Anglo-Norman colonisation of Ireland. This is apparent in the existence of no fewer than seven castles or fortified tower houses. One of the castles is now a small museum. Fine walks go south to St John's Point, and north to Guns Island (accessible at low tide), where seals sometimes gather. Inland the landscape is rich with historic remains for this is St Patrick's country where every hill and valley seems to have links with Ireland's patron saint.
□ Co Down. Map ref 7F3.

904. MOUNTAINS OF MOURNE
Area of Outstanding Natural Beauty

A celebrated landscape of rounded, swelling summits – 15 of them rising above 2000ft (610m) within a 25-mile (40km) circle. The innermost heart of the Mournes is a roadless wilderness of heather, lakes and tumbling streams. The area also includes Rostrevor, Castlewellan and Tollymore Forest Parks, all open to the public, and the Down coast between Newcastle and Warrenpoint. Annalong, with its boats, stone quays, cottages and mountain backdrop, is one of the most picturesque fishing harbours in the British Isles. Another 'must' for visitors is the well-preserved Norman keep guarding the entrance to Carlingford Lough at Greencastle. Opposite Greencastle is the quiet seaside resort of Greenore with its long shingle beach.
□ Co Down. Map ref 7F3.

905. NORTH DERRY
Area of Outstanding Natural Beauty

Vast, empty triangle of dunes and low-lying farmland thrusting out towards Donegal across the neck of Lough Foyle. Facing the Atlantic breakers is Magilligan Strand which is considered to be the longest beach in Ireland, seven miles (11km) of shell-strewn sands, with excellent bass fishing. The loughside mudflats attract large numbers of duck, wild geese and wading birds. Inland to the east rises the spectacular rocky escarpment of Binevenagh Mountain 1260ft (384m).
□ Co Londonderry. Map ref 7E1.

906. SPERRIN MOUNTAINS
Area of Outstanding Natural Beauty

This sparsely populated mountain range stretches for about 40 miles (64km) from west to east and is bounded by the towns of Omagh, Strabane, Cookstown, Dungannon and Magherafelt. The highest point, Sawel, is only 2240ft (684m), but the countryside is hauntingly beautiful, rich in prehistoric standing stones, and threaded by salmon rivers and trout streams such as the Mourne, Ballinderry and Moyola. Here, too, is Gortin Glen Forest Park with its lakes, wildfowl and Sika deer. Of the numerous scenic drives, one of the best climbs is from Desertmartin over Slieve Gallion to lonely Lough Fea.
□ Co Londonderry and Co Tyrone. Map ref 7D2.

907. STRANGFORD LOUGH
Area of Outstanding Natural Beauty

Sheltered by the long arm of the Ards Peninsula, this great sea lough is almost land-locked, being connected to the Irish Sea by the turbulent tidal narrows at Portaferry. Through this half-mile (800m) gap 400 million tons of water pass twice daily with the changing tides. The fierce current here gives the lough its name for Strangford is Norse for 'violent inlet'. With its enormous flocks of wild duck, waders and wintering geese, its 70 islands and basking seals, the lough and its shores are of immense interest to naturalists. The A20 runs close to the water in many places giving good opportunities for bird watching. There is also good sea angling – skate and tope are the main attraction – and sailing. Mahee Island, reached from the shore by a causeway, has the ruins of Nendrum Monastery (see individual entry), destroyed by the Vikings in 974.

The area has all the classic features of a glaciated lowland and the 49 mile (79km) circuit round the lough from Newtownards takes in many of them, especially drumlins, the low, whale-backed hills of boulder clay deposited by the ice sheets. The sinuous coastline of the lough has been produced by the drowning of numbers of these by the sea. Many of the drumlin islands are linked to the mainland by causeways.
□ Strangford Lough lies 10 miles (16km) SE of Belfast. It is circuited by A20, A21, A22 and A25. Map ref 7F2. 7F3.

Co Antrim

Antrim forms the north-east corner of Ireland. Much of it is an irregular upland plateau dropping sharply to the sea on the north and east. Lough Neagh, the Bann Valley and the Glens of Antrim are major landscape features. Belfast is situated where the River Lagan enters Belfast Lough. Tourist office: Antrim 4131.

908. BALLINTOY
Sands, cliffs and downs

From the coast road at Ballintoy there is a view to the west which seems alien to Ireland. The patches of downland sloping seawards to dazzling white chalk cliffs, the beautiful curve of the strand and the sand dunes of White Park Bay, suggest south-east England

Some common Irish place-names and their English meanings

Modern form	Meaning
Ard	Height
Bal	Place or town
Curragh	Marsh or plain
Dun	Castle or fort
Enis	Island or water meadow
Kel	Church
Lis	Enclosure
Lough	Lake
Seari	Old
Tipper	Well

rather than Ireland. This beautiful stretch of coast is owned by the National Trust. A rich area for naturalists and geologists with faults, landslips, raised beaches and fossils. The cliff path looks across the bay to Sheep Island, breeding ground for many sea birds. The bay is noted for its birds of prey including buzzards, kestrels and peregrines. A mile-long (1.6km) nature trail, shows the flora of sand and chalk as well as geological features. The ready supply of flints in the chalk helped support a relatively large prehistoric population and numerous remains have been found here. The nearby hamlet of Portbraddan, nestling in the cliffs, has the smallest church in Ireland. The ruin of Dunseverick Castle is perched on the edge of a cliff. The castle marks the northern end of the oldest road in Ireland, used by Celts to make the crossing to Scotland. A precipitous road leads to the small harbour of Ballintoy. To the east of the village is the extraordinary Carrick-a-Rede rope bridge which spans a wide chasm between the mainland and a steep rocky island. The bridge, used in summer by local fishermen, swings some 8oft (24m) above the sea.

□ Ballintoy is on B15 off A2, White Park Bay runs along the A2 to W of Ballintoy. Map ref 7E1.

909. CUSHENDUN
Scenic and architectural variety

This attractive village on the North Antrim coast has two claims to fame: one geological, the other architectural. The 10 miles (16km) along the narrow road from Fair Head past Murlough Bay and Torr Head to Cushendun takes the traveller through a remarkable variety of landscapes in a short distance. The rocky, treeless plateau of Fair Head changes into a narrow belt of open chalk downland which drops to the wooded slopes of Murlough Bay. The coastal slopes here are formed from a landslip of chalk and basalt. Then, at Cushendun, there are sea caves cut in Old Red Sandstone conglomerate. Here Scotland's Highland Border Fault (with the Southern Upland Fault it encloses Scotland's Midland Valley) can be traced across the sea south-westwards into Northern Ireland as it comes onshore at Cushendun. The architectural interest springs from the fact that the village was largely built by Welsh architect

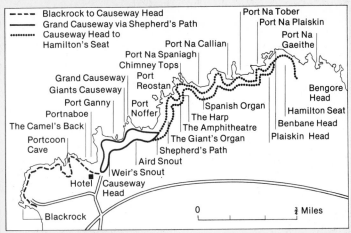

The Causeway Coast of Co Antrim, showing the three main walks and the places of interest you can see from them

Clough Williams-Ellis who created Portmeirion in North Wales.

□ 12 miles (19.3km) E of Ballycastle off A2. Map ref 7F1.

910. GIANT'S CAUSEWAY
Strange rock formation

This promontory of symmetrical basalt columns ranks among the world's leading scenic land forms. It is cut into three bays running from Port Ganny to Port Noffer. Although formed by the slow cooling of volcanic lava (see Chapter 6), legend has it that the causeway was built by the Irish giant Finn MacCool trying to reach his Scottish enemy. Similar, less grand structures are found on Scotland's Isle of Staffa at Fingal's Cave. The rock formations have been given fanciful names: the Giant's Organ at Port Noffer rises to about 4oft (12m). There are also the Giant's Grandmother and the Wishing Chair. Three main walks are: Blackrock to Causeway Head 1½ miles (2.4km), taking in Portcoon Cave; the Grand Causeway along Shepherd's Path 2 miles (3.2km) which allows you to examine the causeway at close quarters; and the 5 mile (8km) circular walk from Causeway Head to Hamilton's Seat. The North Antrim Cliff Path continues to Dunseverick Castle, 4½ miles (7.2km) past Bengore Head, the highest point on the Causeway. The main walks in the area of the Causeway are indicated on the map above.

□ B146 from Portrush or Bushmills, off A2, to Causeway Head car park. Map ref 7E1.

911. GLENARIFF FOREST PARK
Forest glens

The park is situated amidst the famous Glens of Antrim and includes forest, recreation areas and several small lakes and rivers. Early settlers found Glenariff heavily forested and when the land was cleared it revealed a marshy valley floor while upper hillslopes were covered with scree and peat. Only the middle slopes could be cultivated and a system of 'ladder' farming was developed where each holding ran upslope so that all had a fair proportion of good and bad land. The beautiful seminatural broadleaved woodland beside the Glenariff river and its waterfalls is managed solely for conservation and is a nature reserve and area of scientific interest. One of the first manufacturing industries in Ireland may have started with Neolithic man's axe factory at Tievebulliagh, just north of Glenariff.

□ Off A43 Ballymena to Waterfoot road. Map ref 7F1.

912. PORTRUSH
Headlands and sea caves

On a long peninsula jutting into the Atlantic, Portrush is famous for its golf courses and sea fishing from the rocks. Walks to the tip of the headland, Ramore Head, give fine views of the Donegal mountains, Rathlin Island and the Mull of Kintyre. There is a nature reserve by Lansdowne Green where the rocks contain the spiral patterns of fossil ammonites. Boat trips are available to the nearby Skerries and the Giant's Causeway. White Rocks, three miles (4.8km) from Portrush, at the eastern end of East Strand, can also be seen by boat. These chalk cliffs are riddled with caves. Non-sailors can reach Cathedral Cave by a steep path from the road or walk from Portrush. Two huge rock columns support the roof of the cave which runs 2oo ft (6om) into the cliff. Other curious formations include the Priest Hole; the Giant's Head, which looks like a face staring out to sea; the Lion's Paw and the Wishing Arch. Nearby is Dunluce Castle, a romantic ruin, poised above the sea on a craggy rock. The present castle dates from around 1300. It was ruined after a storm in 1639.

□ Portrush is N of Coleraine on A2 and A29. Map ref 7E1.

913. RATHLIN ISLAND
Nature reserve and cliffs

The island is L-shaped, about six miles (10km) long and one mile (1.6km) across. Almost completely treeless its cliffs present an unusual combination of colour and rocks, the black and white of basalt and chalk. They are rich in caves. Some have magnificent interiors, their walls and pillars of white limestone resembling a cathedral. Most can only be entered by boat. In the Stone Age the island had an axe 'factory' at Brockley. Axe heads of porcellanite, identified as Rathlin-made, have been found in many parts of the British Isles. The cliffs which form almost the entire 16 mile (25.7km) coastline are the breeding places of huge numbers of seabirds – an estimated 20,000 guillemots alone. West Lighthouse is one of the best spots to see them. The islanders depend on fishing, particularly for lobsters, and cattle and sheep for their livelihoods.

□ Situated in the Waters O'Moyle, eight miles (12.8km) from the mainland resort of Ballycastle. Motorboat service in fine weather from Ballycastle Pier. Crossing takes about 50 mins. Map ref 7E1.

914. SHANE'S CASTLE
Nature reserve

The Shane's Castle Reserve, on Lough Neagh, the largest freshwater lake in the British Isles, is managed by the RSPB. There is a nature trail and an interesting range of habitats with deer, red squirrels, badgers and foxes in the woods, and flowers, ferns, mosses and liverworts by the streams. There are also large numbers of birds and wildfowl and in winter many seaducks. Two public hides. Information centre at the castle.

□ Off A6 to NW of Antrim on edge of Lough Neagh. Map ref 7E2.

Co Armagh

This is a county of gentle hills and the setting of many events in the epic history of Ireland. The city of Armagh, once the seat of the Ulster kings, has long been an important ecclesiastical centre. Tourist office: Armagh 524052.

915. OXFORD ISLAND
Nature trail

Oxford Island Nature Reserve is on the south-east corner of Lough Neagh, the largest freshwater lake in Britain. It is now a peninsula rather than an island due to the lowering of the water-level in the lough. There are sheltered bays which attract large numbers of wildfowl, especially in winter; reed-beds which provide a haven for one of the largest colonies of great crested grebes; wet meadows, where in summer you may be lucky enough to hear the rare corncrake; and areas of young woodland. The Nature Centre houses an exhibition about the wildlife of the reserve and its conservation. The nature trail itself is nearly two miles (3km) long (there is a short cut) and includes an observation hide.

□ Near Craigavon. Map ref 7E2.

Honeycomb columns of solid basalt, formed by slow-cooling volcanic lava, created the Giant's Causeway. Arrows show rock contracting into an hexagonal pattern.

Ireland

Co Down

In the south are the Mountains of Mourne with Slieve Donard rising from the sea. Slieve Croob tops another range of hills in the centre of the county and in the east the Ards peninsula forms a barrier between the sea and land-locked, island-dotted Strangford Lough. Tourist office: Belfast 46609.

916. CASTLEWELLAN FOREST PARK
Mountain viewpoint

The park lies in the northern foothills of the Mountains of Mourne. Highest point in the forest is Slievenaslat 901ft (275m) from which there are fine views of the surrounding countryside. The main features of the park are the castle, a 100 acre (40 hectares) lake stocked with brown and rainbow trout, five other small lakes and the arboretum.
□ Just N of A25 at Castlewellan. Map ref 7F3.

917. DROMORE
Motte and bailey castle

Dromore is sited where the main road linking Lisburn with Newry crosses the Lagan Valley. As part of the Anglo-Norman conquest many motte and bailey castles were built in the 12th century and Dromore can boast a fine survival, perhaps the best preserved in Ulster. It was built on a defensive site above an entrenched bend of the River Lagan. The medieval town which grew up under its protection remained small until the 18th century.
□ Eight miles (13km) SW of Lisburn just off the A1 which now by-passes the town. Map ref 7F3.

918. MOUNT STEWART
Garden fantasy

A very large garden landscaped in the 18th century and largely replanted and redesigned in the 20th century by the Marchioness of Londonderry. She filled Italian terraces with permanent plants, made a Spanish garden, a fantastic topiary garden and commissioned from a local craftsman, strange and amusing statues and ornaments. There are many rare and beautiful plants. The garden is on the eastern shore of Strangford Lough. Open daily from Apr-Sept, except Fri. Tel: Greyabbey 387.
□ On A20 S of Newtownards. Map ref 7F2.

919. MURLOUGH NATURE RESERVE
National nature reserve

Northern Ireland's first nature reserve was established in 1967. Seven hundred acres (282 hectares) of sand dunes extend for about three miles north-east of the Royal County Down Golf Course. The oldest dunes, inland from the sea, date back at least 5000 years.
□ Entrances at Slidderyford and Twelve Arches Bridge on A2 between Dundrum and Newcastle. Map ref 7F3.

920. NENDRUM
Early monastery

An old monastic site whose location on Mahee Island in Strangford Lough could not save it from destruction in the 10th century. Tradition has it that Nendrum was founded by St Mochoi in the 5th century, but the earliest firm archaeological evidence comes from 200 years later. Excavations have revealed a remarkably complete plan of an early monastic settlement containing several circular houses, a church, graveyard and a round tower (now reduced to a stump) enclosed within three walls. The impressive monastic remains, which can be visited at any time, were important in establishing the secular as well as the religious role of monasteries in 'Dark Age' Ireland.
□ 12 miles (19km) SE of Belfast off A22 to road bridge onto Mahee Island. Map ref 7F2.

921. ROWALLANE GARDENS
Rare trees and shrubs

Rare trees, shrubs and herbaceous plants in 50 acres (20 hectares) divided into a series of gardens. The rhododendrons, azaleas, magnolias and cherries are outstanding. Open throughout the year daily. Tel: Saintfield 510721.
□ 11 miles (17.7km) SE of Belfast, one mile (1.6km) S of Saintfield on A7. Map ref 7F3.

922. SLIEVE DONARD
The easiest way up Northern Ireland's highest mountain

Slieve Donard, 2796ft (852m) where the mountains of Mourne rise over the rest of Ulster before they come down to the sea, is a popular mountain with walkers. From the top you can see over a score of other peaks. It is also the easiest of the higher mountains of the British Isles to walk. From sea cliffs at its base to wild valleys viewed from the summit, the mountain has great beauty. The ascent takes 2½ hours, climbing through woods, past deep green pools, gorse-fringed cascades, blocks of granite and rough brown heather. The path is well-trodden. It starts from Donard car park at the south end of Newcastle. Following the right-hand bank of the Glen River to the first bridge, it crosses this and continues along the left bank. When the path is almost ready to leave the forest, another bridge leads back to the right bank again. A fence is climbed over a stile, and a rough track taken up the right hand side of the burn – to where it eventually fords the stream and climbs uphill. At the col between Slieve Commedagh and Slieve Donard you are now at the Mourne Wall, the boundary of the water catchment. Wide enough to be walked upon, it leads eastwards to the summit cairn.
□ Newcastle is 31 miles (50km) S of Belfast on T2 (A24). Map ref 7F3.

923. ULSTER FOLK MUSEUM AND TRANSPORT MUSEUM
Buildings of old Ulster

The open-air section of the museum consists of old reconstructed buildings from all over Ulster. There is a mill house, weaver's house, forge, flax mill and spade mill. There are demonstrations too of 19th century-style reaping and mowing with original farm machinery. Open daily all year. Sun afternoon only. Tel: Holywood 5411 for details.
□ Cultra Manor, Holywood. On A2 Belfast-Bangor road, about seven miles (11km) from centre of Belfast. Map ref 7F2.

Co Fermanagh

The county's outstanding feature is the river Erne and island-strewn Upper and Lower Lough Erne. Enniskillen, the chief town, stands between the two lakes. Elsewhere the county is hilly. The Marble Arch area is noted for its limestone scenery. Tourist office: Enniskillen 4361.

924. CASTLE COOLE
Neo-classical house

For admirers of neo-classical architecture this is a house of rare, if cold, perfection, surviving scarcely altered since it was built and finished in 1789-c1820, for the 1st and 2nd Earls of Belmore. James Wyatt modified slightly earlier plans by the Irish architect Richard Johnston and designed all the interiors. Among the many fine rooms is a great circular saloon. The furniture made for the house remains in situ, including the splendid contents of the saloon and the state bed, with its elaborate Regency draperies. The castle is owned by the National Trust and is open on afternoons daily (except Fri) Apr-Sept. Tel: Saintfield 510721 for details.
□ 1½ miles (2.4km) SE of Enniskillen off A4. Map ref 7D3.

925. LOUGH ERNE
Fishing and sailing

The Erne waterways are less well-known for boating than the famous Shannon, but they are just as beautiful and interesting. They offer 300 sq miles (777 sq km) of navigable water and 135 miles (217km) of cruising through canalised and natural river, open and island-studded sheltered loughs. Take your own boat on a trailer, or go to almost any boatyard and they will hire out dinghies for a day or longer.
□ Lower Lough Erne is NW of Enniskillen, Upper Lough Erne to the SE. Map ref 7D3.

926. MARBLE ARCH
Limestone arch and disappearing rivers

This name relates to a remarkable landform, a natural arch of white carboniferous limestone spanning the Cladagh River where it emerges from its one mile (1.6km) long underground journey through the mountainside. At various points this subterranean water course can be viewed down deep vertical shafts such as Cradle Hole, 100ft (30m) deep, where the limestone has collapsed.
□ Take the T53 (A32) out of Enniskillen then minor road W to Wheathill. Alternatively take the N16 (A4) to Blacklion and take minor road E to Wheathill. Map ref 7D3.

Co Londonderry

Here the scenery is of hill, glen and river. To the south are the Sperrin Mountains, to the north the Atlantic coasts are fringed with surf-washed beaches. Derry, overlooking a broad tidal curve of the River Foyle, is the chief town. Tourist office: Londonderry 65151.

927. DOWNHILL CASTLE
Rural mansion

For those who like something out of the ordinary. The 'Earl-Bishop' Frederick Augustus Hervey, Earl of Bristol and Bishop of Derry, travelled Europe collecting statues and pictures and built a series of eccentric houses to contain them. Downhill was built up above the sea in the late 18th century, but was gutted by fire in 1851. The bleak shell of the great house remains and, at the edge of a windswept landscape which was once the park, an exquisite circular temple, the Mussenden Temple, survives untouched, on a dizzy site at the edge of the cliffs. Inside, a fine room contains contemporary furniture. The temple is open on afternoons daily (except Fri) Apr-Sept.
□ Four miles (6.4km) W of Coleraine off A2. Map ref 7E1.

928. MAGILLIGAN STRAND
Shellbanks and beach

This seven mile stretch of beach runs from Downhill (see the entry above) to Magilligan Point at the mouth of Lough Foyle. The point is an enormous flat triangle of alluvium and blown sand which juts northwards almost closing the entrance to the lough. The best views of this remarkable terrain are from the basalt cliffs of Binevenagh. A massive Martello tower stands on the point. The strand is the haunt of conchologists who say there are over 120 different kinds of shells to be found.
□ Take A2 to Downhill. Map ref 7E1.

929. ROE VALLEY
Country park

Park consists of a three mile (4.8km) stretch of river banks and woodland. There are car parks, picnic sites, walks and information centre. Activities include canoeing, rock climbing, trout and salmon fishing (permit required). Since the Ice Age the river has cut through the rocks at Carrick, Dogleap and O'Cahan's Rock, to form deep gorges.
□ Off B192 between Dungiven and Limavady. Map ref 7E1.

Co Tyrone

Tyrone is an inland county with mountains, glens, moorlands and plains. Low-lying land borders Lough Neagh in the east. The rest is hilly, rising to the heights of the Sperrins on the Derry border. Tourist office: Omagh 45321.

930. DAVAGH FOREST PARK
Forest drive

The park is situated on the north facing slope of Mt Beleevnamore 12 miles (19km) west of Cookstown. Its main feature is a six mile (9.6km) tarmac scenic drive through mixed conifer forest. From the summit of Mt Beleevnamore there are views to every part of the province. There are also sheltered picnic places, trails and a visitor centre.
□ Access via by-road off A505 Cookstown to Omagh road. Map ref 7E2.

SHANNON HORSE CARAVANS

Horse-drawn caravan holidays and traditional music – two of the many pleasures to be found in the Irish Republic

Republic of Ireland

Co Carlow

The second smallest county in Ireland is green and wooded with streams and soft hills. Through it flows the River Barrow, one of Ireland's most scenic rivers. Carlow town, the county capital, was once an Anglo-Norman stronghold. Tourist office: Waterford 75788.

931. BARROW VALLEY
Scenic river

In the green and wooded country of the Barrow River valley there are a number of attractive villages which can be visited by boat or by car. Muine Bheag (Bagnelstown) is a pleasant place on the river and in Myshall village, a few miles to the east, is one of the gems of the Church of Ireland, the Adelaide Memorial Church of Christ the Redeemer, modelled on Salisbury Cathedral. Borris is a picturesque town at the foot of the Blackstairs Mountains and at Leighlinbridge, seven miles (11.2km) south of Carlow town, the ruins of Black Castle built in 1181 stand by the river. Nearby is Dinn Righ, Hill of the Kings, ancient seat of the Kings of Leinster. All that remains is a large mound. From New Ross to Saint Mullins there is some of the loveliest river scenery in Ireland.
□ The best of the valley lies between Carlow and New Ross. Map ref 8E2.

Co Clare

This is the natural hinterland of Shannon Airport. Clare is rich in antiquities – churches, castles and over 2000 stone or earthen forts. The coast has sandy beaches, mighty cliffs and coves and, in the north, the limestone wilderness of the Burren. Ennis is the county capital. Tourist office: Ennis 21366.

932. THE BURREN
Limestone scenery

The finest example of 'Karstic' limestone scenery in the British Isles. The term 'karst' comes from Yugoslavia where waterless limestone terrain is common, and here in western Ireland, fringed by the Atlantic and boggy lowlands, the waterless plateau of the Burren is an unusual phenomenon. It has all the classic landforms of such scenery including disappearing streams around the slopes of Slieve Elva; completely enclosed depressions, termed 'poljes' (e.g. Carran Depression); broad limestone 'pavements'; bare mountain summits such as Slieve Carran; and numerous periodically flooded depressions or 'Turloughs'. Drive across this limestone desert from Lisdoonvarna eastwards through Caherconnel and Carran to appreciate its treelessness, although botanists will be delighted with its great wealth of rare lime-loving flora. The new Display Centre at Kilfenora helps visitors understand the unique features of this fascinating area. Open daily in the summer. Tel: Kilfenora 30 for details. □ Kilfenora is on the L53 road between Lisdoonvarna and Killinaboy. The L51 from Ballyvaghan to Leamaneagh Castle cuts across the area. Map ref 8B1.

933. MILTOWN MALBAY
Town of painted houses

This small town a little more than one mile (1.6km) from the sea is unusual in that it was planned when town planning as such was unheard of. It is an attractive place with many excellent examples of traditional Irish painted houses. Spanish Point, two miles (3.2km) to the west, has a sandy beach. □ Ten miles (16km) SW of Ennistymon on N67/T69. Map ref 8B1.

934. CLIFFS OF MOHER
Spectacular cliffs

Regarded by many as the finest stretch of coastal cliff scenery in the British Isles. Driving northwards on the N67 from Liscannor the road ascends gently over a featureless grassy plateau with no hint of the dramatic coastline ahead. A signposted path brings you abruptly to the brink of the 600ft (183m) vertical cliffs which run for five miles (8km) along this ironbound Atlantic coastline. Layer upon layer of flagstones, shales and sandstones rise to a thick layer of yellow sandstone which forms an excellent viewing platform near the cliff-top. Climb to O'Brien's Tower, or wander along these breezy cliffs with marvellous views out to the fabled Aran Isles in Galway Bay. □ Three miles (4.8km) NW of Liscannor on the N67 (L54). Map ref 8B1.

Co Cork

Cork has mountains, lakes, river valleys, a rugged coastline with rocky peninsulas jutting far into the Atlantic. In the north and east tracts of undulating limestone country are interrupted by ridges of sandstone with picturesque river valleys between. Tourist office: Cork 23251.

935. ANNES GROVE
Riverside garden

Beautifully set out on slopes overlooking River Awbeg. Includes a formal walled garden, an extensive woodland garden with a notable collection of rhododendrons, exotic plants naturalised along riverside walks. Open mid-Apr to Sept, Sun-Wed in afternoons. □ One mile (1.6km) N of Castletownroche on main Fermoy-Mallow road N72/T30. Map ref 8C3.

936. BALTIMORE
Sailing centre

This is where yachtsmen sailing Irish waters reckon the Atlantic starts: at nearby and aptly-named Roaringwater Bay where the relatively sheltered southern coast becomes the exposed western coast. It offers a choice of sailing according to boat, experience and preference. Boats ranging from Mirror dinghies to a Drascombe Lugger can be hired by the day from the local sailing school. Motor boats from Baltimore run to Sherkin and Clear Islands. □ Seven miles (11km) SW of Skibbereen on L59. Map ref 8B4.

937. GARINISH ISLAND
Italian gardens

When it was purchased in the early years of this century, the intention was to build an Italian style mansion on this tiny islet, with a garden to match. The architect was to be Harold Peto. Unhappily, the house was never started, but the garden was. It is now stocked with a wide range of plants, many of which are too tender to grow outdoors in most parts of the British Isles. □ Ferry from Glengariff Pier Mar-Oct. Map ref 8B4.

938. GLENGARRIF
Village of the rugged glen

A splendid centre to explore the magnificent scenery of Bantry Bay and the Caha Mountains. Long drives can be taken westwards to Castletownbere and then back via the opposite coast of this mountainous peninsula. A shorter drive is over the spectacular Healy Pass, from Adrigole to Lauragh, set like a jewel in the surrounding mountains. Equally enjoyable is a stroll along the wooded coastline of the deeply indented Glengarrif Harbour. □ Take the N71/T65 to Glengarrif then L61 along the N coast of Bantry Bay. Map ref 8A4.

939. KILLEAGH
Limestone valley

The N25 (T12) road runs along a wide limestone valley hemmed in by sandstone ridges to the north and south. Killeagh stands on the Dissour River, once noted for its bleaching properties. The delightful wood of Glenbower stretches up into the hills above the village, a rare example of Irish indigenous forest. The Dissour flows through the trees, partly in a cleft known as Glaunbour, or 'deafening valley'. North-east of Carrigtwohill are natural limestone caves with dripstone formations and at Midleton a stream disappears underground. The road goes on to Youghal, a popular seaside resort with a five mile (8km) beach. □ On the N25 (T12) from Cork to Youghal road. Map ref 8C3.

940. MIZEN HEAD
Ireland's Land's End

Generally regarded as the Land's End of Ireland because it is the most south-westerly point of the Irish mainland. The sandstones and shales of the cliffs exhibit every shade of red and pink and they have been carved by the waves into stacks, walls, buttresses and ledges. Nearby is Barley Cove (between Mizen Head and Brow Head) one of the few extensive sandy beaches along this indented southern coastline. Excellent cliff scenery can be seen along any of the network of roads and paths which crisscross the peninsula, but especially between Brow Head and Streek Head to the south, although the scenery is slightly marred by the abandoned copper mines. □ Access via the L56 south of Bantry or the L57 from Ballydehob. Map ref 8A4.

The River Barrow flows through a scenic stretch of Co Carlow. The river scenery between New Ross and Saint Mullins is as fine as any in Ireland Grandstand view of the Atlantic: the famous Cliffs of Moher, Co Clare

941. OLD HEAD OF KINSALE
Peninsula viewpoint

This bony finger of slates and grits projects some three miles (4.8km) out into the Celtic Sea off Co Cork. The vertical rocks have been etched by waves into cliffs and bays and erosion has almost succeeded in breaching the narrow peninsula at East and West Holeopen Bays. Drive or walk out to the lighthouse for a splendid viewpoint, but eerie in fog as the fog-horn booms. (It was off the Old Head of Kinsale that the Lusitania was sunk.) A few miles north is the fascinating drowned river valley (or ria) of the Bandon River meandering past the picturesque town of Kinsale, with several fine 18th century houses, into the attractive harbour. The monolithic English forts which guard the harbour entrance are worth a visit. Kinsale is a centre for shark fishing. Its inner and outer harbours provide miles of scenic water for the day sailor. Dinghies can be hired locally. So can boats for trips along the coast or up the Bandon River.
□ Take the L42 out of Kinsale to Ballinaspittle, via Western Bridge, and minor road past Old head. Map ref 8C4.

Co Donegal

The north of the county has some of the most spectacular coastal scenery in Ireland and coastal routes such as the 100-mile (161km) circuit of the Inishowen peninsula are outstanding. Bundoran, a popular seaside resort, and Ballyshannon are gateway towns from the south. Behind the coast are hills, moors, glens and lakes and a wealth of archaeological remains. Letterkenny is the chief town. Tourist office: Sligo 5336.

942. ARDS
Forest park

Superb situation on the wild, remote and deeply indented North Atlantic coastline between Bloody Foreland and Malin Head, with the Donegal Highlands at its back, notably Muckish, 2197ft (670m), and the gaunt pyramidal summit of Errigal, 2466ft (752m). In the park itself there are forest walks and spots for picnics.
□ On Sheephaven Bay two miles (3.2km) N of Creeslough on T72. Map ref 7C1.

943. HORN HEAD
Wild headland

A wild peninsula with a spectacular 600ft (183m) cliff. The view from the crest of this awesome cliff is one of boundless Atlantic Ocean, broken only by numerous islands and headlands, and inland of magnificent mountains, especially Muckish and Errigal. To the west of Horn Head is Templebreaga Arch and a blowhole called MacSwiney's Gun, a long cavern in which the sea booms in stormy weather. From the village of Dunfanaghy you can walk around Little Horn to get a magnificent view of the cliffs of the larger peninsula. About one mile (1.6km) east of Port-na-Blagh is Marble Hill, a secluded and beautiful spot with a splendid beach.
□ Take N56 to Dunfanaghy then minor road. Map ref 7C1.

944. MALIN HEAD
Beaches of the geological past

The northernmost point of the Irish mainland, known to millions as a stormy sea area in the shipping forecast. Follow the L79 west along the edge of Trawbreaga Bay and then past the sand dunes of Soldier's Hill and on through the village of Ballyhillin. Here the ancient striped, hedgeless fields of the village run seawards until they are truncated by the abandoned sea cliff of a post-glacial raised beach. Malin Head has probably the best collection of raised shorelines in Ireland. Three – all at different levels – can be seen and Ballyhillin is perched on the crest of the highest of them. They were formed at the end of the Ice Age and after, when the land relieved of the weight of the ice, was uplifted. The watch tower on the headland has splendid views of the rock-bound coast. On clear days the Scottish Hebrides can be seen. To the north is the tiny island of Inishtrahull.
□ Four miles (6.4km) N of Carndonagh. Take the L79 out of Malin. Map ref 7D1.

945. THE POISONED GLEN
Strange valley

This curiously named glen in the heart of Donegal's highest mountains received its reputation from a poisonous plant, the Irish Spurge, which formerly grew on its marshy floor. Its U-shaped profile points clearly to its glacial overdeepening and its smoothly polished bare granite walls glitter in the sunlight and rain alike. From this mysterious cleft, it is easy to drive a short distance east on the L82 before striking westwards on foot to the summit of north-west Ireland's highest peak, Errigal (2466ft; 752m), a stately cone of white quartzite with great encircling skirts of shimmering screes and a jagged summit ridge. The reward for a steep ascent is a magnificent view of Donegal's renowned coastline.
□ Take the L82 from Meenacung to Dunlewy. The Glen runs to the SE of the village. Map ref 7C1.

946. SLIEVE LEAGUE
Cliff/viewpoint

Beyond the little fishing village of Teelin is a mountain track leading over Carrigan Head to the secluded Lough O'Mulligan and the cliffs of Bunglass. Here the view has to be seen to be believed: a magnificent range of cliffs ending in Slieve League, towering 1972ft (601m) above the sea. More adventurous walkers can continue along 'One Man Pass' a narrow ledge with a drop to the sea on one side and to a lonely lake on the other. Having traversed this precarious pathway you are nearly at the summit of Slieve League where there are exceptional views and the remains of a hermitage. Boats can be hired at Teelin for those who wish to see the cliffs from the sea. It may be advisable to find a local guide to show you the cliff walks.
□ Teelin is 7½ miles (12km) W of Killybegs off T72A. Map ref 7C2.

Gaelic is still the everyday language of the Aran islanders in Co Galway

Co Dublin

The county is dominated by the capital, a place of spacious streets and fine buildings, beautifully situated on a crescent-shaped bay which sweeps from the Hill of Howth to Dalkey. To the north of the city are pleasant beach resorts, to the south Dun Laoghaire and Killiney Bay. Tourist office: Dublin 806984 (May-Sept); 807048 (Oct-Apr); for Dublin City 747733.

947. HOWTH
View of Dublin

The peninsula was once an island which is now tied to the mainland by a tombolo of sand built by wave action. There are footpaths around the headland (as well as a road) offering fine views across the sea to the mountains south of Dublin. Howth Castle was a medieval building much reconstructed in the 18th century when formal gardens (now open to the public) were laid out around it.
□ Howth Head forms the northern arm of Dublin Bay and is reached by L86 road. Map ref 3A5.

Co Galway

Galway stretches from Connemara to the banks of the Shannon. It is Ireland's second largest county and its capital, Galway City, stands at the mouth of the Corrib River, a settlement with nearly 1000 years of history behind it. Offshore, across the mouth of Galway Bay, are the Aran Islands. Tourist office: Galway 63081.

948. ARAN ISLANDS
Historic islands

Three islands strung across the waters of Galway Bay. Boat trips to the islands from Galway City are popular, although only Inishmore has a pier. People and goods destined for Inisheer and Inishmaan are ferried to land by *curragh*. The fortress of Dun Aengus (see individual entry) is the greatest single attraction of Inishmore but there are the remains of other forts from Iron Age to medieval times and of early Christian churches on all three islands. Inisheer has the large fort of Creggankeel and tiny Kilgobnet Church, for instance; Inishmaan has Dun Conor fort and some Bronze Age tombs; and Inishmore has Dun Onaght and Dun Oghil forts as well as Dun Aengus and the early churches of Temple MacDuagh and Templenaneeve near Kilmurvey. Kilronan on Inishmore is the largest settlement on the islands. The cottages are neat, the fields laid out between limestone walls and the land itself is in places the result of a remarkable man-made process. Farmers spread sand, seaweed and manure, with any clay or mulch that can be found, on the natural bare limestone surface to create soil. The result is surprisingly fertile land producing good crops.

Ireland

Prehistoric cliff-hanger: Dun Aengus hill fort, Inishmore, Aran Islands

□ Inishmore is 30 miles (48km) SW of Galway. There are regular boat services from Doolin, Co Clare, and from Galway City. There is also a daily air service from Galway from May-Sept. Map ref 8A1.

949. DUN AENGUS
Prehistoric hill fort

This stone-built hill fort has been described as 'one of the most magnificent prehistoric monuments in western Europe'. It stands spectacularly on the edge of a sheer 300ft (92m) cliff on Inishmore (see Aran Islands entry), the most westerly of the three Aran islands that form an isolated natural breakwater in the wide mouth of Galway Bay. Dun Aengus – the prefix 'Dun' is Gaelic for fort or castle – covers 11 acres (4.5 hectares) and consists of three 'concentric' enclosures, defended by stout walls of dry masonry. There is argument as to whether or not its inner enclosure was once circular and has been halved by the collapse of the cliff; or whether it was built with this configuration to take advantage of the excellent defensive rampart provided by the cliff itself. Visitors can walk round the site at any time.
□ Half-a-mile (800m) S of Kilmurvey on Inishmore, Aran Islands. See Aran Islands entry for boat and air service. Map ref 8A1.

950. PORTUMNA
Forest park

Portumna, where the Shannon enters Lough Derg at its northern end, is a popular angling centre. Within the forest park there are walks and nature trails, wildfowl ponds and stands for viewing wildlife, which includes deer. Nature trail leaflets are available at the information centre.

□ Entrance one mile (1.6km) from Portumna on the Ennis road. Map ref 8C1.

951. ROUNDSTONE
Coast road and corals

This coastal resort, beautifully situated on Roundstone Bay, is a favourite of artists and botanists. On the Ballyconneely road about two miles (3.2km) from Roundstone, at the foot of Errisbeg Mountain, are the beaches of Dog's Bay and Gurteen Bay which sit back to back, either side of a shell-sand spit, joining a granite island to the mainland. This is made from the microscopic shells of tiny creatures which formerly lived in deep water offshore. Both bays have sparkling white shell-sand and numerous shells. Errisbeg, which rises to 987ft (301m) north of the town, gives fine views. Its ascent is easy. Unusual and rare plants grow on the slopes of Errisbeg, including *Erica Mediterranea*. The coast road beyond Dog's Bay runs along the shores of Ballyconneely Bay to Mannin Bay. Here the so-called 'coral' beach is not an animal product like true coral but is of vegetable origin, derived from a calcareous seaweed, *Lithothamnion*, which thrives on the sea-floor beneath the clear waters of western Connemara.
□ Minor road L102 S, off the T71 Maam Cross to Clifden road. Map ref 8A1.

952. YEATS COUNTRY
Literary landscape

William Butler Yeats (1865-1939), Ireland's greatest poet, is not associated with any one particular area in the way that Hardy is with Dorset. Nonetheless he drew powerful inspiration for his work from the Irish countryside. The landscape of Ireland, particularly that of the west, is a constant thread through his writings. Two areas in particular are now regarded as 'Yeats country'.
Sligo. As a child Yeats stayed here with his maternal grandparents, as a poet he returned to write about places such as Lough Gill and Drumcliff. And it is at Drumcliff that he is buried, with a gravestone bearing his own epitaph:
'Cast a cold eye
  on life, on death,
  Horseman, pass by!'

Yeats grave, Drumcliff, Co Sligo

Gort, Co Galway. In this pleasant small Irish town Yeats stayed, along with other Irish writers, at Coole Park, the home of Lady Gregory. There they fostered a mutual enthusiasm for Irish literature which encouraged writers such as Yeats and Sean O'Casey and led to the founding of Dublin's Abbey Theatre in 1904. Little now remains of Coole Park other than a huge beech tree carved with the initials of Lady Gregory, Yeats and other literary figures. Close to Gort is Ballylee Castle, sometimes known as Ballylee Tower after the book of poems, *The Tower*, which Yeats wrote while living there in the 1920s. The building had been built in the 16th century and cost Yeats just £35 when he bought it in 1917. After being allowed to decay in the years after his death, the castle has now been renovated and is open to visitors during summer months as a Yeats museum.
□ Drumcliff is five miles (8km) N of Sligo, Lough Gill immediately SE of the town. Gort is 18 miles (29km) N of Ennis, Ballylee Castle is five miles (8km) NE of Gort. Map ref 7C3, 8B1.

Co Kerry

South Kerry has some of the finest and best known scenery in Ireland – the Lakes of Killarney, Carrantuohill, the Ring of Kerry and, offshore, the rocky Skelligs. North Kerry is less dramatic, a pleasant undulating lowland stretching away to the Shannon estuary. Tourist office: Tralee 21288.

953. CARRANTUOHILL
The easiest way up Ireland's highest mountain

This walk is the easiest way up the Republic of Ireland's highest mountain: the 3414ft (1040m) Carrantuohill. The highest point of the MacGillycuddy Reeks, this mountain is every bit as serious as Snowdon, Scafell Pike or Ben Nevis – if not more so. Rescue facilities are not as assured as in North Wales; the massif is near enough to the Atlantic to mean frequent cloud cover at short notice; and this is a region of Old Red Sandstone with its characteristic sharp ridges and sheer corries, much of it little explored. The popular approach is from the north via Hag's Glen and the Devil's Ladder. More than any other mountain climb featured in this book, some hill walking experience helps here. There is another route to the top from Black Valley to the south, but it has not the character of the one described. Nor has it the test-piece of the 'Ladder' which if it intimidates you means you should not be on the mountain in the first place. For the summit ridge is 'big country'.

From the Dunloe to Glencuttane road an access road passes Corran Tuathail Youth Hostel. A short distance away a footbridge crosses the Gaddagh River. Follow this to a 'green road' which pierces the glen to the twin lakes of Callee and Gouragh, where the scenery is tremendous. The Devil's Ladder is the gash running to the col south-west of the lakes, and after passing between these keep Carrantuohill on your right during the approach. Climb the left hand side of the stream while ascending the Ladder up grass, clay and rocks. From the saddle the summit cross (and windmill which powers the bulbs which illuminate it) beckons. Make for it following the cairns in a north-westerly direction after your ascent of seven miles (11km) and five or six hours.
□ 12 miles (19km) SW of Killarney. Map ref 8A3.

954. CUMMERAGH VALLEY
Corries and lakes

A rarely travelled back road gives you an opportunity to see some of Ireland's finest glacial corries and their accompanying lakes. Along this road you will see a magnificent mountain panorama unfolding to the right. The large lakes of Namona, Cloonaughlin and Derriana are held in by enormous crescent-shaped glacial moraines, with that around Lough Derriana being particularly impressive. Its southernmost arm is so massive that it has dammed up a tiny marginal lake, Lough Nellinane high up between its outer slope and the rocky hillside. The work of ice – scouring, plucking and polishing – is to be seen around these large corries, carved in the massive red and purple layers of Old Red Sandstone.
□ Near Waterville. Leave the main N70/T66 at Waterville and take the minor road to Dromod. Map ref 8A3.

955. DERREEN
Woodland garden

Notable for its collection of New Zealand tree ferns this garden on the southern shore of the Kenmore River was established over 110 years ago. The setting is magnificent with many fine trees and shrubs. Open from Apr-Sept on Sun, Tues and Thurs afternoons. Tel: Lauragh 3.
□ On L62 SW of Kenmore, ½ mile (800m) from Lauragh village on a small peninsula in Kilmackillogue Harbour. Map ref 8A3.

956. GALLARUS ORATORY
Drystone chapel

This Dark Age chapel is the most perfectly preserved early Christian building of its kind in the British Isles. The walls, between 3-4ft (1m) thick, were built of dry stone, almost entirely without mortar, in a technique similar to that deployed in the Bronze Age construction of the burial chamber at Newgrange (page 335). Its high ridged roof looks like an upturned boat. The chapel is approached through lanes lined with lush fuchsia hedges.
☐ Five miles (8km) NW of Dingle along unclassified road. Map ref 8A3.

957. LAKES OF KILLARNEY
Scenic splendour

This magnificent park embraces most of the lake district and its better known attractions. A short, comprehensive drive can start at Muckross Abbey, then to Muckross House which houses the Kerry Folklife Museum (open daily except Mon in winter). The next stop is Torc Waterfall, 60ft (18m) high and surrounded by trees. At Torc Bridge, where there is a Park Information Centre, take the winding path up to the waterfall where the river falls through a series of sandstone crags from the Devil's Punch Bowl high on the side of Mangerton Mountain. From here you get a tremendous view of the lakes which occupy large glacial depressions at the foot of the mountains. The wooded limestone shores of the smaller Middle and Lower Lakes have been dissolved into strange formations and mysterious caves. Continue along the N71 to Ladies View for one of the best views of the Killarney valley and its lakes.
☐ Killarney National Park (Bourne Vincent Memorial Park): Main entrance 2½ miles (4km) from Killarney on the main N71/T65 road to Kenmare. Map ref 8A3.

958. MACGILLYCUDDY'S REEKS
Dramatic mountain pass

The seven mile (11.3km) mountain track through the awesome valley known as the Gap of Dunloe starts from Kate Kearney's cottage, originally a coaching inn where you could buy illegal 'poteen'. The track takes you between the Macgillycuddy's Reeks, with Carrantuohill (3414ft; 1040m) the highest mountain in Ireland among the peaks, and Tomies and the Purple Mountain. This great U-shaped gash, 1500ft (457m) in depth, was the work, not of a local mountain glacier, but of a huge ice-sheet centred over Kenmare. You can walk through the Gap, or make the journey by pony and trap, or on horseback past a string of dark mysterious tarns. Details of jaunting car and boat trips from Tourist Information Office at Killarney. Tel: Killarney 31633.
☐ Minor road off the T67 at Beaufort leads to the Gap of Dunloe. Map ref 8A3.

959. PORTMAGEE
Seabirds and sea views

Three miles (4.8km) south of the village is Coomanaspig Pass, 1100ft

Beehive hut on Slea head, Co Kerry, westernmost point of mainland Ireland

(335m), one of the highest and most spectacular viewpoints in Ireland accessible by car. Continue to St Finan's Bay (sandy beach, fuchsia lanes), then walk north along rugged coast for grandstand view of Puffin Island. Here can be seen not only puffins, but Ireland's largest colony of Manx shearwaters (10,000 pairs), together with fulmars, storm petrels, choughs and ravens. Also glorious views of distant Skellig Rocks, Blasket Islands and Dingle Peninsula.
☐ Eight miles (12.8km) SW of Cahirciveen. Map ref 8A3.

960. ROSS CASTLE
Launch place for the lakes

The castle, now a ruin, is sited on a peninsula which extends into Lough Leane, the lower of the Killarney lakes. Owners can launch their own boats with prior permission. Tel: Killarney 32252 for this. Innisfallen Island is near the northern end of Lough Leane and about one mile (1.6km) offshore from Ross Castle. Evergreens flourish all over the island and holly is particularly luxuriant. The ruins of Innisfallen Abbey (AD 600) are near the island's landing stage. Boats and boatmen can be hired at Ross Castle.
☐ One-and-a-half miles (2.4km) from Killarney town centre off Killarney-Kenmore road. Map ref 8B3.

961. SKELLIG ISLANDS
Ancient island monastery

The Skelligs are three rocky islands that rise from the Atlantic like peaks of drowned mountains. It would be hard to imagine a more remote position for these jagged pinnacles of grit and shale: seven to eight miles (11-13km) out in the ocean off Ireland's south-west coast. Great Skellig rises to 700ft (213m) and provides the bleak setting for the best preserved ancient monastery site in Europe, reached from the landing jetty by a stone stairway which is still intact after 1000 years. This Dark Age monastery site, spread over a number of levels, contains beehive-shaped huts, oratories, cemeteries, stone crosses, holy wells and the church of St Michael. It has survived partly because of its isolation and because, unlike some other early monasteries (e.g. Nendrum, see page 328), it was built of stone. On the western side of the

island small terraced walls nursed patches of earth used as gardens or small fields. Little Skellig, the second largest gannetry in the North Atlantic, has over 20,000 pairs of gannets. The nearest mainland viewing point for the Skelligs is Bolus Head, a pleasant day's walk from Waterville. In summer boats to Great Skellig operate from Valentia Island and other places on the Kerry coast. The trip takes 1½-2 hours each way.
☐ Seven-eight miles (11-13km) W of Bolus Head. Map ref 8A3.

962. SLEA HEAD
Cliff coast drive

The most westerly point of the Irish mainland overlooking the drowned valley of Dingle Bay. The coast road winds precariously along the cliffs to Slea Head and on to Ballyferriter. From the head you can see the Blasket Islands. Centuries ago this headland was cut off from the rest of the peninsula by a defence system. The area is full of prehistoric and early Christian remains, the most notable being at Fahan where there is a concentration of beehive huts, known as clochans, as well as souterrains and standing stones.
☐ Follow minor road from Dingle along coast. Map ref 8A3.

963. VALENTIA ISLAND
Scenic island

This rocky island offers magnificent sea-scapes, tropical vegetation, breathtaking cliffs. It is an excellent centre for sea fishing and diving. There are fine views from Geokaun Mountain (880ft; 268m), which lies to the north of the island, overlooking Knightstown, the 'capital' of Valentia. These include Glenleam, with its huge rhododendron

banks and fuchsia glades, Valentia Harbour, Dingle Bay and the Blasket Islands. Boat trips can be arranged from Knightstown harbour to Beginish and Church Islands and the Skelligs.
☐ Minor road off the N70 (Ring of Kerry Road) at Portmagee where a bridge spans the narrow channel to the island. Map ref 8A3.

Co Kildare

This, the flattest of the Irish counties, is the centre of the horse country with the Curragh races and the bloodstock sales at Kill. The north, beyond Naas, is bog country, while the south has the Curragh plain and the outer foothills of the Wicklows. Tourist office: Kildare 97636.

964. CASTLETOWN HOUSE
Georgian style mansion

A huge early 18th century house built for Thomas Conolly, a self-made Speaker of the Irish House of Commons. Part designed by the Florentine architect Galilei during a brief Irish visit, part by the Irish architect Edward Lovett Pearce. What has been described as the 'magnificent monotony' of the central block is like a Baroque town palace transposed to Ireland, and to either side colonnades curve to wings in the Palladian manner. Inside the most memorable features are the cool white Rococo plasterwork of the great staircase, and the long gallery elaborately redecorated in the Pompeian style in the 1780s. The vista north of the house terminates in the extraordinary Conolly's Folly (open to those of the public who can find their way to it). Super-imposed arches, like a fragment of a Roman aqueduct, pile up to a huge crowning obelisk, with hallucinatory effect. It is open daily except Tues from Apr-Sept; in winter only during afternoons on Suns.
☐ Just north of Celbridge 12 miles (19km) W of Dublin off L2. Map ref 8E1.

965. TULLY
Japanese gardens

The gardens are in the grounds of the National Stud. They were laid out by Lord Wavertree's Japanese gardner, Eida, from 1906-1910. As perfect miniature gardens, they symbolise the life of man through all its stages, from the cradle to the grave. The gardens have some of the oldest bonsai in Europe. Open daily Easter-Oct and Sun afternoons. Tel: Kildare 21251.
☐ One mile (1.6km) SE of Kildare. Map ref 8E1.

Castletown House, 18th century mansion near Celbridge, Co Kildare

Ireland

Kilkenny Castle, Co Kilkenny. Castle and town were founded by the Normans

Co Kilkenny

Kilkenny has two of Ireland's most beautiful waterways, the Nore and the Barrow. These and the hills of Booley and Slievedaragh give the area quiet beauty. With its narrow streets and arched passages Kilkenny city has an old world atmosphere. Tourist office: Kilkenny 21755.

966. KILKENNY
County town

The town of Kilkenny was essentially the creation of the Anglo-Normans who regarded towns as centres of civilisation, commerce and political power. This political role caused many towns to be attacked or deserted when Norman influence began to wane. But Kilkenny was lucky. Not only does the castle survive (although partly reconstructed) but so, too, do probably more late-medieval buildings than can be found in any other Irish town. Evidence of its continuing importance and prosperity as a market and administrative centre can be seen in the way that 18th century buildings were incorporated in the old medieval walled city. Fragments of the walls survive in the old town. So does the typical Norman rectangular street pattern.
□ 30 miles (48km) N of Waterford. Map ref 8D2.

Co Laois

Portlaoise is the capital of the county, an historic place which was settled by the English in the 16th century. The remains of their castles can be seen everywhere. The Rock of Dunamase and its ruined fortress, the Timahow Round Tower and Abbeyleix are among the attractions. Tourist office: Mullingar 8761.

967. ABBEYLEIX
Woodland gardens

Beautiful woodland gardens with a fine collection of plants, trees, shrubs and magnolias. Monk's Bridge over the River Nore, dating from the 13th century, is still in use. Lily pond. Open Easter-Sept afternoons only. Tel: Abbeyleix 31227 for details.
□ 60 miles (96.5km) from Dublin on N8/T16 to Cork. Map ref 8D1.

Co Leitrim

Leitrim stretches for over 50 miles (80.5km) from Longford to the sea at Tullaghan where it has a coast of just a couple of miles. Lough Allen virtually divides the county in two. Carrick-on-Shannon, the county town, is on one of the ancient crossing places of the river. Tourist office: Sligo 5336.

968. LOUGH ALLEN
Lake of the Shannon

Seven miles (11.2km) long and three miles (4.8km) wide this is one of three great lakes of the River Shannon. A circuit of the lake can be made from Drumshanbo on its southern shore to Dowra, through Drumkeerin and back to Drumshanbo. The lough is noted for big pike. Boats can be hired in Drumshanbo.
□ Drumshanbo is N of Carrick-on-Shannon. Map ref 7C3.

Co Limerick

The Shannon is the county's northern boundary and on its other three sides it is bounded by a semi-circle of mountains and hills. Limerick city has grown from a settlement founded by the Danes. To the south-east of it is Adare reputedly the most picturesque village in Ireland. Tourist office: Limerick 47522.

969. ADARE
Thatched village

Adare is one of the most picturesque villages in Ireland and its thatched cottages and wide main streets give it a marked English character. Most Irish villages seem to have developed haphazardly, and only those built by landlords close to the gates of their estates – or 'demesnes' – appear to have any preconceived plan. Adare is such a village. Although its long history of settlement is evident in the remains of a 13th century castle, an abbey and two friaries, the village as it now stands owes most of its finest buildings to the efforts of the Dunraven family in the early 19th century. The manor house and grounds of the Dunraven demesne are open daily from Apr-Oct, Sun afternoons only. Closed Sat.
□ 10 miles (16km) SW of Limerick on N21/T28. Map ref 8C2.

970. CUSH
Ancient farming

A complex of ancient fields and enclosures on the western slopes of Slievereagh. Six enclosures or 'raths' averaging 65ft (20m) in diameter are joined together in a settlement where 70 rotary querns, glass beads and an abundance of iron slag have been found. Around the raths is a field system, marked out by earth banks and ditches, of the same late Iron Age/early Christian period.
□ Seven miles (11km) SE of Kilmallock off L28 at Kilfinnane. Map ref 8C2.

Co Louth

The smallest county in Ireland has two areas of exceptional beauty: the Cooley Peninsula where wild, heather covered mountains rise from the sea and in the south part of the Boyne Valley. The village of Louth, south west of Dundalk, once important, gave its name to the county. Tourist office: Dublin 806984/807048.

971. MELLIFONT
Cistercian abbey

The abbey ruins are those of the first Cistercian house – and therefore of classical European form rather than in the Celtic tradition – to be founded in Ireland. The monastery was founded in 1142 and the church consecrated in 1157. Mellifont can be the starting point for an attractive 10-mile (16km) walk to and from the burial chamber of Newgrange (see page 335). Leave Mellifont and head via Obelisk Bridge for the somewhat overgrown Navan-Drogheda canal towpath to Slane. Three miles (5km) further east lies Newgrange and the other burial mounds of Brugh na Boinne. Return to Mellifont via the road north from T26.
□ Four miles (6.4km) NW of Drogheda off T25. Map ref 7E4.

972. MONASTERBOICE
Monastic settlement

A monastic settlement possibly dating back as far as the end of the 5th century and founded by St Buithe. The remains are comprehensive: two churches, a round tower, two early grave slabs, a sun-dial and three fine sculptured crosses. One of these known as the Cross of Muireadach, is the finest of all early Irish crosses and was erected in the 10th century. The key to the tower can be obtained from the house at the gate of the settlement.
□ Five miles (8km) N of Drogheda on N1/T1. Map ref 7E4.

Co Mayo

County Mayo stretches from Lough Corrib and Killary Harbour in the south to Erris and Killala Bay in the north. It lies at the heart of Ireland's 'Western World'. Castlebar is the county capital. Tourist office: Westport 269.

973. ACHILL ISLAND
Ireland's largest island

This island joined to the mainland by a bridge is the largest off the Irish coast.

It is a unique combination of golden sands, moors, mountains and towering cliffs. The sea cliffs of Croaghaun Mountain (2193ft; 668m) on its western tip are the highest cliffs in northwest Europe, with a sheer drop of almost 2000ft (610m). This remote spot can be reached from Dooagh village via Lough Acorrymore. An easier walk is from Dooagh to Keem Bay where harmless basking sharks can sometimes be seen. The golden beach at Keel curves away to the Minaun cliffs where the famous Cathedral Rocks have been fretted by the waves into the pillars and arches of a great Gothic cathedral. Dugort, on the northern coast is the place to start a climb up Slievemore Mountain, 2204ft (612m). Alternatively you can walk the seven miles (11.3km) around its base. On the eastern side is the deserted village of Slievemore, abandoned in the Great Famine. Boats from Dugort visit the seal caves under Slievemore. There are also boat trips from Achill Sound around the coast and to various islands.
□ N59 to Achill Sound then 10 miles (16km) west to Dooagh. Map ref 7A3.

974. CLARE ISLAND
Island in the bay

Set at the mouth of the island-studded Clew Bay, this island steeped in legends and history offers only one hotel and a welcome from its tiny population of about 160 people. The southern coast is almost entirely bounded by cliffs up to 100ft (30m) high. Knockmore Mountain on the west side drops dramatically from 1550ft (472m) to sea level, terminating in sheer cliffs up to 300ft (91m) high which run about three miles along the coast. It is worth walking around Grainne Ui Mhaille's castle although it is not generally open to visitors. It stands above the little harbour on the east coast, the home of the ferocious Grace O'Malley, Sea Queen of the West, in the 16th century.
□ Clew Bay. Boat trips from Roonagh Point daily, four miles (6.4km) S of Louisburgh on the T39 and L100. Map ref 7A4.

975. CONG
Canal that lost its water

This historic village stands on the narrow neck of land between Lough Corrib and Lough Mask. Its dry canal is a melancholy monument to man's folly – and a vivid reminder that limestone is a permeable rock through which water soaks freely. In the mid-19th century in an attempt to link the two loughs millions of tons of carboniferous limestone were dug out by hand. The task took five years. But today the canal wharf, bridges and locks stand unused, just as they have been since they were built. For the day the canal was opened the water flowed in for only a short distance. Then it disappeared underground. There is a four mile (6.4km) walk along this canal-that-never-was. There are over forty caves around the village and among the most accessible are Kelly's Cave and Captain Webb's Hole, ½ mile (800m) east on the L101; Pigeon Hole, ½ mile (800m) north of Cong Sawmill on the L101. Here there is a car park, forest

walk as well as a cave with an underground river running through it.
□ Six miles (10km) S of Ballinrobe on the L98 and L101 roads, via Neale. Map ref 7B4.

976. KILLARY HARBOUR
The finest fjord in Ireland

If you want to see Ireland's answer to a Norwegian fjord then Killary Harbour in the beautiful west of Ireland will not be disappointing. Take the road from Westport beneath the frowning crags of Devil's Mother (2131ft; 649m) to the idyllic oasis of trees and flower gardens to be found at the isolated village of Leenane or Leenaun, where the full sweep of the burrowing Atlantic waters can be viewed. Alternatively take the L100 from Louisburgh southwards as it wends past wild Doo Lough cradled in a gash in the south Mayo mountains. Towering peaks rise on all sides and it is difficult to believe that the enclosed waters of Killary are indeed tidal. The shores of the fjord can be followed on foot out to the open sea, but if you want hidden beaches near the fjord mouth then follow the minor road round the northern flanks of the majestic Mweelrea (2668ft; 813m) which leaves the L100 at Cregganbaun and creeps round to the spectacular Atlantic coast at Killary Lodge.
□ Take the N59/T71 S out of Westport. Map ref 7A4.

977. TOURMAKEADY
Lake fishing centre

The Irish-speaking village of Tourmakeady is an excellent centre for fishing and touring. In a beautiful situation at the foot of the Partry Mountains (highest peak Benwee 2239ft; 682m) and on the western shores of Lough Mask. Adjacent to the village there are forest walks, a waterfall and nature trail.
□ Take minor road out of Westport through Partry Mountains or skirt the northern shores of Lough Mask from Ballinrobe, approx 11 miles (17.6km). Map ref 7B4.

Co Meath

From Tara, in the heart of the county, the high kings of Ireland once ruled. The countryside is rich in such reminders of the past and a visit to the Boyne Valley is like a course in Irish history from prehistoric tumuli to Norman castles. Tourist office: Dublin 806984/807048.

978. NEWGRANGE
Prehistoric cemetery

This is the name given to the most famous of a series of Neolithic passage graves in a 'prehistoric cemetery' set on a ridge above the River Boyne. It is a great mound or cairn, 42ft (12.8m) high and composed of hundreds of thousands of water-worn river pebbles. Twelve huge standing stones surround the cairn and, inside, a 62ft (19m) long passage leads to a central chamber which has intricate rock carvings displaying the whole repertory of megalithic art. There are two other mounds nearby at Knowth and Dowth. The whole site is known as Brugh na Boinne, or the Boyne Valley Cemetery. New-

grange is open to visitors daily May-Sept, closed Mons the rest of the year.
□ Six miles (9.6km) SW of Drogheda off L21. Map ref 7E4.

979. TARA
Capital of the Irish kings

The hill of Tara, although little more than 500ft (154m), dominates the area and is one of the most famous Irish historical sites. It is the traditional seat of the kings of Tara and the centre of a pagan cult in the Iron Ages. The many earthworks and man-made mounds on the hill have been given romantic names (e.g. Fort of the Kings, Royal Seat, King's Chair etc) for which there is no proof of accuracy. Most of these monuments belong to the Celtic Iron Age, but the burial mound known as 'The Mound of the Hostages' has been dated to 2000 BC by radio-carbon techniques. The site can be visited at any time.
□ Seven miles (11km) E of Trim off N3/T35. Map ref 7E4.

Co Offaly

Offaly lies near the very centre of Ireland. To the west flows the Shannon and near its banks is the old monastic city of Clonmacnois. Tullamore is the principal town and lies in the north of the county. Tourist office: Mullinger 8761.

980. CLONMACNOIS
Monastic settlement

One of central Ireland's most characteristic landforms is the esker, a long sinuous ridge of sand and gravel which snakes across the lowland bogs. Formed when glacial melt-streams honeycombed the former ice-sheets, eskers represent the sediments deposited in the sub-glacial ice-tunnels. These sediments were left behind when the ice-sheets disappeared. In the earliest historic times the eskers provided dry routeways through the peat bogs and the ancient Pilgrim's Road runs westwards along an esker to the historic monastic and cathedral ruins of Clonmacnoise in a lonely and beautiful setting on the east bank of the Shannon. It was founded in the 6th century by St Ciaran and became famous as a centre of scholarship and craftsmanship as well as religion. But it suffered so severely under Viking raiders and later the English that it was abandoned in the 16th century. Yet its importance can be gauged by the variety of the remains. Here, in varying stages of disrepair, are one cathedral, seven churches, two Round Towers, three crosses and the largest collection in Ireland of early gravestones.
□ 15 miles (24km) S of Athlone off N62/T32 at Ballynahowen. Map ref 8C1.

Co Roscommon

Roscommon stretches from the Arigna Mountains in the north to low-lying Lough Ree in the south with the majestic Shannon flowing along the county's eastern boundary. The Lough Key Forest Park near Boyle has a fine lakeside setting. Tourist Office: Mullinger 8761.

981. LOUGH KEY
Forest park

Facilities include a camping area and caravan park with shop and restaurant. A popular place for boating, cruising, fishing and swimming. Also bog garden, deer compound, forest walks and nature trail (booklet available on site). Tel: Cootehall 7 for details of cruising. For boats, enquire at shop.
□ Two miles (3.2km) E of Boyle, seven miles (11.2km) NW of Carrick-on-Shannon on T3. Map ref 7C3.

Co Sligo

When William Butler Yeats wrote about 'The Land of Heart's Desire' he had the beauty of the Sligo countryside in mind. Mountains, seas and lakes combine to make a poet's landscape. Sligo town lies in a valley between two mountains. Tourist office: Sligo 5336.

982. CARROWKEEL
5000 year old village

A Neolithic settlement and cemetery in a fantastic landscape of limestone platforms and precipices in the Bricklieve Mountains. The village consists of a cluster of nearly 50 stone rings on a bare rocky platform 800ft (243m) above sea level. Such a collection of Neolithic dwellings, 4000 to 5000 years old, is unrivalled in the British Isles.
□ 15 miles (24km) S of Sligo. Follow routes T3 and L11 to Ballymote. Proceed along L11 towards Boyle, branching off for Carrowkeel at *The Traveller's Rest*. Map ref 7C3.

Co Tipperary

In the north Ireland's largest inland county is a land of plains, lakes – it has Lough Derg, largest of the Shannon lakes – and river valleys, with high mountains in the south. Tourist offices: North Tipperary, Nenagh 31610; South Tipperary, Cashel 61333.

983. CAHIR
Castle and colourful houses

This small old-world town, straddling the River Suir at the eastern end of the Galtee Mountains, provides excellent examples of traditional Irish painting of houses and cottages. The colours used are often unlikely combinations of pinks, dark green and browns – almost 'fairground-style' – but surprisingly effective for all that. Each household mixes its own paints and chooses the colours to blend with those already adopted by their neighbours. A genuine survival of an Irish tradition. Cahir Castle with its massive keep, high enclosing walls and spacious courtyard is the focal point of the town. It is open daily June-Sept and is floodlit all year.
□ 12 miles (19km) SE of Tipperary on N24/T13. Map ref 8C2.

984. GLEN OF AHERLOW
Secluded glen

This fertile glen is spread between the Galtee mountains and the Slievenamuck hills to the north. Formerly an important pass between the plains of

Tipperary and Limerick it has been the scene of many ancient battles and the retreat of dispossessed and outlawed Irishmen who took refuge in the numerous caves on the Aherlow side of the Galtees. At the head of the glen near the village of Galbally, almost on the Co Limerick border, are the ruins of the Franciscan Moor Abbey. On the northern slopes of the glen, on the Slievenamuck hills, is a 16ft (5m) statue of Christ which was put there in 1950. A walk along the ridge is a rewarding way of exploring the glen.
□ Access on minor roads to the W of the N24/T13 Cahir to Tipperary road. Map ref 8C2.

985. KNOCKMEALDOWN'S VEE ROAD
Scenic drive

The remarkably engineered Vee Road, named from its hairpin bends on the northern slopes of the Knockmealdown Mountains (2609ft; 795m) is one of the most scenic drives in southern Ireland. From Clogheen the road climbs the forested mountainside until it breaks out on to open moorland. There are superb views northwards over the narrow limestone vale of Mitchelstown to the imposing Old Red Sandstone and Silurian massif of Galtymore (3016ft; 919m), one of Ireland's highest mountains. Behind you the conical outliers of Sugarloaf Hill overlook the narrow mountain pass of The Gap where a tiny lake, Bay Lough, occupies a glacial corrie, now overflowing with wild rhododendrons. South of the pass the road descends gently to the Blackwater river valley where, just 10 miles (16km) from the sea at Dungarvan, this mighty river makes its anomalous southward turn at Cappoquin. Instead of following an easy limestone corridor to the sea, the river turns back to flow in wooded gorges through successive sandstone ridges *en route* to its estuary at Youghal.
□ Tipperary/Cork border. Take the L34 south from Clogheen. Map ref 8C3.

986. ROCK OF CASHEL
Acropolis of Ireland

In the seemingly endless plains of central Ireland, the Rock of Cashel comes as something of a surprise: one of the most historic and visually exciting places in the British Isles. This small upfold of Carboniferous Limestone rising 300ft (92m) above the plain was utilised in pre-Christian times by the early Irish as a citadel for their Munster kings' palace. The splendid grouping of grey limestone buildings dominated by the ruined cathedral and round tower has enormous aesthetic appeal and has drawn comparisons with Athen's Acropolis, notwithstanding their very different architectural character. The rock and its ruins are floodlit in summer. From the rock itself there are splendid views over the surrounding lowlands, which are known as the Golden Vale – here is some of the richest farmland in Ireland. Cashel is the market town for the area. The rock is open from June-Aug daily. Closed on Mons in winter.
□ Eight miles (13km) E of Tipperary on N74/T36. Map ref 8D2.

Ireland

Co Waterford

The north is mountainous with the Comeragh and Knockmealdown ranges the most prominent. Between them and the coast there are gentler landscapes with castles, cathedrals, river valleys and well-kept plantations. The coast has fine beaches and sheltered coves. Tourist office: Waterford 75788.

987. ARDMORE
Best of the Round Towers

A coastal monastic site with perhaps the finest example of the 100 or so Round Towers which survive in Ireland. These tapering stone cylinders date from the period of the Norse raids between the 10th and 12th centuries. Sometimes reaching as high as 106ft (33m) as at Kildare they were watch towers, places of refuge and stores for monastic treasures. The 12th century cathedral at Ardmore is among the most impressive of early Christian buildings in Ireland. The site can be visited any time.
☐ Five miles (8km) E of Youghal off T12/N25. Map ref 8D3.

988. CARRICK CASTLE
Elizabethan mansion

For Ireland, an almost unique survival: a gabled Elizabethan manor house, built in about 1600 by the 10th Earl of Ormonde, chief of the great Anglo-Irish clan of the Butlers. The original late medieval castle survives as a ruin, attached to the house. Inside there is a long gallery and the remains of fine plasterwork. The whole is like a transplant from the Cotswolds, and acquires an exotic and unlikely quality in its Irish landscape setting, at the edge of the picturesque little town of Carrick-on-Suir. The house is open on request. There are no guided tours.
☐ 15 miles (24km) NW of Waterford off A24. Map ref 8D2.

Co Westmeath

Westmeath is an inland county pleasantly endowed with low hills. In the north-east they command good views over lake-dotted landscapes. Mullingar is the county capital. Tourist office: Mullingar 8650.

989. FORE ABBEY
Benedictine priory

Snugly situated in a valley hemmed in by jagged limestone cliffs is a 9th century church and the remains of a medieval walled town, including a fine gateway. Here, too, are the only authenticated remains of a Benedictine priory in Ireland so that the richness and variety of remains, allied to their setting, make this one of the most attractive sites in this part of the country. Keys are available at the Post Office in Fore village.
☐ 15 miles W of Kells (also known as Ceanannas) on L142. Map ref 7D4.

Co Wexford

A countryside of low hills, river valleys, lush pastures, well-kept thatched cottages and sandy beaches. To the north it is bounded by the Wicklow Hills, to the west by the River Barrow and Blackstairs Mountains. Wexford is the chief town. Tourist office: Wexford 23111.

990. SALTEE ISLANDS
Bird islands

These islands are Ireland's most famous bird sanctuary with a population of over three million birds during late spring and early summer. There are two islands, Lesser and Great Saltee, the latter being of greater interest. It has one of the three gannet colonies in Ireland, and is the only one off the south-east coast.
☐ The Saltees lie off Kilmore Quay from where there are boat trips to the islands in summer. Map ref 8E3.

991. MOUNT LEINSTER
Mountain viewpoint

The road to the summit of this high mountain was built to service the giant TV transmitter which stands on the 2610ft (795m) summit, and is extremely steep. Visitors are recommended to leave their cars at the gate to the summit road and finish the climb on foot. The Blackstairs Mountains are an isolated group so the summit is a magnificent viewpoint, not only over the surrounding lowlands, but north to the high Wicklow Mountains. From Bunclody the road strikes westward up the beautiful forested valley of the Clody River before emerging on the high, windswept granite moorlands. It then snakes up the ridge to the summit, with breathtaking views of the Barrow and Slaney valleys, to the west and east respectively.
☐ The mountain is on the border between Wexford and Carlow counties. Access via a minor road off the N80/T16 just NW of Bunclody. Map ref 8E2.

Co Wicklow

County Wicklow, just south of Dublin, is called the 'Garden of Ireland'. Its coast is mostly low and sandy while the granite mountains of central Wicklow are cut by deep glens and wooded valleys. Here is some of the finest scenery in the east of Ireland. Wicklow, the county town, overlooks a wide crescent-shaped bay. Tourist office: Dublin 806984/807048.

992. AVONDALE
Forest park

Planned walks, nature trails and picnic place in the beautiful valley of Avonmore. Avondale House (home of Charles Stewart Parnell) is open weekdays, May-Sept. Car park (small charge).
☐ Just S of Rathdrum. Map ref 8F1.

993. GLENDALOUGH
Wild beauty and rich history

The most picturesque of all the Irish monastic sites. It lies at the head of a secluded valley containing two lakes and is surrounded by the Wicklow Mountains. Dark Age and Medieval remains abound. The oldest church, although much restored, is Templenaskellig which is at the foot of a sheer cliff and can only be reached by boat. The trip, giving wonderful views of Glendalough Valley, takes 15 minutes. Other churches in varying stages of ruin on the old monastic site on the valley floor include the 10th century cathedral and the tiny 11th century St Kevin's Church, named after the saint said to have founded the monastery here in the 7th century. The imposing Round Tower, 110ft (33.5m) high, is still almost perfect after 1000 years. The valley site is scenically attractive with many footpaths leading through the wooded slopes around the lakes.
☐ Three miles (5km) W of Laragh off L107. Map ref 8E1.

994. GLEN OF IMAAL
Amphitheatre in the hills

The Glen of Imaal is a vast natural amphitheatre nearly five miles (8km) long and three miles (4.8km) wide. It is surrounded by hills which, on three sides, rise to over 1000ft (305m). The River Slaney, which flows into the sea at Wexford, rises on Lugnaquilla, which stands at 3039ft (926m) to the east of the glen.
☐ Minor road via Donard off the N81/T42 Hollywood to Baltinglass road. Map ref 8E1.

995. MOUNT USHER GARDENS
Riverside garden

Many rare trees and shrubs planted in a natural setting in this privately owned garden by the Vartry River where it tumbles down over an impressive series of small weirs. Open daily all year, but Suns May-Sept afternoons only.
☐ Three miles (4.8km) N of Wicklow at Ashford. Map ref 8F1.

996. POWERSCOURT DEMESNE
Waterfall and gardens

In the Deer Park of the fine mansion of Powerscourt is one of the highest single-leap waterfalls in the British Isles. Its setting is magnificent, nestling in a hollow of the Wicklow Mountains. The Dargle River pours down into a sylvan glen over a 400ft (122m) cliff before entering a deep pool surrounded by fallen boulders. A fascinating spot for a picnic, with time to explore the very contrasting landscaped gardens of Powerscourt itself, one of the finest formal gardens in Europe, with large terraces descending to a circular lake and, to one side, a Japanese garden. In all a magnificent example of an aristocratic garden laid out with taste and imagination. The mansion burned down some years ago. The gardens open from Easter-Oct daily. The waterfall is open all year.
☐ SW of Enniskerry, off the T43A. Map ref 8F1.

997. ROUNDWOOD
Rivers and waterfalls

Reputed to be the highest village in Ireland at 780ft (237m) above sea level. The scenery and fishing for brown trout are the two main attractions. There are boats for hire to fish in the reservoir. A short distance west of the village are the beautiful Loughs, Dan and Tay. Devil's Glen, about five miles (8km) south-east of Roundwood off the minor road to Ashford, is a deep chasm with craggy sides which nurses the Vartry River after it has fallen almost 100ft (30m) into the Devil's Punch Bowl. The thickly forested ravine of the Devil's Glen is an excellent example of a glacial meltwater channel which was cut by the torrents flowing from the snow-capped summits of the Wicklows. Restrained by the edges of the lowland ice sheets the waters cut spectacular rocky gorges in the margins of the Vartry Plateau as they tried to escape southwards.
☐ 12 miles (19km) S of Enniskerry on the main T81 road. Map ref 8F1.

998. RUSSBOROUGH
Palladian mansion

The most sensational surviving example of the Anglo-Irish aristocracy's favoured method of keeping up with their much richer English counterparts in the 18th century. A comparatively small house built c 1740 for the Earl of Miltown, made to seem three times its size by stringing out wings, walls, stables, arches and obelisks to either side. The result is a sensationally beautiful stage set, looking over to the Wicklow Mountains. Inside, room after room is decorated with fine Rococo plasterwork, and the great Beit collection of pictures, furniture, porcelain and bronzes, of international repute. The house is open on afternoons at weekends and bank holidays from Easter-Oct and also on Weds June-Sept: woodland garden open when in flower. Tel: Naas 65239 for details.
☐ Two-and-a-half miles (4km) S of Blessington off N81/T42. Map ref 8E1.

999. VALE OF AVOCA
Bright waters meet

Two miles north of Avoca village is The Meeting of the Waters in this beautiful valley. Here the Rivers Avonmore and Avonbeg join to form the Avoca River, a place made famous by Thomas Moore's poem of the same name. Near the confluence is the tree, or what is left of it, beneath which the poet spent many hours resting. The Vale of Avoca is especially pretty in late spring when wild cherry is in blossom. This district is rich in mineral deposits, particularly copper, lead, zinc and sulphur. At nearby Woodenbridge the goldsmiths of ancient Ireland obtained much of their gold from Croghan Kinsella, to the south-west of the village. In 1796 the finding of a nugget started a minor gold rush. To the north of Avoca is Avondale Forest Park.
☐ Seven miles (11.3km) NW of Arklow, on the T7. Map ref 8F1.

1000. WICKLOW
Sailing and sands

This county town overlooking a wide crescent-shaped bay was, like many ports and towns on Ireland's eastern coast, based on a Viking settlement (see page 48). Its harbour is not the prettiest in Ireland, but it provides good safe day-sailing and there are one-day dinghy sailing courses in the town. Wicklow Head, two miles (3.2km) to the south is a fine view point. Brittas Bay, six miles (9.6km) south of the town has a three mile (4.8km) stretch of dunes and beach.
☐ 30 miles (48km) S of Dublin on N11/T7. Map ref 8F1.

Acknowledgements

The contributors to this book are, appropriately, as diverse as the countryside itself. Some are academics who coped manfully with the journalistic pressures of short deadlines; some are journalists who were subject to academic scrutiny of the most rigorous kind. This fusion of skills was required, we believe, to bring before a wider public the knowledge which previously has been confined largely to specialist sources.

The names of our major contributors and consultants have been listed at the front of this book; those of the photographers and artists whose work appears in the book are given on p. 342. But the scale and complexity of the book is such that even these lengthy lists do not cover all the organisations and individuals to whom we are indebted.

In a few cases material first published in *The Sunday Times Magazine* has been reproduced in this book, although rarely in unaltered form. Such material includes contributions by Hunter Davies, a former editor of the Magazine, and Caroline Silver, equestrian correspondent of *The Sunday Times*. We would also like to acknowledge help from Roland Adburgham, Bill Cater, Noel Chanan, Veronica Horwell and George Rosie.

We are particularly grateful to John Fowles for his foreword. At his request the fee for this has been paid to the Kenneth Allsop Memorial Trust in aid of Steep Holme, the island in the Bristol Channel bought to commemorate Kenneth Allsop, broadcaster, author, dedicated conservationist and former Sunday Times journalist, who died in 1973.

Many specialist organisations helped us both compile the book and to check its accuracy. If any errors have survived a stringent series of checks and double-checks, then the responsibility lies with the book's editors rather than the following organisations whose help we now gratefully and gladly acknowledge: the Nature Conservancy Council; the Countryside Commission; the Royal Society for the Protection of Birds; the Council for the Protection of Rural England; the National Trust (and also the National Trust for Scotland); the Department of the Environment; the Ministry of Agriculture (especially Elizabeth Hoffman and her colleagues in the Economics Department); all the national park authorities; the Forestry Commission; the British Tourist Authority (in particular Barbara Feathers); the national tourist boards of England, Wales, Scotland, Northern Ireland and the Republic of Ireland; the regional tourist boards within England and Wales; the Meteorological Office; the Council for Small Industries in Rural Areas; the National Monuments Board; the Civic Trust; the WATCH environmental group; the National Farmers' Union; the National Farmers' Union of Scotland; the Irish Farmers' Association; the Ulster Farmers' Union; Massey-Ferguson (UK) Ltd; the Association of Agriculture; the Royal Highland Agricultural Society; Nottingham University School of Agriculture; the Irish Horse Board; the Irish Pig and Bacon Commission; the Shire Horse Society; the Agricultural Engineering Association; the Royal Agricultural Society of England; the Milk Marketing Board; the Cotswold Hybrid Pig Company; the National Pig Breeders' Association; University of Reading Museum of English Rural Life; the Countryside Museum; the Rare Breeds Survival Trust; the Geological Museum, Institute of Geological Sciences; the Royal Horticultural Society; Gascoigne, Gush and Dent Ltd; H.M. Coastguard; Royal National Lifeboat Institution; National Maritime Museum, Greenwich; Trinity House; Northern Lighthouses Board; Commissioner of Irish Lights; and the Irish Coastguard.

Many individuals within these organisations bore the brunt of our inquiries and we hope they will understand that lack of space inhibits a more personal acknowledgement. We would, however, especially wish to thank Michael Murless; John Habgood of the Norfolk Reed Growers' Association; thatchers W.R. Farman, Norfolk, and George Dray, Devon; wheat-straw grower David Hurford, Devon; blacksmiths H.G. Middleton and Sons, Devon; gamekeeper Alan Smith, Suffolk; Michael Leyburn; Hazel Waugh; Yvonne Adams; and Harold Hillier.

Clive Crook was greatly helped in the design of this book by Pedro Silmon. The diagrams and maps – unless otherwise stated – were the work of John Grimwade and David Worth. Additional picture research was provided by Anne Horton.

Inevitably a general book of this kind has drawn upon some information in specialist publications. Those which we have found most useful are listed in the bibliography on pages 339–341 and more specific acknowledgments are made in appropriate parts of the text. In particular we are grateful to Yale University Press for allowing us to reproduce on pages 80–85 the essay on country houses written by Mark Girouard for *The Sunday Times Magazine* but derived from his book, *Life in the English Country House*, first published in 1978. The maps on page 193 are reproduced by permission of the Ordnance Survey. The Saracen monument on pages 70–71 is by Mervyn Blatch from *Parish Churches of England in colour* (Blandford Press).

It is neither politeness nor duty which compels us to acknowledge the role of our publisher, Macdonald and Jane's. Without their imagination (and money) it would have been impossible to produce a book of either this scale or what we hope to be such high levels of art, photography and text; without their tolerance, as deadlines began to slip, quality would also have been impaired. Particular thanks are due to Susan Egerton-Jones and Alan Coombes.

Finally, but most important of all, is our debt to *The Sunday Times*. The book was only possible through the willingness of Harold Evans, the editor of *The Sunday Times*, and Ron Hall, the editor of the Magazine, to allow so many of their staff to be diverted to the project. We are also grateful for the help of Michael Rand, art director of *The Sunday Times Magazine*, and Robert Ducas, the head of the Times Newspapers office in New York. We hope that they, and all the other individuals and organisations whose help we have acknowledged here, believe the end-product to have been worth the effort.

Defenders of the Countryside

A guide to official and voluntary organisations concerned with the conservation of the countryside of the British Isles and its wildlife.

Official organisations

British Waterways Board Melbury House, Melbury Terrace, London NW1 6JX
Public body set up by the Transport Act 1962. The following year the Board took over the ownership of the nationalised inland waterways which it has managed ever since. These comprise some 2,000 miles of canals and navigable rivers – mostly in England but including several in Scotland and Wales.

Countryside Commission John Dower House, Crescent Place, Cheltenham, Glos., GL50 3RA
Principal statutory body concerned with country matters. Provides facilities for enjoyment of the countryside in England and Wales. Designates national parks and AONBs. Submits proposals for long-distance footpaths and bridleways. Encourages provision of country parks and picnic sites.
There is a separate Committee for Wales at 8 Broad Street, Newtown, Powys.

Countryside Commission for Scotland Battleby, Redgorton, Perth, PH1 3EW
Objects similar to those of the Countryside Commission.

Forestry Commission HQ: 231 Corstophine Road, Edinburgh, EH12 7AT, London Office: 25 Savile Row, London W1X 2AY Established 1919. Responsible for promoting the interests of forestry in Great Britain. The Commission has also developed the recreation potential of some of its forests, establishing forest parks to which the public are admitted.

Nature Conservancy Council 19/20 Belgrave Square, London SW1X 8PY
Established by the Nature Conservancy Council Act 1973, and taking over some of the functions of the Nature Conservancy, the Council is responsible for the conservation of flora, fauna, geological and geophysical features throughout Great Britain, and for establishing, maintaining and managing National Nature Reserves. At present the Council's 164 NNRs cover well over 300,000 acres. Land not being managed as a nature reserve but of special interest as a wildlife habitat can also be notified to a local planning authority as a 'Site of Special Scientific Interest' (SSSI). To date, over 3,356 SSSI's have been notified.

Water Space Amenity Commission 1 Queen Anne's gate, London SW1H 9BT
Established under the Water Act 1973. Forms a link between the national water and recreational interests.

Voluntary organisations

An Roinn Tailte Ant Seirbhis Foraoise & Fia-Dhulra (The Department of Fisheries, Forest and Wildlife Services) 22 Upper Merrion Street, Dublin 2

An Taisce (The National Trust for Ireland) 126 Lower Camden Street, Dublin 2

Association for the Preservation of Rural Scotland 20 Falkland Avenue, Newton Mearns, Renfrewshire, G77 5DR
Aims and activities similar to those of the CPRE.

Botanical Society of the British Isles c/o Dept of Botany, British Museum (Natural History), Cromwell Road, London SW7 5BD
Supports measures to conserve flowering plants and ferns. Publishes a code of conduct for the conservation of wild plants. Present membership: around 2,500.

British Butterfly Conservation Society Tudor

House, Quorn, Leicestershire LE12 8AD
Formed 1968. Promotes conservation of British butterflies. Present membership: around 1,350 – many of whom are actively engaged on carrying out habitat surveys for the Society.

British Mountaineering Council Crawford House, Precinct Centre, Booth Street East, Manchester M13 9RZ
Promotes the interests of British mountaineers and mountaineering in all its aspects, including access to climbing areas and conservation of mountain countryside.

British Naturalists' Association Willowfield, Boyneswood Road, Four Marks, Alton, Hants
Supports schemes for improvement of wildlife, and promotion and maintenance of national parks, nature reserves and conservation areas.

British Trust for Conservation Volunteers HQ: Zoological Gardens, Regent's Park, London NW1 4RY. Scottish Office of the National Conservation Corps: 70 Main Street, Doune, Perthshire
Runs and finances a voluntary field force, the National conservation Corps, composed of volunteers who devote spare time to practical conservation chores. They welcome volunteers from those who are physically fit and over 16 years of age.

British Trust for Ornithology Beech Grove, Tring, Hertfordshire
Promotes ornithology in the British Isles with particular emphasis on field work. Co-ordinates work of British bird observatories and bird-watchers in national surveys, nest records and bird censuses.

Civic Trust 17 Carlton House Terrace, London SW1 5AW
Founded 1957. Encourages the protection and improvement of the environment in town and country. Makes awards for good development. Has initiated hundreds of street improvement schemes. Encourages tree planting and removal of landscape eyesores. Administers the Architectural Heritage Fund, which provides loan capital to local building preservation trusts. Is prominent in promoting environmental legislation, such as the Civic Amenities Act 1967, which established for the first time the concept of the 'Conservation Area' as opposed to individual buildings.

Committee for Environmental Conservation (CoEnCo) 29–31 Greville Street, London EC1N 8AX
Formed 1969. Encourages the best use of natural resources. Considers matters of national importance affecting the environment by providing a forum at which problems may be examined by the major conservation organisations.

Commons, Open Spaces and Footpaths Preservation Society 166 Shaftesbury Avenue, London WC2H 8JH
Founded 1865. Aims to preserve commons (over 1½ million acres in Britain) and village greens for public use, to advise on the securing and preserving of public open spaces, to obtain public access to open country and to preserve footpaths and bridleways.

Conservation Society 12 London Street, Chertsey, Surrey KT16 8AA
Formed 1966. Aims at limitation of human population and introduction of national policies based on recognition of the finite extent of natural resources.

Council for National Parks 4 Hobart Place, London SW1W 0HY
Founded 1977. Composed of representatives from voluntary amenity, conservation and recreation bodies. Aims to preserve the natural beauty of National Parks.

Council for Nature Zoological gardens, Regent's Park, London NW1 4RY
Set up in 1958. Is the national representative body for the voluntary natural history movement in the UK. Has hundreds of associates and affiliated bodies including County Naturalists Trusts, field clubs, etc. By co-ordinating the efforts of thousands of naturalists it has become a potent force for nature conservation, active in advocating such measures as the Conservation of Wild Plants and Wild Creatures Act 1975.

Council for the Protection of Rural England (CPRE) 4 Hobart Place, London SW1W 0HY
Formed in 1926 to improve and protect the rural scenery and amenities of the English countryside. Keeps a close watch on legislation affecting the planning and protection of the countryside.

Council for the Protection of Rural Wales 14 Broad Street, Welshpool, Powys, SY21 7SD
Aims and activities similar to those of the CPRE.

Country Landowners' Association 16 Belgrave Square, London SW1X 8PQ
Formed 1907. Protects and promotes the interests of private owners of agricultural and rural land in England and Wales. Has more than 46,000 members – though half are owner-occupiers with less than 100 acres apiece.

County Naturalists Trusts
Every county in England and Wales has a Naturalists' Trust which establishes and manages nature reserves, organises meetings and visits for its members and publishes newsletters. Details of membership and addresses of the Trusts' Honorary Secretaries are available from the Society for the Promotion of Nature Conservation (SPNC), The Green, Nettleham, Lincoln, LN2 2NR.

Fauna Preservation Society Zoological Society of London, Regent's Park, London NW1 4RY
Founded 1903 to safeguard wild animals and their habitats throughout the world and to bring about the creation of more national parks for this purpose. Takes active interest in British Isles fauna and in 1977 played a major part in establishing otter havens in England and Wales.

Field Studies Council Director and Information Office: Preston Montford, Montford Bridge, Shrewsbury SY4 1HW. London Office: 9 Devereux Court, Strand, London WC2R 3JR
An independent charity organisation encouraging the pursuit of field work and research in all branches of knowledge whose essential subject matter is out of doors. Runs wide range of courses at its own residential centres in England and Wales.

Friends of the Earth 9 Poland Street, London W1V 3DG
Founded in the UK in 1970 to urge understanding of the need for conservation and preservation of natural resources. Acts as a pressure group to promote environmentally sound legislation, the prevention of pollution and degradation of the environment.

Greenpeace Colombo Street, London SE1 8DP
International conservation body which supports vigorous policy of non-violent direct action in defence of the environment. Prominent in campaigns against nuclear energy, whaling, and the killing of grey seals in Scotland.

Irish Wildlife Conservancy c/o Royal Irish Academy, 19 Dawson Street, Dublin 2

Men of the Trees Crawley Down, Crawley, Sussex
Founded 1922. A charitable society advocating the planting and protection of trees in Britain and throughout the world.

National Trust 42 Queen Anne's Gate, London SW1H 9AS
Founded 1895. Owns and safeguards for the nation considerable areas of the most beautiful countryside in England, Wales and Northern Ireland, together with over 400 miles of unspoilt coast, 100 gardens and some 200 historic buildings open to visitors.

National Trust for Scotland 5 Charlotte Square, Edinburgh, EH2 4DU
Objects similar to those of the National Trust.

Otter Trust Earsham, near Bungay, Suffolk
Promotes the conservation of otters. Instrumental in setting up otter havens in England and Wales. Owns a 47-acre Norfolk fen where otters occur, in addition to the Trust's own 23-acre HQ at Earsham.

Ramblers' Association, 123 Wandsworth Road, London, SW8.
Founded 1935. Encourages rambling and mountaineering, care of the countryside, preservation of natural beauty, protection of footpaths, and provision of access to open country. Watchdog for ramblers' rights throughout Britain – including the 103,000 miles of public paths in England and Wales. Membership: 30,000.

Royal Society for the Protection of Birds HQ: The Lodge, Sandy, Bedfordshire, SG19 2DL
Founded 1889. Gained a Royal Charter in 1904. Seeks to encourage protection and conservation of wild birds. Manages over 70 reserves throughout the UK. Also investigates and combats contraventions of the protection of Birds Acts. Membership: well over 260,000.

Scottish Field Studies Council Forelands, 18 Marketgate, Crail, Fife, KY10 3TL
Educational body set up to provide teachers, students and amateurs with opportunities to increase their knowledge of countryside topics.

Scottish Rights of Way Society 32 Rutland Square, Edinburgh, EH1 2BZ
Aims to defend and acquire rights of way in Scotland.

Scottish Wildlife Trust 8 Dublin Street, Edinburgh, EH1 3PP
Set up in 1964 to prevent destruction of natural habitats and wildlife throughout Scotland. Has established over 40 nature reserves in past 12 years.

Society for the Promotion of Nature Conservation (Association of Nature Conservation Trusts) The Green, Nettleham, Lincoln, LN2 2NR
Voluntary organisation founded in 1912 and incorporated by Royal Charter in 1916. Promotes nature conservation and protection of flora and fauna by establishing nature reserves representing typical habitats. Acts as the National Association of the 40 County Conservation and Naturalists' Trusts, including the Scottish Wildlife Trust and the Ulster Trust for Nature Conservation. Total national membership stands at over 120,000. Over 1,000 nature reserves are owned, leased or managed by the Trust.

Society for the Protection of Ancient Buildings 55 Great Ormond Street, London WC1 N3J
Founded in 1877 by William Morris. Its main concern is the repair and protection of Britain's architectural heritage, both ecclesiastical and secular. Has been instrumental in preserving thousands of buildings, from barns and dovecotes to Fountains Abbey in Yorkshire.

The Soil Association Walnut Tree Manor, Haughley, Stowmarket, Suffolk 1P14 3RS
Founded 1946. Voluntary body which believes that organic husbandry is the best means of building up soil fertility to produce better crops of high nutritional value leading to better health.

Tree Council 35 Belgrave Square, London SW1X 8QN
Established 1974. Aims to promote the planting and good cultivation of trees in great Britain, and acts as a forum for organisations concerned with trees.

Ulster Trust for Nature Conservation, c/o Inver Cottage, 67 Huntley Road, Banbridge, Co Down.

Trees for Ireland 9th Floor, Fitswilton House, Wilton Place, Dublin 2

Watch c/o The Society for the Promotion of Nature Conservation, 22 The Green, Nettleham, Lincoln.
The Watch Trust for Environment Education is a charity sponsored by the SPNC and The Sunday Times. Its objects are to educate young people in an understanding and appreciation of nature and the environment.

Wildfowl Trust The New Grounds, Slimbridge, Glos., GL2 7BT
Founded by Sir Peter Scott in 1946. The Trust is concerned with the study of wildfowl in the wild and in captivity. Maintains seven wildfowl reserves in England and Scotland, of which Slimbridge is the most famous.

Wildlife Youth Service of the World Wildlife Fund Wildlife, Wallington, Surrey
Encourages young people between the ages of 5 and 18 to play a greater part in nature conservation. Organises holiday adventure camps, field study projects, nature trails, film shows and lectures.
Woodland Trust Butterbrook, Harford, Ivybridge, Devon
Established as a registered charity in 1972. Aims to conserve, restore and re-establish trees (especially broadleaved trees), plants and all forms of wildlife in the UK.
World Wildlife Fund Panda House, 29 Greville Street, London EC1N 8AX
International charitable organisation founded in 1961. Primarily concerned with raising money for the conservation and safeguarding from extinction of particular species of wild animals and plants. In the past 17 years WWF has contributed £16 million to 2,000 conservation projects in 135 countries, including Britain.

In addition to the national organisations of Great Britain and Ireland there are countless smaller groups actively engaged in conservation at local and regional level. It is impossible to list them all here, but among the most vigorous are:—
Dartmoor Preservation Association 4 Oxford Gardens, Mannamead, Plymouth PL3 4SF
Founded 1882. Dedicated to preserving the wildness and true character of Dartmoor. Was successful in opposing the construction of a reservoir at Swincombe which would have drowned the wild heart of the moor.
The Exmoor Society Parish Rooms, Dulverton, Somerset
Technically a branch of the CPRE, but almost exclusively concerned with conservation of the Exmoor National Park. Set up in 1958 to fight (successfully) Forestry Commission proposals to afforest one of the wildest parts of Exmoor.
Friends of the Lake District Gowan Knott, Kendal Road, Staveley, Kendal, Cumbria LA8 9LP
Society of some 7,000 members whose special concern is to protect the landscape and natural beauty of the Lake District and Cumbria as a whole.
Society of Sussex Downsmen 93 Church Road, Hove, Sussex BN3 2BA
Founded 1923. Main objective is conservation of the Sussex Downs.

Further reading

Chapter 1
Britain before Man, Institute of Geological Sciences, HMSO.
Britain's Structure and Scenery, L.D. Stamp, Collins.
The Face of the Earth, G.H. Drury, Penguin.
Fenland: Its Ancient Past and Uncertain Future, Sir Harry Godwin, Cambridge University Press.
Fossils, H.H. Swinnerton, Collins.
Geology and Scenery in England and Wales, A.E. Trueman. Revised edition, J.B. Whittow and J.R. Hardy, Penguin.
Geology and Scenery in Ireland, J.B. Whittow, Penguin.
Geology and Scenery in Scotland, J.B. Whittow, Penguin.
On the Rocks – A Geology of Britain, Robert Muir Wood, BBC Publications.
Outline of Historical Geology, A.K. Wells and J.F. Kirkaldy, Murby.
Rocks, David Dineley, Collins.
Rocks and Pebbles, T.V. Østerguard and J.B. Whittow, Penguin.
The Story of the Earth, Institute of Geological Sciences, HMSO.
Organisations
Institute of Geological Sciences, Geological Museum, Exhibition Road, London SW7 2DE. Publications of the Institute are obtainable at the museum and HMSO. The museum also arranges a programme of lectures, films and field studies.

Chapter 2
Anglo-Saxon England and the Norman Conquest, H.R. Loyn, Longman
Deserted Medieval Villages, Maurice Beresford and J.G. Hurst, Lutterworth Press.
English Landscapes, W.G. Hoskins, BBC Publications.
Fields in the English Landscape, Christopher Taylor, Dent.
A Guide to Ancient Sites in Britain, Janet and Colin Bird, Paladin.
A Guide to the Prehistoric and Roman Monuments in England and Wales, Jacquetta Hawkes, Chatto and Windus.
Guide to Prehistoric England, N. Thomas, Batsford.
Guide to Prehistoric Scotland, R. Feachem, Batsford.
Handbook to the Roman Wall, J. Collingwood-Bruce, (12th edition by I.A. Richmond), Newcastle-on-Tyne.
The Industrial Archaeology of Britain, R. Buchanan, Pelican.
Ireland – A General and Regional Geography, T.W. Freeman, Methuen.
Iron Age Communities in Britain, Barry Cunliffe, Routledge and Kegan Paul.
Landscapes of Britain, Roy Milward and Adrian Robinson, David and Charles.
The Making of the English Landscape, W.G. Hoskins, Hodder and Stoughton/Penguin.
The Making of the English Landscape: series of county and regional surveys edited by W.G. Hoskins and Roy Milward, Hodder and Stoughton.
The Making of the Scottish Landscape, R.N. Millman, Batsford.
Medieval England: An Aerial Survey, M.W. Beresford and J.K. St Joseph, Cambridge University Press.
Medieval Monasteries of Great Britain, Lionel Butler and Christopher Given Wilson, Michael Joseph.
Prehistoric and Early Christian Ireland: A Guide, E.E. Evans, Batsford.
The Prehistoric Peoples of Scotland, S. Piggott, Routledge Kegan Paul.
The Reclamation of Exmoor Forest, C.S. Orwin and R.J. Sellick, David and Charles.

Roads and Tracks of Britain, Christopher Taylor, Dent.
Roman Britain, I.A. Richmond, Penguin.
Rural Settlement in England, Brian Roberts, Dawson and Archon/Penguin.
The Shell Book of Inland Waterways, H. McKnight, David and Charles.
Town and Country in Roman Britain, A.L.F. Rivet, Hutchinson.
The World's Landscapes – Ireland, A.R. Orme, Longman.
Organisations
The English Tourist Board, 4, Grosvenor Gardens, London SW1W 0DU. The board publishes a number of leaflets on various historic trails.
Roman Heritage Trails: A booklet 'Discover Roman Britain' has details of nine trails linking Roman sites. There are also leaflets on three of the trails which go into greater detail. These are the Brigantian (North), Coritanian (Midlands) and Saxon Forts Shore Trail (South East).
Norman Heritage Trails: 'Discover Norman Britain' details nine trails which cover nearly 200 Norman sites including cathedrals, churches, castles, museums, monuments and battle sites.
The Civil War Heritage Trail: a map-folder features over twenty civil war battle sites and places of interest in Bucks, Berks, Beds, Herts and Oxon.
Captain James Cook Heritage Trail: this trail is in a map-folder and takes the visitor on a tour of the north-east through some of the most scenic countryside in England.
Cassette Trails: The English Tourist Board produced three cassette tape trails for motorists. There are two in Northumbria: Trail One is Northumberland, Trail Two, County Durham. Both trails are about 250 miles (402km) long. The tapes give directional instructions, cover points of interest on route and present interviews with well-known local people. The third trail is in Somerset and North Devon and covers 150 miles (241km) of coastal scenery and moorland. The first two are obtainable from the Northumbria Tourist Board, 9, Osborne Terrace, Jesmond, Newcastle upon Tyne, Tyne and Wear, NE2 1NT: the third from the West Country Tourist Board, 37, Southernhay East, Exeter, Devon EX1 1QS.
Wales Tourist Board, Brunel House, 2 Fitzalan Road, Cardiff, CF2 1UY, publishes 'Wales, A Glimpse of the Past – A Tourist's Guide to the Industrial Trails, Slate Quarries, Mines and Mills'.
Scottish Tourist Board, 23 Ravelston Terrace, Edinburgh, EH4 3EU, publishes 'Scotland: In Famous Footsteps'. These trails are based on Mary Queen of Scots, Robert Bruce, Burns, Boswell and Johnson. The board also publishes 'Scotland 1001 Things to See'.

Chapter 3
Buildings of England (series) Nikolaus Pevsner, Penguin.
The Concise Oxford Dictionary of English Place Names, E. Eckwall, Oxford.
English Church Architecture through the Ages, Leonora and Walter Ison, Barker.
English Place Name Elements, A.H. Smith, Cambridge University Press.
English Villages, John Burke, Batsford.
English Villages, F.R. Banks, Batsford.
Historic English Inns, A.W. Coysh, David and Charles.
Houses in the Landscape, John and Jane Penoyre, Faber and Faber.
Inns and their Signs, E.R. Delderfield, David and Charles.
The Life and Sport of the Inn, M. Brander, Gentry Books.
Life in the English Country House: a Social and Architectural History, Mark Girouard, Yale University Press.
The Living Village, Paul Jennings, Hodder and Stoughton.
Market Towns of England, Gary Hogg, Batsford.

339

Ordnance Survey Place Names on Maps of Scotland and Wales, HMSO.
Patterns of English Building, Alec Clifton-Taylor, Faber and Faber.
Your House: the Outside View, John Prizeman, Hutchinson.
(Many books listed under Chapter Two are relevant to topics such as villages and market towns which are covered in Chapter Three.

Chapter 4
Benningfield's Butterflies, Gordon Benningfield and Robert Goodden, Chatto and Windus.
The Birdlife of Britain, Philip Burton and Peter Hayman, Mitchell Beazley.
The Birds of Britain and Europe, Herman Heinzel, Richard Fitter and John Parslow, Collins.
Birds of the Wayside and Woodland, T.A. Coward, Frederick Warne.
British Birds of Prey, Leslie Brown, Collins.
The Broads, E.A. Ellis, Collins.
British and Irish Orchids, D.M. Turner Ettlinger, McMillan Press.
Butterflies, E.B. Ford, Collins.
The Concise British Flora in Colour, W. Keble Martin, Ebury Press and Michael Joseph.
The Englishman's Flora, Geoffrey Grigson, Paladin.
A Field Guide to the Birds of Britain and Europe, R. Peterson, G. Mountford and P.A.D. Hollom, Collins.
A Field Guide to the Butterflies of Britain and Europe, L.G. Higgins and N. Riley, Collins.
A Field Guide to the Insects of Britain and Northern Europe, M. Chinery, Collins.
A Field Guide to the Trees of Britain and Northern Europe, A. Mitchell, Collins.
Food for Free, Richard Mabey, Collins.
Grass and Grasslands, Ian Moore, Collins.
Grasses, C.E. Hubbard, Penguin.
Guide to the Mammals of Britain and Europe, Maurice Burton, Elsevier Phaidon.
Hedges, E. Pollard, M. Hooper and N.W. Moore, Collins.
Insect Natural History, A.D. Imms. Collins.
The International Book of Trees, Hugh Johnson, Mitchell Beazley.
Life in Lakes and Rivers, T.T. Macan and E.B. Worthington, Collins.
The Moths of the British Isles, R. South, Collins.
Mountain Flowers, John Raven and Max Walters, Collins.
Mushrooms and Toadstools, John Ramsbottom, Collins.
Mushrooms and Toadstools in Colour, Else and Hans Hvass, Blandford Press.
Natural History in the Highlands and Islands, F. Fraser Darling, Collins.
Nature Conservation in Britain, Dudley Stamp, Collins.
Trees, Woods and Man, H.L. Edlin, Collins.
The Unofficial Countryside, Richard Mabey, Collins.
Wild Flowers of Britain, Roger Phillips, Ward Lock.
The Wild Flowers of Britain and Northern Europe, Richard Fitter, Alastair Fitter and Marjorie Blamey, Collins.
Wild Flowers of Chalk and Limestone, J.E. Lousley, Collins.
Wild Orchids of Britain, V.S. Summerhayes, Collins.

Chapter 5
Agriculture, James A.S. Watson and James A. More, Oliver and Boyd.
British Agriculture, J. Donaldson, Atchley.
Craft Workshops in the English Countryside, Council for Small Industries in Rural Areas.
Crafts and Rural Industries – Wales, Wales Tourist Board.
Discovering Farm Museums and Farm Parks, Shirley Toulson, Shire Publications.

English Husbandry, Robert Trow Smith, Faber and Faber.
Farms and Farming, Rowland W. Purton, Routledge and Kegan Paul.
Farming for Profit, Keith Dexter and Derek Barber, Penguin.
Great Farmers, James A.S. Watson and May Elliott Hobbs, Faber and Faber.
New Agricultural Landscapes, Countryside Commission.
New Agricultural Landscapes: a discussion paper, Countryside Commission.
New Agricultural Landscapes: issues, objectives and action, Countryside Commission.
Pick Your Own – Where to Go, National Farmers' Union.
Stay on a Farm, British Tourist Authority.
Thatching and Thatched Buildings, Michael Billett, Robert Hale.
A Visitor's Guide to Scottish Craft Workshops, Scottish Development Agency, Small Business Division.
Organisations
The Association of Agriculture, Victoria Chambers, 16–20 Strutton Ground, London, SW1 publishes a monthly bulletin which lists farms holding open days from April to October.
Council for Small Industries in Rural Areas, Queen's House, Fish Row, Salisbury, Wiltshire SP1 1EX, publishes textbooks and information on many rural crafts.
The National Farmers' Union, Agriculture House, Knightsbridge, London SW1X 7NJ.
Scottish Development Agency, Small Business Division, 102 Telford Road, Edinburgh, EH4 2NP.

Chapter 6
Beaches and Coasts, C.A.M. King, Arnold.
Beside the Seaside, A. Smith, Allen and Unwin.
Book of the Seaside, Automobile Association, Drive Publications.
The Coast of England and Wales in Pictures, J.A. Steers, Cambridge University Press.
The Coastline of England and Wales, J.A. Steers, Cambridge University Press.
The Coastline of Scotland, J.A. Steers, Cambridge University Press.
The English Coast and the Coast of Wales, J.A. Steers, Collins/Fontana.
Flowers of the Coast, I. Hepburn, Collins.
The Hamlyn Guide to the Seashore and Shallow Seas of Britain and Europe, A.C. Campbell, Hamlyn.
Lighthouses of England and Wales, Derrick Jackson, David and Charles.
The Pebbles on the Beach, Clarence Ellis, Faber and Faber.
The Sea Coast, J.A. Steers, Collins.
The Sea Shore, C.M. Yonge, Collins.
Seashore Life, Gwynne Vevers, Blandford Press.

Chapter 7
Backpacking, Peter Lumley, Teach Yourself Books.
Backpacking in Britain, Robin Adshead and Derrick Booth, Kaye and Ward.
The Hike Book, Jack Cox, Lutterworth.
No Through Road, Automobile Association/Readers Digest.
Rambling and Youth Hostelling, Ramblers' Association and Youth Hostels Association, Know The Game Books.
The Walker's Handbook, H.D. Westcott, Penguin.
Walking, Hiking and Backpacking, Anthony Greenbank, Constable.

Classic Rock, Ken Wilson, Hart Davis, MacGibbon.
Climbing for Young People, Anthony Greenbank, Harrap.
Mountaineering, Alan Blackshaw, Kaye and Ward/Penguin.
Rock Climbing, Peter Livesey, EP Sport.

Safety on Mountains, Central Council for Physical Recreation, Mountain Leadership Training Board.
Where to Climb in the British Isles, E.C. Pyatt, Faber.

Fly Fishing, Maurice Wiggin, Teach Yourself Books.
The Pursuit of Stillwater Fish, Brian Clarke, A.C. Black.
Sea Angling, Trevor Housby, Teach Yourself Books.
Sea Angling for Beginners, Alan Young, Pan.
Where to Fish, The Field.

Better Riding, Lt. Colonel 'Bill' Ford, Kaye and Ward.
Eventing: the book of the three-day event, Caroline Silver, Collins.
Official Handbook, Association of British Riding Schools.
Where to Ride, British Horse Society.
Where to Ride in Ireland, Irish Horse Board.

The Beginner's Guide to Sailing, Donald Law, John Gifford.
Dinghy Sailing, Ken Duxbury, Pelham Books.
Family Cruising, T.L. Kinsey, Stanley Paul.
Sailing, Peter Heaton, Penguin.
Sailing, Robin Knox-Johnson, Collins.
Small Boat and Dinghy Sailing, John Chamier, Pelham Books.

The Beginner's Guide to Canoeing, Alan Byde, Pelham Books.
Know the Game – Kayak Canoeing, EP Publications.

Ordnance Survey Map Catalogue, HMSO.
Ordnance Survey Maps – a descriptive manual, J.B. Harley, HMSO.
Organisations
Backpackers Club, 20 St Michaels Road, Tilehurst, Reading, Berkshire.
Camping Club of Great Britain and Ireland Ltd, 11 Lower Grosvenor Place, London, SW1.
Country Commission for Scotland, Battleby, Redgorton, Perth.
Forestry Commission, 231 Corstophine Road, Edinburgh EH12 7AT. Publishes a wide variety of useful literature including 'See Your Forests' a series of complete guides to forest walks, picnic places, wayfaring, fishing and horse riding in forests in England, Wales and Scotland.
Girl Guides Association, 17-19 Buckingham Palace Road, London, SW1.
Outward Bound Trust, 14 Oxford Street, London W1.
The Ramblers' Association, 123 Wandsworth Road, London, SW8. Publishes lists of all path guides for ten regions.
Forest Service, Department of Agriculture, Dundonald House, Belfast BT4 3SB, publishes leaflets on forest parks and their facilities in Northern Ireland.
Forest and Wildlife Service, 22 Upper Merrion Street, Dublin 2, publishes 'The Open Forest – a guide to areas open to the public'. The booklet covers the forest parks of the Republic of Ireland.
Scottish Sports Council, 1 St Colme Street, Edinburgh.
The Scout Association, 25 Buckingham Palace Road, London SW1.
The Sports Council, 70 Brompton Road, London SW3.
Young Explorers' Trust, 238 Wellington Road South, Stockport.
Youth Hostels Association, Trevelyan House, 8 St Stephen's Mill, St Albans, Herts.
Irish Youth Hostels Association, 39 Mountjoy Square, Dublin 1.
Scottish Youth Hostels Association, 7 Glebe Crescent, Stirling FK8 2JA.
Royal Yachting Association, Victoria Way,

Woking, Surrey GU21 1EQ, publishes booklets on the following subjects: Motor Cruising Training Manual Basic Course; Motor Cruising Training Manual, Inland Waders; Motor Cruising Training Manual, Coastal Waters. The Association also has a 'Learn to Sail' list of establishments, sailing schools and clubs, including courses for power boat enthusiasts.

The British Canoe Union, Flexel House, 45 High Street, Addlestone, Weybridge, Surrey KT15 1JV, publishes a coaching handbook.

Inland Waterways Association, 114 Regents Park Road, London NW1.

Association of British Riding Schools, Chesham House, 56 Green End Road, Sawtry, Cambridgeshire PE17 5UY.

British Horse Society, National Equestrian Centre, Kenilworth, Warwickshire CV8 2LR.

Irish Federation of Sea Anglers, 137 Leinster Road, Rathmines, Dublin.

National Federation of Sea Anglers, 26 Downsview Crescent, Uckfield, Sussex.

Scottish Federation of Sea Anglers, 8 Frederick Street, Edinburgh.

Welsh Federation of Sea Anglers, 2 Coed Bach, Highlight Park, Barry, Glamorgan.

The Angler's Co-operative Association, Midland Bank Chambers, Westgate, Grantham. A body set up to fight pollution.

The National Anglers' Council, 5 Cowgate, Peterborough. The sport's main link with the Government. It is pledged to work with all other organisations for the benefit of angling.

The National Federation of Anglers, Haigh House, Green Lane, Derby. The biggest and most important national voice in coarse angling with a membership of around 500,000.

Chapter 8
AA Guide to Stately Homes, Museums, Castles and Gardens, Automobile Association.
The Flower Garden in England, Richard Gorer, Batsford/Royal Horticultural Society.
The Garden – a Celebration of One Thousand Years of British Gardening, John Harris (Ed), Mitchell Beazley.
The Garden: an Illustrated History, Julia S. Berrall, Penguin.
Garden Kalendar, Gilbert White, The Scolar Press.
The Gardens of Britain, a Series of Six Regional Guides, Batsford/Royal Horticultural Society.
Gardens of England and Wales Open to the Public, National Gardens Scheme.
Gardens to Visit, Gardeners' Sunday.
The Growth of Gardens, Richard Gorer, Faber and Faber.
Historic Houses, Castles and Gardens in Great Britain and Ireland, ABC Historic Publications.
Historic Houses and Gardens in Wales, Wales Tourist Board.
St Michael Book of Great Gardens in Britain, Peter Coates, Marks and Spencer.
Scotland's Gardens, Scotland's Gardens Scheme.
The Shell Guide to Gardens, Arthur Hellyer, Heinemann.
Visit an English Garden, English Tourist Board.
Organisations
Gardeners' Sunday, White Witches, Claygate Road, Dorking, Surrey.
National Gardens Scheme, 57 Lower Belgrave Street, London SW1W 0LR.
Scotland's Gardens Scheme, 26 Castle Terrace, Edinburgh EH1 2EL.
The Royal Horticultural Society, Horticultural Hall, Vincent Square, London SW1.

Chapter 9
Climate and the British Scene, Gordon Manley, Collins.
Climatological Atlas of the British Isles, HMSO.
The Drought in the South West, Frank Booker and James Mildren, Department of Economic History, University of Exeter, Exeter Industrial Archeology Group.
The English Climate, H.H. Lamb, English University Press.
Mammals of Britain: their tracks, travels and signs, M.J. Lawrence and R.W. Brown, Blandford.
Nature through the Seasons, Richard Adams and Max Hooper, Penguin.

Chapter 10
Countryside Planning, A.W. Gilg, David and Charles/Methuen.
Derelict Britain, J. Barr, Penguin.
The Destruction of the Country House, Roy Strong, Marcus Binney and John Harris, Thames and Hudson.
Epitaph for the Elm, Gerald Wilkinson, Hutchinson.
Green and Pleasant Land: Social Change in Rural England, Howard Newby, Hutchinson.
Man and Environment, Robert Arvill, Penguin.
New Lives, New Landscapes, Nan Fairbrother, The Architectural Press.
Policies for Landscape under Pressure, A.W. Gilg, Northgate Publishing.
Survival of the English Countryside, Victor Bonham-Carter, Hodder and Stoughton.
Tomorrow's Countryside, G. Christian, John Murray.
Tomorrow's Landscape, Sylvia Crowe, The Architectural Press.
Vanishing Britain, Roy Christian, David and Charles.
The Vanishing Wildlife of Britain, Brian Vesey-Fitzgerald, MacGibbon and Kee.

General
Akenfield, Ronald Blythe, Penguin.
Bartholomew Gazetteer of Britain, John Bartholomew.
Book of the Countryside, Automobile Association, Drive Publications.
The Country Diary of an Edwardian Lady, Edith Holden, Michael Joseph.
Discover Northern Ireland, Ernest Sandford, Northern Ireland Tourist Board.
The Highlands and Islands, F. Fraser Darling and J. Morton Boyd.
Historic Houses, Castles and Gardens, ABC Historic Publications.
Historic Monuments in the care of the State, HMSO.
In the Country, Kenneth Allsop, Hamish Hamilton.
Museums and Galleries in Great Britain and Ireland, ABC Historic Publications.
Nicholson's Guide to Great Britain, Robert Nicholson Publications.
The Past All Around Us, Readers' Digest.
Properties Open, National Trust.
The Shell Guides to England, Ireland, Scotland and Wales, Michael Joseph.
Stately Homes, Museums, Castles and gardens in Britain, Automobile Association.
A Walk along the Wall, Hunter Davies, Weidenfeld.
A Walk around the Lakes, Hunter Davies, Weidenfeld.
Organisations
The Geographical Association, 343 Fulwood Road, Sheffield S10 3BP. Publishes British Landscapes Through Maps series. Each booklet describes an area depicted on one or more Ordnance Survey Maps. Areas covered unclude Cornwall, Doncaster, Oxford and Newbury, East Kent, the Lake District, Strathpeffer and Inverness, Norwich, Fishguard and Pembroke, Snowdonia, Worcester District.

Tourist information

The tourist organisations listed below publish a wide range of literature and information on their respective countries and areas. 'Tourist Information Centres in England, Scotland, Wales and Northern Ireland' is a booklet which gives the addresses and telephone numbers of all the regional and local tourist information offices throughout the United Kingdom. It is published by the English Tourist Board.

British Tourist Authority, 64 St James's Street, London SW1A 1NF.

<u>National Tourist Boards</u>
English Tourist Board, 4 Grosvenor Gardens, London SW1W 0DU.
Irish Tourist Board, Baggot Street Bridge, Dublin 2.
Isle of Man Tourist Board, 13 Victoria Street, Douglas, Isle of Man.
Northern Ireland Tourist Board, River House, 48 High Street, Belfast BT1 2DS.
Scottish Tourist Board, 23 Ravelston Terrace, Edinburgh EH4 3EU.
Wales Tourist Board, Brunel House, 2 Fitzalan Road, Cardiff CF2 1UY.

<u>Regional Tourist Boards (England)</u>
Cumbria Tourist Board, Ellerthwaite, Windermere, Cumbria.
Northumbria Tourist Board, 9 Osborne Terrace, Jesmond, Newcastle upon Tyne, Tyne and Wear NE2 1NT.
North West Tourist Board, The Last Drop Village, Bromley Cross, Bolton, Lancashire BL7 9PZ.
Yorkshire and Humberside Tourist Board, 312 Tadcaster Road, York, North Yorkshire YO2 2HF.
Heart of England Tourist Board, PO Box 15, Worcester, Worcestershire WR1 2JT.
East Midlands Tourist Board, Bailgate, Lincoln, Lincolnshire LN1 3AR.
Thames and Chilterns Tourist Board, 8 The Market Place, Abingdon, Oxfordshire OX14 3HG.
East Anglia Tourist Board, 14 Museum Street, Ipswich, Suffolk 1PI 1HU.
London Tourist Board, 26 Grosvenor Gardens, London SW1 0DU.
West Country Tourist Board, Trinity Court, 37 Southernhay East, Exeter, Devon EX1 1QS.
Southern Tourist Board, Old Town Hall, Leigh Road, Eastleigh, Hampshire SO5 4DE and Isle of Wight Tourist Board, 21 High Street, Newport, Isle of Wight PO30 1JS.
South East England Tourist Board, Cheviot House, 4–6 Monson Road, Tunbridge Wells, Kent TN1 1NH.

<u>Regional Tourist Boards (Wales)</u>
Mid Wales Tourism Council, The Owain Glyndwr Centre, Machynlleth, Powys.
North Wales Tourism Council, Civic Centre, Colwyn Bay, Clwyd LL29 8AR.
South Wales Tourism Council, Darkgate, Carmarthen, Dyfed.

<u>Regional Tourist Boards (Scotland)</u>
Borders Regional Council, Tourism Division, Regional Headquarters, Newtown St. Boswells.
Central Regional Council, Tourism Department, Viewforth, Stirling FK8 2ET.
Dumfries and Galloway Tourist Association, Douglas House, Newton Stewart DG8 6DQ.

Fife Tourist Authority, Fife House, North Street, Glenrothes KY7 5LT.
Grampian Regional Council, The Leisure, Recreation and Tourism Department, Woodhill House, Ashgrove Road West, Aberdeen AB9 2LU.
Highlands and Islands Development Board, PO Box 7, Bridge House, Bank Street, Inverness.
Lothian Regional Council, Department of Recreation and Leisure, 40 Torphichen Street, Edinburgh EH3 8JJ.
Strathclyde Regional Council, Department of Leisure and Recreation, McIver House, Carogan Street, Glasgow G2 7QB.
Tayside Regional Council, Department of Recreation and Tourism, Tayside House, 26–28 Crichton Street, Dundee DD1 3RD.
Note: Some of the offices listed above answer written and/or telephone inquiries only.

Regional Tourist Boards
(Republic of Ireland)
Athlone, 17 Church Street.
Cashel, Town Hall.
Cork, Tourist House, Grand Parade.
Dublin, 14 Upper O'Connell Street and 51 Dawson Street.
Dun Laoghaire, 1 Clarinda Park North.
Ennis, Bank Place.
Galway, Aras Failte, Eyre Square.
Kilkenny, The Pabade.
Killarney, Town Hall.
Letterkenny, Derry Road.
Limerick, 62 O'Connell Street.
Mullingar, Dublin Road.
Nenagh, Kickham Street.
Skibbereen, 14/15 Main Street.
Sligo, Stephen Street.
Tralee, 32 The Mall.
Waterford, 41 The Quay.
Westport, The Mall.
Wexford, Crescent Quay.

Photographers and artists

Chapter 1
Photographs: 10 Institute of Geological Sciences. 12 (Top) Adam Woolfitt/Susan Griggs; (Bottom) J.W. Roberts. 13 Robert Freson. 15 Aerofilms. 16 (Top) Michael Sheil/Susan Griggs; (Bottom) Robert Freson. 17 Denis Waugh. 18, 19 IGS. 21 (Top) English Tourist Board; (Bottom left) Adam Woolfitt/Susan Griggs; (Bottom right) English Tourist Board. 22 David Reed. 24 Adam Woolfitt/Susan Griggs. 25 Michael Sheil/Susan Griggs. 26 Alan Le Garsmeur. 27 Denis Waugh.
Artwork: 11, 13, 14, 15, 17, 18, 19 John Grimwade. 20 David Worth. 22, 23 Michael Turner. 26 Dee McLean. 27, 28, 29, 31 Pavel Kostal/Artbag. 30 (Top) John Grimwade; (Bottom) Pavel Kostal/Artbag.

Chapter 2
Photographs: 32–33 Robert Freson. 34 Spectrum. 36 (Top left) Steve Herr; (Bottom left) Georg Gerster/John Hilleson. 36–7 Robert Freson. 38 David Reed. 38 Michael Sheil/Susan Griggs. 40–41 Donald McCullin. 41 David Lavender. 43 Bord Failte. 44 (Top left) Spectrum; (Middle) Aerofilms; (Bottom) Robert Freson. 45 (Top) Robert Freson; (Bottom) Denis Waugh. 46 Aerofilms. 47 John Prizeman. 49 (Top) Ken Griffiths; (Bottom) Robert Freson. 50 Michael Sheil/Susan Griggs. 52–3 Robert Freson. 54 (Top) Denis Waugh; (Bottom) Andy Williams/Robert Harding Associates.
Artwork: 39 David Worth. 46 Ken Lewis.

Chapter 3
Photographs: 56–7 Robert Freson. 58 (Top) Adam Woolfitt/Susan Griggs; (Bottom) Aerofilms. 59 Robert Freson. 60 (Top) Denis Waugh; (Bottom) Robert Freson. 61 (Top) Denis Waugh; (Bottom) English Tourist Board. 62 (Left) David Lavender; (Right) Robert Harding Associates. 63 Robert Freson. 64 Denis Waugh. 66–7 Robert Freson. 67 (Top) Adam Woolfitt/Susan Griggs; (Bottom) David Reed. 69 David Reed. 70–71 Edwin Smith; National Monuments Board; Oxford County Library. 72 Robert Freson. 74 David Reed. 75 Robert Freson. 76–7 John Prizeman. 78 Robert Freson. 79 Civic Trust. 80 Denis Waugh. 81 Yale University Press. 82 Malcolm Aird. 83 (Top) National Monuments Record; (Bottom left) Lucinda Lambton Library; (Bottom right) Nature Conservancy Council. 84 Country Life. 85 National Monuments Record.
Artwork: 64–5 David Baxter. 68–9 Ken Lewis.

Chapter 4
Photographs: 86, 87 Tony Evans. 90 Robert Freson. 113 Denis Waugh. 116 Ian Yeomans/Susan Griggs. 118 Mike Sheil/Susan Griggs.
Artwork: 88–89, 92–93 Peter Barratt, Artist Partners. 94–95 Josephine Ranking, Garden Studio. 96–97 Clare Martin. 98–99 Graham Allen, Linden Artists. 100–101 Norman Weaver, Artist Partners. 102–103 John Francis, Linden Artists. 104–105 Peter Barratt, Artist Partners. 106–107 Clare Martin. 109 John Francis, Linden Artists. 110–111 John Rignall, Linden Artists. 112 Phillip Rymer, Garden Studio. 114–115 Ian Garrard, Linden Artists. 116–117 John Francis, Linden Artists. 118–119 Richard Orr, Linden Artists.

Chapter 5
Photographs: 120, 121 David Lavender. 124 Adam Woolfitt/Susan Griggs. 125 (Top) Julian Calder/Susan Griggs; (Bottom) Adam Woolfitt/Susan Griggs. 127 Robert Freson. 128 David Lavender. 129 (Top) Donald McCullin; (Bottom) John Prizeman. 130 Pamela Toler. 133, 136 Ken Griffiths. 137 Denis Waugh. 138 Tony Evans. 140 (Top) Tony Evans; (Middle) Noel Chanan; (Bottom) Adam Woolfitt/Susan Griggs. 141 Ken Griffiths. 142, 143 Robert Freson. 144 (Top) Denis Waugh; (Bottom) Tony Evans.
Artwork: 122, 123 Ken Lewis. 130 David Penny. 132, 133, 134 Jake Tebbit. 135 Hargrave Hands. 139 Ken Lewis.

Chapter 6
Photographs: 146, 147 Robert Freson. 148, 149 (Above left) David Lavender; (Above right) Aerofilms; (Bottom) Robert Freson. 150 David Reed. 151 Don McCullin. 152 Adam Woolfitt/Susan Griggs. 154 Don McCullin. 155 John Whittow. 156 Aerofilms. 157 (Top) Robert Freson; (Bottom) Richard Shirtcliffe. 158 Robert Freson. 159 Aerofilms. 161, 162 David Reed. 163 Robert Freson. 165 Tony Evans. 171 IGS.
Artwork: 152 John Grimwade. 153 David Worth. 156 (Top) John Grimwade; (Bottom) David Worth. 158, 159, 160 David Worth. 163 John Grimwade. 164, 165 David Worth. 166, 167, 168, 169, 170 Gillian Platt, Garden Studio. 171 IGS.

Chapter 7
Photographs: 172–3 Ken Griffiths. 174 Robert Freson. 176, 179 Robert Freson. 181 Donald McCullin. 184 Spectrum. 185 Adam Woolfitt/Susan Griggs. 187, 189 Robert Freson. 191 Robert Freson.
Artwork: 198–199 Diane Tippell.

Chapter 8
Photographs: 194, 195 Robert Freson. 196 Robert Freson. 197 Arthur Hellyer. 201 (Top) Ken Griffiths; (Bottom left) Robert Freson; (Middle right) David Lavender; (Bottom right) Robert Freson.

Chapter 9
Photographs: 204–5 Robert Freson. 206–7 Adam Woolfitt/Susan Griggs. 209 Denis Waugh. 212–3 Noel Chanan.
Artwork: 208, 209, 214 David Worth. 215 John Grimwade.

Chapter 10
Photographs: 216–7 Robert Freson. 221 Tony Evans. 224–5 (Top) Tony Evans; (Bottom left) Robert Freson; (Bottom right) Adam Woolfitt/Susan Griggs. 228–9 Denis Waugh.
Artwork: 222–223 Janet Marsh.

1000 DAYS OUT
Maps: by David Worth.
242 West Country Tourist Board. 244 (Top) Robert Freson. 244 (Bottom) Aerofilms. 245 Clare Martin. 246 Robert Freson. 248 (Left) Denis Waugh. 248 (Right) Dorset County Museum. 249 Clive Crook. 250 (Top) Robert Freson. 250 John Etches. 251 (Top) Noel Chanan. 251 Clare Martin. 252 Somerset Rural Life Museum. 253 David Reed. 254 Walton Adams. 255 (Top) Trust Houses Ltd. 255 Spectrum Colour Library. 256 Clare Martin. 258 (Top) Ian Yeomans/Susan Griggs. 258 John Grimwade. 259 (Top) South East England Tourist Board. 259 Robert Freson. 261 National Trust. 262/3 Aerofilms. 262/3 Aerofilms. 264 Anthony Howarth/Susan Griggs. 267 National Trust. 268 Black Star. 269 Thomas A. Wilkie. 270 Gloddfa Ganol Mountain Tourist Centre. 271 Festiniog Railway Company. 272 Bruno de Hamel. 274 Steve Benbow. 276 (Top) National Trust. 277 (Top) Cooper Bridgeman Library. 277 Picturepoint. 278 Planet News. 280 Eric Turrell. 281 Avoncroft Museum of Buildings Library. 282 (Top) Robert Freson. 284 Robert Freson. 285 David Reed. 286 Michael Holford Library. 287, 288, 291, 292 David Reed. 293 Julian Calder/Susan Griggs. 294 British Tourist Authority. 296 A.F. Kersting. 298 British Tourist Authority. 299 (Top) British Tourist Authority; (Bottom) British Tourist Authority. 300 David Dore. 301 David Reed. 303 Robert Freson. 304 Steve Herr; English Tourist Board. 306 David Reed. 307 Sparrow Hill Museum, Rochdale. 308 Newcastle upon Tyne City Library. 310, 312 Robert Freson. 314 Adam Woolfitt/Susan Griggs. 315 (Top) 315 (Middle) Anthony Howarth. 315 (Bottom) Adam Woolfitt/Susan Griggs. 316 Forestry Commission. 317 Adam Woolfitt/Susan Griggs. 319 Michael Sheil/Susan Griggs. 320 National Trust for Scotland. 323 (Left) Farrell Grehan/Susan Griggs. 323 (Right) George Gerster; (Bottom) Anthony Howarth/Susan Griggs. 324 Michael Sheil. 326 British Tourist Authority. 327 British Tourist Authority. 329 John Hillelson. 339, 331, 332, 333, 334, 335 Bord Failte.
Half-title page: Tony Evans.
Back cover: Owlpen Manor and Dinas Forest, Denis Waugh; Dorset Coast, Robert Freson.

345

347